Human Motivation and Emotion

Human Motivation and Emotion

ROSS BUCK

UNIVERSITY OF CONNECTICUT

John Wiley & Sons, Inc.
New York London Sydney Toronto

Library of Congress Cataloging in Publication Data:

Buck, Ross.
  Human motivation and emotion.

  1. Motivation (Psychology). 2. Emotions. I. Title.
[DNLM: 1. Motivation. 2. Emotions. BF683 B922h]
BF683.B823   155.4   75-37893
ISBN 0-471-11570-3

Printed in the United States of America

10 9 8 7 6

To William, Maria, Jenney,

and all the children

PREFACE

This book is a broad introduction to the psychological literature on motivation and emotion, with an emphasis on human studies or animal experiments with direct applications to humans. Homeostatic drives such as hunger and thirst are only briefly covered to illustrate the workings of physiological mechanisms and to demonstrate cognitive influences on motivation. The broad coverage of this book is based upon the assumption that there are many different approaches and a rich diversity of techniques for studying motivational and emotional phenomena, and that the understanding of human motivation and emotion requires consideration of a variety of these viewpoints and methodologies.

Plan of the book.

The first chapters are devoted to the physiological bases of human behavior. Most treatments of the physiology of motivation have emphasized animal behavior because most studies in the area have used animal subjects. However, there is much clinical information on humans which, although it can seldom be used to rigorously test hypotheses about the physiological bases of behavior, can illustrate the role of physiological processes in human behavior. This book attempts to make full use of such data, considering for example the results of lobotomies; self-stimulation in humans; the use of implanted electrodes in humans to control pain, aggressive behavior, and epileptic seizures. It also covers (in Chapter 4) work of the control of physiological processes in humans via biofeedback and mediation, and the clinical implications of this work.

The next group of chapters considers major research trends in specific areas of motivation and emotion, including emotional expression and nonverbal communication, aggression, sex and competence. These chapters do not assume that the reader has read the physiological chapters. Each chapter considers its topic from an evolutionary perspective, with the chapter on aggression in particular covering ethological studies relevant to human behavior. Each chapter also considers its topic from the viewpoint of the development of the individual, for example the influence of social learning experiences associated with sex-role development, and the exposure to models in the mass media.

The next two chapters cover cognitive approaches to motivation and emotion, with the first considering the motivational implications of a number of cognitive theories, including balance theory, dissonance theory, social comparison theory, and attribution theory. The next chapter covers the application of cognitive theory, particularly dissonance and attribution theory, to such "traditional" motivational states as hunger, thirst, pain, and stress. The final chapter analyzes social influences on human motivation and emotion, stressing group aggression and moral behavior, with particular reference to Milgram's experiment and studies of factors causing the inhibition of helping behavior in emergencies.

Suggestions on using the book.

Just as there are many approaches to studying motivation and emotion, there are many ways in which a course in the subject might be taught. Some instructors might wish to emphasize physiological bases, while others might wish to stress the cognitive and social aspects of motivation and emotion. To help accommodate different approaches, an appendix is provided covering neuroanatomy and other technical matters useful for a fuller understanding of specific physiological mechanisms. The appendix is designed as an introduction to this material and is presented at a level of complexity similar to that found in an introductory textbook in physiological psychology. Those wishing further details on the topics covered in Chapters 2 and 3 can use this appendix, others may wish to use Chapters 2 and 3 as they are, while still others may prefer to skip the physiological material entirely. The later chapters do not assume knowledge of physiological mechanisms.

Treatment of social issues.

Although this book is written from the experimental point of view, a number of social issues are touched upon. These include the use of brain implants for the treatment of mental disorders in humans, the effects of exposure through mass media to violence and sexual materials, sex roles and emotional expression, helping behavior in emergency situations, biofeedback, and meditation. The book does not take a specific stand on any of these issues, but it does attempt to provide a background in empirical research upon which consideration and discussion of these issues may be based.

Acknowledgments.

The bulk of this book was written while at Carnegie-Mellon University, and thanks are due to the graduate and undergraduate students in my motivation, physiological, personality, and social psychology courses there who indicated by their enthusiasm—or lack of enthusiasm—what aspects of motivation are of the most general interest and who suggested how to present material which, although important, is not of such intrinsic interest. I also wish to thank my colleagues, particularly Robert E. Miller, who provided valuable comments on much of the manuscript, and Benjamin Kleinmuntz and B. von Haller Gilmer, who gave valuable advice on the process of writing a book. The comments and advice of George Mandler, Kenneth E. Moyer, Roger N. Johnson, Kenneth MacCorquodale, Devendra Singh, and other conscientious reviewers are also much appreciated. Needless to say, they are in no way responsible for any deficiencies in this book, but their comments have added to its strengths.

A number of secretaries have aided in the preparation of this manuscript, including Lou Beckstrom, Betty Boal, and Marian Bodnar. In particular, Lila Weiner provided much expert assistance during the early phase of the project, and Lucy Tilton has been most helpful in the past year at the University of Connecticut.

I wish above all to thank my wife, Marianne, without whose support and encouragement through difficult times this book could never have been completed.

Ross Buck

Storrs, Connecticut
September 1975

CONTENTS

Human Motivation and Emotion

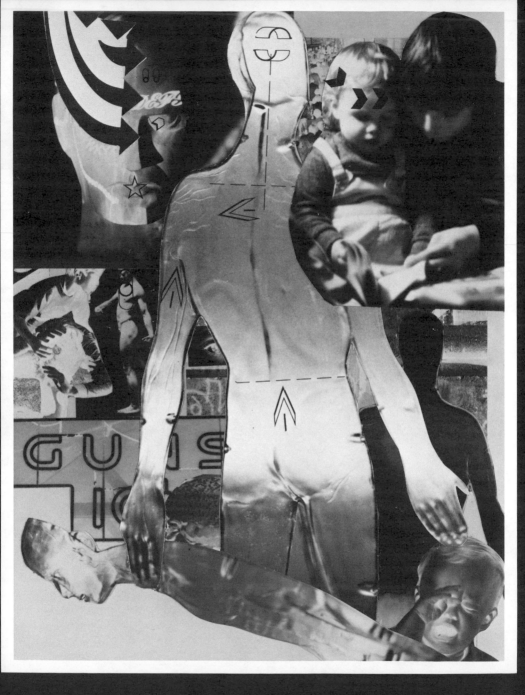

CHAPTER ONE

INTRODUCTION

Different individuals often behave differently in a given situation. One child may adapt easily and happily to his first day at school, another may refuse to leave his mother's side. One college student may have great difficulty controlling his weight as the school year progresses while his roommate may have no such problem. Also, a given individual may behave in different and seemingly contradictory ways in different situations. A person may shoot down helpless women and children one day and be a loving husband and father another. The concepts of motivation and emotion attempt to explain such differences in behavior from individual to individual and from situation to situation.

Since there are no obvious external explanations for these differences in behavior, one concludes that unseen internal events—motives and emotions—must account for them. The problem with internal events, of course, is that they are not directly visible and are therefore difficult to study. That does not mean that they cannot be studied. Indeed, there are many ways that one might study them. One might look into the history of the individual to determine whether or not something happened to him in the past that affected his behavior differently from another individual. Perhaps the unhappy child on the first day of school suffered some separation from his parents, while the happy child did not. Or, one might look into the heredity of the individual. Perhaps the unhappy child has an inherited tendency to be anxious and frightened. Alternatively, one might look at the present situation. Perhaps the mother of the unhappy child unwittingly does something that makes it difficult for the child to leave her. Or one might look for differences in the physiological mechanisms associated with the behavior. Perhaps the child was excited by some event unrelated to school, and the physiological response to that excitement contributed to his fear when he realized that his mother was leaving. Or conceivably, the unhappy child may have suffered some kind of brain damage that caused him to be unusually anxious and fearful.

The difficulty with unseen internal events is not that they cannot be studied, but that they can be studied in so many ways. Herein lies the complexity and the fascination of the study of motivation and emotion: there are many possible approaches to the subject matter, and there is no way to decide beforehand which approach is more meaningful and appropriate in a given instance.

Each approach to motivation and emotion is characterized by a more or less unique research tradition and set of methodological techniques. Each approach can be thought of as a separate "system," with its own conceptual and methodological frame of reference and an internal structure of criteria and principles, the "rules of the game," which make it possible for that system to function. However, these principles limit the range of the approach, just as the rules limit the number of possible moves in a game. Each approach has its blind spots: there are aspects of behavior with which it cannot deal. An individual analyzing behavior from one point of view misses the true complexity of the causation of behavior.

The people working within a given approach often fail to recognize that there are other valid ways of looking at behavior besides their own. At worst, they may make their position absolute by defining the subject matter according to their own interests and calling anything that does not fit this definition meaningless or absurd. More commonly, they simply ignore work that does not seem immediately relevant to their own. However, it is essential for the ultimate understanding of behavior that these approaches be open to cross-fertilization by new and different questions, interpretations, and methodological techniques, so that the differences between them can stimulate new syntheses of understanding.

The science of psychology has reached a point where the methods and results of quite different approaches to behavior are becoming relevant to one another. This trend is seen clearly in the study of human motivation and emotion. An adequate psychology of human motivation and emotion requires the simultaneous consideration of areas of psychology that have long been separated by different research traditions and techniques. Some of the factors affecting human behavior are approached most easily from a physiological point of view, some lend themselves to a cognitive analysis, some reflect social or situational influences, and so forth. The same overt behavior may be motivated by one kind of influence in one case, and a quite different influence in another. For example, an aggressive act (killing a helpless person) might be the result of a physiological abnormality (i.e., a brain tumor) or social pressure (i.e., the order of a superior military officer). No one approach to aggressive behavior can adequately explain all aggressive behavior. To have a true appreciation of the complexity of human motivation, one must have some understanding of a variety of approaches to motivation and the methods that they employ.

A Developmental-Interactionist View of Motivation and Emotion

DEFINITIONS

It is perhaps customary to begin a book on a subject with a definition of what the subject is. This is more difficult than one might first imagine. Just as there are many approaches to studying motivation and emotion, so there are many ways of defining those terms. Each definition may be useful within its own system or frame of reference.

There is probably no single "essence" that appears in all of the things labeled "motivation" or all of the things labeled "emotion." The aggressive behavior induced by a brain tumor and that induced by social influences may have nothing in common except the superficial outward similarity of the behaviors: the "motivational" processes upon which similar acts are based may have nothing in common. Nevertheless, it is meaningful to label these behaviors "aggressive" and to speak of the processes upon which they are based as kinds of "aggressive motivation." As the philosopher Ludwig Wittgenstein has suggested, things named by the same word need not have anything specific in common beyond informal similarities or "family resemblances." The relationships and similarities between the different uses of a word are like the twisted fibers of a thread: no one fiber goes through the whole thread, and one given fiber may be a considerable distance from another given fiber, but because of their relationships with the fibers close to them, the fibers form a continuous whole. So it is with general terms like "motivation" and "emotion." One usage of such a term may have nothing in common with another usage of the same term, but because of the web of meanings of all the various usages, the term is meaningful in a general way.

Motivation and emotion have traditionally been separate areas of concern within psychology. Motivation has usually been defined in terms of the determinants of *behavior;* that is, motivation has often been seen as the process by which behavior is activated and directed (Young, 1961). In contrast, emotion is generally defined in terms of states of *feeling* (Strongman, 1973). Both motivation and emotion have often been contrasted with processes of thought or cognition.

Recent research has demonstrated that it is impossible to separate the activation and direction of behavior, subjective feeling, and cognition. All of these processes play integrated and interacting roles in motivation and emotion. Rather than placing the concepts of motivation and emotion into deceptively neat definitional categories, we shall present a descriptive schema of how feeling, cognition, and behavior are interrelated processes involved in motivational and emotional phenomena. In the summary to each chapter, the content of that chapter will be related to this schema.

THE DESCRIPTIVE SCHEMA

This book will suggest a developmental-interactionist view of motivation and emotion in which cognitive and physiological factors interact in producing behavior after undergoing relatively independent developmental histories. The detailed analysis of how this occurs is the major subject of this book, but some general outlines can be drawn now.

Figure 1.1 illustrates the schema, with the process beginning with an internal or external affective stimulus (i.e. a stimulus that has emotional or motivational implications). Internal affective stimuli might include abnormal brain activity associated with some pathological state, a low blood sugar level caused by fasting, high levels of sex hormone at the onset of puberty, and so on. External affective stimuli might include the sight of an enemy or a lover, the presence of a novel object to a child, or an order from an authority figure.

These stimuli impinge upon a "filter" which represents the unique characteristics and learning experiences of the individual. The filter includes innate mechanisms common to the species or inherited by the individual, and any relevant learning experienced by the individual. The latter may involve classically conditioned associations as well as direct or vicarious social learning experiences about the stimulus situation and the individual's social role in that particular situation. The filter determines the impact of the affective stimuli for the particular individual in that particular situation.

The impact of the affective stimuli is felt at both a cognitive and a physiological level. On the cognitive level, the individual understands and interprets the stimuli on the basis of his past experience and present social role. On the physiological level, his nervous and endocrine systems work to adapt the body to the changed circumstances created by the affective stimuli. The cognitive and physiological responses interact with one another: the subjective experience of one's physiological reaction is an important source of information for the cognitive interpretation of the situation, and that cognitive interpretation itself may come to require bodily adaptation.

This interaction between cognitive and physiological responses determines the person's reportable emotional experience and his overt behavior, according to this schema. That behavior is also affected by the display rules learned by the subject in that situation: in one situation the person may freely express his reactions to the affective stimuli, in another he may inhibit them.

The subject's overt response may feed back to alter the original affective stimuli, and it may also alter the ongoing process of cognitive understanding. For example, if an angry person attacks, the enemy may flee. The successful attacking response may both reinforce the labeling of the affective state as "anger" and alter the original external stimulus to the affect.

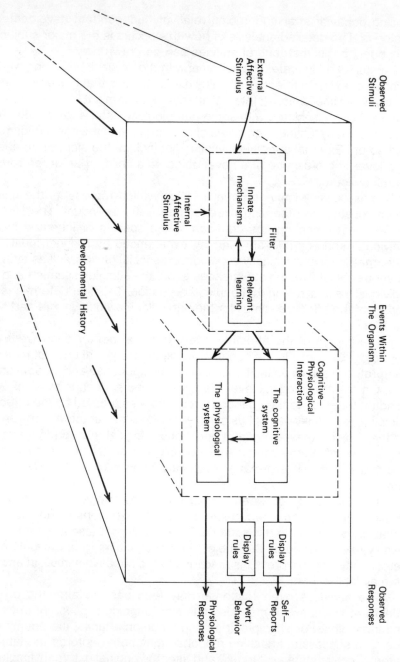

FIGURE 1.1   Human motivation and emotion: a descriptive schema.

The overt behavior of the individual is generally the major source of information to others about his affective state, although it is possible that an observer might attempt to assess his subjective experience or cognitive state by asking for self-reports (i.e. "Did that guy make you angry?" "Why did you act like that?"). Both overt behavior and self-reports may be influenced by the display rules. Under exceptional circumstances, the observer may assess the physiological state of the individual through special equipment. This schema includes the developmental history of the individual as a third dimension along which all of the factors described above—innate mechanisms, learning experiences, the cognitive system, and the physiological system—develop relatively independently of one another. For example, the nature of the cognitive understanding of an affective stimulus may change greatly as a child grows into young adulthood. Childish fears evaporate, new fears and concerns become manifest. His physiological reactions and perhaps certain innate mechanisms may also change as he goes through the period of puberty. All of these changes may contribute to the emotional turmoil that is often associated with adolescence, although not in any simple way. The overt behavior, self-reports, and physiological responses which are the observable manifestations of motivation and emotion are always the result of a complex interaction that takes place within the organism, mediated at most times by the learned display rules.

LEVELS OF OBSERVATION

As the schema suggests, there are three major levels for observing and measuring motivational and emotional states: the overt-behavioral level, self-report level, and physiological level. For example, if one is investigating the effects of fear-arousing situations, one might choose to measure escape and avoidance behavior or to ask the responder how fearful he feels or to measure the responder's state of physiological arousal. It is sometimes argued that, since overt behavior, self-report, and physiological responses presumably reflect the same affective process, they should vary together. For example, a person who shows strong avoidance behavior should also report feeling very fearful and he should have large physiological reactions. However, measures from these various levels of affective response often do not vary together. A person who reports feeling great fear may for example manifest smaller physiological responses than a person who admits feeling little fear. The whole question of the relationships between motivational and emotional events measured at different levels of observation is important and intriguing, and we shall return to it in Chapter 7. For the present, we shall briefly review some of the major recent trends in the study of motivation and emotion, which have resulted in a revolution in thinking about the basis of human and animal behavior.

Recent Developments in the Study of Motivation and Emotion

Psychologists have made significant advances in the understanding of emotional and motivational phenomena in the years since World War II. The fields in which these advances have been made can be grouped generally into the following: physiological approaches to behavior, ethology, the study of cognitive development and functioning, and the study of situational and social influences. What follows is a brief description of some of these advances. They will be considered more fully at appropriate places in this text.

PHYSIOLOGICAL APPROACHES TO BEHAVIOR

Brain Mechanisms and Behavior   A wide variety of techniques has been developed over the past decades to study brain functions, including new methods for recording the chemical and electrical activity of the brain, for temporarily or permanently deactivating or lesioning brain areas, and for stimulating the brain either electrically or chemically. The usual experimental technique is to alter brain activity in some way, often by lesioning or stimulating a particular brain area, and then to observe the effects of that manipulation on behavior. Thus, an experimenter might stimulate the brain of a fully fed animal in the presence of food and observe that the animal eats. Lesioning of the same brain area might cause a cessation of eating and starvation. Such observations suggest that that brain area is involved in hunger motivation.

The use of these techniques has greatly increased our understanding of the brain. However, it should be stressed that this knowledge is still primitive and fragmentary: the brain remains an immensely complex riddle, notwithstanding some popularized accounts which tend to overstate our understanding of, and ability to control, the brain (cf. Valenstein, 1973, for a discussion of the popular view of brain research).

Despite our lack of basic understanding of the brain, the fragmentary knowledge gained from animal research has been used, and sometimes perhaps misused, in clinical applications to humans. The widespread use of frontal lobotomy—the cutting off of parts of the frontal lobes from the rest of the brain—followed a report that such operations might reduce anxiety in monkeys. A bold psychiatrist attempted the operation on 20 mental patients and published an enthusiastic report of the effects. It was only after many years, and tens of thousands of operations, that it became clear that frontal lobotomies have a wide variety of detrimental effects (Rylander, 1973; Valenstein, 1973). The new techniques of brain recording, stimulation, and lesioning, plus the new knowledge gained from animal experimentation, have contributed to what Rylander (1973) calls a "renaissance of psychosurgery." A growing number of workers have attempted to apply these new techniques to humans, particularly in the control of muscular tremor, intractible pain, epileptic seizures, psychiatric disorders, and aggression. Some of these attempts have been clearly successful. Others, particularly those involved in the control of psychiatric disorders and aggression, have stirred much controversy. We shall consider this further below.

The Growth of Psychophysiology   The typical psychophysiological experiment reverses the procedure of the typical experiment on brain mechanisms outlined above. Instead of manipulating the physiological event and observing its effects on behavior, the psychophysiologist usually causes some cognitive, emotional, or behavioral event to occur and observes the resulting physiological changes (Sternbach, 1965). For example, an experimenter might tell a person that he is going to receive a painful electric shock and observe the subsequent changes in heart rate, blood pressure, skin conductivity, and so forth. An important aspect of such experiments is that they can, and usually do, employ human rather than animal subjects. They can therefore study the complex interactions between cognitive, social, and situational variables and physiological responding.

The physiological changes studied by the psychophysiologist are usually measured and recorded by a polygraph, a general-purpose machine capable of amplifying a variety of electrical signals from the body and recording them onto moving paper, magnetic tape, or special processing equipment. The development of relatively inexpensive and highly reliable polygraphs, plus the standardization of recording techniques, has done much to contribute to the growth of psychophysiology.

Biofeedback   Also contributing to the interest in psychophysiology has been the discovery that, if people are given information (feedback) about certain physiological responses, they can often learn to alter those responses to some extent. It is difficult to distinguish or make fine discriminations about most events going on in the interior of the body. Our skin, skeletal muscles, tendons, and so on are well endowed with sensory nerves which transmit much information, so that we can tell, for example, where our hand is when we are not looking at it. In contrast, our internal visceral organs (stomach, lungs, intestines, etc.) have relatively few sensory nerves. We can rarely feel food in the stomach or the peristaltic movements of the intestines or the speed of the heart.

Experiments in biofeedback have suggested that a person given feedback by a polygraph can learn to speed or slow his heart, raise or lower his blood pressure, alter peristaltic activity, alter patterns of electrical activity in the brain, or control the activities of certain skeletal muscles that are normally difficult to control. Many of these physiological responses are involved in the reaction to stress and emotion, and they contribute to certain organic disorders, including some kinds of ulcers, headaches, high blood pressure, and so forth. It is possible that biofeedback techniques may come to have significant clinical and therapeutic applications. It would be quite significant, for example, if a person could learn to control his heart rate or blood pressure voluntarily. There have been many reports—some encouraging, some discouraging—about the potential usefulness of biofeedback techniques for the treatment of different disorders. We shall consider some of these in Chapter 4.

Developments in Psychopharmacology   Developments in technique and methodology have also contributed to the understanding of the chemical basis of behavior, and indeed of life itself. In the late 1940s and early 1950s, important hormones were isolated, synthesized, and put to clinical use, and a wide variety of psychoactive drugs has been developed. The mode of action of many of these hormones and drugs is poorly understood. Most have come into use by means of pragmatic clinical test: they have been found to produce certain effects in animals or humans, and after an evaluation of their safety, major effects, and side effects, they have been certified for use.

In recent years, more has become known about the mode of action of many of these drugs, although they are still far from being fully understood. Some of this knowledge has emerged from basic research in cellular processes and the chemistry of living tissues. Knowledge of the mode of action of psychoactive drugs has great theoretical and practical importance: it both illuminates the biochemistry of the normally functioning nervous system and it makes it possible that much more specific and effective drugs, with fewer side effects, can be developed.

ETHOLOGY

During the course of evolution, some behavior patterns are adaptive to the survival of a species, while others are maladaptive. According to the theory of evolution, individuals showing the adaptive behavior patterns tend to have higher survival rates and are more likely to reproduce themselves than other individuals, so that during the course of evolution each species evolves a characteristic set of behavior patterns just as it evolves a particular physical appearance. Ethology involves the study of this evolution of behavior, often through the prolonged observation of animal and human behavior in naturally occurring situations. This emphasis upon the evolution of behavior and the methodology of naturalistic observation represents a new approach to the study of innate or instinctive behaviors, and the ethologists have contributed an increased appreciation of the complexity of animal behavior and the analogies and possible relationships between human and animal behavior.

The Social Behavior of Nonhuman Primates   This contribution is particularly evident in the study of the social behavior of nonhuman primates, particularly monkeys and apes. For many years, our conception of the social behavior of these creatures derived from the observation of animals confined in zoos (Ardrey, 1966). Such animals show a great deal of bizarre sexual behavior, which led many to conclude that a strong sexual drive is the source of attraction underlying the social organization of monkeys and apes. However, studies of groups of animals in the wild, using the techinique of naturalistic observation, did not find an exaggerated concern with sex (cf. Carpenter, 1965). Instead, it became clear that a complex social organization exists in groups of monkeys and apes which is quite useful to the survival of the species. Also, these animals showed unexpected intelligence and sophistication in the wild, demonstrating the ability both to use and apparently to make tools. In addition, experiments showed that the social skills of monkeys require much social experience in infancy and early childhood in order to develop into normally socialized adults. Monkeys deprived of early social experience show striking abnormalities. More recent experiments have shown that at least one kind of ape, the chimpanzee, has significant symbolic and linguistic capabilities. All of these observations have narrowed the apparent gap between human social behavior and that of the monkeys and apes.

With this new perspective, some began to take the view that social behavior arose in the evolution of the primate line as an adaptation to the prevailing conditions of life, that, in the primate, behavior patterns associated with social behavior evolved just as did their excellent eyes, brains, and efficient grasping hands. This raised the question of the extent to which human social behavior may be based upon built-in mechanisms acquired during the course of evolution. Some have suggested that much human social behavior, from aggressive and sexual acts to complex sociopolitical structures and practices, reflect our ancient mammalian and primate biological heritage.

Human Social Evolution   Drawing upon the new understanding of the social behavior of nonhuman primates, plus new fossil evidence about human evolution, more or less detailed scenarios of human social evolution have been suggested (cf. Washburn, 1961; Lorenz, 1966; Morris, 1967). Such a scenario must begin by a consideration of the geological changes that created the environment in which human evolution occurred (see Figure 1.2). Sixty million years ago, the earth was covered by tropical forests and swamps. (The climate was much more constant that it has been in recent times: there were no spasms of glaciation comparable to those that have occurred within the past few million years.) In these lush surrounding, forest-dwelling monkeys and apes evolved. About 30 million years ago, the earth's temperature began to fall gradually, perhaps as a

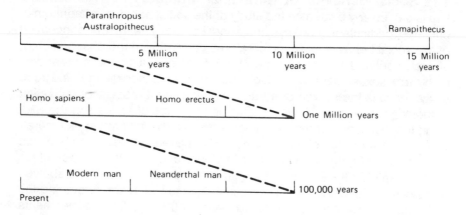

FIGURE 1.2   An outline of human evolution. At present the fossil record of human evolution is incomplete. Almost no fossil evidence exists for some of the most important stages. For example, there is little evidence regarding the evolution of the ground-dwelling ape. A few bones of the human-like primate *Ramapithecus*, dating from about 15 million years ago, have been found in Africa and India. A 10-million-year gap then occurs in the fossil record until the appearance of the hominid *Australopithecus* in eastern and southern Africa. *Australopithecus* lived between 1 and 5 million years ago, and apparently made and used pebble tools. They may have lived near other species of prehumans, such as *Paranthropus*. A recent find has been made of "1470 Man," a possibly tool-using creature of the genus *Homo* who lived about 2.8 million years ago (Leaky, 1973). The next sure link in the hazy chain of human evolution is *Homo erectus*, who used fire and traveled from a probable origin in Africa throughout Africa and Asia. *Homo erectus* lived about 750,000 years ago. *Homo sapiens* appeared about 250,000 years ago. Neanderthal is an extinct subspecies of *Homo sapiens* who lived throughout Europe 75,000 years ago, leaving evidence of a complex culture and religion. Modern human beings appeared about 40,000 years ago, although another recent find in Africa of an apparently modern human may be 100,000 years old. The site of this find contained fragments of chipped bone suggestive of an ability to count and a ceremonial infant burial suggesting a belief in an afterlife.

result of changes in wind currents associated with mountain-building activities. About 12 million years ago, the earth's climate became drier and drought ravaged many of the tropical forests. The forests shrank away toward the equator, where they remain today. With the forests went the forest-dwelling apes, whose numbers dwindled with the size of their habitat. Today only four species of forest ape exist: the gibbon, the orangutan, the gorilla, and humanity's closest living relative, the chimpanzee.

It is thought that as the forests receded, some apes gradually became adapted to life on the drier savannahs. These ground apes must have lived a most difficult and dangerous life. They did not have the ability to digest the tough grasses of the savannah, as the specialized herbivores could, and they did not have the speed, strength, and natural weapons of the specialized carnivores. They did have the primate's good vision, good brain, efficient grasping hands, the ability to make simple tools, and, perhaps most important, social organization.

The environment of the savannah created a situation where adaptation was extremely difficult and poorly adapted individuals soon perished. For these reasons the process of evolutionary change was unusually rapid. The upright posture, changes in the hands, and the increase in the complexity of the brain occurred, and some have suggested that certain kinds of social organization developed. For example, it has been suggested that the rigors of the hunt and the increasing dependence of the infant led to the emergence of the sex roles: the physically stronger males, unencumbered by pregnancy, went out on the hunt while the females protected and educated the infants and young. Since those individuals who were best adapted to these roles tended to have a higher survival rate, it is argued that this could have resulted in the development or exaggeration of differences in temperament between male and female humans.

This scenario of human social evolution, and others like it, have attracted much interest and controversy. Many of their suggestions seem plausible at first glance, although it is difficult to imagine how a single biologically based process common to the heritage of all peoples could account for the great diversity of social structures found around the world. Also, these suggestions are difficult or impossible to evaluate by objective evidence. Little evidence of social structure survives to allow examination by anthropologists, although some limited conclusions can be deduced from fossil tools, evidence of dwelling places, graves, and so forth.

Nonverbal Communication   One of the basic aspects of social life is the process of communication between individuals. The new interest in animal social organizations and their possible parallels with human society have contributed to the study of how animals and humans communicate with their fellows. Ethologists have demonstrated that much animal communication takes place by nonverbal behaviors, gestures, and facial expressions and that there are intriguing similarities between certain human gestures and expressions and those used by monkeys and apes. At the same time, clinical and social psychologists and psychiatrists have showed a renewed interest in human nonverbal communication, and important methodological advances have been made. It is becoming clear that the ability to accurately send and receive nonverbal messages is basic to the social life of both animals and humans.

COGNITIVE PSYCHOLOGY

Thus far this brief survey of recent developments in the study of motivation and emotion has emphasized the built-in "nonrational" determinants of behavior that are based upon biological mechanisms. However, advances have also been made in the understanding of rational determinants of behavior: the cognitive functions that involve the reception and processing of information and knowledge about oneself and the environment. During the 1930s and 1940s academic psychology was dominated by approaches stemming from Watson's behaviorism, which rejected cognitive variables as permissible subjects of study for science. It was argued that psychologists should confine their study to observable events, such as physical stimuli and overt responses. Since then, techniques have been developed which clearly demonstrate that it is possible and highly fruitful to study cognitive variables, given the proper methodology. For example, the development of the computer led to theories of information processing and flow which have been applied to cognitive psychology, and the computer itself has been used as a model to stimulate the human information processing system (Simon & Newell, 1956).

Piaget's Theory   One of the major influences upon contemporary cognitive psychology is Jean Piaget's analysis of cognitive development in children. Piaget first became interested in the special nature of the reasoning of children when he worked with Binet on the development of the first "intelligence" tests (Brown, 1965). Binet was interested in measuring individual differences in intelligence, which was measured in terms of how many questions a child failed on a standard test. Piaget noted that the children who got a wrong answer often had a reason for that answer, but the child's reasoning was faulty from the point of view of an adult. Piaget began to develop new kinds of measuring techniques to study the nature of the reasoning employed by the young child, and this led him to a different concept of intelligence and an analysis of children's thinking which has had an enormous influence upon contemporary developmental psychology.

Cognitive Theories in Social Psychology   Even during the dominant behavioristic trend of the 1930s and 1940s, the concerns of social psychologists with attitudes, values, group communication, and so on were uniquely suited for study at the cognitive level of analysis. Cognitive theories thus flourished in social psychology at a time when they were weak in other fields. These theories included Fritz Heider's balance theory and attribution theory and Leon Festinger's social comparison theory and cognitive dissonance theory. These investigators pioneered new techniques of experimentation and measurement which demonstrated that purely cognitive motives (i.e., a need for understanding, for cognitive consistency, for a sense of justice, etc.) can have widespread effects upon human behavior.

Cognitive-Physiological Interactions   It has become apparent that cognitive functions interact with the built-in physiological and biological determinants of behavior, although the detailed analysis of this interaction has only begun. Building upon the new theories and techniques for studying cognitive and physiological processes, Stanley Schachter, Richard Lazarus, and others have shown that cognitions interact with physiological states—physiological measures can be altered by manipulating cognitions, the subjectively experienced emotion can be altered by cognitive and physiological manipulations, and so forth. The notion of an interaction between cognitive and physiological factors is at the heart of Schachter's theory of emotion, which has been applied to a wide variety of emotional and motivational phenomena from obesity to threat to romantic love.

SOCIAL AND SITUATIONAL INFLUENCES

To this writer, the most significant single finding in psychology since World War II is the extent to which human behavior is subject to social and situational influences. The power of these influences has been greatly underrated in our culture among professional students of human behavior as well as laymen. We tend to see most human behavior as originating from motivational states within the individual. However, experiments by Solomon Asch, Stanley Milgram, and others have shown that social and situational pressures have unexpectedly powerful influences upon behavior. Asch showed that many people would give an obviously incorrect perceptual judgment in conformity to the judgments of others. Milgram found that most people would give what they thought to be extremely strong and painful electric shocks to a helpless and protesting victim in obedience to the orders of an experimenter.

These findings have added a basic new dimension to our conception of human nature. It appears that most normal people are quite capable of participating in cruel and perhaps murderous behavior under certain conditions. However, the same individuals are also capable of unusual self-sacrifice, courage, and generosity under other conditions. This is the paradox that is suggested by the findings on the importance of social and situational influences in human behavior: given the right circumstances, the same individual may act like a hero, a coward, a sadist, or a martyr. We shall return to the role of social influence at several points in this book.

Summary

Any human behavior must be seen as an outcome of a complex interaction between one's physiological state, biological heritage, the cognitions about oneself and the environment that has developed over the life of the individual, and present social and situational pressures. It is impossible to determine the nature of this interaction by observing a given kind of behavior with one given methodology: many kinds of behavior must be studied using a wide variety of approaches and methods. The following chapters will describe some contemporary approaches to the study of human motivation and emotion.

CHAPTER TWO

ADAPTATION, STRESS AND AROUSAL

Great strides have been made during recent years in studying the physiological bases of motivation and emotion. Psychologists and physiologists have developed techniques of electrical stimulation and recording that have unlocked many secrets of the nervous system. More recently developed techniques of chemical stimulation and assay hold promise of more advances, particularly in light of the rapidly increasing knowledge in basic biochemistry. However, only the tip of the iceberg has yet been revealed.

This chapter will consider the physiological systems responsible for the maintenance of orderly bodily functions—chiefly the autonomic nervous system and the endocrine system. According to Cannon's emergency theory and Selye's theory of adaptation, these systems respond in times of stress to arouse the body for emergencies. Also, as recent studies in psychosomatic medicine have demonstrated, these reactions can contribute to disease if the stress is too severe or continued over a long period of time. The chapter shall also examine the role played by the autonomic and endocrine systems in motivation and emotion, with particular reference to the controversy between the James–Lange theory of emotion and Cannon's theory and its possible resolution in Schachter's self-attribution theory. We shall then consider arousal theory, which grew out of Cannon's emergency theory and which involves the analysis of central nervous system mechanisms: the reticular activating system and the diffuse thalamic system.

Before we begin, let us define some terms that identify the gross structures of the nervous system. The *central nervous system* consists of the brain and spinal cord. The *peripheral nervous system* includes all of the nerves entering and leaving the brain and spinal cord: the sensory nerves entering from various sense organs and the motor nerves leaving to various effectors such as the muscles and glands. The peripheral nervous system is divided into the *somatic nervous system*, including the sensory nerves from most receptors and motor nerves serving the skeletal muscles, and the *autonomic nervous system*, including the sensory and motor nerves serving heart, glands, and smooth muscles of the viscera. We will begin by looking briefly at the somatic nervous system, although most of our concern will be with autonomic functioning.

The Peripheral Nervous System

THE SOMATIC NERVOUS SYSTEM

In the spinal nerves, motor nerves emerge from the spinal cord in the ventral root, (toward the front of the body) and sensory nerves enter in the dorsal root (see Figure 2.1). The sensory nerves carry information from receptors throughout the skin, muscles, and tendons that are sensitive to stretch, pressure, pain, and temperature. The receptors convert this information to nerve impulses which are carried to the central nervous system. The motor nerves carry instructions from the central nervous system to the skeletal muscles. The instructions include commands for gross voluntary movements, for precise and finely articulated skilled movements, and for largely unconscious postures and gestures. These sensory and motor systems are integrated at several points in the central nervous system, including the spinal cord, cerebellum, and cerebral cortex. A good deal is known about this remarkable system that lets us walk without thinking about our legs, touch our forefingers together without looking at them, and learn complex and intricate skills, although we would go too far afield if we discussed them here. Even the simple act of contracting a muscle involves a complex servomechanism that integrates sensory information and motor commands (see Merton, 1972).

THE AUTONOMIC NERVOUS SYSTEM

The autonomic nervous system is particularly important in the physiological regulation of emotion and motivation. It is, along with the endocrine system, one of the mechanisms by which the central nervous system regulates the internal environment of the body. The central nervous system affects the autonomic nervous system largely through the hypothalamus, a region of the brain which we shall consider in detail in the next chapter. One function of the autonomic nervous system is to help maintain homeostasis, a constant internal environment within the body that supports life. Another function involves adaptation, or preparing the body for emergencies and stress by activating bodily defense mechanisms. These functions of homeostasis and adaptation are largely involuntary and unconscious.

The autonomic nervous system contains two branches, the *sympathetic nervous system* and the *parasympathetic nervous system*. Most autonomically innervated structures are affected by both branches, and the actions of the two branches are usually antagonistic. Thus, sympathetic activation dilates the pupils while parasympathetic stimulation constricts them. Table 2.1 lists most of the autonomically innervated structures and the effects on them of sympathetic and parasympathetic stimulation. The sympathetic branch is activated primarily by the posterior hypothalamus, while the parasympathetic is activated primarily by the anterior hypothalamus.

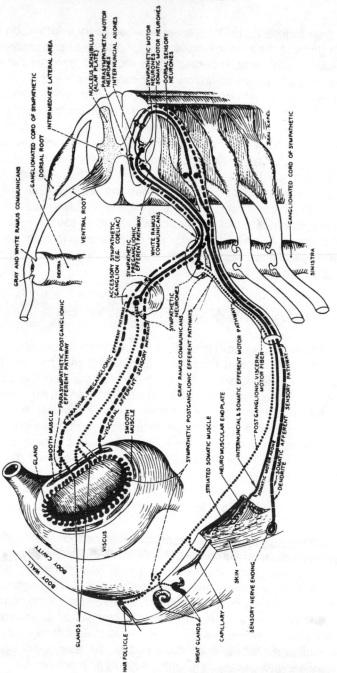

FIGURE 2.1   Somatic and autonomic motor pathways. From H. S. Rubenstein, *The study of the brain*. New York: Grune and Stratton, 1953. Copyright © 1953 by Grune and Stratton. Reprinted by permission of the publisher.

TABLE 2.1   SOME EFFECTS OF AUTONOMIC STIMULATION.

EFFECTOR	SYMPATHETIC STIMULATION	PARASYMPATHETIC STIMULATION
1. Iris of eye	Dilation	Constriction
2. Lacrimal Glands	?	Secretion—tears
3. Salivary Glands	Sparse, thick, viscous secretion.	Profuse, secretion
4. Lungs (Bronchia)	Relaxation, dilation	Contraction
5. Heart	Increase heart rate	Decrease heart rate, vagal arrest
6. Blood Vessels:		
Skin and mucosa	Vasoconstriction	Some vasodilation?
Skeletal muscle and viscera	Vasoconstriction and vasodilation	?
7. Stomach and intestines	Motility and tone decreased, sphincters contracted, secretion inhibited (?).	Motility and tone increased, sphincters relaxed, secretion stimulated.
8. Sweat Glands	Secretion	Not innervated
9. Pilomotor Musc.	Contraction	Not innervated
10. Adrenal Medulla	Discharge of epinepherine and norepinepherine	Not innervated
11. Fat Deposits	Fat & fatty acids released into blood	Not innervated
12. Liver	Glucose released into blood	Not innervated?
13. Spleen	Contraction	Not innervated
14. Pancreas	Not innervated	Secretion, including insulin
15. Urinary Bladder	Relaxation of wall, contraction of sphincters	(Contraction of wall, relaxation of sphincters
16. Sex Organs	Loss of erection	Erection

The parasympathetic and sympathetic nervous systems are active in a dynamic state of balance in which the actions of one may be stronger than those of the other. Because of their antagonistic effects, it is sometimes meaningful (although oversimplified) to speak of sympathetic or parasympathetic "dominance." When the sympathetic is dominant, the sympathetic effects shown in Table 2.1 are manifest and the parasympathetic effects are inhibited, and vice versa.

Synaptic Transmission in the Autonomic Nervous System

A nerve cell influences other cells by secreting small amounts of chemical transmitter substances into the space separating it from the other cell. This space is called the synapse and the chemical substances are called *synaptic transmitters*. (See the Appendix, especially Figure A.1, for a discussion of the process of synaptic transmission). One of the major differences between the sympathetic and parasympathetic nervous systems lies in these synaptic transmitters. The synaptic transmitter in the parasympathetic nervous system is acetylcholine (ACh), a chemical that is quickly neutralized by the enzyme acetylcholinesterase (AChE) released by the nerve cell. Synaptic transmission using ACh as the synaptic transmitter is termed *cholinergic* transmission.

The major synaptic transmitter in the sympathetic nervous system is a chemical once called noradrenalin since it is also secreted by the inner portion of the adrenal gland (the adrenal medulla). The modern name for this substance is norepinepherine. Norepinepherine is not neutralized as quickly as is ACh, and it exists in considerable quantities outside the sympathetic nervous system nerve cells. In fact, norepinepherine and a closely related substance epinepherine (once called adrenalin) are both hormones released from the adrenal gland into the general circulation when stimulated by the sympathetic nervous system. Once in the bloodstream, these two hormones have effects on the body which are generally similar to the effects of sympathetic nervous system stimulation. Synaptic transmission using norepinepherine as the transmitter substance is termed *adrenergic* transmission

It has been suggested that the release of epinepherine and norepinepherine from the adrenal medulla provides a long-lasting chemical backup to the sympathetic nervous system. Sympathetic stimulation effects the body quickly, within seconds, but it is not designed to have long-lasting effects. The release of epinepherine and norepinepherine into the bloodstream may be a slower-acting but longer-lasting way to cause the same bodily changes. These changes appear to be important in preparing the body for emergency situations.

Cannon's Emergency Theory of Emotion   The   physiologist W.B. Cannon based his emergency theory of emotion on his extensive investigations into the functioning of the autonomic nervous system. Cannon argued that, in general, the parasympathetic branch has evolved to serve vegetative functions such as digestion and the buildup of energy reserves, while sympathetic activation prepares the physiological defense mechanisms of the body in what Cannon called the "fight of flight reaction" (Cannon, 1915, 1932). Cannon noted that when the sympathetic nervous system is dominant, breathing is faster and deeper, there is less secretion of mucus in the air passages, and the bronchioles of the lungs dilate. He suggested that these reactions function to increase the amount of oxygen coming into the body to fuel metabolism. At the same time, heart rate and the volume of blood pumped with each beat increase, certain blood vessels constrict, and blood pressure rises. This may function to divert blood from the inhibited viscera and intestines to the heart, brain, and skeletal muscles, increasing their blood supply. The sympathetic nervous system also acts to release norepinepherine and epinepherine from the medulla of the adrenal gland into the blood stream. These substances reinforce the sympathetic activation. For example, epinepherine functions to release stores of sugar from the liver, thus increasing the energy available to the muscles. "All of these changes," wrote Cannon, "are directly serviceable in rendering the organism more effective in the violent display of energy which fear or rage may involve" (Cannon 1932, p. 228).

The functions Cannon ascribes to the sympathetic nervous system are termed catabolic, in that they deplete energy reserves stored within the organism. The opposite functions are ascribed to the parasympathetic nervous system: the anabolic restoration of stored supplies. Such a buildup of energy stores takes place during sleep, when the parasympathetic nervous system is dominant. Heart rate, stroke volume, and blood pressure decrease, and the blood tends to be diverted to the viscera. In the gastrointestinal tract, digestive processes are increased and reserves of glycogen are built up in the liver from blood sugar. Mucus is produced in the mouth, nose, throat, and lungs (Sternbach, 1966).

A rapid onset of sympathetic arousal caused by sudden, intense stress can produce a compensatory flood of parasympathetic activation. This can result in involuntary defecation and urination, slowing or even stopping of the heart, and fainting. Fainting is caused by sudden drop in the blood supply to the brain due to the slowing of heart rate, dilation of blood vessels in the viscera, and consequent drop in blood pressure.

Cannon's theory has been criticized for presenting an incomplete and oversimplified picture of the functioning of the autonomic nervous system. For example, Arnold (1960) has argued that physiological events of the fight or flight reaction are debilitating rather than invigorating to the organism. Also, as we shall see, many autonomic functions long regarded as automatic and involuntary may in fact be quite modifiable and potentially controllable. We shall return to Cannon's theory and more recent conceptions of autonomic functioning later in the chapter.

When Cannon was analyzing the role of the autonomic nervous system in homeostasis and adaptation, he was not aware that another system, the endocrine system, also participates in these functions. Cannon felt that the adrenal gland was important because of the sympathetic-like effects of norepinepherine and epinepherine from the adrenal medulla. We now know that the outer layer of the adrenal gland, the adrenal cortex, is also essential in the maintenance of homeostasis and the adaptation to stress. Unlike the adrenal medulla, which is under nervous system control, the adrenal cortex is controlled chemically.

The Endocrine System

The *endocrine* or ductless glands release chemical substances, called hormones, into the bloodstream. The central nervous system controls the endocrine system by way of neurochemical feedback loops involving the hypothalamus and the pituitary gland. The essential components of this feedback process have been described by Scharrer (1966). The central nervous system receives and integrates information affecting endocrine functions. This may include sensory information from the environment, interoceptive information from the body, feedback from hormones in the bloodstream, and built-in behavior patterns and biological rhythms which may differ from species to species. The central nervous system then exerts appropriate control over the endocrine system, largely through the connection between the hypothalamus of the brain and the pituitary gland. The pituitary secretes hormones into the bloodstream, some of which cause other endocrine glands to secrete particular hormones. The central nervous system apparently senses the presence of these hormones, most often through the hypothalamus which is very liberally supplied with blood vessels. As the concentration of hormones builds up, the pituitary and thus the other endocrine glands are "turned off."

An illustration of the feedback system involving the pituitary and adrenal cortex is presented in Figure 2.2. Information about a stressful event

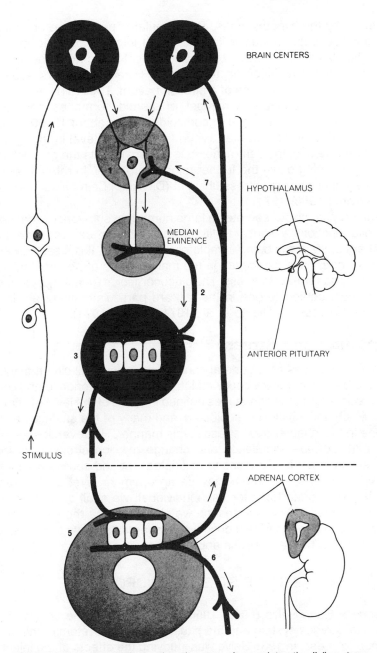

FIGURE 2.2   The pituitary-adrenal system. Appropriate stimuli (i.e. stress stimuli) activate neurosecretory cells in the hypothalamus (1), causing them to release corticotropin releasing factor (CRF) via short blood vessels (2) into the anterior lobe of the pituitary gland (3). Pituitary cells then release adrenocorticotropic hormone (ACTH) into the bloodstream (4). The ACTH stimulates the cells of the adrenal cortex (5) to secrete corticoid hormones into the bloodstream (6). The level of corticoids in the bloodstream in turn regulate CRF production (7). From S. Levine, "Stress and behavior," Copyright © 1971 by Scientific American, Inc. All rights reserved.

is received by the hypothalamus. This stimulates neurosecretory cells to release corticotropin releasing factors (CRF) into the local bloodstream which stimulates the release of adrenocortical-tropic-hormone (ACTH) into the general circulation. In the rat, ACTH release occurs about 10 seconds after the occurrence of a stressful event. The ACTH acts on the adrenal cortex to secrete a number of steroid hormones collectively termed corticoids. The release of corticoids occurs about 15–60 minutes after a stressful event in the rat. When the corticoid level in the blood is appropriately raised, the central nervous system inhibits the production of CRF, thus shutting down the further release of ACTH. In rats this occurs at least an hour after the stressful event (DiGiusto, Cairncross, and King, 1971; Levine, 1968; 1971).

The adrenal cortex secretes a large number of substances that serve metabolic functions essential to life. Some of these are still unidentified and others are far from being completely understood. It is clear, however, that these hormones participate in the maintenance of homeostasis and in the bodily adaptation to stress. The glucocorticoids (primarily hydrocortisone in man, corticosterone in the rat) are particularly important in the response to stress (Di Giusto et al., 1971; Levine, 1971).

Adaptation and Stress

We shall treat stress as a general concept embracing all circumstances, good and bad, that require bodily adaptation by the autonomic and endocrine systems. Stress is sometimes defined in terms of the level of stimulation to which an individual is subjected, and many of the studies we shall examine in this chapter treat stress in this manner. However, it should be noted that too *little* stimulation and change may be stressful to some individuals in that it is experienced as unpleasant and causes autonomic and endocrine arousal. There may be an optimum level of stimulation which is most comfortable for each individual: we shall consider this in detail in Chapter 8. For the present, we shall examine the nature of the autonomic and endocrine repsonse which adapts the body to stress, and the relationship between stress and disease.

SELYE'S STRESS SYNDROME

The work of Hans Selye (1950; 1956) has illuminated the action of the autonomic nervous system and the pituitary–adrenal system in the bodily response to stress. In 1935 Selye was studying the effects of the injection of certain hormones in rats. They became sick and showed similar symptoms, including enlarged adrenal glands, shrunken thymus glands and lymph nodes, and ulceration in the stomach. Selye initially thought that the effects were due to the nature of the hormone, but he found that, strangely, the effects were greater when he used impure preparations of the hormone. Finally, he injected formalin, a simple irritant, and found the same effects. Selye deduced that the common element in the hormone preparations and formalin was that they were both impurities that irritated the organism. He then put animals in other situations that caused severe strains on the body, such as resisting cold, drugs, and diseases. He found the same effects, which he called the "stress syndrome." He concluded that the symptoms he discovered were due to a nonspecific bodily reaction that is common to all stress (Selye, 1956).

To Selye, stress occurs to the extent that normal homeostatic regulatory mechanisms of the body fail to adapt to a situation. Any situation may be stressful if the organism is unable to easily adapt to it. Selye's analysis resembles Cannon's emergency theory but extends it by showing the role of the endocrine system as well as the autonomic nervous system.

Selye (1956) distinguishes three states in the response to stress (see Figure 2.3). The first, acute stage is the *alarm reaction*. The initial shock phase of the alarm reaction is characterized by a drop in bodily resistance to the stress. It involves autonomic arousal and discharge of norepinepherine and epinepherine from the adrenal medulla, as well as an increasing release of ACTH and corticoids. If the stress is too severe, the organism may die during the shock phase of the alarm reaction. If the stress is not that severe, but continues, the second countershock phase of the alarm reaction is initiated. The ACTH and corticoid response cause the characteristic signs of the stress syndrome to appear, including adrenal enlargement, shrinkage of the thymus and lymph nodes, and ulceration. During the countershock phase, the resistance to the stress increases above normal as more specific local defenses are prepared. Selye suggests that the events of the alarm reaction function to maintain life while these "local adaptive responses" are organized.

The second stage in the response to stress is the *state of resistance*. The most appropriate local channel of defense against the stress has been organized and the generalized stress response is no longer necessary. Corticoid activity falls to almost normal levels and the symptoms of the stress syndrome disappear. For example, a man who enters a cold environment may, after a period of suffering, acquire physiological responses that help him adapt to chronic cold. Such local adaptive responses may successfully eliminate the source of stress. However, if irritation persists for a very long time, the ability of the local adaptive responses to contain the stress and respond to new stress eventually break down, in which case the final *stage of exhaustion* occurs. The

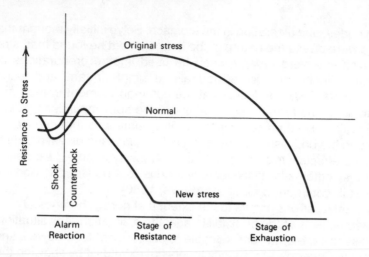

FIGURE 2.3 The general adaptation syndrome. Under prolonged stress, initial shock and countershock reactions may be followed by a stage of resistance and then a stage of exhaustion that culminates in death. Adding a new stress to the original one may accelerate the process. The Physiology and Pathology of Exposure to Stress by Selye; figure on p. 55. North Holland Publishing Company: 1950. Reprinted by permission of the publisher.

pituitary-adrenal system is again activated, corticoid level rises, and the symptoms of the stress syndrome reappear. This reaction may prolong survival for a time, but gradually the resistance to the stress declines. Recovery is no longer possible if the stress continues, and death eventually follows.

This final decline in resistance may actually be due in part to the reappearance of the pituitary and adrenal hormones. The high corticoid level may itself come to be stressful after the organism is sufficiently weakened. Selye uses the term "disease of adaptation" to describe a disorder that results as much from the body's attempts to deal with stress as it does from external agents such as infection (Selye, 1956, pp. 66–67). For example, ACTH and corticoids may increase the secretion of gastric acid and pepsin in the stomach and alter the stomach's resistance to these secretions, resulting in ulceration (Di Giusto et al., 1971).

Work on the medical application of the pituitary-adrenal hormones has proceeded since the mid-1930s. It was spurred in the United States during World War II by the (false) rumor that German fliers were being given adrenal-cortical hormones to resist the effects of fatigue and low oxygen. In the late 1940s, ACTH and the adrenal corticoid cortisone were finally isolated in sufficient quantities for clinical tests. Reports of the successful treatment of widely different disorders soon followed, stirring considerable excitement in the medical community. Unrelated diseases with different patterns of symptoms, including acute asthma, rheumatoid arthritis, pneumonia, and rheumatic fever, often showed dramatic relief of symptoms following treatment with cortisone and ACTH (Gray, 1950).

Unfortunately, this initial optimism was tempered because of the unusually severe side effects of the hormones. High blood pressure, headaches, confused mental states ranging from moodiness to psychosis, and lowered resistance to infection were encountered as some of the side effects of large prolonged doses. Also, the hormone treatments did not cure the disease but only removed the symptoms. When the treatment was discontinued, the symptoms usually returned (Keeton, 1967). Nevertheless, the effects of the hormones demonstrated the participation of the pituitary–adrenal system in a wide variety of disorders and they seriously challenged the long medical practice of compartmentalizing particular diseases with particular causes. As we shall see, the effects of this challenge to medical philosophy are still being felt.

HORMONAL RESPONDING AND FEAR

Recent studies on the behavioral effects of ACTH and the adrenal hormones shed light on how autonomic and endocrine responding works in helping the organism to cope with fear-inducing situations. Fear is often investigated experimentally by studying escape and avoidance behavior. As a typical experiment, let us assume that an animal is put in a shuttle box which is divided into two compartments. Each compartment has a grid floor which can be electrified, delivering a painful shock. A signal such as a light or sound is activated, and a few seconds later the grid on which the animal is standing is electrified. The shock arouses the animal, and he runs about. Most animals soon escape the painful shock by running into the opposite compartment. Presently, the signal is sounded again and that compartment is electrified, and the animal must cross into the original compartment to escape. Eventually, most animals learn to cross into the opposite compartments as soon as the signal is presented, thus avoiding the shock completely. If the shock is then discontinued, so that the animal is not shocked when it fails to respond to the signal, the avoidance response will usually stop or extinguish gradually.

Di Giusto, Cairncross, and King (1971), in a review of studies on the hormonal effects on fear responding, suggest that the fast-acting sympathetic–adrenal medulla system may facilitate the initial acquisition of appropriate responses to fearful situations. For example, Wynne and Solomon (1955) found that sympathectomy (destruction of the sympathetic nervous system) retarded the learning of escape and avoidance responses. However, this system may become less important once the animal has learned an avoidance response, because sympathectomy and destruction of the adrenal medulla do not appear to affect avoidance performance once initial learning has taken place (Moyer and Brunell, 1959; Moyer and Korn, 1965).

There is no conclusive evidence that ACTH or the glucocorticoids affect acquisition, but they do have strong effects on the extinction, of avoidance responses. Murphey and Miller (1955) demonstrated slower extinction when animals were injected with ACTH, and Miller and Ogawa (1962) reported the same effect in adrenalectomized rats. A series of studies by De Weid and his colleagues (1966; 1967) indicated that, while ACTH does indeed slow the extinction of avoidance responding, the glucocorticoids appear to facilitate extinction. These results and others led Di Giusto et al (1971) to suggest that ACTH prolongs the occurrence of fear-motivated behavior, probably by enhancing fear motivation itself. Thus, while the sympathetic–adrenal medulla system may facilitate the initial acquisition of behavior that effectively copes with fear, ACTH may contribute to the motivation of such coping behavior once it has been acquired (see Table 2.2). The glucocorticoids from the adrenal cortex may then provide a switch-off mechanism, in some way counteracting the effects of ACTH so that unnecessary coping behavior may be extinguished (Weiss, McEwen, Teresa, Silva, and Kalkut, 1969). Whatever their mechanism of action, ACTH and glucocorticoids are related to effective avoidance behavior once the avoidance response has been acquired (cf Brain, 1972: Davidson and Levine, 1971).

TABLE 2.2   EFFECT OF PERIPHERAL MECHANISMS ON THE ACQUISITION AND EXTINCTION OF ESCAPE AND AVOIDANCE BEHAVIOR.

	EFFECT ON ACQUISITION	EFFECT ON EXTINCTION	POSSIBLE FUNCTION
Sympathetic-Adrenal Medulla	Facilitates	No effect	Facilitates acquisition of coping behavior
ACTH	No effect	Inhibits	Maintain coping behavior once acquired
Glucocorticoids	No effect	Facilitates	Allow unnecessary coping behavior to drop out

NOREPINEPHERINE AND EPINEPHERINE IN ANGER AND FEAR

It should be recalled that norepinepherine is the major transmitter substance of the sympathetic nervous system and that both epinepherine and norephinepherine are released into the bloodstream by the adrenal medulla. A number of studies have suggested that norepinepherine secretion may be related to anger and aggression, while epinepherine may be associated with fear and anxiety (Schildkrault and Kety, 1967). The physiological effects of injections of epinepherine and norepinepherine are generally quite similar, but there are some differences. For example, norepinepherine produces a large rise in diastolic blood pressure and a fall in heart rate, while epinepherine produces a large rise in systolic blood pressure and a rise in heart rate (See the Appendix). The first experiments demonstrating the roles of these substances in anger and fear used these cardiovascular measures and others to study epinepherine and norepinepherine indirectly.

Ax (1953) and J. Schachter (1957) put subjects in situations designed to elicit fear or anger while they took a variety of physiological measures. For example, Ax insulted his subjects with a rude and arrogant polygraph operator to elicit anger and frightened them with unexpected shocks and sparks in the measuring apparatus. Both studies suggested that the physiological response to the fear situation was generally similar to the response caused by an injection of epinepherine, while the response to the anger situation was more like that caused by norepinepherine. Funkenstein, King, and Drolette (1957) put their subjects in provoking situations and rated their response as overtly angry or anxious and depressed. The angry subjects had norepinepherine-like patterns of physiological response, while the anxious subjects had epinepherine-like patterns.

More recent studies have taken direct measures of epinepherine and norepinepherine. Elmadjian, Hope, and Lamson (1967) found greater increases in norepinepherine in hockey players active in a game, while players watching the game showed more epinepherine. The same investigators found high norepinepherine in psychiatric patients during aggressive outbursts and high epinepherine in patients during staff conferences. Finally, Silverman and Cohen (1960) found that, when deliberately provoked prior to a stress experience in a centrifuge, persons who openly showed anger had increased norepinepherine in their urine, while those who showed anxiety had elevated epinepherine. Interestingly, one subject who reacted with anxiety in the centrifuge stress situation and anger in a different situation showed high epinepherine in the former situation and high norepinepherine in the latter (Silverman, Cohen, Shmavonian, and Kirshner, 1961).

Funkenstein (1955), summarizing the finding of assays of the adrenal medulla of different animal species, reported that norepinepherine seems to predominate in the adrenal medulla of predatory animals such as lions, while epinepherine predominates in domestic animals, social animals like the baboon, and animals whose survival depends on flight, such as the rabbit. He also stated that norepinepherine is dominant in the adrenal medulla of young children, but that epinepherine becomes dominant at a later age, leaving us to ponder what relationships there might be between young children and lions *versus* rabbits, cattle, baboons, and adults.

This relationship between epinepherine-norepinepherine and fear and aggression seems fairly well established, but the mechanisms underlying the relationship are not yet understood. It may well be a secondary result of a process in the central nervous system. Gellhorn (1967) has suggested that parasympathetic dominance may be related to a high epinepherine-to-norepinepherine ratio and fear, and that sympathic dominance may underlie a low epinepherine-to-norepinepherine ratio and aggression and that this balance may be determined in the hypothalamus.

Stress and Disease

We have considered several ways by which the body responds to stressful circumstances. Figure 2.4 presents a summary of these reactions. A stressor, acting through central nervous system mechanisms, affects the hypothalamus. The hypothalamus initiates responding in the autonomic nervous system, affecting the body within seconds both directly through autonomic motor fibres and indirectly through the release of epinepherine and norepinepherine from the adrenal medulla. The hypothalamus also causes the release of ACTH from the pituitary. The ACTH response is slower than the autonomic response, but it is more lasting. As the ACTH builds up it releases glucocorticoids from the adrenal cortex. The glucocorticoids build up gradually and appear to reach a ceiling. Further ACTH cannot liberate more glucocorticoids above this ceiling level, but it may prolong the secretion of glucocorticoids. The glucocorticoids provide the muscles with long-term access into the energy stores of the body, and they may also aid in the conversion of epinepherine in the adrenal medulla (Wurtman and Axelrod, 1965). These reactions are of central importance to psychosomatic medicine, the branch of medicine concerned with the interaction of psychological and somatic factors in disease. For the emergency "fight or flight" reactions that apparently proved so useful through the course of evolution may at times be maladaptive, particularly for humans. People who habitually fight or flee from their problems often wind up in jails or mental hospitals. In others the physiological reactions associated with the emergency response may put the body under strain which can lead to illness and even death.

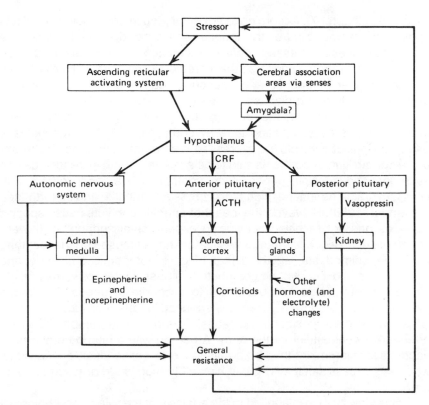

FIGURE 2.4   Summary of the bodily response to a stressor. See text for explanation.

PSYCHOSOMATIC MEDICINE

The relationship between stress and bodily symptoms has long been recognized. In 1628, William Harvey wrote that, "Every affection of the mind that is attended with either pain or pleasure, hope or fear is the cause of an agitation whose influence extends to the heart" (Quoted in Hunter and McAlpine, 1963). However, psychological factors in disease were long minimized by scientific medicine, perhaps in part as a reaction against early concepts of disease that blamed illness upon malevolent spiritual powers (Kaplan, 1972). After Freud, the importance of emotion in producing mental and physical symptoms was more widely accepted. Franz Alexander (1950) combined Freud's theory and Cannon's studies of autonomic functioning in his analysis of psychosomatic disease.

One of the cornerstones of Freud's theory is the process of repression, in which the individual avoids a conflict by forcing it into unconsciousness (See Chapter 7). According to the theory, such unconscious conflicts appear in dreams, slips of the tongue, and other disguised forms. The presence of these repressed conflicts is signaled to the conscious person by anxiety. Alexander suggested that chronic anxiety caused by repressed conflicts trigger autonomic and endocrine reactions which can lead to organ dysfunction and disease.

Alexander confronts the problem of why people get some symptoms and not others by suggesting that, by some still unknown mechanism, different kinds of conflicts are expressed in different symptoms. For example, a certain kind of conflict is said to be associated with increased gastric secretion and possible peptic ulcer, another with asthma, others with colitis, migraine headache, high blood pressure, arthritis, and so forth (see Alexander, 1950). However, the idea that specific conflicts cause specific illnesses has not received convincing experimental support. In the absence of such evidence, many investigators have focused on the fact that, as Selye pointed out, anything that triggers autonomic and endocrine responses could if continued contribute to illness. In this view, the physiological system reacts nonspecifically to a source of stress. The organ system affected, and the illness experienced by the individual, is determined by the predispositions and habits of the particular person: the stress affects the weakest link of the body. A person with a high natural rate of gastric secretion might thus be predisposed to peptic ulcer, an individual who uses excess salt may dispose himself to high blood pressure, and so forth.

This view has been applied to the analysis of the role of psychological factors in a wide variety of disorders. Alexander focused upon a relatively small number of psychosomatic disorders such as peptic ulcer, asthma, and so on in which psychological factors seemed to be the major cause of the disease. However, this suggests a misleading distinction between psychologically caused illnesses and other illnesses in which, by implication, psychological factors are relatively unimportant. The more recent conceptions of psychosomatic medicine have emphasized the interaction of somatic and psychological factors in all illnesses (Engel, 1967). This interaction is seen clearly in the effects of life changes on illness patterns.

LIFE CHANGES AND ILLNESS

Numerous studies dating from the late 1950s demonstrated that disease involves more than the exposure to bacteria and virus, improper diet and exercise, metabolic malfunctions, and so forth. Even when such conditions are the immediate causes of illness, it appears that they are most effective in producing illness when the bodily defenses of the individual are weakened. Selye's analysis suggests that such weakening occurs when the defenses have been engaged in adapting to stress over a long period of time. However, when the defenses of the body are mobilized by sudden crisis, disease should decline for a short time.

One of the first suggestions that various illnesses are related to stress was the discovery of illness clusters: within a few years an individual may experience a wide range of illnesses of various causes involving a variety of bodily systems (Hinkle and Wolff, 1958). These illness clusters seem to be related to the individual's adaptation to his current life situation (Hinkle et al., 1958; Wolff, 1962). One of the most common events calling for adaptation by the individual is a change in one's life. Such changes may be seen by the individual as positive (a raise, marriage, an outstanding personal achievement, etc.) or negative (the death of a friend or family member, divorce or separation, being fired, etc.). Studies have related such life changes to the occurrence of a wide variety of illnesses, including cancer, coronary disease, tuberculosis, skin disease, hernia, and so on (cf. Hinkle, 1961; Graham and Stevenson, 1963; Wyler, Masuda, and Holmes, 1971).

In an attempt to quantify the concept of life change, Holmes, Rahe and their colleagues developed the Social Readjustment Rating Scale (SRRS), upon which judges rated the amount of readjustment necessitated by 43 life events (Holmes and Rahe, 1967). Studies using different age and cultural groups as judges and different methods of scaling the judgments showed considerable agreement about the seriousness of these life events (Komaroff, Masuda, and Holmes, 1968; Harmon, Masuda, and Holmes, 1971; Ruch and Holmes, 1971). Table 2.3 shows the ratings given by 211 college students and 394 older adults (Ruch and Holmes, 1971). Using the rating values derived from the SRRS, a questionnaire called the Schedule of Recent Experience (SRE) which quantifies the recent life events of an individual was developed (Rahe, Meyer, Smith, Kyaer, and Holmes, 1964). Studies with this scale have indicated that people are more likely to develop a wide variety of illnesses in the year following a time of life change and that greater life change is associated with more serious illnesses (cf. Rahe, McKean, and Arthur, 1966; Wyler, Masuda, and Holmes, 1971). This appears to be the case whether the life change is perceived as being positive or negative, although overwhelming negative life changes may be particularly dangerous (cf. Schmale and Engel, 1967).

Several studies have used the SRE to predict illness among the personnel of naval ships during 6–7-month combat cruises. The crews of three heavy cruisers, the attack aircraft carrier *Ranger,* and the battleship *New Jersey* were studied in this way (Rahe, 1968; Rubin, Gunderson, and

TABLE 2.3   RANKING AND ITEM SCALE SCORES OF THE TOTAL ADULT AND ADOLESCENT SAMPLE ON THE SOCIAL READJUSTMENT RATING SCALE.

Life event	Adult group		Adolescent group	
	Rank of arithmetic mean value	Arithmetic mean value	Rank of arithmetic mean value	Arithmetic mean value
Death of spouse	1	100	1	69
Divorce	2	73	2	60
Marital separation	3	65	3	55
Jail term	4	63	8	50
Death of a close family member	5	63	4	
Major personal injury or illness	6	53	6	50
Marriage	7	50	9	50
Fired from work	8	47	7	50
Marital reconciliation	9	45	10	47
Retirement	10	45	11	46
Major change in health of family member	11	44	16	44
Pregnancy	12	40	13	45
Sex difficulties	13	39	5	51
Gain of a new family member	14	39	17	43
Business readjustment	15	39	15	44
Change in financial state	16	38	14	44
Death of a close friend	17	37	12	46
Change to a different line of work	18	36	21	38
Change in number of arguments with spouse	19	35	19	41
Mortgage over $10,000	20	31	18	41
Foreclosure of mortgage or loan	21	30	23	36
Change in responsibilities at work	22	29	20	38
Son or daughter leaving home	23	29	25	34
Trouble with in-laws	24	29	22	36
Outstanding personal achievement	25	28	28	31
Wife begins or stops work	26	26	27	32
Begin or end school	27	26	26	34
Change in living conditions	28	25	24	35
Revision of personal habits	29	24	35	26
Trouble with boss	30	23	33	26
Change in work hours or conditions	31	20	29	30
Change in residence	32	20	30	28
Change in schools	33	20	34	26
Change in recreation	34	19	36	26
Change in church activities	35	19	38	21
Change in social activities	36	18	32	28
Mortgage or loan less than $10,000	37	17	31	28
Change in sleeping habits	38	16	41	18
Change in number of family get-togethers	39	15	37	22
Change in eating habits	40	15	40	18
Vacation	41	13	39	19
Christmas	42	12	42	16
Minor violations of the law	43	11	43	12

Arthur, 1969; 1971b; 1972). Such subject populations are uniquely suited for research on disease because all the sailors aboard a ship are exposed to a similar environment, complete and objective medical records can be kept for all aboard, and life change scores can be taken at the beginning of the cruise prior to the occurrence of illness. These studies showed that sailors who reported more life change in the 18 months prior to the voyage had more sick call visits on the voyage (See Figure 2.5). A related finding was that the number of sick call visits declined in the times of sudden crisis. This was noted on one of the cruisers when it was in the Mediterranean when the 1967 Arab-Israeli war broke out, on the *Ranger* when it was ordered into the Sea of Japan following the capture of the *Pueblo* by North Korea, and on the *New Jersey* when it was ordered into the Western Pacific following the downing of a U.S. patrol plane by North Korea (Rubin, Gunderson, Arthur, 1971a). Rubin et al. note that it is difficult to ascertain whether these declines in sick call visits were due to reductions in actual illness or to decreases in illness reporting. However, the finding is consistent with the notion that a sudden crisis which mobilizes the resources of the body decreases the incidence of disease for a short period of time.

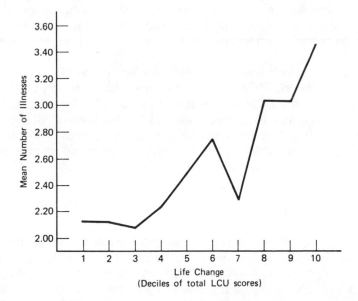

FIGURE 2.5   Relationship between life change (LCU deciles) and illness incidence. Drawn from data presented in R. T. Rubin, E. K. E. Gunderson, and R. J. Arthur, "Life stress and illness patterns in the navy—V. Prior life change and illness onset in a battleship's crew." *Journal of Psychosomatic Research*, 1971, 15, 89–94. Copyright © 1971 by Pergamon Press, Inc. Reprinted by permission.

We have seen how the antonomic and endocrine systems participate in the bodily response to stress. We shall now examine the role that these systems play in a larger context. Since they occur outside the central nervous system, antonomic and endocrine reactions are regarded as peripheral factors. The next section will consider the general role of peripheral factors in motivation and emotion.

Peripheral Factors in Emotion and Motivation

One of the oldest arenas for debate in psychology is that between peripheral and central theories of emotion and motivation. The generally older peripheralist positions maintain that the sources of motivation and emotion lie in peripheral signals—dryness of the mouth for thirst, stomach contractions for hunger, visceral and somatic sensation for emotion. Recent studies have shown that these peripheral cues are not necessary for the proper regulation of food and water intake or for emotional expression. The dominant view at present is that motivation and emotion originate in central nervous system mechanisms. However, peripheral events undoubtedly contribute to the subjective experiences normally associated with motivational and emotional states, and they may serve as important cues to the central mechanisms about the state of the body (cf Cofer and Appley, 1964).

A classic and instructive example of this kind of debate is the controversy between the W. B. Cannon and the James–Lange theory of emotion. We have encountered Cannon's ideas on the role of antonomic responding. He felt that these responses were a part of the heritage of evolution, functioning to maintain homeostasis and aid adaptation. The James–Lange theory did not address the adaptive role of these responses but used them to explain emotional experience.

THE JAMES–LANGE THEORY OF EMOTION

The James–Lange theory was proposed independently by the American psychologist William James (1884) and the Danish physiologist Carl Lange (1885). The central ideas were that somatic and visceral changes occur when an emotional stimulus is perceived and that "our feeling of these same changes as they occur IS the emotion" (James, 1968, p. 19). Thus, we do not cry because we are sorry. We see something that makes us cry, and our feeling of the crying is the sorrow. We see a bear, tremble, and run, and our feeling of the trembling and running is fear.

James argues that without these somatic and visceral changes, the perception of an emotional stimulus would be purely cognitive and unemotional. "We might see the bear, and judge it best to run . . . but we could not actually *feel* afraid" (1968, p. 19). Thus, the theory considers peripheral somatic and visceral responses to be necessary to add an emotional quality to the perception of an event.

James stated that the ultimate test of his theory would be to study persons deprived of their peripheral sensation. If such a person "recognized explicitly the same mood of feeling known . . . in his former state, my theory of course would fall. It is, however, to me incredible that the patient should have an *identical* feeling, for the dropping out of the organic soundingboard would necessarily diminish its volume in some way" (James, 1968, p. 36).

CANNON'S CRITIQUE OF THE JAMES–LANGE THEORY

In 1927, Cannon reviewed the experimental and clinical work relevant to the James–Lange theory, and he found five basic objections to it (cf. Cannon, 1968). We shall consider these objections in turn, together with more recent experimental evidence.

Total Separation of the Viscera from the Central Nervous System Does Not Impair Emotional Behavior   Sherrington (1900) isolated the viscera and most of the muscles from the brains of dogs by a high spinal transection. He found no apparent change in the emotional behavior of the animals. Cannon, Lewis, and Britton (1927) found a similar result after they destroyed the sympathetic nervous system of cats. In the presence of a barking dog, the cats would show most of the typical signs of rage behavior—hissing, growling, baring of teeth, lifting of the paw to strike. The only missing feature was erection of the hair, which is directly innervated by the sympathetic nervous system.

James's supporters countered that, although these studies demonstrated that the viscera are not necessary for emotional *behavior,* they did not prove that these animals actually *experienced* emotion (Perry, 1926; Schachter, 1964). It is possible that the animals were acting out emotional behavior that they had learned before the operation without really feeling emotional. For example, we have seen that Wynne and Solomon (1955) found that sympathectomy retarded the acquisition of avoidance responding. However, if the sympathectomy was performed after the avoidance response was learned, it had no effect on extinction. The sympathectomized animals' performance of a previously learned avoidance response was similar to the performance of normal animals, suggesting that visceral arousal may facilitate the acquisition, but not the maintenance, of emotional behavior.

Studies on humans are critical to decide this issue. Cannon cited Dana's (1921) report of a number of clinical cases, including a woman who broke her neck in a fall. The injury produced complete loss of sensation from the neck down, but she reported apparently normal emotions of affection, joy, annoyance, and grief and showed no change in personality. This finding is clearly opposed to the predictions of the James–Lange theory, although Dana admits that the normal mental condition of this patient was rather unique. On the other hand, a patient with a unilateral sympathectomy reportedly "found that his previous and customary sensation of shivering while listening to a stirring passage of music occurred in only one side and he could not be thrilled in the sympathectomized half of his body" (Delgado, 1969, pp. 134–135). The latter observation seems to indicate that sympathectomy does alter subjective experience.

Hohmann (1962; cited in Schachter, 1964) interviewed 25 patients who had suffered injuries to the spinal cord and asked them to compare their emotional experience before and after their injury. He found that such patients did generally report decreased emotional experience. The higher the spinal lesion, and consequently the greater the loss of visceral sensation, the greater was the reported decrease in subjective emotional experience. Interestingly, some of the patients reported that they acted emotionally without feeling it. One said, "I get thinking mad, not shaking mad, and that's a lot different," and another reported " . . . it's sort of a cold anger. Sometimes I act angry when I see some injustice. I yell and cuss and raise hell, because if you don't do it sometimes, I've learned people will take advantage of you, but it just doesn't have the heat to it that it used to. It's a mental kind of anger." (Schachter, 1964, pp.74–75).

All in all, it appears from these studies that peripheral visceral and somatic changes are not necessary for the maintenance of previously learned emotional behavior, although they may facilitate the acquisition of such behavior. Also, these changes may not be essential to all emotional experience, but they do seem to underlie some kinds of emotional experience,

The Same Visceral Changes Occur in Diverse Emotional States and in Nonemotional States
Cannon's second point was that the same kinds of visceral responses occur in widely different situations and that they cannot therefore account for the wide range of emotions that are experienced. The diffuse sympathetic adrenal medulla response, he argued, is quite similar in such different emotional and nonemotional states as fear, anger, exposure to heat or cold, physical exertion, and fever. The advocates of James's position responded that the differences between states may be created by the skeletal muscles rather than the viscera (Angell, 1916; Perry, 1926).

Recent studies have suggested that there may be some differences in the patterns of visceral and skeletal muscle change due to different emotions. Wolf and Wolff (1947) studied a patient with an abdominal fistula and observed that motility, secretion, and dilation of the blood vessels occurred during anger, so that the stomach lining became red and inflamed. During anxiety or depression, there were decreases in these measures so that the lining appeared pale. Shagass and Malmo (1954) and Malmo, Kohlmeyer, and Smith (1956) reported an interesting relationship between the content of psychiatric interviews and the pattern of skeletal muscle activity. In four patients (all women) hostile interview content was associated with increased tension in the forearm and in three of these cases sexual interview content was associated with muscle tension in the leg. Other studies reviewed above have indicated that norepinephrine secretion may be related to anger and aggression and that epinephrine secretion may be related to fear and anxiety (Schildkraut and Kety, 1967).

It appears that the physiological response to emotion may not be as simple and unitary as Cannon assumed. However, it is also true that very few consistent differences in the patterns of physiological response to different emotional states have emerged, and it is questionable that they could wholly account for the distinctions in the subjective quality of emotion.

The Viscera Are Relatively Insensitive Structures   Cannon's third point was that the viscera are poorly endowed with sensory fibers (having only one for about every ten visceral motor fibers) and that we are unaware of most events in the viscera. However, this point does not prove that the viscera are incapable of contributing to emotional experience.

Visceral Changes Are Too Slow To Be a Source of Feeling
Cannon pointed out that visceral responses have a long latency and that both emotional experience and expression can occur after intervals too short to provide feedback from peripheral visceral structures. A study by Newman, Perkins, and Wheeler (1930) found that one kind of emotional experience was reported immediately after an emotional stimulus was presented. They also found reports of a developing experience that occurred from 3 to 15 seconds after the exposure of the stimulus. They suggested that the later, more complete, experience depends on visceral feedback.

Together with the doubts raised with Cannon's first objection about the necessity of visceral changes in emotional experience, this seems to indicate that some kind of emotional experience is possible without peripheral visceral feedback. However, it appears that complete emotional experience normally involves visceral feedback.

The Artificial Induction of Visceral Changes Known to Occur in Specific Emotions Fails to Produce That Emotion   Injections of epinepherine produce physiological effects generally similar to those of natural sympathetic nervous system arousal. Cannon argued that the James–Lange theory implies that emotion should be experienced when epinepherine is injected.

Maranon (1924; reported in Schachter, 1964) studied the effects of epinepherine injections in 210 patients. When asked what they experienced, about 71% reported only physical symptoms such as palpitation, tremor, and tightness in the throat and chest. The rest reported emotion, but it had a detached "as if" quality. They said "I feel as if afraid," "I feel as if awaiting a great joy," or "as if moved." A few subjects did seem to show genuine emotion, usually sorrow. This occurred when the patients discussed actual emotional events, such as the death of a parent or the illness of a child.

Cannon felt that Maranon's result contradicted the James–Lange theory. His argument is somewhat unconvincing, however, both because epinepherine has little effect on parasympathetic or somatic functioning and because some of Maranon's subjects apparently *did* experience emotion.

Cannon concluded in his critique that the effects of peripheral visceral and somatic changes on emotional experience are in fact quite small. The returns from James's "organic sounding board" are very faint indeed, he wrote. "The processes going on in the (viscera) are truly remarkable and various; their value to the organism, however, is not to add richness and flavor to experience, but rather to adopt the internal economy so that in spite of shifts of outer circumstance the even tenor of the inner life will not be profoundly disturbed" (Cannon, 1968, p. 51).

SCHACHTER'S SELF-ATTRIBUTION THEORY

In a 1927 discussion of emotion, Bertrand Russell reflected upon an experience he had had with an injection of epinepherine given by a dentist. He stated that he felt the same bodily reactions he would feel when experiencing a strong emotion, but he didn't really experience an emotion. He felt *as if* he was angry, or frightened, or excited, but he knew he wasn't because he knew that there was no *reason* to be. The epinepherine in itself was not sufficient to cause a full-blown experience of emotion because a cognitive element was lacking. Russell concluded that there are two kinds of determinants of emotion: physiological changes and appropriate cognitions. "In normal life," he wrote, "there is already a cognitive element present . . . But when (epinepherine) is artifically administered, this cognitive element is absent, and the emotion in its entirety fails to arise" (Russell, 1961, pp. 226–227). This insight is the basis of Schachter's theory and experiments on the determinants of emotion. Schachter suggests that emotion has a cognitive aspect and a physiological aspect and that, when either the cognitive or physiological aspect are missing, the emotion will be incomplete.

Schachter and Singer (1962) studied the effects of different cognitions on the reactions to an injection of epinepherine. Some of their subjects were injected with epinepherine, others with a saline placebo. Among the epinepherine-injected subjects, some were informed correctly about the drug's effect by being told that "your hand will start to shake, your heart will start to pound, and your face may get warm and flushed." Other subjects were misinformed about the effects and were led to expect numbness, itching, and a slight headache. A third group was told nothing about any side effects. All of these subjects were in a state of epinepherine-induced arousal, but only the informed group had an appropriate cognitive explanation or attribution about that arousal: they knew it was produced by the drug. The uninformed subjects, on the other hand, felt the arousal but had no explanation for it.

To see whether the emotions of the uninformed subjects could be manipulated experimentally, Schachter and Singer provided different kinds of explanations for the arousal in different conditions. All subjects waited with another person who supposedly had also received an injection. Actually, the person was a model employed in the experiment. In one condition, the model behaved in a happy, boisterously euphoric manner, throwing paper airplanes, shooting wads of paper, playing with a hula hoop, and so forth. In the other condition, the model began acting angry and aggressive while filling out a questionnaire and finally tore it up in rage and stalked out of the room. The experimenters examined the overt behavior and self-reports of the subjects to determine the extent to which they were influenced by the model. As expected, the uninformed subjects acted and reported feeling more euphoric or angry, depending on the condition, than did the informed subjects.

This result was complicated by the fact that the placebo conditions were not significantly different from the uninformed epinepherine conditions (Shapiro and Crider, 1969). However, the elegance of Schachter's theory has overshadowed the inelegance of his results. Schachter and Singer reasoned that the uninformed subjects were in a state of autonomic arousal for which they had no explanation. By giving them different kinds of cognitions by way of the models, different "emotions" were produced. The essential elements of theory are outlined in Figure 2.6. The state of unex-

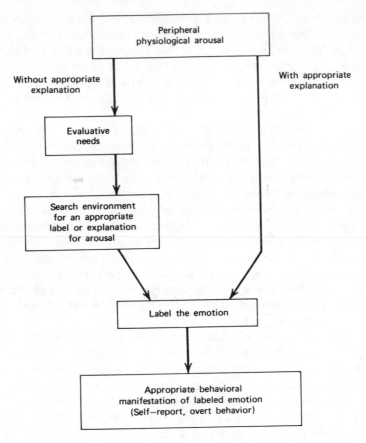

FIGURE 2.6   Schachter's self-attribution theory of emotion.

plained physiological arousal evoked "evaluative needs" in the uninformed subjects (cf. Festinger, 1954 and Chapter 9). They were uncertain
about what caused their arousal and needed to reduce the uncertainty.
They thus searched the immediate environment for an appropriate cognitive attribution or label for their arousal. In the experiment, the model's
behavior provided an appropriate explanation for the arousal, allowing the
subject to label his emotion as euphoria or anger. This reduced his uncertainty and, Schachter suggests, it also determined the quality of the emotion. After this labeling the subjects showed subjective reports and
behaviors appropriate to the labeled emotion.

Perhaps this may explain the partial but apparently incomplete emotional responses of patients with spinal cord damage, who have the cognitive label but not the physiological response, and Maranon's subjects, who

have the physiological response but not the label. When Maranon's subjects were provided with a cognitive label by discussing actual emotional events, some did experience a complete emotion. It may also explain the fast (cognitive?) and slower (visceral?) aspects of the emotional experiences reported by Newman et al., (1930). We will examine experiments that have grown out of Schachter's cognitive-physiological theory of emotion in Chapter 10.

An interesting observation on a patient with a "split-brain" suggests that the individual need not be fully conscious of the reason for the state of arousal to experience an emotion. As discussed more fully in the Appendix, the two cerebral hemispheres are surgically separated from one another in certain cases of epilepsy. Tests have shown that such patients can make verbal reports about information received by the left hemisphere but not by the right hemisphere. Nevertheless, the right hemisphere is apparently capable of generating a complete emotional reaction. In one experiment, a picture of a nude woman was occasionally presented to one hemisphere or the other in the middle of a series of pictures of ordinary objects. This produced an amused reaction regardless of whether it was presented to the left or right hemispheres. However, the reason for the reaction could be verbalized only if the picture was presented to the left hemisphere: "When the picture was flashed to the left hemisphere of a female patient, she laughed and verbally identified the picture as a nude. When it was later presented to the right hemisphere, she said in reply to a question that she saw nothing, but almost immediately a sly smile spread over her face and she began to chuckle. Asked what she was laughing at, she said: 'I don't know . . . nothing—that funny machine.' Although the right hemisphere could not describe what it had seen, the sight nevertheless elicited an emotional response like the one evoked from the left hemisphere" (Gazzaniga, 1972, p.124).

Arousal Theory

Cannon's view of the functions of peripheral physiological events has been widely accepted. In particular, the emergency theory that the sympathetic nervous system responds in a diffuse and unitary way to any emotion-provoking stimulus formed the foundation of arousal and activation theories in psychology (cf. Duffy, 1934; 1957; Lindsley, 1957; Malmo, 1958; 1959; Hebb, 1955). The physiological component of Schachter's theory is essentially an arousal theory.

The central concept of these theories is that an arousal continuum is a fundamental feature of behavior. Arousal varies from a minimum in coma and sleep, through moderate stages, to a maximum in wild excitement.

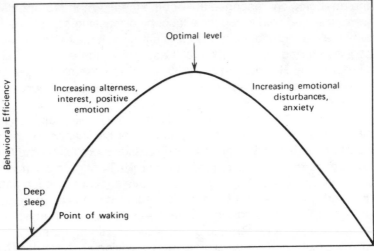

FIGURE 2.7   Hypothetical inverted-U-shaped relationship between behavioral efficiency and level of arousal. Adapted from D. O. Hebb, "Drives and the C. N. S. (Conceptual nervous system)." *Psychological Review*, 1955, 62, 243–254. Copyright 1955 by the American Psychological Association. Reprinted by permission.

Most arousal theorists feel that behavioral efficiency is related to arousal by a function in the form of an inverted U. Behavioral efficiency is low at very low and high arousal, and it is optimal at moderate arousal (See Fig.2.7).

THE PSYCHOPHYSIOLOGICAL MEASURES

One of the most important and fruitful aspects of arousal theory was that it assumed that arousal can be measured directly, by psychophysiological measures that reflect autonomic, somatic, and central nervous system activity. There are a variety of measures of autonomic activity, including *electrodermal* measures (*skin conductance, skin potential*), and measures of the circulatory system *(heart rate, blood pressure,* and *vasomotor responses*). The electromyograph (*EMG*) reflects skeletal muscle tension, and the electroencephalograph (*EEG*) reflects arousal in the central nervous system. These measures are described more fully in the appendix.

Arousal theory assumes that all emotion and motivation involves the same basic continuum of physiological activation and that this continuum is reflected in all of the psychophysiological measures because they are all involved in the same emergency and regulatory functions. Thus, measures of EEG, EMG, skin conductance, and so on should be interchangable indices of arousal which are useful in measuring all motivational and emotional states.

This clear and simple notion has been very useful in stimulating psychophysiological research, and it seems to contain a substantial element of truth. All of these measures do show changes in the direction of arousal in a variety of experimental situations designed to elicit surprise, fatigue, and emotion. However, arousal theory has been seriously questioned in recent years. The actual intercorrelations among the psychophysiological measures are almost always low, although they generally are positive. This suggests that the different measures are responding in unique ways and that the common factor of arousal affecting all of them is relatively small.

Some investigators have attempted to obtain more pure measures of arousal by new methods of scoring the psychophysiological measures that remove the unique factors affecting each measure. For example, Malmstrom, Opton, and Lazarus (1965) noted that heart rate is affected by the breathing cycle, with the heart speeding slightly on inspiration and slowing on expiration (See the Appendix). This *sinus arrythmia* does not affect other autonomic measures such as skin conductance. They attempted to remove this cyclic factor by the peak rate method, which involves counting only those heartbeats that are preceded and followed by slower beats, thus counting only the high points of the heart rate response (Opton, Rankin, and Lazarus, 1966). This resulted in a small increase in the correlation between heart rate and skin conductance.

Another response to the problem of low intercorrelations among psychophysiological measures has been to assume that they reflect important differences in the functional significance of the measures in emotional and motivational states. In this view, artificial attempts to remove the effects of all factors except arousal overlook meaningful differences between the measures. This approach emphasizes the differences between the psychophysiological response to various emotional and motivational states, while arousal theory emphasizes the similarities.

A major example of this approach is the recent series of attempts to interpret the significance of decelerative changes in heart rate in situations where skin conductance measures show no change or change in the direction of arousal. Over 45 years ago, Darrow (1929) reviewed studies showing that looking at simple physical stimuli seemed to cause heart rate deceleration, while stimuli that demanded cognitive processing were associated with acceleration. Lacey (1959; Lacey et al., 1963) noted the same phenomena and suggested that cardiac deceleration functions to facilitate sensory receptivity and thus occurs during "environmental acceptance tasks," when the organism is attending to events in the environment. Cardiac acceleration, on the other hand, functions to lower sensory receptivity and therefore occurs during "environmental rejection" tasks in which environmental stimuli would distract the organism from its cognitive problem-solving activities. Lacey (1967a, Lacey and Lacey, 1968) proposed a detailed physiological model that might underlie such a process, suggesting that fluctuations in heart rate produce fluctuations in feedback to higher centers from the blood pressure receptors in the carotid sinus and aortic arch.

Lacey's hypothesis initiated a spirited controversy in the psychophysiological literature. Many studies demonstrated that tasks involving attention to the environment indeed led to heart rate deceleration with no change or an increase in skin conductance. However, tasks apparently requiring environmental rejection did not necessarily produce cardiac acceleration (Buck, Miller, and Caul, 1969; 1970; Campos and Johnson 1966; 1967; Johnson and Campos, 1967).

This controversy is very much unsettled, but two major points of view seem to be emerging, both of which may contain part of the truth (Jennings, Averill, Opton, and Lazarus, 1971). One is Lacey's idea that heart rate deceleration facilitates attention through its feedback effect on the central nervous system. The other argues that the cardiac changes are closely associated with somatic muscle activity and are *effects* rather than causes of attention shifts. Obrist and his colleagues have noted that heart action is linked metabolically to somatic events because of the needs of the musculature for blood. When the muscles are preparing for action, increased blood flow and thus increased heart rate are called for. They argue that this cardiac-somatic link is of major importance in determining heart rate and that indeed the direction and magnitude of heart rate change is primarily a function of the overall state of the musculature in its preparation for behavior (Obrist, Webb, and Stutterer, 1969; Obrist, Webb, Stutterer and Howard, 1970a, 1970b). Similarly, Elliott (1969; 1972; Elliott, Bankart, and Light, 1970), has found evidence that heart rate accelerations are caused by the "instigation, anticipation and initiation of responses" (1969, p. 225). This cardiac-somatic hypothesis suggests that the heart rate deceleration found in Lacey's environmental acceptance tasks is due to a lessening of overall somatic activity in these situations and that accelerations, when they occur, are due to increased somatic activity. This view clearly regards the cardiac changes as *resulting* from central processes of attention, while Lacey feels that the cardiac changes *determine* attention to some extent.

The two general approaches to the interpretation of the psychophysiological measures which we have considered may each be valuable in its own right. Sternbach (1966) has written, "it is plain that there *is* such a phenomenon as activation . . . but it is also plain that this non-specific response is not all there is to the matter, and that it is no longer particularly useful to think of all emotion or responses to stress as merely those changes which may be labeled as 'activation' " (pp.89–90). Arousal theory is clearly incomplete, but the various psychophysiological measures *are* significantly correlated in most studies, albeit at a low level, and many arousing situations *do* show similar physiological changes, although not all do. Attempts to refine measurement techniques to provide indices of arousal free of unique effects may prove very useful. On the other hand, the approach that emphasizes the differing properties of the measures can lead to greater understanding of both the unique and general aspects of psychophysiological responding.

THE CENTRAL NERVOUS SYSTEM AND AROUSAL

We have been examining the role of peripheral events in arousal theory because they have been the focus of much study, especially in humans, using the psychophysiological measures. Arousal theory has also been applied to the analysis of central nervous system events which are studied in animals by quite different methods. It is a tribute to the usefulness and generality of arousal theory that it can be applied with considerable success to such different realms of investigation. However, as with the analysis of peripheral events, the arousal theory analysis of central nervous system events is incomplete.

The Reticular Activation System   The reticular formation is a collection of nuclei and scattered fiber tracts located in the core of the brainstem extending from the spinal cord to the hypothalamus and thalamus (see Figure 2.8). Its importance for our purposes lies in its involvement in the control of arousal, attention, and sleep. This involvement was illustrated in a now classic 1935 demonstration by Bremer. Bremer cut the brainstem of a cat at the midbrain just above the reticular formation, thus separating the reticular formation from the rest of the brain. He called this operation "cerveau isole." These animals showed an apparently irreversible sleep-like or comatose pattern of response. They displayed synchronized high-voltage slow (8–12Hz) EEG waves similar to those seen during sleep and constricted pupils characteristic of normal sleep (see the Appendix for a discussion of EEG arousal). Only brief and weak EEG arousal could be elicited, even when the animal was stimulated by strong light. In

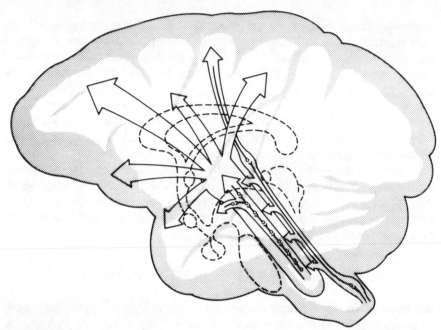

FIGURE 2.8   Ascending reticular activating system schematically projected on a monkey brain. From D. B. Lindsley, "Attention, consciousness, sleep, and wakefulness." In John Field (Ed.). *Handbook of physiology*, Vol. 3. Baltimore: Williams and Wilkins, 1960. Copyright © 1960 by Williams and Wilkins. Reprinted by permission.

contrast, when the brainstem was transected at the spinal cord just below the reticular formation (an operation which Bremer named "encephale isole"), the animal showed normal alternation between periods of aroused and sleep-like activity on the EEG and pupil response, and stimulation elicited apparently normal EEG arousal (Thompson, 1967).

Bremer's observations suggested that the reticular formation may play a part in arousing the rest of the brain. Further support for this notion came in 1949, when Moruzzi and Magoun found that rapid (100–300Hz)stimulation of the reticular formation produced immediate and long-lasting EEG arousal. Such stimulation in a sleeping animal was found to produce waking, often with a start. Subsequent studies showed that the sensory pathways to the brain could be cut without affecting EEG reactivity, but if the reticular formation was lesioned and the sensory pathway left intact, a sleep-like EEG resulted. Also, if a sensory pathway was stimulated before it entered the reticular formation, normal EEG arousal occurred, while if stimulation occurred above the reticular formation, there was no EEG arousal. Activation of the reticular formation thus appears to be necessary for cortical EEG arousal (Lindsley, 1957).

D. B. Lindsley (1951; 1957) suggested from these and other findings that the reticular formation may be the physiological basis for arousal theory's general arousal or activation. The EEG is regarded as one of the most direct measures of arousal, and the reticular formation appears to cause EEG arousal. Lindsley terms the portion of the reticular formation involved in cortical arousal the ascending reticular activating system or ARAS. He argues that the ARAS functions to arouse the brain in all kinds of emotional and motivational situations; thus it is responsible for the "energizing" aspect of emotion and motivation. Other parts of the brain are presumably responsible for the directing aspect, leading to behavior appropriate to the particular emotional or motivational state and situation.

This attractively clear and simple picture of the role of the reticular formation and the unitary nature of general arousal has, like other aspects of arousal theory, been complicated by more recent experimental results. The demonstrations that ARAS activation causes EEG arousal were not followed by convincing experiments showing that it necessarily causes *behavioral* arousal. In fact, number of studies have shown that EEG arousal is not always associated with aroused behavior. Wikler (1952) demonstrated that atropine, a drug that counters the action of the synaptic transmitter acetylcholine (ACh), produces a synchronized sleep-like EEG even in an awake and apparently alert animal. Bradley (1968) demonstrated that such atropinized animals with sleep-like EEGs can be alert and respond without decrement in certain experimental situations. Bradley also showed that the drug physostigmine (which increases the concentration of ACh in the brain by countering the enzyme acetylcholinesterase or AChE) produces EEG arousal in sleeping animals. These experiments demonstrate that EEG arousal and behavioral arousal can be dissociated and that different brain mechanisms may be involved in the arousal of the EEG and the arousal of behavior. From the present data, it appears likely that EEG arousal is caused by a cholinergic mechanism (one that uses ACh as its synaptic transmitter) since drugs that block ACh cause synchronization and drugs that increase ACh cause EEG arousal. However, the relationship of this mechanism to behavioral arousal is complex and is not understood at this time.

Clinical evidence in humans also indicates that the EEG can be dissociated from behavior. Apparently normal EEG activity can occur in comatose patients, and apparently normal behavior can occur with slow synchronized EEG activity (Lacey, 1976b). For example, one patient with severe damage to the reticular formation who appeared to be comatose could reportedly answer complex questions by using a slight arm movement (Lhermitte, Gautier, Marteau, and Chain, 1963; reported in Milner, 1970).

These findings have forced a reevaluation of both the role of the reticular formation and of the unitary nature of general arousal. Lacey (1967b) has suggested that there may be different kinds of arousal: autonomic, EEG, and behavioral arousal. Lacey acknowledges that the assertions of arousal theory may be true in an actuarial sense, in that activation of these three arousal systems may *often* occur simultaneously. The autonomic, EEG, and behavioral arousal systems may often be independently activated, particularly in the intense and aversive situations commonly studied in experiments. However, Lacey argues that it is possible to activate one system without activating the others and that the study of a wider variety of experimental situations will allow the more precise specification of when these arousals do and do not occur together.

It is clear that the ARAS is not a simple, unitary center directing arousal and sleep. On the other hand, it is clear that the reticular formation normally has a role in these processes as an important part of a complex system that is imperfectly understood at this time. Another part of this system is a structure that receives much input from the reticular formation: the diffuse thalamic system.

The Diffuse Thalamic System   The diffuse thalamic system lies above the reticular formation along the midline of the brain, including the intrinsic nuclei of the thalamus. It receives fibers from the reticular formation and some sensory pathways, and it sends fibers to the cerebral cortex by a number of indirect routes.

In some respects, the functions of the diffuse thalamic system seem to parallel those of the reticular formation. High-frequency stimulation of the system produces EEG arousal and lesions produce some behavioral coma and sleep-like EEG. However, these effects are typically not as pronounced as they are when the reticular formation is affected: the EEG arousal is briefer and the coma less profound.

In other respects, the functions of the reticular formation and diffuse thalamic system seem opposed. For example, a single electrical stimulation in the diffuse thalamic system produces a synchronized burst in an aroused EEG, and slow (6–12Hz) repetitive stimulation can change an aroused pattern in the EEG to a synchronized, slow (6–11 Hz) pattern. This EEG synchronization is called a *recruiting response*. Stimulation of the reticular formation with high-frequency current tends to block the recruiting response. According to Andersen and Andersson (1968), the synchronized activity of the recruiting response may be analogous to alpha activity in humans, and the diffuse thalamic system may act as a pacemaker to induce alpha activity in the cortical EEG.

Low-frequency stimulation of the diffuse thalamic system has also produced sleep in cats (Akert, Koella, and Hess, 1952), and some have proposed that the area is a sleep center. Magoun (1963) has suggested that the reticular formation and diffuse thalamic system have essentially opposite functions, with the reticular formation functioning as a waking center, mediating cortical arousal and attention and the diffuse thalamic system being responsible for cortical synchronization and sleep. However, high frequency in the diffuse thalamic system can produce EEG arousal. In fact, one study has reported behavioral arousal and sleep from stimulation in the diffuse thalamic system from the same electrode, depending on whether the frequency of stimulation was fast or slow (Akimoto, Yamogushi, Okabe, and others, 1956).

High-frequency stimulation of the diffuse thalamic system is sometimes done to explore methods of relieving intractible pain in patients by interrupting sensory pathways in the thalamus. Ervin, Mark, and Stevens (1969) report that the subjective experience of such stimulation is not pleasant. It elicits expressions of surprise and dismay: "Stop!" "Good God, what's that?" "I'm falling apart!" The patients have difficulty localizing or describing the sensation, which is sometimes felt on only one side of the body opposite to the stimulation. Patients have compared it to the reaction to fingernails scraping a blackboard, sudden fright caused by a near accident, or nauseating pain caused by a crushed finger (Ervin et al., 1969, p. 56).

Although this diffuse thalamic system stimulation is aversive, the reactions to it are quite different from the negative emotional responses evoked by stimulation in structures that we will examine in the next chapter. They also are markedly different from the effects of stimulation a few millimeters away in the sensory relay nuclei of the lateral thalamus. In these nuclei, stimulation produces only tingling sensations in well-localized points of the body surface (Ervin et al., 1969).

Sharpless and Jasper (1956) have suggested that the diffuse thalamic system may mediate rapid but brief changes in cortical arousal in response to relatively small changes in environmental events. Jasper (1960) suggests further that the projections of the diffuse thalamic system may affect fairly specific portions of the cortex. Sharpless and Jasper see the reticular formation as responsible for long-lasting changes in general arousal that affect the entire cortex as a whole and respond only slowly and crudely to events in the environment. In their view, the reticular formation may maintain a background level of wakefulness while the diffuse thalamic system quickly activates specific areas of the cortex that direct attention to particular aspects of the environment. In this respect the reticular formation has been compared to the channel selector and volume control of a television set, while the diffuse thalamic system is like the fine tuner. Whether or not this is true and how the EEG-synchronizing and sleep-inducing ability of the diffuse thalamic system might be related to its arousal functions are questions that require further study.

Summary

The peripheral nervous system includes the somatic nervous system and the autonomic nervous system. The latter is divided into the sympathetic and parasympathetic branches. Cannon's emergency theory of emotion was based on the idea that general sympathetic arousal functions to prepare the organism for fight or flight. One sympathetic action is to release norepinepherine and epinepherine from the adrenal medulla. There is evidence that epinepherine secretion may be related to fear, while norepinepherine secretion may be dominant during anger and aggression.

The endocrine system consists of ductless glands that release chemical substances called hormones into the bloodstream. The pituitary gland has been called the master gland because it secretes substances that activate the other endocrine glands. It secretes adrenocortical-tropic-hormone (ACTH) to activiate the adrenal cortex, which in turn secretes corticoids into the general circulation. The pituitary-adrenal system was shown by Selye to be involved in the general adaptation syndrome that occurs during stress. It may also be directly involved in the acquisition and extinction of fear-motivated avoidance and escape behavior. The autonomic and endocrine reactions associated with stress may contribute to a wide variety of illnesses, as studies of life change and illness suggest.

The James–Lange Theory maintains that the source of emotion is the peripheral visceral and somatic response to arousing situations. Cannon argued against this point of view, showing that the peripheral responses are not necessary to the expression of emotion. Although there is evidence that peripheral events normally do contribute to the subjective experience of emotion, they are apparently not essential to all kinds of emotion experience, and they are clearly not essential to emotional expression. Schachter suggested that emotion normally involves a combination of physiological arousal and cognitive labels or explanations for that arousal.

Arousal theory derived from Cannon's idea of a diffuse sympathetic response to emergency situations. It argued that peripheral psychophysiological measures should all be affected by the general factor of arousal. This seems to be true, but other unique factors affect each psychophysiological measure more than does the general factor of arousal. The study and understanding of these unique factors should eventually shed more light on the nature of general arousal. It appears that in most cases, peripheral physiological events reflect their own direct role in metabolic functioning. Sometimes, in fulfilling these roles, they reflect central emotional and motivational processes. if proper controls are employed and if care is taken in interpretation, peripheral physiological events can be used to study such central processes as arousal, attention, uncertainty, and so forth.

In a few cases, peripheral physiological events may have effects on higher processes, but this does not appear to be common. There is some evidence that hormones may facilitate the acquisition and extinction of avoidance behavior. Lacey has argued that heart rate has feedback effects which facilitate the acceptance and rejection of environmental events, but this is disputed by others.

The reticular activating system and diffuse thalamic system are central nervous system mechanisms associated with arousal. It appears that cholinergic fibers in the reticular activating system may be responsible for gross changes in EEG arousal, but their relationship with behavioral and autonomic arousal is uncertain. The diffuse thalamic system is associated with more discrete EEG changes, and some have suggested that it is a pacemaker for the synchronized EEG alpha rhythm.

In terms of the schema introduced in Chapter 1, this chapter has been concerned primarily with the autonomic and endrocrine components of the physiological response to affective stimuli: what they are, why they evolved, what bodily functions they serve, and how they may become dysfunctional and damaging to the body. It has also considered the role of the perception and sensation of these visceral and glandular changes in the subjective experience of emotion, culminating in the view that these physiological events combine and interact with cognitive labels and interpretations to produce emotion.

CHAPTER THREE

CENTRAL NERVOUS SYSTEM MECHANISMS OF MOTIVATION AND EMOTION

In this chapter we shall consider the regions of the central nervous system that are most directly linked with emotional and motivational phenomena. These include the hypothalamus, the limbic stysem, and rewarding and aversive areas in the brain. The intent of this chapter is to give an overview of the role of these regions in the regulation of motivation and emotion, drawing upon data from human clinical studies whenever possible.

The Hypothalamus

It is clear that the hypothalamus plays a central role in emotional and motivational processes, but the extent and limits of the role are not well understood. It is known that the hypothalamus exerts direct control over the autonomic nervous system and endocrine system and that lesions and stimulation of the hypothalamus have dramatic effects on food and water seeking, sexual behavior, and emotional behavior. However, the hypothalamus is not the only structure in the central nervous system responsible for these processes. It acts in interaction with higher structures.

The hypothalamus is a collection of nuclei located, as the name indicates, below the thalamus. In the adult human, it is about as large as the end of a man's thumb. Figure A.10 in the Appendix shows the location of the major hypothalamic nuclei. The importance of the hypothalamus in motivation and emotion is dramatically illustrated in the tragic case histories of persons afflicted with hypothalamic diseases. Bauer (1954) has reviewed 60 such cases in which autopsy data were available. Table 3.1 indicates that sexual abnormalities are the most frequent symptom of hypothalamic malfunction. Precocious sexual development involves an early onset of puberty that can affect preschool children or even infants. Eating irregularities, somnolence, disorders of temperature regulation, and psychic disturbances including violent outbursts of rage, abnormal sexual behavior, and compulsive attacks of laughing or crying are also frequent. Reeves and Plum (1969) have described the symptoms in a woman of a tumor restricted to the ventromedial nucleus of the hypothalamus. The woman's symptoms of overeating, rage, and change in endocrine functioning show striking parallels with the results of the animal studies that we shall consider.

It has been suggested that the hypothalamus gathers and integrates information relevant to emotion and motivation from many peripheral and central sources. In some way this information must acquire motivational force, and this force must be translated into behavior. The extent to which the latter processes are based on hypothalamic mechanisms is uncertain, but it seems certain that the hypothalamus has a central role in gathering basic information about bodily functioning and in affecting that functioning

TABLE 3.1   INCIDENCE OF SYMPTOMS OF HYPOTHALAMIC DISEASE IN HUMANS (60 Cases).

SYMPTOMS	NO. OF CASES
Sexual abnormalities	
Precocious puberty	24
Hypogonadism	19
Eating abnormalities	
Obesity	15
Emaciation	11
Abnormal temperature regulation	13
Psychic disturbances	21

Adapted from data presented in H. D. Bauer, "Endocrine and other manifestations of hypothalamic disease." *Journal of Clinical Endocrinology.* 1954, **14,** 13–31. Copyright © 1954 by The Endocrine Society. Reprinted by permission.

via the autonomic and endocrine systems. We shall consider this autonomic role more closely in three areas: the control of eating, sexual behavior, and aggressive behavior.

EATING BEHAVIOR

There are a number of peripheral cues relavant to the control of food intake, including gastric motility, stomach distension, blood sugar level, and metabolic changes associated with eating. The motivational state of hunger was once thought to originate in these peripheral mechanisms. However, experiments have shown that animals can regulate their energy balance even when various mechanisms are eliminated. Most psychologists have concluded that hunger motivation must ultimately depend on central nervous system mechanisms. That does not mean that these peripheral cues are unimportant in the normal regulation of eating. In fact, there are correlations between these cues and hunger sensation and eating behavior. These peripheral cues may thus normally enrich the subjective experience of hunger, and they probably also function as sources of information to the central nervous system about the bodily need for food (Grossman, 1967). The details about how this occurs are not known, but the hypothalamus appears to contain centers that are sensitive to these cues.

The Satiety Center   It has long been known that lesions or tumors in the areas of the hypothalamus can cause gross overeating (hyperphagia) and obesity. Experiments in the 1940s implicated the ventromedial (VM) nucleus in this effect. When the VM nucleus is destroyed, there is an initial response of dynamic hyperphagia in which animals begin to eat up to three or four times their normal intake of food. They quickly increase their weight to two or three times normal. This dynamic stage may last for several months. It is followed by a stage of static hyperphagia in which food intake declines and levels off at a point near normal and the excess weight is maintained (Hetherington and Ransom, 1942; Brobeck, Tepperman and Long, 1943).

Teitelbaum and his colleagues studied this phenomenon during the 1950s and discovered that VM lesioned rats would eat more than normals only if the food was good tasting. If cellulose or bitter quinine were added to the food, the VM lesioned animals ate *less* than normals. If sweet saccharin were added, the VM animals increased their eating more than did normals. Thus, taste seemed usually important in determining the food intake of VM lesioned rats. Other studies show that VM lesioned rats would not work as hard as normals when they had to press a bar to get food reward (Teitelbaum, 1961; Teitelbaum and Epstein, 1963).

These strange findings led to the hypothesis that the food motivation of the VM lesioned rats may actually be *lower* than normal and that they overeat because the VM region of the hypothalamus is a satiety center that normally inhibits eating when enough food has been consumed (Teitelbaum, 1961; Miller, 1964). Thus, the VM lesioned animal is less likely to start eating bad tasting food or work for food because his hunger motivation is low. However, once he starts eating, it is difficult to stop.

If the VM region is indeed a satiety center, one might expect that electrical stimulation of the region would stop ongoing eating behavior. This has in fact been demonstrated (Anand and Dua, 1955) but it is hard to interpret because VM stimulation also appears to be aversive to the animal. Krasne (1962) found that animals would work to turn off a VM stimulus that inhibited eating. Other evidence gives more clear, although indirect, support to the idea of a VM satiety center. Peripheral stimuli that tend to reduce eating, including stomach distension and glucose injections (Sharma, Anand, Dua, and Singh, 1961) as well as appetite depressants (Brobeck, Larsson, and Reyes, 1956) all seem to increase neural activity in the VM region. Also, injections of gold thioglucose, a toxic substance with a molecular structure similar to glucose, was found to damage the VM region and cause effects similar to lesions (Marshall, Barnett, and Mayer, 1955). The latter result suggests that glucoreceptors in the VM hypothalamus absorbed the substance because of its similarity to glucose and were destroyed. All of these studies suggest that the VM region of the hypothalamus is particularly sensitive to information about the organism's need for food. Also, a study by Epstein (1960) used a hypertonic saline solution that presumably excites neural activity and a local anesthetic, procaine, that blocks activity. Injections of the excitatory saline into the VM region depressed feeding as expected, while the inhibitory procaine increased eating.

It seems clear that the VM hypothalamus has a special role in the regulation of food intake. However, as we shall see there also is evidence that it participates in more general motivational functions, including sexual and aggressive behavior. Grossman (1967) has suggested that the effect of VM lesions on food intake may be a special example of a more general motivational effect. He feels that VM lesions may cause a "general lowering of the threshold for all affective responses to the environment" (Grossman, 1967, p. 358). He has shown that VM lesions increase shock-avoidance behavior as well as affecting eating and lowering food-rewarded behavior. VM lesioned rats are quicker to cross a cage to avoid a painful shock. Grossman suggests that the behavior of VM lesioned rats may be due to a greater sensitivity to taste, the unpleasant aspects of having to work for food, the pain of the shock, and indeed any pleasant or unpleasant aspect of the environment (cf. Grossman, 1972).

The Hunger Center   If the VM nucleus has been called a satiety center, the lateral nucleus of the hypothalamus has been labeled a feeding center. Lesions and stimulation in the lateral nucleus generally have effects quite opposite from those in the VM nucleus. For example, in the above-mentioned study by Epstein (1960), procaine anesthetic in the lateral hypothalamus depressed feeding while saline increased feeding, a result precisely opposite to that found in the VM hypothalamus.

The first study showing the importance of the lateral hypothalamus in feeding was done by Brugger (1943). It demonstrated that electrical stimulation in the lateral region elicited vigorous eating and some drinking of both edible and inedible materials. Later, Anand and Brobeck (1951) showed that lesions in this region eliminated eating and drinking. An animal would literally starve to death on a pile of food. Teitelbaum and Stellar (1954) found that if an animal were kept alive by force feeding and drinking, it would gradually recover the ability to eat. It is unclear whether this recovery of function is due to the recovery of hypothalamic tissue or to the taking over of feeding functions by structures outside the hypothalamus. Teitelbaum and Cytawa (1965) have found that the cerebral cortex may be involved in this recovery. Recovered lateral-lesioned rats were subjected to cortical spreading depression, a kind of reversible lesion that depresses cortical functioning for several hours. These animals stopped eating again for many days, suggesting that the disruption of the cortex caused a temporary loss in some way of adapting to the lesion.

A study by Grossman (1960) indicates that eating and drinking can be elicited independently of one another by lateral hypothalamic stimulation. Injections of ACh, the cholinergic transmitter substance, into the lateral region produced drinking while injections of norepinepherine, the adrenergic transmitter, produced eating. This may indicate the presence of two neural systems at the same location in the hypothalamus, a cholinergic system involved in drinking and an adrenergic system involved in eating (see also Baldessarini, 1972).

Summary   Studies of eating behavior have suggested that there may be a satiety center in the ventromedial (VM) hypothalamus that functions to stop eating behavior when enough food has been consumed and a hunger center in the lateral hypothalamus that functions to excite eating behavior. Other evidence suggests that the fibers in the hunger center may be adrenergic.

SEXUAL BEHAVIOR

Both neural and endocrine mechanisms are important in the control of sex. The spinal cord and brainstem contain many of the basic neural reflexes necessary in sexual behavior. Complete transection of the spinal cord does not necessarily abolish reflex responses to genital stimulation, although in humans the experience of genital sensation is lost (Riddoch, 1917). Erection and ejaculation are possible in men after spinal transection, depending on such factors as the patient's general health and the extent of damage to the spinal cord itself (Money, 1961). In female cats with spinal transections, sexual reflexes occur which are unaffected by hormones or the estrus cycle (Bard, 1940).

The Anterior Hypothalamus   The hypothalamus affects sexual behavior through both neural and endocrine mechanisms. The anterior region appears to be an important center in the neural control of sex. Lesions in this area have permanently abolished sexual behavior in male and female rats, cats, and guinea pigs (Sawyer, 1969). The loss of sexual behavior caused by these anterior hypothalamic lesions was not accompanied by atrophy or degeneration in the gonads, and it was not affected by the administration of sex hormones (Milner, 1970). This suggests that it is a neural effect, affecting reflexes necessary for sexual behavior rather than hormones.

Electrical stimulation of the anterior hypothalamus has led to increased male-like sexual activity, sometimes in female animals. Vaughan and Fisher (1962) demonstrated continuous erection, repeated mounting, and a markedly shorter refractory period following ejaculation in male rats. One animal reportedly mounted a female 155 times with 45 ejaculations in seven and one-half hours, another had 20 ejaculations within one hour. Similarly, MacLean and Ploog (1962) reported increased sexual activity in male monkeys with anterior stimulation. Roberts, Steinberg, and Means (1967) reported increased male-like sexual activity among both male and female opossums with anterior region stimulation. Animals of both sexes attempted to mount and copulate with female opossums and a woolly toy dog during stimulation. The similar responses in male and female animals suggests, along with other evidence, that neural circuits for male and female sexual behavior exist in animals of both sexes.

The Ventromedial Hypothalamus   The hypothalamus directs the release of gonad-stimulating (*gonadotropic*) hormones by the pituitary (see the Appendix). The area most important for this direction seems to include the VM region. Robinson and Sawyer (1957) found that electrical stimulation in this area induced ovulation in female cats, while VM lesions in female cats and rabbits abolished estrus and led to atrophy of the ovaries. In contrast to the irreversibility of the anterior region lesions, the effects of the VM lesions are reversible if estrogen is administered to the animal. Rogers (1954) demonstrated a similar loss of sexual behavior and gonadal atrophy after VM lesions in male rats, and it too was reversible with hormonal therapy.

Other Nuclei   In cats and some other species, lesions in the area of the mammillary bodies produce hormone-reversible effects similar to those of VM lesions. However, in female rabbits, lesions in the mammillary region produced irreversible effects similar to those of anterior lesions in the cat. Sawyer (1969) suggests that the VM region is a center for the hormonal control of sex in both the cat and rabbit, while a center for the neural control of sex exists in the anterior region in the cat and the mammillary region in the rabbit (see Figure 3.1). There is other evidence for a posterior hypothalamic center near the mammillary bodies that is involved in the neural control of sexual behavior. Herberg (1963) and Caggiula and Hoebel (1966) found that simulation of a region in the posterior hypothalamus above the mammillary bodies produced vigorous sexual activity in the male rat.

Other evidence bearing on the role of hypothalamic mechanisms in the control of sex have come from studies employing chemical stimulation.

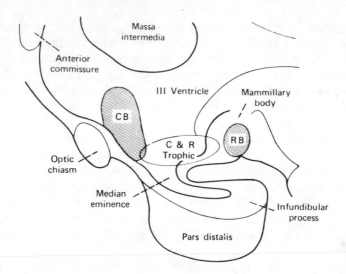

FIGURE 3.1 Location of sex behavioral and gonadotrophic areas in the hypothalamus of the female cat and rabbit. *C & R TROPHIC*: Common area controlling the release of ovulating hormone from the pituitary in both cat and rabbit. *CB* and *RB*: Areas in which lesions permanently abolish estrus in the cat and rabbit respectively. From C. H. Sawyer, "Regulatory mechanisms of secretion of gonadotrophic hormones." In W. Haymaker, E. Anderson, and W. J. H. Nauta (Eds.) *The hypothalamus.* 1969. Courtesy of Charles C Thomas, Publisher, Springfield, Illinois.

Injections of the transmitter substances ACh and norepinepherine have not produced sexual behavior as reliably as the injection of sex hormones. This is a further indication that the hypothalamus must be quite sensitive to the level of circulating hormones. The hormones presumably function to initiate or facilitate activity in circuits involved in sexual behavior, perhaps even acting as synaptic transmitter substances (Milner, 1970).

Fisher (1956;1964) found that male rats displayed exaggerated sexual behavior following injections of the male sex hormone testosterone into the lateral preoptic area of the hypothalamus. The animals attempted to mount unreceptive females and other male rats. Injections of the same substance into more medial (midline) preoptic areas produced maternal-like behavior in male rats. Instead of attempting to mount a female, they would build a nest and attempt to drag the female into it as if she were an arrant rat pup. Testosterone stimulation in the area between the lateral and medial pre-optic regions sometimes produced mixed male-maternal behavior. One rat was observed trying to mount another male rat while carefully carrying a rat pup in his mouth. Fisher suggested that the medial preoptic area in these rats may contain a neural circuit for maternal behavior that is sensitive to the female sex hormone progesterone and is normally activated only in females. However, the introduction of testosterone may artificially activate the center in male rats.

Other evidence for the sensitivity of the hypothalamus to hormones comes from studies of ovariectomized female animals. Sex hormones have produced estrus in such animals when placed in the anterior, preoptic, and lateral areas of the hypothalamus (Sawyer, 1963;1969; Michael, 1962;1965). Michael's study used radioactive forms of female sex hormone estrogen in some animals, and he found evidence that the hormones had been absorbed into more neurons in those animals that showed the strongest sexual behaviors (Michael, 1962).

Recordings of the electrical activity in the hypothalamus have revealed discharges following vaginal stimulation in female cats (Porter, Cavanaugh, Critchlow, and Sawyer, 1957). The activity occurred in the anterior and lateral hypothalamus, particularly in the region of medial forebrain bundle. It occurred only if the cat was in estrus or primed with estrogen. Similar EEG changes have been observed in anterior hypothalamus of rabbits during sexual arousal (Green, 1954).

Summary   Attempts to identify sex centers in the hypothalamus have revealed complex results and species differences that are difficult to reconcile at the present time. At present, it seems that there are two kinds of such centers. Centers of hormonal regulation control the release of gonadotropic hormones, while centers of neural regulation seem to contain or control neural circuits and reflexes responsible for sexual behavior. The ways in which these centers may interact and influence one another are not known. A major center for hormonal regulation seems to be located in the general region of the VM nucleus. Centers for neural regulation seem to exist in the region of the anterior nucleus and preoptic area and in the posterior region near the mammillary bodies. The location of these centers may vary from species to species. It is possible that, as Milner (1970) has speculated, neural sex mechanisms may be distributed on an anterior–posterior dimension along the path of the medial forebrain bundle (MFB) through the hypothalamus.

AGGRESSIVE BEHAVIOR

Some of the earliest evidence of the importance of the hypothalamus in emotion and motivation came from studies of aggressive behavior. In the mid-1920s, Cannon and his colleagues found that decorticate cats could be easily provoked to give a ferocious display of attack, defense, and flight behaviors. The animals hissed and spat, clawed and struggled. They showed evidence of autonomic arousal, including increased heart rate and blood pressure, sweating, and erection of the hair. Cannon called this response sham rage because he assumed that the decorticate animal was incapable of experiencing any subjective emotional response and was merely showing emotional behavior. He used these decorticate animals to study the autonomic and adrenal responses during aggression (Cannon and Britton, 1925). Bard, working in Cannon's laboratory, undertook a systematic investigation of the central nervous system structures necessary for an integrated sham rage response. He found that a complete rage response was possible so long as the posterior hypothalamus remained attached to the brainstem (Bard, 1928). Thus, the entire brain above the posterior hypothalamus could be removed without disrupting the rage response. If the posterior hypothalamus were also destroyed, only isolated components of the rage response could be found. Thus, the animal might hiss, but his hissing was not necessarily accompanied by clawing or scratching.

Bard's result suggests that the posterior hypothalamus may be a center for integrating rage behavior. Some support for this comes from studies reporting that electrical stimulation in this area can produce rage-like behavior, and that lesions may produce some suppression of emotional reactions (cf. Grossman, 1967; MacLean, 1969).

In the same year that Bard published his observations, Hess (1928) reported that electrical stimulation of a different area of the hypothalamus produced well-coordinated rage responses directed against an object of attack. Hess found that the stimulation was most effective in the perifornical region of the hypothalamus surrounding the fornix near the VM nucleus. This observation was confirmed by Hunsperger (1956), who also found a region in the central grey of the brainstem that elicited attack behavior (see Figure 3.2). Stimulation of the central grey was effective even if the perifornical region was lesioned, but perfornical stimulation had no effect if the central grey were lesioned. This and other evidence suggests that rage patterns may normally be channeled from the perifornical region to the central grey (MacLean, 1969).

A number of studies have shown that lesions of the VM nucleus, near the perifornical region, can produce long-term increases in aggressive emotional behavior (Hetherington and Ranson, 1939; Kessler, 1941; Wheatley, 1944). This is puzzling, since stimulation in the same area seems to produce similar emotional behavior. Glusman and Roizin (1960) report attack behavior from VM stimulation, and defensive displays and threats have been found with VM stimulation in cats (Roberts and Kleiss, 1964) and opossums (Roberts, Steinberg, and Means, 1967). It has been suggested that the VM lesions cause sensitivity in Hunsperger's central

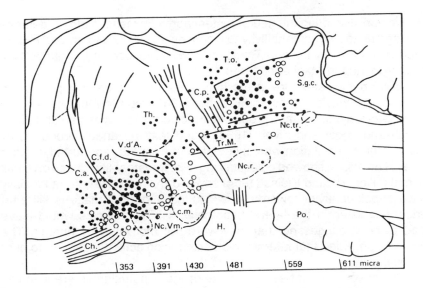

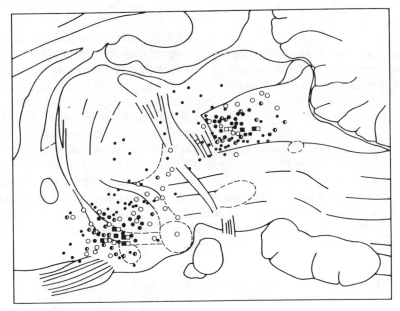

FIGURE 3.2   Electrode placements in the midbrain and hypothalamus from which affective reactions could be elicited. Defensive responses ●, escape ○, escape with defensive movements ◐, attack ■, fright reactions or alternating attack and fright responses ▮. C.a., anterior commissure; C.f.d., descending column of fornix; C.m., mammillary bodies; C.p., posterior commissure; Ch., optic chiasm; H., pituitary (hypophysis); Nc.om., oculomotor nucleus; Nc.r., red nucleus; Nc.tr., trochlear nucleus; Nc.vm., ventromedial (VM) nucleus of the hypothalamus; Po., pons; S.g.c., central gray; T.o., tectum; Th., thalamus; Tr.M., tract of Meynert; V.d'Á., tract of Vicq d'Azyr. From R. W. Hunsperger, "Affektreaktionen auf elektrische Reizung im Hernstamm der Katze." *Helv. Physiol. Acta.* 1956. 14, 70–92. Copyright © 1956 by Schwabe & Co. Reprinted by permission.

grey region, disrupting the neural system normally responsible for defense and leading to a hypersensitivity to incoming stimuli (Glusman and Roizin, 1960; Glusman, Won, and Burdock, 1961; Skultety and Chamberlain, 1965; reported in MacLean, 1969).

Still another structure in the hypothalamus has been implicated in aggressive behavior. Hess and Brugger (1943) reported that stimulation of the lateral hypothalamus produced attack behavior. Wasman and Flynn (1962) and Eggar and Flynn (1963) found that the attack produced by lateral region stimulation was quite different from the rage found in other areas. The animal showed quiet stalking and predatory-like attack on small animals. Roberts and Kleiss (1964) showed that cats that did not initially show attack behavior toward rats would learn to run a maze to kill a rat when stimulated in the lateral hypothalamus. The animals would leave food to hunt, suggesting that they were not motivated by hunger. The authors concluded that lateral region stimulation activates a drive to hunt and kill.

We have seen that several areas of the hypothalamus are involved in aggressive behavior, including the posterior, periformical, VM, and lateral regions. It may be that these regions are responsible for different aspects of aggression. For example, the lateral region seemed associated with a predatory attack quite different from the attack elicited from other areas. Some have suggested that rage behavior shall be broken down into simpler constituents, such as alarm, flight, and rage (Miller, 1961; Roberts, 1958). Other studies have suggested that there may be different regions eliciting attack and defensive behavior (Roberts, 1958; Glusman and Roizin, 1960; Roberts, Steinberg, and Means, 1967). It is possible that different areas of the hypothalamus may eventually be identified more closely with particular aspects of the rage reaction. On the other hand, some psychologists have become convinced that attempts to precisely localize the physiological basis of particular behaviors are misguided. Let us consider two approaches to the interpretation of the role of the hypothalamus in motivation, the classic position of Eliot Stellar and the more recent views of Elliot Valenstein and Glickman and Schiff.

THE ROLE OF THE HYPOTHALAMUS IN MOTIVATION

Stellar's Theory   The evidence for the existence of feeding and satiety centers in the hypothalamus was a major basis for Stellar's (1954) physiological theory of motivation. His schematic diagram representing his position is given in Figure 3.3. He suggested that motivated behavior is a

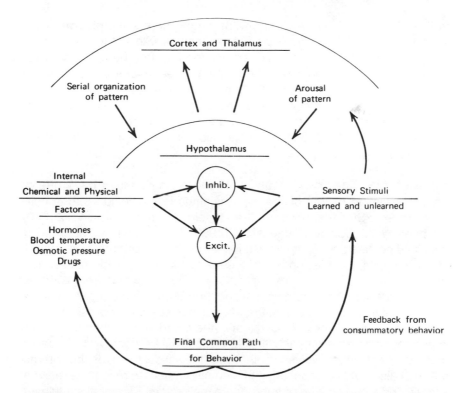

FIGURE 3.3   Schematic diagram of physiological factors controlling motivation. From E. Stellar, "The psychology of motivation." *Psychological Review*, 1954, 61, 5–22. Copyright 1954 by the American Psychological Association. Reprinted by permission.

direct function of the activity of excitatory centers in the hypothalamus. These centers are regulated by inhibitory centers, also in the hypothalamus, which function to suppress the activity of the excitatory centers. Both kinds of hypothalamic centers are affected by information from the internal environment of the body, by sensory stimuli, and by higher brain centers. Stellar thought that the influences of the higher centers are mediated by the hypothalamus; thus he regarded the hypothalamus as the final common path for the expression of emotion and motivation.

Stellar's theory predicts that both excitatory and inhibitory centers should be found in the hypothalamus for each different kind of basic motive. The evidence for this kind of excitatory–inhibitory organization seems to be most persuasive in the case of hunger, with the excitatory hunger center in the lateral hypothalamus and the inhibitory satiety center in the VM region. However, even with hunger there are problems with a simple excitatory–inhibitory explanation. Animals with VM lesions will not eat bad tasting food or work as hard for food. If their hunger drive were working unchecked one might expect them to eat everything voraciously and do anything to get food. With the cases of sex and aggression, the evidence is even more complex. Stimulation of many areas of the hypothalamus have affected these behaviors. There do not seem to be any simple, anatomically distinct hypothalamic centers for the control of sex and aggression.

Valenstein's Theory   Valenstein and his colleagues have offered an interpretation of role of the hypothalamus in motivation that is quite different from Stellar's viewpoint (Valenstein, Cox, and Kakolewski, 1970). To begin with, Cox and Valenstein (1969) note that the evidence for localized centers serving specific drive states have been most persuasive in experiments using lesion techniques, with the feeding and satiety centers being the most striking examples. They suggest that there are indeed localized areas in the hypothalamus concerned with assessing the internal state of the body. For example, the VM nucleus seems to contain glucoreceptors sensitive to the level of sugar in the blood. If one of these centers is destroyed by a lesion, fairly limited effects will be observed. However, motivated behavior involves more than the assessment of the internal milieu. It also involves monitoring of the environment to recognize relevant stimuli, and the execution of appropriate motor acts. Electrical stimulation may activate neural elements involved in any of these functions. Thus, the fact that lesions often produce fairly circumscribed effects associated with specific anatomical locations is not inconsistent with the possibility that electrical stimulation may produce a wider range of effects over a greater anatomical area.

Valenstein, et al., (1970) question the common assumption that electrical stimulation of the hypothalamus activates distinct drive states like hunger and thirst. They point out several problems with this assumption. First, there are many cases where stimulation at the same anatomical site can elicit quite different behavior. For example, Caggiula (1970) and Gallistel (1973) reported the elicitation of male sexual behavior and eating from the same electrode. Second, many of the behaviors elicited by hypothalamic stimulation are species-specific, appearing in some species but not others. Rats will show gnawing and hoarding behavior, roosters will crow, gerbils will show a characteristic foot-thumping behavior. It is hard to believe that there is a drive state analagous to hunger or thirst associated with each of these behaviors. Third, if electrical stimulation activated a strong drive like hunger, one might expect that it would be aversive to an animal and that he would work to turn the stimulation off. In fact, animals will often work to turn such stimulation *on*. Finally, and perhaps most importantly, Valenstein et al. suggest that the results of many studies may be due to the limitations of their testing situations. Usually, if an investigator is interested in studying hunger, he will provide his animals with food and nothing else. Valenstein and his colleagues have shown that if the animal is given a wider range of choice, a number of different behaviors can become associated with the same hypothalamic stimulus.

In one experiment, Valenstein and his colleagues found that if a rat ate in response to stimulation and the food were then removed, another behavior gradually appeared. For example, if water and pieces of wood were provided, the animal came to drink or gnaw on the wood when stimulated. If the food were then reintroduced, the drinking or gnawing behavior were elicited as frequently as the initially preferred eating. When one behavior was elicited by stimulation, a second behavior could almost always be added by removing the goal object of the first behavior for a period of time. In another study, Valenstein et al. (1970) reported that rats who ate in response to stimulation often began to drink instead if the food was changed to another familiar food or even if the shape of the food was changed. This contrasts greatly with the behavior of a rat deprived of food, who will easily generalize to different foods.

To replace the assumption that electrical stimulation of the hypothalamus activates specific drive states, Valenstein et al. (1970) suggest that the stimulation may activate a wired-in hierarchy of behaviors specific to that species of animal. The response that is elicited first is one which, for that particular animal and species, is prepotent, or at the top of the hierarchy. If the goal object for that response is removed, the second response in the hierarchy appears. The occurrence of the second behavior in response to the stimulation seems to reinforce its position in the hierarchy, so that if the goal object for the first response is reintroduced, the second response continues to appear. Valenstein et al. suggest that when the neural substrate underlying a hierarchy of species-specific behaviors is activated by electrical stimulation, the discharge of the substrate by the execution of the behavior is reinforcing. Thus, the occurrence of these responses is reinforcing in itself, apart from their biological consequences.

When electrical stimulation activates a hierarchy of species-specific behavior patterns, the animal's behavior will be based both on the prepotency of the behaviors in the activated system and upon events in the environment. If no goal object associated with a given behavior is present, that behavior will often not occur. Ethologists use the term *releasers* for environmental stimuli whose presence is necessary for the appearance of a behavior pattern (Eibl-Eibesfeldt, 1970). The importance of releasers in determining the behavioral consequences of electrical stimulation is well known. For example, Von Holst and Saint Paul (1962), studying roosters, found that stimulation would elicit ferocious attack on a previously neutral stuffed polecat. If the attack succeeded in knocking over the polecat, the rooster continued to threaten. If the polecat was not knocked over, the rooster would turn and flee. The same stimulation in the absence of any object of attack elicited only restlessness in the roosters (Eibl-Eibesfeldt, 1970).

Valenstein's interpretation of the role of the hypothalamus in motivation is controversial. For example, Wise (1968) has argued that Valenstein's results could have been based on independent neural circuits that are responsible for different behaviors but are physically intertwined. A circuit for one behavior, such as feeding, might have a lower threshold for stimulation than a circuit for another behavior, such as drinking. Initially, the animal might show stimulation-induced feeding. If food were then removed and water made available, continued stimulation might eventually activate the drinking circuit.

Glickman and Schiff's Theory of Reinforcement   Glickman
and Schiff (1967, p. 88) appear to agree with Wise's argument. They suggest that hypothalamic stimulation may produce mixed effects on, say, eating and gnawing behavior, but only because the stimulation invades more than one circuit in the closely packed hypothalamus. In other ways, their theory has parallels with the position of Valenstein et al. Glickman and Schiff point out that theories of reinforcement must go beyond the traditional concern with eating, drinking, and sexual behavior to deal with the rich variety of grooming, gnawing, burrowing, hoarding, and so on behaviors that are found within different animal species. They argue that each species evolves patterns of behavior that are adaptive for that particular species. Adaptive responses are "those which bring the animal into contact with stimuli that are relevant to its survival (approach) and those which remove it from stimuli which are threatening to its survival (withdrawal)." They note from their experiments on curiosity behavior that species that normally must search out and manipulate food and that are not threatened by predators show much curiosity behavior, while species with a simple and easily obtained diet who are threatened by predators do not tend to be curious. Curiosity is more likely to kill a mouse than a cat.

Glickman and Schiff suggest that reinforcement is a mechanism that has evolved to assure responding that is appropriate to that particular species. They do not believe that there is a general reinforcement mechanism that is independent of particular response patterns. Instead, they feel that activation of each neural system in the brainstem and hypo-thalamus which mediates species-specific behaviors is, in itself, reinforc-ing. The "wisdom of evolution" had decreed that the performance of approach sequences are positively reinforcing and the performance of withdrawal sequences are negatively reinforcing.

The Subjective Experience of Hypothalamic Events in Humans

We have seen that the hypothalamus plays a central role in feeding, sexual, and aggressive behaviors, although the interpretation of that role is open to question. One might expect that, since the hypothalamus is so intimately involved in emotional and motivational phenomena, the stimula-tion or destruction of the hypothalamus would be accompanied by vivid subjective experiences. This is not the case. Humans stimulated in the hypothalamus do not generally report the experience of strong feelings or emotions. White (1940) reported that electrical stimulation of the hypo-thalamus of conscious humans did not elicit unusual sensations, emotion-al changes, or alterations of consciousness, although pronounced autonomic changes were observed. Similarly, in a report of 2651 electrode sites in 82 patients, Sem-Jacobson (1968) found relatively few changes in mood and consciousness when he stimulated the area of the hypo-thalamus. In addition, critical diseases of the hypothalamus in humans often produce no subjective emotional reactions. Bauer's (1954) review of 60 cases of hypothalamic disease reported that 21 showed psychic dis-turbances such as rage, abnormal sexual behavior, and compulsive laugh-ing and crying. Unfortunately, Bauer did not differentiate between the outward expression of these disturbances and their subjective experience. Reynolds (1971) has suggested that laughter produced by hypothalamic lesions is entirely compulsive and not associated with the subjective ex-perience of humor, while lesions in the limbic system that produce laughter also make the patient *feel* funny. The latter patient, Reynolds suggested, often reminds one of a person who continually laughs at his own bad jokes.

These results suggest that the emotional and motivational state me-diated by the hypothalamus is incomplete in at least one crucial respect—the subjective experience of the state is largely missing.

The Limbic System

The cerebral cortex which covers most of the visible surface of the brain is called the *neocortex*, or new cortex, because it is the most recent brain structure to appear in the course of evolution. The neocortex has six distinct layers of cells that can be distinguished through a microscope.

Most of the structures making up the *limbic system* are also cortical, or layered, in organization, but they only contain three to five layers of cells. They are phylogenetically older, appearing sooner in evolution, and they are therefore termed paleocortex, or old cortex.

Until recently, many of the paleocortical structures were assumed to serve the sense of smell because they receive projections from the olfactory nerves. These structures were then called the rhinencephalon or smell brain, and this term is still used occasionally. When it was realized that the cortical representations of the autonomic nervous system were located in this region, the paleocortical structures were often termed the visceral brain. The most widely used term for these structures today is the limbic system. This name derived from the word "limbus" or border, and it was used to describe the way the paleocortical structures surround the brainstem (MacLean, 1970).

The appearance of the limbic system in the evolution of the brain marked a significant increase in the ability of animals to cope with new situations. The instinctive fixed action patterns which seem to be organized in hypothalamic and brainstem structures often contain impressively complex sequences of behavior that allow animals to establish territory, hunt, mate, breed, care for the young, and so forth. However, these sequences are generally stereotyped and they cannot adapt easily to new situations. For example, O. Koenig reported difficulty in breeding titmice because the parent birds threw the young out of the nest even though they were healthy and well-fed. It turned out that they were *too* well-fed—they did not gape or open their mouths to their parents because they were not hungry. Failure to gape is evidently a signal in the titmouse that the infant is sick or dead, and the parent reacted accordingly. By forcing the young to eat less frequently, Koenig was able to restore the gaping and raise healthy titmice (Koenig, 1951; reported in Eibl-Eibesfeldt, 1970). With the development of the paleocortical and later neocortical structures, animals become better able to vary their behavior in accordance with environmental events and less dependent on stereotyped fixed action patterns.

The importance of the limbic system to motivation and emotion was suggested in 1937 by the anatomist James Papez, using anatomical considerations almost exclusively. He noted that, whereas the neocortex tends to be connected to the thalamus, the paleocortical structures are reciprocally connected with the hypothalamus. He suggested that this paleocortex–hypothalamus system represents the "anatomical basis for emotion." Papez noted that emotion involves both the experience of a feeling-state and the expression of action and suggested that emotional *expression* is mediated by the hypothalamus since it can occur in decorticate animals. However, he felt that subjective emotional *experience* is a function of the paleocortical structures.

MACLEAN'S CONCEPTUALIZATION OF LIMBIC SYSTEM FUNCTIONING

The limbic system is enormously complex and is only beginning to be understood. One attempt to conceptualize its functions has been offered by MacLean (1968; 1969; 1970), and it provides us with a useful starting point. MacLean suggests that the limbic system can be seen as including three major circuits. The first, labeled 1 on Figure 3.4, is identified with the amygdala and the second, labeled 2, with the septal area. MacLean suggests that the amygdala circuit is concerned with feeling and emotions associated with self-preservation, such as feeding, fighting, and fear. The septal circuit is theoretically concerned with sociability, sex, procreation, and preservation of the species. MacLean notes that both of these circuits receive much input from the olfactory apparatus, presumably because the sense of smell plays such an important role in feeding, fighting, and mating behavior in lower animals (Riss, Halpern, and Scalia, 1969).

The third major pathway, not numbered but visible in Figure 3.4A, is largely bypassed by the olfactory apparatus. It includes the mammillo-thalamic tract connecting the mammillary bodies (M) with the anterior thalamus (A.T.) and the fibers going on to the cingulate gyrus. MacLean (1970) notes that, unlike the other circuits, this pathway is virtually absent in reptiles and develops greatly during evolution reaching its greatest size in humans. He suggests that this circuit may serve social and sexual functions like the septal circuit and that its elaboration during evolution may reflect the shift in emphasis from olfactory to visual regulation of this behavior.

It is impossible to adequately test any general conceptualization on the basis of present knowledge. There are many inconsistent and puzzling experimental findings which may reflect inadequacies or differences in experimental methodologies, measurement techniques, or species differences. But, on balance, there does seem to be evidence that the amygdala hippocampus area is intimately concerned with fearful and aggressive behavior. Stimulation of these structures often causes attack and defensive behavior, while lesioning produces marked taming of aggressive animals and humans (Grossman, 1967). Also, septal stimulation is positively reinforcing and sometimes produces sexual responses in animals and it often produces pleasures in humans, sometimes with sexual overtones. Septal lesions, on the other hand, produce at least transitory emotional reactivity and sometimes viciousness in animals (Grossman, 1967).

CIRCUITS INVOLVING AGGRESSION AND FEAR

The Kluver-Bucy Syndrome   Shortly after Papez suggested the role of the limbic system in emotion, Kluver and Bucy (1937, 1938, 1939)

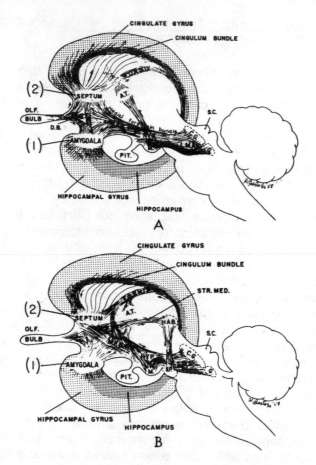

FIGURE 3.4   Schematic drawing illustrating elements of MacLean's conception of the organization of the limbic system. Emphasis is placed upon the importance of the medial forebrain bundle (MFB) as a major line of communication between the limbic system and the hypothalamus and midbrain. *A*, ascending pathways to the limbic system, with emphasis on the divergence of fibers from MFB to the amygdala and septum. These circuits are labeled 1 and 2 because of special attention given to them in text. *B*, descending pathways from the limbic system. A.T., anterior thalamus; C.G., central gray; D.B., diagonal band of Broca; G., tegmentum; HAB., habenula; HYP., hypothalamus; I.P., interpeduncular nucleus; L.M.A., limbic midbrain area of Nauta; M., mammillary body; PIT., pituitary; S.C., superior colliculus. From P. D. MacLean, "Contrasting functions of limbic and neocortical systems of the brain and their relevance to psychophysiological aspect of medicine." *American Journal of Medicine*. 1958, 25, 611–626. Copyright © 1958 by Dun-Donnelly Publishing Co. Reprinted by permission.

made the now classic discovery that striking behavior changes occur when the tips of the temporal lobes are removed. Kluver and Bucy intended to study the role of the temporal lobes in the effects of hallucinogenic drugs. They cut away the tips of the temporal lobes in normally aggressive and intractible rhesus monkeys, removing the amygdala, anterior hippocampus, and much temporal neocortex. To their surprise, the animals showed a dramatic loss of anger and fear. They became tame, friendly, and easily handled, and they approached such normally feared objects as a snake and a burning match. The animals also showed unusual oral behavior, mouthing everything within reach, including metal nails, dirt, feces, the burning match, and the snake. They were also abnormally restless and active. The male monkeys showed hypersexual behavior: they masturbated constantly and attempted to copulate with unreceptive female monkeys, male monkeys, cats, and dogs.

This strange pattern of a loss of anger and fear, orality, unusual hyperactivity, and male hypersexuality has been called the *Kluver-Bucy Syndrome*. Subsequent experiments have demonstrated that the fear and anger reducing effects of the syndrome can be duplicated with lesions restricted to the amygdala and/or hippocampus. Amygdalectomies are particularly effective, and have been shown to reduce aggression even in fierce untamable animals such as the lynx.

Terzian and Dalle Ore (1955) report a constellation of symptoms very similar to the Kluver-Bucy syndrome in the sad case of a 19-year-old man suffering both grand mal and psychomotor epilepsy. Grand mal epilepsy involves seizures with body rigidity and convulsions which interrupt behavior. Psychomotor attacks differ from the more common seizures in that there is a loss of consciousness but activity continues and the patient appears to be conscious. During the attack the patient's behavior may be routine or he may engage in unusual antisocial behavior which may be aggressive or sexual in nature (Coleman, 1956). Psychomotor epilepsy has often been identified with abnormal EEG activity in the hippocampus amydagla region, and is for this reason often called temporal lobe epilepsy.

One of the common methods for the treatment of severe cases of temporal lobe epilepsy that do not respond to drugs has been the surgical removal of the temporal lobe that contains the abnormal EEG activity. This often relieves the attacks with few undesirable side effects. Unfortunately, it did not for the case reported by Terzian and Dalle Ore, and it was decided to remove the opposite temporal lobe as well. The second operation caused the symptoms of the Kluver-Bucy syndrome to appear.

Before the two operations the patient had a "well-preserved memory, a serviceable character, and normal intelligence." However, he had frequent epileptic attacks, some followed by confused states during which he assaulted others and attempted suicide. After the operations there was a "complete loss of emotional behavior." The patient was meek toward the doctors and nurses who had previously been objects of attack, and he could not be provoked to violence. He also became exhibitionistic, proudly displaying his erect penis and masturbating in front of male doctors. He became indifferent to women, in marked contrast to his behavior before the operations. The patient exhibited hyperactivity similar to that seen in the Kluver-Bucy animals, but he did not show unusual oral behavior. He also showed a severe loss of memory, a condition which has been observed in other cases following bilateral hippocampal damage (Scoville and Milner, 1957). He did not recognize and was indifferent to his parents, even though he had been deeply attached to his mother, and he seemed to have forgotten all events of his past life. The operations apparently stopped the psychomotor attacks, but at a tragic cost. The grand mal seizures reappeared several months after the second operation.

More restricted lesions to the amygdala have been found to lessen aggression and rage in humans without the extremely debilitating effects found by Terzian and Dalle Ore. Such effects have been reported by a number of investigators. For example, Heimburger, Whitlock, and Kalsbeck (1966) report some improvement in 23 of 25 patients who underwent amygdalectomy. Narabayashi and his colleagues (Narabayashi, 1961; Narabayashi and Uno, 1966) performed 98 cases of bilateral and unilateral amygdalectomy between 1961 and 1966. One of these developed symptoms of the Kluver-Bucy syndrome. Of 40 cases in which long-term results could be evaluated in 1966, Narabayashi and Uno report lasting calming and taming effects in 27 cases. Sano and his colleagues have attempted to treat rage and aggression more directly by lesioning the posterior hypothalamus. They report "satisfactory calming effects" in all of their 22 patients (Sano, Yoshioka, Ogashiwa, Ishijima, and Ohye, 1966).

A sophisticated technique for creating therapeutic lesions in humans has been reported by Mark and Ervin (1970). For example, Schwab, Sweet, Mark, Kjeliberg, and Ervin (1966) first implanted 48 electrodes in the limbic system to localize the area of the brain that is malfunctioning. By recording from these electrodes, they could pick up the location of abnormal neural firing, and by stimulating through the same electrode, they could at times create a seizure artificially and duplicate the patient's symptoms. This stimulation and recording can be carried out by telemetery, so that the patient is free to move about on the ward without being hindered by wires and without knowing exactly when or where the stimulation will occur. Once the approximate location of the abnormal activity is established, the same electrodes can be used to lesion the area, hopefully stopping the seizures.

The increased use of psychosurgical techniques has been termed a renaissance by some (Rylander, 1973) in the belief that such techniques can effectively treat disorders that have resisted conventional kinds of therapy. However, others have strongly condemned any use of psychosurgical techniques, arguing that they involve an unacceptable assault on the integrity of the individual. Still others have taken a middle position, arguing against a total ban on psychosurgery but at the same time criticizing the practices of some psychosurgeons on both scientific and ethical grounds. We shall examine this controversy in the next chapter. For the present, we shall examine studies using psychosurgical techniques without commenting on these issues.

Stimulation Studies   Strong electrical stimulation in the amygdala–hippocampus regions in animals generally produces rage and attack behavior or fear-like defensive behavior. This effect has been observed in humans as well (Chapman, 1960; Heath, 1964; Delgado, Mark, Sweet, Ervin, Weiss, Bach-y-Rita, and Hagiwara, 1968; Ervin, Mark, and Stevens, 1969). This is illustrated in an interview reported by King (1961), during which the amygdala of an epileptic woman was stimulated. The electrodes were implanted for neurological diagnosis, and the patient was fully conscious and responding to the interviewer when the stimulation was applied.*

Interviewer questions subject about how she feels.

SUBJECT: "I just feel everything is all wrong. Like I can't be a part of anything. Like I didn't belong and everything is a dream or something."

INTERVIEWER: "Did you feel this way before the operation?" (He is referring to the implanting of electrodes.)

SUBJECT: "Yeah, I felt the same way. I didn't want anything and I didn't belong any more." The subject's voice tone was extremely flat and lacking in emphasis. Her facial expression was blank and unchanging.

The region of the amygdala was then stimulated with a 5 ma. current.

INTERVIEWER: "How do you feel now?

SUBJECT (voice much higher in tone): "I feel like I want to get up from this chair! Please don't let me do it! (There is a change to strong voice inflection and marked alteration in facial expression to express pleading.) Don't do this to me. I don't want to be mean!"

INTERVIEWER: "Feel like you want to hit me?"

SUBJECT: "Yeah, I just want to hit something. (Appears and sounds aroused and angry) I want to get something and just tear it up. Take it so I won't (Hands her scarf to interviewer; he hands her a stack of paper, and without further verbal exchange she tears it to shreds) I don't like to feel like this!"

The level of stimulating current was then reduced to 4 ma.

SUBJECT (immediately changing to wide smile):   "I know it's silly, what I'm doing."

INTERVIEWER: "Now feel better?"

SUBJECT: "A little bit."

INTERVIEWER: "Can you tell me any more about how you were feeling a moment ago?"

SUBJECT: "I wanted to get up from this chair and run. I wanted to hit something; tear up something-anything. Not you, just anything. I just wanted to get up and tear. I had no control of myself."

The level of stimulating current was then increased to 5 ma. again.

SUBJECT (voice loud and pleading):   "Don't let me hit you!"

INTERVIEWER: "How do you feel now?"

SUBJECT: "I think I feel a little better like this. I get it out of my system. I don't have those other thoughts (her pre-existing mental symptoms) when I'm like this. . .Take my blood pressure. Make them cut this thing off, it's killing me! Take my blood pressure, I say! (Strong voice inflection and facial appearance of anger.) Quit holding me! I'm getting up! You'd better get somebody else if you want to hold me! I'm going to hit you!" (Raises arm as if to strike.)

The stimulating current was then reduced to 4 ma.

SUBJECT (wide smile and laugh):   "Why does it make me do this? I couldn't help it. I didn't have any control. I wanted to slap your face. I don't like to be done like that." (Voice relaxed: tone apologetic.)

The stimulating current was then shut off and the interview directed toward a detailed review of what had gone on. Some new questions were put:

INTERVIEWER: "Did you see anyone? Your husband?"

SUBJECT: No. I didn't. I didn't even think about my husband."

INTERVIEWER: "Did you feel any pain?"

SUBJECT: "No, it's just a feeling in my body. No pain."

INTERVIEWER: "Would you like to go through that again?"

SUBJECT: "No. It didn't pain, but I don't like the feelings."

INTERVIEWER: "Can you describe them?"

SUBJECT: "I can't describe it, just can act it. I felt better in a way; I wasn't worried any more." (Her mental complaints.)

Limbic Malfunctions and Violent Behavior   We have seen that psychomotor epilepsy involves attacks in which the patient appears to be conscious. The term "psychomotor" was coined in 1935 to describe the association of apparently purposeful behavior with clouded mental states (Green, Duisberg, and McGrath, 1951). Psychomotor attacks usually last for a few seconds or minutes, but they may last for several days. A patient might look at a clock and realize that hours had passed with no recollection of the events that had transpired (Coleman, 1956). Mark and Ervin (1970) report on one man who, driving a large trailer truck, blacked out in Los Angeles and did not wake up until he was near Reno, Nevada. The patient had a similar experience on a motorcycle.

Psychomotor attacks may be associated with bizarre antisocial behavior. The painter Van Gogh suffered from attacks of irrational behavior followed by amnesia. During one of these he cut off one of his ears and sent it to a woman acquaintance (Coleman, 1956). In another case, Mark and Ervin (1970) describe the case of an attractive young woman known as Julia, who had assaulted twelve people by the age of 21. The most serious attack occurred when she was at a movie with her parents at age 18. She felt the familiar sensation of an attack coming on and went to wait in the ladies lounge. She automatically took a knife which she kept for self-protection from her purse. Inside the lounge another girl inadvertently brushed against Julia's arm. Julia struck quickly and viciously with the knife, penetrating the other girl's heart. In a later attack, she drove a pair of scissors into the lung of a nurse. Fortunately, both of Julia's victims survived, but that is not always the case. Mark and Ervin also report on a young girl of 14, called Jennie, who murdered two younger siblings because she could not stand their crying.

Psychomotor epilepsy dramatically demonstrates the action of the limbic system in emotion. MacLean (1970) notes that abnormal EEG activity in limbic structures, particularly the amygdala and hippocampus, is almost always involved in cases like those of Julia and Jennie. In fact, MacLean refers to psychomotor epilepsy as limbic epilepsy. There is evidence that the amygdala–hippocampus portion of the limbic system is particularly susceptible to injury-induced seizure activity. Grossman (1963) injected a cholinergic substance into the amygdala of cats. *One injection* produced abnormal EEG spike and seizure activity that lasted for as long as six months, and behavioral viciousness and rage that lasted for the rest of the animal's life. Injury to these structures in humans is often caused by a lack of oxygen, particularly at birth, head injuries, certain infections, and brain tumors (Mark and Ervin, 1970).

In many cases, brain malfunctions that are hidden and unsuspected may be associated with violent behavior. These malfunctions may not be associated with epileptic attacks or even abnormal scalp EEG's. Their *only* symptom may be violent and impulsive behavior (Stevens, Sachdev, and Milstein, 1968). Mark and Ervin (1970) briefly review the literature linking EEG abnormalities with criminal behavior. They report a wide variety of findings, most appearing to show relationships between certain kinds of crime and EEG abnormalities, others showing no relationships. Mark and Ervin suggest that this variability in results is due to the diversity in the definition of criminal behavior, in EEG techniques and scoring procedures, and in the use of controls and age corrections. In addition, there is evidence that many marked EEG abnormalities may go undetected by EEGs taken from the scalp. Studies using recording electrodes buried in the amygdala and other limbic system structures have revealed abnormal activity that does not appear on the usual scalp EEG (Chapman, 1960; Heath and Mickle, 1960; Mark and Ervin, 1970). In fact, Chatrian and Chapman (1960) reported that abnormal spikes in one part of the amygdala could occur independently of other spikes only a few millimeters away.

Many cases of temporal lobe disease may thus go undiagnosed and improperly treated. The young girl Jennie mentioned above is a good case in point. After her two murders, a thorough medical and psychiatric study was done which found *no abnormality*. Because of her age and the sense-lessness of her crimes, she was referred for depth electrode study of the temporal lobes. The study used a system of remote brain recording and stimulation developed by Delgado in which completely free-moving pa-tients can be monitored and stimulated by wireless telemetery (Delgado et al., 1968). Jennie's depth electrodes revealed normal EEG tracings from the surface of the temporal lobes and the amygdala and abnormal discharges localized in the hippocampus. Since it was known that the patient became violent when she heard a baby's cry, a tape recording of crying was played. This produced seizure activity and an angry, anxious behavioral response. Electrical stimulation of the same region produced seizure activity and a "waving, floating feeling" that Jennie reported ex-periencing before; she had never mentioned it because she thought every-one had such feelings.

Mark and Ervin consider Jennie's case significant for two reasons:

> *First, it shows violent, irrational behavior may be the only overt*
> *symptom of brain disease, especially when the abnormalities are*
> *deep within the brain and do not register on brain wave record-*
> *ings from the scalp, or even from the surface of the brain itself.*
> *Secondly, it proves that we need, but do not yet have, some ac-*
> *curate method of identifying people with deep brain disease,*
> *preferably before they commit any violent act, but certainly, at*
> *least, before they commit more than one (Mark and Ervin, 1970,*
> *p. 121).*

Mark and Ervin suggest four behavioral symptoms that are often present in cases of hidden brain disease: (a) a history of violent physical assault such as child-beating, (b) pathological intoxication in which the drinking of a small amount of alcohol triggers violence, (c) a history of impulsive sexual behavior, and (d) a history of many traffic violations and accidents. Behavior symptoms are also used to diagnose minimal brain dysfunction in children, including hyperactivity, short attention span, emo-tional outbursts, and variability of mood (Stevens et al., 1968). Further understanding of the biochemical and physiological bases of these symp-toms is necessary to develop techniques for the early identification and effective treatment of individuals who are violence-prone because of brain disease.

It should perhaps be emphasized that Mark and Ervin do not argue that all violence-prone individuals are suffering from brain disease. As we shall see in the chapter on aggression, there are many reasons for violence, some of them quite rational. Also it is not true that all those suffering from brain disease are violence prone. They argue that the problem of violence based on brain disease is important, however, because an unknown number of afflicted persons are confined to institutions that are doing nothing to help them, or they are not confined or treated when they are a threat to themselves and to others. Mark and Ervin studied 84 inmates at a medium-security prison with scalp EEGs and the Minnesota Multiphasic Personality Inventory (MMPI), a personality test with scales for the measurement of antisocial tendencies. They found that the 53% of the prisoners who had normal EEGs tended to score high on antisocial traits. The 47% of the prisoners with abnormal EEGs scored in the normal range of the MMPI (LaBrecque, 1972). This suggests that the latter individuals are well enough socialized but that they simply cannot control their behavior during seizure activity. Nothing is being done in the prisons to help these individuals. As Ervin points out, contemporary penologic and rehabilitation programs "cannot possibly teach a person with such organic impairment to control his destructive tendencies (F.R. Ervin, in LaBrecque, 1972, p. 302)".

Environmental Effects   We have seen that stimulation in the amygdala–hippocampus region often produces rage and fear, while lesions in this region have taming effects. Evidently at least some of the structures in this area act in some way to excite fear and aggressive behavior. However, the effects of lesions and stimulation in these regions depend to a great extent on environmental events. An animal stimulated in the amygdala in the absence of any relevant external stimulus will rarely attack the wall just as Von Holst and Saint Paul's (1962) roosters showed attack behavior when stimulated in an aggression-eliciting area only when a stuffed polecat was present. When stimulation-induced attack behavior does occur, it is directed to some extent at appropriate environmental objects. The woman reported by King (1961) who was stimulated in the amygdala during the interview did not at once attack the interviewer. Instead, she asked for a sheaf of papers which she tore up. In almost all cases, behavior seems to be a joint function of events in the brain and events in the environment.

Studies reported by Delgado (1969) illustrate the importance of the social environment in mediating the effect of electrical stimulation of the brain. He used colonies of rhesus monkeys in which the natural dominance of the stimulated animal could be established. He demonstrated that a dominant monkey stimulated in an aggression-eliciting region would usually attack a rival male monkey rather than a favored female or an infant, suggesting that the hostility evoked by the brain stimulation was directed according to the animal's previous experiences in the colony.

In another experiment, Delgado studied the effects of stimulation of an aggression-eliciting area in a single female monkey, Lina, in three different colonies. She was given 120 stimulations in each colony. In the first group Lina was the least dominant of four monkeys. In this group Lina attempted to attack another animal only once, and *she* was the object of attack when stimulation occured on 24 occasions. In the second group, Lina ranked third of the four animals, and stimulation cased her to attack other animals 24 times, while she was attacked only three times. In group three, Lina ranked second in dominance. Here, stimulation evoked 79 attacks from Lina, and she was never attacked at all. Thus, the same brain stimulus that causes a relatively dominant animal to attack others will cause the same animal to be attacked when it is with more dominant animals. Delgado concludes that stimulation of aggressive circuits in his animals "determined the affective state of hostility, but behavioral performance depended upon the individual characteristics of the animal, including learned skills and previous experiences" (1969, p. 128).

CIRCUITS INVOLVING POSITIVE STATES

We saw that MacLean has suggested that a circuit centered in the septal area is concerned with expressive and feeling states conducive to the preservation of the species, such as "sociability and other preliminaries to copulation and reproduction" (1968, p. 84). MacLean suggests that the cingulate gyrus and parts of the hippocampus contribute to this circuit.

Stimulation and lesioning of the septal area produces effects that are markedly different from those produced by manipulations of the amygdala region. Septal lesions in rats produce temporary viciousness and increased reactivity to stimulation (Brady and Nauta, 1953; Grossman, 1967). Such lesions usually speed the acquisition of avoidance responses, suggesting that fear may have greater effects on septal-lesioned animals. Lesions of the amygdala and hippocampus, in contrast, typically retard the acquisition of such avoidance responses (Grossman, 1967).

Stimulation in the septal region of animals is positively reinforcing, in that animals will press a bar rapidly and repeatedly to stimulate this area (Olds and Milner, 1954). Such self-stimulation is sometimes associated with social and sexual responses. Olds has reported that erections occur in about one-third of his rats during self-stimulation and that grooming often occurs after the stimulation (1958; reported in MacLean, 1968). MacLean (1957) reports that septal stimulation can induce afterdischarges in cats with apparently pleasurable grooming reactions and occasional penile erection. MacLean and Ploog (1962) found that the septal area is one of the two centers above the hypothalamus where stimulation elicits penile erection in the squirrel monkey. The other center was in the anterior thalamic region, which MacLean associates with the mammillothalamic circuit that assumes importance in species which, like the squirrel monkey, have a highly developed visual system.

Septal Stimulation in Humans   Stimulation of the septal area of conscious human subjects is usually associated with subjective reports of pleasure, often with sexual overtones. The most extensive study of septal stimulation in humans is that reported by Heath (Heath and Mickle, 1960; Heath, 1964a; 1964b). Between 1950 and 1964, Heath and his associates studied 54 patients with depth electrodes, including 39 chronic schizophrenics, 7 psychomotor epileptics, and 8 nonpsychiatric patients, most with extremely painful diseases such as severe arthritis and advanced cancer. The studies of schizophrenics was based on evidence of malfunctioning in the septal area in schizophrenia. Heath postulated that septal stimulation might restore the schizophrenic's contact with reality and enhance his emotional responsiveness (1964b). Unhappily, septal stimulation did not turn out to have lasting clinical value for schizophrenic patients (Heath and Mickle, 1960).

Heath found that septal stimulation was described as a pleasurable experience by most of his patients, although the reliability of such subjective reports is questionable, particularly with schizophrenic patients. To escape some of these difficulties, stimulation was often delivered during interviews without the patient's knowledge. We saw an example above of the effect of stimulation to the amygdala during an interview. Septal stimulation often produced striking positive changes in the content of the interview. Expressions of depression and despair suddenly changed to expressions of optimism and reports of past or anticipated pleasant experiences. The patients were generally at a loss to explain their sudden change in thinking. For example, Heath reports that one patient, on the verge of tears, "described his father's near-fatal illness and condemned himself as somehow responsible, but when the septal region was stimulated, he immediately terminated this conversation and within 15 seconds exhibited a broad grin as he discussed plans to date and seduce a girl friend. When asked why he had changed the conversation so abruptly, he replied that the plans concerning the girl suddenly came to him" (1964b, p. 225). Another patient, who had been severely depressed for over two years, "smiled broadly and related a sexual experience of his youth within one minute after onset of septal stimulation" (1964b, p. 225).

Heath (1964a) reports that sexual thoughts are often induced by septal stimulation but that objective sexual arousal is rare. Only three male patients, all nonschizophrenic, showed penile erection following septal stimulation. One female epileptic showed a sexual response when ACh was injected into the septal area, her depression being consistently changed to strong pleasure associated with sexual arousal and, frequently, spontaneous orgasm. Interestingly, both this patient and a male patient showed distinct seizure-like EEG activity during orgasm (Heath, 1972). Heath notes that such consistent association between pleasant responses and sexual content is found only in the septal area. Stimulation of other parts of the brain in humans results in expression of pleasure, but the sexual content is usually absent.

Septal stimulation seems to offer significant, although temporary, relief from intractible pain. Heath (1964a) states that the intense physical pain of three cancer patients was immediately relieved with septal stimulation. Ervin et al. (1969) report that stimulation to the principal outflow pathway of the septal area, the medial forebrain bundle (MFB) produces visible relaxation in pain patients. The patients are more communicative and mildly euphoric ("like two martinis"). When the stimulation lasts for 30 to 45 minutes, these positive changes persist for several hours. When the stimulation is carried out longer than this, the patient gradually begins to lose control and looks "slightly drunk."

These findings, and animal experiments that we will discuss below, lead to the suggestion that there is an area of reward or positive reinforcement or a pleasure center extending from the septal area, down the MFB through the lateral hypothalamus, and to the limbic midbrain area.

Positive Responses Elicited Outside the Septal Area   The elicitation of pleasure and sexual arousal in humans is not confined to this septal area–MFB system. In fact, many structures that usually give aversive responses upon stimulation may give rewarding responses at very low current intensities. Bishop, Elder, and Heath (1963) reported that, in one schizophrenic subject, mild stimulation was apparently rewarding in the amygdala, diffuse thalamic system, midhypothalamus, and posterior hypothalamus. More intense stimulation was aversive at all of these sites. There also was evidence that very strong stimulation in the septal area is also aversive.

In other studies, Delgado (1969) has reported that stimulation of the temporal lobes and amygdala region produced pleasurable responses and flirtatious behavior in one male and two female epileptic patients. Also,

Ervin et al. (1969) report that amygdala stimulation in a male epileptic produced a "tremendous" feeling of relief from anxiety and "super relaxation." This patient was one of the few humans reported to have become "addicted" to stimulation; he became severely depressed when amygdala stimulation was discontinued. Patients stimulated in the septal area are not reported to have a continuing need for the stimulation.

Results similar to these occur with animals. As we shall see, the strong tendency of rats to press a bar to stimulate their septal area quickly extinguishes after the current is turned off. Also, rats will work to turn *on* septal stimulation, but they will also work to turn it *off*. Some have suggested that positive and negative sites exist at many points in the nervous system, with the positive sites being more common in some areas (such as the septal area) and less common in others (such as the amygdala). Mild or brief stimulation may turn on only the positive sites in both areas, while strong or prolonged stimulation may begin to affect the negative sites. Whatever the case, the finding that the response to septal stimulation can be negative and that amygdala stimulation can be positive suggests that it is too early to be sure of the exact location of different neural systems in the brain.

MOYER'S CONCEPTUALIZATION OF THE ACTION OF NEURAL SYSTEMS

Many psychologists have interpreted the data we have considered as indicating that there are a variety of built-in neural systems in both animals and man that are substrates for the motivation of different kinds of behaviors. We have considered the views of Valenstein et al. (1970) and Glickman and Schiff (1967). The evidence suggests that there may be circuits responsible for various kinds of fearful avoidance behavior, friendly social behavior, sexual behavior, maternal behavior, aggressive behavior, euphoric behavior, and depressed behavior. Anatomically, these circuits may overlap to some extent. For example, there is evidence that the amygdala contains separate but overlapping anatomical areas serving aggression and fear (Moyer, 1968). These circuits are generally seen as working in a constant interaction with each other and with the environment. Moyer (1970; 1972) has speculated about how such neural systems might operate and interact with each other.

Moyer suggests that a particular neural system may vary along a continuum of activity. The usual state of a neural system is sensitized, or inactive, until activated by an appropriate environmental event. At one extreme, it may be insensitive, in that a normally effective environmental stimulus will not activate it. For example, bilateral removal of the amygdala may cause insensitivity in circuits responsible for certain kinds of aggressive and fearful behaviors. An amygdalectomized monkey may suffer painful attack without retaliating or adequately defending itself.

At the other extreme, a neural system might be so sensitive that it may be spontaneously active, even in the absence of an appropriate environmental stimulus. When a neural system is active, Moyer suggests like Valenstein that its discharge through appropriate overt behavior will be reinforcing. However, the individual will probably not respond in the total absence of an appropriate environmental stimulus. We have considered numerous cases where a neural system may have been artificially excited by chemical or electrical stimulation of the brain. For example, Von Holst and Saint Paul (1962) showed that stimulation of circuits eliciting aggression in roosters when a stuffed polecat was present resulted in only motor restlessness when no appropriate stimulus was present.

Spontaneous activity in a neural system increases the range of environmental stimuli that are appropriate to trigger overt behavior. Von Holst and Saint Paul's roosters showed no attack on the stuffed polecat until the stimulation raised the sensitivity of the aggression circuits. Moyer suggests that spontaneous activity in some aggression systems in humans is accompanied by subjective feelings of anger, aggressive fantasies, and a heightened readiness to react to aggression-eliciting stimuli (See Berkowitz, 1965b). The cases of violence associated with temporal lobe epilepsy may be due to spontaneous activity in aggression circuits caused by abnormal electrical activity in the brain. Such activity causes extreme hyperreactivity to very mild aggression eliciting stimuli. The epileptic patient Julia reacted with vicious attack when another person merely brushed against her arm.

Moyer suggests that the sensitivity of a neural system is dependent upon a large number of factors, including long-term influences such as heredity, disease, early experience, and learning; and short-term influences involving blood chemistry, general arousal, and so forth. We shall consider these in more detail in the chapter on aggressive behavior. In addition, Moyer feels that the neural systems underlying different behavior tendencies have facilitating and inhibiting effects upon one another. He notes that stimulation of septal centers that may underlie some social and sexual behaviors seems to quickly inhibit hostile, fearful, and depressed behaviors. Thus activation of the septal center may inhibit other centers serving aggression, fear, and depression. Also, stimulation that induces fear seems to inhibit certain kinds of aggression. On the other hand, neural activity associated with pain, deprivation, and frustration may tend to excite centers serving aggressive behavior.

Moyer thus feels that behavior is a function of interactions between environmental events and events in the nervous system. The latter in turn are dependent on interactions between different neural systems which in their turn are dependent upon a host of identifiable short and long-term influences. As an example, he suggests that we imagine a young girl who comes home with active aggression circuits (Moyer, 1972). The activity may have originally have been caused by changes in hormonal balance associated with menstruation or by caustic criticisms from a teacher or by rejection by a peer. Moyer suggests that the reason for the activity is not as important as the amount of activity at a given time. The total amount of activity that is present may depend on inherited qualities of her nervous system, the quality of her prenatal care, the amount of oxygen deprivation she suffered at birth, and a host of similar factors in addition to the strength of the original cause of the activity.

The more activity in the girl's aggression circuits, the more likely it is that she will respond aggressively to an appropriate environmental stimulus, and the stronger her response is likely to be. Her response to any particular stimulus will depend on the learning associated with that stimulus. If she has been punished for directing aggression toward her parents, that response may well be inhibited. However, she might be noticeably less friendly and communicative toward them, because activity in the aggression centers may inhibit activity in other circuits. And, if a more appropriate stimulus presents itself, like her little brother, she will probably vent her aggression directly. If no appropriate stimulus is present, she may engage in fantasy aggression.

Rewarding and Punishing Effects of Brain Stimulation

In 1953, James Olds was engaged in studying the reticular formation in rats. He noticed that one animal with an off-target electrode in the septal area would repeatedly return to a place on a table where a stimulus had been applied to the brain (Olds, 1956a). By giving rats a bar with which they could stimulate the septal area, Olds and Milner (1954) found that rats would work very hard, pressing the bar frequently and for long periods of time. They noted that this apparently rewarding brain stimulation made possible extreme control of animal's behavior, "possibly exceeding that exercised by any other reward previously used in animal experimentation."

Subsequent studies by Olds and his colleagues demonstrated that rats would solve a complex maze for rewarding brain stimulation. They would also cross a shock grid to get to a bar to stimulate themselves, tolerating far more painful shocks than 24-hours food-deprived rats would tolerate for food. Rats never seemed to tire of stimulation at certain sites.

One animal stimulated itself at the rate of 2000 responses per hour for 26 hours, slept exhausted for almost 20 hours, and then resumed self-stimulation at the original rate (Olds, 1958).

Some studies showed that rats with electrodes in the MFB region would engage in self-stimulation to the exclusion of satisfying other drives. Food-deprived rats who had free access for one hour a day to both food and a lever to stimulate sites in the lateral hypothalamus ignored the food and lost weight rapidly. Rats with electrodes in different areas took enough time from self-stimulation to eat (Routtenberg and Lindy, 1955). Similarly, food-deprived rats in a T-maze were observed to choose to stimulate the hypothalamus rather than eat, even though they had been without food for as much as 10 days. Other rats would choose food over stimulation in sites outside the MFB area (Spies, 1965).

ANATOMY OF THE REWARD AND PUNISHMENT SYSTEMS

At about the same time that Olds discovered that brain stimulation could serve as a reward, Delgado, Roberts, and Miller (1954) found that stimulation in other areas of the brain is punishing: animals would avoid behavior that caused stimulation of these areas. Subsequent experiments determined the approximate anatomical locus of the rewarding and punishing effects in the rat, and studies with other species have shown generally similar results.

In the rat, the rewarding area seems more extensive than the punishing area. Olds (1961) found that, of 200 electrode sites, 60% produced neither reward nor punishment. Most of these sites were in the cortex and thalamus. 35% of the electrodes gave positive effects, and only 5% produced punishment. In the cat on the other hand, punishing effects seem more common. Placements are generally quite close to those producing rewarding effects, and many sites that produce rewarding effects with brief, mild stimulation also produce punishing effects with stronger or more prolonged stimulation. Stimulation of most of the limbic system appears to be rewarding, particularly in the septal area. Stimulation of the amygdala has produced both rewarding and punishing effects. Wurtz and Olds (1962) found that the medial nuclei of the amygdala tended to be rewarding and the lateral nuclei punishing. Similar mixed results have been obtained from the hippocampus (Ursin, Ursin, and Olds, 1966).

The medial forebrain bundle (MFB), coursing through the lateral hypothalamus, seems to produce the strongest reward effects. Olds and Olds (1963) noted that stimulation to the medial hypothalamus was much less rewarding, and stimulation to the periventricular system (PVS) was found to be punishing. This is interesting in the context of the other studies we have considered suggesting that the septal MFB area is associated with positive affects and the VM hypothalamus and perifornical to central gray regions are implicated in aggression. Some have concluded that reward effects are mediated by the MFB and punishing effects by the PVS (Stein, 1964). These two systems were diagramed by Le Gros Clark in 1938, long before their behavioral significance was suspected. His diagrams are presented in Figure 3.5. The MFB and PVS appear to occupy about the same area in the figure, but actually they run parallel to one another, with the MFB lateral to the PVS.

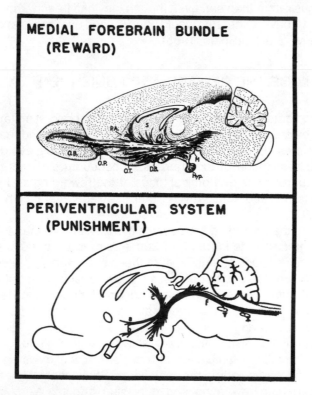

FIGURE 3.5   Schematic diagrams representing the medial forebrain bundle (MFB) and periventricular (PV) system in a generalized and primitive mammalian brain. A partial labeling of the features includes: *UPPER* —A., anterior commissure; Ch., optic chiasm; D.B., diagonal band of Broca; Hyp., pituitary (hypophysis); P.A., parolfactory area; S., septal area. *LOWER*—a., paraventricular nucleus; b., supraoptic nucleus; c., dorsomedial thalamus; d., posterior hypothalamus; e., tectum; f., motor nuclei and cranial nerves. From W. E. Le Gros Clark, J. Beattie, G. Riddoch, and N. Dott, *The hypothalamus.* Edinburgh: Oliver and Boyd, 1938. Copyright holder could not be located.

THE NATURE OF THE MOTIVATION UNDERLYING SELF-STIMULATION

A number of theories have attempted to explain the nature of the motivational state underlying the rewarding and punishing effects of brain stimulation (Olds and Olds, 1965; Deutsch and Deutsch, 1966; Milner, 1970). Some, like that of Olds, view reward and punishment as primary motives, and suggest that motivational phenomena may be described under a hedonistic pleasure versus pain dualism. Others see rewarding and punishing effects as secondary results of the excitation and inhibition or specific drives (Grossman, 1967). These theoretical issues are unlikely to be resolved in the near future.

The motivational state underlying self-stimulation must be extremely strong and compelling in some respects since animals will work so hard and go through so much to obtain the stimulation. It was initially thought that the stimulation might create a vividly pleasurable experience, and the rewarding areas were called pleasure centers (Olds, 1956a). Some worried that if such stimulation were available to human beings, they would seek stimulation-induced ecstasy to the exclusion of all other concerns. However, studies of brain stimulation in humans did not produce the frantic behavior commonly seen in animals (see below).

More thorough study showed that there are puzzling differences between rewarding brain stimulation and rewards like food and drink which satisfy real physiological needs. If rewarding brain stimulation is withheld for a short time, animals often appear to lose interest in it (Deutsch, 1972). This phenomenon manifests itself in several ways. First, rats will quickly stop pressing a bar after the current is turned off, thus the self-stimulation response has relatively low resistance to extinction. Second, more aperiodic reinforcement schedules which produce steady responding for food or water do not produce responding for brain stimulation (Gallistel, 1964). Finally, an animal may not perform a learned response like running a maze if too much time has elapsed between trials. Gallistel (1969) found that a rat quickly ran a straight runway to get to a stimulating lever if he was released immediately after a stimulation. However, if the animal was held for five munutes and then released, the rat would usually not run at all. Recall that a rat would tolerate severe and painful shock in such a runway to obtain a rewarding stimulation. Others have found that rats require a free stimulus as an *hors d'oeuvre* before they will perform behavior previously rewarded by stimulation.

Some psychologists have argued that the effects of rewarding brain stimulation are fundamentally similar to the effects of other rewards and that the apparent differences in response to brain stimulation depend on differences in delay of reinforcement, the nature of the response, and other properties of the typical self-stimulation experiment (see Gibson, Reid, Sakai, and Porter, 1965). However, others feel that the motivational state underlying self-stimulation is different in important respects from natural motives. For example, Deutsch (1963;1972) has argued from the above findings that brain stimulation itself produces the drive for brain stimulation. He suggests that each stimulus has the double function of rewarding the previous response and creating the drive for the next response. When too much time elapses between reinforcements, the drive for brain stimulation decays, and the animal loses interest. Deutsch points out that this loss of interest will not happen if a real drive like hunger is present along with the brain stimulation. The response of *hungry* rats running for brain stimulation seems indistinguishable from the response of hungry rats running for food (Olds, 1956b). Deutsch suggests that the presence of the hunger somehow prevents the decay of the drive for brain stimulation.

SELF-STIMULATION IN HUMANS

We have seen that electrical stimulation often induces reports of pleasure in humans and that the effects of such stimulation has been studied in interview situations. Self-stimulation has also been attempted in humans, with mixed results.

Bishop, Elder, and Heath (1964) tested the self-stimulation behavior of two patients, a psychomotor epileptic and a schizophrenic. They were given a key and instructed, "If it feels good, press until you want to stop." Self-stimulation behavior occurred readily, but both men continued to press the key at the same rate regardless of stimulus intensity or reinforcement schedule. In fact, they kept responding at the same rate even after the stimulus was turned off. Figure 3.6 shows typical variations in the response of a rat to changes in stimulus intensity, reinforcement schedule, and extinction and the *lack* of variation in the response of the two men to such changes. On being asked why they continued to press the bar for zero current, the schizophrenic invariably replied that it "felt good," and the epileptic would say that he was trying to cooperate, and since he had been placed in front of a lever, he assumed that he was supposed to press it!

Sem-Jacobsen (1968) reports a similar experience with an overcooperative patient who noticed that a visiting physician showed great interest whenever he smiled during stimulation. He then began to smile during stimulation that had not previously elicited any response. The patient was strongly cautioned against this, and he consequently stopped smiling even

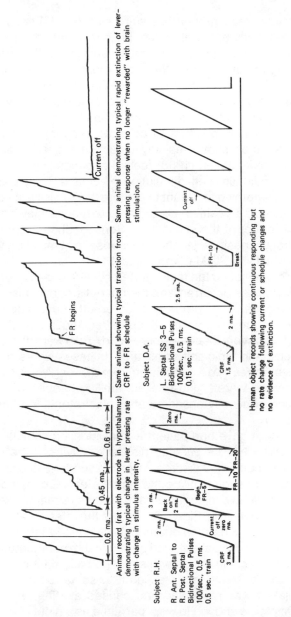

FIGURE 3.6   Comparative rat and human self-stimulation records. From M. P. Bishop, S. T. Elder, and R. G. Heath, "Attempted control of operant behavior in man with intracranial self-stimulation." In R. G. Heath (Ed.), *The role of pleasure in behavior*. New York: Hoeber, 1964. Copyright © 1964 by the Hoeber Medical Division, Harper and Row Publishers. Reprinted by permission.

when moderately pleasurable areas were stimulated. These results emphasize that the study of the effects of brain stimulation, as well as other kinds of experimentation with humans, is subject to the effects of the person's perception of his role in the experiment and the demand characteristics of the situation (Rosenthal, 1966; Orne, 1962).

Even when human subjects seem to self-stimulate only because of the subjectively felt characteristics of the stimulation, the motivation underlying self-stimulation appears to be quite complex. It cannot be assumed that the subject stimulates only to gain emotional reward and avoid punishment. Sem-Jacobsen (1968) feels that curiosity may be the dominant factor that maintains self-stimulation in humans. The person may feel an indefinable something and want to explore it, even if it is mildly unpleasant. In other cases, a positive, pleasurable response may be secondary to some other effect of the stimulation. Sem-Jacobsen reports that one apparently strongly positive, laughing response to stimulation was caused by a muscle twitch that tickled the subject.

Sem-Jacobsen found the fastest rate of self-stimulation on occasions when afterdischarges occurred and the patient's consciousness was impaired. In such cases, the current was turned off to avoid convulsion, but rapid self-stimulation continued without effect until the afterdischarge ceased and the patient became more alert. Afterward the patient was unable to explain the rapid self-stimulation. In cases where patients have stimulated themselves into a convulsion from a strongly positive electrode site they afterward were "lying relaxed, smiling happily, contrary to the restless fighting frequently observed after electrotonic treatment" (Sem-Jacobsen, 1966).

Heath (1964b) gave one patient a transistorized stimulator that was worn on the belt while he pursued his daily activities. The patient was suffering from narcolepsy, a disorder involving sudden attacks of sleeping. He was given buttons to stimulate the septal area, hippocampus, and the tegmentum in the limbic midbrain area. Counters revealed the number of presses given to each area. Figure 3.7 shows the relative rate of response in these three areas. The tegmentum button induced intense discomfort and a look of fear in the patient, and after initial experimentation he fixed the button so that it could not be pressed. The patient found hippocampal stimulation mildly aversive, but pressed it to some extent for 10 weeks. Septal stimulation was rewarding and caused alerting, allowing him to control his symptoms enough to work part-time as a night club entertainer. Friends recognized that the septal buttom promptly awakened him, and when he fell asleep too rapidly they occasionally pushed it for him. The patient reported that the septal button made him feel as if he was building up to a sexual orgasm, but he was unable to reach orgasm despite fre-

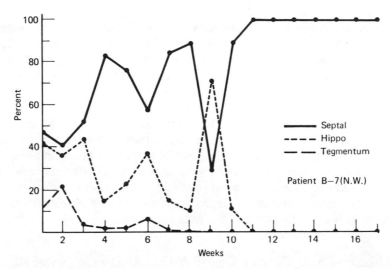

FIGURE 3.7   Comparative records of self-stimulation from sites in the septal area, hippocampus, and tegmentum in a patient with narcolepsy and cataplexy. From R. G. Heath, "Pleasure responses of human subjects to direct stimulation of the brain: Physiologic and psychodynamic considerations." In R. G. Heath (Ed.), *The role of pleasure in behavior.* New York: Hoeber, 1964. Copyright © 1964 by the Hoeber Medical Division, Harper and Row publishers. Reprinted by permission.

quent and sometimes frantic button pushing. He reported that this was frustrating and produced a nervous feeling.

Another patient, a psychomotor epileptic, was allowed to self-stimulate a variety of sites for a six-hour period (Heath, 1964b). The most frequent pressing was to a point in the medial thalamus, not because it produced pleasure, but because it made the patient almost able to recall an elusive memory. He could not quite grasp the memory and pressed the button repeatedly, up to 1100 times in an hour, to pursue it. This created considerable frustration and anger. The patient found that he could relieve the frustration by stimulating positive sites in the septal area and limbic midbrain area. He sometimes coupled the thalamic stimulation with stimuli to the more pleasurable sites. This patient also had two electrodes in the amygdala that produced moderate pleasure and one in the hippocampus that produced aversion and a sick feeling.

Heath (1964a; 1964b) reports that his findings with humans are generally consistent with animal findings in suggesting that sites yielding reward are found in the septal area and other limbic system structures, the MFB through the lateral hypothalamus, and the lateral limbic midbrain area. He notes that positive responses in the septal area often have sexual content while those in the lateral hypothalamus and limbic midbrain area yield positive responses without sexual content: "This is a good feeling." "Drunk feeling." "Happy button." Stimulation of the periventricular system and the medial limbic midbrain area induces discomfort and pain. Stimulation of the amygdala and hippocampus sometimes yield pleasure and sometimes punishment, depending in part on the intensity of the stimulation.

The motivation for self-stimulation in humans appears to be complex indeed, involving much more than a simple pursuit of pleasure and avoidance of pain. It does seem that strong subjective experiences of pleasure can be induced, some with sexual overtones and some without. However, the stimulation does not induce irresistable ecstasy, and, although the patient may wish the stimulation to be repeated, there is little evidence of addiction to brain stimulation in the published reports.

THE PHARMACOLOGY OF REWARD AND PUNISHMENT

There are a number of indications that the reward and punishment systems in the central nervous system can be pharmacologically differentiated, perhaps because the natures of the transmitters involved in the two systems are different. The understanding of the pharmacology of these systems is extremely important. Such understanding will contribute to the explanation of the mechanisms of action of known psychoactive drugs, and it may lead to the development of much more specific and effective drugs for the treatment of affective disorders. We shall consider two hypotheses which, although they are speculative and quite possibly wrong in many details, may indicate in broad outline the nature of the actions of different chemical substances in the rewarding and punishing areas of the brain.

The Catecholamine Hypothesis of Affective Disorders   Through the use of fluorescence techniques, neurons containing the catecholamines norepinepherine and dopamine and the indole amine serotonin have been discovered and traced through the brain. Many such cells can be found in the brainstem, and their axons have been seen to extend into the hypothalamus and limbic system structures (Kety, 1970). It is probable that these amines are the transmitter substances in these cells, and we have considered the process of adrenergic transmission in the last chapter and in the appendix.

Kety (1970) has outlined the history of the interest in the psychological significance of the amines, beginning with the discovery of lysergic acid diethylamide (LSD) in 1943. It was found that LSD inhibits the action of serotonin, and this led to speculation that the inhibition of serotonin in the central nervous system may be responsible for the hallucenogenic effects of LSD. Subsequent studies found that the tranquilizer reserpine depletes the level of serotonin and norepinepherine and that certain stimulant substances increase the levels of serotonin and norepinepherine in the brain.

Since then, there has been increasing evidence that drugs that deplete or inactivate norepinepherine in the brain (such as reserpine) produce sedation or depression, while drugs which increase norepinepherine (such as amphetamine) have exciting, antidepressant effects (Schildkraut and Kety, 1967). Some of these drugs and their effects are summarized in Table 3.2. Kety has stated that "practically every drug which has been found effective in altering affective states in man has also been found to exert effects on catecholamines in the brain in a way which would be compatible with the possibility that these amines are involved in the mediation of these states and in the actions of the drugs which affect them" (1970, p. 65). He suggests that one of the most effective treatments for depression in humans, electroconvulsive shock treatments, may also have its effect through the stimulation of the secretion of brain norepinepherine.

These findings have led to the "catecholamine hypothesis of affective disorders" (Schildkraut, 1969). This states that "some, if not all, depressions may be associated with a relative deficiency of norepinepherine at functionally important adrenerglc receptor sites in the brain, whereas elations may be associated with an excess of such amines" (Schildkraut and Kety, 1967, p. 28).

There is evidence that affective states other than depression are based in part upon the amines (Baldessarini, 1972). Displays of rage elicited from brain stimulation of the amygdala or lesions of the brainstem in cats have been increased or decreased by drugs which potentiate or block the action of norepinepherine (Reis and Gunne, 1965; Reis and Fuxe, 1969). Similarly, male mice in overcrowded conditions are more aggressive with artificially increased amine levels and less aggressive with decreased levels (Welsh and Welsh, 1969).

Amine metabolism also seems to be associated with sleep. Inhibition of serotonin leads to insomnia, while increased serotonin appears to increase slow wave sleep (Jouvet, 1969). Norepinepherine may be important in REM (rapid eye movement) or paradixical sleep that is often associated with dreaming. REM sleep seems to increase the synthesis of norepinepherine, and Kety (1970) suggests that REM sleep may function to replenish supplies of brain norepinepherine.

Moderate stress seems to increase the turnover of norepinepherine: the rate at which it is synthesized and utilized. More severe stress leads to the depletion of brain norepinepherine (Kety, 1970; Baldessarini, 1972). In one interesting study, stress in pregnant rats was observed to result in a sustained increase of norepinepherine turnover in the brains of their

TABLE 3.2   SUMMARY OF THE PHARMACOLOGICAL OBSERVATIONS COMPATIBLE WITH THE CATECHOLAMINE HYPOTHESIS OF AFFECTIVE DISORDERS.

DRUG	EFFECTS ON MOOD IN MAN	EFFECTS ON BEHAVIOR IN ANIMALS	EFFECTS ON CATECHOLAMINES IN BRAIN (ANIMALS)
Reserpine	Sedation Depression (in some patients)	Sedation	Depletion (intracellular deamination and inactivation)
Tetrabenazine	Sedation Depression (in some patients)	Sedation	Depletion (intracellular deamination and inactivation)
Amphetamine	Stimulant	Stimulation Excitement	Release norepinephrine (? onto receptors) Inhibits cellular uptake (and inactivation) of norepinephrine
Monoamine oxidase inhibitors	Antidepressant	Excitement Prevents and reverses reserpine-induced sedation	Increases levels
Imipramine	Antidepressant	Prevents reserpine-induced sedation Potentiation of amphetamine effects	Inhibits cellular uptake (and inactivation) of norepinephrine ? Potentiates action of norepinephrine (as in periphery)
Lithium salts	Treatment of mania		? Increases intracellular deamination of norepinephrine ? Decreases norepinephrine available at receptors
α-Methyl-paratyrosine	Sedation (transient) with hypomania upon withdrawal	Sedation (in some studies)	Inhibits synthesis

From J. J. Schildkrant and S. S. Kety, "Biogenic amines and emotion." *Science,* 1967, **156,** 21–30. Copyright © 1967 by the American Association for the Advancement of Science. Reprinted by permission.

offspring (Huttunen, 1971). Another interesting and important development has been the finding that the amines may modify the activity of hypothalamic neurons that regulate the functioning of the pituitary gland and, ultimately, the endocrine system (Baldessarini, 1972).

Stein's Hypothesis on the Pharmacology of Reward and Punishment
One of the most provocative findings in this area for our purposes is the evidence that self-stimulation may be based on adrenergic neural systems. The area eliciting the strongest self-stimulation effects, the MFB, is a major pathway for ascending amine-containing fibers (Baldessarini, 1972). Wise and Stein (1969) found that self-stimulation is inhibited by reserpine and alpha-methylparatyrosine (A-MPT), which deplete brain catecholamines. On the other hand, amphetamine and MAO inhibitors which increase the effect of the amines also facilitate self-stimulation.

Stein (1968) has taken the fact that self-stimulation appears to be based upon an adrenergic system and combined it with evidence that the effects of punishment may be mediated by a cholinergic system in which ACh is the transmitter substance. From these data Stein has evolved a speculative but quite interesting hypothesis.

Stein argues that an adrenergic reward system exists in the MFB. Adrenergic drugs will increase the rewarding qualities of that system as measured by self-stimulation, and adrenergic blocking agents will decrease the reward. Also, Stein feels that the periventricular system (PVS) contains a cholinergic punishment system. He and his colleagues have found evidence that anti-ACh drugs such as atropine, when injected into the brain, cause increases in behavior that has been suppressed by punishment, extinction, or satiation. A rat that has learned to press a bar for food rewards and that has pressed until he has eaten enough and is satiated will begin to press again if atropine is administered. The animal may not eat, and he will continue to press even if given food from another source. The atropine seems to increase the lever-pressing behavior that had been suppressed by satiation. Also, rats given atropine will tolerate more punishment, taking more shock and bitter quinine, and they will begin to perform behavior that had been extinguished. On the other hand, drugs potentiating the effects of ACh, such as the anti-AChE drug physostigmine, appear to have effects opposite to those of the anti-ACh drugs. With the former, the effects of punishment and extinction seem to become more pronounced and aversive.

Stein suggests that the adrenergic MFB reward system and the cholinergic PVS punishment system interact through limbic system structure and particularly the amygdala. The theory is illustrated in Figure 3.8. Normally, behavior is inhibited by the action of the PVS. A rewarding stimulus

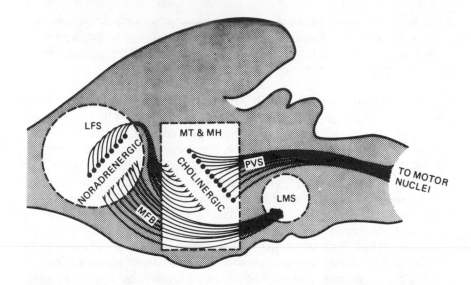

FIGURE 3.8   Diagram representing hypothetical relationships between reward and punishment mechanisms inferred from chemical stimulation experiments. A rewarding stimulus releases behavior from periventricular system (PVS) suppression by the following sequence of events: (1) Activation of the medial forebrain bundle (MFB) by stimuli previously associated with reward (or the cessation of punishment) causes release of norepinepherine into suppressor areas in limbic forebrain structures (LFS). The amygdala may function as such a suppressor area. (2) The action of norepinepherine inhibits activity in the LFS suppressor areas, thus reducing their cholinergically mediated excitation of the medial thalamus and hypothalamus (MT & MH). (3) Decreased activity in the MT and MH lessens activity in the PVS, thereby reducing its inhibitory influence on behavior. From L. Stein, *Reciprocal action of reward and punishment mechanisms*. Washington, D.C.: U. S. Government Printing Office, 1968.

causes activation in the MFB which releases norepinepherine into the amygdala and other limbic structures. This inhibits them, and their inhibition causes a lessening of the cholinergic excitation of the medial hypothalamus and thalamus. This decreases activity in the PVS, reducing its inhibitory influence on behavior.

Summary

The hypothalamus has a central role in gathering basic information about bodily functioning from receptors sensitive to glucose, hormone levels, and so forth. It also serves as the immediate control of the functioning of the autonomic and endocrine systems. However, the hypothalamus acts in the service of higher brain centers in fulfilling these functions. In humans, electrical stimulation of the hypothalamus does not give rise to the subjective experience of emotional or motivational states, although pronounced autonomic responses do occur.

Studies of eating behavior have suggested that the ventromedial (VM) hypothalamus may function as a satiety center to stop eating behavior, while the lateral hypothalamus may be a hunger center which excites eating behavior. Attempts to define centers related to sexual activity have suggested that two kinds of such centers may exist. Centers of hormonal regulation control the release of gonadotropic hormones from the pituitary, while centers of neural regulation control neural circuits and reflexes responsible for sexual behavior. Centers for neural regulation have been identified in the anterior, preoptic, and posterior areas of the hypothalamus, although their exact location may vary from species to species. A major center for hormonal regulation is in the VM region.

Several areas of the hypothalamus seem to be involved in aggressive behavior, including the posterior, VM, perifornical, and lateral regions. These areas may be associated with different kinds of aggression: the lateral region seems most closely associated with a kind of predatory attack, the other regions with generalized rage reactions or attacks on animals of the same species. The types of aggression and their physiological bases are far from being understood.

We have considered several theories about the nature of the role of the hypothalamus in motivation, including those of Stellar, Valenstein, and Glickman and Schiff. The role played by this small, densely packed group of nuclei at the base of the brain is still far from being understood.

The limbic system is a more complex group of structures that appeared later in evolution than the hypothalamus. Electrical stimulation of the limbic system differs from that applied to the hypothalamus in a crucial respect: such stimulation often produces strong subjective experiences in humans, a result consistent with Papez' suggestion that, while the hypothalamus mediates emotional *expression,* the limbic system mediates emotional *experience.* These experiences tend to vary from region to region in ways compatible with the results of animal studies: certain areas evoke fear and/or aggression at moderate levels of stimulation, while other areas evoke positive, sometimes sex-related, experiences. MacLean has suggested that the amygdala-hippocampus circuit is associated with feeding, aggression, and fear and that the septal circuit is associated with sex and sociability. Much evidence tends to support this view but there is enough contradictory data to indicate that it is too early to be sure of the exact location of different neural systems in the brain.

Despite this, there have been many attempts to apply the increasing knowledge of brain mechanisms to the clinical manipulation of human motivation, emotion, and behavior. Some of these seem clearly beneficial, such as the treatment of intractible pain or neurological disease. Others are controversial, such as the attempts to control aggression or treat homosexuality. We shall examine some of the ethical and practical problems raised by these attempts in the next chapter. However, it does appear that a significant and perhaps a very large proportion of violent crimes may be related to limbic malfunctioning and that current programs of rehabilitation may be useless in such cases.

The discovery of the rewarding and punishing effects of brain stimulation by Olds was the catalyst for much of the research we have considered in this chapter. The nature of the motivation underlying the high rates of self-stimulation, however, is unclear. The understanding of this motivation, and the neurochemical systems associated with it, would represent a major breakthrough in the analysis of the physiological bases of motivation.

In terms of the schema introduced in Chapter 1, this chapter concerned the central nervous system components of the physiological response to affective stimuli. It showed some ways in which innate mechanisms are involved in the reaction to affective stimuli. It also demonstrated how central nervous system events can be internal affective stimuli in their own right, so that an individual's reaction to an otherwise mild external stimulus may be heightened. This is shown dramatically when brain abnormalities or the artificial manipulation of brain structures produces extreme hyperactivity with uncontrolled violence.

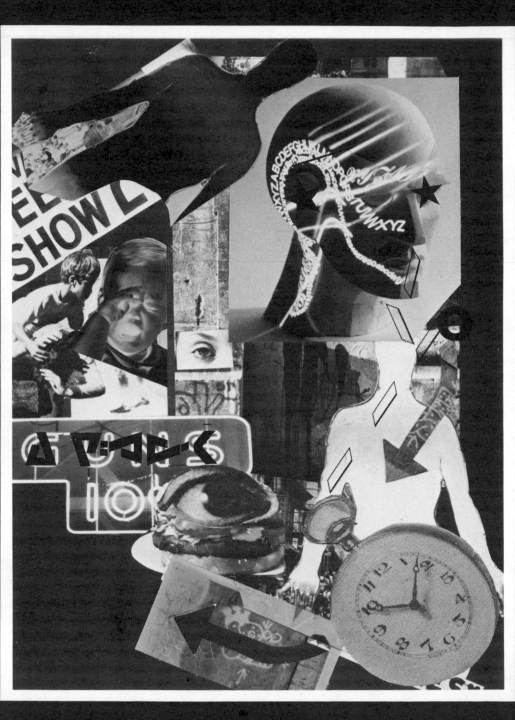

CHAPTER FOUR

CONTROL OF PHYSIOLOGICAL RESPONDING

In recent years there has been an increasing appreciation of the plasticity of the physiological processes involved in emotion and motivation. In particular, physiological processes long regarded as automatic have been shown to be controllable, given appropriate learning experience. These findings have challenged our conventional beliefs about the nature and capabilities of the body. This chapter will examine how the autonomically mediated visceral and glandular responses involved in motivation and emotion can be altered by learning. We will consider the classical conditioning of autonomic responding, interoceptive classical conditioning, the instrumental conditioning of autonomic events, and demonstrations of the control of autonomically mediated events in humans. We will also examine the implications of these phenomena for the understanding and treatment of disease.

Classical Conditioning of Physiological Events

DEFINITION

Classical conditioning involves the use of an unconditional stimulus (UCS), such as meat powder, that naturally evokes an unconditioned response (UCR), such as salivation. If a previously neutral stimulus (i.e., a bell or light) is properly paired with the UCS, it comes to elicit a response similar to the UCR (See Figure 4.1). The previously neutral stimulus is termed the conditioned stimulus (CS) and the response it evokes is the conditioned response (CR). If the CS is then presented again and again without the reinforcing UCS, the CR gradually disappears or is extinguished.

EXPERIMENTS

It has long been recognized that physiological functions can be modified by classical conditioning procedures. Indeed, in Pavlov's original demonstration, the conditioned response was salivation. Similarly, it has long been known that events in the environment can become conditioned stimuli that evoke the physiological, behavioral, and presumably subjective responses associated with emotion. Such conditioned emotional responses have been a subject of experimental study for years (e.g., Estes and Skinner, 1941) and many personality theorists have argued that emotions are acquired through classical conditioning procedures (e.g., Miller and Dollard, 1941; Mowrer, 1960). These theories were strongly influenced by a classic experiment reported in 1920 by J. B. Watson. Watson demonstrated the development of conditioned emotional responses in an

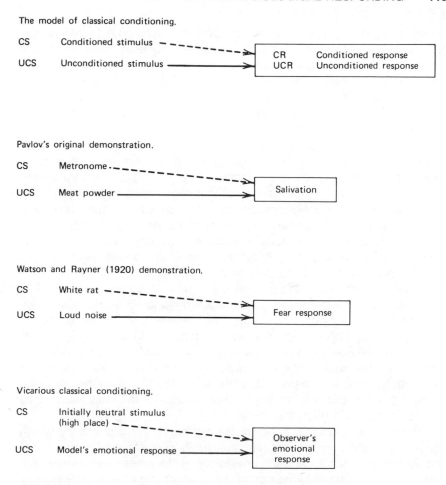

FIGURE 4.1   Examples of exteroceptive classical conditioning.

eleven-month old infant, Albert (Watson and Rayner, 1920). At nine months, the experimenters had demonstrated that Albert responded to a loud noise with a fear response of crying and withdrawal behavior, but that he rarely if ever responded fearfully in other situations. Thus, the noise was a UCS evoking a UCR of fear. At eleven months, Albert was shown a white rat, the CS, for the first time. As he reached out for it, a loud noise was sounded behind his head. After seven such presentations, Albert showed a complete fear reaction (CR) to the sight of the rat alone. His fear later generalized to other furry objects and small animals (Watson and Rayner, 1920).

This suggests that, if a person has repeated unpleasant (or pleasant) experiences in a certain kind of situation, he will come to exhibit the physiological, behavioral, and/or subjective responses associated with unpleasant (or pleasant) emotional states when that situation is repeated. For example, a child's common experience of joy on bright sunny days might lead to a lifting of his spirits on similar days as an adult, and his frustration on rainy days could lead to a greater tendency toward depression during such weather.

It is important to note that the individual need not experience a situation directly for conditioning to take place. A number of studies have shown that vicarious classical conditioning is possible. Bandura (1969) has demonstrated that many forms of learning, including the acquisition of conditioned emotional responses, can occur by simply observing others (*models*) undergo an experience. In the vicarious learning of a conditioned emotional responses, the model's emotional response serves as an unconditioned stimulus eliciting the unconditioned emotional response from the observer. When a child observes that his mother, or an actor on television, is frightened, this can elicit a fearful response in the child. A neutral stimulus present when the model's emotional response occurs can become the conditioned stimulus for the observer's emotional response (see Figure 4.1). This kind of an analysis can account for the development of a wide variety of human fears and joys. If a child's mother is afraid of high places, her insecurity could cause her child to be uneasy whenever he is with her near a high place. Like Watson's loud noise in the presence of the rat, the mother's insecurity in the presence of the high place could lead to fear of high places in the child.

In essence, classical conditioning illustrates the process by which many neutral stimuli or events may eventually come to control emotional and motivational states and the physiological responses associated with them. The potential usefulness of this kind of learning analysis of emotional and motivational phenomena has increased significantly in recent years. It has been found that, not only can environmental events become conditioned stimuli evoking emotion-related physiological changes, but one physiological change can function as a CS or UCS eliciting other physiological events, so that virtually every bodily function is potentially modifiable by learning. In addition, contrary to previous belief, instrumental conditioning procedures can alter autonomically mediated physiological events. Let us first examine how internal physiological events can function either as conditioned or unconditioned stimuli in classical conditioning.

Interoceptive Classical Conditioning

DEFINITION

In standard exteroceptive classical conditioning, the CS and UCS are events in the external environment. Thus, the CS might be a bell or light or tone, the UCS an airpuff to the eye, meat powder, or electric shock (see Figure 4.1). In interoceptive classical conditioning, in contrast, either the CS, the UCS, or both are applied directly to an internal visceral surface (see Figure 4.2). Thus, while exteroceptive classical conditioning involves the standard sensory apparatus, interoceptive conditioning uses the sensory system that monitors the body's internal environment. This system is relatively unsophisticated in comparison with the exteroceptive sensory apparatus; the viscera are supplied with fewer nerves, and, in humans, most visceral processes occur outside of conscious awareness. Despite this, classical conditioning using interoceptive conditioned and unconditioned stimuli has been demonstrated repeatedly, particularly by psychologists and physiologists in the Soviet Union.

EXPERIMENTS

Razran (1961) has summarized and discussed a number of studies of interoceptive conditioning that have appeared in the Russian literature. These include experiments both on animals, typically dogs, and human subjects. In animals, the interoceptive stimulation is often delivered by fistulas formed in the viscera, or by surgical exteriorization of the viscera. In humans, patients with preexisting fistulas have volunteered to serve as subjects, and healthy persons have served by swallowing rubber balloons which may have electrodes attached. Figure 4.3, reproduced from Razran's paper (1961, p. 65), shows an experiment using the balloon-swallowing technique. Typical CSs and UCSs for interoceptive conditioning experiments include inflating an inserted balloon with air or water, irrigating the viscus directly with jets of air, water, or chemical stimuli, scratching the viscus, and administering an electric shock to the viscus. A wide variety of responses may be measured. The responses monitored in the experiment illustrated in Figure 4.3 included the EEG, vasomotor responses, gastric movements, blinking, and visual sensitivity.

In one of the animal experiments reported by Razran, the CS was inflation of the duodenum of a dog. Shock to the paw was the UCS, which elicited a paw-withdrawal response as the UCR. The dog showed the paw-withdrawal CR to the duodenum inflation on the fifth trial. After 129

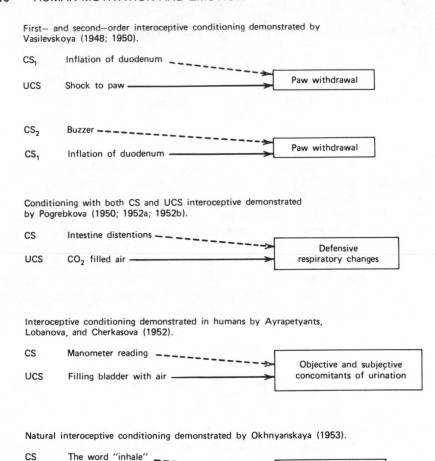

First— and second—order interoceptive conditioning demonstrated by Vasilevskoya (1948; 1950).

CS₁   Inflation of duodenum ------→ Paw withdrawal

UCS   Shock to paw ───────────→ Paw withdrawal

CS₂   Buzzer ------→ Paw withdrawal

CS₁   Inflation of duodenum ───────→ Paw withdrawal

Conditioning with both CS and UCS interoceptive demonstrated by Pogrebkova (1950; 1952a; 1952b).

CS   Intestine distentions ------→ Defensive respiratory changes

UCS   CO₂ filled air ───────────→ Defensive respiratory changes

Interoceptive conditioning demonstrated in humans by Ayrapetyants, Lobanova, and Cherkasova (1952).

CS   Manometer reading ------→ Objective and subjective concomitants of urination

UCS   Filling bladder with air ──────→ Objective and subjective concomitants of urination

Natural interoceptive conditioning demonstrated by Okhnyanskaya (1953).

CS   The word "inhale" ------→ Peripheral vasoconstriction

UCS   Inhalation ───────────→ Peripheral vasoconstriction

FIGURE 4.2   Examples of interoceptive conditioning, in which either the conditioned stimulus (CS), unconditioned stimulus (UCS), or both are applied to an internal visceral surface.

reinforced trials, the shock was discontinued and the duodenal inflation was preceeded by a buzzer. After 18 such trials, the buzzer came to evoke paw-withdrawal, even though the buzzer had never been directly associated with the shock. Thus, second-order conditioning, in which a second conditioned stimulus (CS₂) is associated with a previously conditioned stimulus (CS₁) but never with the original unconditioned stimulus, has been successfully demonstrated with an interoceptive CS₁ (Vasilevskoya, 1948; 1950; reported in Razran, 1961).

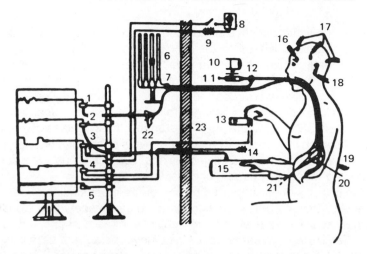

FIGURE 4.3   Instrumentation used in the swallowing technique for studying interoceptive conditioning in humans. The apparatus illustrated was used to study the interaction of interoceptive events, the EEG, blood volume, blinking, and visual sensitivity. A partial labeling of the features includes: (1) Record of gastric movements; (2) record of arm plethysmogram; (3) marker of light stimulus; (4) subject's report of interoceptive and/or visual sensations; (5) time; (6) burettes to introduce solutions into the stomach through opening of stopcocks (7) and (12); (11) syringe to draw out the liquid contents of the stomach; (13) response key; (15) volume plethysmograph;(17) and (18) EEG electrodes; (19) and (21) electrodes and leads of gastric balloon; (20) gastric balloon; (23) partition between experimenter and subject. From G. Razran, "The observable unconscious and the inferable conscious in current Soviet psychophysiology." *Psychological Review*, 1961, 68, 81–147. Copyright 1961 by the American Psychological Association. Reprinted by permission.

In another animal experiment, Razran reported a case in which both the CS and UCS were interoceptive. The UCS was the ventilation of dogs' lungs with air containing 10% carbon dioxide. This produced defensive respiratory changes as the UCR. The CS was the rhythmic distention of loops formed in the dogs' intestines at the rate of 90–100 distentions per minute at 60–80 mm Hg. pressure. When paired with the UCS, the CS produced respiratory CRs after 3 to 6 trials, and the animals readily learned to discriminate the CS from unreinforced distentions occurring at 15 per minute at 55–60 mm Hg. pressure. The CRs proved to be highly resistant to extinction. Interestingly, Razran noted that, as experimentation continued, the dogs seemed to become adapted to breathing the high carbon dioxide UCS. However, some of the animals even then continued to show aversive reactions to the CS (Pogrebkova, 1950; 1952a; 1952b; reported in Razran, 1961).

Razran cites an experiment by Markov (1950) which gives some insight into how interoceptive stimulation is experienced by humans. Electric shocks were delivered to the stomachs of healthy human subjects (including Markov himself) through electrodes mounted on a swallowed balloon. As the shocks increased in intensity, there was a long period in which no sensations were reported. This was followed by a period of dull, poorly localized diffuse sensations, followed finally by clear and well-localized sensations of acute pain. Presumably, most studies of interoceptive conditioning involve low or moderate levels of stimulation that are not perceived or are barely perceived by the subject. Thus, interoceptive conditioning must be a largely unconscious process.

This conclusion is supported by one of the most striking experiments reported by Razran (1961). It was conducted by Ayrapetyants, Lobanova, and Cherkasova (1952) on human subjects, three persons with urinary bladder fistulas who volunteered for the study. The apparatus is illustrated in Figure 4.4. Recordings were made of bladder compression, the rate and amount of urine secretion, respiratory, vascular, and electrodermal changes, and the time and intensity of the subjects' urination urges. Bladder compression was indicated on a manometer with a conspicuous dial that was visible to the subject. Unknown to him, the manometer could be

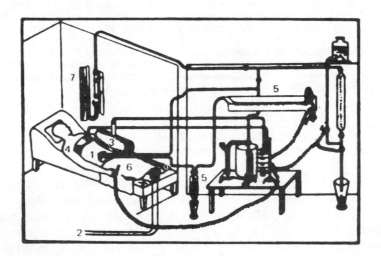

FIGURE 4.4   Apparatus for interoceptive conditioning of human subjects with urinary bladder fistulas. (1) urinary bladder fistula; (2) skin conductance electrodes; (3) volume plethysmograph; (4) respiration cuff; (5) registration of urination; (6) subject's report of sensations; (7) manometer watched by subject. Adapted from G. Razran, *Op. Cit.* Copyright 1961 by the American Psychological Association. Reprinted by permission.

detached and the readings varied by the experimenter independently of the actual bladder compression. In effect, the manometer reading was a conditioned stimulus associated with the UCS of filling the bladder with air.

Successful conditioning to the sham readings was demonstrated readily for all subjects. When the reading was high, they reported intense urination urges, accompanied by most or all of the objective reactions of urination, high intrabladder pressure, and other responses, even though the bladder was empty (see Figure 4.5). In addition, with low readings on the manometer, inflows of air which normally produced the urination urge and its accompaniments were insufficient. To be fully effective, the inflows had to be greatly increased, sometimes doubled, over their normally effective levels (Ayrapetyants, Lobanova, and Cherkasova, 1952; reported in Razran 1961). Thus, not only did the interoceptive conditioning appear to be unconscious, but it altered in some way the subjects' normal response to internal stimuli associated with the urination urge that are presumably consciously perceived.

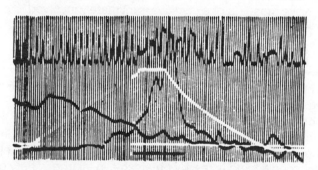

FIGURE 4.5   Interoceptive urinary conditioning in humans. Black lines from above represent: pneumogram, skin resistance, intrabladder pressure, subject's report of urinary urge. Upper white line is the conditioned stimulus—the experimenter moving upward the reading of the manometer. The lower white line is for the unconditioned stimulus—filling the bladder with air—which was not used on this trial. The bladder was empty. From G. Razran, *Op. Cit.* Copyright 1961 by the American Psychological Association. Reprinted by permission.

In addition to these experimental demonstrations, Razran presented evidence that interoceptive conditioning occurs naturally. Okhnyanskaya (1953) reported that inhalation elicits vasoconstriction in the arm as an unconditioned response. Similar vasoconstriction also occurs to the word "inhale" when no inhalation takes place. Evidently the word "inhale" has become a CS because of its natural association with the UCS of inhalation. Razran cites several similar examples which appear to demonstrate natural interoceptive conditioning.

Other Russian studies cited by Razran indicated that semantic stimuli can become conditioned stimuli in classical conditioning. More importantly, they showed that this conditioning was more easily transferred to semantically related words than phonetographically related words. For instance, if the subject was conditioned to salivate to the word *skripka* (violin), he showed more transfer to words like *gitara* (guitar) and *struna* (string) than to *skrepka* (paper clip) and *strizhka* (hair cutting). Furthermore, if salivation was conditioned to the word *horosho* (good) and extinguished to the work *plokho* (bad) and if the subject was then presented with different words or sentences, he would tend to salivate to the novel stimuli to the extent of the goodness of their meaning along a good-bad continuum. One subject, a 13-year-old boy, salivated only one or two drops to sentences like "my friend is seriously ill," "the pupil broke the glass," and "the Fascists destroyed many cities," while he salivated 17–23 to sentences like "the children are playing well," and "the Soviet Army was victorious" (Razran, 1961, p. 101). These studies make the important point that the cognitive meaning of a stimulus is intimately involved in conditioning.

IMPLICATIONS

Razran points out a number of characteristics of interoceptive classical conditioning that have exciting theoretical implications. First, as we have seen, interoceptive events are not consciously perceived at moderate levels of stimulation, and conditioning involving interoceptive stimuli must therefore be largely unconscious. Despite this unconscious character, interoceptive conditioning is readily obtainable in a large variety of experimental situations. Second, Razran suggests that interoceptive conditioning is less easily extinguished than exteroceptive conditioning. Thus it is more irreversible, and an interoceptive CS_1 can readily function to condition a response to a novel stimulus in second-order conditioning. Third, the nature of the processes on which interoceptive stimuli are normally based is fundamentally different from the large and diverse variety of exteroceptive stimuli. Interoceptive events are based upon recurring bodily functions that are always carried around with the organism. They are always available for conditioning, and they are ever-present afterward to reflect the effects of the conditioning. Also, the individual can never escape the interoceptive stimuli within him, as he can escape and avoid such external events as furry objects and small animals.

Because of these considerations, interoceptive conditioning must be, as Razran suggests, an "almost built-in function that is constantly generated and regenerated in the very process of living and action" (1961, p. 97).

A unique, complex, and largely unconscious system of conditioned visceral reactions must be built up during the life of each organism. We carry around within us a large variety of stimuli that are unconscious, or at least dull, diffuse, and hard to identify and label. These include stimuli associated with respiratory activity, postural responses, events in the menstrual cycle, food moving in the stomach, the autonomic and endocrine responses associated with stress, and so forth. The interoceptive conditioning studies imply that these internal events can become conditioned stimuli associated with an endless variety of exteroceptive UCSs. Consider a child who repeatedly receives a particularly strong display of warmth and affection from his mother while eating. Assuming that the display of warmth is a UCS eliciting both feelings and physiological responses of comfort in the child, one would expect that the stimulus complex associated with eating would eventually become conditioned to comfort responses. Part of this stimulus complex is interoceptive, such as the physiological events associated with eating and digesting. Thus, the child may come to derive an unusual amount of comfort from eating. Alternatively, consider a child whose parents repeatedly argue and fight at the table, eliciting the feelings and physiological responses of fear while eating. Theoretically such feelings should become conditioned to the stimulus complex associated with eating. Eventually the individual could deal with the exteroceptive aspects of the stimulus complex by simply avoiding them. If his parents had Early American furniture in the dining room, for example, he may come to find such furniture unpleasant, and avoid it. This solution is not possible for the interoceptive aspects of the stimulus complex, however. The individual cannot escape the physiological events of eating and digesting even if they have come to elicit unpleasant feelings and maladaptive physiological events.

Thus, visceral responses can become ever-present and inescapable conditioned stimuli capable of modifying other visceral functions in a wide variety of ways. The visceral accompaniments of eating can come to evoke the internal changes associated with emotional states. Similarly, the visceral accompaniments of emotion can become capable of modifying vital organs so as to produce functional disturbances such as asthma, hypertension, or constipation (Razran, 1961). Interoceptive conditioning thus adds a new dimension to the analysis of conscious and unconscious processes, with important implications for personality theory in general and psychosomatic medicine in particular. In fact, interoceptive conditioning is at the center of the Soviet experimental study of psychosomatic medicine, or, in their terms, corticovisceral psychology (Brozek, 1964).

The interoceptive classical conditioning findings introduced by Razran's paper have not been followed up systematically in the United States, and there has been no attempt to draw out the full theoretical implications of the Russian research. In part, this may be because American psychologists have been more interested in studying the effects of brain stimulation on conditioning and on visceral processes. It may also be due to the fact that the findings Razran reported on interoceptive conditioning did not in themselves cause a theoretical controversy in the United States. Another aspect of Razran's review which did fuel a controversy has been followed up in the United States with extremely productive results. This concerned the instrumental, as opposed to the classical, conditioning of visceral functions.

Instrumental Conditioning of Visceral Functions

DEFINITION

In classical conditioning, an unconditioned stimulus that already elicits the response to be learned serves to reinforce the learning. This reinforcement is not contigent upon the learner's behavior: the dog's salivary response does not determine whether or not he receives meat powder on a given trial. In instrumental conditioning, the reinforcement occurs only when the learner makes a correct instrumental response. In instrumental reward conditioning, the learner receives some reward when he makes a correct response. For example, if a dog is being conditioned to have a high (or low) heart rate, the reward would be presented only at times that his heart rate is high (or low). In instrumental escape or avoidance conditioning, an instrumental response terminates or avoids a noxious stimulus such as an electric shock. Thus an animal might be given a shock which is terminated when his heart rate is high (or low). Because of the contingency between the reinforcement and the learner's behavior, instrumental conditioning is often thought to be voluntary, while classical conditioning is involuntary or automatic (Miller, 1969).

American learning theorists have long held the view, stated by Skinner (1938), that visceral behavior mediated by the autonomic nervous system may be modified by "classical, but not instrumental, training methods" (Kimble, 1961, p. 100). According to Miller (1969), this view is based more on cultural bias than experimental fact. He traces a long-held belief in the inferiority of the autonomic nervous system that dates back to the writings of Plato. The belief is founded today on a number of widely held assumptions about autonomic functioning. For example, Cannon (1932) concluded that the sympathetic branch of the autonomic nervous system fires as a unit and is thus incapable of finely differentiated responding.

Others have argued that since the autonomic nervous system is primarily a motor system, lacking afferent function, and since it does not interact directly with the external environment, it must be incapable of instrumental learning (Smith, 1954; quoted by Katkin and Murray, 1968).

These beliefs and assumptions were challenged when Razran (1961) reported that a Russian psychologist, Lisina, had succeeded in demonstrating instrumental conditioning of vasodilation in human subjects. Five subjects were subjected to electric shock, which normally produces vasoconstriction in the blood vessels of the arms. However, vasodilations also occurred occasionally, and when they did the shock was terminated, thus reinforcing the instrumental response of vasodilation. After 80 such reinforcements, no increase in vasodilation was evident. The subjects were then allowed to watch the records of their vasomotor responses on the plethysmograph. With such feedback, they were eventually able to transform their vasoconstriction responses to vasodilations. Razran stated that this demonstrated that autonomic responses can be modified by instrumental conditioning techniques and that such modification may be possible only when cognitive mediation is present (Razran, 1961).

When Lisina's report became available in English (1965), the importance of the mediation became more evident. Lisina stated that her subjects learned to use such somatic devices as relaxing the skeletal muscles and changing the depth of their respiration to gain voluntary control over their vasomotor responses (Katkin and Murray, 1968). This suggested that Lisina's study had not in fact demonstrated the direct instrumental conditioning of vasodilation. In Skinner's (1938) analysis of autonomic conditioning, he acknowledged that humans can bring autonomic functions under voluntary control. An actor, for example, can learn to cry real tears. But Skinner argued that this control is exerted by voluntary mediating responses that are conditioned or unconditioned stimuli for autonomic responses. Such mediating responses may be somatic or cognitive in nature (Katkin and Murray, 1968).

Somatic mediation occurs when the subject learns to make skeletal-muscular responses that are conditioned to an autonomic response. This may have occurred in Lisina's experiment. By watching the feedback from the plethysmograph, her subjects could have soon learned what postural, breathing, and other skeletal muscle adjustments were necessary to control their vasomotor responses. Similarly, subjects in a heart rate conditioning experiment could learn to control their heart rate indirectly by learning to alter appropriately their respiration and activity.

Cognitive mediation occurs when the subject learns to make internal symbolic responses that are conditioned to autonomic responses. For example, a subject might learn to have anger-arousing thoughts which increase his skin conductance responding, or placid, relaxing thoughts that decrease such responding.

Either somatic or cognitive mediation may thus result in indirect changes in autonomic response that are apparently due to instrumental conditioning. In order to establish definitely the instrumental conditioning of autonomic functions, the possibility of somatic and cognitive mediation must be removed. Obviously, this poses a difficult and demanding experimental task.

MILLER'S EXPERIMENTS

Even before Razran's (1961) report of Lisina's experiment, Neal Miller was interested in demonstrating the instrumental conditioning of autonomic functions. Miller's formulation of learning theory made no distinction between classical and instrumental conditioning, arguing that they are basically similar processes based on similar neural mechanisms (Miller and Dollard, 1941; Miller, 1951; 1959). This view demanded that autonomic responses modifiable by classical conditioning methods must also be modifiable by instrumental conditioning methods (Miller, 1969). Miller and his colleagues were well aware of the stringent controls necessary to demonstrate instrumental conditioning of autonomic functions. They used the rat as their major experimental subject, an animal presumably bereft of substantial cognitive abilities. To eliminate somatic mediation they used curare, a drug that blocks the motor end plates of all skeletal muscles. This paralyzes the subject completely without eliminating consciousness in humans and without interfering with the autonomic control of visceral responding. Artificial respiration is required to maintain breathing, so that artifacts due to breathing can be controlled.

Miller's first positive results were obtained with an experiment on salivation in dogs that were not paralyzed by curare. Miller and Carmona (1967) rewarded one group of thirsty dogs with water when they showed spontaneous salivation, and another group when they showed no salivation for a long period of time. As expected, the group rewarded for salivating showed an increase, while those rewarded for not salivating showed a decrease, in salivation over the 40 days of training. The results could not be due to classical conditioning because the changes were in opposite directions. However, the animals rewarded for increases appeared to be more active than the other animals, who seemed drowsy. This suggested that somatic mediation was occurring: the animals may have learned to become more active in one group, indirectly increasing salivation, and less active in the other, thus decreasing salivation. To counter such move-

ments, the dogs were paralyzed with curare. Unfortunately, the curarization elicited continuous, copious salivation that was so viscous that it
gummed up the recording apparatus (Miller, 1969).

At the same time, Trowill (1967) was working on the conditioning of
heart rate in curarized rats. He found, by trial and error, an appropriate
dose of curare and a respiration rate that held the heart rate of the
paralyzed animals fairly constant over a 2–4 hour experimental session.
The animals were rewarded by electrical stimulation of rewarding areas of
the brain, half receiving rewards for fast heart rates, half for slow rates.
The groups showed small, but significant heart rate changes in the rewarded directions.

To improve the training techniques, Miller and DiCara (1967) first
rewarded small heart rate changes, and then progressively larger changes
in the correct direction. Through this shaping, the rats learned large heart
rate increases and decreases that averaged 20 percent in either direction
(see Figure 4.6). In addition, this study showed that the rats could learn a
discrimination between the presence or absence of a time-in stimulus (a

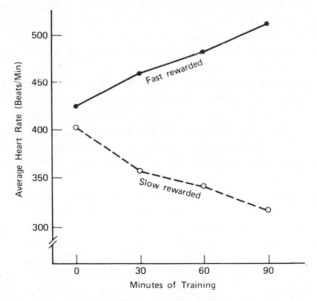

FIGURE 4.6   Instrumental learning by heart in groups rewarded for fast or
for slow rates. Each point represents the average of beats per minute during
five minutes. From N. Miller and L. V. DiCara, "Instrumental learning of heart
rate changes in curarized rats: shaping and specificity to discriminative stimulus." *Journal of Comparative and Physiological Psychology*, 1967, 63, 12–19.
Copyright 1967 by the American Psychological Association. Reprinted by permission.

flashing light and tone). The reward for a heart rate response in the correct direction was given only in the presence of the time-in stimulus. After the discrimination training, the rats changed significantly in the predicted direction only when the time-in stimulus was presented.

Subsequent studies demonstrated that basic similarities exist between the learning of visceral responses and the learning of skeletal responses. DiCara and Miller (1968a) tested whether or not learned changes in heart rate could be retained without further practice. After recovery from the curare, trained rats were returned to their home cages. Three months later, they were curarized again and given nonreinforced test trials. The rats demonstrated retention by showing significant changes in the previously rewarded direction. In addition, DiCara and Miller (1968b) demonstrated that rats could learn instrumental heart rate increases and decreases to escape and avoid shock as well as to obtain brain stimulation reward. Finally, Hothersall and Brener (1969) demonstrated extinction of the heart rate changes following nonreinforcement. Thus, many of the basic laws of learning that apply to the instrumental conditioning of skeletal responses, including acquisition, discrimination, retention, extinction, and escape and avoidance learning, also apply to visceral learning.

Up to this point, the experiments we have cited involve learned changes in heart rate, with the paralysis of the skeletal muscles by curare used to rule out somatic mediation. As Miller (1969) points out, it is conceivable that motor cortex activity might affect autonomic functions even when overt skeletal muscle movement is rendered impossible (Black, 1966). Perhaps the rats learn to send out impulses from the motor cortex that would have caused movement had the end plates of the motor nerves not been inactivated by curare. These impulses could conceivably affect autonomic responses by either inborn or classically conditioned connections.

Reasoning that such motor cortex activity would probably have general effects upon all autonomic functions, Miller and his colleagues set out to demonstrate that instrumental learning could specifically affect one autonomic function without altering others. Miller and Banuazizi (1968) demonstrated that one visceral response (change in heart rate) could be learned independently of another (change in intestinal contractions). One group of curarized rats was trained to increase (or decrease) intestinal contractions. Heart rate and intestinal contractions were recorded from all animals. The animals rewarded for increases or decreases in intestinal contractions showed such changes without affecting heart rate, and the converse was true for animals rewarded for increases or decreases in heart rate.

In another experiment, Miller and DiCara (1968) showed that the rate of urine formation in the kidney could be quickened or slowed by instrumental conditioning without altering heart rate or blood pressure. They found evidence that these changes were mediated by changes in renal blood flow: the greater the rate of blood flow to the kidneys, the faster the urine formation. Apparently, the animals in fact learned to alter the blood flow to the kidneys, presumably by vasomotor changes in the renal arteries. These vasomotor changes were highly specific, as shown by the fact that the groups rewarded for increases and decreases did not differ in their vasomotor responses measured in the tail.

In other studies, Carmona, Miller, and Demierre demonstrated the instrumental escape-avoidance conditioning of changes in the stomach wall that were presumably mediated by vasomotor responses (Miller, 1969). DiCara and Miller (1968c) showed instrumental reward conditioning of vasomotor responses in the tail, and DiCara and Miller (1968d) demonstrated escape-avoidance conditioning of increases or decreases in blood pressure that were independent of heart rate.

To test the limits of the specificity of vasomotor learning, DiCara and Miller (1968e) tested the blood vessels in the pinnae of the rat's ears. These are thought to be innervated by the sympathetic branch of the autonomic nervous system, which Cannon (1932) believed to fire as a unit. Thus, vasodilation in the right ear should be accompanied by vasodilation in the left ear as well. DiCara and Miller rigged the experiment so that the curarized rat would receive rewarding brain stimulation only when there was a difference between the two ears in vasomotor responding. To their delight (and surprise) the experiment worked. Rats rewarded for relative vasodilation in the left ear, or relative vasodilation in the right ear, all showed the rewarded response. In addition, they performed this feat without affecting the vasomotor responses in the left and right forepaws.

These findings on the specificity of visceral learning appear to rule out the effects of somatic mediation by means of the motor cortex as far as is possible (Katkin and Murray, 1968). It seems very doubtful that the motor cortex could have such fine-grained control of visceral processes. The issue of cognitive mediation is more difficult to dispose of. Much depends on how one defines "cognitive." Some psychologists would deny that any cognitive process occurs in rats, others would argue that instrumental conditioning *per se* requires some kind of cognitive operations.

There is evidence that the instrumental conditioning requires more complex neuroanatomical structures than does classical conditioning, whether or not one labels their functions as cognitive in nature. A number of studies suggest that the intact neocortex is necessary for instrumental conditioning, but not for classical conditioning. A study by DiCara, Braun, and Pappas (1970) indicates that this is true in the case of visceral responses as well as more conventional instrumental responses. They trained different groups of normal and neodecorticate rats to alter their heart rate or intestinal activity through either instrumental or classical conditioning procedures. The neocortical lesions disrupted the instrumental, but not the classical, conditioning of these responses.

The problem of mediation is even more difficult to deal with when considering the instrumental conditioning of visceral responses in humans. But regardless of these questions of interpretation, there can be no doubt that the experiments by Miller and his colleagues demonstrate that autonomically mediated visceral and glandular functions are more readily modifiable by learning than was previously thought possible. The implications of this fact alone are considerable.

Recently a number of investigators, including Miller and his colleagues, have had difficulty replicating some of the findings on instrumental autonomic conditioning in curarized animals (DiCara, 1975). In particular, the baseline heart rate of curarized rats in recent studies has been 10 to 20% higher than the baseline rate in previous studies, and it is less variable and not as amenable to change. The reason for this is unclear. Miller has suggested that changes in some unknown factor, such as the supply of rats, the precise parameters of respiration, or the purity of the curare, may be causing this high baseline heart rate (Miller and Dworkin, 1974). Wilson and DiCara (1975) have suggested that the high heart rate may be caused by the stressfulness of the curare-induced immobilization of the animal and that the problem may be attenuated by adapting the animal to curare before beginning the experiment. A recent experiment has apparently repeated the earlier findings of learned heart rate increases and decreases in curarized rats (Gliner, Horvath, and Wolfe, 1975). Hopefully, the reasons for the failures in replication will soon be clarified so that the conditions underlying instrumental autonomic learning can be fully explored.

The Control of Autonomic Responses in Humans

THE PROBLEM OF MEDIATION

In a comprehensive review of studies that purported to show the instrumental conditioning of autonomic functions, Katkin and Murray (1968) divided the literature into those studies showing pure instrumental conditioning in which the problem of mediation is adequately dealt with and studies showing control of autonomic functions without removing all doubts that mediating factors—previous relationships between autonomic responses and somatic or cognitive events—might actually underlie the effects. The series of studies by Miller and his colleagues reported above are the only demonstrations of pure instrumental conditioning of autonomic activity, according to Katkin and Murray. The other group of studies, including all experiments using human subjects, do not conclusively rule out the possibility that the apparent instrumental conditioning of autonomic responses might actually be an epiphenomenon associated with somatic and cognitive mediators.

Katkin and Murray argued that the curarization employed by Miller's group, plus the impressive demonstrations of the specificity of visceral learning, rule out the possibility of somatic mediation as far as is possible. They did not mention cognitive mediation in discussing the Miller group's studies; apparently they made the (unstated) assumption that cognitive mediation is possible only in humans. Among human subjects, they argued that an individual's thinking activity can produce arousing or calming thoughts that elicit previously conditioned autonomic responses. If those responses are reinforced, the individual might simply learn to think the appropriate kind of thought, leading to apparent instrumental conditioning of the autonomic response. They concluded that any definitive demonstration of instrumental conditioning of autonomic responses in humans would "require unconscious subjects to eliminate cognitive mediation and complete curarization to eliminate somatic mediation" (Katkin and Murray, 1968, p. 66)

Katkin and Murray spoke of the many studies that do not meet these rather strict criteria as demonstrating the "control," as opposed to the "conditioning," of autonomic responses. They pointed out the possibility that, for the practical purpose of learning to control autonomic processes, the proper use of cognitive and somatic mediators may greatly enhance efficiency.

Crider, Schwartz, and Shnidman (1969) criticized the criteria for instrumental autonomic conditioning employed by Katkin and Murray. They argued that there is no evidence that somatic and cognitive mediators can, in fact, produce the autonomic effects required by Katkin and Murray's argument and that it is therefore more parsimonious to conclude that direct instrumental conditioning of autonomic responding has been demonstrated in the human studies. In reply, Katkin, Murray, and Lachman (1969) contended that the issue involves the theoretical predispositions of the researchers involved in the controversy, rather than questions of fact, but they nevertheless concluded that "the evidence on instrumental autonomic conditioning in humans remains far less convincing than the evidence available from animal studies"(Katkin, Murray, and Lachman, 1969, p. 462).

DEMONSTRATIONS OF AUTONOMIC CONTROL IN YOGIC EXERCISES

Regardless of the eventual outcome of the controversy over mediation, which may turn out to be largely semantic, it is increasingly clear that humans can bring under control a large number of autonomically mediated functions previously regarded as involuntary. Such control has long been popularly associated with Eastern religious disciplines such as the Yoga systems of India. In fact, there is evidence that some of the Yogic exercises are accompanied by significant autonomic changes and that some practitioners of Yoga (Yogis) can attain considerable autonomic control (Hardt, 1970).

In an experiment conducted in 1933, M. A. Wenger noted that the performance of a student from India in a muscle relaxation experiment far exceeded the performance of other subjects. The student reported that he used a Yogic method of exercise to achieve the relaxation, and Wenger resolved to travel to India to investigate. The journey was finally made during the 1950s (Wenger and Bagchi, 1961). The observations by Wenger and his colleagues on 43 male and two female Yogis or students of Yoga demonstrated that marked autonomic changes occur during some of the exercises.

One of the most impressive demonstrations they observed was that by a Yogi who could reliably produce perspiration on his forehead, accompanied by increases in systolic blood pressure and skin temperature of the arm, plus other autonomic changes. The man had lived in cold mountain caves for parts of two winters, usually alone and clad only in animal skins. To escape being distracted from his meditation by the cold, he practiced concentrating on warmth, visualizing himself in extremely hot situations. He reported that, over a six-month period, he gradually succeeded in producing sensations of warmth, and that later, in moderate temperatures, the same practices produced perspiration as well. Wenger and Bagchi (1961) suggested that the Yogi used voluntary cognitive mediating responses involving visual imagery to produce previously conditioned autonomic responses.

Wenger, Bagchi, and Anand (1961) investigated the claims by three Yogis that they could stop their hearts voluntarily. They found that electrocardiogram and plethysmographic records indicated that the heart did *not* stop. However, the Yogis did succeed in causing the heart to pump very little blood, making the ordinary signs of heart action disappear. Cardiac sounds could not be detected with a stethoscope, and the palpable radial pulse disappeared at times. It is possible that the Yogis accomplished this by reducing the venous return to the heart by means of extreme breath and muscle control (Wenger and Bagchi, 1961).

Other Yogis studied by Wenger and his associates demonstrated such phenomena as marked voluntary slowing of the heart, voluntary regurgitation, and the ability to suck fluids into the bowel and bladder via tubes through the anal and urethral sphincters (Wenger and Bagchi, 1961; Wenger, Bagchi, and Anand, 1961).

Although they did not observe any fire walkers directly, Wenger and Bagchi (1961) reported that the practice occurred commonly in certain locations in India and that, although it requires courage and confidence, it does not seem to require special training in Yogic exercises. Westerners have accomplished the feat on a number of occasions, and it seems that a combination of factors, including very brief contact with the embers, a steady and deliberate pace, a covering of ashes over the embers, and tough feet, are responsible for the lack of pain and blistering (Dalal and Barber, 1969). Plantar sweating may also play a part (Coe, 1957), and it is possible, although not proven, that some degree of voluntary control over plantar sweating might be desirable, if not necessary, for fire walking.

It is sometimes implied that the Yogic demonstrations of bodily control must be accompanied by an altered state of consciousness or trance state, and in fact there is evidence that Yogic meditation is accompanied by EEG changes that may reflect changes in consciousness. However, although the demonstrations of bodily control and autonomic changes achieved through Yogic exercises are impressive, they do not in themselves indicate that any altered state of consciousness is necessary for this control. First, the demonstration of unusual psychophysiological abilities is not considered to be necessarily related to meditation in India. The goal of meditation is a spiritual one: the attainment of Samadhi, or union with Supreme Reality. According to Dalal and Barber (1969), many of the demonstrations of bodily control are made by men who have not seriously studied a system of Yoga in the strict spiritual sense. Second, autonomic control has been manifested by persons outside the Yogic traditions. Lang (1970) reported that one of the secrets behind the famous escapes of Harry Houdini, the magician, was that he taught himself to hold a key suspended in his throat and regurgitate it at will. He learned to control his normally involuntary gag reflex by long practice with a piece of potato attached to a string. Similarly, a Russian mnemonist studied by the Soviet psychologist A. Luria could control his heart rate over a range of 40 beats per minute, and he could simultaneously raise his skin temperature in one hand and lower it in the other (Lang, 1970). Finally, experiments have shown that most people can readily learn voluntary control over autonomically mediated responses if given feedback about the response. Let us consider these experimental demonstrations in some detail.

EXPERIMENTAL DEMONSTRATIONS OF AUTONOMIC CONTROL

In recent years, a great many well-controlled experiments have shown that autonomic control can be demonstrated among ordinary subjects, given proper training techniques. The essence of the technique lies in giving the learner some form of direct and immediate feedback about the autonomic response. The response is monitored by physiological sensors, and the relevant information is immediately relayed to the learner in an easily understood form. This has become known as biofeedback.

Katkin and Murray (1968) reviewed experimental studies demonstrating the control of electrodermal responding, peripheral vascular responding, and heart rate using different forms of biofeedback. These have demonstrated increases (Van Twyer and Kimmel, 1966) and decreases (Johnson and Schwartz, 1967) in the rate of spontaneous skin conductance responding; increases and decreases in the rate of spontaneous vasonconstrictions (Snyder and Noble, 1965; 1966); reductions in heart rate variability (Hnatio and Lang, 1965; Lang, Sroufe, and Hastings, 1967); and heart rate acceleration and deceleration (Brener and Hothersall, 1966; Engel and Chism, 1967; Engel and Hansen, 1966).

More recently David Shapiro and his colleagues at Harvard Medical School have shown that human subjects can learn to modify their blood pressure, and they have demonstrated considerable specificity in this learning. In one study, either a rise or a fall in blood pressure was rewarded by a flashing light. After 20 flashes the (male) subject was rewarded by a three-second exposure of a picture of a nude female. A significant difference in blood pressure emerged between the rise and fall groups during the experimental session, without a corresponding difference in heart rate (Shapiro, Tursky, Gershon, and Stern, 1969). In a subsequent study using similar procedures, Shapiro, Tursky, and Schwartz (1970) demonstrated the emergence of a significant difference in heart rate without a corresponding difference in blood pressure. In addressing themselves to the problem of cognitive mediation in their discussion of these studies, Shapiro, Tursky, and Schwartz (1970) point out that in order to interpret such findings in terms of cognitive mediation, one would have to assume that "certain thoughts elicit directional changes specific to blood pressure in one case or to heart rate in another" (p. 422), an assumption that they feel is not justified at this time.

CONTROL OF EEG ACTIVITY

A related series of experiments employing biofeedback techniques concerns the ability to control electroencephalographic (EEG) activity. The

EEG, of course, involves changes in the higher brain centers in the central nervous system, rather than the autonomic nervous system. Nevertheless, the results of studies employing EEG responses are generally similar to those of studies of visceral learning.

In animal experiments, Miller and Carmona instrumentally conditioned bidirectional changes in EEG activity among noncurarized cats and curarized rats (Miller, 1969); Black demonstrated alterations of theta wave activity in dogs; and Fox modified visual cortex activity in both animal and human subjects by means of instrumental conditioning techniques (DiCara, 1970).

In research with human subjects, particular attention has been focused on factors involved in determining the abundance and control of a particular kind of electrical activity in the brain: alpha waves. Alpha waves are oscillating electrical potentials with a frequency of between 8 and 12 Hz and an amplitude of up to 50 microvolts. They are most prominent when recorded from electrodes placed on the back of the head (Kamiya, 1968).

There are a number of intriguing things about alpha waves. First, they seem to be associated with a particular kind of conscious state, a kind of relaxed alertness. Second, they are particularly abundant in Yogis and Japanese Zen monks during meditation. Third, it appears that they can be controlled by many people using biofeedback techniques.

Kamiya (1962) has shown that subjects can learn to discriminate between the presence and absence of their alpha activity. He told his subjects simply that they were to guess whether they were in state A (alpha present) or state B (alpha absent) when a signal sounded, and he then told them whether they were right or wrong. A majority of subjects were able to reach a significiant proportion of correct guesses within seven one-hour sessions. When asked to describe the differences between the two states, the subjects characterized the alpha-absent states as involving visual imagery, while the alpha-present states involved "not thinking," or "letting the mind wander." The alpha state was commonly experienced as a pleasant feeling of calmness, tranquility, and alertness devoid of concrete visual images (Kamiya, 1968).

The descriptions of the alpha state closely resemble subjective descriptions of Yoga and Zen meditation, and a number of studies have investigated EEG activity during meditation. Most of these agree that both Yoga and Zen meditation are associated with unusually abundant and high amplitude alpha activity (Anand, Chhina, and Singh, 1961; Kasamatsu and Hirai, 1966; Okuma, Kogu, Ikeda, and Sugiyama, 1957; Wenger and Bagchi, 1961; although Das and Gastaut, 1955, found fast activity in Yogis during meditation). In addition, occasional trains of lower frequency (5 to 7 Hz) theta activity have been reported among Zen monks (Kasamatsu and Hirai, 1966). Recently Wallace (1970) studied physiological effects of transcendental meditation among 15 American college students who had practiced the technique for from 6 months to 3 years. He reported increased regularity and amplitude of alpha activity during meditation and, in four subjects, he found large-amplitude alpha waves replaced at times by theta waves in a pattern similar to that found in the Zen monks by Kasamatsu and Hirai (1966).

There is also some evidence that alpha blocking is altered during meditation. Normally, alpha activity is blocked when a novel stimulus is presented to a subject. If the stimulus is presented repeatedly, the alpha blocking ceases to occur, or becomes habituated. Anand et al. report that for some Yogis, normal alpha blocking does not take place when the Yogi is stimulated by light, noise, a hot glass tube, or a vibrating tuning fork during meditation. Two Yogis showed persistent alpha activity even while their hand was submerged in ice water for 45–55 minutes (Anand et al., 1961). Alpha blocking is apparently affected in different ways during Zen and transcendental meditation. Kasamatsu and Hirai (1966) reported that there was no *habituation* of the alpha blocking response when a click stimulus was repeatedly presented to Zen monks during meditation. The monks reported that the repetitive stimuli were perceived more clearly than they would be in a normal waking state, and it is possible, given the EEG responses and the reported experiences of the monks, that they were responding to each click as a wholly unique event (Kasamatsu and Hirai, 1966: Reported in Hardt, 1970). Similarly, Wallace (1970) reported no habituation of alpha blocking to repeated sound and light stimuli in most of his subjects during transcendental meditation.

In addition to the EEG responses, other physiological processes are altered by meditation. The Zen monks showed decreases in respiration, oxygen consumption, and spontaneous skin conductance responses, and slight increases in heart rate and blood Ph during meditation (Kasamatsu and Hirai, 1966; reported in Wallace, 1970). Yogis showed decreases in respiration, increased skin resistance, and no changes in heart rate and blood pressure during meditation (Bagchi and Wenger, 1957; Wenger and Bagchi, 1961; Wenger et al., 1961). Wallace (1970) reported decreased oxygen consumption, increased skin resistance, and decreased heart rate during transcendental meditation.

It thus appears that the practice of meditation is associated with fairly consistent patterns of physiological responses, and particularly with an abundance of EEG alpha waves. It is therefore of great interest that alpha waves can be controlled, given auditory or visual biofeedback. Kamiya (1968) used auditory feedback to train his subjects to control their alpha waves. When alpha waves were present, a tone was sounded to the subject. The subject was told only that "certain mental states produced the tone," and that he was to remain motionless and try to keep the tone on. At the end of each minute-long trial, the subject was told the percent of time the tone had been on. After five such trials, his task was to keep the tone off (i.e., reduce alpha activity) for 5 one-minute trials. Eight of the ten subjects were able to control the tone, and thus their alpha activity, after 40 such tests. Kamiya also found that most subjects given auditory feedback are able to increase or decrease the frequency (in Hz) of the alpha wave itself. Similar results have been reported from several laboratories, including one experiment using a light as feedback (Hart, 1968). Brown (1974) even set up a toy train and a racing car set run by alpha waves, as demonstrations.

Many seized upon the relationship between alpha activity and meditation, on the one hand, and the apparent increases in alpha activity with feedback, on the other, as evidence that alpha feedback could facilitate the learning of meditation ("turn on the power of your mind" read one advertisement for an alpha feedback device), or at least provide a unique and pleasant high. These hopes have been disappointed by studies using control groups which do not receive feedback. Such groups have been found to produce alpha rhythms during rest that are as abundant as those of groups receiving feedback (Lynch and Paskewitz, 1971). Thus, although people can learn to increase and decrease alpha rhythms with biofeedback, they apparently cannot increase alpha past the level they would spontaneously have if resting. There is no evidence that alpha feedback can facilitate the learning of meditation.

However, as Sterman (1973) points out, other brain rhythms have been increased over their spontaneously occurring levels with biofeedback, and some of them may have important therapeutic applications. We shall next consider some of the direct implications that the new-found knowledge on physiological control has for psychosomatic medicine and some of the recent experimental attempts to apply this knowledge to medical problems.

Physiological Control and Psychosomatic Medicine

THEORETICAL IMPLICATIONS

The Russian studies of interoceptive conditioning, taken together with previous knowledge regarding the classical conditioning of emotional responses and the more recent demonstrations of instrumental conditioning and control of autonomically mediated visceral and glandular events, lay a theoretical and practical foundation for a new approach to the understanding and treatment of psychosomatic disease. It may be that many bodily and behavioral abnormalities arise through accidental classical or instrumental conditioning. If this is so, it should be possible to unlearn them.

Psychosomatic medicine in the United States draws upon the intellectual traditions of Cannon and Freud (Mirsky, 1960) while that discipline in Russia is based mainly upon Pavlovian conditioning (Brozek, 1964). At first glance, there seems to be little similarity between the two approaches. For example, the terms used in psychosomatic medicine in the United States and Russia are quite different, making communication difficult. However, closer inspection may reveal that the phenomena described by the different terms are often the same. For example, in a paper on the psychoanalytic theory of somatic disorders, Engel and Schmale (1967) define the term "conversion" as involving the achievement of mental representation of a bodily part or system. They regard conversion as a basic mechanism in the development of a wide variety of psychosomatic symptoms, acting both directly and through complications involving the bodily reactions to the conversion. Examination of their discussion suggests that the process of achieving a mental representation in conversion may involve a process much like classical or instrumental conditioning and that complications might often arise through higher order interoceptive conditioning. Hopefully, similarities in conceptualization such as this will eventually overcome the differences in terminology.

From the recent literature on autonomic conditioning, it is clear that both classical and instrumental conditioning can lead to the learning of abnormal bodily symptoms. Since classical conditioning demands nothing beyond a repeated association between some internal or external event and a reinforcing UCS, its effects may be more widespread. Instrumental conditioning of autonomic functions requires that the occurrence of some autonomic response be followed fairly directly by some reinforcing event, and thus it probably occurs less often during normal life than does classical conditioning. We have commented on how interoceptive classical conditioning in particular must be an almost built-in feature of life. We carry around within us a very complex but relatively unchanging and inescapable array of interoceptive stimuli that can become associated with both external events and other internal processes. If we repeatedly experience an event that causes an abnormal bodily change in a particular kind of situation, both the exteroceptive and interoceptive aspects of that situation should later tend to produce that same bodily change. If a child repeatedly experiences fear while eating, both the exteroceptive and interoceptive aspects of the stimulus complex associated with eating will tend to produce fear. The simple association of the eating and the fear should suffice. On the other hand, for instrumental autonomic conditioning, an autonomic response must produce reinforcement. This might occur when a child gets special attention that he needs only when he is sick to his stomach, or pale, or has a headache. The visceral and glandular events associated with the symptoms could be directly reinforced by the attention.

THERAPEUTIC APPLICATIONS OF BIOFEEDBACK

If the studies on physiological control suggest how some psychosomatic symptoms may develop, they also suggest how they may be treated: through techniques of unlearning or extinction and through attempts to control physiological responses in such a way as to have therapeutic effects. Theoretically, any symptom under neural control is a good candidate for therapeutic training if it is clear that a certain direction of change is medically advisable and if the changes can be monitored to provide feedback (DiCara, 1970).

There have been a large number of attempts to apply biofeedback techniques in therapy settings, covering an impressive range of disorders. These clinical studies are encouraging, but must be viewed with some caution. No study reported thus far has met the rigorous criteria required to prove conclusively the effectiveness of a therapeutic technique (Miller, 1974).

Cardiovascular Disorders   One of the most important clinical studies thus far is that carried out by Bernard Engel and his colleagues. They have attempted to treat cardiac arrythmias, organic disorders in which normal heart rhythm is disrupted, by instrumental training involving cardiac feedback. Weiss and Engel (1971) studied eight patients with potentially dangerous arrythmias caused by premature ventricular contractions. In the feedback sessions, the patient lay in his bed watching a display of three lights: one red (slow), one green (fast), and one yellow (correct). When the red light was on, a slowing of the heart would turn on the correct yellow light; when the green light was on, a speeding of heart rate was required.

Each patient went through ten 34-minute training sessions in which he learned to speed the heart, then ten sessions in which he learned heart rate slowing. He then learned to alternately speed and slow the heart for 1–4 minute periods throughout the session. Such bidirectional training may facilitate the learning of voluntary control (Miller, 1974). The patient then learned to control heart rate variability. When the rate was too fast, the red light came on; when it was too slow, the green light came on. This feedback contingency gave the patient prompt feedback each time he had a preventricular contraction: in such cases an abnormally fast beat (red light) would be followed by an abnormally slow beat (green light). (see Figure 4.7).

All of the patients learned these tasks to some extent, and five showed a reduced rate of preventricular contractions. Four of these were successful enough that they were weaned from the feedback: the feedback was gradually phased out. The patient was encouraged to become aware of his preventricular contractions through his own sensations and learn to control them without feedback. These four patients showed reduced rates of preventricular contractions which were maintained in follow-up studies following the training (Engel and Bleeker, 1974).

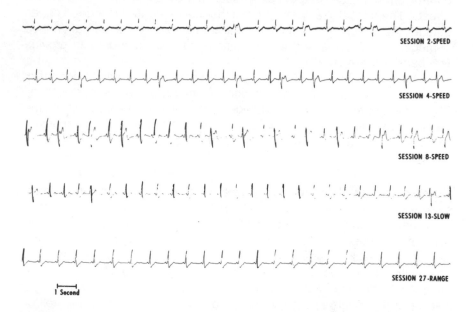

FIGURE 4.7   EKG records during conditioning, showing an increase in preventricular contractions (PVCs) during speeding conditioning and a decrease in PVCs during slowing and range conditioning. From T. Weiss and B. T. Engle, "Operant conditioning of heart rate in patients with premature ventricular contractions." *Psychosomatic Medicine*, 1971, 33, 301–321. Copyright 1971 by the American Psychosomatic Society. Reprinted by permission.

Another major example of clinical research is the series of studies on the control of hypertension carried on by David Shapiro and his colleagues (1969). Seven patients with essential hypertension—high blood pressure without known cause—were given feedback sessions in which they were rewarded for decreases in blood pressure. The reward consisted of a light and tone given at the end of each trial on which blood pressure decreased. After 20 such rewards, the subject was shown a scenic color slide and promised five cents. Meaningful decreases in blood pressure was demonstrated in five of the seven patients.

Headache   Most headaches can be classified as tensionassociated with chronic tension in the skeletal muscles of the neck and head, vascular (migraine-type) headaches apparently associated with the dilation of blood vessels in the brain, or a combination of the two (Lachman, 1972; Martin, 1972). Both tension and migraine headaches have been the focus of therapeutic studies using biofeedback.

Budzynski, Stoyva, and Adler (1970) reported a successful application of EMG feedback in treating tension headaches. They trained patients to relax the frontalis muscle in the forehead with lights controlled by the EMG record. When the patient relaxed his muscles, a green light came on. With increased tension, a yellow, then a red light came on. Five patients trained in muscle relaxation with feedback in two laboratory sessions per week for eight weeks, and they were encouraged to practice at home as well. All patients showed improvement, particularly those who had initially had more severe headaches. A second study used 18 patients randomly assigned to one of three treatment groups: a valid feedback group, an incorrect feedback control group who were instructed to relax and concentrate on a signal not associated with their EMG activity, and a no treatment control group. Results indicated that the valid feedback group showed a signifcant reduction in headache activity when compared to the control groups. Five of the six valid feedback patients showed significant declines in headaches during training, and three of these reported few headaches in a follow-up conducted 18 months later (Budzynsky, Stoyva, Adler, and Mullaney, 1973).

A possible feedback therapy for migraine headache was discovered when, by chance, a research subject noticed that her sudden recovery from a migraine headache coincided with a flushing in the hands and a 10°F increase in hand temperature within two minutes. Such hand warming is presumably based on an increase in blood flow to the hands caused by a dilation of the local blood vessels (Sargent, Green, and Walters, 1973).

A pilot study was organized using 28 subjects: 22 with probable migraine headaches, 6 with tension headaches. The patients were given devices measuring the differential temperature of the forehead and the hand and instructed to try to warm the hand relative to the forehead. The patients practiced on their own time and kept their own records. Results suggested that 63% of the migraine sufferers were improved, compared with only 33% of the tension headache sufferers, suggesting that the handwarming technique may be effective only with vascular headaches. Wickramasekera (1973) has reported success in treating migraine with the handwarming technique after the EMG feedback technique had failed.

Gastric Disorders   Noxious conditioning has been reported as a treatment for vomiting by Lang and Melamed (1969). The patient was a nine-month old boy who repeatedly vomited his entire meal after eating. At the beginning of training, he weighed less than 12 pounds, was in an advanced state of dehydration and malnutrition, and he was not expected to live. No organic cause of the condition was apparent. The therapists took EMG readings along the infant's esophagus to detect the first signs of vomiting. A computer was programmed to deliver an electric shock to the leg whenever the activity appeared and to continue the shock until vomiting ceased. The infant ceased to vomit after the first few meals with this therapy, and at last report he was healthy (Lang, 1970).

Other investigators have reported the treatment of fecal incontinence (Engel, Nikoomanesh, and Schuster, 1974) and functional diarrhea (Furman, 1973) using biofeedback. In an interesting study, Welgan (1974) reported that ulcer patients can learn to control the secretion of gastric acids by means of biofeedback. Twenty patients with duodenal ulcers were fitted with a nasogastric tube so that stomach contents could be drawn out through a tube in the nose. The acidity of the fluid was measured and the patients rewarded with a tone for decreases in acidity. Results indicated that there were significant declines in acid concentration and volume. It seems likely, however, that large scale clinical applications of this process must await technical advances that provide faster, more reliable, and more comfortable methods of measuring stomach acidity.

Epilepsy   There have been several reports of positive results using biofeedback to alter the abnormal electroencephalograph (EEG) rhythms in epilepsy. Lang (1970) reported that F. M. Forster treated an epileptic patient who developed seizures when exposed to a light flickering at a certain rate. A computer-controlled feedback system presented the patient with a light flickering at a rate progressively closer to the critical one and simultaneously analyzed his EEG to detect an incipient seizure. Upon detecting a seizure, the computer turned off the light and stopped the seizure by presenting auditory clicks. Eventually, the treatment was effective in eliminating the seizures (Lang, 1970). Randt, Korein, Carmona, and Miller have attempted with some success to train epileptic patients to suppress certain abnormal brain waves (reported in Miller, 1969).

The most promising studies of epilepsy treatment have been those of M. B. Sterman (1973). Sterman discovered that learning to increase a certain EEG rhythm—12 to 16 Hz. recorded from the sensory-motor cortex area—made cats resistant to drug-induced seizures. This sensory-motor rhythm (SMR) could be detected in normal humans as well, and its incidence could be increased through biofeedback. Sterman then began working with four epileptic patients whose seizures were not controlled by drugs. They were given 30–60 minute training sessions at least three times per week, in which the presence of SMR was signaled by a light and tone. After a few weeks, the frequency and duration of SMR bursts began to increase, and after three months the abnormal EEG patterns had decreased and the patients experienced fewer and milder seizures. When training was discontinued for three patients, they experienced a return to the pretraining level of seizure activity within six weeks. When training was reinstituted, the seizures rapidly diminished. One patient was provided with a home feedback unit after 10 months of training to maintain the feedback. (See also Sterman, Macdonald, and Stone, 1974).

Results similar to those of Sterman were reported by Finley (1974), whose single patient increased his SMR percentage from 10% to 64% in 34 training sessions while his seizure rate decreased by a factor of ten. Incorrect feedback was given to this patient for one week, and the seizure rate increased fivefold. Kaplan (1974) also found fewer seizures in two of three patients, although no biofeedback-related EEG activity could be demonstrated. She interpreted the clinical improvement as being due to relaxation rather than a specific result of biofeedback training.

Relaxation Therapy   Stoyva, Budzynski, and their colleagues have investigated the value of EMG biofeedback as an adjunct to behavior therapies based upon relaxation. They consider three therapeutic techniques that are centered on the idea that deep muscle relaxation can allay anxiety: Jacobson's Progressive Relaxation, (Jacobson, 1938; 1970), autogenic training (Schultz and Luthe, 1959; Luthe, 1969), and systematic desensitization in behavior therapy (Wolpe, 1958; Wolpe and Lazarus, 1966). Budzynski and Stoyva (1969) pointed out that these therapeutic techniques have a common problem in training patients to relax really deeply. Tense patients in particular have a difficult time relaxing. They may often have a poor idea of what real relaxation feels like, and they may actually increase their tension while striving to relax. In addition, the therapist has difficulty in determining whether the patient is truly relaxed. Budzynski and Stoyva attempted to overcome these problems by providing an EMG feedback system for both patient and therapist.

Budzynski and Stoyva (1969) found that patients could achieve deep relaxation more quickly when provided with the feedback. They then used EMG feedback in conjunction with systematic desensitization in behavior therapy. The desensitization technique involves having the patient imagine a stressful scene while relaxing. Theoretically, the relaxation is physiologically incompatible with a fear response, thus so long as the patient is really relaxed while imagining the scene, the fear response to the scene is extinguished. If the patient begins to become anxious, he must immediately stop imagining the scene and relax. It is desirable for him to stop imagining the scene as quickly as possible. Budzynski and Stoyva found that EMG activity preceeded a self-report of anxiety by about 5–15 seconds for most patients. They tentatively suggested from this that the EMG feedback may be a more sensitive indicator of anxiety than the patient's self-report (and perhaps his self-perception) and that it thus may be a more efficient indicator for the purposes of desensitization.

Other Applications   We have touched upon only a few of the potential theraputic applications of the biofeedback technique. Other investigators are exploring the use of biofeedback in relieving spasmatic torticollis, a stubborn condition in which the head is turned to the side (Cleeland, 1973; Brudny, Grynbaum, and Korein, 1974); Reynaud's disease, in which certain peripheral blood vessels are painfully constricted (Schwartz, 1973); and so forth. One additional application must be mentioned. J. Basmajian (1972) reports working with a group of music professors recording the EMG activity of the lip and cheek muscles of wind-instrument players. The patterns of EMG activity have been found to vary with the skill of the players. In addition, subjects with multiple electrodes have been able to activate local areas of the lip and cheek muscles using feedback. Basmajian suggests that performance may be improved by training inexperienced players to make EMG patterns similar to those of proficient players. This suggests a whole area of potential biofeedback application: the study and direct modification of skilled human performance.

Placebo Effects   Although these studies on the theraputic potential of biofeedback are impressive, they must be viewed with some caution. Even if the technique works effectively, it is impossible at this stage to determine whether or not it is superior to other available treatments. Also, none of the therapy studies to date fully meets the rigorous methodological criteria necessary to establish the effectiveness of a theraputic technique without question. One of the major unresolved issues in this area is the question of whether hidden aspects of the biofeedback therapy situation might be responsible for the positive changes seen, rather than the biofeedback training itself. In particular, some of the therapeutic success found in these studies may be placebo effects due to the patient's hopes and expectations, the suggestions given him by the therapist and therapeutic situation, the attention that the patient receives, and so on (Miller, 1974).

Placebo effects are frustrating to biofeedback and other medical researchers because the improvement in the patient's disorder is not due to the specific therapeutic procedures and techniques employed but are instead due to unknown and unspecified factors, such as the characteristics of the particular patient and therapist, their expectations about change, and so forth. This makes it difficult to assess the usefulness of specific theraputic procedures.

The standard research design that controls for placebo effects in drug research is the blind design, in which some patients are given an ineffective drug (a placebo) and others the drug under investigation. In the single-blind design the patient does not know the drug is a placebo; in the double-blind design neither the patient *nor the therapist* are aware who has the placebo until the end of the experiment. If a group who receives the placebo improves as much as those who received the real drug, the improvement is assumed to be due to placebo effects.

The blind experiment is expensive and time-consuming, and the administration of known ineffective treatments to patients raises ethical problems. Also, the classic blind experiment is impractical to apply in many biofeedback studies because it is too easy for the patient to realize that he is getting placebo feedback. If a person is given random schedule of lights supposedly indicating muscle relaxation, he can easily discover that the feedback is phony by tensing the muscles involved. Thus a less satisfactory kind of control procedure must suffice. For example, we saw that Budzynski et al. (1973) approximated a single-blind design by giving incorrect feedback to certain patients—asking them to concentrate on a signal not associated with their EMG activity. However, this required a different set of instructions, and therefore different patient expectations, from the valid feedback condition. It is concievable that the difference in reported headaches could be due to this difference in expectations.

Although placebo effects make it more difficult to study the effectiveness of specific treatments, they are interesting phenomena in their own right and illustrate how higher cognitive processes can influence bodily functioning. In some cases placebo effects themselves have been used to attempt to cause therapeutic changes, but this practice has certain dangers. We shall return to the therapeutic uses and abuses of the placebo effect in Chapter 10.

PSYCHOSURGERY AND PHYSIOLOGICAL CONTROL

A more direct and drastic way of modifying the physiological systems that underlie behavior is through psychosurgery: surgery performed to alter emotional reactions, social behavior, personality characteristics, and so on of human beings. We reviewed some of this work in the last chapter, including the studies by Heath and his colleagues on septal stimulation, the work by Mark, Ervin, et al. on aggression, and the tragic case history of the young man reported by Terzian and Dalle Ore. The practice of psychosurgery has been at the center of a growing controversy as the techniques of surgical control become more refined and the temptation to apply these techniques to behavioral and emotional problems in humans increases.

Much of this controversy concerns the use of psychosurgery to control aggressive behavior. As is discussed in Chapter 3, operations involving amygdalectomy and posterior hypothalectomy have been used by some to calm and "tame" human beings, particularly mentally retarded people and patients with temporal lobe epilepsy (cf. Narabayashi, 1972; Balasubramanian and Ramamurthi, 1970; Mark and Ervin, 1970; Heimburger et al., 1966). Hundreds of persons, many of them children, have been involved in these programs.

Some have reacted to such operations with outrage, charging that the use of psychosurgical procedures to alter aggression is an assault upon the will and dignity of the individual and could become tools of social and political repression (cf. Chorover, 1974). In a defense of psychosurgery, Mark (1974) agrees about the potential for abuse but argues that, since the individuals involved in warranted psychosurgical procedures are unable to control their aggressive outbursts and indeed may later be remorseful to the point of suicide, the operation could give a person more rather than less control of his behavior.

Elliot Valenstein (1973) has presented an extensive critical examination of psychosurgery and the complex scientific and ethical issues involved. He has pointed to several issues in the present practice of psychosurgery that would seem to require justification by the practioners.

> 1.   *Too little is known about human brain functioning to predict the results of psychosurgery with certainty.* One of the most obvious objections to psychosurgery is that the brain acts to a great extent as a whole and cannot be compartmentalized into parts whose precise function is known. One critic has argued that no brain activity occurs in isolation and that the destruction of any given area has unpredictable and potentially disasterous results

(Chorover, 1974). Mark (1974) responds that it is true that, in a sense, the brain responds as a whole, but it is also true that there is a partial specialization of function according to structure: certain structures do govern particular behaviors, which is what makes psychosurgery possible. Valenstein (1973) takes a middle ground on this question, pointing out the difficulties of transferring knowledge of brain functioning derived from experiments with animals to humans, and noting that similar brain alterations may produce widely differing reactions in two individuals. As a result, he states, "the prediction of postoperative changes (from psychosurgery) will always fall short of what would be desirable" (1973, p. 325).

2. *Many psychosurgeons have a tunnel view of animal research.* Psychosurgeons have almost always based their techniques and sites of operation directly upon information gained from animal research. However, aside from the difficulties of generalizing from animal studies to humans, their view of the animal research itself is often focused upon the seemingly beneficial effects of an operation, ignoring evidence of important deficits. As an example, Valenstein cites an operation used by Roeder, Orthner, and Muller (1972) to treat adult male homosexuals who sought sexual contact with young or teenage boys. These investigators were struck by animal research indicating that destruction of the VM nucleus of the hypothalamus may at times eliminate hypersexual behavior in animals. On the basis of these results, they made unilateral lesions in the VM nucleus of 20 male patients over a 10 year period. We have seen that there is indeed animal research suggesting that destruction of the VM nucleus will reduce and often eliminate sexual behavior. However, the VM nucleus is also involved in the regulation of many critical autonomic and endocrine functions, and VM lesions in animals are associated with the development of obesity and with irritability and aggression as well as sexual changes. As Valenstein notes, the idea of destroying a large part of the VM nucleus would be a frightening thought to most knowledgeable scientists. He also notes that, although Roeder et al. report that homosexual impulses vanish after the operation, this may be due to a general lowering of sexual drive.

3. *Less drastic treatments than psychosurgery may be available in some cases.* Although many psychosurgeons themselves argue that psychosurgery should be used only when all other treatment fails (i.e. Mark, 1974), Valenstein notes that there is seldom any explicit documentation of previous treatments and it is thus impossible to form an independent judgment about whether other treatments were adequately explored. Also, some have employed psychosurgical techniques in disorders where other treatments are clearly available. In this regard, Valenstein cites the use of surgery to control aggression in hyperactive children without an adequate exploration of drug treatments. He also cites a study by Moan and Heath (1972) in which septal stimulation was used as a reward to alter the sexual orientation of a male homosexual. Valenstein notes that behaviorally oriented therapeutic techniques are available which have been successful in altering sexual orientations without electrode implantations.

4. *The reporting of the results of psychosurgery is often incomplete and/or biased.* One of the most troubling of Valenstein's criticisms of psychosurgery is that the results of the operation are often difficult to evaluate objectively because of incomplete or biased reports of results. He states, "The 'evidence' often consists of the subjective impressions of those who cannot help but be concerned about the correctness of their decision to undertake psychosurgery as well as often being ego-involved in establishing the success of the particular surgical method employed" (1973, p. 296). He notes that the results of surgery are often reported using the categories "improved" and "no change": There is often no category of "made worse." Also, there are several cases in which persons other than the psychosurgeons make much less optimistic evaluations of the condition of a patient or group of patients. He states that "this is not to imply that the results have been consciously distorted, but in the absence of objective criteria and adequate experimental controls, it is very easy to find improvement when one looks for it and to attribute it to the particular psychosurgical procedure used." (p. 296).

Valenstein strikes a middle ground between those who would outlaw psychosurgery and the enthusiasts who would increase its application to emotional and behavioral problems. It is possible to select data that seem to provide support to either extreme position: there is evidence that some patients have been helped by psychosurgery, and there is evidence of some abuse of psychosurgical procedures. He advocates increased restraints and review procedures that would protect the patient from an over-zealous or ambitious surgeon but states that "we should resist those individuals who relate past abuses only for the purpose of gaining support for their position that broad categories of experimental medicine should be outlawed. Such a solution would stultify research and close the door to future progress that might be based on new findings or principles that are unknown at present" (p. 337).

Summary

We have considered several ways by which autonomically mediated visceral and glandular reponses can be altered by learning. Vicarious or direct classical conditioning can cause a previously neutral external stimulus or event to evoke the physiological responses associated with emotion and motivation. Interoceptive classical conditioning shows how internal bodily events can come to evoke such responses. The latter are particularly important because they show how internal events that are largely unconscious, always present, and impossible to escape can come to evoke emotional and motivational phenomena.

In classical conditioning an existing response to one stimulus is attached to a new stimulus by the association of the two stimuli. In instrumental conditioning, a response is made more likely to a given stimulus or event by reinforcing the animal whenever that response occurs in the presence of that stimulus or event. Miller's experiments demonstrated that autonomic responses such as heart rate, vasomotor responses, and salivation can be altered by instrumental conditioning. Other studies demonstrated the instrumental conditioning of physiological responses in humans via biofeedback, in which the subject is given feedback about normally unconscious autonomic, somatic, or central nervous system activities.

The studies of classical conditioning suggest how many potentially disruptive physiological responses associated with emotional and motivational states may be acquired by an individual. Such responses may also be acquired by instrumental conditioning, but this is probably less likely. However, the instrumental conditioning procedures do suggest ways that pathological physiological responses might be treated: through biofeedback an individual might learn to alter his heart rate, blood pressure, stomach acidity, muscle tension, etc. directly.

It is as yet too early to determine whether or not learning through biofeedback will become an important therapeutic technique, but some present indications are encouraging, and the possibilities are exciting. If therapeutically significant changes in bodily functioning can be reliably demonstrated using these techniques, it will have far-reaching practical consequences.

A more direct way to alter the physiological systems underlying emotional and motivational phenomena is though psychosurgery. A variety of surgical techniques developed in animal studies have been applied in humans to control socially undesirable sexual and aggressive behavior as well as neurological disorders. These techniques have provoked much controversy, both on scientific and ethical grounds.

In terms of our schema, this chapter has considered how physiological events covered in previous chapters can be influenced by learning: the physiological response of one person to an affective stimulus may differ from that of another because of different learning experiences. In addition, physiological responses can come to affect other physiological reactions through interoceptive conditioning. This chapter has also discussed ways in which dysfunctional physiological responses may be altered, including biofeedback procedures and psychosurgery.

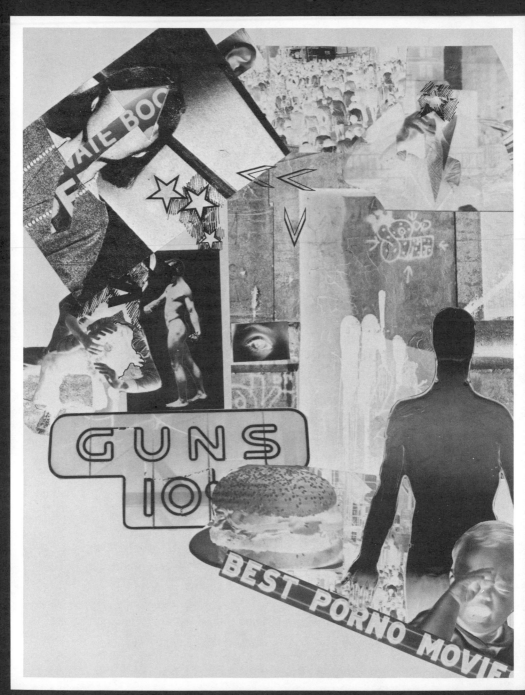

CHAPTER FIVE

AGGRESSION

The phenomenon of aggression has been studied in both humans and animals using a rich varity of approaches, so that the literature in the field is both extensive and diverse. Because of this, the complex processes involved in emotional and motivational expression are particularly well illustrated in the case of aggression. In this chapter we shall examine the controversy between those who stress the importance of biological versus environmental determinants of aggressive behavior. As we shall see, much of this controversy results from confusion between different kinds and levels of analysis of aggression. Let us begin with a question that is unanswerable, but that nevertheless has had and continues to have great importance in influencing the conduct of human affairs.

Is Human Nature Good or Evil?

The controversy between those who regard human nature as basically good and those who see it as fundamentally evil has arisen many times in history, and it has had important social and political consequences. The controversy has been resurrected recently in debate about the basis of aggression and, perhaps because of its ultimate political implications, the debate has been heated.

PHILOSOPHICAL BACKGROUND

This controversy had important effects on history in Europe during the seventeenth and eighteenth centuries. The theory of the divine right of kings was being challenged, particularly in England, and philosophers were looking for a new theoretical basis for governmental authority. It was found in the idea of a social contract that was established between individuals (cf. Russell, 1945, pp. 623–633). The reason for, and nature of, this contract depended upon how the philosopher viewed the state of nature that existed prior to the social contract. In *Leviathan* (1650), Thomas Hobbes argued that all are motivated by the instinct for self-preservation to dominate others while maintaining their own freedom. The resulting war of all against all made life in the state of nature "nasty, brutish, and short." *Home homini lupus*, proclaimed Hobbes: Man behaves like a wolf toward other men. Hobbes felt that the social contract was established out of fear as a kind of peace treaty to end this universal war. He argued that the basic task of the state is to establish and maintain law and order and that the state is most efficient at this task when sovereignty is delegated to a central authority, preferably an absolute ruler.

In contrast to Hobbes' theory, John Locke (1632–1704) held that, in the state of nature, people lived together without leaders according to reason and natural law, much like a community of virtuous anarchists. For Locke, this natural law had a divine origin. This more positive concept of human nature was the basis of the relatively equalitarian and democratic political philosophies of Locke and David Hume, and it contributed to both the French and American revolutions. Indeed, as Bertrand Russell (1945) has pointed out, this concept of human nature survives in much modern liberalism, although it has lost its theological basis and thus its logical foundation.

DARWIN'S THEORY

The controversy arose again in the late nineteenth century with the impact of Darwin's theory of evolution. In *Origin of Species* (1859) and *The Descent of Man* (1872) Darwin proclaimed that the force behind evolution was the "struggle for existence": living things multiply faster than nature can provide for them; thus some offspring from a given generation will die before reproducing themselves. The offspring that survive will tend to be those who are best adapted to their particular environment. Thus the fittest survive, and given time turtles develop shells, deer run faster, giraffes' necks become longer.

Less obvious than these physical adaptations are the behavioral adaptations that can evolve just as surely as the giraffe's neck. For example, infant monkeys would not survive long if they were not strongly attached to their mothers. Thus, there is a *selection pressure* favoring the survival of monkeys with strong tendencies for attachment or affection at birth. We saw in Chapter 3 that species tend to show curiosity and exploratory behavior only if such behavior is adaptive for them, that is only if a selection pressure favors curious animals. Similarly, if it were adaptive for a species to be aggressive, there would be selection pressures favoring animals with strong aggressive tendencies and the species would come to manifest much aggressiveness.

Rightly or wrongly, Darwin's theory gave new credence to the Hobbesian view of human nature. The idea of the struggle for existence and the survival of the fittest gave rise to social and political notions that Darwin himself regretted. Social philosophers misinterpreted the theory as implying an active intraspecies rivalry or competition in nature: Tennyson's "nature red in tooth and claw." This suggested a similar natural and inevitable competition between humans, in which only the fittest human beings were worthy of survival. Particularly in the United States, an ideology of Social Darwinism was used as a scientific justification for a *laissez-faire* economic system and a rationalization for the exploitation of colonial and native American populations (cf. Hofstadter, 1959).

Darwin's dictum that "Man still bears in his bodily frame the indelible stamp of his lowly origin" gave impetus to the tendency to find the causes for human behavior in innate factors or *instincts*. An instinct is generally seen as an innate tendency to action that is aroused by a limited range of stimuli. The concept has been used since antiquity to apply to innate behavior patterns in animals, and Darwin's theory encouraged its use with human behavior as well. During the late nineteenth and early twentieth centuries there was extensive and often uncritical use of the instinct concept (cf. Cofer and Appley, 1964).

During the 1920s, there was a strong reaction among psychologists against the use of the instinct concept, particularly in the United States. At the same time, there was a resurgence in the use of environmental explanations of behavior. The originator of behaviorism, J. B. Watson, stated in 1930 that there were no human instincts and that indeed the development of the same infant into a lawyer, artist, beggar, or thief could be accomplished by purely environmental manipulations. Theories that stressed innate determinants of behavior fell into disrepute, and the use of the instinct concept among American psychologists virtually disappeared.

ETHOLOGY

The concept of instinct remained in use among ethologists. Ethologists study the biology of behavior: the adaptive behavior patterns that develop during the course of evolution that we alluded to above. Their major technique of study is the systematic observation of animals in natural settings.

Ethologists maintain that innate or instinctive components of an animal's behavior, often technically called *fixed action patterns*, can be established without doubt through the *deprivation experiment*. The deprivation experiment is accomplished by (a) raising an animal in isolation from all others of the same species to prevent any possible imitation and by (b) making it impossible for the animal to learn the behavior in question through trial and error (Eibl–Eibesfeldt, 1970, p. 20). For example, Grohmann (1939) raised pigeons in small cages so that they could never see other pigeons or flap their wings. When their normally reared siblings could fly, he released the isolated pigeons and found they could fly well. This way of demonstrating instinctive components in behavior has given the concept of instinct a more precise basis.

In 1966, the work of the pioneer ethologist Konrad Lorenz was published in English with the title *On Aggression*, and it soon became a best seller. This work, and others that have followed it, have again stirred controversy among environmentalists. Again rightly or wrongly, Lorenz' views have been associated with Social Darwinism and a fundamentally Hobbesian view of human nature (Montagu, 1968). Let us consider Lorenz' theory in some detail, and then turn to some of its critics.

Theories of Aggression as Innate

LORENZ' THEORY OF AGGRESSION

Why Aggression is Useful   One of Lorenz' points in *On Aggression* is to show that aggressive behavior is normally useful and functional to the survival of a species. He made this point in opposition to the concept of aggression developed by Sigmund Freud. In Freud's early theorizing, he argued that all behavior is ultimately energized by *sexual instincts*. However, in part because Freud was profoundly affected by the cruelty and destruction of World War I, he came to believe that self-destructive *death instincts* were opposed to the sexual or life instincts. In *Beyond the Pleasure Principle*, written in 1920, Freud proposed that aggressive behavior resulted when the self-destructive death instincts were deflected to outer targets by the sexual instincts (cf. Jones, 1961). Thus, Freud felt that aggression is the result of a process that is fundamentally opposed to the preservation of life.

Lorenz notes that, from the point of view of evolutionary theory, such a destructive process is unlikely. Animals with strong death instincts would tend to die out, leaving the field to their sexier relatives. Instead, Lorenz argues that aggresive behavior has survived because it is normally adaptive and helps to preserve the species. The survival value of interspecies aggression—aggression between members of different species—is fairly obvious: the more aggressive the individual, the more likely he is to survive the contest and reproduce. The usefulness of intraspecies aggression between members of the same species is less evident, and Lorenz cites several possible functions.

One function was suggested by Darwin: aggressive contests over sexual partners tend to select the strongest of the rivals for reproduction. If this strength is useful to the species, such aggression has survival value.

A second function of intraspecies aggression is that it tends to evenly distribute the animals of a given species over the available environment. Ethologists have found that individuals in many species have a high readiness to fight when in familiar surroundings but that this aggressiveness lessens as the individual moves out into unfamiliar places. As a result, each individual will tend to establish a familiar *territory* within which it is aggressive and others are less aggressive. The territory is defined by animals' relative readiness to fight. The net effect is that individuals will spread themselves evenly over the available area. Such a distribution is adaptive unless a species has a social organization that requires that individuals stay together.

Aggression is also adaptive within a social species, according to Lorenz. Social life in higher vertebrates is almost invariably accompanied by a pecking order or *dominance order*, so that each individual comes to know who is stronger and who is weaker than himself. The dominance order is ultimately based upon the threat of violence, but, once the ranking is established, it acts to decrease fighting. In a potential confrontation, a less dominant animal will submit rather than fight. Washburn and DeVore, observing baboon troops living in the wild, reported much fighting among adolescent animals who had not yet established a dominance order but relatively little among animals with established dominance relationships (cf. DeVore, 1965).

The Equilibrium Between Killing Power and Inhibitions   Another of Lorenz' points is that some of the checks and balances normally imposed by evolution upon highly aggressive animals are missing in humans. He notes that the result of intraspecies aggression in animals is rarely debilitating or fatal. Animals may fight furiously, but serious wounds and deaths are rare. Many species have apparently evolved inhibitory mechanisms to stop intraspecies aggression before it becomes really dangerous. These often involve *appeasement gestures*, which are gestures of submission that can stop an ongoing attack. A beaten dog or wolf turns his head away, offering his vulnerable neck to the victor; a jackdaw offers the unprotected base of his skull; other species have similar behaviors. In all cases, the attacker stops and the fight is over.

According to Lorenz, the species that have the most highly developed inhibitions of aggression are those with the most dangerous natural weapons. He reasons that animals with natural weapons but without inhibitions would kill each other off in intraspecies fights. The animals with inhibitions would tend to be more successful in surviving such fights. Thus, among animals with dangerous natural weapons, such as the teeth of the wolf or the beak of the raven, there is a selection pressure favoring animals with strong inhibitions against intraspecies aggression. This is not the case for relatively harmless species such as the rabbit, dove, and primate. There is rarely any opportunity for a member of one of these species to inflict serious injury quickly upon one of its own kind with its natural weapons, so there is no selection pressure favoring natural inhibitions of killing. In the unnatural situation of captivity where the beaten animal cannot escape, there may be no way to stop the fight and it may be killed slowly. Lorenz notes with irony that when caged in pairs the symbol of peace, the dove, may slowly and mercilessly kill its cagemate. Although it has been shown that many primates have extensive repertoires of submissive gestures and behaviors (Hamburg,1971), Lorenz apparently feels that primate inhibitions are not as fast-acting or reliable as those of animals with more deadly natural weapons.

Some anthropologists have suggested that human beings are aggressive because they evolved from carniverous, predatory, hunting apes. Lorenz feels that the opposite is the case: humans are aggressive because they developed from relatively harmless, omniverous creatures that lacked natural weapons and thus had no particular selection pressure to develop strong inhibitions of intraspecies aggression. The invention of artificial weapons upset the natural equilibrium between killing power and inhibitions. It was like suddenly giving a dove the beak of a raven, and there was no time for inhibitions to arise through natural selection. Lorenz notes that the possible inventors of pebble tools, the Australopithecines, may have used their tools to kill their fellows (Leaky, 1961). Also, Sinanthropus pikinensis, the first known user of fire, may have used the fire to roast his fellow man.

Lorenz feels that humankind would have destroyed itself at an early stage if it had not been that the same capacity to reason that led to the invention of weapons also led to the ability to know the consequences of one's actions. An individual would come to realize that if he killed other members of his group, the group as a whole would be weakened and more vulnerable. Thus, reason tended to inhibit aggression within the group. However, reason did not achieve security from fighting between different groups. In fact, Lorenz suggests that the more warlike groups may have survived most successfully. This resulted in a selection pressure for militant enthusiasm, an inborn readiness to defend the social norms and rites of one's group against other groups possessing different norms and rites. Lorenz argues that those societies that best defended their norms and rites survived and that therefore militant enthusiasm was bred into the human race as a consequence of a kind of natural selection of human societes.

The Discharge of Aggressive Drive   Another major point that Lorenz advocates in his theory is that "present-day civilized man suffers from insufficient discharge of his aggressive drive" (1966, p. 235). Lorenz argues that the more aggressive humans survived the rigors of prehistoric life most successfully and that therefore an excess of aggression has been bred into the human race. This high level of aggressive drive, combined with a lack of natural inhibition, makes human beings into a most dangerous and self-destructive species. Lorenz feels that it is possible to find constructive outlets for this aggressive drive. In particular, he suggests that sporting contests between nations may be beneficial in providing a harmless discharge or *catharsis* for the aggressive drive.

This idea rests upon Lorenz' theory of drive, which is used by many of the ethologists. The basis for instinctive behavior is seen to be an "accumulation of a central nervous system excitatory potential" (Eibl-Eibesfeldt, 1970, p. 59). The discharge of this excitatory potential is normally inhibited by "higher cortical controls." The inhibition can be removed at the biologically appropriate moment by an *innate releasing mechanism.* It is postulated that the innate releasing mechanism at first responds unselectively to many stimuli, but that with normal experience only biologically appropriate stimuli become *releasers* capable of disinhibiting the accumulated excitatory potential.

If no appropriate releasers are available to discharge the excitatory potential, it will theoretically continue to accumulate and may eventually find expression on inappropriate releasing stimuli. For example, in the case of aggression, "the constant endogenous accumulation of excitatory potential continues to lead man to seek a discharge for this drive, and in ignorance of the biological conditions he projects his periodically occuring anger outward—in his personal daily life to those who are next to him, for instance, the spouse, and in a larger group, possibly against minorities or neighboring peoples" (Eibl-Eibesfeldt, 1970, p. 59).*

The physiological mechanism by which excitatory potential accumulates is not known, although Eibl-Eibesfeldt (1970) suggests that it may involve increases in the level of catecholamines in the central nervous system (see Chapter 3). However, there is no direct evidence for this. The question is important, for as we shall see, the concept of the accumulation of an aggressive drive has been strongly criticized.

CRITICISMS OF LORENZ' THEORY

Lorenz' theory has been closely examined and criticized by a wide variety of behavioral scientists, and a brief examination of their major objections reveals significant differences in basic assumptions about the determinants of aggressive behavior.

Biologically appropriate releasers can also lead to aggression: according to Lorenz, the appropriate releasers for the expression of militant enthusiasm are (a) a threat to the social unit emanating from (b) a hated enemy. The response can be greatly heightened by the urging of (c) an inspiring leader, especially in the presense of (d) many other individuals manifesting militant enthusiasm.

Do Instincts Exist in Humans?   One of Lorenz' strongest critics is M. F. Ashley Monagu, who has assembled into the book *Man and Aggression* (1968) a number of critical reviews by behavioral scientists of Lorenz' theory and the somewhat similar but less systematic notions of Robert Ardrey. Montagu argues that Lorenz' attempt to attribute instincts to humans is, like previous attempts, a failure. "Man is man because he has no instincts, because all he is and has become he has learned, acquired, from his culture, from the man-made part of the environment, from other human beings" (Montagu, 1968, p. 9). He argues that humans evolved as social and cultural creatures and that the selection pressures working in human evolution have worked *against* the retention of instinctive behaviors. In fact, Montagu argues that humankind's closest animal relatives, the great apes such as the gorilla and chimpanzee, do not have instincts.

Other critics of Lorenz are not as convinced as Montagu that instinctive factors play no part in human aggression. Berkowitz, for example, feels that social scientists have too long denied, minimized, or ignored the importance of built-in determinants of human behavior (1969a). However, Berkowitz argues that Lorenz' use of the term "instinct" in *On Aggression* is loose and oversimplified. For example, when Lorenz states that "militant enthusiasm is instinctive and evolved out of a communal defense response," he goes well beyond the bounds of the precise technical definition of instinct (Berkowitz, 1969a, pp. 378–379).

The Role of Learning in Human Aggression   Another objection to Lorenz' theory is that it neglects the importance of learning in human aggression. To Montagu, "the notable thing about *human* behavior is that it is learned. Everything a human being does as such he has had to learn from other human beings" (1968, p. xii). Berkowitz notes that even behaviors based on innate factors can be modified by learning.

The Accumulation of Aggressive Drive   Lorenz' idea that aggressive energy can accumulate and thus appear spontaneously has been criticized. J. P. Scott (1968) attacks Lorenz on physiological grounds, arguing that there are no known chemical or physiological changes in aggression that correspond to the decrease in blood sugar that contributes to the accumulation of hunger. Scott notes that there are areas of the brain that contain neural circuits important in the excitation and inhibition of aggressive behavior (see Chapter 3), but he feels that these are normally activated by environmental stimuli rather than internal events. He argues that it is difficult to see how a mechanism for accumulating aggression could have evolved: "Fighting is an emergency reaction, and it is hard to imagine how natural selection would lead to the development of a mech-

anism of continuous internal accumulation of energy which would un-
necessarily put an animal into danger" (Scott, 1968, p. 53). Similarly,
Berkowitz (1969a) argues that many aggressive behaviors that appear to
be spontaneous are really evoked by environmental stimuli.

The Draining-off of Aggressive Drive   Lorenz' related idea that
accumulated aggressive energy can be harmlessly drained off in sports
events or other substitute activities has been strongly cirticized. Lorenz'
notion is a form of the "catharsis hypothesis" which has been advanced
as an explanation of human emotional behavior since ancient Greece.
There are two aspects to this hypothesis. One is that catharsis occurs
vicariously: that aggression can be drained off simply by observing aggressive behavior in others. This was the idea expressed by Aristotle when he
wrote in *Poetics* that "tragedy serves to purge the passions." The other
form of the catharsis hypothesis is that actually engaging in aggressive
behavior will reduce subsequent aggressive behavior (Doob and Wood,
1972; Konecni and Doob, 1972). Lorenz appears to accept both forms of
this hypothesis in his idea that aggressive drive can be reduced in substitute activities such as sporting events.

   Much of the criticism of Lorenz has focused on his support of the
notion of vicarious catharsis. There is little anecdotal evidence that observing sporting events reduces aggressive tendencies, and considerable
evidence that the opposite may be true. There are innumerable examples
of fights breaking out at high school basketball and football games in the
United States and in soccer matches in England and other countries. In
fact, a recent war between El Salvador and Honduras was caused by a
soccer game (Lever, 1969). To test the hypothesis that aggressive sports
increase aggressive tendencies in the audience, Goldstein and Arms
(1971) assessed hostility among male spectators before and after a football game and a competitive but less aggressive gymnastics meet. They
found evidence that hostility increased following the football game regardless of whether the spectator's team won or lost. No such hostility increase was found after the gymnastics meet.

   As we shall see, the social learning view of aggressive behavior leads
to predictions directly opposed to the notion of vicarious catharsis. Social
learning theory suggests that observing aggressive behavior will often
increase subsequent aggressive tendencies. Lorenz did not consider this
point of view or the many relevant experiments in his prescription for
reducing the aggressive drive in humans.

THE ETHOLOGICAL STUDY OF HUMAN BEHAVIOR

Lorenz' work and the work of other ethologists has greatly increased our appreciation of the complexities of animal behavior and the fascinating analogies between animal and human behavior. However, these analogies should serve only as a starting point for the ethological analysis of human behavior. As Tinbergen has suggested, the *methods* of ethology, as well as the *results* of ethology, must be applied to man (Tinbergen, 1968). There has been an increasing number of studies in human ethology, due in part to interest in the results of the ethologists and in part to recent awareness of the limitations of observations made only in laboratory-experimental settings.

It is impossible to subject humans to the kind of deprivation experiment used by ethologists to establish that a behavior pattern is instinctive. However, Eibl-Eibesfeldt (1970) points out that the existence of some instinctive behaviors in humans can be established by the observation of children born deaf and blind. These unfortunate children live in constant darkness and silence and have no means of normal imitation. Despite this, they show complex expressive movements—laughing, crying, cuddling, stomping the foot when angry, pushing and turning away when rejecting something—that are similar to those of healthy children. Eibl-Eibesfeldt argues that these behaviors could not be learned and that they demonstrate without doubt the existence of at least some instinctive behavior patterns in humans.

Other studies have found that stimuli important in the release of aggressive behavior patterns in animals seem to have analagous effects in humans. For example, a large number of experiments have shown that humans are very sensitive to social spacing. People tend to keep a certain distance between themselves and others. The size of these body-buffer zones varies from individual to individual, from culture to culture, and from situation to situation (Hall, 1959; 1966; Sommer 1969). One becomes uncomfortable and possibly angry when strangers violate one's space and embarrassed when one inadvertently violates the space of someone else. Felipe and Sommer (1966) observed the escape behavior of people when another person invaded their space by sitting down too close to them. In one study, the victim was a coed sitting alone in a largely empty university library. A female experimenter sat down beside the subject, moving the chair within three inches of the subject's chair so that there was about 12 inches separating their shoulders. If the subject moved her chair away, the experimenter pursued her by adjusting her own chair. The experimenter did not acknowledge the subject's presence at any time. Results indicated that 70% of the subjects whose personal space was violated in this way left the room within 30-minute experimental session as compared with less than 30% of subjects whose personal space was not violated. The investigators found similar results among male mental patients sitting alone on the park-like ground of a mental hospital.

Another clever experiment carried out in a natural setting showed that a major threat gesture among primates—the direct stare—also upsets human beings. The investigators either stared or did not stare at drivers stopped at the red light at an intersection. They then timed the speed that the car crossed the intersection when the light turned green. Drivers who were stared at crossed the intersection faster than drivers who were not stared at, suggesting that the former were escaping from an uncomfortable situation (Ellsworth, Carlsmith, and Henson, 1972).

It should be pointed out again that similarities between human and animal behavior do not prove that they are based on identical processes. More research is needed to determine the nature of these possibly innate processes in both animal and human behavior.

Environmental Theories of Aggression

Environmental theories of aggression assume that aggression is the result of external circumstances, such as frustration or the learning of aggressive habits. We shall consider the frustration-aggression hypothesis and Bandura and Walters' social learning theory of aggression.

THE FRUSTRATION-AGGRESSION HYPOTHESIS

The Role of Frustration The frustration-aggression hypothesis originated in Freud's early theorizing, before he posited a death instinct in 1923. It was adopted by a group of learning theorists at Yale University during the 1930s. In 1939, Dollard, Doob, Miller, Mowrer, and Sears published *Frustration and Aggression,* in which they argued that the "occurrence of aggressive behavior always presupposes the existence of frustration and, contrariwise, the existence of frustration always leads to some form of aggression." Thus, aggression is the inevitable consequence of frustration. The authors defined frustration in terms of the interference with a goal response: if an organism making a pattern of responses that has been reinforced in the past is thwarted so that it is not reinforced, it is frustrated.

The initial assertion of a one-to-one relationship between frustration and aggression was soon softened. Critics pointed out that, in some cultures such as that of Bali, aggression is *not* the usual response to frustration (Bateson, 1941) and that responses such as regression may also occur to frustration (Barker, Dembo, and Lewin, 1941). In 1941, Miller conceded that aggression is not the inevitable consequence of frustration; however, he still argued that it is the natural dominant response to frustration and that nonaggressive responses will occur only if aggression has been unrewarded or punished in the past. Also, he still argued that frustration is the inevitable antecedent of aggression: if aggression occurs, the organism must have been frustrated in the past.

More recent evidence indicates that factors other than frustration can cause aggression. One such factor is *imitation*. If a child sees someone behaving aggressively, he may tend to imitate that aggression regardless of whether or not he has been frustrated. This finding is central to Bandura and Walter's (1963) social learning theory of aggression, which we shall consider next. All in all, the frustration-aggression hypothesis has been greatly qualified in the years since it was first proposed. Berkowitz has offered as a contemporary statement: "A frustrating event increases the probability that the thwarted organism will act aggressively soon afterward." (1969b, p. 2) This version clearly acknowledges that frustration is only one of a number of possible antecedents to aggression, and that aggression is only one of a number of possible responses to frustration.

Behavioral Catharsis   We have seen that there is reason to question the notion of vicarious catharsis: the idea that observing aggression may reduce aggressive tendencies. The other form of the catharsis hypothesis suggests that the active expression of aggression will lessen later aggressive behavior. This notion of "behavioral catharsis" was accepted by Freud in his early theorizing and it was adapted from psychoanalytic theory by the frustration-aggression theorists. Dollard et. al. wrote "the occurrence of any act of aggression is assumed to reduce the instigation to aggression." (1939, p. 50) This position is still being defended by some frustration-aggression theorists, and we shall consider it in more detail below.

BANDURA AND WALTERS' SOCIAL LEARNING THEORY OF AGGRESSION

The Role of Imitation   A major feature of Bandura and Walters' theory is the importance it places upon *observational learning,* and particularly upon the imitation of *social models.* Previous learning theory approaches to personality had difficulty accounting for the formation of novel responses—responses that had never occurred and could not have been directly reinforced. Bandura and Walters argue that the child acquires most novel responses through the imitation of social models. For example, a child can learn how to use a gun by watching televised models using guns, even if has no toy gun to practice with. Bandura and Walters also suggest that the observation of social models may have inhibitory or disinhibitory effects upon responses that a child has already learned. Thus watching an aggressive model use a gun might disinhibit a different aggressive response, such as hitting a sibling.

As a demonstration that novel aggressive responses can be acquired through observational learning, Bandura, Ross, and Ross (1963) exposed nursery school children to an adult model who exhibited specific aggressive responses with a large inflated plastic bobo doll. The adult sat on the doll and punched it, hit it with a wooden mallet, tossed it up and down, and kicked it; all the while uttering such distinctive vocalizations as "sock him," "hit him down," and "pow." In different conditions, the children saw a real-life model, the same model on film, or a film of an adult dressed up like a cat. There was also a control condition with no model.

After they saw the model, the children were allowed to play with attractive toys. They were then mildly frustrated by being obliged to leave these toys and go to a room which contained, among other things, a bobo doll. Their play was observed and both imitative aggressive responses similar to the responses similar to the responses previously exhibited by the model, and nonimitative aggressive responses, were counted.

The results of the experiment are summarized in Table 5.1 As expected, the children who observed a model exhibited more imitative aggressive responses than those who saw no model. The nature of the model made little difference. The real life model, filmed model, and costumed model conditions all resulted in more imitative aggression than did the no-model control condition, although the costumed model was somewhat less effective then the real life and filmed models.

Bandura and Walters argue that children can learn a complex repertoire of novel aggressive responses through such exposure to aggressive models. Such exposure can also inhibit or disinhibit previously learned responses. As Table 5.1 indicates, the children exposed to an aggressive

TABLE 5.1   MEAN AGGRESSION SCORES.

MODEL CONDITION	IMITATIVE AGGRESSION		NONIMITATIVE AGGRESSION	
	GIRLS	BOYS	GIRLS	BOYS
Real life	14.2	28.4	26.3	42.1
Filmed	9.0	23.8	29.2	39.3
Costumed	7.8	16.2	27.5	71.8
No model	1.8	3.9	17.8	40.4

Adapted from data presented in A. Bandura, D. Ross, and S. Ross, "Imitation of film-mediated aggressive models." *Journal of Abnormal and Social Psychology,* 1963, **66,** 3–11. Copyright 1963 by the American Psychological Association. Reprinted by permission.

Reinforcement patterns have been found to alter aggressive behaviors in nonlaboratory settings. For example, aggression in nursery schools can be reduced if the teachers ignore aggression whenever possible and reward nonaggressive, cooperative behavior (Brown and Elliott, 1965). Such techniques of behavior modification based on the reinforcement principle have been successfully adapted to control aggression in a wide variety of settings. There is also evidence that naturally occuring social reinforcement effectively shapes aggressive behavior. Patterson, Littman, and Bricker (1967) carefully observed aggressive acts and their consequences during nursery school play over a period of months. The past rewarding or punishing reactions of the potential victim—crying and compliance or retaliation and counterattack—were found to influence the rate, type, and target of aggression as time went on.

Parenthetically, it should be noted that sex differences in aggression are found in these modeling experiments. Boys were consistently more likely to show aggression toward the bobo doll in all conditions of the Bandura, Ross, and Ross study, including the no-model condition. (See Table 5.1). In the Bandura (1965b) study, Figure 5.1 shows that boys were more likely to perform aggressive responses when given no incentive, particularly in the model-punished condition. Also, there was apparently a sex difference in the initial observational learning of aggressive responses. Boys were better able to reproduce the model's aggressive responses than girls when asked and rewarded for doing so. It may be that the boys were more careful and attentive observers of the model's aggressive behavior.

Some suggest that this apparent sex difference in the attention paid to an aggressive model is based on learning, while others argue that constitutional factors are more important. Bandura (1965a) suggests that if one has been rewarded in the past for producing a certain kind of behavior, one will come to anticipate further rewards for reproducing that behavior and will therefore pay particular attention when that behavior is being performed by others. Thus, assuming that boys receive more social rewards for showing aggressive behavior than girls, they should be expected to attend more to, and learn more from, aggressive models. On the other hand, as Hamburg (1971) points out, there is a consistent sex difference in chimpanzees, gorillas, and other primates in the attention paid to the aggressive displays of adults. Males pay more attention to aggression than females. This difference appears in infancy and seems to be unlearned. This observation, if generalized to humans, suggests that there may be a built-in sex difference in the tendency to model aggressive behavior. We shall return to this question in the next chapter.

The Role of Frustration   Bandura and Walters suggest that the presence of frustration may often increase the probability that aggression will occur in a given situation. First, frustration may increase general arousal, which in turn increases the intensity of all responding including aggressive responding. Also, many persons learn to respond aggressively when they are frustrated. However, Bandura and Walters do not feel that frustration necessarily leads to aggression, arguing that children can learn nonaggressive and even constructive responses to frustration.

As an example, they cite a study by Davitz (1952) in which five groups of four children each were rewarded for aggressive and competitive behavior in brief training sessions, while five other groups were rewarded for constructive and cooperative behavior. Later the children were given candy and shown a movie. At the climax of the movie, the film was suddenly stopped and their candy was taken away. After this rather frustrating experience the children were observed in a free play situation. The children in the groups taught to be aggressive were judged to respond to the frustration in a more aggressive and less constructive way than those in the groups taught to be cooperative.

To recapitulate, Bandura and Walters argue that most new aggressive responses were learned through imitation, and that reinforcement determines whether or not these learned responses will be performed. If a child makes imitative aggressive responses in a given situation and if these responses are rewarded, he will tend to respond aggressively in similar situations in the future. Many persons may learn to respond to frustrating situations with aggression, not because frustration necessarily leads to aggression but because aggressive responses to frustration are often imitated and rewarded. Social values in some societies may encourage aggression as a response to frustration, while other societies may encourage more constructive behavior.

Bandura and Walters' theory has important social implications. We saw in the last section that Lorenz predicts that observing aggression will control aggressive behavior through vicarious catharsis. Bandura and Walters predict the opposite. If children learn aggressive behavior so easily by imitating aggressive models, one way to control aggression in a society is to restrict the exposure of children to such models. Also, if social values encourage aggression as a response to frustration, another way to control aggression is to alter such values. These implications have led to much scientific and political debate over the possible role in encouraging aggression in American society of one highly visible source of aggressive models and values: the mass media.

THE MASS MEDIA AND AGGRESSION

The great amount of violence on the mass media has often attracted the attention of social critics, with television being singled out because its contents are so easily available to children. Violence on television has gradually increased since the medium began, with no sign of any significant decrease in response to recent criticism. It has recently been estimated that, between the ages of 5 and 15, the average child in the United States witnesses the destruction of over 13,400 persons on television (Liebert, Neale, and Davidson, 1973).

Geen (1972) cites the following incident adapted from a 1971 news story:

> Police are investigating possible parallels between a recent "Hawaii Five-O" television program and a multiple slaying. The gunman was armed with two rifles and was dressed in Army fatigues with a bag of candy in the pocket. He reportedly yelled and laughed hysterically as he moved through a factory, killing five workers. Three others, including a policeman and the gunman, were wounded. The police have been unable to establish a motive for the shooting, but they note that many elements resembled the television program, including the gunman's clothing, method of operation, and candy. Receipts indicated that one rifle and ammunition were purchased shortly after the broadcast.

Since the early 1960s, evidence has been accumulating that under certain circumstances, aggressive behavior depicted in films or television can increase subsequent aggressive behavior. A large number of studies and recently an investigation by the Surgeon General of the United States have been directed toward this problem.

Early Laboratory Experiments   An early demonstration that aggressive behavior may be increased in adults through filmed violence was made by Walters and his colleagues. Walters, Llewellyn Thomas, and Acker (1962) and Walters and Llewellyn Thomas (1963) required subjects to give electric shocks to another person as punishment for errors on a learning task. The subject chose the intensity of the shock. Actually, the other person was not being shocked and the number of "errors" was fixed. The experimenters were really interested in the effects of different films on the intensity of shock the subject chose to give. In one condition, the subject saw a knife fight from the movie *Rebel Without a Cause,* in another he saw a neutral educational film. Results indicated that subjects who had seen the aggressive film gave more intense shocks than did subjects who had seen the neutral film.

The Role of Anger   Feshbach (1961) argued that such vicarious aggressive displays would increase aggression only in nonangered subjects. He suggested that aggressive films would have cathartic effects among angered subjects. This hypothesis was tested by Berkowitz and his colleagues who found that, on the contrary, the aggression-arousing effect of filmed violence was stronger when the subject was angry.

In Berkowitz' experiments, some subjects were angered by being insulted or shocked harshly by another person while others were not angered. Some subjects were then shown a film clip from the movie *Champion,* which depicts a boxer receiving a severe beating. Other subjects saw a nonaggressive control film. The subjects were then tested for aggression by having them judge the creativeness of a house-plan ostensibly designed by the other person. Actually, all subjects evaluated the same house plan. The judgment was given in the form of electric shocks to the other person: the worse the job of the house plan, the more shocks the subject should give up to a maximum of eight. Results indicated that subjects who were angered and saw the aggressive film gave more shocks and longer shocks than angered subjects who saw the nonaggressive film. This effect was strongest when the other person was associated with the film, either because he was a boxer (Berkowitz 1965a) or because his name was similar to that of the beaten fighter (Berkowitz and Geen, 1966; Geen and Berkowitz, 1966).

The Role of Justification   Bandura and Walter's theory suggests that observed violence may have its effect both through imitation of the aggressive model and through disinhibition of the usual socialized restraints on aggressive behavior. Berkowitz argues that the latter disinhibitory effect is greater for justified violence than it is for unjustified violence. He found that the boxing film produced more aggression when the violence was depicted as justified (i.e. the losing fighter was a villain receiving his just desserts) than if the loser was the hero (Berkowitz, 1964). Meyer (1972) found that this holds for presentations of real violence (a film of a North Vietnamese soldier being executed by stabbing by a South Vietnamese soldier) as well as fictional violence. Meyer's results, shown in Figure 5.2, indicated that angry subjects returned more shocks and more intense shocks to the anger instigator after watching real or fictional violence presented as justified than did subjects who watched the same

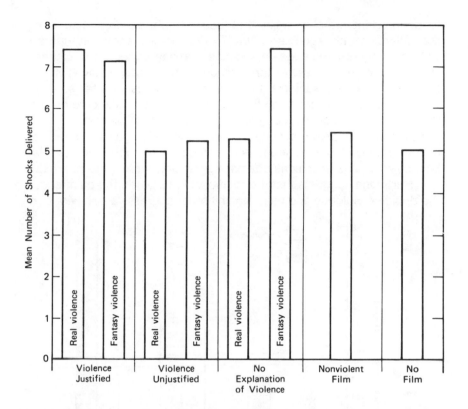

FIGURE 5.2   Mean number of shocks returned by each group. Adapted from data presented in T. P. Meyer, "Effects of viewing justified and unjustified real film violence on aggressive behavior." *Journal of Personality and Social Psychology*, 1972, 23, 21–29. Copyright 1972 by the American Psychological Association. Reprinted by permission.

violence presented as unjustified. When no instructions were given regarding the justifiability of the violence, the fictional violence still led to increased aggression while the real violence did not.

The Role of Pain Cues   It is possible that extremely intense and painful violence may sometimes serve to increase inhibitions against aggression. Goranson (1970) reports that when subjects were told that the losing fighter in the boxing film later died of his injuries, they were less aggressive following the film than were other subjects. Goranson's study was done on college students, most of whom presumably have relatively strong inhibitions against aggression. Hartmann (1969) studied male adolescents confined to an institution for delinquents. The subjects were angered or not angered and then exposed to a film of a fist fight that focused on the attacker, a film that focused on the pain and suffering of the victim, or a nonaggressive film. The results are shown in Figure 5.3. Both nonangered and angered subjects who saw either of the aggressive films were more aggressive than subjects in the nonaggressive film condition. Also, angered subjects showed more aggression after seeing the victim's pain than after seeing the attacker's assault. This difference was in the opposite direction among nonangered subjects. Hartmann feels that the tendency for pain reactions to raise inhibitions against aggression is counteracted in his experiment by the presence of anger and the relative lack of socialized inhibitions against aggression among his subjects.

Hartmann suggests that the relationship between the painfulness of the depicted violence and the disinhibition of aggressive behavior can be

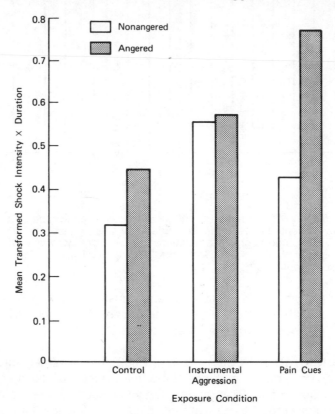

FIGURE 5.3   Mean transformed shock intensity x duration for subjects viewing the control film, instrumental aggression film, and the pain cues film. From D. P. Hartmann, "Influence of symbolically modeled instrumental aggression and pain cues on aggressive behavior." *Journal of Personality and Social Psychology*, 1969, 11, 280–288. Copyright 1969 by the American Psychological Association. Reprinted by permission.

represented by an inverted U-shaped curve: the pain reactions excite aggression up to a point, but when they become too intense they begin to inhibit aggression (see Figure 5.4). The effect of anger or a lack of socialized inhibitions is to displace the curve upward and to the right. Some experiments by Zimbardo and his colleagues suggest that under certain conditions which he terms "deindividuation," there may be an almost complete loss of inhibitions against aggression, even among presumably socialized people. We shall discuss their findings below.

The Role of Arousal   There is another way by which an aggressive film might produce an increase in subsequent aggressive behavior. Possibly the excitement of the film produces arousal in the subject. If the subject is angry, this arousal may produce more aggression either because the dominant aggressive responses are energized by arousal as Bandura and Walters' (1963) theory suggests or because the subject may label the additional arousal as anger as Schachter and Singer's (1964) theory suggests (see Chapter 2). On the other hand, it may be that aggressive cues in the film are necessary for increased aggression to occur.

Berkowitz directed an experiment to test this possibility. Angered and nonangered subjects were shown either an exciting but nonaggressive

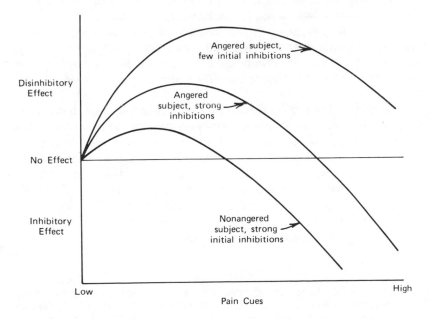

FIGURE 5.4   Theoretical relationship between pain cues on film and the inhibition or disinhibition of aggressive behavior. Adapted from a suggestion by Hartmann (1969).

film about the running of the first four-minute mile, or a nonexciting film about canal boats in England. Although the exciting film was rated as more arousing than the nonexciting film, it did not lead to increased aggression, suggesting that aggressive cues in the film are necessary to cause an increase in aggression (Buck, 1965).

On the other hand, a recent study suggests that arousing films with erotic content can increase aggressive behavior. Zillman (1971) found that a film with highly arousing sexual content but no hint of violence caused increased aggression among angered male subjects as compared with a nonaggressive travel film and even a violent boxing film. He concluded that the increase in aggression was due to the arousing aspects of the erotic film.* Doob and his associates have also emphasized the role of arousal in the disinhibitory effects of aggressive films (Doob and Climie, 1972; Doob and Kirshenbaum, 1973). The relative importance of aggressive cues and arousal in the disinhibition of aggressive behavior through films is an important issue that has yet to be clarified.

Berkowitz and LePage (1967) reported a finding that seemed to indicate that aggressive cues without any accompanying arousal could increase aggressive behavior. They found that angered subjects were more aggressive in the presence of weapons (a shotgun and a .38 revolver) than when no weapons were present. However, other investigators have not been able to repeat this finding (Buss, Booker, and Buss, 1972), and Page and Scheidt (1971) suggested that it may have been based on sophisticated experimental subjects who guessed the purpose behind the presence of the guns. Although this latter possibility has been disputed by Berkowitz (1971a), the reality of the weapons effect appears to be in doubt.

The Surgeon General's Report   The experimental results that we have considered clearly demonstrate support for the basic predictions of social learning theory regarding the role of imitation, disinhibition and reinforcement in the expression of aggressive behavior. However, it is not possible to make sweeping conclusions about the effects of media violence on the basis of these studies alone. The major criticism leveled against these studies is their artificiality. As Singer (1969) has pointed out, the laboratory settings and the often complicated procedures in the experiments are very different from the usual course of events in real life.

Recent studies on the relationship between sexual arousal and aggression have found conflicting results. Jaffe, Malamuth, Finegold, and Feshbach (1974) found increased aggression following sexual arousal, Baron (1974) found decreased aggression in aroused subjects.

Whereas an actual television program or movie involves a more or less complex sequence of ideas and events of which violence is only one feature, most of the studies we have considered employ an unusually clear-cut and intense violent episode isolated from the rest of the play. Similarly, the aggressive responses measured in these experiments are often far removed from what is normally considered to be aggression. Finally, the possibility cannot be discounted that the experimental subject may guess the purpose of the experiment and act accordingly: a subject who sees an aggressive film may simply guess that the experimenter wants him to be aggressive.

The question of the effect of media violence have fueled two United States Senate investigations—the Kefauver hearings of 1951 and the Dodd hearings of 1961–1962—neither of which came to any definite conclusion. The experiments of Bandura, Walters, Berkowitz, and others helped to initiate another investigation in 1969 by the office of the Surgeon General. In the course of the investigation, a number of experimental and survey studies were commissioned specifically to study the effects of televised violence on children. The experimental studies attempted to circumvent some of the artificiality of previous experiments by using entire television programs rather than excerpts, measuring the effects of the programs in the real-life nursery school environment, and measuring the occurrence of constructive and prosocial behaviors as well as aggressive behavior. The survey studies were designed to further avoid the charge of artificiality by measuring variables close to life, such as actual viewing preferences and peer ratings of aggressiveness.

One of the experimental studies involved showing nursery school children a diet of either aggressive cartoons, neutral nature films, or prosocial films which were segments of *Misterogers Neighborhood* that emphasized cooperation and coping with fears and frustration (Stein and Friedrich, 1972). The children were exposed to 12 twenty-minute episodes from the diet over a four-week period. Behavior observations in the nursery school began in a three-week baseline period before the diet was shown, ran through the four-week stimulation period, and continued for two weeks. The results of the experiment were complex, but there was evidence that the violent diet stimulated aggressive behavior among children who were initially above the median in aggressive behavior. There was also evidence that exposure to *Misterogers Neighborhood* increased prosocial behavior in children from families of lower socioeconomic status, while the violent diet seemed to increase prosocial behaviors among high-status children (Stein and Friedrich, 1972).

In another study, children were shown an aggressive portion of *The Untouchables* or a control film of a track race. The aggressive film was found to lead to increased aggression (Liebert and Baron, 1971). In addition, the facial expressions of some of the children were recorded, and it was found that boys who showed expressions of pleasure or interest in the aggressive film were more aggressive than boys who showed disinterest. This relationship was not found among girls (Ekman, Liebert, Friesen, Harrison, Zlatchin, Malmstrom, and Baron, 1971).

Considering the results from all of the experimental studies, the Surgeon General's report makes the following carefully qualified conclusion: "Televised violence may lead to increased aggressive behavior in certain subgroups of children, who might constitute a small proportion or a substantial proportion of the total population of young television viewers." (p. 123) According to the report, the children most likely to react to televised violence with aggressive behavior are those who are initially more aggressive.

The survey studies were correlational in nature, and it is more difficult to establish conclusively causal relationships with correlational studies than it is with experimental studies. However, the data from the survey studies were consistent with the interpretation that viewing violence causes aggressive behavior. One study found a positive relationship between a measure of exposure to televised violence in eight-year-old boys and peer rating of aggressiveness ten years later (Lefkowitz, Eron, Walder, and Huesmann, 1971; Eron, Huesmann, Lefkowitz, and Walder, 1972). These authors ascertained the favorite televised programs of the same group of rural New York state children in the third grade, eighth grade, and the year after high school graduation. Peer ratings of aggressiveness were also taken. Among boys but not girls, high exposure to televised violence in the third grade was related to high ratings of aggressiveness at age 18 (see Figure 5.5). A study by McLeod, Atkin, and Chafee (1971a; 1971b) also found a positive relationship between past and current violence viewing and measures of aggression in both boys and girls. Several other studies reported positive relationships between the preference for violent programs and aggression.

Considering all of the survey results, the report concludes that "there is a modest relationship between exposure to television violence and aggressive behavior." (pp. 177–178) Taken together, the experimental and survey results are both consistent with the idea that there is a causal relationship between viewing violence on television and aggressive behavior, and they both suggest that this relationship may exist only for children who are predisposed to be aggressive.

The Determinants of the Preference for Violence   A common explanation for why people choose to watch violence is that such

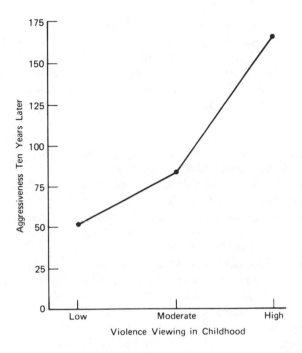

FIGURE 5.5   Relationship between boys' violence viewing at age 8 and their interpersonal aggressiveness as measured 10 years later. Drawn from data presented by Eron, Huesmann, Lefkowitz, and Walder, 1972. From Albert Bandura, AGGRESSION: A Social Learning Analysis, (c) 1973. Reprinted by permission of Prentice-Hall, Inc. Englewood Cliffs, N. J.

watching helps to drain off aggressive tendencies. As we have seen, the studies commissioned and evaluated by the Surgeon General's investigation appear to establish that this vicarious catharsis hypothesis is seldom if ever true and that in fact the opposite is often the case. This leaves us with the question of why violence on television and in motion pictures is so popular.

There is undoubtedly no simple answer to this question, and very little research has yet been done on it. We saw above that Bandura (1965a) suggests that those who learn to expect rewards from aggressive behavior may be more likely to attend to aggressive behavior in others, and some ethologists suggest that there may be biologically programmed preferences for displays of aggression in some species. Both of these positions may be correct—there is very little relevant research. Another possibility is that watching violence can function as a way to cope with fears and anxieties about violence. Fenichel (1939) and Klausner (1966) have discussed counterphobic behavior, in which an individual voluntarily exposes himself to feared situations as a way of mastering the fear.

Boyanowsky, Newtson, and Walster (1972) tested the hypothesis that viewing violence may be a form of counterphobic behavior following the tragic stabbing murder of a woman student at a large midwestern university. Two motion pictures happened to be playing near the campus at the time: *In Cold Blood,* based on the murder of a family by two psychopaths, and *The Fox,* the story of a lesbian relationship. Two days after the stabbing, attendance at *In Cold Blood* increased significantly from the previous week, while attendance at *The Fox* changed only slightly. The investigators also called randomly selected women students from the victim's dormitory and from a comparable control dormitory. The caller gave the student a choice between a free ticket for *The Fox* or *In Cold Blood.* There was no difference between the two movies immediately following the murder: 41% of those in the victim's dormitory versus 58% in the control dormitory chose *In Cold Blood.* One week later however, 72% from the victim's dormitory compared to 48% of the control subjects chose the violent film. There was thus an increase in the preference for *In Cold Blood* after an interval following the murder, particularly among persons who had a relationship with the victim.

The authors interpret the increased preference for the violent film as indicating an attempt to reduce fear and anxiety. They suggest that watching the violence produces an effect analagous to *desensitization* in behavior therapy. Desensitization is a technique developed to lessen fear by presenting a feared stimulus in mild doses while the subject relaxes (Wolpe, 1958; Lazarus, 1963). There have been reports that severe fear following combat has been successfully treated by exposure to film and sounds of combat which are graded in intensity (Schwartz, 1945; Saul, Rome and Lenser, 1946; reported in Bandura, 1973). Also, there is evidence that children who watch much television show smaller autonomic responses to televised violence then do children who watch little television (Cline, Croft, and Courrier, 1972). Although the latter results may be interpreted in several ways—it is possible, for example, that the parents of children who watch little television are less tolerant of aggression than parents of heavy watchers—it is consistent with the idea that viewing violence may lessen fears about violence.

SOCIAL LEARNING THEORY AND BEHAVIORAL CATHARSIS

We have seen that there is very little support for the vicarious catharsis hypothesis: observing aggression appears generally to increase aggressive tendencies rather than reduce them. The other form of the catharsis hypothesis suggests that aggressive behavior will lessen later aggression.

This is the version adapted from psychoanalytic theory by the frustration-aggression theorists.

Physiological Studies   This version of the catharsis hypothesis has been studied by Hokanson and his colleagues in one of the few systematic investigations of the effects of aggression on a physiological measure. Hokanson found that an insult which increased aggressive tendencies also increased systolic blood pressure. He reasoned that, if aggressive behavior results in a cathartic reduction of aggressive tendencies, there should be a faster reduction of the heightened blood pressure following aggressive behavior than following nonaggressive responses. A series of studies supported this reasoning: verbal and physical aggression toward an anger instigator led to a relatively rapid return of elevated systolic blood pressure to the initial resting level (Hokanson and Burgess, 1962a, 1962b; Hokanson, Burgess, and Cohen, 1963; Hokanson and Shetler, 1961).

These initial studies employed both male and female subjects, but sex differences were not systematically investigated. Hokanson and Edelman (1966) studied sex differences in the physiological recovery patterns following different kinds of responses to a frustrator. The subject was told that he and a partner could choose to give each other a shock, a reward, or no response on each trial. The subject and partner were seated in different rooms and the partner's responses were actually controlled by the experimenter. The partner went first and consistently gave the subject a shock. The subject then chose to give the partner a shock, reward, or no response. Systolic blood pressure was taken before and after the partner's response, before and after the subject's response, and then for 20-second intervals until reading reached the pretrial level. Another trial was then begun for a total of five trials.

Results indicated that, for males, systolic blood pressure recovered more quickly following an aggressive counterresponse than following a reward or no response. However, females showed the opposite result: They recovered more quickly after they had *rewarded* the partner. Other experiments have also suggested that aggression has a tension-reducing effect among males only. Baker and Schaie (1969) and Gambaro and Rabin (1969), using male subjects, found evidence of faster physiological recovery following aggression, while Holmes (1966) and Vantress and Williams (1972) found no such effect using female subjects. There is evidence that guilt over aggression may reduce the tension-reducing effect of aggressive behavior: highly guilty subjects show less tension reduction following aggression than low-guilt subjects among both males (Gambaro and Rabin, 1969) and females (Schill, 1972).

To explain these findings, Hokanson (1970) proposed that a subject will show arousal reduction if he is able to make a response that he has learned will avoid aggression from others. Males learn that counteraggression will generally turn off a peer's aggressive behavior, while females are rewarded for passive, nonaggressive counterresponses.

To test this notion, Hokanson, Willers, and Koropsak (1968) put male and female subjects in a situation similar to that of Hokanson and Edelman, except that only reward and punishment responses were permitted and a different physiological measure—vasoconstriction in the finger—was taken. The vasoconstriction measure recovers more quickly, allowing a large number of trials. On the first 32 baseline trials, the subject was rewarded or shocked by the partner on a random basis regardless of the subject's response. On the next 60 conditioning trials, the subject was rewarded for sex-inappropriate behavior. Females were rewarded after they shocked the partner and shocked after they rewarded the partner; males received shocks after they shocked and rewards after they rewarded. For the last 32 extinction trials, the partner's behavior became random again.

The results are presented in Figure 5.6. On the baseline trials, sex-appropriate behavior led to faster vascular recovery: males recovered more quickly after they shocked the other and females showed faster recovery after rewarding the other. This result is similar to those in the previous experiments. During the conditioning phase, this gradually changed, and the subject began to show faster vascular recovery after he made the response never followed by shock from the partner. Females began to show faster recovery following aggression, and they increased significantly in the number of shocks they gave to the partner. Males began to show faster recovery following rewarding responses, and they increased their rewarding behavior slightly. During the extinction trials, the original characteristic behavioral and vascular responses tended to return.

This experiment indicated that, in a relatively brief training period, the cathartic arousal-reducing effects of one respone were extinguished while a different response acquired arousal-reducing qualities. The data suggest that *any* response that avoids aggression from the other can acquire arousal-reducing qualities.

To test the limits of his hypothesis, Stone and Hokanson (1969) provided a third response alternative: self-shock. The subject could, if he wished, respond to the partner by shocking himself with a shock less severe than that given by the partner. During the baseline phase, self-shock was rare and associated with long vascular recovery. During a conditioning phase, self-shock was rewarded by friendly responses from

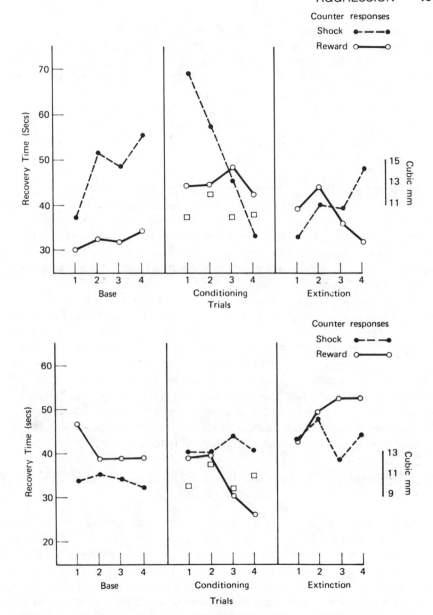

FIGURE 5.6   Summary of plethysmographic data for female subjects (*upper*) and male subjects (*lower*). From J. E. Hokanson, K. R. Willers, and E. Koropsak, "The modification of autonomic responses during aggressive interchange." *Journal of Personality*, 1968, 36, 386–404. Copyright © 1968 by Duke University Press. Reprinted by permission.

the other while all other responses were answered by shock. The self-shock response increased in frequency and became associated with cathartic fast vascular recovery. In a subsequent study, Hokanson and Stone (1969) demonstrated that the less intense the self-shock, the sooner it became associated with fast vascular recovery.

Hokanson's studies show that aggression per se does not necessarily lead to a reduction in arousal after one has been attacked. Apparently, almost any response will reduce arousal if the subject has learned that the response will be instrumental in avoiding further attack.

Behavioral Studies   Studies investigating the effect of aggression on subsequent aggressive behavior have provided uneven support for the hypothesis of behavioral catharsis. There is evidence that engaging in aggressive behavior not directed against a frustrator may increase rather than decrease subsequent aggression. Thus Mallick and McCandless (1966) found that aggressive play increased subsequent aggression in frustrated children.

When the aggressive behavior is directed against a frustrator, some studies have noted a decrease in later aggression toward that frustrator (Bramel, Taub, and Blum, 1968; Doob and Wood, 1972; Konecni and Doob, 1972). For example, Konecni and Doob gave angered subjects an opportunity to shock their attacker, shock an innocent person, or no chance to give shocks. All were then given an opportunity to shock the attacker. Subjects who had previously shocked the attacker or an innocent person gave fewer shocks to the attacker than persons who had given no shocks. Interestingly, subjects who had given no shocks also gave a large number of shocks to an innocent scapegoat who had not attacked them.

THE LIMITS OF A SOCIAL LEARNING ANALYSIS OF AGGRESSION

Social learning theorists have amassed an impressive array of evidence that human aggression is greatly influenced by imitation and reinforcement. However, the investigators who link aggression with innate factors have equally impressive evidence. As we saw in Chapter 3, humans can show aggressive behaviors that appear to be primarily the products of brain abnormalities or electrical stimulation of the brain. A patient sitting quietly when stimulation was applied to the amygdala "was out of contact, then she made a series of angry grimaces which included lip retraction and baring of the teeth, the ancient 'primate threat display.' " She then lunged suddenly in an attack against the wall (Mark and Ervin, 1970). Such observations indicate that neural circuits exist which in some way mediate some kinds of aggressive behavior and that these circuits can be activated abnormally.

While physiological events can apparently be the direct cause of some aggressive behavior, it is also true that learning and environmental factors influence even physiologically based aggression. Animals respond quite selectively following brain stimulation. They do not strike out automatically: their reaction is affected both by previous experience and events in the environment (See Chapter 3). This seems true with humans as well. Consider the tragic case of Charles Whitman. On the night of July 31, 1966 Whitman wrote a letter which stated in part:*

> I don't understand what it is that compels me to type this letter
> . . . I don't really understand myself these days. I am supposed
> to be an average, reasonable, and intelligent young man. How-
> ever lately (I can't recall when it started) I have been a victim of
> many unusual and irrational thoughts. These thoughts constantly
> recur, and it requires a tremendous mental effort to concentrate
> on useful and progressive tasks . . . After my death I wish that
> an autopsy would be performed on me to see if there is any vis-
> ible physical disorder. I have had some tremendous headaches
> in the past and have consumed two large bottles of Excedrin in
> the past three months.
> It was after much thought that I decided to kill my wife, Kathy,
> tonight after I pick her up from work . . . I love her dearly, and
> she has been a fine wife to me as any man could ever hope to
> have. I cannot rationally pinpoint any specific reason for doing
> this. I don't know whether it is selfishness, or if I don't want her
> to have to face the embarrassment my actions would surely
> cause her. At this time though, the most prominent reason in my
> mind is that I truly do not consider this world worth living in, and
> am prepared to die, and I do not want to leave her to suffer
> alone in it. I intend to kill her as painlessly as possible. . . .
> (Quoted in Johnson, 1972, p. 78).

Later that night Whitman killed his wife and mother, and the next morning he shot 38 people from a tower at the University of Texas, killing 14. An

*From Johnson, R.N.: AGGRESSION IN MAN & ANIMALS. Philadelphia, W.B. Saunders Company, 1972. Reproduced with the permission of the publisher and author.

autopsy revealed a malignant tumor the size of a walnut near the amygdala (Sweet, Ervin, and Mark, 1969).

Assuming that this tumor was the immediate cause of Whitman's shooting spree, it is possible that a person with less thorough training in aggression might have had a different response to the same tumor. Bandura (1973) has pointed out many elements in Whitman's development that could have disposed him to violent action:*

> *Whitman was raised in an atmosphere of familial violence. Like his father, who repeatedly beat his wife and displayed a "fanatic" interest in guns, Whitman was known to assault his wife and others with a minimum of provocation. From early childhood he also shared his father's fondness for firearms. As a marine recruit he was courtmartialed for insubordination and fighting.*
> *Upon discharge he had occasional brushes with the law in connection with aggressive activities . . . Contrary to journalistic accounts, Whitman's record was not that of a meek altar boy suddenly gone berserk (Bandura, 1973, p. 180).*

Theories of aggression that emphasize innate factors, such as those of Lorenz and other ethologists, and theories that emphasize environmental factors, such as that of Bandura and Walters, may be all substantially correct but incomplete. Each theory may apply to one aspect of the phenomenon of aggression but miss other aspects which are covered by other theories. In an analysis of theories of child development, Baldwin (1967) has noted that different theories often do not overlap: "The theories generally talk past each other; each is concentrated on some particular area of child behavior and development to the exclusion of many of the questions which other theories regard as fundamental" (Baldwin, 1967, p. 583). Theories of aggression also appear to have this "patchwork quilt" quality: Each is valid and useful when applied to a restricted set of phenomena but invalid when generalized beyond that set. This suggests that it is misleading to think of the theories as competing with one another. Theories are rarely incompatible but they are often designed to explain different sets of phenomena and are thus irrelevant to one another.

The topic of aggression may usefully be seen as encompassing a number of qualitatively different sets of phenomena, each of which re-

---

* *Albert Bandura, AGGRESSION: A Social Learning Analysis, © 1973. Reprinted by permission of Prentice-Hall, Inc. Englewood Cliffs, N.J.*

quires an analysis of its own. Along these lines, several authors have suggested schemes to classify different kinds of aggression. While tentative, these schemes provide systematic ways to organize the diverse phenomena that we label "aggression."

Different Kinds of Aggression

LORENZ' TYPOLOGY

Lorenz (1966) distinguishes six types of innate aggression. Three of these usually occur between members of different species. *Predatory aggression* involves the attack of the predator upon the prey. *Mobbing* occurs when the prey counterattacks in force against a predator. Such attacks occur when birds attack a cat or owl by day and when geese gang up on a fox. The *critical reaction* is the desperate fight of an animal who cannot escape from a source of danger. This particularly violent form of aggression can occur when an animal is cornered or when it is surprised by an enemy a short distance away. Lorenz notes that many big game hunting accidents have occurred when a large animal is surprised by a hunter at close range.

The other types of aggression distinguished by Lorenz typically occur between members of the same species, and we have considered some of them above. *Territorial aggression* involves the increased readiness of an animal to fight when he is on familiar ground. *Rival fights* occur when animals (generally males) vie for sexual partners. *Brood defense* involves the defense of the young, and it may be a form of critical reaction where the animal is prevented from escaping the danger because of innate bonds to the young.

FESHBACH'S TYPOLOGY

Feshbach (1964; 1971) makes quite a different distinction between kinds of aggression. He defines *instrumental aggression* as aggressive behavior directed toward the achievement of nonaggressive goals, as when a child learns to get his way by bullying smaller children. In contrast, *hostile aggression* is behavior with the goal of injuring an animate or inanimate object. Thus injury to the object is an end in itself rather than a means to another end.

Conceptually, there are important differences between instrumental and hostile aggression. As we shall see in the next section, instrumental aggression can be based entirely upon learned habits and expectations, while hostile aggression theoretically involves emotional factors as well. However, it is often difficult to separate the role of instrumental and emotional factors in a given aggressive act. A parent who severely spanks a child may be engaging in instrumental behavior aimed at developing inhibitions against undesired behavior, but emotional factors—anger and hostility—might also be involved and the parent might really want to hurt the child at that moment. The real intentions of the aggressor are often obscure to the observer and they may be obscure even to the aggressor himself.

MOYER'S TYPOLOGY

Moyer (1968) has offered an analysis which in many respects combines and extends the typologies of Lorenz and Feshbach. Moyer classified eight kinds of aggression according to the stimulus situation which elicits them. His analysis is summarized in Table 5.2. Moyer specified the releaser which elicits each kind of aggression and the general environment in which the aggression occurs. He also points out that each of these kinds of aggressive behavior may have a different physiological basis, and he makes tentative suggestions based on available knowledge about the neural and endocrine basis of each kind of aggression (see Avis, 1974, for a review of the pharmacological bases of several kinds of aggression).

TABLE 5.2   MOYER'S TYPOLOGY OF AGGRESSION.

TYPE OF AGGRESSION	RELEASING STIMULUS	ENVIRONMENT
1. Predatory	Natural prey.	Any setting.
2. Inter-Male	Strange male conspecific (inhibited by appeasement gestures).	Any setting.
3. Fear Induced	Any threat.	Confining: aggression preceeded by attempt to escape.
4. Territorial	Any threat.	On established territory.
5. Maternal	Any threat.	Presence of young.
6. Irritable	Any attackable object.	Any stressor: frustration, deprivation, pain.
7. Instrumental	Any attackable object.	Any setting.
8. Sex-related	Object normally producing a sexual response.	Any setting.

Predatory aggression involves an attack by a predator upon its natural prey. The range of stimuli that elicits this type of aggression is quite narrow, although the predatory response can occur in virtually any environment. The topography of the predatory response is often distinct from other kinds of aggressive responses. A mouse-killing rat, for example, will kill by a clean bite through the spinal cord at the back of the neck. Non-predatory rats can be trained to kill and eat mice, but they never learn to use the neck-biting predatory response (Moyer, 1972).

The lateral nucleus of the hypothalamus may be particularly involved in predatory aggression. As we saw in Chapter 3, stimulation of the lateral hypothalamus often elicits stalking and attack in predatory animals such as cats. Perhaps significantly, less intense stimulation of the lateral hypothalamus also elicits eating, and there may be some relationship between the role of this area in eating and predation. Simulation and lesions in the amygdala also affect predatory aggression, suggesting to Moyer that the lateral hypothalamus functions in predation may be controlled by the amygdala. Moyer notes that hormonal manipulations do not seem to affect predatory aggression greatly.

Intermale aggression, similar to Lorenz' rival fight, is elicited by a strange male of the same species. The attack-inhibiting appeasement gestures that play such a major role in Lorenz' theory are thought by Moyer to be unique to intermale aggression.

The male sex hormone testosterone is particularly important in intermale aggression: testosterone increases aggressiveness in immature and castrated male mice and rats which normally show little aggression. Testosterone has little effect on aggression in adult female rats. The neural basis of intermale aggression is unclear, but there is evidence that early experience with sex hormones may have widespread effects on neural mechanisms underlying all sex-related behavior, including aggressive behavior. We shall consider this topic in the next chapter.

Fear-induced aggression is similar to Lorenz' critical reaction. Moyer defines it as aggression that is preceded by attempts to escape. He points out that it is difficult to determine that fear-induced aggression rather than some other kind of aggression is being studied in many experiments because the animal is generally given no opportunity to escape.

Moyer reasons that any physiological manipulation that reduces fear should reduce fear-induced aggression. As it turns out, a number of such manipulations affect both fear and aggression, and it is difficult to determine whether the changes in aggression are due to the manipulation of circuits directly responsible for aggression or are secondary to changes in fear. Thus lesions in the amygdala and temporal lobes have been found to reduce both fear and aggression, while stimulation of these regions tends to increase both fear and aggression. Lesions and stimulation in the septal area tend to have the reverse result, with stimulation decreasing and lesions increasing fear and agression (see Chapter 3). More research is needed to determine whether the neural mechanisms underlying fear-induced aggression can be differentiated from those underlying other types of aggression. The effects of hormones on fear-induced aggression are not well understood.

Territorial and *maternal aggression* are characterized by the environment in which the aggression occurs. Moyer notes that very little is known about the physiological bases of these kinds of aggression, although there is evidence that both neural and hormonal mechanisms may be involved.

Irritable aggression involves attack without attempts to escape the object being attacked. It can range from extreme rage to half-hearted displays of annoyance. Moyer suggests that irritable aggression is increased by pain, deprivation, frustration, and indeed perhaps any stress. It may be analagous to Feshbach's hostile aggression.

Although Moyer cites evidence that the structures underlying fear-induced and irritable aggression may be different to some extent, the general finding that the amygdala, temporal lobes, and septal area are involved in fear-induced aggression may be applied to irritable aggression as well. In addition, stimulation and lesions in the vicinity of the VM (ventromedial) nucleus of the hypothalamus and stimulation of the central grey of the midbrain appear to elicit irritable aggression (see Chapter 3, Figure 3.2).

Irritable aggression is also influenced by hormonal factors. Irritability is a common symptom of disturbances of endocrine balance, such as hypofunction or hyperfunction of the adrenal cortex or thyroid gland. Increased irritability is often found during the premenstrual period when large hormonal changes are taking place (Dalton, 1964). Moyer cites a study of female prisoners indicating that 62% of crimes of violence were committed in the premenstrual week (Morton, Addition, Addison, Hunt, and Sullivan, 1953).

Moyer cites considerable evidence suggesting that male sex hormones increase irritable aggression. The androgen dehydroisoandrosterone (diandrone) has been found to increase self-confidence and aggressiveness in adolescents with feelings of inferiority and to lead to irritability and rage in aggressive patients (Sands and Chamberlain, 1952; Sands, 1954). Conversely, castration reduces aggressiveness in animals, and there is clinical evidence that castration reduces antisocial behavior in sex criminals (cf. Hawke, 1950; LeMaire 1956). Also, the effects of androgens may be inhibited or masked by estrogens (Suchowsky, 1969). For example, the estrogen stilboestrol has been found to reduce aggression as well as hypersexual behavior in men (Dunn, 1941; Sands, 1954).

Instrumental aggression, in contrast to the other kinds of aggression, does not have a definable physiological basis. If aggressive behavior is reinforced, an animal (or human) will tend to repeat that behavior when in a similar situation, regardless of the state of the neural and hormonal systems that may underlie other kinds of aggression. Moyer's conception is similar to Fesbach's definition of instrumental aggression as being directed toward the achievement of nonaggressive goals. As an example of instrumental aggression, Moyer suggests a member of Murder Incorporated who kills without anger or passion but simply for pay.

Moyer also proposes an eighth kind of aggression, *sex-related aggression,* in which the target of aggression is the same stimulus that produces sexual responses. He feels that such aggression may well be in a category separate from the others, but he notes that almost nothing is known about it.

We noted above that the different theories of aggression that we have been considering may each cover a restricted part of the whole range of phenomena that are labeled "aggression." Each theory may be valid when applied to that restricted range of phenomena, but invalid if generalized too far. Moyer's typology provides a framework by which we can see the relationships and differences among this patchwork of theories. Bandura and Walters' social learning theory of aggression, and the great volume of research and theory that have stemmed from it, seems to deal mainly with instrumental aggression. Their concern with the imitation of social models and the social reinforcement of aggressive behavior seems to be best suited to the analysis of how an individual comes to see aggressive behavior as an appropriate and rewarded kind of behavior in the pursuit of other goals. Their theory is not so useful when we inquire about aggression as an end in itself, or the effects of stress and emotion on aggression, or the physiological and phylogenetic bases of aggression.

The frustration-aggression hypothesis, with its emphasis upon frustration as an important determinant of aggression and its support of the notion of behavioral catharsis, may be a theory of a kind of irritable aggression. We have seen above that some studies have found support for behavioral catharsis: engaging in aggressive behavior sometimes reduces subsequent aggression. Other studies do not support this finding, and some find the opposite result. It may be that with irritable aggression, something akin to behavioral catharsis may occur. Irritable aggression involves a goal to injure, and when the aggressor perceives that the target has been injured sufficiently there may be less instigation to further irritable aggression. It is important to note that this reduction in the instigation to aggression would apply only to irritable aggression. If the aggressive response is successful in the pursuit of goals other than those of injuring the target, social learning theory would suggest that aggression would be rewarded as an instrumental response in that situation and the instigation to instrumental aggression would be increased. Thus engaging in aggressive behavior may simultaneously decrease the instigation to irritable aggression and increase the instigation to instrumental aggression.

Konrad Lorenz' theory, with its emphasis on rival fights, appeasement gestures, and built-in inhibitions of aggression, may be primarily a theory of intermale aggression. Other ethologists and anthropologists who argue that man is aggressive because he evolved from a predatory hunting ape may be basing their thinking on predatory aggression. Each of these theories may be useful in organizing observations and making predictions when it is applied to a restricted range of phenomena, but none of the theories can alone account for the whole diverse range of aggression. Also, none of the theories we have examined thus far has touched on another kind of basis of aggressive behavior which, for human beings, may be the most important of all: social bases of aggression. We shall consider the social bases of aggression—how aggressive acts may be caused by social and situational pressures—in Chapter 11.

Summary

We have considered the philosophical problem posed by human aggression as one that is often phrased in terms of good versus evil. There is a common tendency to regard human nature as destructive and aggressive versus constructive and sociable. However, as we shall see, human sociability—our tendency to form groups, attach ourselves to common symbols, obey the expectations of authority figures, and so on—may underlie much destruction and violence. We shall consider such socially based aggression below.

In this chapter, we explored the idea that human destructiveness is an innate carryover of our animal heritage, considering in particular Lorenz' theory of aggression and the idea that humans lack natural inhibitions of aggression. We also considered the criticisms of Lorenz' theory, centering on the ideas that learning is more important than innate factors in human behavior and that the catharsis notions advanced by Lorenz and others are at least greatly oversimplifed and probably incorrect.

These issues were considered further in the discussion of environmental theories of aggression, including the frustration-aggression hypothesis and Bandura and Walters' social learning theory of aggression. We saw that Bandura and Walters' theory predicts that the vicarious viewing of violence may well increase aggressive tendencies, a prediction directly opposed to the vicarious catharsis notion of Lorenz and others. Many studies, particularly those commissioned by the Surgeon General's office, have tended to support the social learning point of view: watching media violence seems to increase aggressive tendencies, at least among persons who by temperament, training, or mood of the moment are ready to be aggressive.

Impressive though the evidence supporting the social learning analysis of aggression is, there are some instances of aggressive behavior which seem to be based at least in part upon other mechanisms, such as the aggression evoked by brain stimulation. It may well be that there are different kinds of aggressive behavior that have nothing in common with one another outside a superficial outward similarity. Each theory may cover a specific kind of aggression adequately, but to appreciate the wide range of factors that may underlie behavior labeled as aggressive, a "patchwork quilt" of different theoretical approaches is required. This is true in the analysis of many phenomena other than aggression, both inside and outside the realm of human motivation and emotion. We considered several typologies of aggression, including those of Lorenz, Feshbach, and Moyer, which suggest the nature and scope of this patchwork quilt. We also suggested an additional determinant of aggressive behavior in humans—social and situational factors.

In terms of the schema introduced in Chapter 1, this chapter has been most concerned with the innate mechanisms involved in the response to affective stimuli and with the process by which social learning experiences can alter the response to such stimuli. However, all of the mechanisms proposed in the schema can be seen to be operating in aggression: for example, Bandura and Walters argue that frustration is a general reaction that may increase any strong response tendency. This could involve a state of frustration-induced physiological arousal which is cognitively labeled in accordance with the persons previous experiences and expectations in that situation.

IVATE BOOTH
EEP
SHOW 25¢
ADULTS ONLY
GEORGEOUS GIRLS
ADULT
TOPLESS GO GO
SEX SYMB
BEST PORNO MOVIES"

CHAPTER SIX

SEX

There has been considerably less psychological research directed toward the study of sex than the study of aggression. This is particularly true of the study of human sexual behavior. As a result, there are real gaps in our understanding of human sexual behavior, and because of sensitivity about sexual matters those gaps are not easily filled. Despite this, there has been much theorizing about sex, and some have even suggested that sex is a basic drive from which all other motives are derived.

Developments in the Study of Sex

THE NINETEENTH CENTURY

It is difficult today to appreciate the extent that sexuality was distrusted and feared in Western cultures during the nineteenth century. Masturbation was widely thought to cause disease, insanity, and even death. It was improper to name many parts of the body—one could not even speak of the legs of tables and chairs. Adults were warned not to be suggestively demonstrative toward children—one writer stated that "the coarse hugging, kissing, etc. which the children are sure to receive in great abundance from ignorant and low-minded domestics are certain to develop a blind precocious sexualism of feeling and action, which tends directly to all the evils I have mentioned, on the maturity of those offspring, and sometimes in sudden disease and death to little ones." (Hough, 1849; quoted in Sunley, 1955).

It was against this background that the objective study of sex began. Sexual behavior was seen to be based upon inherited sexual instincts present in both animals and humans. Darwin's theory, with its emphasis on evolution through the reproduction of the fittest, suggested to some that the sexual instinct was the driving force in evolution. Darwin also increased interest in human instincts and in the common features of animal and human behavior. At about the same time, physicians such as R. von Krafft-Ebing and Havelock Ellis began to study systematically human sexual phenomena and write on sexuality in children and sexual "perversions."

FREUD'S THEORY

Sigmund Freud was a transitional figure, refining the Darwinian ideas, the early conceptualizations of human sexuality, and other intellectual influences of the day into a comprehensive theory of human motivation and behavior (cf. Cofer and Appley, 1964; Jones, 1953–1957). We shall first consider Freud's theory of instinct or drive, which was modeled after the contemporary conception of the sexual instinct (Burnham, 1972). We shall then outline Freud's theory of psychosexual development.

Freud's Theory of Instinct*   Freud came to recognize two general-al kinds of instincts, the *death instincts* and *life instincts.* The latter included instincts of self-preservation, such as those of hunger and thirst, and sexual instincts.

In *Instincts and Their Vicissitudes* (1915), Freud posited four distinguishing characteristics of instincts: a source, an impetus, an aim, and an object. The *source* of an instinct is an internal bodily event. As noted in the consideration of interoceptive classical conditioning in Chapter 4, such events differ from external stimuli in that they are recurring and inescapable. The *impetus* of an instinct is its force or pressure and thus the demand it makes on the energy of the individual. The *aim* of an instinct is to remove this internal stimulation. Freud assumed that instincts are basically conservative, seeking to reduce tension to its lowest level: "An apparatus which would even, if this were feasible, maintain itself in an altogether unstimulated condition" (Freud, 1915). The *object* of the instinct is anything that satisfies the aim of the instinct. Although the instinct itself is inherited and relatively inflexible, the object that satisfies the aim of the instinct may change (or undergo *displacement*) any number of times.

The aim of an instinct must usually be accomplished indirectly. In the presence of hunger, for example, the aim is to reduce the internal stimulation associated with hunger pangs. The newborn infant has no way to deal with these internal stimuli—Freud suggests that it can only have hallucinations about relieving the hunger pangs which do not help at all. However, its distress arouses caretakers who feed the child and reduce its discomfort. Such experiences, Freud suggests, enable the infant to associate instinctual gratification with objects in reality—the caretaker, the breast, the refrigerator—which serve indirectly to satisfy the aims of the instinct.

The original objects of some instincts, and particularly the sexual instincts, can never be acceptably used to satisfy the aims of the instinct. In such cases the individual must find other objects that can appropriately reduce the tension. For example, the mother is the original object of the sexual instinct, according to Freud. During the normal course of psychosexual development, displacement to socially approved objects oc-

---

* *It should be noted that Freud used the German word* Trieb, *or moving force, which was translated into English as instinct. He used another word,* Instinkt, *when speaking of animal behavior. Freud's intention would have been more accurately conveyed had the term "drive" been used in the original translation (Cofer and Appley, 1964, p. 598).*

curs. The individual acquires a masculine or feminine sex role and eventually takes a person of the opposite sex to both satisfy the sexual instincts and the social goal of reproduction.

The Course of Psychosexual Development   The sources of the sexual instincts are the *erogenous zones* of the body, including the mouth, anus, and genitals. All of these structures are lined with mucous membranes and are abundantly supplied with sensory receptors and blood vessels. With stimulation, vasocongestion occurs and they become engorged with blood and produce intense sensations. Freud suggested that sensations from the erogenous zones have a common "itching" quality and that stimulation creates a need for further stimulation. Such stimulation may be provided by thumb-sucking, eating, rubbing the mouth or anus, retaining and passing a stool, masturbation of the genitals, and so forth.

According to Freud, sexual instincts based on the different erogenous zones appear successively in the life of the young child. At five or six, this process ceases and the basic personality of the child has then been formed. If normal development has occurred, these infantile forms of the sexual instincts become organized at puberty to serve the mature reproductive function.

1.   ORAL STAGE.   The first stage in the development of mature sexuality is the oral stage, in which the tissues of the mouth and lips are the major source of pleasurable stimulation. The infant finds that the tactile stimulation associated with sucking, chewing, and biting are both related to the satisfaction of hunger and pleasurable in themselves. He also associates objects—at first the breast, and later food, the mother, and other feeding-related stimuli—with this pleasurable and satisfying stimulation. Freud felt that either too much satisfaction or too little satisfaction of the infant's oral eroticism could lead to the *fixation* on objects appropriate to the oral stage. Too much oral satisfaction may result in an oral-passive adult who is overly dependent on others, overwhelmed by authority, and preoccupied with food. Too little satisfaction leads to an oral-aggressive, sarcastic, and pessimistic personality.

2.   ANAL STAGE.   During the second year, the child's increasing control over excretory functions gives him his first experience with mastering an instinctive impulse. At this time, anal

stimulation becomes his most important source of sensual pleasure. The object that the child produces—feces—becomes extremely important to him, as does his parents' attitude toward this creation. According to Freud, threat and frustration during toilet training can lead to anal fixation. The child may learn to hold back the feces. Through displacement, this may develop an anal-retentive character, distinguished by stubborness, stinginess, and excessive cleanliness. Alternatively, the frustrated child may learn to expel the feces at inopportune moments, perhaps developing the anal-expulsive traits of destructiveness, disorderliness, and cruelty.

3.   PHALLIC STAGE.   In the third or fourth year, genital stimulation and masturbation gradually come to dominate the child's sensual life. According to Freud, this immature masturbation is accompanied by fantasies reflecting the child's conception of his genital organs and his relationship with his parents. At the beginning of the phallic stage, both boys and girls have developed strong sexual feelings toward the mother. This early attachment is based upon the erotic oral and anal stimulation provided by the mother In the natural course of nursing, bathing, toileting, and so forth. When the phallic period begins, the child wishes for similar stimulation of the genitals.

In the phallic period, the course of psychosexual development of boys and girls diverges, largely because of the different appearance of the external genitalia. The boys begins to feel rivalry with the father for the mother's affections, and this turns to intense jealousy and hatred that conflicts with his love for the father. At the same time, he fears his powerful father. He notices that girls do not have penises and assumes that they have been castrated. This leads to fears that the father will realize the son's desire for the mother and cut off the boy's penis. This fear, or *castration anxiety,* along with the son's conflict between love and hatred for his father, create the emotional turmoil of the *Oedipus complex.* The normal way that this intense conflict is resolved is that the boy *identifies* with his father—he strives to become as much like his father as possible. This serves two functions for the child. It relieves him of his fear of castration, and it enables him to enjoy the mother vicariously through the father.

Girls also begin the phallic period with intense love for the moth-. er. However, when a girl notices that boys have penises and she does not, she experiences a disappointing blow to self-esteem and sense of inferiority for which she blames her mother. She turns to the father because he has the valued penis which she hopes to share. At the same time, the girl develops *penis envy:* She envies men and desires a penis for herself. Freud suggests that this wish is often displaced into the wish to have a baby, particularly a boy baby. To pursue this goal and to enjoy her father vicariously, the girl identifies with her mother. This *Electra complex* is the female equivalent of the male Oedipus complex. It does not involve as intense conflict and fear as the Oedipus complex, so that identification is not as complete.

This identification with the same-sex parent accomplishes two important functions in personality formation. One is the development of *sex-role identity.* In becoming like the same-sex parent, the child takes on the behavior patterns culturally ascribed for his sex. The other is the development of the *conscience,* which we shall consider in the chapter on moral development.

4. LATENCY PERIOD. At the end of the phallic stage, at about 5 or 6, the child enters a latency period in which sexual instincts are temporarily quiescent. At this point, Freud feels that the basic personality has been formed. The fears, conflicts, and desires that determined its formation are repressed and become unconscious. Thus the child remembers nothing about the intense feelings of the phallic period.

5. GENITAL STAGE. At puberty, the physical maturation of the sexual apparatus reawakens sexual desires. In this stage the young person must go beyond the selfish and infantile gratifications of those desires he had obtained by stimulating his own body. He must develop loving relationships with others if his needs are to be maturely satisfied, and this involves learning to satisfy the needs of others. Recent theorists, both inside and outside the psychoanalytic tradition, have emphasized the growth of independence, self-reliance and self-esteem during this period of psychosexual development. Notably, Erikson has

pointed out that the adolescent must find an *identity* or role in life, based upon his experiences of family relationships, his perception of himself in the eyes of others, and the social roles available to him (Munroe, 1955).

The Role of Repression   If the child's psychosexual development goes wrong, fixations, conflicts, and fears interfere with the adult's ability to function maturely. Freud felt that infantile desires and conflicts are *repressed* or become unconscious because they would cause unbearable anxiety and guilt were they conscious. However, these repressed wishes continue to strive toward consciousness and fulfillment. They appear in consciousness in disguised forms: in dreams, slips of the tongue, unreasonable fears and desires, infantile object choices, and, if sufficiently intense, in severe neurotic symptoms. Thus a young man with repressed hatred of his father might become unreasonably hostile to authority, or a woman might become unable to experience sexual satisfaction because of penis envy.

All of these feelings continue to affect the person only because they are repressed and unconscious. If the adult could bring them into consciousness, he could deal with them in mature rather than childish ways and they would disappear. The goal of psychoanalysis is to bring these repressed feelings into consciousness, to "make the unconscious concious." This is not easily done because of the anxiety and guilt aroused by the repressed material. To circumvent these defenses, Freud used the technique of free association, in which the patient relaxes and tries to relate everything that comes to mind as he thinks about his present life, dreams, childhood, and so forth. The psychoanalyst, with his knowledge of the symbolic language of the unconscious, attempts to interpret these associations and encourage the patient to relive, gain insight into, and eventually overcome his repressed conflicts in the close theraputic relationship.

The Impact of Freudian Theory   Many have pointed out that there are significant weaknesses and contradictions in Freud's theory and have expressed doubt about the validity of its fundamental assumptions. For example, many feel that the Oedipus-Electra complex was at most an attribute of the Viennese Victorian era when Freud worked rather than a universal human experience. This is not the place for a detailed critique of Freudian theory, however (see Hall and Lindzey, 1970, for a critique of the theory). Freud's ideas have been outlined because they represented a fundamentally different approach to the phenomenon of human sexuality and had a profound influence on later work. First, they made the scientific study of sex possible, and indeed necessary, if one is to appreciate the full range of human behavior. Second, Freudian theory prompted a new view on the morality of sexual expression which is still very much in vogue. The logic of the Freudian position suggested that restraints and inhibitions on sexual behavior can be unhealthy to the individual. Some have argued that, if repression is ultimately caused by fears and anxieties about the expression of sexuality, it can and should be eliminated by eliminating such restraints and all other vestiges of the Victorian prudishness of the nineteenth century. Both of these influences are seen in the work of Alfred C. Kinsey and his associates.

THE KINSEY STUDIES

The first large-scale study of human sexual behavior was carried out by Alfred C. Kinsey and his associates beginning in 1938. Their first major report, *Sexual Behavior in the Human Male,* was published by Kinsey, Pomeroy, and Martin in 1948 and the second, *Sexual Behavior in the Human Female,* by Kinsey, Pomeroy, Martin, and Gebhard in 1953. Their pioneering work is still being carried out by the Institute for Sex Research, founded by Kinsey at Indiana University (cf. Pomeroy, 1972).

The data in the "Kinsey Reports" were gathered from interviews of 5300 men and 5940 women. The subjects were of widely varying socio-economic levels. All were volunteers and most were recruited through social groups (Parent-Teacher Associations, churches, work groups, etc.) and personal contacts. Subjects were given searching two-hour interviews by highly experienced interviewers. Detailed information was obtained concerning the subject's sex education, sexual maturation, history of masturbation, heterosexual, homosexual, and animal encounters, marital history, and nocturnal sex dreams. The interviewers were given considerable latitude in the ordering and wording of the questions, enabling them to fit the interview to the particular subject. This practice was criticized by some who pointed out that such practices could allow the interviewers to unintentionally bias the data. However, Kinsey et al. argued persuasively that flexibility was necessary in obtaining the trust and confidence of the subject.

The first report on male sexual behavior attracted widespread public attention and sparked much controversy. The data indicated a high incidence of practices widely regarded as indecent and unnatural, including extramarital intercourse, masturbation, and homosexual activity. Also, some of the discussion in the reports seems to imply a permissive attitude toward such activities. Kinsey et al. (1948) argued that the condemnation of such practices often reflects prejudiced moral judgments and that sexual suppression may often have more psychologically undesirable effects than engaging in these "unnatural" acts. Critics charged that these opinions were themselves unwarranted moral judgments that were not supported by the data. Many worried that they would unduly encourage the "youth who is in search of authoritative justification for the unrestrained satisfaction of his sexual urges" (Terman, 1948, p. 372).

Other criticisms of the reports centered on the sampling method used by Kinsey and his colleagues, and these were quite serious. Some of the statements in the reports (such as their titles) implied that their results could be widely generalized. However, as many pointed out, Kinsey's sample did not come close to representing the population of the United States or any other known population. For example, approximately 64% of the males and 75% of the females in the sample attended college, versus less than 15% of the U.S. population of that time (Hobbs and Lambert, 1948; Hyman and Barmack, 1954). Also, 78% of the sample males over 20 were single, while only 30% of this group was single in the general population. As Hobbs and Lambert (1948) point out, these and other problems of sampling and definition could have seriously inflated the estimates of male homosexuality made in the 1948 report.

Kinsey et al. countered that other methods of sampling have their own disadvantages, particularly in the sensitive area of sex research. A statistically correct probability sample would undoubtedly choose a large number of persons who would refuse to participate in the interview or answer all questions truthfully. Kinsey et al. felt confident that their own subjects were cooperative and reasonably truthful, and they were able to cite some evidence for this from special checks on accuracy. However, their method of sampling does invite the possibility of sampling errors of unknown magnitude. Also, it is quite possible that there are systematic differences in sexual behavior between people who would agree to cooperate in a study involving sex and people who would refuse to cooperate. This is a common problem in sex research, and we shall encounter it again.

Whatever their deficiencies, the Kinsey et al. reports were clearly superior to previous studies of sex (cf. Cochran, Mosteller, and Tukey, 1953, for a close examination of the strengths and weaknesses of the 1948 report; and Lieberman, 1971, for a compilation of the reviews of the Kinsey reports). They pioneered a new tradition of objective study of sexual phenomena and made later methodological advances possible.

THE MASTERS AND JOHNSON STUDIES

W. H. Masters and Virginia E. Johnson carried the objective tradition a step further by engaging in the systematic study of the act of human sexual intercourse and orgasm. As they noted, a "massive state of ignorance" has always existed about human sexual physiology, and they began their studies in 1954 to increase basic knowledge of the anatomy and physiology of the human sexual response. In 1959 the project was coordinated with a clinical program dealing with sexual inadequacy. Masters and Johnson and their colleagues at the Washington University School of Medicine in St. Louis spent years developing and using new techniques of observing and recording the responses of human beings to various kinds of genital stimulation. The results were presented in book form in 1966 in *Human Sexual Response* and in 1968 in *Human Sexual Inadequacy.*

The first subjects of the Masters and Johnson studies were 118 female and 27 male prostitutes, who aided in the design of laboratory techniques used in later studies. The later, major sample was recruited largely from the academic community associated with the medical school. As of July 1965 it consisted of 312 men ranging in age from 21 to 89, and 382 women from 18 to 78. The sample included 276 married couples (Masters and Johnson, 1965).

Prospective subjects were given extensive interviews and physical examinations, and those selected for participation were given a thorough orientation program so that they felt secure and confident about the research facilities and instruments. They were then studied during a number of complete and incomplete orgasmic cycles. Genital stimulation was applied by automanipulation, artifical coition, or natural coition. Gross behavior was observed and sometimes filmed, subjects were interviewed before, during, and after stimulation, and many physiological measures

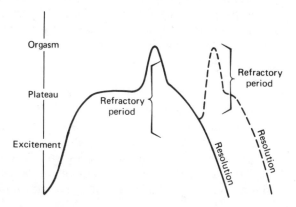

FIGURE 6.1   The male sexual response cycle. From W. H. Masters and V. E. Johnson, "The sexual response cycles of the human male and female: Comparative anatomy and physiology." In B. Lieberman (Ed.) *Human Sexual Behavior.* New York: Wiley, 1971. Copyright © 1971 by John Wiley and Sons, Inc. Reprinted by permission of the publisher.

were taken. At least 7500 female cycles and 2500 of the simpler male cycles were studied this way.

The Masters and Johnson studies established many basic facts and exposed many misconceptions about human sexual functioning. For example, they greatly clarified the nature of the female orgasm. Masters and Johnson noted that as recently as 1957, a psychosomatic gynecology textbook stated that women have no interest in or capacity for orgasmic response (Hall, 1969). Their studies indicated that, on the contrary, women have great capacity for orgasm which, unlike the male orgasm, may be repetitive and vary greatly in intensity and duration. They also overturned Freud's notion that an orgasm arising from clitoral stimulation is different from one arising from vaginal stimulation. Their studies showed that the female orgasm is physiologically identical whether it arises through clitoral stimulation, vaginal stimulation, fantasy, or any other kind of effective stimulation.

The Nature of Sexual Arousal

THE SEXUAL RESPONSE CYCLE

Masters and Johnson (1965) distinguish four successive phases in the human sexual response cycle. These phases are diagrammed for males in Figure 6.1 and for females in Figure 6.2. They found essential parallels

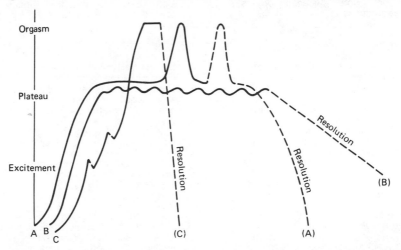

FIGURE 6.2   The female sexual response cylce. From W. H. Masters and V. E. Johnson, *Op. Cit.* Copyright © 1971 by John Wiley and Sons, Inc. Reprinted by permission of the publisher.

between the bodily reactions of males and females during these phases. These parallels are illustrated in Table 6.1.

TABLE 6.1   SEXUAL RESPONSE CYCLE—PELVIC VISCERA.

MALE	FEMALE
EXCITEMENT PHASE	
Penile erection (3 to 8 seconds)	Vaginal lubrication (5 to 15 seconds)
↑↓ as phase is prolonged	↑↓ as phase is prolonged
Thickening, flattening, and elevation of scrotal integument	Thickening of vaginal walls, flattening and elevation of major labia
↑↓ as phase is prolonged	↑↓ as phase is prolonged
Moderate testicular elevation and size increase	Expansion of inner $2/3$ vaginal barrel and elevation of cervix and corpus
↑↓ as phase is prolonged	↑↓ as phase is prolonged
PLATEAU PHASE	
Increase in penile coronal circumference and testicular tumescence ($1/2$ to $1 \times$ enlarged)	Orgasmic platform in outer $1/3$ of vagina
Full testicular elevation and rotation (30 to 35 degrees)	Full inner $2/3$ vaginal expansion, uterine, and cervical elevation
Purple cast to corona of penis (inconsistent, even if orgasm is to ensue)	"Sex-skin" discoloration of minor labia (constant, if orgasm is to ensue)
Mucoid-like emission (Cowper's gland)	Mucoid-like emission (Bartholin's gland)
ORGASMIC PHASE	
Ejaculation	Pelvic Response

1.   Contraction of accessory organs of reproduction
   a.   Vas deferens
   b.   Seminal vesicles
   c.   Ejaculatory duct
   d.   Prostate
	1. Contractions of uterus from fundus toward lower uterine segment

2. Relaxation of external bladder sphincter	2. Minimal relaxation of external cervical os (nullipara)
3. Contractions of penile urethra $8/10$ second for 2 to 3 contractions (slowing thereafter for 2 to 4 more contractions)	3. Contraction of orgasmic platform $8/10$ second for 4 to 8 contractions (slowing thereafter for 2 to 4 more contractions)
4. External rectal sphincter contractions (2 to 4 contractions at $8/10$-second intervals)	4. External rectal sphincter contractions (2 to 4 contractions at $8/10$-second intervals) External urethral sphincter contractions [2 to 3 contractions at irregular intervals (10 to 15%)]
RESOLUTION PHASE	
1. Refractory period with rapid loss of pelvic vasocongestion	1. Ready return to orgasm with retarded loss of pelvic vasocongestion
2. Loss of penile erection in primary (rapid) and secondary (slow) stages	2. Loss of "sex-skin" color and orgasmic platform in primary (rapid) stage Remainder of pelvic vasocongestion as secondary (slow) stage

TABLE 6.1 (CONTINUED)   SEXUAL RESPONSE CYCLE—GENERAL BODY REACTIONS.

MALE	FEMALE
EXCITEMENT PHASE	
Nipple erection (30%)	Nipple erection
	Sex-tension flush (25%)
PLATEAU PHASE	
Sex-tension flush (25%)	Sex-tension flush (75%)
Carpopedal spasm	Carpopedal spasm
Generalized skeletal muscle tension	Generalized skeletal muscle tension
Hyperventilation	Hyperventilation
Tachycardia (100 to 160/min)	Tachycardia (100 to 160/min)
ORGASMIC PHASE	
Specific skeletal muscle contractions	Specific skeletal muscle contractions
Hyperventilation	Hyperventilation
Tachycardia (100 to 180/min)	Tachycardia (110 to 180/min)
RESOLUTION PHASE	
Sweating reaction (30 to 40%)	Sweating reaction (30 to 40%)
Hyperventilation	Hyperventilation
Tachycardia (150 to 180/min)	Tachycardia (150 to 180/min)

From Tables 1 and 2 in Masters and Johnson, *Op. Cit.* Copyright © 1971 by John Wiley and Sons, Inc. Reprinted by permission of the publisher.

Excitement Phase   The excitement phase develops quickly or slowly in response to sexual stimulation. The stimulation may be of virtually any nature and modality, and it could include erotic tactual, auditory, olfactory, or visual stimuli, or stimuli present only in fantasy. Ethologists have noted among many species of animals that certain releasing stimuli are particularly effective in inducing sexual excitement within that species. For example, the bright plumage of many birds, such as the peacock, functions to attract sexual partners. Some ethologists suggest that there are particularly effective sexual releasing stimuli among humans as well. Eibl-Eibesfeldt (1970) notes that advertisements often make use of sexual releasers because of their attention-getting qualities. Others might argue that these releasing stimuli might be effective sexual stimuli purely because of learning.

Among the first bodily reactions of the excitement phase are penile erection in the male and vaginal lubrication in the female. Nipple erection occurs in the female and occasionally in the male breast. The female breast begins to enlarge because of *vasocongestion:* The blood supply is increased and less blood is removed through the veins, and the tissue therefore becomes engorged with blood. Similar vasocongestion thickens the male scrotal integument and the female vaginal wall. As the excitement phase progresses, further vasocongestion enlarges and elevates the testes in the male and expands and extends the vaginal barrel and elevates the cervix and corpus in the female.

Plateau Phase   If effective sexual stimulation is continued, the individual enters the plateau phase of the response cycle. There is lessened receptivity to extraneous stimuli, and sexual tension is intense—the body undergoes considerable physiological strain. Both superficial and deep vasocongestion increase. Masters and Johnson regard this vasocongestion as the primary physiological response of both male and female humans to sexual stimulation.

The bodily reactions of the plateau phase outside the pelvic region include the continued vasocongestive increase in the size of the female breasts and tumescence of the pigmented areolae surrounding the nipples. A vasocongestive sex-tension flush often appears on the skin of females and less often on males. This measles-like rash appears first on the midline of the chest and may spread upward to the face, neck, and forehead and in females downward to the abdomen, thighs, and lower back. The appearance and extent of the flush seem to be associated with very high levels of sexual tension. There are also numerous voluntary and involuntary skeletal muscle reactions and generalized muscle tension during the plateau phase, and heart rate, respiration rate, and systolic blood pressure are markedly increased.

In the pelvic region, the plateau phase is associated with further deep vasocongestion. In the male, the coronal circumference of the penis is increased and the testes are further enlarged, elevated, and rotated. In women, vasocongestion produces an orgasmic platform in the outer third of the vagina, reducing its diameter by as much as 50%. The expansion of the inner 2/3 of the vagina and the cervical and uterine elevation are completed. If sexual tension is high, the coronal area of the penis may acquire a purple cast and, in women, a marked reddening occurs in the minor labia. This discoloration of the labia is inevitably followed by orgasm if stimulation is continued.

Orgasmic Phase   The male orgasmic experience involves contractions associated with ejaculation, the female experience involves the sensations of powerful contractions of the uterine musculature and the orgasmic platform (See Table 6.1). The subjective intensity of the orgasm is apparently related to the duration of these contractions. There is considerable variation in the duration and intensity of orgasmic reactions in women, both between different women and in the same woman on different occasions. There is apparently less variation in the male orgasmic reaction.

Resolution Phase   The male orgasm is followed by a refractory period in which erection is at least partially lost and sexual tension is lowered to the level of the excitement phase. The female maintains a high level of tension following orgasm and if stimulation continues she is usually capable of immediate and repeated return to orgasmic experience (Figure 6.2, pattern A). After orgasm, the resolution phase involves a more or less gradual dissapation of sexual tension. This dissipation generally proceeds more gradually in females. If stimulation is terminated before orgasm, an extended and perhaps frustrating resolution phase ensues (Figure 6.2, pattern B).

SEXUAL AROUSAL AND AROUSABILITY

The state of sexual tension described by Masters and Johnson involves the current level of sexual excitement. Whalen (1966) has distinguished this transient level of sexual excitation, which he calles *sexual arousal,* from *sexual arousability,* which he defines as the propensity for arousal, or the "rate at which an individual approaches maximal sexual arousal." Thus individuals differ in arousability if one is more easily aroused than another. Figure 6.3 illustrates the growth of arousal in three individuals with high, medium, and low arousability.

Extending Whalen's conceptualization slightly, one might say that arousability is determined both by the number of stimuli that produce sexual arousal and by the effectiveness of those stimuli (i.e. the amount

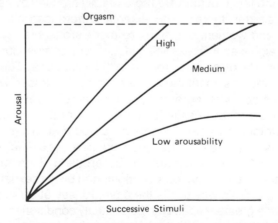

FIGURE 6.3   The growth of arousal in individuals of high, medium, and low arousability produced by a series of consecutive sexual stimuli. In two instances arousal reaches maximum and orgasm occurs. From R. E. Whalen, "Sexual motivation." *Psychological Review*, 1966, 72, 151–163. Copyright 1966 by the American Psychological Association. Reprinted by permission.

of increase in arousal that they produce) and also by the number and effectiveness of stimuli that inhibit sexual arousal. A highly arousable individual may not become aroused in a particular situation because arousing stimuli are absent and/or inhibiting stimuli are present. However, this is less likely to happen with a highly arousable individual than it is with an individual of low arousability. Whalen suggests that arousability is determined in part by physiological factors such as hormonal level, and in part by experience in associating sexual arousal with a variety of stimuli.

The concept of arousability allows us to inquire about the nature and causes of individual differences in the tendency to become sexually aroused. We have discussed the similarities and differences between sexual arousal in males and females above. Let us now discuss gender differences in arousability.

GENDER DIFFERENCES IN SEXUAL AROUSABILITY

The Kinsey Data   One of the striking results in the 1953 Kinsey et al. report was that females reported having fewer orgasms than males. The Kinsey researchers considered this to be a basic difference between the sexes, and they attempted to explain it. They argued that the anatomical basis and physiological accompaniments of orgasm are essentially the same for males and females and that these do not contribute to the sex difference in orgasm frequency. Instead, they concluded that the difference is due to the fact that men are more readily aroused by sexual stimuli. Using Whalen's terms, there are no essential differences in sexual arousal between men and women, but men are more arousable.

Kinsey et al. based this reasoning in part on a comparison of the male and female reports of sexual arousal in 33 situations. The interviewer asked the respondents about the arousal they experienced when observing the opposite sex, viewing erotic pictures, reading romantic literature, and so forth. In 29 of these situations, men reported experiencing higher arousal than women. The researchers assumed that this result reflected true differences in arousal, rather than possible sex differences in the perception of when it is acceptable to be aroused. They argued that it indicates that the male is more often conditioned by his sexual experience. In attempting to explain why this is the case, Kinsey et al. suggested only that males have a greater capacity to be sexually conditioned than women.

This explanation was criticized for being insufficient and farfetched (Hyman and Barmack, 1954). There are a number of other plausible explanations for why females may have lower arousabiity than males. For example, the sexual code in U.S. society is more restrictive for the female, perhaps causing more stimuli to be associated with sexual inhibition among women. Also, there may be sex differences in the physiological systems underlying arousability. Males could conceivably be physiologically more arousable than females even if the physiological capacity for sexual arousal and orgasm in females is equal to, or greater than, that of males.*

The Role of Masturbation   Two associates of the Institute for Sex Research, W. Simon and J. Gagnon, have advanced an interesting hypothesis about psychosexual development which is relevant to the question of sex differences in arousability (1969). They note that Kinsey et al. found that, by the age of 16, almost all males have experienced orgasm, brought about almost always by masturbation. In contrast, only 2/3 of the females report having masturbated, and those who do generally began at a later age and masturbated much less frequently. About ½ of the women who masturbated did so only after they had experienced orgasm in petting or coitus. More recent studies have found generally similar results (Arafat and Cotton, 1974).

Simon and Gagnon suggest that this difference in masturbation is initially due to a physiological difference in arousability and that differential experience with masturbation tends to perpetuate this difference. They argue that a "biologically-rooted incentive" to become sexually aroused exists more strongly in males than females, at least during adolescence. The increased hormonal levels in puberty seem to create a fairly intense drive in adolescent males that leads to a high propensity to masturbate even in the face of considerable guilt and anxiety. In contrast, women report few feelings of sexual deprivation in adolescence, suggesting that their drive to become aroused is not as intense (Kinsey et al., 1953).

Simon and Gagnon suggest that the long period of masturbation and related fantasy among adolescent males in U.S. society allows them to associate sexual arousal with a wide variety of stimuli. The masturbatory act "can be conceptualized as in activity in which the actor is, in effect, training himself to invest symbols with affect" (Simon and Gagnon, 1969, p. 16). As a consequence, these males develop the ability to respond sexually to a wide variety of visual, tactual, fantasy, etc., stimuli: they "eroticise a large part of the world." In contrast, the relative sexual inactivity of adolescent females may prevent them from learning many things about how to be aroused and responsive. It is noteworthy that coital interest in marriage peaks much later in females than in males, and that

---

*The greater arousability of men could possibly be due to the greater concentration of androgens in men. See below.

many women do not experience orgasm until they have had considerable coital experience. This may be because the female takes more time to become fully free from sexual inhibitions, but it could also be because the female must "learn how to be sexual" to some extent.

Simon and Gagnon suggest that, while adolescent males in U.S. culture are developing what in Whalen's terms would be strong sexual arousability, adolescent females are being trained in an area where males receive almost no training: the rhetoric of romantic love and the handling of intense interpersonal relationships. From their perspective, dating and courtship are activities in which males train, or attempt to train, females about sexuality while they themselves are obliged to come to terms with forming stable affect-laden relationships. Simon and Gagnon note with Erikson that the late adolescent's involvement in relationships involving sex is intimately associated with the process of identity experimentation, and it is an area where the adolescent is particularly unprotected and vulnerable. Success or failure in these experiments may have consequences that reach far beyond the sexual sphere, deeply affecting the developing self-concept and sense of competence. We shall return to this point below.

Physiological Determinants of Arousability

In considering the factors that influence the development of sexual arousability in animals and humans it is again convenient to distinguish the role of physiological factors and environmental or social factors, although it is often difficult to see this distinction in overt behavior. As with aggression, a given overt act may be a function of physiological factors, environmental factors, or a combination of the two.

HORMONAL MECHANISMS

As Whalen suggests, sex hormones affect the neural and muscular structures underlying sexual arousability. In addition, they play a role in the development and organization of these structures. We shall consider the latter effects after briefly outlining the basic hormonal and neural mechanisms underlying sexual behavior.

The gonads—the male testes and female ovaries—are relatively inactive in childhood. At puberty they are stimulated by gonadotropic hormones from the pituitary that cause them to increase the secretion of their own hormones. The androgen testosterone is secreted by the testes and estrogen and progesterone by the ovaries (see the Appendix). The secretion of these hormones declines gradually after adolescence in males and is reduced in females at menopause. The pituitary also stimulates the production of cortical sex hormones from the adrenal cortex.

The sexual behavior of lower mammals is closely controlled by these hormones, particularly in females. The sexual receptivity of many female mammals is closely associated with the estrus cycle, with greatest receptivity occurring near the time of ovulation when the potential for fertilization is greatest. The estrus cycle is in turn controlled by the ovarian hormones. Ovariectomy abolishes the estrus cycle and sexual receptivity among many species, including rodents, carnivores, and ungulates. They can be reinstated if ovarian hormones are administered artificially. In monkeys and apes, the effects of ovariectomy are less marked, and spayed females may occassionally be receptive. Among humans, the effects of both ovariectomy and menopause are highly variable, with many women reporting no loss in sexual desire (Beach, 1947; 1969).

The latter results suggest that arousability in women is not closely associated with levels of ovarian hormones. There is evidence that it may instead be related to levels of androgens from the adrenal cortex (cf. Money and Ehrhardt, 1972). Schon and Sutherland (1963) report on the removal of the pituitary gland in women with advanced cancer. In such cases hormones essential to life are replaced, but the hormones which activate the adrenal androgens and ovarian hormones are not. Such women show a marked decrease in sexual desire and behavior which the authors attribute to the lack of adrenal androgens. Similarly, women with adrenalectomy for cancer show declines in sexual desire and responsiveness (Waxenburg, Drellich, and Sutherland, 1959). Conversely, women treated with androgens often show an increase in sexual desire and responsiveness, even though they may be seriously ill (Foss, 1951; Money, 1961; Salmon and Geist, 1943). Recent studies with female rhesus monkeys show results consistent with this clinical evidence. Treatment with the pituitary-adrenal inhibitor dexamethasone and adrenalectomy were found to suppress sexual receptivity in female monkeys, and this effect could be reversed by the administration of androgens (Everitt and Herbert, 1969; 1970; 1971).

Increases and decreases in androgens also result in increases and decreases in male sexual behavior (cf. Hart, 1974). Copulation is eliminated in male rats following castration, although the decline is more gradual than the elimination of receptivity in female rats following ovariectomy. The decline is slowest in mature and sexually experienced male rats. Experience alters the effects of castration among males of other species, including dogs (Beach, 1969) and cats (Rosenblatt, 1965). Rosenblatt found that testosterone injections reinstated sexual behavior in castrated male cats only if they were sexually experienced before castration. Among apes, some males seem to be able to retain potency after castration, although they are not capable of orgasm or ejaculation. The effects of castration among men show great individual differences, but in most cases there is a gradual loss of sexual capacity. Bremer (1959), in a study of 157 males legally castrated in Norway, found that asexualization occurred shortly after castration in 74 cases and within a year for 29 others. The remaining 54 showed reduced sexual drive and activity. Androgen therapy of castrated human males generally restores normal sexual responsiveness and ability (Beach, 1947; 1969; Money, 1961).

From all of these results, Whalen (1966) suggests that the androgens may be associated with arousability in both men and women. The exact mode of this action of androgen is unclear. It could act peripherally by increasing the sensitivity of the external genitalia, or it could act directly upon central neural centers responsible for sexual arousability.

NEURAL MECHANISMS

Many of the events of the sexual response cycle described earlier in the chapter are reflexes controlled at the level of the spinal cord. Spinal transection does not disrupt the estrus cycle or many coital responses of female dogs and cats (Beach, 1947; Cofer and Appley, 1964). Among males, erection and ejaculation can occur in spinal rats, rabbits, and dogs. Genital stimulation of men with spinal cord injury elicits erection, pelvic thrusts, and ejaculation. Similar erection and pelvic thrusting may be elicited from male infants, suggesting that it is an unlearned reflex behavior pattern (Kinsey et al., 1948).

We saw in Chapters 2 and 3 that areas of the hypothalamus and limbic system have been implicated in the control of sexual behavior. The anterior hypothalamus seems to be an important center in the neural control of sex, and the ventromedial nucleus is involved in hormonal control. Limbic structures are also involved, and MacLean (1970) has suggested that a circuit including the mammillothalamic tract has evolved in higher mammals along with the shift from olfactory to visual control of sexual behavior.

The destruction of higher brain centers is more disruptive of copulatory patterns in males than in females, at least among subprimates. Destruction of the neocortex does not abolish coital activity in female rats, rabbits, cats, or dogs, although their reactions may not be as well-timed or integrated as those of intact animals. In male rats, dogs, and cats, neocortical damage is highly disruptive. This may be because the neocortex is more important in male sexual behavior whereas females are more controlled by hormones. Alternatively, the difference may be due to the more active role played by the male in copulation. Neocortical destruction may simply make it more difficult for an animal to engage in any complex behavior, and this may disrupt male sexual behavior more than female (Beach, 1947; 1969).

HORMONAL EFFECTS ON NEURAL MECHANISMS

Small amounts of hormones are secreted by the gonads from before birth. These play a major role in determining whether the adult brain responds in a male or female manner (cf. Beach, 1965; Finger and Mook, 1971). Many experiments over the past decade have studied the effects of hormone administration and/or gonadectomy in early life. Figure 6.4 illustrates some of the findings of these studies.

If genetic female animals are exposed to testosterone at an appropriate age before or shortly after birth, they will fail to develop normal female patterns of sexual behavior in adulthood (Column C). This has been demonstrated with female rats, guinea pigs, dogs, and monkeys. Such masculinized female rats fail to show normal sexual behavior even when given estrogen or progesterone in adulthood (Column C). If they are given androgens in adulthood (Column B), they display male sexual behaviors (i.e. mounting) to a greater extent than females not masculinized in infancy (Column A).

Male rats normally show little reaction to the injection of female sex hormones (Column D). However, if they are castrated shortly before birth, they will tend to show female sexual responses (i.e. lordosis) when given female hormones (Column E) or if implanted with ovarian tissue (Column F).

These findings have been interpreted as indicating that neural substrates potentially exist for both masculine and feminine behavior patterns, at least in many mammalian species, and that the presence of testosterone during early development suppresses the female substrate. Testosterone in infancy also increases adult male sexual behavior, either by stimulating the development of masculine brain substrates, or by increasing the sensitivity of the external genitalia, or both (Finger and Mook, 1971; cf. Beach, Noble, and Orndorff, 1969; Hendricks, 1969). The critical period at which testosterone has these effects varies from species to species, but for many animals and probably for man it occurs before birth.

The way in which early testosterone exerts these effects is not yet well understood. It may act in part by determining the thresholds at which the brain responds to hormonal stimulation. Thus there is evidence that

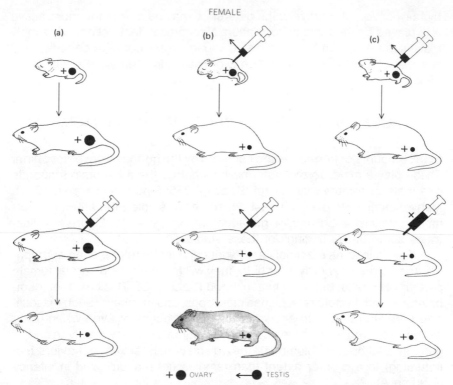

FEMALE

FIGURE 6.4 A summary of studies of hormonal effects. Masculinized female rats were produced by injection of testosterone at birth. In column (a) a normal female is injected with male hormones when mature; the animal exhibits some male sexual behavior. In column (b) the female is injected with male hormone in infancy; when reinjected at maturity it exhibits full male sexual behavior, and it fails to exhibit female sexual behavior even when injected with female hormone [Column (c)]. Feminized male rats were produced by injection

early testosterone depresses the adult response to progesterone and estrogen. It may also act by causing structural changes in the developing brain. Davidson and Levine (1972) suggest that such changes might conform to either a "one-anlage" model in which a single undifferentiated mechanism in the fetal brain develops in a feminine direction unless influenced by testosterone to develop in a masculine direction, or a "two-anlage" model in which testosterone causes the development of a male mechanism and simultaneous suppression of a female mechanism. In the latter case, the suppressed mechanism is retained into adulthood and may be activated by unusual circumstance, such as the introduction of hormones of the opposite sex or stimulation of the brain. Thus the animal is potentially

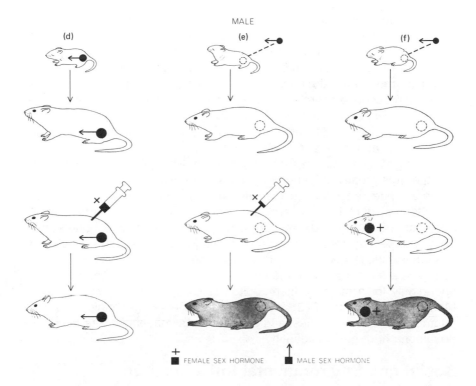

of estrogen and progesterone or by ovary implants only when the males had been castrated at birth and thereby deprived of testosterone during the critical first days of life. In column (d) a normal male is unaffected by the injection of female hormones at maturity. In column (e) a castrated male is similarly inject-ed; it then assumes the female's sexual posture. In column (f) the same behavior is produced by implanting an ovary. Adapted from S. Levine, "Sex dif-ferences in the brain." Copyright © 1966 by Scientific American, Inc. All rights reserved.

bisexual. Although they cite some studies supporting the two-anlage hypothesis, Davidson and Levine indicate that the evidence is not yet conclusive and the question is still unsettled.

Some imperfect analogies exist between these studies with animals and the condition of humans in certain cases of hermaphroditism. Herma-phroditism is produced in genetic females by the presence of excess androgen during fetal development. The excess androgen may come from the mother. More often, it comes from the adrenogenital syndrome—the adrenal cortex of the fetus produces excess androgen instead of corti-sone. In such cases, the external genitalia at birth may be indistinguishable from those of normal males, although ovaries are present internally. With early diagnosis and surgical and hormonal treatment, such an individual can grow up as a normal female (Money, 1968).

Male hermaphroditism occurs when a genetic male fails to produce or properly utilize androgen before birth. In the testicular feminizing syndrome (or more aptly, the androgen insensitivity syndrome), the individual does not respond to androgens. Such persons have no ovaries, abdominal testes, a short vagina but no uterus, and a female external appearance (Williams-Ashman and Reddi, 1971). They can often achieve satisfactory adjustments as females (Money, 1968).

The gender identity of such individuals may be quite confused or quite definite. It is greatly influenced by nonphysiological factors, such as the external appearance of the genitals, the physique, the attitudes of the parents during childhood, and the reactions of peers, particularly at adolescence. Gender identity is not necessarily related to genetic sex, hormonal sex, or gonadal sex. In Money's words "it is just as likely that a genetic female hermaphrodite with ovaries will have been ostensibly raised as a female and want to change to male as vice versa; and correspondingly for a male hermaphrodite" (1968, p. 85). In a recent book, Money and Ehrhardt (1972) have shown how neural mechanisms, prenatal and postnatal hormones, and environmental influences interact in the development of gender identity.

Social and Environmental Influences on Arousability

While human sexual arousability has a clear physiological basis, it is at the same time affected by powerful learning and social influences. The rigid hormonal control over arousability becomes progressively less rigid in higher animals, with humans being least affected by the presence or absence of hormones. At the same time, the substrates of sexual behavior in the brain have become susceptible to excitation and inhibition from a wider range of stimuli. In humans, these substrates can "be activated by stimuli possessing no biologic sexual significance and their excitability may be so depressed by extraneous factors that they sometimes fail to respond in biologically adequate situations" (Beach, 1947, p. 310).

SOCIAL LEARNING THEORY

We have defined sexual arousability as being positively related to the number and effectiveness of stimuli that produce sexual arousal and as being negatively related to the number and effectiveness of stimuli that inhibit sexual arousal. One way of analyzing how stimuli come to have excitatory and inhibitory effects on sexual arousal is through Bandura and Walters' (1963) social learning theory. As we saw in the last chapter, this theory emphasizes the processes of imitation and reinforcement in the development of behavior patterns.

One of the relatively few laboratory studies demonstrating the imitation of sexually relevant behavior was carried out by Walters, Bowen, and Parke (1963). Male college students were shown a movie of a series of pictures of nude males and females with a moving spot of light superimposed on the film. The students were told that the spot of light indicated the eye movements of a previous subject. Half the students saw the light moving over the nude bodies, the other half saw the light move mostly over the background. The students than looked at similar pictures while their own eye movements were recorded. Those who had seen the previous subject appear to look at the bodies themselves spent more time looking at the bodies, and less time looking at the background, than students exposed to the more inhibited subject.

Cross-cultural studies give many examples of the importance of social learning in sexual arousability. What is highly arousing in one culture may be neutral or actually repulsive in another. Thus, different cultures may prefer thin or corpulent physiques, shiny white teeth or black pointed teeth, natural feet or deformed crippled ones (cf. Ford and Beach, 1951). Bandura and Walters pointed out as an example that the female breast is a culturally conditioned sex object in U.S. society which has no unique sexual significance in other cultures.

Unlike many cultures, there is little socially sanctioned opportunity for an individual in U.S. culture to observe explicit sexual behavior in others, or even to hear about or read explicit descriptions of sexual behavior. Young people, in particular, have little access to such materials, and thus little sanctioned opportunity to learn about sexual behavior by direct modeling and imitation. This is an interesting contrast with aggressive behavior, where a young person can watch an average of eight aggressive episodes an hour on television (Murray, 1973).

PORNOGRAPHY: THE MASS MEDIA AND SEX

As with aggression, the great power of the mass media as instruments of social learning has brought their potential influence upon sexual behavior under government scrutiny. The United States Commission on Obscenity and Pornography was established by Congress in 1967 to, among other things, "study the effects of obscenity and pornography upon the public, . . . its relationship to crime and other antisocial behavior, and to recommend such legislative . . . action as the Commission deems necessary to regulate effectively the flow of such traffic, without in any way interfering with constitutional rights" (Public Law 90–100, Oct. 3, 1967). A number of studies were contracted by the Commission, and the report was released in 1970. We shall briefly review the results of some of these studies and the conclusions of the Commission.

Attitudes about Pornography

One of the findings of the Commission was that there is a striking heterogeneity of opinion about pornography and sex in general within the United States. In a national sample, Abelson, Cohen, Heaton, and Suder (1970) asked people the title of magazines in which they had seen material which they considered pornographic. A few mentioned such widely distributed and popular magazines as *Ladies Home Journal* and *Reader's Digest.* Others apparently define virtually nothing as pornographic.

Abelson et al. found that opinions about the effects of pornography also varied widely. Relatively few (2%) spontaneously mentioned pornography as one of the two or three most serious problems facing the country. As Table 6.2 indicates, many feel that pornography has socially desirable effects (provides information about sex, improves sex relations for some) but many also feel it has undesirable effects (leads to a breakdown in morals, makes people sex crazy). There is apparently no substantial public consensus about any effect. Studies of professionals and other presumed experts show a similar diversity of opinion. One study surveyed police chiefs and professionals in child guidance, social work, psychology, psychiatry, and sociology. When asked whether they thought reading obscene books plays a significant role in causing juvenile delinquency, 58% of the police chiefs said yes and 31% said no. In contrast, 12% of the professionals said yes and 77% said no (Beninghausen and Faunce, 1965; reported in the Commission Report, 1970). A survey of psychiatrists and psychologists revealed that, although about 80% majority of those who responded reported no experience with cases in which pornography caused antisocial behavior, some (16.8%) did report such experience. When asked if they thought persons exposed to pornography are more likely to engage in antisocial sexual acts, 14% agreed and 84% disagreed.

The Users of Pornography

Abelson et al. (1970) found that over 90% of men and 80% of women report experience with erotic material at some time during their lives. This experience is infrequent for adults—about once a year—but considerably more frequent among adolescents. Abelson et al. defined persons who reported having read or seen five or more erotic depictions in the past two years as having "high recent experi-

TABLE 6.2   PRESUMED EFFECTS OF EROTICA: ALL ADULTS FROM A NATIONAL SAMPLE.

[Question: "On this card are some opinions about the effects of looking at or reading sexual materials. As I read the letter of each one please tell me if you think sexual materials do or do not have these effects." (Q. 55; multiple responses)]

PRESUMED EFFECTS	HAS THAT EFFECT: (N = 2486)		
	YES	NO	NOT SURE NO ANSWER
Sexual materials excite people sexually	67%	17%	16%
Sexual materials provide information about sex	61%	27%	12%
Sexual materials lead to a breakdown of morals	56%	30%	14%
Sexual materials lead people to commit rape	49%	29%	22%
Sexual materials provide entertainment	48%	46%	6%
Sexual materials improve sex relations of some married couples	47%	32%	22%
Sexual materials make people bored with sexual materials	44%	35%	21%
Sexual materials lead people to lose respect for women	43%	41%	16%
Sexual materials make men want to do new things with their wives	41%	28%	32%
Sexual materials make people sex craxy	37%	45%	18%
Sexual materials provide an outlet for bottled up impulses	34%	46%	20%
Sexual materials give relief to people who have sex problems	27%	46%	26%

From H. Abelson, R. Cohen, E. Heaton, and C. Slider, "Public attitudes toward and experience with erotic materials." *Technical reports of the Commission on Obscenity and Pornography.* Vol 6. Washington, D.C.: U.S. Government Printing Office, 1970.

ence" with erotica. This group included 26% of adult males, 11% of adult females, 36% of adolescent (ages 15 to 20) males, and 38% of adolescent females. These persons tend to be young (the age of highest consumption are 21 to 29 for men, 18 to 20 for women) and comparatively well educated, living in large- or medium-size metropolitan areas. They are generally more likely than others to accept principles of freedom of expression and to have liberal attitudes about sex. They are heavier consumers of media in general (newspapers, magazines, movies, etc.) and are more active socially and politically than others. Abelson et al. suggest from this that exposure to erotica is one element in a life style characterized by high media consumption and social and community activity. Such persons may be more "likely to have encountered sexual stimuli in the normal course of social participation" (Commission Report, p. 98). This interpretation is supported by a survey study of American college students (Berger, Gagnon, and Simon, 1970) and a national survey of Sweden (Zetterberg, 1970).

Abelson et al. observe that this picture of the user of pornography is quite different from the common image of sexually unsatisfied middle-age men who "furitively avail themselves of erotic materials as a substitute for authentic sex experience" (1970, p. 42). However, the survey definition of highly experienced consumers was too broad to reveal the characteristics of really habitual users, and several investigators were commissioned to study directly the characteristics of patrons of adult bookstores and movie theaters (Nawy, 1970; Winick, 1970a; 1970b). Such persons were observed to be predominately white, middle-class, middle-aged married males. Interviews of patrons suggested that they had fewer sexually related experiences in adolescence than other males. However, they reported being more sexually oriented in adulthood. Their frequency and satisfaction of intercourse were similar to those of other males, but they reported having a greater number of partners and engaging in a greater variety of activities.

Nawy (1970) speculated that strong adult interest in pornography may stem in part from conflicts about sexual behavior in childhood and adolescence. Goldstein, Kant, Judd, Rice, and Green (1970; 1971) suggest a similar conclusion. They found that both heavy users of pornography and institutionalized sex offenders (rapists and pedophiles) reported *less* exposure to pornography in adolescence that did control males. This difference was particularly large with respect to adolescent exposure to movies and pictures of sexual intercourse. Goldstein et al. suggest that "it appears that sex deviates and users are noticeably lacking in experience, during their adolescent years, with stimuli representing our culture's definition of 'the normal sex act' " (1971, pp. 7–8).

The sex offenders reported a continuing low exposure to pornography into adulthood while users changed to show much greater exposure than controls. The users also reported a high rate of adult masturbation. Among the controls, 87% reported that they engaged in masturbation associated with erotica in adolescence, but only 37% carried this practice on into adulthood. Among users of pornography, the comparable figures are 86% and 78%: The incidence of masturbation did not decline as much in adulthood (Kant and Goldstein, 1970).

From these data, Goldstein et al. suggested that the users' adult interest in pornography may be a compensation for limited adolescent experience with pornography and sexual matters in general. In their words, "it appears that unresolved sexual conflicts in adolescence relate to adult sexual patterns in which erotica is a necessary stimulant . . . to obtain gratification. In the normally developed male, the adolescent use of erotica . . . declines, and the sexual partner becomes the primary source of arousal and gratification" (1970, p. 59).

An interesting aspect of this position is that it implies that more adolescent experience with pornography may actually be helpful in normal sexual development. Goldstein et al. feel that a "reasonable exposure to erotica" in adolescence is a surface manifestation of normal sexual interest and curiosity which eventually leads to a socially acceptable pattern of adult sexual behavior. Little exposure in adolescence may reflect a restrictive atmosphere in which sexual curiosity is unduly discouraged.

Before the "adult" establishments begin to sell their wares only to those *under* 21, some possible difficulties with the Goldstein et al. data should be pointed out. Representative sampling is a particularly difficult problem in sex research, and the data of Goldstein et al. must be questioned on these grounds. They were unable to induce many patrons of adult establishments to participate in interviews and had to obtain their sample of users largely through advertisements. The resulting sample of users seemed to be biased toward the well-educated and more affluent. Also, they initially drew a sample of 133 controls, but could induce only 63 of these to complete the interview. Ten of these were eliminated because of technical problems with the interview and two more were eliminated because they "belonged to a deviate group." Thus, only 38% of the original sample of controls was included in the data. Under these circumstances the findings of Goldstein et al. must be viewed with much caution: Their samples could be wildly unrepresentative of the population of users and controls. Nevertheless, their interpretations are interesting and seem compatible with the findings in other studies of little adolescent sexual experience among adult users of pornography.

Commission studies of adolescent experience with pornography also seem generally compatible with the notions of Goldstein et al., and they suggest another reason why very low adolescent exposure to pornography may be associated with disrupted sexual development. The most common source of pornographic materials in adolescence is a friend of the same age. "This exposure occurs in a social situation where materials are freely passed around . . . The experience seems to be more of a social one than a sexual one" (Commission Report, 1970, p. 21). There is evidence that adolescents who are less active socially have less exposure to pornography. One might speculate from this that young people with low acquaintance with pornography may often be those with poor interpersonal relationships which in turn contribute to later problems of sexual development.

The Effects of Pornography   The most immediate and obvious effect of exposure to pornography is a transitory affective response that may or may not involve sexual arousal. The intensity and nature of this response varies widely, depending on such factors as the characteristics of the particular viewer, the nature of the theme presented, the form of presentation, and so forth. Often the affective response is ambivalent, particularly if the subject is not experienced with pornography. He may feel guilt and disgust in addition to sexual excitement and fascination.

Commission experiments indicated that persons are more likely to be sexually aroused by pornography if they are younger, sexually experienced, college educated, and religiously inactive. The studies cast some doubt upon the suggestions of Kinsey et al. (1953) that women are less aroused by erotic stimuli than men. They showed that men generally report erotic stimuli to be more arousing than do women, but that when asked to report the physiological responses to sexual arousal (erection, vaginal lubrication, genital sensations, etc.) there was no great difference between men and women. This result was found for unmarried college-age people (Mosher, 1970), married college students (Kutschinsky, 1970), and middle-aged married couples (Mann, Sidman, and Starr, 1970).

There is evidence that viewing pornography is associated with transitory increases in sexual behavior in some persons. In one study, Mann et al. (1970) studied 85 couples who had married for at least 10 years. Fifteen couples were assigned to a control group. The remainder were asked to submit daily reports of their marital sexual behavior for four weeks. They then viewed a variety of either erotic or nonerotic films once a week for four weeks. They continued to submit daily reports through the film-viewing period and for an additional four weeks. Assuming that the daily reports were accurate, the erotic films did not significantly alter the attitudes of the subjects about sexual practices: they did not become more or less innovative or inhibited. Also, there were no sustained changes in sexual behavior attributable to the erotic films. However, the subjects viewing the erotic films were more sexually active on the nights following their viewing of the films.

This general result has been repeated in a number of studies. Table 6.3 summarizes the effect of erotic stimuli on masturbation and Table 6.4 summarizes their effect on heterosexual coitus. In general, these studies indicate that, following exposure to erotic materials, frequencies of masturbation or coitus increase among a minority of persons, decrease among a smaller proportion, and do not change in a majority. This tendency toward an increase in sexual behavior is transitory and appears to diminish within 24–48 hours. Exposure to erotic material does not systematically effect the reported incidence of unusual or innovative sexual practices.

The Committee Report concluded that an increase of sexual activity followed exposure to erotic material in a minority, and that it constituted a "temporary activation of individuals' preexisting patterns of sexual behavior" (p. 25).

Pornography and Criminal Behavior   A number of studies contracted by the Commission found "no evidence to date that exposure to explicit sexual materials plays a significant role in the causation of delinquent or criminal behavior among youth or adults" (p. 27). This conclusion was based on the following findings from the studies: (1) The reported

TABLE 6.3   MASTURBATORY FREQUENCY 24 HOURS BEFORE AND AFTER EXPOSURE TO SEXUAL STIMULI.

POPULATION	N	NO CHANGE	DECREASED	INCREASED	
Married Danish males, 22–34[1] (Kutschinsky, 1970a)	42	79%	7%	14%	No
Married Danish females, 18–28[1] (Kutschinsky, 1970a)	28	89%	0	11%	test
Single German males, 19–27[2] (Sigusch, et al., 1970)	50	66%	6%	28%	No
Single German females, 19–27[2] (Sigusch, et al., 1970)	50	82%	4%	14%	test
Single German males, 19–27[2] (Schmidt and Sigusch, in press)	128	59%	11%	30%	(.001)
Single German females, 19–27[2] Schmidt and Sigusch, in press)	128	82%	4%	14%	(.01)
Single German males, 19–29[2] (Schmidt, et al., 1969)	99	68%	5%	26%	(.001)
Single Canadian males, 18–25[2] (Amoroso, et al., 1970)	60	65.5%	8.6%	25.8%	(.05)
Single American males, 18–20[2] (Mosher, 1970a)	194	81%	7%	7%	(NS)
Single American females, 18–20[2] (Mosher, 1970a)	183	90%	1%	2%	(NS)
Single American males, 18–30[2] (Davis and Braucht, 1970a)	121	72%	—	28%	(.001)
Married American males, 30–59 (Mann, et al., 1970)	48	—	—	4%	(NS)
Married American females, 30–64 (Mann, et al., 1970)	32	—	—	2%	(NS)

From *Report of the Commission on Obscenity and Pornography,* Washington, D.C.: U.S. Government Printing Office, 1970.

[1] Subjects included some unmarried but coitally experienced persons.

[2] Subjects included both coitally experienced and inexperienced persons.

experience of delinquent and nondelinquent youth with pornography seems to be essentially similar; (2) studies of the increased availability of pornography following its legalization in Denmark showed that the increase in pornography was accompanied by an apparent decrease in the incidence of sexual crime; (3) studies of the relationship between sexual crimes and the availability of pornography in the United States are inconclusive; (4) finally, as we have seen, male sex offenders report less adoles-

TABLE 6.4   COITAL FREQUENCY 24 HOURS BEFORE AND AFTER EXPOSURE TO SEXUAL STIMULI.

POPULATION	N	NO CHANGE	DECREASED	INCREASED	
Married Danish males, 22–34[1] (Kutschinsky, 1970a)	42	71%	2%	26%	No
Married Danish females, 22–34[1] (Kutschinsky, 1970a)	28	68%	0	32%	test
Single German males, 19–27[2] (Sigusch, et al., 1970)	50	80%	4%	16%	(NS)
Single German females, 19–27[2] (Sigusch, et al., 3 erap	50	82%	6%	12%	(NS)
Single German males, 19–27[2] (Schmidt and Sigusch, in press)	128	76%	9%	15%	(NS)
Single German females, 19–27[2] (Schmidt and Sigusch, in press)	128	81%	5%	14%	(.001)
Single German males, 19–29[2] (Schmidt, et al., 1969)	99	71%	11%	17%	(NS)
Single Canadian males, 18–25[2] (Amoroso, et al., 1970)	60	77.6%	10.3%	12.1%	(NS)
Single American males, 18–20[2] (Mosher, 1970a)	194	91%	4%	2%	(NS)
Single American females, 18–20[2] (Mosher, 1970a)	183	95%	2%	3%	(NS)
Single American males, 18–30[2] (Davis and Braucht, 1970a)	121	82%	11%	7%	(NS)
Married American males, 30–59 (Mann, et al., 1970)	48	—	—	36%	(.01)
Married American females, 30–64 (Mann, et al., 1970)	32	—	—	28%[3]	(.01)

From *Report of the Commission on Obscenity and Pornography,* Washington, D.C.: U.S. Government Printing Office, 1970.

[1] Subjects included some unmarried but coitally experienced persons.

[2] Subjects included both coitally experienced and inexperienced persons.

[3] Percent increase of experimental over control Ss. Additional tests found that mean sexual activity levels on film viewing nights exceeded those for the rest of the four-week period at high levels of significance for males ($T = 5.31$, $= 48$, $p < .001$) and females ($T = 4.19$, $= 48$, $p < .001$).

cent experience with pornography than other adult males. Based on these studies, "the Commission cannot conclude that exposure to erotic materials is a factor in the causation of sex crime or sex delinquency" (p. 27).

Recommendations of the Committee   On the basis of the empirical findings, the majority of the Commission concluded that pornography does not pose a major social problem, and that indeed much of the problem regarding pornography stems from the "inability and reluctance of people in our society to be open and direct in dealing with sexual matters" (p. 47). They argue that this tends to restrict the legitimate flow of accurate information about sex. Such information is needed, particularly in adolescence, to help the individual to understand himself and his feelings. If such information cannot be obtained openly from legitimate sources, the individual will seek it through clandestine sources which may well provide inaccurate and distorted information. The Commission recommended increased effort in sex education as a way of obviating the need for pornographic materials. It also recommended the repeal of all legislation prohibiting the sale of sexual materials to consenting adults, although it supported legislation prohibiting the distribution of pornography to minors and the public display and unsolicited mailing of sexual materials.

A minority of 3 of the 18 Commissioners issued a vigorous dissent from these conclusions. They gave a detailed critique of the empirical research, citing such problems as the overreliance on verbal self-reports, the failure to match groups on relevant criteria in some cases (by comparing rapists with college students rather than other criminals, for example), the lack of longitudinal and clinical studies, the lack of studies of young adolescents, problems with basing all interpretations on volunteers who agreed to report sexual histories or submit to pornography, alleged bias in reporting data and forming conclusions among the majority of the Commissioners, and so forth. They felt that the failure to find a causal relationship between exposure to pornography and sex crimes was due to the inherent difficulty of conclusively proving causal relationships between social science variables. Feeling that proving a causal relationship between exposure to pornography and criminal behavior is both impossible and unnecessary, they argue that the question of the legalization of pornography must be judged on moral grounds. From their point of view, pornography degrades and debases sex and should be subject to stricter laws, and they point out that a substantial majority of Americans favor stricter laws.

This controversy boils down to a question of values which cannot be settled by research findings alone. The value of the right to free expression for a minority is apparently in conflict with other moral values in a majority, and such a conflict can be settled only through political and judicial processes. At best, the findings of empirical studies can illuminate and clarify the issues in such controversies. The same basic issue is involved in the question of whether or not violence on the mass media should be subject to censorship, although it should be noted that the amount of media portrayal of violence is vastly greater than the portrayal of sex and it is much more available to children.

Summary

Sexual motivation is a strong, at least partially biologically based process which has been connected in theory with the motivation of much normal and aberrant human behavior. The objective study of human sexual motivation has been hampered by sensitivity and embarassment more than the study of other human motives, and this makes the conclusions from such studies more tentative. The fact that many persons refuse to take part in studies of sex makes it difficult even to be sure of the typical course of normal sexual development, the typical range of sexual experience, and so forth. However, there have been great strides in the understanding of human sexual motivation during this century.

We briefly considered the role of sexual motivation in Freud's theory, largely because of its historical importance in pointing out the possibly central role of sexual motives in both normal and abnormal human behavior. The details of Freud's theory have not been generally accepted by American psychologists, but the theory did make the objective study of sex possible and indeed necessary for a full understanding of human behavior.

The first major step in the objective study of sex was the "Kinsey Report," which reported the results of interviews conducted among large numbers of persons. However, the sampling procedures of the Kinsey studies have been questioned, throwing the generalizability of their results into considerable doubt. The Masters and Johnson investigations were the first which systematically studied the act of human intercourse and orgasm.

One of the important distinctions in the analysis of sexual behavior (which is applicable to other motivational and emotional states as well) is that between sexual arousal—the transient level of sexual excitation—and sexual arousability—the propensity for sexual arousal. There is little evidence of any important difference between men and women in the nature of sexual arousal, but there is some evidence that males are more arousable than females. It is unclear whether the latter phenomenon is attributable to physiological factors (i.e. androgen concentrations) or learning experiences (i.e. those associated with masturbation) or both. Hormone levels and neural mechanisms are involved in both sexual arousal and sexual arousability, and there is evidence that the early experience with sex-related hormones may cause the development or inhibition of male and female neural substrates.

Learning has an increasingly important role to play in sexual behavior as one goes up the phylogenetic scale. In humans, the importance of observational learning and imitation brings up the problem of the role of social models in sexual learning. Studies of pornography have shown that such exposure to sexual models is a common experience of adolescents, and there is some evidence that a continuing strong interest in pornography in adults may be associated with relatively little adolescent exposure to pornography. However, these studies are flawed by the reluctance of many "normal" persons to participate in a study involving sex. Other studies showed transient increases in sexual behavior following exposure to pornography. There does not appear to be any conclusive evidence that exposure to pornography per se is harmful.

In terms of the schema introduced in Chapter 1, this chapter has again shown how innate mechanisms and physiological factors interact with learning and cognitive factors in the determination of behavior. It has also introduced the distinction between arousal and arousability. In terms of the schema, arousal may be seen as the transient level of excitation in the physiological system. Arousability is the extent to which affective stimuli cause such arousal after being filtered by innate mechanisms and the individual's learning experiences.

CHAPTER SEVEN

THE DEVELOPMENT AND EXPRESSION OF EMOTION

We have seen in the last two chapters that there is disagreement about the extent to which aggressive and sexual behaviors should be expressed or inhibited. Many regard sexual and aggressive tendencies as stemming from innate drives or instincts which, if they are not expressed, may build up strength and have unhealthy consequences. A major source of this view is Freud's theory that neurotic symptoms result from repressed sexual and aggressive impulses. More recently, ethologists have argued that the basis for instinctive behavior is an "accumulation of central nervous excitatory potential" (Eibl-Eibesfeldt, 1970, p. 59) which, if not adequately discharged, may find expression upon inappropriate objects. Similarly, Alexander (1950) has suggested that the blocking of the expression of emotion can become a source of stress within the body, causing peripheral nervous and hormonal effects that can result in psychosomatic illnesses (see Chapter 2). Similar views have given rise to a wide range of psychotherapeutic techniques designed to purge the emotions.

Others feel that the open expression of emotion is not necessarily beneficial and that it indeed may be harmful both to the individual and society. Berkowitz (1971b; 1973) worries that encouraging open sexual and aggressive expression may create conditions where socially undesirable behaviors may be disinhibited and rewarded. For example, he feels that the therapy techniques based upon the free expression of aggression within the therapy session (which he terms ventilative therapies) may cause undesirable transfer to situations in which aggression is not appropriate.

This controversy, like others we have considered, is based to a great extent upon values and moral judgments. However, as before it is possible that empirical studies can illuminate and clarify the issues involved. Let us consider the available data on emotional expression and inhibition.

The Development and Expression of Emotion in Primates

ONTOGENY OF EMOTION IN RHESUS MONKEYS

The rhesus macaque monkey lives in small groups which are highly adaptive to the individual monkey and without which he probably could not long survive. Life within these small groups demands much coordination of individual behavior which in turn requires cooperation and communication between individuals. Ordinarily, this coordination of behavior is successful: there is typically little conflict within the primate group and the group is capable of engaging in cooperative ventures adaptive to all. There are many striking examples of cooperation within monkey groups. Large adult males will often work together in driving off predators, leaving weaker females and juveniles in safety. Monkeys also learn from one another, and group habits or traditions may become established. A particularly interesting example of this was observed in a group of rhesus monkeys on Koshima Island in northern Japan. The animals were fed wheat and began to gather it by laboriously picking out pieces of grain from sandy earth. A young female apparently found that if a handful of the material were dropped into a nearby stream, the wheat floated and could easily be scooped up. She communicated this to the other monkeys, and soon the tradition of throwing material into the stream and scooping up the wheat spread throughout the group. At last report 19 of 49 monkeys in the area began using this invention (Kawai, 1965; Kawamura 1963; Itani, 1958).

Rhesus monkeys are highly aggressive, volatile, and irascible animals. One might ask what enables them to cooperate with one another in such peace and harmony. The answer might well have a bearing on the social behavior of that most dangerous primate, *Homo sapiens*. Harry Harlow and his associates at the University of Wisconsin have extensively studied the ontogeny of emotion in the rhesus monkeys, using as the major experimental design the deprivation experiment.*

Studies of Contact Comfort   Harlow's first deprivation studies in primates were not really designed to be deprivation experiments. Harlow was interested in the development of the intense attraction of the infant to the mother. The most widely accepted theory of the time was that the mother acquired reward properties because her presence was associated with the satisfaction of strong homeostatic drives, particularly the hunger drive. Psychoanalysts emphasized that the mother's breast became associated with both the satisfaction of hunger and the oral gratification. Learning theorists felt that the mother acquired secondary reward properties just as any stimulus does when it is associated with the satisfaction of a homeostatic (primary) drive (Dollard et al., 1939).

Harlow did not doubt the importance of homeostatic drives or the mechanism of secondary reinforcement, but he felt that mother love must also be based at least in part on "more picturesque and less pragmatic" unlearned motives (Harlow, Gluck and Suomi, 1972). He noted that newborn monkeys often could not survive if raised in a bare wire cage, even though they were well fed. However, if they were given a small scrap of terrycloth the survival rate increased significantly. The infant would cling

* The term "ontogeny" is used in biology to refer to the history of the development of an organism.

tightly to the cloth and would scream in loud protest when the cloth was removed to be cleaned. Harlow came to suspect that the infant had a real need for contact comfort: bodily contact with a soft, skinlike surface. He suggested that bodily contact may be an "unlearned nativistic force" that is importantly involved in the development of the infant's love for its mother and its attachments with other monkeys.

To test whether contact comfort was more important in the development of love than was nursing, Harlow and Zimmerman (1958) constructed two surrogate mother monkeys. One was made of bare wire, the other covered with cloth. Both could be fitted with a removable nursing bottle on the thoracic midline. In half the cases, the cloth mother nursed and the wire mother did not; in the remainder, the conditions was reversed. To insure proper experimental control, each infant was isolated from other monkeys and raised, as it were, by the surrogates.

Experiments showed that the infants clung to the cloth mother regardless of whether they nursed from the wire or cloth mother. Furthermore, older infants seemed to gain trust and confidence from the cloth mother. If placed in a large strange playroom, they would rush and cling to the cloth mother. As they held the mother, they gradually seemed to lose their fear and finally began to play and enjoy the playroom. The wire mother could not instill such apparent feelings of confidence, even if it had been the source of milk to the infant.

Harlow concluded that contact comfort is a variable of overwhelming importance in the development of mother love and that the variable of nursing is comparatively unimportant (Harlow, 1959).

At this point Harlow had a laboratory full of young surrogate-reared monkeys who had grown up isolated from other monkeys and were raised instead with a wire mother, a cloth mother, or some combination of the two. He then put these isolates in a breeding program to gain more young subjects. The breeding program was, in his words, "frighteningly unsuccessful." The isolate monkeys were incapable of normal sexual behavior. Some were willing enough, but they could never seem to get things together properly. Their behaviors resembled the infantile sexual responses of very young monkeys. Other monkeys, particularly those raised only with wire mothers, were wildly fearful and destructive. Many could not even be housed with other monkeys, let along engage in sexual behavior. Some engaged in strange, self-destructive behavior, such as biting and tearing at their own flesh. The large canine teeth of some males had to be removed to prevent them from goring themselves to death (see Figure 7.1). A few female isolates who were successfully impregnated proved to be child beaters when their first infants were born. Five of 38 primiparous isolate mothers killed their infants, a sixth infant was removed following serious maiming, and the remainder of the mothers showed much brutal infant abuse and neglect which is most uncharacteristic of rhesus monkey mothers (see Figure 7.2). Harlow had inadvertently created a laboratory full of highly neurotic monkeys (cf. Harlow, 1962).

FIGURE 7.1   Self-destructive behavior in an isolated male rhesus monkey. (Courtesy Harry F. Harlow, University of Wisconsin Primate Laboratory. From Harlow, McGaugh, Thompson, 1971, Fig. 5.1.)

FIGURE 7.2   Punitive behavior toward an infant in an isolated female rhesus monkey. (Courtesy Harry F. Harlow, University of Wisconsin Primate Laboratory. From Harlow, McGaugh, Thompson, 1971, Fig. 5.3.)

A Model of Ontogeny   The isolated monkeys had been raised in an environment which provided relatively few opportunities for learning fearful and aggressive behavior, yet they displayed if anything more fear and aggression than normally reared monkeys. Harlow had not expected

this: indeed at one point he was suggesting that the cloth surrogates provided rather good mothers—patient, stolid, never getting angry or rejecting the infant (Harlow, 1959). However, as it turned out the experiment was a deprivation experiment in the ethologists' sense (Eibl-Eibesfeldt, 1970) and it strongly implied that the monkeys' fearful and aggressive reactions, as well as their affectional reactions, are based on innate mechanisms. Harlow turned from the study of mother love to the fuller study of the development of affection, fear, and aggression in rhesus monkeys.

Careful observation suggested that the capacity for affection is present in the infant monkey at birth, but there is little evidence of fear or aggression. The very young monkey shows curiousity about everything and fear of nothing, and the mother's protective presence is essential to his survival. After a few weeks, the infant begins to react with apparent fear to some stimuli. Harlow suggests that neural structures underlying fear begin to mature at this point. At six months, fear responses are well established, but aggression has not fully appeared. The six-month-old monkey exhibits many isolated components of aggressive behavior during play—threat, grimacing, submissive gestures, biting, and so on—but it is not until the end of the first year that play occasionally becomes really violent and abusive. A dominance ordering emerges from these initial aggressive bouts, and fighting subsequently declines and is largely replaced by gestures of threat and submission. Harlow feels that the appearance of aggression, like that of fear, is due to the maturation of genetically determined neural structures (cf. Deets and Harlow, 1971).

Harlow thus argues that neural structures underlying affection, fear, and aggression develop in a fixed maturational sequence. However, the way that the animal learns to deal with and use these emotions depends upon social experience. Normally, fear appears only after the infant has had plenty of time to become acquainted with, learn to trust, and form affectional bonds with other monkeys. For this reason he does not fear other familiar monkeys. Aggression does not fully appear until even more experience in interacting with other monkeys has been gained.

Deprivation Experiments   Harlow and his colleagues conducted a series of deprivation experiments to test this model (cf. Deets and Harlow, 1971). The general results are summarized in Table 7.1. One group of infants was isolated for the first three months of life. These infants typically showed signs of emotional shock upon being removed from the isolation chamber. Many engaged in autistic behavior—lying prone while clutching the head and body with the arms and legs. One died and another had to be force-fed to survive. After a week they were introduced to other infants in playrooms. They continued to show some autistic behavior but most

TABLE 7.1   SUMMARY OF EXPERIMENTS ILLUSTRATING THE EFFECTS OF SOCIAL DEPRIVATION ON FEARFUL AND AGGRESSIVE BEHAVIORS.

PERIOD OF ISOLATION	SOCIAL BEHAVIOR AT END OF ISOLATION PERIOD	LATER SOCIAL BEHAVIOR
0–3 months	Initial autistic behavior, gradually make good adjustment	Essentially normal
0–6 months	Low affiliation High fear Low aggression	High fear, high aggression directed at inappropriate targets (young and adult monkeys)
0–12 months	Very high fear, autistic behavior. Almost no social behavior	Very high fear, low levels of aggression developing to high levels
6–12 months	Normal levels of fear, high aggression	Some affiliative behavior, normal fear, high aggression
18–26 months	Initial high levels of social behavior, gradually make normal adjustment	Essentially normal

Adapted from Deets and Harlow (1971).

eventually made a good adjustment. Apparently, some fear of strange situations had matured in the three months that they were in the isolation chamber, but it was not enough to prevent contact and eventual affiliation with peers.

A second group of infants was isolated from birth to six months of age, at which time the maturation of fear should be complete. The infants' adjustment with other monkeys should in this condition be severely affected by strong fear responses. As anticipated, the isolates in this condition rarely approached other monkeys, and play was virtually nonexistent. Autistic behavior and other fearful responses were common. The isolates did not show the threats and occasional attacks that are seen in six-month-old normal monkeys.

This kind of reaction was seen even more strongly in animals isolated from birth to 12 months of age. These animals were socially devastated, engaging in almost continuous autistic self-clutching and other bizarre withdrawn behaviors and showing almost no social interaction. Thus among animals isolated during the first 6 to 12 months to life, fear seemed to block all social behavior, both affiliative and aggressive in nature.

Although these animals showed less aggression than normals immediately following their isolation period, in later tests many showed heightened and inappropriate aggression. At 3 years and 4½ years of age, these isolates were placed with a variety of unfamiliar animals—one-year-old juveniles, age-mates, and fully grown adults. At three years of age, the six-month isolates showed heightened aggression which was often directed at inappropriate targets—they attacked the juvenile brutally and made suicidal assaults on the adult. The 12-month isolates at age 3 made threats but no attacks, but at 4½ they were as aggressive as the six-month isolates. Thus, early isolation apparently slows but does not prevent the maturation of aggressive behavior.

Further data show that these six- and 12-month isolates continue to be hyperfearful and hyperaggressive in adulthood. They also engage in inappropriate sexual behavior, largely because they attack and flee from potential mates. Some isolates were confined at 18 months of age with a monkey of the opposite sex. This "therapeutic" experience, which lasted an average of 17 months, had virtually no effect on sexual behavior.

These data suggest that isolation from other monkeys during the period in which conspecific attachments are normally formed and fear is maturing makes the monkey forever fearful of social contact. The effect appears to be irreversible. Harlow reasons further that if the isolation is delayed until after fear has matured, but before aggression has matured, the animal should show disturbances of aggression but not fear. This was illustrated by a study in which animals were isolated between the sixth and twelfth month of life. As predicted, these animals were not unduly fearful but they were highly aggressive. The normal animals were not able to cope with the aggressive isolates: the normal animals became distressed while the isolates appeared to be at ease. This heightened aggression continued into adolescence among these isolates.

If isolation is delayed until all emotional responses are well established, it should have few if any permanent effects. This was supported in a study which isolated the monkeys between the age of 18 and 26 months. Social tests made before and after isolation revealed a transitory increase in all social behavior—sex, play, threat, submission and so on—immediately following the isolation. Within a week, social behavior had returned to the normal preisolation level.

Ontogeny of Emotion in Humans   Deets and Harlow (1971) point out that human infants show evidence that fear is absent during the early months of life. Most infants show active affiliative behavior—smiling, laughing, responding to hugging, and so on—with familiar or strange adults. Also, the very young infant does not show prolonged protest if separated from familiar adults. At about six months of age, the attachment to significant figures becomes apparent—the infant shows distress when separated from the mother and begins to show distress with strangers. This fear of strangers develops gradually during the latter half of the first year of life. This is consistent with the notion that "social affiliation and attachments are established in the human infant before fear of unfamiliar stimuli becomes manifest" (Deets and Harlow, 1971, p. 22). Unfortunately, there is little systematic data on the aggressive behavior of infants and toddlers younger than four or five years of age, the period when maturation and early experience may do much to determine the aggressive behavior of the individual, although many exasperated parents will testify to the impressive aggressive capacities of two- and three-year-olds.

Harlow's data demonstrate convincingly and dramatically that total isolation from conspecifics during early life can have a devastating effect on later social behavior. One might ask why this is the case. What does the monkey gain from experience with other monkeys that is so irreplaceable in later life? Part of the answer may well be, as Harlow suggests, that the isolated individual fears other animals and can never overcome this fear. Others have suggested that the isolated animal never develops the ability to communicate accurately with other animals, and that this lack of communicative skill is one reason for the social deficit (Mason, 1961). Let us consider the role of communication in monkey social behavior.

EMOTIONAL COMMUNICATION IN PRIMATES

Communicative Facial Expressions and Gestures   In *Expression of the Emotions in Man and Animals* (1872) Darwin drew attention to the fact that many animals have evolved a rich variety of expressive behaviors: behaviors that appear to serve as signals that are adaptive to the species. A major example is the pattern of threat and submissive behaviors that seem to regulate intraspecies aggression in many species (see Chapter 5). Emotional behavior in primates is accompanied by a particularly striking repertoire of facial expressions, gestures, calls, and other expressive behaviors. Such behaviors may make possible the emotional communication between individuals which is crucial to the coordination of behaviors within the primate group.

The chimpanzee, which is the closest relative to man of all the living primates, has been observed in the wild by Jane Van Lawick-Goodall and her associates (1965; 1968). The chimpanzee lives in large, loosely organized groups, with small temporary subgroups forming apparently on the basis of friendships between the animals. Chimpanzees have been observed to use, and even make, simple tools. For example, Van Lawick-Goodall (1965) photographed one as it chewed a handful of leaves to manufacture a sponge to soak up water from a depression in a tree trunk. Others were seen to select a twig or grass stalk, poke it into a termite mound, pull it out and eat the clinging insects. An animal suffering from diarrhea was observed to pick leaves to clean itself. Other chimpanzees, particularly ones raised in the open savannah, were seen to use sticks to attack a stuffed leopard (Kortlundt, in Eibl-Eibesfeldt, 1970).

Van Lawick-Goodall reported that it took some time for her to appreciate the complexities of communication between wild chimpanzees. They have several greeting gestures, including embracing and kissing when meeting someone they know. Another gesture is similar to sexual presenting and is used by other apes and baboons: the greeting animal, male or female, turns its posterior toward the other. Another gesture is called shaking hands; a lower animal extends a hand palm up, a common gesture of begging. The higher-ranking animal reaches out, palm down, in a touch which seems to calm the other (see Figure 7.3). Lower-ranking chimpanzees have also been seen to bow to other animals (Van Lawick-Goodall, 1965; 1968; Eibl-Eibesfeldt, 1970).

Some of the gestures used by chimpanzees may be inborn behavior

FIGURE 7.3   "Shaking hands" in chimpanzees. Van Lawick-Goodall (1965) observed that the submissive animal on the left may have feared for her infant, who is out of sight, when the 12-year-old dominant male approached, and that she lifted her hand as a way to ask for reassurance. The dominant animal's touch appeared to calm her. (Drawing by Herr Hermann Kacher, in I. Eibl-Eibesfeldt, LOVE & HATE, Holt, Rinehart, Winston, 1971. From a photograph by J. and H. van Lawick-Goodall, in NATIONAL GEOGRAPHIC, Vol. 128, No. 6, December 1965, pp. 802–831)

patterns common to all chimpanzees and perhaps common to other primates, including man. Eibl-Eibesfeldt (1970) notes that there are many analogies between the expressive behaviors of chimpanzees and those of man, including threatening facial expressions and postures, holding the hand palm up in supplication, stomping the foot and shaking the fist in anger, nodding, and hugging. Whether or not these behaviors have a common root in inborn behavior patterns is uncertain: we shall consider this further below. However, some of the expressive behavior of chimpanzees is apparently not totally inborn, for it shows local variations in form and meaning. Van Lawick-Goodall (1968) observed that a movement like lifting a baby onto the mother's back was a signal for the infant to mount the mother, while Kortlandt (1967) found the same gesture to be a warning signal between males (Eibl-Eibesfeldt, 1970). Apparently "cross-cultural" studies of chimpanzees are needed to determine what expressive behaviors have universal meaning.

Measuring the Facial Communication of Affect in Primates

R. E. Miller and his colleagues developed an experimental situation to measure the communication of affect by means of facial expression in rhesus monkeys. They taught two monkeys to press a bar within a few seconds after a light came on in order to avoid a painful electric shock. After both animals had thoroughly learned this avoidance task, they were paired in such a way that one, the "sender," could see the light but had no access to the bar. The other "observer" monkey could use the bar but could not see the light. The observer could see the televised image of the head and a facial region of the sender, who was in another room. If the sender made a facial reaction when he saw the light and if the observer could perceive and accurately interpret this reaction, the observer could press the bar which would avoid the shock for both of them. Miller found in several experiments that normal rhesus monkeys could solve this task with little difficulty (Miller, Murphey, and Mirsky, 1959; Miller, Banks, and Ogawa, 1962, 1963; Miller, Banks, and Kuwahara, 1966).

One might ask how isolated monkeys would do at this task. We noted that Mason (1961) suggested that the social inadequacy observed in isolated monkeys may be due in part to an impairment in the ability to communicate with other monkeys. The isolates may lack the communicative skills which normally facilitate social interaction. As Mason put it:

> *Orderly and harmonious intraspecies social relationships in rhesus monkeys are highly dependent upon previous socialization experience. Among the specific factors which are responsi-*

ble for orderly social interactions, species-specific gestures ap-
pear to be of particular importance . . . The behavior of restrict-
ed monkeys suggests that the effective development of these
elementary forms of social co-ordination and communication is
dependent upon learning. It is probable that the absence of
these social skills contributed to the turbulent relations between
socially restricted monkeys (Mason, 1961, p. 290).

To test Mason's hypothesis, Miller, Caul, and Mirsky (1967) obtained three 12-month isolates from Harlow's laboratory. They put them in the communication task in all possible combinations with three normal monkeys of the same age. In the initial training phase, where they were not paired with other monkeys, the isolated monkeys learned the avoidance task as quickly as did the normals. Thus, their ability to learn did not seem to be impaired. However, when paired with other monkeys, the isolates were clearly deficient both as senders and as receivers of communication. As observers they were completely incapable of using the facial expressions of sender monkeys to perform the appropriate response, regardless of whether the sender was a normal monkey or another isolate (see Figure 7.4). When isolate senders were paired with normal observers, the normals showed a large number of avoidance responses at the appropriate time when the light was on (Figure 7.4A). However, the normals also made many responses at inappropriate times: they pressed the bar between trials when the light stimulus was not on, perhaps because the isolate senders made many disturbed and fearful facial expressions throughout the testing session whether the light was on or not. The number of intertrial responses was weighed in computing whether significant communication occurred for each session. As Figure 7.4B shows, there were a large number of significant sessions only when normal senders were paired with normal observers.

Miller et al. concluded that their study supports Mason's hypothesis that the lack of opportunity to acquire communication skills is a major factor in the social deficit of monkeys reared in isolation. "It was strikingly apparent from this experiment that the monkeys deprived of social relationships during the first year of life do not utilize social information as do normals even after 3–4 years of social opportunities following the isolation period" (Miller et al., 1967, p. 239).

The Development of Emotional Expression in Humans

These studies illustrate nicely the interaction between constitutional and

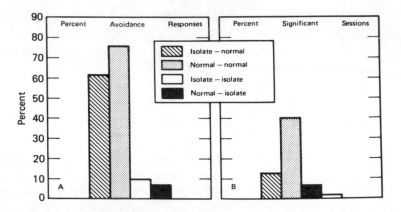

FIGURE 7.4   Behavior of receivers during communication tests between pairs of rhesus monkeys. From R. E. Miller. W. F. Caul, and I. A. Mirsky, "Communication of affects between feral and socially isolated monkeys." *Journal of Personality and Social Psychology*, 1967, 7, 231–239. Copyright 1967 by the American Psychological Association. Reprinted by permission.

environmental factors: both the maturation of innate physiological mechanisms and social experience are apparently required for the normal development of emotional expression. There is evidence in humans also that innate mechanisms exist, as evidenced by the very early appearance of characteristic modes of emotional responding in infants. However, the eventual expression of this temperament is strongly influenced by socialization.

TEMPERAMENT IN HUMANS

The Concept of Temperament   Temperament shall refer to innate emotional dispositions, based presumably upon neural and hormonal mechanisms. There is evidence from animal literature that temperament can be inherited. For example, animals have been bred for aggressiveness and emotionality: by selectively breeding the most aggressive and least aggressive of a pool of initially similar animals, strains differing in aggressiveness have been developed. Similar techniques have been used in developing strains of emotional (or fearful) and nonemotional animals (Gray, 1971).

The Longitudinal Study of Temperament in Humans   Thomas, Chess, and Birch (1970) have studied the temperament of infants beginning at birth. They used parent interviews and observation of the child to identify temperamental traits. In pilot studies, they identified nine characteristics that could be reliably scored for very young children: (1) motor activity, (2) rhythmicity, (3) distractibility, (4) approach-withdrawal, (5) adaptibility, (6) attention span and persistence, (7) intensity of reaction, (8) threshold of responsiveness, and (9) quality of mood (see Table 7.2). They found that children develop a characteristic temperament as early as two or three months of age.

TABLE 7.2   CATEGORIES USED TO DESCRIBE TEMPERAMENTAL CHARACTERISTICS

CATEGORIES OF PERSONALITY INDEX	TYPE OF CHILD		
	EASY	SLOW TO WARM UP	DIFFICULT
Activity level (Proportion of active periods to inactive ones)	Varies	Low to moderate	Varies
Rhythmicity (Regularity of hunger, elimination, sleep)	Very regular	Varies	Irregular
Distractibility (Degree to which extraneous stimuli alter behavior)	Varies	Varies	Varies
Approach-Withdrawal (Response to a new object or person)	Positive approach	Initial withdrawal	Withdrawal
Adaptability (Ease of adapting to changes in environment)	Very adaptable	Adapts slowly	Adapts slowly
Attention Span-Persistence (Time devoted to and effect of distraction on an activity)	High or low	High or low	High or low
Intensity of Reaction (The energy of response)	Low or mild	Mild	Intense
Threshold of Responsiveness (Intensity of stimuli required to evoke a response)	High or low	High or low	High or low
Quality of Mood (Friendly, pleasant behavior vs unfriendly, unpleasant behavior)	Positive	Slightly negative	Negative

From A. Thomas, S. Chess, and H.G. Burch, "The origin of personality." Copyright © 1970 by Scientific American, Inc. All rights reserved.

Thomas et al. then turned to the longitudinal study of 141 children from birth. In 1970, the study had been in progress for over a decade, and it had established that the child's original temperament usually persists over this time. They cite two particularly striking examples of this persistence:*

> Donald exhibited an extremely high activity level almost from birth. At three months, his parents reported, he wriggled and moved about a great deal while asleep in his crib. At six months he "swam like a fish" while being bathed. At 12 months he still squirmed constantly while he was being dressed or washed. At 15 months he was "very fast and busy"; his parents found themselves "always chasing after him." At two years he was "constantly in motion, jumping and climbing." At three he would "climb like a monkey and run like an unleashed puppy." In kindergarten his teacher reported humorously that he would "hang from the walls and climb on the ceiling." By the time he was seven Donald was encountering difficulty in school because he was unable to sit still long enough to learn anything and disturbed other children by moving rapidly around the classroom.
>
> Clem exemplifies a child who scored high in intensity of reaction. At four and a half months he screamed every time he was bathed, according to his parents' report. His reactions were "not discriminating—all or none." At six months during feeding he screamed "at the sight of the spoon approaching his mouth." At nine and a half months he was generally "either in a very good mood, laughing or chuckling," or else screaming. "He laughed so hard playing peekaboo he got hiccups." At two years his parents reported: "He screams bloody murder when he's being dressed." At seven they related: "When he's frustrated, as for example when he doesn't hit the ball very far, he stomps around, his voice goes up to its highest level, his eyes get red and occasionally fill with tears. Once he went up to his room when this occurred and screamed for half an hour" (Thomas et al., 1970, p. 104).

Not all children in the study showed this basic constancy of tempera-

* From A. Thomas, S. Chess, and H.G. Burch, "The origin of personality." Copyright © 1970 by Scientific American, Inc. All rights reserved.

ment. Some changed significantly with time, perhaps because of circumstances in the child's environment, perhaps because inconsistency in temperament is itself a basic attribute of some children.

Thomas et al. found that the nine characteristics they identified tend to fall in three clusters, shown on Table 7.2. Approximately 40% of the children fell in the easy category, 15% displayed a temperament termed slow to warm up because they tended to withdraw and were slow to adapt, and 10% of the children were classified as difficult. The rest of the children —35%—could not be described in any of these categories.

The authors note that the effects of the environment in general, and socialization in particular, depend upon the temperament of the individual child. They point out, for example, that the child's temperament determines his response to various child-rearing styles. They suggest that there is no single approach to child rearing or education that will work with all children. The difficult child requires unusually objective and consistent treatment that takes the child's temperament into account. The slow-to-warm-up child needs time to adapt to new environments to help him overcome his natural tendency to withdraw, but he also requires encouragement to try new experiences or he may reject anything new. For example, one boy at age 10 lived on a diet consisting primarily of hamburgers, applesauce, and medium-boiled eggs. Thomas et al. also feel that it is important to harmonize the demands of the environment with the child's temperament. They point out that a demand which conflicts too strongly with a child's temperament is likely to cause great stress. For example, it is extremely difficult for an active child to endure a long automobile trip without frequent stops to allow him to run around and let off steam, and a persistent child should not be called away from an activity without adequate warning.

SEX DIFFERENCES IN TEMPERAMENT

The results of the Thomas et al. study suggest strongly that characteristic modes of emotional response are present in early life and that they often persist at least into late childhood. Other evidence suggests that there are general sex differences in temperament. In particular, males tend to be more aggressive than females and females are more passive and nurturant than males.

The Evidence for Sex Differences in Temperament   The degree to which sex differences in emotional behavior in human adults is based upon "wired-in" differences in temperament or differences in socialization is exceedingly difficult to determine, because both the temperamental difference and the socialization pressures are in the same direction.

The conclusion that some part of this difference involves innate differences in temperament that are not based upon socialization comes from several sources. First, as we saw in Chapter 6, male sex hormones are often associated with increased aggressive behavior in many species of animals, including humans. Also, among virtually all vertebrates and particularly among primates, male animals are more aggressive than females (cf. Scott, 1958a). For example, Harlow and his associates have noted very large sex differences in the rough and tumble play of young monkeys. This roughhousing, wrestling, and sham-biting behavior seems particularly important in the socialization of monkey aggressive behavior, and it is much more common among males than females. Harlow suggests that the sex difference in rough and tumble play is innate, and that it plays an important part in the shaping of adult monkey sex roles (Harlow, McGaugh, and Thompson, 1971).

That these differences in animals occur also in humans is suggested by the common finding that young boys are more aggressive than young girls (see Chapter 5). For example, we saw that one of Bandura's studies suggests that boys are more attentive to displays of aggression than are girls. It is not certain, of course, that these differences reflect wholly biological factors. Sex-role socialization begins very early and is pervasive: For example Lewis (1972) has noted that before six months of age mothers have more physical contact with male offspring than with females, perhaps because the boys are more fretful than girls. However, after six months the boys receive less physical contact than girls. Lewis suggests that this may be a result of the mother's wish that the boy be encouraged to be independent, and that he get out and explore and master his world. Perhaps as a result, by one year of age boys spend less time near the mother, venture farther from the mother, and look at and talk to their mother less than do girls.

Temperament and Cultural Sex Roles   Some might conclude that the argument that there are sex differences in temperament implies a tacit justification for sexual discrimination. This is not the case. If one accepts the principle of giving social rewards on the basis of achieved characteristics (education, skill, relevant prior performance, etc.) rather than acquired characteristics (family background, race, sex, religion, etc.), such discrimination is clearly without justification. Also, there is a range of individual differences in temperament within both sexes: there are aggressive females and passive males. Such persons tend to be particularly victimized by the inflexible adherence to sexual stereotypes, and they may be obliged to express themselves in disguised, and presumably less satisfactory, ways.

This is illustrated by the longitudinal study reported by Kagan and Moss (1962) which studied the stability of a number of kinds of behavior between childhood and adulthood. The study began in 1929 and ended in 1954 when the subjects were young adults. A summary of their results is shown in Figure 7.5. Passive and dependent behaviors in childhood were found to predict similar behaviors in adults among females but not males. Conversely, heterosexual behavior in adolescence (dating behavior) and childhood aggressive behavior were related to similar adult behavior among males but not females. Other behaviors, such as achievement strivings, sex-appropriate behavior, and spontaneity, were relatively stable in both males and females.

Kagan and Moss attribute this pattern of results to an interaction between temperament and cultural sex-role training. Passive and dependent behavior is often encouraged in females but punished in males, while the opposite is true of aggressive and sexual behavior. Thus, the aggressive behavior of a temperamentally aggressive boy will be discouraged much less than that of a temperamentally aggressive girl, and it will thus persist in the boy but not the girl. Achievement strivings, sex-appropriate

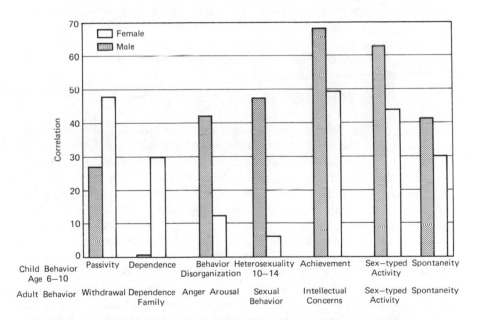

FIGURE 7.5   Summary of relations between selected child behaviors and similar adult behaviors. From J. Kagan and H. A. Moss, *Birth to Maturity*. New York: Wiley, 1962. Copyright © 1962 by John Wiley & Sons, Inc. Reprinted by permission of the publisher.

behavior, and spontaneity are encouraged among both males and females. Kagan and Moss suggest from this that, in order for a behavior to be stable from childhood to adulthood it must be congruent with social expectations.

When there is a conflict between the child's temperament and cultural expectations, the temperament cannot be expressed in direct and obvious ways. However, Kagan and Moss found evidence that temperament may find expression in less direct substitute behaviors, which are more socially acceptable (and perhaps less satisfactory) than the most directly expressive behaviors. For example, aggressive behavior in young girls predicted dependency conflict, intellectual competitiveness, and "masculine" interests in adult women, and passivity in boys was associated with sexual anxiety, noncompetitiveness, and social apprehension in adult men.

Nonverbal Communication of Emotion in Humans

We saw from the studies on monkeys that the ability to communicate emotion accurately is particularly important in the coordination of the behaviors of individuals. This seems to be true of human beings as well; recent research has shown that nonverbal behaviors may be as important to human communication as they are to the communication of other primates, and there is evidence that the ability to communicate accurately is related to a variety of social and emotional behaviors.

THE VARIETIES OF NONVERBAL BEHAVIOR

It is not possible here to give a comprehensive review of the large and rapidly growing literature of human nonverbal behavior, but some attempt should be made to indicate its scope. We shall concentrate on studies of the nonverbal communication of emotion by means of facial expression in humans. It should be noted that the communicative and social-regulatory functions of a wide variety of other human nonverbal behaviors have been pointed out in recent years. Duncan (1969) has suggested that the three nonverbal modalities which have received the most attention include the following: *Kinesics* is the study of body movements such as facial expressions, gestures, eye movements, posture, and so forth. The great current interest in kinesics is traceable in large part to the pioneering studies of Birdwhistell (1970). *Proxemics* is the study of the social and personal use of space. We referred to some studies of proxemics in Chapter 6 in the discussion of the territorial behavior of man (cf. Hall, 1959; 1966; Sommer, 1969). *Paralanguage* includes voice qualities, nonfluencies of speech, and nonlanguage sounds like yawning and grunting.

Behaviors in all of these categories are believed to be involved in the smooth regulation of human social behavior, although they may or may not be concerned with emotion or affect. For example, Weiner, Devoe, Rubinow, and Geller (1972) have discussed the role of nonverbal behavior in the flow of verbal communication. As a part of their analysis they hypothesize about the function of the orientation of the palms of the hands of a person who is speaking:

> *Palms up is equivalent to uncertainty or to "I think" or "I believe" or "It seems to me" in a verbal statement, and adds for the addressee the message that the issue need not be pursued since uncertainty is indicated. Palms down indicates an assertion with the speaker again communicating that the subject matter is not open to question—equivalent verbal statements are "clearly," "absolutely," "without doubt," etc. Palms out (i.e. facing toward the addressee) is a statement of assertion and is equivalent to the statement, "I shall say it" or "Don't interrupt."* (Weiner et al., 1972, p. 211).

The reader might like to evaluate the validity of these hypotheses by his own observations.

The study of all of these kinds of nonverbal behavior will undoubtedly add to the understanding and appreciation of the complexities of human communication and interaction. We must restrict our present attention, however, to the communication of emotion by means of facial expressions and gestures.

STUDIES OF FACIAL EXPRESSIONS AND GESTURES

Early Studies   It is natural to inquire about the extent to which the experiments we have covered on monkeys have implications about human social behavior. It seems reasonable to expect that the ability to send and receive nonverbal messages is important in human social behavior as well.

The experimental investigation of the facial-gestural expression of affect in man began in the 1920s. In 1929 Landis published a classic experiment. Landis photographed his subjects as they went through a series of 17 situations, which included looking at pornographic pictures, smelling ammonia, listening to music, decapitating a live rat, receiving a strong electric shock, telling a lie, looking at pictures of people with skin diseases, and so forth. He selected the more expressive photographs and asked 42 judges to describe the emotion being portrayed and the situation that might have evoked it. He reported that the emotions and situations described by the observers were completely irrelevant to the actual situations and introspective reports of the subjects. He concluded that it is impossible to name an emotion accurately on the basis of facial expression alone.

The negative results of Landis and some other early investigators unfortunately tended to depress interest in the area (cf. Ekman, Friesen, and Ellsworth, 1972). However, it now appears that these negative findings were due to inappropriate experimental methodology. Ekman et al. (1972) have summarized a number of criticisms of Landis' experiment and other early studies. For example, they note that Landis' subjects may have been motivated to inhibit and mask the natural facial display of emotion. Landis' subjects knew they were being photographed and knew that Landis was interested in facial expression. In fact, their faces were marked with burnt cork to facilitate the measurement of facial movements, and every time they made a facial movement, Landis took a picture of them. On top of this, all of Landis' subjects knew him personally. It is perhaps not surprising that they did not behave naturally in such a situation.

Landis' situation may have been so stressful that it masked any differential effects of the 17 tasks. Landis felt that the different tasks should elicit disgust, astonishment, sexual excitement, and anger, but the effect of the experimental situation itself may have overwhelmed such differences. Also, as Ekman et al. point out, many of Landis' subjects showed frequent smiles. Landis was sure that they were not feeling happy, and he saw the smiles as evidence that the smile is a meaningless expression. However, these smiles could have indicated embarrassment or stress. A motion picture of the subjects showing the facial context of the smiles might have made this clear.

More recent experiments have established beyond doubt that significant communication of affect through facial expression occurs in humans. Some of these studies have used as stimuli candid magazine photographs in real emotion-arousing situations, others have used posed facial expressions (cf. Ekman et al., 1972). We shall not consider all of these studies, but we shall outline studies derived from Tomkins' (1962; 1963) theory of emotion, cross-cultural studies, and studies that have used spontaneous facial expressions as stimuli. We shall also describe a technique for scoring the specific cues used in the facial communication of emotion.

Tomkins' Theory of Primary Affects   The question of whether facial expressions and gestures associated with emotion are culture-specific or universal to man has long attracted much controversy. Darwin (1872) argued for the universality of facial expression and even conducted the first study on the recognition of emotion from facial expressions on photographs. He showed photographs of facial expressions to 15 persons and reported that 14 correctly guessed the approximate emotional state of the subject (Darwin, 1872, p. 186; reported in Izard, 1968).

Others have emphasized cultural differences in emotional expression (e.g. LaBarre, 1947; Birdwhistell, 1970). In a very influential early study, Klineberg (1938) pointed out a number of differences between Western emotional expression and that found in Chinese literature. He found, for example, that surprise may be signaled by standing on one foot or sticking out the tongue and that worry could be expressed by handclapping. Klineberg himself felt that some emotional expressions are universal and he gave many examples of cultural similarities in his paper, but his demonstration of cultural differences was emphasized by others, perhaps because it was consistent with the then-dominant behaviorism and environmentalism (Izard, 1968).

Those who have agreed with Darwin that there are some universal features in the facial expression of emotion have proposed a number of theoretical bases for this universality (e.g. Allport, 1924; Asch, 1952; Huber, 1931). Some have emphasized the role of evolution, others the existence of innate physiological programs, others the role of learning experiences universal to all human development (Ekman et al., 1972). These explanations are not, of course, mutually exclusive. One of the most influential theories has been that of Tomkins (1962; 1963). He postulated that there are innate neural (probably subcortical) programs that link evoking stimuli to certain *primary affects*—fear, anger, sadness, disgust/contempt, shame, surprise, interest, and happiness. He argued that each primary affect is associated with a distinguishable facial display which is universal for the human species. *Secondary affects* are derived from primary affects, and the facial expressions associated with them may be combinations of the expressions from the primary affects involved: thus smugness may be a combination of anger and happiness.

Studies derived from Tompkins' theory have been directed at the study of the universality of the primary affects and the components of the facial displays associated with them. Most of this work has involved the use of posed photographs, although recent studies have begun to use motion pictures and videotapes of spontaneous expressions as well. For example, a number of studies using posed photographs of emotional expressions have found that seven of Tomkins' primary affects—all save shame—consistently emerge when observers are asked to categorize posed photographs (Ekman et al., 1972). Ekman et al. suggest that these seven emotion categories are a minimal list, although not necessarily an exhaustive list, of those that can be judged from posed photographs. However, it is possible that a quite different set of categories may emerge from the study of spontaneous facial expressions in motion (cf. Eibl-Eibesfeldt, 1970; 1972).

Cross-cultural Studies   One of the ways to support the claim of the universality of facial expressions and primary affects is to demonstrate that facial expressions are categorized in the same way in different cultures. Such a demonstration would be particularly convincing if the cultures selected were isolated from one another. Thus, Ekman and his colleagues studied the recognition of photographs of posed facial expressions in two preliterate cultures—the Sadong of Borneo and the Fore of New Guinea—as well as five literate societies—the United States, Brazil, Argentina, Chile, and Japan (Ekman, Sorenson, and Friesen, 1969; Ekman et al., 1972). They selected as stimuli 30 standard photographs of the posed facial expressions of Caucasians from a total of 3000, guided by the facial affect scoring technique (FAST) which shall be described below. Each photograph theoretically was an unambiguous depiction of one of six primary affects. Observers were asked to categorize each photograph by selecting a word from a list of the six affects: happy, fear, disgust/contempt, anger, surprise, and sadness. They found that observers in both the literate and preliterate cultures were able to categorize the emotions as predicted more often than chance. However, the agreement was higher in the literate cultures. Also, the preliterate groups successfully tested were not totally isolated from outside influences: many in the Sadong sample had seen movies in a commercial center a day's walk from the village, and in the Fore sample only those more influenced by contacts with Westerners seemed able to complete the task because of problems with instruction and translation.

To avoid these problems and still study the most isolated of the Fore villagers, Ekman and Friesen (1971) constructed a different task. They told their subjects a brief story ("his child died and he felt sad"), showed them a set of three photographs of faces, and asked them to choose the face that was appropriate to the story. For their sample they selected only the most isolated subjects—those who had seen no movies, did not speak or understand English or Pidgin, had never lived in a Western town or government settlement, and had never worked for a Caucasian. The sample included 189 adults and 130 children of both sexes. This experiment was more successful and demonstrated that a large percentage chose the expected photograph. The only exception was fear, which was discriminated from sad, angry, disgusted, and happy faces but not from surprised faces.

Ekman and Friesen asked nine of the isolated New Guineans to show how their own face would look if they were the person described in the story. Videotapes of the resulting expressions were shown to 34 American college students, who were able to judge accurately poses of happiness, anger, disgust/contempt, and sadness, but not surprise and fear.

The findings of Ekman and his associates are corroborated in a study by Izard (1971), who studied nine literate groups from England, France, Germany, Greece, Japan, Sweden, Switzerland, the United States, and Africans living in France. Izard also asked his subjects to judge posed photographs. Taken together, these studies indicate that photographs and in one case videotapes of posed emotional expressions are categorized in similar ways in widely different cultures.

Eibl-Eibesfeldt (1970; 1972) has used a quite different technique to study universal elements in facial expression. He has filmed facial behavior as it occurs in natural settings in a wide variety of literate and preliterate cultures. To obtain candid films, Eibl-Eibesfeldt used a lens fitted with a mirror prism which makes it possible to film to the side, with the camera and the attention of the cameraman seeming to point away from the actual subject. Combining this technique with the fast- and slow-motion analysis of behavior sequences, regularities in behavior become apparent that are not normally noticed. For example, Eibl-Eibesfeldt noticed that a person eating alone often glances up and scans the horizon, a behavior also shown by baboons and chimpanzees. He suggests that it may be an innate alert behavior against enemies that has remained even though human beings are now generally safe while eating.

Eibl-Eibesfeldt has filmed in Europe, Kenya, Tanzania, Uganda, India, Siam, Bali, Hong Kong, New Guinea, Japan, Samoa, the United States, Mexico, Peru, and Brazil. He has paid most attention to mother-child behavior, greeting, flirting, praying, and begging behavior. He reports wide agreement between cultures in the expressions and gestures associated with such behaviors, using many photographs from films to illustrate these similarities.

Eibl-Eibesfeldt does not make the assumption derived from Tomkins' (1962; 1963) theory that specific facial displays are associated with innate primary affects. He feels that there are a number of invariant components of facial expression—fixed action patterns—which can be superimposed upon one another to yield a complex and culturally variable expression. For example, he has found that the eyebrow-flash is a common expression during greeting and flirting which may be an innate greeting expression (See Figure 7.6). He feels that such universal elements may be combined in culturally variable ways to arrive at complex greeting displays.

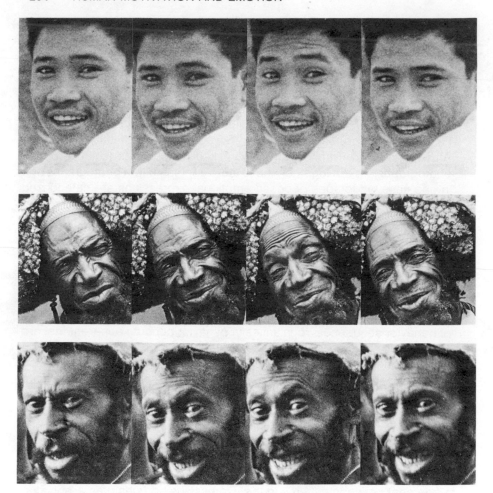

FIGURE 7.6   Eyebrow-flash during greeting. Upper row: Balinese of the island of Nusa Penida. Middle row: Paupa, Huri tribe near Tari (New Guinea).
Lower row: Paupa, Woitapmin tribe near Bimin (New Guinea). Similar observations have been made of subjects from Samoa and France. (Courtesy Profes-
sor I. Eibl-Eibesfeldt. From Eibl-Eibesfeldt, 1970, Fig. 265.)

The Facial Affect Scoring Technique (FAST)   One of the ma-
jor problems with the study of nonverbal communication in general, and
facial expression in particular, is deciding what to measure. There are no
generally accepted units of facial expression: usually investigators have
improvised their own units and/or have used global measures of expressiveness. A set of meaningful units would make it possible to study the
nature and timing of the specific facial cues important in communication.
Several scoring techniques have been proposed in recent years (Blur-

ton-Jones, 1969; 1971; Ekman, Friesen, and Tomkins, 1971; Grant, 1969). Ekman et al. (1971) call their method the facial affect scoring technique (FAST), and we shall consider it briefly.

FAST involves scoring movement in three facial areas, the eyebrow/ forehead, the eyes/lids, and the lower face. It employs an atlas of photographic examples which define movements in each area which, theoretically, distinguish between six of the primary affects: happiness, sadness, surprise, fear, anger, and disgust. Coders view each of the areas of the stimulus face separately and classify the type and duration of each movement according to the atlas. Thus, a coder looking at the eyebrow/forehead region can compare any response he sees with eight criterion photographs of that area in the atlas and can assign a code number to that response. There are 17 criterion photographs of the eyes/lids and 45 photographs of the lower face. The criterion photographs for the emotion of surprise are illustrated in Figure 7.7.

Since the criterion photographs are linked with different emotions, formulas can be used to derive the frequency and duration of occurrence of each emotion in each of the three regions of the face. Thus, the output of FAST is a series of scores for happiness, sadness, surprise, and so on separately for the eyebrow/forehead, the eyes/lids, and the lower face (Ekman et al., 1972).

Ekman and his colleagues have begun experiments designed to test the validity of FAST. In one, Ekman, Friesen, and Malmstrom (1970) showed American and Japanese subjects a film of autumn leaves and a stress-inducing film of sinus surgery. Unknown to the subjects, their facial behavior was videotaped and the FAST technique was applied. The results revealed a great difference in the facial behavior elicited by the two films. The stressful film showed much more behavior described by FAST as surprise, sadness, disgust, and anger and less behavior described as happiness.

This study also yielded data relevant to the hypothesis of the universality of facial expression. A detailed analysis showed that the occurrence of the six kinds of emotion in the three facial areas was quite similar for the Japanese and American sample. Thus, the two samples showed a similar distribution in the frequency and duration of facial expressions indicating happiness, sadness, surprise, and so forth.

It should be noted that, as Ekman et al. (1972) point out, these results provide only an initial validation of the theory that the six emotions in FAST are primary emotions linked with particular facial expressions. It may be that the facial expressions specified by FAST as reflecting a specific emotion may in fact often appear during other emotions and may often not appear during the appropriate emotion. For example, it may be that the furrowed forehead seen in Figure 7.7 is not inevitably linked with surprise.

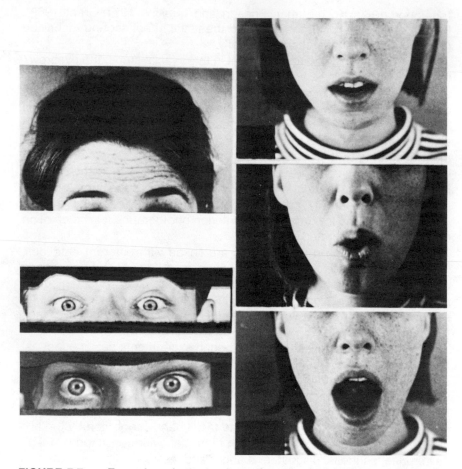

FIGURE 7.7   Examples of criterion items from the facial affect scoring technique (FAST) showing the brow/forehead, the eyes/lids, and the lower face items for surprise. (Ekman, P., Friesen, W. V., Ellsworth, P., "Emotion in the Human Face" 1972, Fig. 1.)

Indeed it seems similar to Eibl-Eibesfeldt's photographs of the eyebrow-flash greeting illustrated in Figure 7.6. Perhaps it is an innate greeting expression that often appears during surprise. On the other hand, perhaps Ekman, Friesen, and Tomkins are right and the kind of gestures photographed by Eibl-Eibesfeldt occur only when there is an element of surprise in the greeting.

Further research is underway that hopefully will establish whether or not the theory of primary affects is valid and if so whether or not the FAST photographs are correct representations of the associated facial expressions. Even if the theory is found wanting, however, FAST will likely remain useful because it represents a careful, sophisticated, and practical approach to the measurement of the units of facial expression.

Studies of Spontaneous Facial Expressions   Several studies have investigated communication through spontaneous facial expressions by using global measures of expressiveness. Some of these have recorded facial expressions in standard interview situations. For example, Ekman (1965) gave senders an interview in which the interviewer was initially hostile and threatening. The interviewer then explained the purpose of his hostility, apologized, and praised the sender for his performance under stress. A large number of still photographs of the senders' face was taken throughout the interview. Later, a random sample of photographs from the stressful and relief phases of the interview were given to 35 judges, who rated how pleasant or unpleasant the sender felt when the picture was taken. Photographs from the stressful phase were rated as significantly more unpleasant than those from the relief phase.

Howell and Jorgenson (1970) also gave a standardized interview with stressful and relief phases. They took one-minute motion pictures of the head and shoulders of the sender during each part. Judges later rated film clips taken from the stressful phase as more unpleasant than those from the relief phase.

Other studies of spontaneous expressive behavior in humans have used methodologies deriving directly from R. E. Miller's experiments on monkeys. Lanzetta and Kleck (1970) gave male senders 20 trials in which a red signal light was followed in a few seconds by a shock, and a green light was followed by no shock. Unknown to the senders, their facial expressions were videotaped for 12 seconds as they were anticipating shock or no shock. Observers (including the sender himself) viewed the videotapes and attempted to judge whether the sender was anticipating a shock or no shock. The observers should have guessed correctly 50% of the time by chance alone. The actual percentage of correct judgments ranged from 55% to 83%, with a median of 62%. Using a similar situation, Gubar (1966) also found significant communication.

INDIVIDUAL DIFFERENCES IN SENDING ACCURACY

Sex Differences   All of the studies of spontaneous facial expressiveness cited above found evidence of substantial individual differences in expressiveness between different senders. Another experiment suggested that there may be a sex difference in expressiveness. Buck, Savin, Miller, and Caul (1969; 1972) presented male and female senders with a series of 25 color slides arranged in five categories: sexual pictures of seminude males and females, scenic pictures of pleasant landscapes, maternal pictures of young mothers and children, disgusting pictures of severe burns and facial injuries, and unusual pictures of strange photographic effects. After each slide, the sender rated his emotional reaction to it along a pleasant–unpleasant scale. An observer watched with a hidden television camera (without audio) as the sender looked at and briefly talked about his reaction to the slide. The observer attempted to judge which of the five kinds of slides the sender was looking at. Chance judgment in this case would be 20%. The observer actually judged a mean of 40% of the slides correctly when a female was sender, but only got 25% correct (not significant) when a male was sender. The observer also rated how pleasant or unpleasant the sender's emotional response was on each slide, and his ratings were correlated with the sender's ratings to obtain the pleasantness measure of communication accuracy.* The average pleasantness measure for female senders was +.48, that for males was +.22. Thus there was evidence that, at least among the college student population tested, females are more accurate senders than males. This result was replicated in another experiment using similar methods (Buck, Miller, and Caul, 1974).

Physiological Differences   Several experiments also revealed an interesting and quite unexpected negative relationship between sending accuracy and physiological responding. Buck et al. (1969; 1972) and Lanzetta and Kleck (1970) both found that accurate senders had less of a skin conductance reaction to the emotional stimuli in the experiments than did the less accurate senders. This finding was replicated by Buck et al. (1974), who also found evidence that sending accuracy is negatively related to the sender's accelerative heart rate response on the slide trials. Furthermore, Miller (1973) found evidence of a negative relationship between sending accuracy and heart rate responding in medical school students. In other words, expressive individuals who make facial expressions that can be accurately judged by observers seem to have *smaller* physiological responses than do less expressive individuals. This relationship is illustrated in Figure 7.8. It indicates that the more accurate senders showed fewer skin conductance responses to the slides. It also shows

* The pleasantness measure is a correlation coefficient that can vary from − 1.00 (perfect negative relationship between sender's and observer's ratings) through zero (no relationship between ratings) to + 1.00 (perfect positive relationship between ratings). The higher the positive value of the measure, the better the communication.

...rted that "the greater the visible signs of ...sponse on the galvanometer" (quoted in ...lan, 1959). A similar observation was made ...dis (1932) found that, among 100 delinquents, ...motional that gave the fewest electrodermal ...d Solomon (1934) suggested that low electrod-... a sign of a "basic deficiency or disturbance in ... (quoted in Eysenck, 1967, p. 171). In 1935, H. E. ..."externalizer" to describe a person high in overt ... and low in skin conductance responding, and the ... describe one who has little overt expression but ...ctrodermal changes (Jones, 1935). The appropriate ...7.8 are labeled using Jones' terminology.

Jones first studied electrodermal responding in in-..., 1960). Few such responses could be obtained in early ...ome investigators had concluded that some part of the ...ervous system underlying the response was immature at this ..., Jones found that electrodermal responses could be elicited ... disturbing and mildly unpleasant stimuli, although their thresh-...er and the response smaller than those in older children. Also, ...ed that if the infant showed signs of external disturbance, such ... electrodermal responding tended to decrease. He hypothesized ... increase in the control of the overt display of emotion in older ... may be related to the increase in electrodermal responding with ...n older children, the increase of inhibition and of apparent emotion-...trol may not imply a diminished emotionality but merely a shift from ... to inner patterns of response" (Jones, 1950, p. 161).

Jones then studied children of preschool and nursery school age, and ...und that, with some individuals, consistent patterns of physiological and ...vert expressiveness could be demonstrated:*

> These patterns are of at least three sorts, as represented by the "externalizer," who displays a somewhat infantile pattern of marked overt but reduced or infrequent galvanic responses; the "internalizer," who reverses this relationship; and the "generaliz-

* From Jones, H. E. The longitudinal method in the study of personality. In Personality development in children. I. Iscoe and H. W. Stevenson (Eds) Chicago: University of Chicago Press, 1960. Copyright © 1960 by the University of Chicago. Quoted by permission.

that females te
tance respo
frequent
studie
sk

Emo

TH

The negative
accuracy and ph
explain it, Buck et
dependently found w
tween electrodermal
expression of emotion ha

back as 1920, Prideaux repo
emotion . . . the less the
Learmonth, Ackerly, and Ka
by Waller (1919–1920). La
it was the most overtly
responses, and Darrow a
ermal responding may b
emotional organization
Jones used the term
emotional expression
term "internalizer" t
large or frequent el
portions of Figure

Jones' Theory

fants (cf. Jones
infancy, and
sympathetic n
age. Howeve
in infants by
old was hig
Jones not
as crying
that the
childre
age: "
al co
oute

fo
o

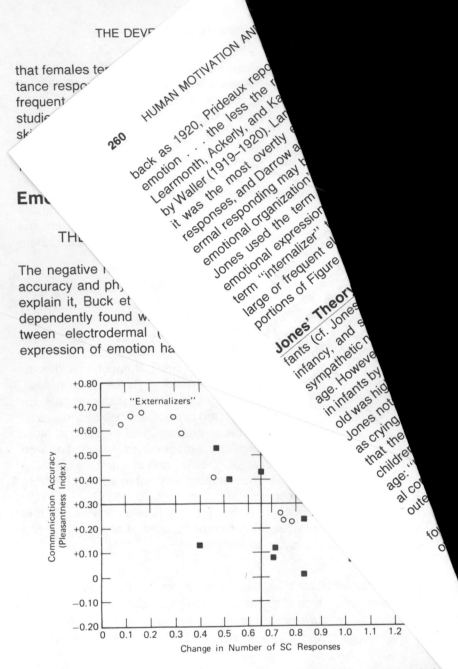

FIGURE 7.8   Relationship between communication accuracy and sender's skin conductance response. From R. Buck, V. J. Savin, R. E. Miller, and W. F. Caul, "Nonverbal communication of affect in humans." *Journal of Personality and Social Psychology*, 1972, 23, 362–371. Copyright 1972 by the American Psychological Association. Reprinted by permission.

*er," who tends to respond with a total discharge both overt and
internal. There was also evidence in a few cases of what might
be termed a compensating or reciprocal type of response. Such
individuals exhibited marked overt and marked galvanic reactions, but not on the same stimuli; their emotional expression
tended to be selective, so that a heightened discharge in one
direction was usually accompanied by a reduced discharge in
the other (Jones, 1960, p. 163).*

Thus, for everyone except the generalizer, an overt response was accompanied by a reduced electrodermal response. Some children seemed
consistently to be internalizers within the range of stimulus situations that
Jones provided, others showed a consistent externalizing mode of response, while still others showed an externalizing mode of response to
some stimuli and an internalizing mode of response to others.

*These results generated the following hypothesis: The relatively
undifferentiated emotional dynamic of infancy is extroversive in
nature, involving generalized movements and low thresholds for
vocal expression in crying. . . . As the infant passes into early
and later childhood, overt emotional expression tends to bring
disapproval and punishment rather than succorance. The internal avenues of discharge are not disapproved or inhibited; to an
increasing extent these hidden channels carry the efferent load
of major as well as minor emotional changes. The wider range
of emotional patterns which now appears may be due partly to
genetic factors and partly to differences in parental discipline
and other conditions of the child's social environment (Jones,
1960, pp. 14–15).*

Jones then turned to the study of extreme high and low electrodermal
reactors (Jones, 1936). He used adolescents aged 11 to 18. Jones found
that high reactors manifested striking motor restraint: they were quiet,
reserved, well controlled, and deliberative. Their mood levels seemed to
be relatively constant. They were given favorable assessments in social
characteristics, being judged as calm, poised, good natured, cooperative,
and responsible. In contrast, the low reactors were characterized as being
active, talkative, and animated. This uninhibited expressiveness was combined with apparently maladjustive social characteristics: they were

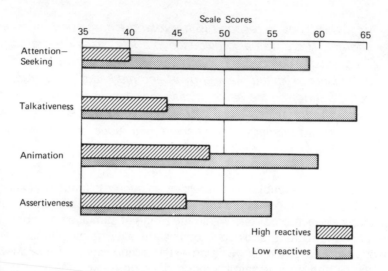

FIGURE 7.9   A comparison of high and low electrodermal (skin conduc-tance) reactors in social behavior. From H. E. Jones, "The study of patterns of emotional expression." From FEELINGS AND EMOTIONS edited by M. Reym-ert. Copyright 1950. Used with permission of McGraw-Hill Book Company.

judged to be impulsive, attention seeking, and bossy (see Figure 7.9). Jones suggested that the low reactors seemed to be engaging in a mala-daptive, infantile mode of response.

A follow-up of Jones' studies suggested a much different evaluation of the adaptive value of the pattern of overt emotional responding as-sociated with high and low electrodermal activity. Block (1957) studied 20 high reactors and 20 low reactors from a sample of 70 medical school applicants. Their electrodermal responding was measured and each appli-cant was then interviewed by a psychologist. In this study, it was the high reactors who were judged to be maladjusted, even though they seemed to show the same reserved and responsible behavior. Psychologists judged the high reactors to be "withdrawing; worrying individuals who turn their anxieties toward internal routes of expression," while the uninhibited low reactors were seen as "independent, aggressively direct, and relative-ly non-conforming" (Block, 1957, p. 13).

The reason for the difference between the Jones and Block studies in the relative evaluation of high and low reactors is not clear. In both cases, the evaluations were made by trained psychologists. Perhaps behavior seen as adaptive and appropriate for young adolescents may be judged to be inappropriate in medical school students, and vice versa. The same behavior judged to be reserved and responsible in an adolescent may be seen as showing undue submission and caution in a medical student; the response seen as impulsive and bossy in an adolescent may be aggressively direct in a medical student.

More recent experiments have supported the general notion of a negative relationship between overt and physiological responding. Learmonth et al. (1959) correlated the skin potential responses of 20 student nurses to scores on personality tests (the Rorschach and MMPI). They concluded that the fluctuation in potential "seems to be less in those individuals whose personality structures are most consistent with the free expression of feeling" (p. 155). Similarly, Crider and Lunn (1971) found electrodermal lability to be negatively related to measures of extraversion and impulsivity, and Eysenck (1967) has summarized a number of studies which suggest a negative relationship between extraversion and electrodermal responding. Finally, as we shall see in Chapter 10, the reanalysis of several of R.S. Lazarus' experiments by Weinstein et al. (1968) indicates that subjects high in denial show more autonomic arousal than subjects low in denial.

We have seen that a great variety of studies employing a wide diversity of subject populations and experimental approaches has suggested that the overt display of emotion is often associated with little physiological responding, particularly electrodermal responding. Persons who show little overt display tend to have larger or more frequent physiological responses. This relationship is not a simple one. As Jones' studies show, the same individual might show an internalizing mode of response in one situation an externalizing mode of response in another, and that some (generalizers) may show both overt and physiological responding. Even among extreme physiological reactors and nonreactors, it is as yet unclear whether it is "healthier" to use an internalizing or an externalizing mode of response. Also, although Jones and others seem to assume that the inhibition of overt responding directly *causes* increased physiological responding, no one has actually proved that the relationship is a casual one. No study yet answers the important question of *why* the inhibition of overt emotional responding is associated with increased physiological responding.

Sex Differences in Response Modes   In considering the meaning of externalizing and internalizing response modes, Jones (1960) suggested that, if overt emotional expression brings social disapproval, the overt responding will be inhibited and this will somehow cause an increase in the use of hidden "internal avenues of affect discharge." Although this explanation does not specify the mechanism by which inhibition causes increased physiological responding, it does shed light on the finding illustrated in Figure 7.8 that there is a tendency for males to be internalizers and females to be externalizers, at least when responding to emotionally loaded color slides. In U.S. culture, overt emotional responding is more likely to evoke disapproval when manifested by young boys than girls. Boys may thus learn to inhibit and mask overt emotional displays. And this may in some way be associated with increased skin conductance responding.

A review of experiments of sex differences in electrodermal responding reveals that many studies show greater skin conductance responding among males than females (cf. Prokasy and Raskin, 1973). Graham, Cohen, and Shmavonian (1966) and Shmavonian, Yarmat, and Cohen (1965) report greater skin conductance responding in males than females in classical conditioning situations involving shock. Also, Craig and Lowrey (1969) report more skin resistance changes for males than females in a task involving watching another person receiving shocks, and McCracken (1969) reports higher skin conductance levels in males than females when listening to time-compressed speech. Interestingly, males showed *less* response than females on more overt indicants of affect. In both the Craig and Lowrey and McCracken studies, males rated themselves as experiencing less stress than did females, even though males had greater electrodermal responding.

Thus, in a number of emotional-arousing situations, males show an internalizing mode of response, showing relatively little overt reaction but a large physiological response, while females show the opposite, externalizing mode of response. It should be noted that this does not seem to hold in aggressive situations. As we say in Chapter 5, females show less tendency to commit physical aggression than do males, and they seem to manifest greater increases in blood pressure when aggressive. There is also evidence that females show greater skin conductance responding than males when required to give shocks to another person (Buck, 1972; see Chapter 9). Thus in aggressive situations, males seem to use an externalizing and females and internalizing mode of response. This is consistent with Jones' position, since aggression is inhibited in girls more than it is in boys. It also suggests again that the same individual can show an externalizing mode of response in one situation and an internalizing mode of response in another.

Personality Differences in Response Modes   One personality measure found to be related to externalizing and internalizing response modes is Eysenck's (1959) extraversion–intraversion scale. We saw that Crider and Lunn (1971) found greater electrodermal activity among persons scoring high in intraversion. Buck et al. (1972) found among females that accurate senders scored high in extroversion. Buck et al. (1974) distinguished between externalizers and internalizers according to both their facial expressiveness and physiological responding and found that internalizers scored higher in introversion than externalizers.

Buck et al. (1974) also found that internalizers had lower self-esteem than externalizers and that they were more likely to describe their emotional response to the color slides in impersonal terms, not referring to themselves or their own feelings. When looking at a picture of a landscape, for example, an internalizer was likely to say "that's a nice picture," while an externalizer would probably say "that makes me feel good." Perhaps persons using an internalizing mode of response are less likely to acknowledge to others, either verbally or nonverbally, that they are affected by an emotional stimulus.

Response Modes and Bodily Stress   It may well be that internalizing and externalizing response modes are relevant to the problem of the psychological causation of illness. It is known that emotional problems underlie or at least contribute to a wide variety of somatic illnesses, but little is understood about the bodily mechanisms involved. The negative relationship between overt emotional expression and physiological responding could illustrate the functioning of a part of this mechanism. The increased level of physiological responding involved in the internalizing mode of response may well be stressful to the internal economy of the body (see Chapter 2).

It is interesting in this regard that an interview study of 20 patients with psychosomatic illnesses found that 16 were similar to the internalizing subjects in the Buck et al. (1974) experiment in that they could seemingly not put their own private experiences into words (Nemiah and Sifneos, 1970). The patients fully recounted events that happened to them and their own actions, but there was a nearly total absence of material relating to their own thoughts, feelings, and attitudes. The authors suggested that this "striking incapacity for the verbal description and expression of feelings" does not occur with neurotic patients:

> *(The goal of the psychiatrist) is to have the patient express and describe, freely and in detail, the nature, quality and intensity of his inner feelings and fantasies. From his experience with psychoneurotic patients, the psychiatrist has learned that merely giving the patient the opportunity to talk about his troubles will usually draw forth from him a wealth of affect-laden material . . . (In contrast, the patient with psychosomatic illness) tends*

> *to minimize affect and emotional involvement . . . The way to*
> *the patient's inner, private life seems to be blocked up by an im-*
> *pregnable wall (Nemiah and Sifneos, 1970, p. 155–156).*

As a result of this inability to express emotion, the psychosomatic patient is hard to work with in the traditional psychotherapy setting. The authors conclude that psychosomatic illness often involves a problem of emotional communication.

Related to this is the possibility that the lessened expressiveness among males that we have encountered may be associated with physiological stress which in turn contributes to the shorter lifespan of men and the greater incidence of such disorders as heart disease, peptic ulcer, and gastrointestinal cancer. The finding that men tend to be internalizers and women externalizers in some emotional situations is consistent with this notion. However, these possibilities must be investigated by further research before any definite conclusions can be drawn.

INTROVERSION-EXTRAVERSION AND EMOTIONAL EXPRESSION

There is a theory that is very different from that of Jones that also has implications about emotional expression. We have seen that Eysenck's extraversion-intraversion scale has shown relationships with sending ability and electrodermal responding and that it has differentiated persons using an internalizing mode of response from those responding in an externalizing fashion. It would be instructive, then, to inquire into the theoretical basis of Eysenck's scale.

Eysenck first became convinced of the usefulness of the introvert–extravert dimension in the course of large-scale factor analytic studies begun during World War II. Psychiatric ratings and life history information were available for large numbers of soldiers suffering from neuroses. These were subjected to factor analysis and two major variables which were substantially independent of one another were extracted. These were identified as neuroticism–stability and extraversion–introversion. The neuroticism dimension seemed to involve the degree of emotionality of an unstable kind. The externalizer-internalizer dimension involved the degree of sociability, impulsiveness, activity, liveliness, and excitability.

Eysenck (1970) argues that these variables are basic to personality and that their importance has been recognized from antiquity in Galen's typology of melancholics, cholerics, sanguines, and phlegmatics. Cholerics and melancholics are inclined to strong emotion, and are thus high in

FIGURE 7.10   Diagram showing Galen's typology (*inner circle*) and Eysenck's description of the Introvert–Extravert and Unstable–Stable (Neurotic–Stable) personality dimensions (*outer circle*). From Eysenck, H. J. THE BIOLOGICAL BASIS OF PERSONALITY. 1967. Courtesy of Charles C. Thomas, Publisher, Springfield, Illinois.

neuroticism, while phlegmatics and sanguines are more stable. Also, melancholics and phlegmatics tend toward introversion, and sanguines and cholerics toward extraversion (see Figure 7.10).

In 1957, Eysenck brought the learning theory concepts of cortical excitation and inhibition into the theory. He posited that in the introvert, excitatory potentials are generated more easily, and inhibitory potentials less easily, than in the extravert. This makes the introvert more subject to conditioning from the environment than the extravert. In 1967 he posited that this difference rests upon differences in the ascending reticular activating system (ARAS—see Chapter 2). He suggested that the ARAS has a lower threshold of activation in the introvert than the extravert, and that is why it is easier to generate an excitatory potential, and harder to generate an inhibitory potential, in the introvert. Eysenck thus feels that the basic difference between introverts and extraverts is an innate, presumably hereditary, physiological difference.

Because the introvert is more easily conditioned than the extravert, he is more susceptible to the process of socialization. Eysenck considers the process of socialization to be a process of conditioning. He thinks of the conscience as "a cluster of classically conditioned fear reactions" (Gray, 1972, p. 197). Everything being equal, an introvert should be more completely conditioned and thus socialized than an extravert, and this results in many of the behavioral and psychological differences between introverts and extraverts. For example, if an introvert becomes neurotic he tends to show signs of oversocialization: the dysthymic neuroses such as phobias, reactive depression, obsessive and compulsive disorders, and high anxiety. If an extravert becomes neurotic he tends to react with hysterical or psychopathic symptoms suggestive of undersocialization.

One important implication of this position relevant to our present interest is that introverts should have a higher level of physiological arousal than extraverts. Some of the strongest evidence for this hypothesis is that, as we have seen, electrodermal responding is greater among introverts than extraverts. Eysenck (1967) also summarizes a study in which heart rate was higher in introverts (Claridge and Harrington, 1963a). The only other physiological response specifically related to intraversion-extraversion in Eysenck's 1967 book is the EEG, which Eysenck predicts will show faster activity for introverts than extraverts. The literature on this question is complex and confusing: Gale, Coles, Kline, and Penfold (1971) point out seven studies that support Eysenck's prediction (Claridge and Harrington, 1963b; Gale, Coles, and Blaydon, 1969; Gottlober, 1938; Hume, 1968; Marton and Urban, 1966; Mundy-Castle, 1955; and Savage, 1964) and six, including their own, which do not support it (Broadhurst and Glass, 1960; Costa, Cox, and Kateman, 1965; Fenton and Scotton, 1967; Glass and Broadhurst, 1966; Henry and Knott, 1941).

A basic postulate of Eysenck's theory is that introverts condition more rapidly than extraverts. The data on this point too has been conflicting. Eysenck and Levey (1972) have concluded that introverts condition more rapidly only under certain conditions: when the CS is weak, when there is a short CS-UCS interval, and under conditions of partial reinforcement (see Chapter 4). This admission has serious consequences for the theory, which posits that introverts and extraverts condition differently during the process of socialization. It seems highly unlikely that the conditioning associated with socialization would follow the precise stipulations laid down by Eysenck and Levey.

Gray (1972) has recognized this critical theoretical problem and seeks to alleviate it by suggesting that the introvert is more susceptible to punishment rather than generally more conditionable. In doing so, he proposes an extension of Eysenck's theory about the physiological basis of extraversion and introversion. Basing his reasoning upon the apparently extraverting effect of the barbiturate drug sodium amobarbital, Gray speculates that the physiological site of action of this drug involves the hippocampus and part of the septal area which seems to act as a pacemaker for the hippocampal theta rhythm (4.8 *hz* electrical activity that is recorded from the hippocampus). He proposes that the theta rhythm response indicates the functioning of a neural system which is normally activated by frustration or nonreward. This theta response is presumed to be associated with the inhibition of whatever behavior had been associated with such punishment of frustration. The more activity in this system, the more effective such punishment would be in inhibiting behavior. Gray proposes that the more activity in the system, the more an individual is

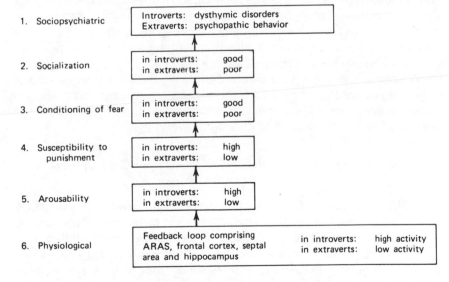

FIGURE 7.11   Gray's proposed modification of Eysenck's theory of introversion–extraversion. From J. A. Gray, "The psychophysiological nature of introversion–extraversion: A modification of Eysenck's theory." In V. D. Nebylitsyn and J. A. Gray (Eds.) *Biological Basis of Individual Behavior*. New York: Academic Press, 1972. Copyright © 1972 by Academic Press, Inc. Reprinted by permission of the publisher.

susceptible to punishment, and the more introverted he will be.

The ARAS may be involved in increasing activity in this septal-hippocampal system, so that Eysenck's proposal that the ARAS underlies introversion extraversion may be correct but incomplete. Gray also suggests that the septal-hippocampal system is represented at a higher level in the frontal cortex.

Gray's modification of Eysenck's theory is diagrammed in Figure 7.11. Activity in the septal-hippocampus system is associated with high arousal and high susceptibility to punishment. This in turn leads to easy fear conditioning and, assuming that socialization involves mostly the conditioning of fear responses, this leads to good socialization. The result is an introverted individual.

Gray's explanation is highly speculative and its adequecy has yet to be tested. It might be noted that Eysenck and Gray are concerned with the same kind of relationship that Jones (1950) noted in the literature of externalizing–internalizing: that the free expression of emotional behavior is often negatively associated with physiological responding. However, they interpret this relationship in a way directly opposite to Jones' explanation. Jones suggests that rigorous socialization experiences cause physiological arousal. Eysenck and Gray say that innate physiological mechanisms associated with high arousal cause socialization to be more effective. Jones' explanation implies that learning and experience determine the physiological response, Eysenck's and Gray's explanations imply the opposite. These are very different explanations for the same kind of empirical relationship. At present, there does not appear to be enough evidence about the causal relationships between the physiological and overt expression of emotion to choose between them.

NONVERBAL SENDING ACCURACY IN CHILDREN

Sex Differences   One potential source of such evidence is the study of the development of emotional expression and physiological responding in children. As an example, the basis of the sex and personality differences in sending accuracy has been clarified by the study of communication accuracy in young children. It was reasoned that, if girls are superior senders in early childhood, it would tend to support the hypothesis that their greater expressiveness as adults is based on innate, unlearned factors of some kind. On the other hand, if no sex difference exists in young children, it would tend to support the notion that the difference in adulthood is based upon the sex-role learning.

Buck, Worthington, and Schiffman (1973; Buck, 1975) developed a technique for measuring sending ability in children from the experiments on the spontaneous reactions of adults to emotionally loaded color slides. Children ages four to six were shown 16 slides in four categories: familiar people were pictures of the child himself and his friends at nursery school, unfamiliar people were pictures of persons unknown to the child, unpleas-

FIGURE 7.12   Examples of stimuli used to evoke facial responces in young children: a, familiar; b, unfamiliar; c, unusual; d, unpleasant (Photos a, b, c, by R. Buck; d, Sybil Shelton/Monkmeyer)

ant slides were pictures found to be mildly unpleasant to children, and unusual slides were strange photographic effects (see Figure 7.12). The child rated his reaction to each slide along a pleasant–unpleasant scale on a specially constructed rating scale.

Videotapes of the child's reactions, showing his upper chest and face, were taken by a hidden camera. These were observed by the child's mother and by groups of 10–14 undergraduate observers. The observers attempted to guess what kind of slide the child watched on each trial and how pleasant or unpleasant his reaction was. Results indicated that, although there were marked individual differences between children in their tendency to send accurate nonverbal messages in this situation, overall communication was statistically significant both when the mother was observer and when the undergraduates were observing.

The results seemed most consistent with the hypothesis that the sex difference in sending ability is based upon sex-role learning. There was no evidence of a large sex difference in sending accuracy in these children. There was no difference when the mother was observing, although the undergraduates were found to guess the kind of slide being viewed by the girls more frequently than they did those viewed by the boys. The authors suggested that this may indicate the initial emergence of the eventually greater sending accuracy of women.

Personality Differences   To explore the meaning of the individual differences in sending accuracy that were observed in the children, a scale was constructed from the results of previous experiments that had investigated internalizing versus externalizing modes of response to emotion. The scale consisted of a series of statements about attributes previously found to distinguish externalizers from internalizers. Thus, different items asked whether the stimulus person "plays alone most of the time," "often shows aggression," "is co-operative," and so forth. This scale was given to teachers in the nursery school who knew all of the children in the study, and their ratings of the children on each item were correlated with the children's sending ability.

The results were quite clear. Sending accuracy was positively related to a number of attributes previously found to distinguish externalizers, such as high activity level, direct expression of hostility, and being an extravert. Sending ability was negatively related to many of the attributes of internalizers, such as cooperation, emotional control, and solitary play (See Table 7.3). The pattern of relationships between sending accuracy and the teachers' ratings depicted the more expressive children as being more sociable and having many friends, although they were also impulsive, aggressive, bossy, and hard to get along with. This picture of the

TABLE 7.3   ITEMS FOUND TO BE RELATED TO COMMUNICATION AC-CURACY IN YOUNG CHILDREN.

A. Items positively correlated with sending accuracy.

Often shows aggression.
Has a high activity level.
Has many friends at the school.
Expresses his feelings openly.
Is impulsive.
Is often difficult to get along with
Expresses his hostilities directly
Tends to be rebellious and nonconforming.
Is bossy.
Often dominates other children.
Is an extravert.

B. Items negatively correlated with sending accuracy.

Plays alone much of the time.
Is shy, fear strangers.
Keeps to himself.
Is emotionally inhibited.
Controls his emotions.
Is quiet and reserved.
Is cooperative.
Is an introvert.

outgoing but impulsive externalizer and the responsible but inhibited internalizer is quite consistent with the results of previous experiments (see above).

This finding that personality patterns closely resembling those of the internalizer–externalizer and the introvert–extravert are found to be associated with nonverbal expressiveness in young children is consistent with the hypothesis that such patterns are unlearned. Thus, this study is consistent with the notion that the sex difference in sending accuracy in adults is based upon sex-role learning, while the personality difference may well be based upon unlearned factors. More research is needed, however, before these hypotheses are accepted or rejected with any certainty.

At the beginning of this chapter we asked whether it is healthier to inhibit emotion or to express it directly. We can now see that there is no simple answer to this question. Whether an internalizing or externalizing mode of emotional expression is considered even by trained psychologists to be healthy or not may depend partly upon who is doing the expressing, as well as the situation in which the expression is occurring.

The direct effects of emotional expression on bodily functioning are unclear. We have seen that there is a very interesting negative relationship between emotional expression and physiological responding, but the mechanisms underlying this relationship is unknown. However, it does appear that large physiological responses which may be disruptive to the internal bodily economy are often accompanied by an inability to accurately communicate one's emotional state to others via nonverbal expressions and gestures. Perhaps one does not have to act out his feelings overtly to deal with his emotions without internal stress. Perhaps it is enough if one is expressive enough to accurately communicate his feelings to those around him, so that they can understand him and act appropriately. This form of emotional expression—accurate emotional communication—may well be healthy for both the individual and society.

Summary

We have been treating emotions and motives as processes taking place within the organism which are normally hidden to the observer unless special measurement techniques are used. In this chapter we considered the process of emotional expression, asking in part whether the free outward expression of emotions and motives may be associated with different internal processes than the inhibition of outward expression.

Consideration of the development of emotional expression in nonhuman primates revealed that the production and recognition of some expressions may be innate. However, the correct use of these expressions in the regulation of social behavior appears to require early experience in social relationships with other monkeys. In rhesus monkeys, it appears that an infant must establish friendly affectional relationships with other monkeys before the emotions of fear and aggression develop. Otherwise, these negative emotions seem to color the animal's later relationships with other monkeys. The reason for the disruption in social relationships is unclear, but it may involve in part a disruption in the animal's ability to send and receive accurate emotional messages with other monkeys.

The analysis of the development of emotional expression in humans suggests a similar interaction between innate factors and learning experiences. There is evidence of individual differences in temperament which seem to be innate, but the expression of these factors is altered by learning. For example, there is evidence of individual differences in nonverbal expressiveness which are related to sex in adults but not preschool children. These differences may be related to temperamental factors in young children, while in adults the differences may be due to both temperament and sex-role learning: males may be taught to inhibit the free expression of emotion more than females.

Research on the communication of emotion via facial expression suggests that certain facial displays appear and are correctly recognized in widely different cultures. Other studies suggest that persons high in nonverbal sending accuracy show less evidence of autonomic arousal than persons low in sending accuracy. The reason for the latter finding is unclear: the widely differing explanations of H. E. Jones and H. T. Eysenck are considered.

This chapter again emphasizes how innate factors interact with learning in the determination of behavior: appropriate social experiences are necessary for certain innate mechanisms to function properly. This chapter also emphasizes the fact that the various observable manifestations of emotion and motivation—self-reports, physiological responses, and overt behavior—do not necessarily have a simple relationship with one another. Depending upon the particular display rules learned in a given situation, the self-report and overt response to emotion may be inhibited or exaggerated. This may be associated with physiological changes as well. A person who shows an appropriate and communicative facial display often has a smaller skin conductance response than a person with a less communicative display. The nature and determinants of the relationships between overt behavior, physiological responding, and self-report are poorly understood, and research is only beginning to be directed toward this question.

CHAPTER EIGHT

COMPETENCE

The Darwinian tradition fostered the notion among many psychologists that motivation must ultimately be related to the survival of the species. There was a tendency to argue that the bodily functions most essential to survival—the homeostatic needs of hunger, thirst, sex, and so on—must be the most basic kinds of motives. Thus, a concept of motivation emerged in which the satisfaction of hemeostatic needs is primary, while other motives are secondary, derived from the homeostatic primary drives.

In recent years it has become clear that much behavior is not related to the satisfaction of homeostatic drives and that in fact the homeostatic drives are relatively unimportant in complex animal and human behavior. Such drives as hunger, thirst, temperature regulation, and so on are highly interesting and important phenomena in their own right, but they are no longer seen as prototypes for all motivational phenomena.

Much of the disenchantment with drive theory derived from the analysis of exploratory and stimulus-seeking behavior. From this a new conceptualization has emerged which is still consistent with the basic Darwinian notion in arguing that motivation is related to species survival. However, in addition to the homeostatic needs, it is now recognized that the need for the organism to adapt to, learn about, and control the environment may be a built-in basis for behavior. The general term for the ability to know and deal adaptively with the environment is *competence*.

In this chapter we shall examine the classical drive theory and the studies of exploratory and stimulus-seeking behavior that called it into question. We shall then examine two approaches to explaining exploratory behavior: the concept of an optimal level of stimulation and White's concept of competence. We shall then consider Piaget's theory of cognitive development and its relation to competence. Finally, we shall examine one of the most extensively studied of human motives, the achievement motive, which can be considered to be a specific form of competence.

Exploration and Stimulus-Seeking

THE CHALLENGE TO CLASSICAL DRIVE THEORY

Classical Drive Theory   During this century, much of the thinking of academic psychologists about motivation has been organized around the concept of drive (cf. Cofer and Appley, 1964). The drive concept was introduced in 1918 by R. S. Woodworth, at a time when psychologists were attacking the unrestricted usage of the then dominant instinct theory. It formed an essential part of the learning theory identified to a great extent with researchers from Yale University and the University of Iowa: Clark

Hull, Neal Miller, O. H. Mowrer, and Kenneth Spence. In this section we shall briefly overview the basic tenets of classical drive theory. The reader is advised to consult Cofer and Appley (1964) for a more complete examination of the positions of these theorists.

Drive theory is based ultimately upon the biological *needs* of the organism. *Primary drives* are internal biological disturbances which result from natural tissue needs, such as those for food, water, air, sex, pain avoidance, temperature regulation, and so forth. The existence of a need is signaled to the organism as a relatively strong, persistent internal stimulus that energizes the animal's behavior. For example, the need for food causes an internal disturbance to which the animal responds at first with random activity. The drive, and thus the activity, persists until food is found and the need is reduced. This satisfaction, or *drive reduction,* serves to *reinforce* those responses that have most closely preceded its occurrence by strengthening the association between those responses and the stimuli in that situation. The next time that that need is aroused in that situation, the process is repeated. Since certain responses in a given situation lead more quickly and consistently to the satisfaction of the drive than do other responses, those responses tend to be reinforced more than others. The animal comes to perform responses that have been reinforced in the past: that is he performs those responses that have most quickly and consistently resulted in drive reduction.

As an exemple, let us imagine a rat that has been deprived of food and placed in the start box of a T-maze. The animal's general behavior is energized by the hunger drive, so that he is theoretically more active than a satiated rat. Eventually, he finds food pellets in the goal box at the end of the right alley. The resulting drive reduction reinforces the response of turning right, so that this response is associated with the stimulus complex of the T-maze. If the animal is put back into the start box, he will have a slightly greater tendency to turn right than before, and if he is similarly rewarded the right turn will be further reinforced. In this way, the animal learns the *habit* of turning right in the T-maze. Whereas the drive has *energized* the animal's behavior, the habit comes to *direct* behavior.

The evolutionary usefulness of this system is evident. The drive state energizes the animal's behavior. When the drive is reduced the responses contributing to this drive reduction are reinforced and eventually incorporated into habits. The habits direct behavior efficiently to the previously effective source of drive reduction whenever behavior is subsequently energized by that drive. It might be noted that there are tissue needs that do not have drive-inducing qualities in most species. Thus, no drive state arises in man in the presence of air with insufficient oxygen. In fact, oxygen deprivation often has euphoric effect, a fact which makes it particularly dangerous for fliers, miners, and others obliged to work in situations in which oxygen might become scarce. Similarly, dangerous doses of radiation do not stimulate avoidance behaviors as burns do. Apparently no mechanism for signaling the existence of these needs to the organism has evolved in most species, perhaps because such mechanisms do not normally confer a significant adaptive advantage.

The reinforcement of primary drives can lead to acquired or *secondary drives* via the process of classical conditioning. Neutral stimuli in the environment that are consistently associated with the reinforcement of a primary drive can come to be reinforcing in themselves. Thus, if a certain light is turned on whenever an animal is fed, it may become reinforcing in itself and the animal may press a bar or learn a maze to turn it on even without being fed. We saw in the last chapter that this notion of secondary drive was used by learning theorists to explain why an infant develops love for its mother: the mother is associated with the gratification of the hunger drive.

Any primary or secondary drive contributes singly or in combination to an undifferentiated *general drive state*. This state is assumed to interact with habit strength in determining an organism's performance. For example, Hull felt that generalized drive (D) has a multiplicative relationship with habit (sHr) in producing the excitatory potential (sEr) which underlies behavior (Cofer and Appley, 1964). This formulation may be written:

$$D \times sHr = sEr$$

It assumes that, if drive has a zero value, excitatory potential will be zero and there will be no behavior. In other words, like Freud's theory of instinct, this conception implies that when all bodily needs are met, the organism should theoretically have no drives and should therefore be more or less inactive until the next drive state comes along (Hebb, 1955).

Exploration and Reinforcement　　Drive theory has not fared well

on this implication that the animal should be relatively inactive in the absence of drives. In the early 1950s, a number of investigators began to show that healthy animals are not inactive when their bodily needs are met. They explore their environment and appear actively to seek out stimulation. In fact, the opportunity for exploration has been shown to be an effective reinforcement in the learning of a habit.

Some of the first observations of this kind were made by Harlow and his associates, who gave rhesus monkeys an assembled mechanical puzzle made of metal locks. The animals disassembled the puzzle and showed increasing adeptness with practice (Harlow, 1950; Harlow, Harlow, and Myer, 1950). Such manipulatory behavior was observed in infant monkeys as young as 20–30 days of age (Harlow, Blakek, and McClearn, 1956). Harlow argued that this manipulatory behavior is intrinsically motivating and is independent of the classical primary drives of hunger, thirst, sex, and so on and of secondary reinforcement based on those drives. In fact, there was evidence that the addition of a food reward in the puzzle *decreased* manipulatory behavior. If a raisin were placed in a part of the puzzle that was unfastened in a late stage of manipulation it interfered with the efficient solution of the puzzle. Also, after a monkey had received the raisin for solving the puzzle, his subsequent interest in manipulating the puzzle decreased.

Other experiments showed that the opportunity for exploration can act as a reinforcement. Montgomery and his colleagues carried out a series of studies which showed that rats would learn such conventional tasks as a Y-maze and a black-white discrimination for the reward of exploring a checkerboard maze (Montgomery, 1951; 1954; 1955; Montgomery and Segall, 1955; Zimbardo and Montgomery, 1957). Rats also learned to go to novel stimuli such as a goal box with an unusual paint scheme and texture in the walls (Chapman and Levy, 1957), and a goal box containing novel objects (Berlyne and Slater, 1957). Rhesus monkeys have learned and performed complex tasks for extended periods of time with the only reward being a brief opportunity to look out into the room. This reward was particularly effective if another monkey or a toy train were provided in the room (Butler, 1953; 1958; Butler and Harlow, 1957). All of these observations suggest that, under many circumstances and particularly in the absence of strong primary drives, animals will show activity and will even work to increase the amount and variety of external stimulation impinging upon them.

Studies of Sensory Deprivation   Another   kind   of   evidence against the implications of the classical drive theory came from the dramatic experiments on sensory deprivation in humans. The first experiment of this kind was reported by Bexton, Heron, and Scott (1954). They employed college student subjects to lie in a cot for 24 hours a day in a partially sound-deadened room wearing translucent goggles which prevented pattern vision and gloves with cardboard cuffs which reduced tactile stimulation (see Figure 8.1). The students were paid twenty dollars a day to do literally nothing.

The subjects showed a variety of emotional and perceptual effects which suggested that continued sensory deprivation is highly aversive. Very few were able to long tolerate this situation after an initial period of sleep, and they terminated the experiment despite what at that time was a generous wage. Prior to termination, they showed boredom, restlessness, irritability, and an apparent hunger for stimulation. Some subjects

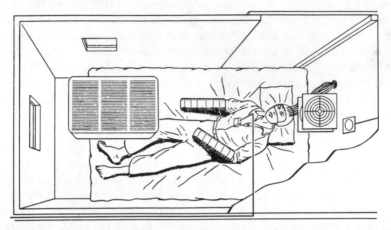

FIGURE 8.1   Diagram of the sensory deprivation situation used in the Bexton, Heron, and Scott experiment. From W. Heron, "The pathology of boredom." Copyright © 1957 by Scientific American, Inc. All rights reserved.

could choose to listen to a recorded talk for 6-year-old children on the dangers of alcohol, or a recording of an old stock market report. The subjects asked to listen to such normally boring material repeatedly. Some of the subjects reported vivid hallucinatory experiences, such as a "procession of squirrels with sacks over their shoulders marching 'purposefully' across a snow field and out of the field of 'vision,'" and "a miniature rocket ship discharging pellets that kept striking his arm."

A great volume of research on sensory deprivation has followed from the Bexton et al. (1954) experiment (cf. the review by Zubek, 1969a). The results show many complexities and inconsistencies which seem attributable to individual differences among subjects and procedural and methodological variations in different experiments. For example, the initial reports of hallucinations during sensory deprivation stirred great interest because of their possible relevance to clinical phenomena and to psychoanalytic and physiological theories (Zuckerman, 1969). However, no comprehensive explanation of the hallucinations has emerged. Some experiments found a low incidence or complete absence of these phenomena, and other studies have found unexpectedly that they can be obtained after very short isolation experiences. Some have argued that they are caused by the subject's set or expectation to have hallucinations, although this is strongly disputed. According to Zuckerman (1969), interest in the hallucinatory phenomena has diminished because of these problems.

There is evidence that prolonged sensory deprivation leads to a remarkable divergence of EEG, autonomic, and behavioral indices of arousal (see Chapter 3). The EEG in many subjects shows a general slowing of activity, with progressively lower frequencies in the alpha range and an increase in temporal theta rhythms. Although some subjects show little EEG change, others show a considerable slowing both during isolation and for a time following isolation. This slowing of the EEG has been tentatively attributed to disturbances in the ARAS due to the decrease in the level and variety of sensory input. Prolonged deprivation also causes increases in electrodermal responding and heart rate and decreases in blood pressure and respiration, along with many restless movements and reports of generally negative affect (Zubin, 1969b).

Explanations of Exploratory Behavior

THE CONCEPT OF OPTIMAL STIMULATION

Theoretical Bases   All of these observations suggest that the organism both needs, and will work for, an increase in stimulation under certain circumstances. This tends to cast doubt upon theory that behavior is always directed toward drive reduction, unless of course one argues that there is a drive to explore and seek stimulation. It is a tribute to the usefulness and resiliency of the drive concept that this theoretical path has been taken by many investigators. However, this step demands a major reformulation of drive theory. Before, drive reduction was assumed to involve a decrease in the level of stimulation impinging on the organism, and it was implied that a total lack of stimulation would be a desirable state. However, the concept of an exploratory drive demands that, under some circumstances, drive reduction involves an increase in stimulation. Some theorists have handled this problem by suggesting that there is an optimal level of stimulation, above which the reduction of stimulation is rewarding and below which the increase of stimulation is rewarding.

Some of these theorists have dropped the traditional assumption that drive reduction always involves a decrease in the level of stimulation impinging on the organism and have retained the assumption that behavior is always directed toward drive reduction. An example of this approach is Berlyne's (1960) theory. Berlyne defines drive as a "condition whose termination or alleviation is rewarding" (1960, p. 167). Thus, by definition an increase in drive cannot be reinforcing. Berlyne explains curiosity, exploratory behavior, and the effects of sensory deprivation by assuming that the relationship between drive and the variety and complexity of stimulation is curvilinear: both very low levels of stimulation and very high levels of stimulation are associated with high drive. Thus, a low level of stimulation is associated with a high drive state, the reduction of which is reinforcing.

Other theorists have retained the assumption that drive varies directly with organismic stimulation but dropped the assumption that only decreases in drive are rewarding. This position is exemplified by Hebb (1955), who approaches the problem from the point of view of arousal theory. In the company of other arousal theorists, Hebb argues that arousal is synonymous with the concept of generalized drive. As we saw in Chapter 2, arousal theory posits that there is an optimal level of arousal (see Figure 2.7). Hebb suggests that there is an optimal level of drive (or arousal) such that, when drive is at a high level, a response that decreases drive will be reinforced and that, when drive is at a low level, a response that increases drive will be reinforced. Thus, both increases and decreases in drive may be reinforcing depending on the initial state of the organism.

This general concept of an optimal level of stimulation or arousal has been adopted by many contemporary theorists as a way of explaining exploratory behavior and the need for stimulation (cf. Zuckerman, 1969; Suedfeld, 1969). The theories differ on a number of points, one of the most important being the definition of exactly what aspect of stimulation is involved in the optimal level. Some are couched in terms of simply the number of incoming stimuli, while others take the variety, meaningfulness, and information content of the stimulation into account as well.

Individual Differences in the Optimal Level of Stimulation

The increased importance of the concept of optimal stimulation has encouraged interest in the nature of individual differences in this variable. A number of investigators have suggested that people differ in their characteristic optimal level of stimulation, with individuals high in the need for stimulation characterized as "swingers" who seek out complex and interesting stimuli, enjoy working in the din of music and voices, and live in a general uproar because of their need to vary their environment and maintain a high level of excitement. In contrast, persons low in the need for stimulation have been characterized as "bores" who need absolute quiet in order to work and who manage their lives in a meticulously regular, predictable manner (Sales, 1971; Zuckerman, 1969).

There are interesting analogies between the notion of individual differences in stimulation and several other major lines of research, including Eysenck's work on extraversion–introversion and Russian work on I.P. Pavlov's neurological typology. Although it is too early to be certain, it is possible that these analogies reflect a basic personality dimension of major importance. However, this area is plagued by unusually difficult problems of measurement, and thus far the theories have been more exciting than the data has been convincing.

Pavlov's typology was developed from his observations of individual differences in the classical conditioning of dogs. It is based upon three dimensions of activity within the central nervous system: the strength, mobility, and equilibrium of the opposing forces of inhibition and excitation. Of these, the dimension of strength has been further developed at the Moscow laboratory of B.M. Tepov, and it has received the greatest amount of attention from Western psychologists (cf. Gray, 1964). Fortunately, much of the work is now available in English in excellent sources (Nebylitsyn, 1972; Nebylitsyn and Gray, 1972).

In essence, it is thought that a given stimulus produces a greater excitation in the weak type of nervous system than it does in the strong. The stronger the nervous system, the less the excitation produced by a given stimulus. The weak type is therefore relatively reactive to stimulation and the strong type is relatively resistant to stimulation (Strelau, 1970). As a result, the strong type is insensitive to weak stimuli but is adept at dealing with strong stimuli, while the weak type is effective in dealing with weak stimuli but cannot cope with intense or massed stimulation (Sales, 1971).

The concept of the strength of the nervous system has stirred considerable interest in England because of its apparent similarity with Eysenck's concept of extraversion–introversion. As we saw in the last chapter, the extravert is assumed to be less arousable and susceptible to conditioning than the introvert. Eysenck (1966) suggested that the extravert resembles the strong type who does not react to stimulation, while the introvert resembles the reactive weak type. This contention has been questioned by some who regard the similarity as more apparent than real (Strelau, 1970; Nebylitsyn, 1972) and by some experiments which do not confirm Eysenck's hypothesis or suggest that, in fact, extraverts may have a tendency toward a weak nervous system (Mangan and Farmer, 1967; White, Mangan, Morrish, and Siddle, 1969; Zhorov and Yermolayeva-Tomina, 1972). At present the relationship between extraversion–introversion and strength of the nervous system appears to be in doubt, despite the interesting theoretical parallels.

The strength of the nervous system also has potential relevance to the concept of individual differences in the need for stimulation (Sales, 1971). Unfortunately, studies in this area are complicated by the lack of any simple, reliable, and generally accepted measures of either the strength of the nervous system or the need for stimulation. The most reliable measure of the strength of the nervous system used in Soviet laboratories, called the "method of extinction with reinforcement of the photochemical reflex," is laborious and time-consuming. Other methods involve the measurement of reaction times, electrodermal responses, EEG rhythms, and various sensory functions (Teplov, 1972). These measures do not always yield similar results. For example, Ippolitov (1972) tested the ability of sensory thresholds to measure strength, on the theory that weak types should have lower sensory thresholds than strong types. He measured sensory thresholds for vision, hearing, and the cutaneous modalities; strength was measured by the photochemical reflex. Results indicated that all three sensory thresholds were correlated with strength as expected, with strong individuals having higher thresholds. However, there were a considerable number of disparities between measures of the same individual: a person with a high threshold on one measure might have a low threshold on another. This was the case even though Ippolitov had initially discarded all subjects whose thresholds were unstable.

A number of investigators are working to develop and validate measures of the need for stimulation, some of them based upon the Russian research. For examples, Petrie (1967) and Sales (1971) have used the kinesthetic aftereffects task, which has been interpreted as a measure of an individual's tendency to augment or reduce incoming stimulation. Theoretically, a "reducer" on this task tends to damp down incoming stimulation and thus should have a strong type of nervous system and be high in the need for stimulation. Studies have shown that kinesthetic aftereffect reducers react favorably to such complex stimuli as an experimentally created psychedelic party (Sales, 1972). Also, reducers report more exposure to complex and intense social situations, show high levels of talking in a group discussion, exhibit high activity when left in an empty room for seven minutes, and show other evidence of being high in the need for stimulation (Sales, 1971; 1972).

Unfortunately, the kinesthetic aftereffects procedure has been found to have questionable reliability, and research findings using it have been inconsistent. Consequently, Sales and Throop (1972) suggested that measures of strength of the nervous system could be employed to measure the need for stimulation. Using an auditory threshold measure, Sales, Guydosh, and Iacono (1974) showed that high threshold (high need for stimulation) subjects were relatively unresponsive to simple stimuli and showed evidence of having greater desire for social stimulation.

Other investigators have attempted to develop projective and questionnaire measures of the need for stimulation (Maddi, 1961; Maddi, Propst, and Feldinger, 1965; Garlington and Shimota, 1964). For example, Zuckerman, Kolin, Prince, and Zoob (1964) developed the sensation-seeking scale (SSS) to quantify the construct of optimal stimulation level. It employs a diversity of items pertaining to the preference for the novel and unfamiliar, for danger and thrills, for extremes of sensation, and so forth. It has been used to investigate individual differences in the tolerance for sensory deprivation, with somewhat mixed results (cf. Myers, 1969), and has been related to a variety of personality measures (cf. Zuckerman, Bone, Neary, Mangelsdorff, and Brustman, 1972).

Myers and his colleagues have developed an instrument specifically designed to investigate sensory deprivation tolerance. It contains five subscales, each covering susceptibility to a potentially negative aspect of the sensory deprivation experience: quiet-dark-cell phobia, chronic worry, sociability, activity need, and thrill-seeking. The latter two scales relate most directly to the need for stimulation as it has usually been defined. The investigators found that volunteers for a six-day sensory deprivation experiment tended to be low in quiet-dark-cell phobia and activity need and high in thrill-seeking. Of these volunteers, the subjects who quit the experiment early were those higher in quiet-dark-cell phobia and higher in thrill-seeking than those who stayed. Thus, persons high in thrill-seeking tended to volunteer for the experiment but had little staying power. A subsequent factor analysis of this scale revealed that the activity need subscale was related to liking for contact sports in a factor named Vigor, which seemed to be a kind of need for stimulation with a healthy cast. The thrill-seeking subscale was highly loaded on a factor named Thrill, which was related to an insolence and sociopathy scale, among others. Myers suggests that this factor has a high sociopathic flavor and may relate to the view of sociopathy as a pathological stimulus-seeking behavior. The Zuckerman et al. SSS scale was loaded upon both the Vigor and Thrill factors (Myers, 1969).

Hopefully, future research will clarify the nature of the need for stimulation and lead to the development of valid and generally accepted measuring instruments. As Myers' result suggests, the need for stimulation may well be complex and multidimensional, so that no single measure will be able to capture all of its ramifications. However, the concept seems naturally suited to the theorizing about optimal levels of stimulation, and it has the potential for integrating the great body of Soviet research on strength of the nervous system with Western approaches to the study of individual differences.

EFFECTANCE MOTIVATION AND THE CONCEPT OF COMPETENCE

Another approach to the explanation of exploration and stimulus-seeking behavior does not use the concept of optimal stimulation as a central explanatory principle. Instead, it posits that exploration, stimulus seeking, and a wide variety of related behaviors are intrinsically rewarding. For example, Harlow (1953) considers such behaviors to be based upon innate propensities which are released by appropriate environmental stimuli such as a novel object, a puzzle, a new place, and so forth. It is easy to imagine how innate exploratory tendencies could be adaptive to some species. We saw in Chapter 3 that Glickman and Schiff (1967) noted that species who must search out food and are not threatened by predators show more curiosity behavior than species with an easily obtained diet who are threatened by predators.

In 1959, Robert W. White published an influential paper in which he attempted to gather together some of the important things that were missing from drive theory and also the psychoanalytic instinct theory. He reviewed the trends in psychology that we have considered and also related developments in psychoanalytic ego psychology and concluded that these developments compel a serious reconsideration of the whole problem of motivation. He argued that tendencies to explore, manipulate, and seek stimulation have properties very different from those of classical homeostatic drives or psychoanalytic instincts and that these properties have not been adequately considered in previous approaches to motivation.

Some exploratory and stimulus-seeking activity may be directed toward the maintenance of some optimal level of stimulation and novelty for the organism, but White goes further and points out that these behaviors have another common property: they have an effect upon the environment. He cites a classic study of children's play by Gross (1901), who attached great importance to the child's "joy in being a cause" in altering and dealing with the environment. The behaviors shown by a growing child begin with "sucking, grasping, and visual exploration and continues with crawling and walking, acts of focal attention and perception, memory, language and thinking, anticipation, the exploring of novel places and objects, effecting stimulus change in the environment, manipulating and exploiting the surroundings, and achieving higher levels of motor and mental coordination" (White, 1959, p. 317). White proposes that these and similar behaviors all involve the "effective interaction with the environment" and that they be gathered together under the general heading of *competence.* He argues that these actions are directed, selective, and persistent and that they are motivated by an intrinsic need to deal with the environment, which he terms *effectance motivation.*

To illustrate such behavior, White turned to the work of a Swiss psychologist who had had relatively little impact on American psychology at that time: Jean Piaget. Piaget (1952) closely observed and reported on the behavior of his own three children. For example, he gave his son

Laurent, age 10 months, a piece of bread to examine. Laurent dropped the bread many times, broke off pieces, and let the pieces fall. He seemed to watch the motion of the falling body with great interest. The next day, he resumed his research with other objects:

> *He grasps in succession a celluloid swan, a box, and several other small objects, in each case stretching out his arm and letting them fall. Sometimes he stretches out his arm vertically, sometimes he holds it obliquely in front of or behind his eyes. When the object falls in a new position (for example on his pillow) he lets it fall two or three times more on the same place, as though to study the spatial relation; then he modifies the situation. At a certain moment the swan falls near his mouth; now he does not suck it (even though this object habitually serves this purpose), but drops it three times more while merely making the gesture of opening his mouth (Piaget, 1952, p. 269; quoted in White, 1959, p. 319).*

White argues that this kind of behavior is not directed toward the fulfillment of any particular goal, but is associated with a general need to deal with the environment:*

> *If the behavior gives satisfaction, this satisfaction is not associated with a particular moment in the cycle. It does not lie solely in sensory stimulation, in a bettering of the cognitive map, in coordinated action, in motor exercise, in a feeling of effort and of effects produced, or in the appreciation of change brought about in the sensory field. These are all simply aspects of a process which at this stage has to be conceived as a whole. The child appears to be occupied with the agreeable task of developing an effective familiarity with his environment. This involves discovering the effects he can have on the environment and the effects the environment will have on him. To the extent that these results are preserved by learning, they build up an increased competence in dealing with the environ-*

* From White, R.W. Motivation reconsidered: The concept of competence. Psychological Review. 1959, 66, 297-333. Copyright 1959 by the American Psychological Association. Quoted by permission.

*ment. The child's play can thus be viewed as serious business,
though to him it is merely something that is interesting and fun
to do (White, 1959, p. 320–321).*

White feels that effectance motivation is neurogenic—energized by
the natural activity of the nervous system. Strong homeostatic drives may
take precedence over effectance motivation—one must eat to live—although White notes that children will often be so absorbed in play that they
refuse to eat or visit the bathroom. He characterizes effectance motivation
as "what neuromuscular system wants to do when it is otherwise unoc-
cupied or is gently stimulated by the environment" (p. 321).

White's notion of effectance motivation is quite similar to the kind of
motivation thought to underly cognitive development in the theories of
Jean Piaget.* We have seen that exploratory and stimulus-seeking behavior in animals has been explained as a result of the individual's need to
adapt to the environment. Piaget views the development of a cognitive
representation of the outside world and oneself as a kind of adaptation to
reality. He sees internal and external stimuli as potential sources of information to the individual. During development, the individual learns to transform, process, and integrate this information in such a way as to give
meaning to the external environment and his own internal bodily state.

Piaget's concerns are related to *epistemology,* the branch of philosophy which investigates the origin, structure, and validity of knowledge. In
this section, as well as the next chapter, we will examine what Kelley
(1973) has termed psychological epistemology, the process by which the
individual comes to know the environment and himself, and how he evalu-
ates the truth of that knowledge. This will not address the central and
perhaps insoluble problem of epistemology of whether our knowledge is
really accurate. (Bertrand Russell has pointed out that it is impossible to
refute a person who believes that the world was created five minutes ago,
complete with memories and records.) Instead, we will be concerned with
the epistemology of average persons, how they become convinced that
their knowledge is accurate, and how this affects their behavior.

Piaget's Theory of Cognitive Development

Jean Piaget was trained as a biologist, and this early orientation left its
mark on his theorizing. He sees a basic analogy between the development
of cognitive functions and the adaptation of the organism to its environ-

---

* *The term "cognition" has been defined in various ways. We shall define it
generally as a unit of knowledge about the environment or about oneself.*

ment, noting that both processes involve an interaction between the organism and the external world. Piaget feels that the cognitive system "constructs its own structure" in the course of adapting to the external world. We shall first examine Piaget's basic theory about the development of structures of behavior and knowledge which relates to the studies of curiosity and exploratory behavior considered above. We shall then illustrate this theory while examining the successive periods of cognitive development.

THE CONSTRUCTION OF REALITY

According to Piaget, the knowledge of a child is not a simple representation of the external world as seen by an adult. The adult representation of reality must be gradually developed, and it is this process that Piaget seeks to illuminate. He argues (1971) that knowledge does not arise solely from the object (the world) or solely from the subject (the child) but from interactions between the object and subject. In particular, the subject must act on the object—the child must act on the world—before he can come to know it: "In order to know objects, the subject must act upon them, and therefore transform them; he must displace, connect, combine, take apart, and reassemble them" (Piaget, 1971, p. 704). It is only with long practice with such *transformations* that it becomes possible for the child to come to know what belongs to himself as an active subject, what belongs to the object, and what belongs to the action.

Assimilation and Accommodation   The major concepts that Piaget uses to analyze this process are *assimilation* and *accommodation*. Assimilation is a general biological process that involves the "integration of external elements into evolving or completed structures of an organism" (Piaget, 1971, pp. 706–707). Just as food undergoes assimilation when it is chemically transformed and integrated into the substance of the organism, so reality data are transformed in such a way that they become incorporated into the structure of the subject (Piaget and Inhelder, 1969. p. 5).* The relationships and connections inherent in reality data are not incorporated into the subject in any simple way: the subject becomes aware of such connections only to the degree that he can assimilate them. Thus the organizing activity of the subject, like the process of the digestion of food, is necessary. The degree of assimilation is determined by the

* This structure in the infant consists of action-schemes, and in the older child it involves the operations of thought. Piaget considers the latter to be interiorized actions which can be performed physically or mentally.

existing structure: in general, if the reality data are not too discrepant from the previously established structure, those data are assimilable. Reality data are, in effect, filtered through the existing structure in the process of assimilation. Once assimilated, they may modify and enrich the existing structure.

This modification of the assimilatory structure to fit the elements it assimilates is termed accommodation. Accommodation is a kind of cognitive adaptation: the structure used by the subject to deal with reality is progressively modified to fit reality. Thus, new elements are added to the structure through assimilation, and the structure itself is changed through accommodation. As Baldwin (1967) explains it:

> *Assimilation describes the capacity of the organism to handle new situations and new problems with the present stock of mechanisms; accommodation describes the process of change through which the organism becomes able to manage situations which are at first too difficult for it (Baldwin, 1967, p. 176).*

The subject must be able to assimilate a new situation to some degree before accommodation is possible. If a situation is partially, but not completely, assimilated, Piaget considers experience with that situation to be a food or *aliment* for the structure. Such a situation demands some accommodation—it is a challenge. Such situations are assumed to motivate the organism: the relevant behaviors or mental operations are activated by the intrinsic qualities of the situation.

As an example of this process in an infant, Baldwin (1967) suggests an eight-month-old child who cannot pick up a marble, although he can pick up a slightly larger object such as a block. Accommodation will not begin until the child can assimilate marbles sufficiently to begin to try to pick them up. The object must appear to him to be graspable. Once the child begins to try to pick up marbles he may try persistently and repeatedly. Gradually, he acquires the ability to pick up marbles—this is the process of accommodation. Once the ability is acquired, accommodation has occurred and the marbles are fully assimilated with respect to picking them up. Piaget feels that at this point an *equilibrium* has been established between assimilation and accommodation. Now the task is no longer challenging and it loses its ability to be intrinsically motivating. The child no longer seems to be interested in picking up marbles precisely because the behavior can be performed easily and effectively (Baldwin, 1967).

In other words, the aspects of a situation that are assimilable but not completely assimilated intrinsically motivate the appropriate behaviors in the infant. Similarly, aspects of a situation that are assimilable (meaningful) but not completely assimilated (not completely understood) activate appropriate mental operations in an older child. Children develop unorganized belief systems which contain inherent conflicts and contradictions. Experiences in which these contradictions occur set up forces to harmonize the child's ideas into a more coherent system through assimilation and accommodation.

Equilibration   Piaget calls this process *equilibration* because it results in an equilibrium between assimilation and accommodation. When this equilibrium has been achieved, the situation has been mastered and the newly assimilated behaviors or mental operations become available as a tool for assimilating new things. Some new aspect of the situation may now become assimilable and begin to motivate behavior toward mastering it. In this way, novel (but not too novel) situations serve as aliment or food for further growth.

Elkind (1971) has conceived this equilibration process in terms of *cognitive growth cycles*. He suggests that every mental ability goes through a growth cycle characterized at the outset by stimulus-seeking behavior. Such stimulus-seeking is particularly evident when the child becomes absorbed in repetitive behavior. Elkind gives the following excellent example:*

> *I watched the child intently without disturbing her at first, and began to count how many times she repeated the exercise; then, seeing that she was continuing for a long time, I picked up the little arm chair in which she was seated and placed chair and child upon the table; the little creature hastily caught up her case of insets, laid it across the arms of the chair and gathering the cylinders into her lap, set to work again. Then I called upon the children to sing; they sang, but the little girl continued undisturbed, repeating her exercise even after the short song had come to an end. I counted forty-four repetitions; when at last she ceased, it was quite independently of any surrounding stimuli which might have distracted her, and she looked around with a satisfied air, almost as if awakening from a refreshing nap (Montessori, 1964, pp. 67–68; quoted in Elkind, 1971, p. 3).*

*From Montessori, M.J. Spontaneous activity in education. *Cambridge, Mass.: Robert Bentley, Inc., 1964. Copyright © 1964 by Robert Bentley, Inc. Quoted by permission.*

Like Piaget, Elkind feels that cognitive growth cycles are motivated by intrinsic growth forces and that these are largely dissipated when the cycle is complete and a new cognitive structure is formed. At this point, extrinsic motives and emotions take over the activation and utilization of the new ability.

The equilibration process, or the process of cognitive growth, proceeds in a step-by-step manner. At each level of development, the child encounters new problems which cause a new phase of challenging assimilatory distortions. These are gradually matched by accommodations until an equilibrium has been achieved. The child develops an increasingly broad, organized and ultimately abstract structure of behaviors and mental operations to accommodate his wider and increasingly meaningful experience. In this way, the child gradually constructs an inner representation of reality through his experiences with reality.

THE STAGES OF DEVELOPMENT

Piaget analyzes this development as a series of stages, each of which involves a qualitatively different style of mental functioning. We shall briefly examine these stages and some of the major events associated with them.

Sensory-Motor Period   The first stage of cognitive development is the sensory-motor stage, which occupies approximately the first 18 months of life. Piaget believes that the newborn infant has no *a priori* notions about the strange world he is thrust into. He is aware of his sensory experiences but has no way to organize or make sense of them: the initial experience of a newborn infant has been described as a "booming, buzzing confusion." As the infant's experience in this new world accumulates, consistencies occur, and these consistencies in experience form the basis for cognitive growth.

According to Piaget, one of the most important developments of the sensory-motor period is that the infant begins to behave as if the external world consists of stable and permanent objects. At first, the infant acts as if the existence of an object depends upon him perceiving it:*

> *The universe of the young baby is a world without objects, consisting only of shifting and unsubstantial "tableaux" which ap-*

---

* From Piaget, J., and Inhelder, B. The psychology of the child. *New York: Basic Books, 1959. Copyright © 1959 by Basic Books, Inc. Quoted by permission.*

> *pear are then totally reabsorbed, either without returning, or reappearing in a modified or analagous form. At about five to seven months when the child is about to seize an object and you cover it with a cloth or move it behind a screen, the child simply withdraws his already extended hand or, in the case of an object of special interest (his bottle, for example), begins to cry or scream with disappointment. He reacts as if the object had been reabsorbed (Piaget and Inhelder, 1969, p. 14).*

An older infant (seven to nine months) will begin to look under the screen when the object is placed there, as if he realizes that it still exists. However, he will still not behave fully as if the object is stable and permanent. Piaget suggests the following experiment:

> *Hide an object in A to the right of the child, who looks for it and finds it; then, before his eyes, remove and hide the object in B to the left of the child. When he has seen the object disappear in B (under a cushion, say), it often happens that he looks for it in A, as if the position of the object depended upon his previous search which was successful rather than upon changes of place which are autonomous and independent of the child's action (Piaget and Inhelder, 1969, p. 14).*

Eventually, the infant comes to seek the object soley in terms of where it was placed, and at a later stage he will begin to show the use of simple inferences in his quest for the object. For example, if an infant picks up a screen in search of an object and finds an unexpected cushion, he will immediately move the cushion as well.

Many other developments take place during the sensory-motor period. The child becomes able to coordinate and integrate information from different sensory modalities, and begins to act as if the different modalities were sources of information about the same object. For example, if the infant's mother moves her lips and the father speaks, an older infant shows signs of surprise while a younger one does not. Also, the infant begins to learn about spatial and temporal relationships and causality. A young infant, having learned that pulling a string on his crib causes movement in a dangling rattle, may continue to pull the string to affect other objects yards away, or he may try to turn on an electric light by squinting at the light switch. An older infant will not make these mistakes.

At the end of the sensory-motor period, the child has acquired all of the basic sensory and motor skills for exploring the environment. When he encounters a novel object, he uses the same behaviors to explore it that an adult would use: he picks it up, hefts it, looks at it and listens to it, feels it, shakes it, smells it, bites it, and so forth. However, Piaget feels that true mental life—cognitive and conceptual representations of reality—has not yet fully begun. The child, he believes, does not yet have the ability to represent an object or event internally in symbolic form. This ability, which Piaget calls the *semiotic function,* begins to become manifest at about one and one-half to two years. Its existence is conclusively demonstrated by several behavior patterns that require symbolic representation. One of these is *deferred imitation,* in which the child imitates a model who is no longer present. For example, one 16-month-old girl witnessed a playmate's tantrum, and an hour or two later after the playmate's departure, she laughingly imitated the tantrum. Another such behavior pattern is *symbolic play,* in which the child pretends that one object is another, absent, object. For example, one little girl, who had recently been impressed by the bells in an old church steeple, stood ramrod stiff at her father's desk making a deafening noise. " 'You're bothering me, you know. Can't you see I'm working?' 'Don't talk to me,' replied the little girl. 'I'm a church' " (Piaget & Inhelder, 1969, p. 59).

The semiotic function allows the representation of events and objects not perceived at the moment. This allows the internalization or interiorization of the child's actions into symbolic form, and this ushers in the next period of cognitive development.

Preoperational Period   Once the groundwork has been laid by the development of such basic sensory-motor schemes as the object concept and the semiotic function, the child begins a long period in which his internal cognitive representation of reality gradually becomes organized according to logical principles: He acquires the ability to use logical operations in guiding his behavior.* The first phase of this process is the preoperational period, which is a period of preparation during which the child usually appears to behave logically. However, special tests devised by Piaget and his associates reveal serious gaps in logical reasoning.

One of these tests is the famous conservation of liquids problem. The child is shown two identical glasses, *A* and *B*, and an equal amount of water is poured into each. A taller, thinner glass *C* is then produced, and

---

* Operations are defined as "transformations of reality by interiorized actions that are grouped into coherent, reversible systems (joining and separating, etc.)" (Piaget & Inhelder, 1969, p. 93).

the water is poured from glass *B* into glass *C*. The child is then asked which contains more water, glass *A* or glass *C*. During the preoperational period, the child will attempt to solve the problem by inspecting the glasses. If he notes that the column of water in glass *C* is higher than that in glass *A*, he will say that *C* has more water. If he notes that the width of the column of water is greater in glass *A* than glass *C*, he will say that *A* has more water. The same child may switch back and forth, saying that *A* or *C* has more water depending upon the dimension he is attending to at the moment.

In contrast, older children will say at once that the amount of water is equal in *A* and *C*. The perceptual approach to the problem is replaced in older children by statements based on simple logical operations: "Nothing has been taken away or added." "You can put the water in *C* back into *A*." "The water is higher but the glass is narrower, so it's the same amount." (Piaget and Inhelder, 1969, p. 98). The ability to use these logical operations characterizes the next phase of cognitive development.

The process by which the child gradually comes to organize his representation of reality by logical principles involves *decentering*. Decentering has many important influences on the child's cognitive and social development. The young preoperational child is *egocentric,* unwittingly captive within his own point of view (Brown, 1965). He centers everything on his own body much as medieval man centered the universe on the earth. The child must come to understand the objective relationships between his own body and actions and the objects and events of the world. This is difficult, for the world of the child is large and complex. It contains, for example, other persons who have points of view that are different from that of the child. At first, the child is not aware of other points of view. He must experience a Copernican revolution in his own thinking to understand that he is not the center of the world and that the world appears different to other persons.

The egocentrism of the preoperational child is illustrated by his inability to predict the appearance of an object from another point of view. Piaget and Inhelder (1948) constructed a three-dimensional model with three mountains: a small green one to the right as one faced the scene at point *A,* a larger brown one behind it and to the left, and a still-larger grey one in the background. The model was photographed from other points of view (*B, C, D,* etc.). For the test, a doll was placed at these different points of view and the child was asked to choose the photograph that showed the model as the doll would see it. Children over seven were able to choose the correct perspective, but younger children attributed their own point of view to the doll, whatever the doll's position (Brown, 1965).

The process of decentering thus involves the differentiation and coordination of multiple perspectives of reality. This has implications for social and moral development as well as cognitive development, as we shall see in Chapter 11.

Concrete Operational Period   About the age of six to eight years, the child acquires the ability to use the logical operations required by the conservation of liquid and other simple conservation problems, and he becomes aware that the universe appears different from different points of view. However, his abilities to reason are still limited to concrete logical operations centered on real objects. He has not attained the ability to reason about abstract or formal propositions and hypotheses that are removed from the actual observation of concrete objects.

This deficit is concretely illustrated by another problem-task, this one employed by Inhelder and Piaget (1958):

> You present the child with five jars A through E containing colorless liquids. The combination of A, C, and E produces a yellow color; B is a bleaching agent and D is pure water. The child has seen the color but not the method of obtaining it. The problem presented to him (with G. Noelting) is to discover the combination that will produce the color and to determine the roles of B and D (Piaget and Inhelder, 1969, p. 134).

A young adolescent (age 12–14 years) who is able to use formal operations will attack this problem by working out, mentally or on paper, all the possible combinations of the liquids and then by methodically testing these combinations two-at-a-time, three-at-a-time, four-at-a-time, and all five together. The concrete operational child will not work out all of these possible combinations. He may try all of the two-at-a-time combinations, and all five together, but he will not usually think of combining the three-at-a-time or four-at-a-time. In other words, he has difficulty in imagining and planning combinations of the liquids in an abstract way.

The end of the concrete operational period is the end of childhood and the beginning of adolescence. Thinking becomes liberated from the concrete and the person acquires the ability to deal in nonpresent possibilities and potentialities. "The subject becomes capable of reasoning correctly about propositions he does not believe, or at least not yet; that is, propositions that he considers pure hypotheses. He becomes capable of drawing the necessary conclusions from truths which are merely possible, which constitute the beginning of hypothetico-deductive or formal thought" (Piaget and Inhelder, 1969, p. 132).

Formal Operational Period   The adolescent has developed the basic cognitive skills that he will use as an adult. He has the ability to use formal logical operations which permit him to consider alternatives and entertain different possibilities. At the same time, his social role in many cultures requires him to make decisions about his future life: his education, marriage, career, and so forth.

The new intellectual power first present during adolescence, plus the rapid physiological and bodily changes beginning at puberty, plus social factors present particularly in industrialized societies, all contribute to the identity crisis of adolescence. We saw above that adolescence is a period of crisis in sexual identity. In addition, the multitude of specialized careers available in industrialized societies create a danger of confusion about one's occupational identity. Piaget sees the affective changes of adolescence as due primarily to these social demands, along with the maturation of formal operational cognitive skills (cf. Piaget and Inhelder, 1969, p. 169).

Psychoanalyst Erik Erikson (1950) has emphasized the role of the physiological revolution of puberty in creating a need to find a sense of continuity in life. Erikson describes adolescents as "primarily concerned with what they appear to be in the eyes of others as compared with what they feel they are, and with the question of how to connect the roles and skills cultivated earlier with the occupational prototypes of the day." (1950, p. 261). He feels that, at least in European and American society, adolescence is a time of psychosocial moratorium in which society gives the individual freedom to try out different roles and identities in a relatively protected atmosphere. Often at this stage the emotional need for continuity (plus, Piaget would add, the new formal operational cognitive skills) leads young people to overidentify with certain individuals, groups, or ideological doctrines. We shall discuss this tendency further in the section on moral development in Chapter 11.

We have seen that cognitive development appears to be motivated in part by intrinsic interest in situations that are incompletely assimilated. The conflicts and contradictions in such situations create forces to alter the cognitive system. This interest in situations which are different (but not too different) from expectation is quite compatible with White's concept of effectance motivation. Piaget suggests moreover that this intrinsic motivational force, by fostering the development of a cognitive system that is adaptive and consistent with the individual's experience with reality, is responsible for the organization of our knowledge of ourselves and the external world.

Although this intrinsic effectance motivation may be considered to be undifferentiated in children, it may be profitable to distinguish various adult motives that are related to effectance. These might include needs for understanding, construction, mastery, achievement, and so forth. However, these adult motives do not have a simple origin in effectance. As in the case of other biological propensities, such as those for aggression and sex, the effectance motive is profoundly affected by learning and social influences. We shall now consider one of the adult motives related to effectance motivation and competence: the achievement motive.

Achievement Motivation

Achievement motivation has been the focus of several highly successful research programs, beginning with the efforts of D.C. McClelland, Robert Atkinson, and their associates at Wesleyan University in the late 1940s and early 1950s. The initial investigations derived from Henry Murray's (1938) concept of human motivation. One of the universal human needs Murray recognized was the need to achieve, which he defined as the striving to "overcome obstacles, to exercise power, to strive to do something difficult as well and as quickly as possible" (Murray, 1955). McClelland (1953) defined the need to achieve (or need achievement) as involving "success in competition with some standard of excellence" (pp. 110–111). Thus, the need to achieve might be considered a differentiated and focused extension of effectance motivation in which the idea of success in overcoming obstacles or in competing with difficult standards is emphasized.

THE MEASUREMENT OF ACHIEVEMENT MOTIVATION

The Thematic Apperception Test   The measurement of the need to achieve also derived from Murray's work. Morgan and Murray (1935) devised the Thematic Apperception Test, or TAT, in which a subject is shown a series of ambiguous pictures. The subject's task is to make up a story about the persons or things portrayed in the picture: what is happening, what will happen, and so forth. The fundamental assumption behind the test is that motivation influences fantasy, and that underlying motives are therefore revealed in the content of the story.

McClelland and Atkinson (1948; Atkinson and McClelland, 1948) demonstrated that the effects of food deprivation were reflected in the content of TAT stories. The stories of men deprived of food for 16 hours showed more references to food deprivation and activities instrumental in obtaining food than the stories of nondeprived men. McClelland and Atkinson developed a system for scoring food-deprivation-related imagery by comparing the stories of deprived and nondeprived men.

In an analogous way, McClelland, Atkinson, and Clark (1949) developed a system for scoring achievement motivation by comparing the stories of male college students whose need to achieve had been aroused with the stories of relaxed or nonaroused students. They used special TAT-type pictures designed to encourage achievement themes. The need to achieve was aroused by leading the students to believe that they had failed on a test of important intellectual and leadership abilities. It was assumed that this would cause a deprivation of success analogous to the deprivation of food. In the relaxed condition, students took the same test but were told that the test, rather than they themselves, was being evaluated. The relaxed and aroused stories showed many differences which were incorporated into the scoring system for the need to achieve. For example, aroused subjects wrote more stories in which there was concern over competition with some standard of excellence (i.e., they expressed more pride or disappointment over goal attainment, set definite standards of good performance, mentioned unique accomplishments, etc.). This kind of theme was categorized as "achievement imagery," and rules for recognizing it were formulated. Other such categories included "environmental obstacles," "affective states" relevant to success or failure of goal attainment, "instrumental activity" relating to the attainment of a goal, and so forth (cf. Atkinson, 1958, for the manual for scoring achievement motivation, affiliation motivation, and power motivation).

Other Measures   The system for the content analysis of TAT-type stories was adapted to score achievement themes in other kinds of written material, such as children's stories, folk tales, fiction, and so forth. We shall see that this enabled McClelland et al. to investigate the level of achievement motivation in cultures and societies of the past. Also, Atkinson (1958) found that persons high and low in the need to achieve differ in their graphic expression, or, more prosaically, their style of doodling. For example, individuals high in need achievement show more S-shaped lines, more single unattached lines, and fewer multiwave lines than persons low in need achievement. French developed another test of achievement motivation in her (1956) French Test of Insight. In this, subjects are given a number of verbal statements about the actions of different persons and are asked to give the most likely reasons for such actions. Other measures of achievement motivation have used incomplete story and doll play techniques (Crandall, 1963).

It is noteworthy that the instruments that have had the most success in predicting achievement behaviors are projective tests. Tests that have directly asked the subject whether or not he is motivated toward achievement have been less successful (de Charms, Morrison, Rietman, and McClelland, 1955; LeVine, 1966). The high social desirability of achievement motivation apparently contaminates attempts to measure it through direct self-reports. However, the reasons why relationships exist between the fantasy measures of need achievement taken by these projective instruments and achievement behaviors are far from clear (see de Charms, 1968, for a discussion of this problem). McClelland and Winter (1969) suggest that the projective tests measure what people spontaneously think about, and that the things that are thought about frequently are more likely to spill over into behavior.

Atkinson moved to the University of Michigan and McClelland to Harvard after their initial studies of achievement motivation. They then followed different but mutually reinforcing lines of investigation, with Atkinson developing a theoretical model of achievement motivation and McClelland collecting empirical data to test theoretical notions and to clarify further the nature of need achievement (de Charms, 1968). We shall examine Atkinson's model briefly, and then consider the results of some of the many ingenious studies of achievement motivation.

ATKINSON'S MODEL OF ACHIEVEMENT MOTIVATION

The Basic Model   Atkinson (1957) sees achievement motivation to be a result of an approach–avoidance conflict between the *hope of success* (T_S) and the *fear of failure* (T_{AF}). *Resultant achievement motivation,* or the resultant tendency to approach or avoid an achievement related activity (T_A) is:

$$T_A = T_S - T_{AF} \qquad (1)$$

The hope of success and the fear of failure are further conceptualized as involving the following: a motive to achieve success (M_S) or avoid failure (M_{AF}), the subjective probability of success (P_s) or failure (P_f), and the incentive value of success or pride (I_s) or the incentive value of failure or shame (I_f). Thus, the hope of success involves a combination of $M_S \times P_s \times I_s$ and the fear of failure involves $M_{AF} \times P_f \times I_f$. Combining these into Equation (1) gives:

$$T_A = (M_S \times P_s \times I_s) - (M_{AF} \times P_f \times I_f) \qquad (2)$$

In this model, the need to achieve is M_S and is seen as a relatively stable personality disposition to strive for success. It is generally measured by one of the projective measures of need achievement described above. M_{AF} is a relatively stable personality disposition to avoid failure, and is often measured by one's score on the Mandler and Sarason (1952) Test Anxiety Questionnaire (TAQ). The other factors, P_s, I_s, P_f, and I_f, are seen to be environmental or situational determinants of achievement behavior that vary from situation to situation (Weiner, 1970). P_s and P_f, the subjective probability of success and failure, are assumed to total unity: $P_s + P_f = 1.00$. Thus, if a person is fairly certain of success ($P_s = .85$) he will also be fairly certain that he will not fail ($P_f = .15$). I_s (pride) and I_f (shame) are assumed to be determined by P_s and P_f: $I_s = 1 - P_s$ and $I_f = 1 - P_f$. Thus, if a person is quite certain of success ($P_s = .85$) he will feel little pride if he succeeds ($I_s = 1 - .85 = .15$) but he will feel great shame if he fails ($P_f = .15$; $I_f = 1 -. 15 = .85$).

By taking these definitions into account and by making simple mathematical transformations of Equation (2), the model of achievement tendency can be represented:

$$T_A = (M_S - M_{AF}) [P_s \times (1 - P_s)] \tag{3}$$

This indicates that the resultant achievement tendency is a function of need achievement, the motive to avoid failure, and the subjective probability of success in that particular situation. If $M_S > M_{AF}$, the individual will tend to approach achievement-related activities, while if $M_{AF} > M_S$, he will tend to avoid them. There are other implications of this model, and the reader might enjoy working them out and consulting Atkinson (1957; 1964) or Atkinson and Feather (1966) for further details.

These equations represent the magnitude of achievement tendency in a given situation. However, Atkinson notes that actual achievement behavior is overdetermined: it may be instigated by many sources of motivation besides achievement motivation, such as monetary rewards, social reinforcement, prestige associated with goal attainment, and so forth. These nonachievement-related sources of motivation are characterized as *extrinsic motives*. Thus, a student may strive for high grades in school for such extrinsic rewards as to get into college, to please his parents, to get the car Saturday night, and so forth. Conversely, a student might deliberately get lower grades—a gentleman's C—to please his peers. This deliberate avoidance of achievement may be particularly prevalent among women, and we shall consider it further below.

Atkinson adds extrinsic motivation to Equations (1), (2), and (3) for a more complete representation of the tendency to approach or avoid achievement-related behavior:

$$T_A = (M_S \times P_s \times I_s) - (M_{AF} \times P_f \times I_f) + \text{extrinsic motivation} \tag{4}$$

An Addition to the Model   Atkinson's model has been extremely useful in stimulating research and in explaining many phenomena related to achievement motivation, and it has been supported by the evidence of many studies (cf. Atkinson, 1964; Atkinson and Feather, 1966; Weiner, 1970; 1972). However, the original model had an important weakness in that it was stimulus-bound: the individual was considered inactive until an external stimulus engages a motive and instigates behavior (Atkinson, 1964). However, we have seen that there is much evidence that the individual is active in the absence of external stimuli. To account for this persistence of behavior, Atkinson and Cartwright (1964) postulated that motivation has a kind of inertia. Once goal-directed behavior is aroused it will tend to persist until the goal is attained. The strength of the tendency to act will be a function of the tendency aroused in the immediate stimulus situation, as in Equation (4), plus the inertial tendency (T_{Gi}):

$$T_A = (M_S \times P_s \times I_s) - (M_{AF} \times P_f \times I_f) + T_{Gi} + \text{extrinsic motivation}$$
(5)

T_{Gi} is the strength of the previously aroused but unsatisfied tendency to approach or avoid an achievement-related goal.*

The revised model predicts that interruption or failure will have different effects upon the subsequent achievement behavior of persons high and low in resultant achievement motivation. Specifically, failure should increase the achievement tendencies of persons high in resultant achievement motivation but decrease the achievement tendencies of persons low in resultant achievement motivation. Let us take an illustration adapted from Winer (1970).

Assume that for individuals whose M_S is higher than their M_{AF}, $M_S = 2$ and $M_{AF} = 1$. Conversely, for persons whose M_{AF} is higher than their M_S, assume that $M_S = 1$ and $M_{AF} = 2$. Assume further that the individuals do a task on which they perceive that the probability of success is 3 in 10 ($P_s = .30$). The resulting tendency to approach this initial task is given in the top half of Table 8.1.

TABLE 8.1   STRENGTH OF ACHIEVEMENT MOTIVATION BEFORE AND AFTER A SUCCESS OR FAILURE EXPERIENCE.

	$M_S > M_{AF}$ $(M_S \times P_s \times I_s) - (M_{AF} \times P_f \times I_f) +$ $T_{Gi} = T_A$	$M_{AF} > M_S$ $(M_S \times P_s \times I_s) - (M_{AF} \times P_f \times I_f)$ $+ T_{Gi} = T_A$
Task One	$(2 \times .3 \times .7) - (1 \times .7 \times .3) + 0 = .21$	$(1 \times .3 \times .7) - (2 \times .7 \times .3) + 0 = -.21$
Task Two		
Following success	$(2 \times .4 \times .6) - (1 \times .6 \times .4) + 0 = .24$	$(1 \times .4 \times .6) - (2 \times .6 \times .4) + 0 = -.24$
Following failure	$(2 \times .2 \times .8) - (1 \times .8 \times .2) + .21 = .37$	$(1 \times .2 \times .8) - (2 \times .8 \times .2) - .21 = -.37$

Adapted from B. Weiner, "New conceptions in the study of achievement motivation." In B. A. Maher (Ed.) *Progress in Experimental Personality Research.* Vol. 5. New York: Academic Press, 1970. Copyright © 1970 by Academic Press, Inc. Reprinted by permission.

* Atkinson defined T_{Gi} as the strength of the approach motivation ($M_S \times P_s \times I_s$) of a failed or interrupted task. Weiner (1970) presents evidence that T_{Gi} is better defined as the resultant approach–avoidance motivation ($M_S \times P_s \times I_s$) $-(M_{AF} \times P_f \times I_f)$ or T_A, of a failed or interrupted task. We shall use Weiner's definition.

Suppose that some subjects have a failure experience on this initial task, while others have a success experience. This experience should alter the perceived probability of success. Assume that the failure experience lowers the perceived probability of success by .10 so that now P_s = .20 among subjects who failed, while the success experience raises the perceived probability of success by the same amount so that now P_s = .40 among subjects who succeeded. This would also change the values of I_s, P_f, and I_f, as seen in Table 8.1. Also according to the revised model of Atkinson and Weiner, after failure the T_A of the failed task will be added as the inertial tendency T_{Gi}.

The resulting tendency to approach a second task is given in the bottom half of Table 8.1. It will be observed that the failure experience leads to greater achievement tendencies than the success experience among persons whose $M_S > M_{AF}$, but greatly decreases the achievement tendencies of persons whose $M_{AF} > M_S$. Weiner (1965) and others have reported data agreeing with this revised model, showing that failure dampens subsequent performance among subjects with low resultant achievement motivation, while enhancing the performance of subjects with high resultant achievement motivation (cf. Weiner, 1970; 1972).

It should be noted that this revised model assumes that inertia affects subsequent behavior only after interruption or failure. Success has little effect in this model, beyond causing small increases in the subjective probability of success. This appears to be a significant weakness in the model, for success in fact often has substantial effects on subsequent performance which cannot be predicted from this model (cf. Weiner, 1970, p. 86).

Applications to Other Motives   While it has its limitations, Atkinson's model has been quite useful in stimulating research on achievement motivation. There are suggestions that this kind of analysis may be usefully applied to other human motives. For example, affiliation motivation may be described in terms of a resultant affiliative tendency involving the need for affiliation and the fear of rejection. Similarly, aggression may be seen in terms of resultant aggressive tendencies which involve aggressive needs and aggressive inhibitions. It remains to be seen whether Atkinson's model will be applied extensively to these areas.

STUDIES OF ACHIEVEMENT MOTIVATION

McClelland's research has been directed toward examining individual differences in the need to achieve, or M_S in Atkinson's model. McClelland reasoned that one's level of need achievement must have important implications for scholastic and occupational choice and success and that the number of individuals with a high need to achieve within a given society will influence the prosperity and economic success of that society. Thus, his research examines problems that have important practical and social implications. We shall examine the characteristics of a person who is high in the need to achieve and then consider McClelland's highly imaginative hypothesis relating achievement motivation and economic development, the teaching of the need to achieve, and the question of sex differences in achievement motivation.

The Nature of the Person High in Need Achievement   An entrepreneur is a person who "exercises some control over the means of production and produces more than he can consume in order to sell it for individual or household income" (Brown, 1965, p. 451). McClelland has found a strong relationship between high need for achievement and entrepreneurial behavior. Thus, he reports that entrepreneurial business executives scored higher than professionals with similar social and educational backgrounds in several nations, including the United States, Italy, and Communist Poland (McClelland, 1961). Also, many of the college students originally tested for need achievement in 1947 were followed up in 1961. The occupations of those in business were classified as entrepreneurial (sales, managing a business) or not entrepreneurial (personnel, credit, office managers). It was found that 83% of the entrepreneurs versus only 21% of the nonentrepreneurs had been high in need achievement 14 years earlier (McClelland, 1965b).

On the basis of such studies, McClelland and Winter (1969) characterize the person with a high need achievement (McClelland abbreviates need achievement as *n* Ach):*

> *Laboratory studies of individuals with high* n *Ach show that in general they behave like successful, rationalizing, business entrepreneurs. That is, they set moderately difficult goals for themselves, neither too easy nor too hard, so as to maximize the likelihood of achievment satisfaction. They are more than normally interested in concrete feedback on how well they are doing. In this respect they seem to be particularly like businessmen who, more than professionals, get concrete feed-*

---

* From McClelland, D. C., and Winter, D. G. Motivating economic achievement. New York: Free Press, 1969. Copyright © 1969 by Free Press, Inc. Quoted by permission.

back in concrete performance terms as to their relative success or failure. They like assuming personal responsibility for problems, because in that way they can get a sense of achievment satisfaction from completing a task, whereas they cannot if success depends on luck or circumstances beyond their control, or if they are working exclusively on someone else's problem. Finally, those with high n *Ach generally show more initiative and exploratory behavior, continually researching the environment to find tasks that they can solve to their satisfaction (McClelland and Winter, 1969, p. 11).*

This description emphasizes that a person with a high need to achieve is oriented toward success in a very particular kind of task: one with concrete feedback and a sense of personal responsibility. The desire for concrete feedback may dispose the achievment-oriented individual to regard growth and expansion as the most direct and satisfying indication of success. McClelland and Winter note that this concern for growth may become irrational and self-defeating. Nevertheless, they apparently regard the need to achieve as a highly positive social and economic force, identifying it with the "desire to improve" (p. 10) and suggesting that it can and should be taught to students and businessmen. Much of their high regard for the need to achieve stems from its apparent relationship to economic growth and expansion in society.

Achievement Motivation and Economic Growth   In his 1904 book *The Protestant Ethic and the Spirit of Capitalism,* the German sociologist Max Weber argued that the Protestant Reformation in Western Europe produced a vigorous new character type among both workers and entrepreneurs, which was ultimately responsible for the development of industrial capitalism. The Protestant world view, stressed particularly by the Calvinist sects, was that one's highest command was to perform the duties of one's calling. Good works, monastic withdrawal, and the strict observance of the rites of the church were not as important in assuring salvation as simply doing one's best at whatever station in life God had assigned. The hard work encouraged by this world view tended to bring economic prosperity, which was interpreted by the Calvinists as a sign that one was doing well at the calling and was one of the elect predestined for salvation: God helps those who help themselves. At the same time, the individual could not relax and enjoy his prosperity on the pleasures of the flesh: expending one's fortune on wine, women, and song was rather severely frowned upon and interpreted as a sure sign of damnation. One of the few things a properly ascetic Protestant could do with his money was to reinvest it in the calling, thus plowing it back into further expansion of business.

McClelland (1961) agrees with Weber's thesis and advances a psychological model to explain and extend it. He attempts to show that Protestantism increased economic development by increasing the need for achievement among its followers. At the same time, he tries to demonstrate that other periods of economic expansion have been caused by high levels of the need to achieve.

McClelland begins his analysis with the childhood origins of achievement motivation. A 1953 study by Winterbottom contrasted the attitudes of the mothers of boys high and low in the need for achievement. She found that the mothers of boys high in need achievement expected their sons to be independent and self-reliant at an earlier age than mothers of lows. For example, the mothers of highs expected their sons to "try hard things for himself," "do well in competition," and "know his way around the city" at an earlier age, and they reported fewer restrictions on the child than did the mothers of lows.

McClelland (1961) suggested that the Protestant ideology would tend to encourage parents to stress independence and mastery at an early age. This, he thought, led to higher levels of the need for achievement which in turn contributed to the spirit of capitalism. He argued that this can be generalized to other cultures and other kinds of economies: certain cultural values, some of which are found in Protestantism, encourage early independence training and thus the need to achieve. This in turn causes economic development, such as the rise of capitalism in Western Europe. This thesis is presented in Figure 8.2.

McClelland and his associates have engaged in an impressive num-

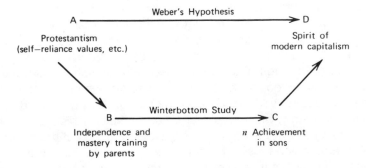

FIGURE 8.2   Diagram of the hypothesized relationships between Protestantism, the need for achievement, and the spirit of capitalism. From D. C. McClelland, *The achieving society*. Princeton: Van Nostrand, 1961. Copyright © 1961 by Van Nostrand Reinhold Co. Reprinted by permission.

ber and range of studies of various aspects of this hypothesis in nations all over the world. McClelland is fully aware of the great difficulties encountered by cross-cultural research on the relationships between such complex factors as economic development and personality: he notes that there is some confusion, flaw, or alternative explanation in nearly every finding. However, he argues that the overall direction of his results is consistent with the thesis that certain cultural values encourage the need to achieve and that this need is one important factor affecting economic development.

Some of McClelland's most interesting studies have involved the comparison of national levels of achievement motivation with the economic development of a society. A moment's reflection will suggest some of the difficulties involved in such a study: How does one measure the achievement motivation of a society? What is a valid index of economic growth? To complicate matters further, McClelland specifies that high need for achievement should *precede* times of economic development in a society. The current level of the need for achievement should not necessarily be associated with economic development. Thus, the measure of the need for achievement must be made at a time preceding the measure of economic development.

One of McClelland's studies investigated the relationship between need achievement and economic development in 23 modern societies. McClelland reasoned that cultural values encouraging the need for achievement should appear in children's stories and that a high level of achievement imagery in such stories should be related to later economic development. The need for achievement was thus measured by a content analysis of children's stories published in that society in 1925 and 1950. Economic development was measured in several ways, one of which was the production of electricity in kilowatt hours per capita. McClelland predicted that nations with a high level of need achievement in 1925 would have a larger increase in electrical production between 1929 and 1950 than nations low in the need for achievement. He did not predict any relationship between electrical production and the 1950 level of the need for achievement.

These expectations were supported: There was a statistically significant correlation of +.53 between the level of need achievement in 1925 children's books and the 1929–1950 increase in electrical production. Also, the correlation between electrical production and the 1950 level of need achievement was only +.03, which was not significant. These predicted relationships remained through a number of analyses designed to minimize such possible contaminating factors as differences in resources, war damage, and so forth.

Other studies attempted to study the relationship between achievement motivation and economic development in past societies. The results were impressive. For example, McClelland measured economic development in ancient Greece by the size of the area that had trade with Greece, and the need to achieve by content analyses of ancient Greek literature. The results are shown in Figure 8.3. A high level of the need for achievement preceded the rise and flowering of Greek civilization around 500–400 B.C., a fall in need achievement preceded the fall of Greek civilization. Similarly, an initial high level and fall of achievement imagery in Spanish literature preceded a period of economic growth and subsequent decline in Spain during the late middle ages (see Figure 8.4). In this case, economic development was measured by the amount of shipping cleared to the New World from Spanish ports. Also, rises and declines in achievement imagery in English literature between 1500 and 1800 paralleled economic rises and declines (as measured by coal imports at London) 50 years later (see Figure 8.5). McClelland notes that the increase in achievement imagery in the 1700–1750 period was associated with the Protestant revival of John Wesley and the rise of Methodist, Quaker and other nonconformist Protestant groups.

McClelland's analysis has been extended to cultures in which exten-

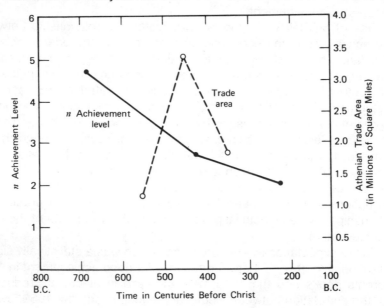

FIGURE 8.3   Average need achievement level plotted at midpoints of periods of growth, climax, and decline of Athenian civilization as reflected in the extent of her trade area. From D. C. McClelland, *Op. Cit.* Copyright © 1961 by Van Nostrand Reinhold Co. Reprinted by permission.

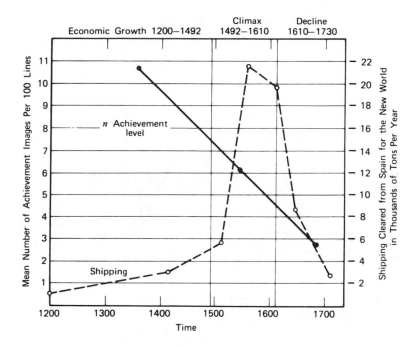

FIGURE 8.4   Average need achievement level in literature at midpoints of periods of economic growth, climax, and decline in medieval Spain. From D. C. McClelland, *Op. Cit.* Copyright © 1961 by Van Nostrand Reinhold Co. Reprinted by permission.

sive written records have not survived, by using Aronson's (1958) graphic expression measure of achievement motivation. This has been applied to the decorative designs applied to the pottery of ancient cultures. For example, this technique was applied to the civilization of pre-Inca Peru for the years between 800 B.C. and 700 A.D. McClelland (1961) reports that evidence of high need for achievement in the designs on funeral urns were followed by economic growth as measured by the volume of public building, while two low levels of need achievement were followed by the conquest of Peru by outside civilizations. Also, Davies (1969) has applied this technique to the bronze age Minoan civilization on Crete. He found the early Minoan period (2600–1950 B.C.) to be associated with a rise and peak in designs suggestive of high need for achievement. This preceded the flowering of Minoan civilization (1950–1650 B.C.). The number of designs suggesting need achievement fell after this early period, with the apparent decline in the need for achievement preceding the fall of Minoan civilization between 1600 and 1400 B.C.

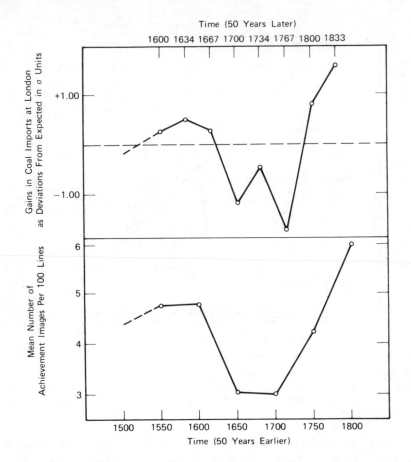

FIGURE 8.5   Average need achievement levels in English literature (1550–1800) compared with rates of gain in coal imports at London 50 years later. From D. C. McClelland, *Op. Cit.* Copyright © 1961 by Van Nostrand Reinhold Co. Reprinted by permission.

Achievement Motivation Training Courses   This evidence that the need to achieve may be related to economic growth and development in a society invited speculation about whether or not it is possible to increase the level of need achievement. McClelland (1965a) has presented a theory of motive acquisition, which argues against the notion that motivation is immutable and gives a theoretical rationale for courses designed to change motivation. He and his associates have also set up classes in the United States and in India which have attempted to teach the need to achieve.

The nature of these classes is described by McClelland and Winter (1969). The goal of the class is to help the trainee to think and act like a successful entrepreneur. It begins with a general orientation to need achievement (or the entrepreneurial spirit) and how it is related to individual performance and success and to national economic growth. Following this, the trainees are trained to think the kinds of thoughts found in the TAT thought samples of people with a high need for achievement. For example, they write TAT-type stories, score them, write new, more achievement-oriented stories, and so forth. This theoretically enables them to recognize achievement-oriented thoughts.

The trainees are then encouraged to apply this new knowledge and understanding of achievement-oriented thinking to their behavior. This is done through lectures, discussions, demonstrations, the study of case histories of successful entrepreneurs, and so forth. The trainees also play at applying achievement thinking in simulated business situations where they can get an idea of how to use achievement strategies without actual risk. For example, in a simulation called "The Business Game," the participant is required to submit a contract to build a certain number of items from tinker toy pieces. He is allotted a certain amount of time to decide how many pieces he wants. The profit payoff depends on the number of items built but the number of extra pieces is deducted from the profit. The individual can compete with other players or against his own past performance.

The next step is to transfer these thoughts and games to the real-life situation and goals of the participant. The trainee writes an autobiography to obtain better self-knowledge, he is encouraged to make specific goals for the future and formulate practical plans for meeting those goals, and so forth. All of this is accomplished with individual counseling sessions and group sessions in which all of the trainees participate. It is hoped that the participants will get to know each other and begin to regard the training group as a new reference group on which they can depend for help in the future.

These training courses have been attempted on an experimental basis with several kinds of groups: American businessmen, Indian businessmen, and underachieving male high school students. The study of American businessmen was conducted on a group of middle-level executives participating in a four-week management development course (Aronoff and Litwin, 1966). Sixteen men participated in a special five-day achievement training course, while a matched group of men was untrained. The rates of advancement (promotions and raises) of the men were determined for a two-year period prior to the course and for two years following the course. It was found that the men who participated in the achievement course showed significantly greater advancement in their occupations compared to the nonparticipants.

The studies using businessmen from India began in 1963 with 34 businessmen from the Bombay area. In 1965 McClelland reported that, whereas only 27% of these men had been classified as unusually active in business before the course, 67% were unusually active after the course. In a randomly chosen control group, 18% had been unusually active before 1963 and 27% had been active since 1963 (McClelland, 1965a).

A more ambitious study was begun in 1964 in the small cities of Kakinada and Vellore. A third city, Rajahmundry, served as a control. Among the trained groups, 18% were classified as unusually active in business in the two years before the course (1962–1964), while 51% were unusually active after the course (1964–1966). In the untrained control groups, the comparable figures were 22% and 25%. Thus, the course participants showed a greater increase in business activity. Specifically, they began to work longer hours, make more definite attempts to start new businesses, make more specific capital investments, employ more workers, and have larger percentage increases in the gross income of their firms. There was also evidence of effects on the economic standards of the communities involved. McClelland and Winter (1969) estimate that the course was responsible for the mobilization of 376,000 rupees of new capital investments and about 135 new jobs in the cities in which the courses were held. They conclude that the courses made a significant improvement in the entrepreneurial performance of the trainees and had a noticeable economic effect on their communities.

Both of these projects with businessmen used as trainees persons who were probably strongly oriented toward achievement in the first place. There is evidence that the courses may not be as successful among populations not initially oriented toward achievement. Kolb (1965) ran an achievement training program with underachieving boys at a summer camp and assessed the effects of the course on their subsequent grades over a two-year period. He found that the course improved the academic performance of middle-class boys, but not boys from a lower-class background. Kolb suggests that the middle-class boys were able to maintain the things they had learned from the course more successfully because they returned to a home environment which reinforced and encouraged achievement behavior.

Sex Differences in Achievement Motivation   The reader may have noticed that virtually all of the studies we have summarized on achievement motivation have used males as subjects. In fact, the relatively few studies on achievement motivation which have employed female subjects suggest that there are significant differences in the nature of achievement motivation among men and women. Thus, Weiner (1972) notes that achievement striving may be a more complex phenomenon among women than among men, because achievement behavior in women conflicts with the traditional female role. It is known from studies conducted in the United States (Sears, Maccoby, and Levin, 1957) and cross-cultural studies (Barry, Bacon, and Child, 1957) that boys generally receive more training and encouragement for achievement than girls. In fact, it is possible that this conflict causes a "fear of success" in women which complicates the relationship between the motive for success and the fear of failure which seems to successfully account for much of the achievment behavior of males.

This motive to avoid success has been analysed by Horner (1966; 1969) who defines it as the fear that success in competitive situations may lead to negative consequences, such as unpopularity and loss of femininity. She considers the motive to avoid success to be a stable personality attribute analogous to Atkinson's M_S and M_{AF} and acquired early in life along with other sex-role expectations and behaviors (Horner, 1969). To study it, she asked male and female college students to write about a male or female student who was at the top of the class in medical school. She found that over 65% of the female students wrote stories containing evidence of the fear of success: thus, they wrote that the successful women was lonely, unpopular, guilty, unhappy, and so forth. In contrast, only 10% of the males showed any evidence of the fear of success in their stories about the successful male: the great majority saw his success in exclusively positive terms. Horner has also shown that men and women low in the fear of success work better when in competition, while women high in the fear of success work better when alone. Furthermore, women high in the fear of success tend to aspire to traditional female careers—schoolteacher, nurse, housewife, and so forth—despite high academic abilities, while women low in fear aspire to further graduate study and nontraditional careers.

Summary

This chapter began by considering the phenomenon of stimulus-seeking and exploratory behavior, and how this phenomenon did much to unseat the classical drive theory which dominated American psychology between the 1920s and the 1960s. Related human studies of sensory deprivation and the need for stimulation were also reviewed.

Several explanations for exploratory behavior were considered, including the notion of an optimal level of stimulation and R. White's notion of effectance motivation, which is quite similar to the kind of motivation thought by Jean Piaget to underly the process of cognitive development. Piaget's theory was considered in some detail because of the insight that it gives into the process of the development of the cognitive system. According to Piaget, behaviors and experiences that enrich the cognitive system are intrinsically rewarding to the child. Behaviors and experiences that do not enrich the cognitive system (because they are too simple or too complex) are not intrinsically rewarding, and extrinsic rewards are thus required to motivate such behavior. The same behavior may thus be strongly rewarding to a child one week and passé the next.

Effectance motivation is considered to be undifferentiated in children, capable of motivating many kinds of behavior. In adulthood, various motives may be related to effectance, one of which is achievement motivation. Research on achievement motivation is reviewed, particularly studies of achievement motivation and economic growth, and studies of sex differences in achievement motivation.

In terms of the schema presented in Chapter 1, this chapter has emphasized the course of development of one of the systems involved in motivation and emotion: the cognitive system. It is relevant to human motivation and emotion in two ways. First, the development and functioning of the cognitive system itself involves certain kinds of motives. We have considered the role of effectance motivation in the construction of the cognitive system; in the next chapter we shall consider forms of adult cognitive motivation. Second, the cognitive system is involved in the interpretation and labeling of noncognitive motives and emotions. We have seen how the child constructs an inner representation of reality through his experiences with reality. It is likely that the child also constructs an inner representation of emotional reality through his experiences with the subjective feelings, verbal labels, positive or negative consequences, and so on, associated with emotional situations. We shall examine this process more closely in Chapter 10.

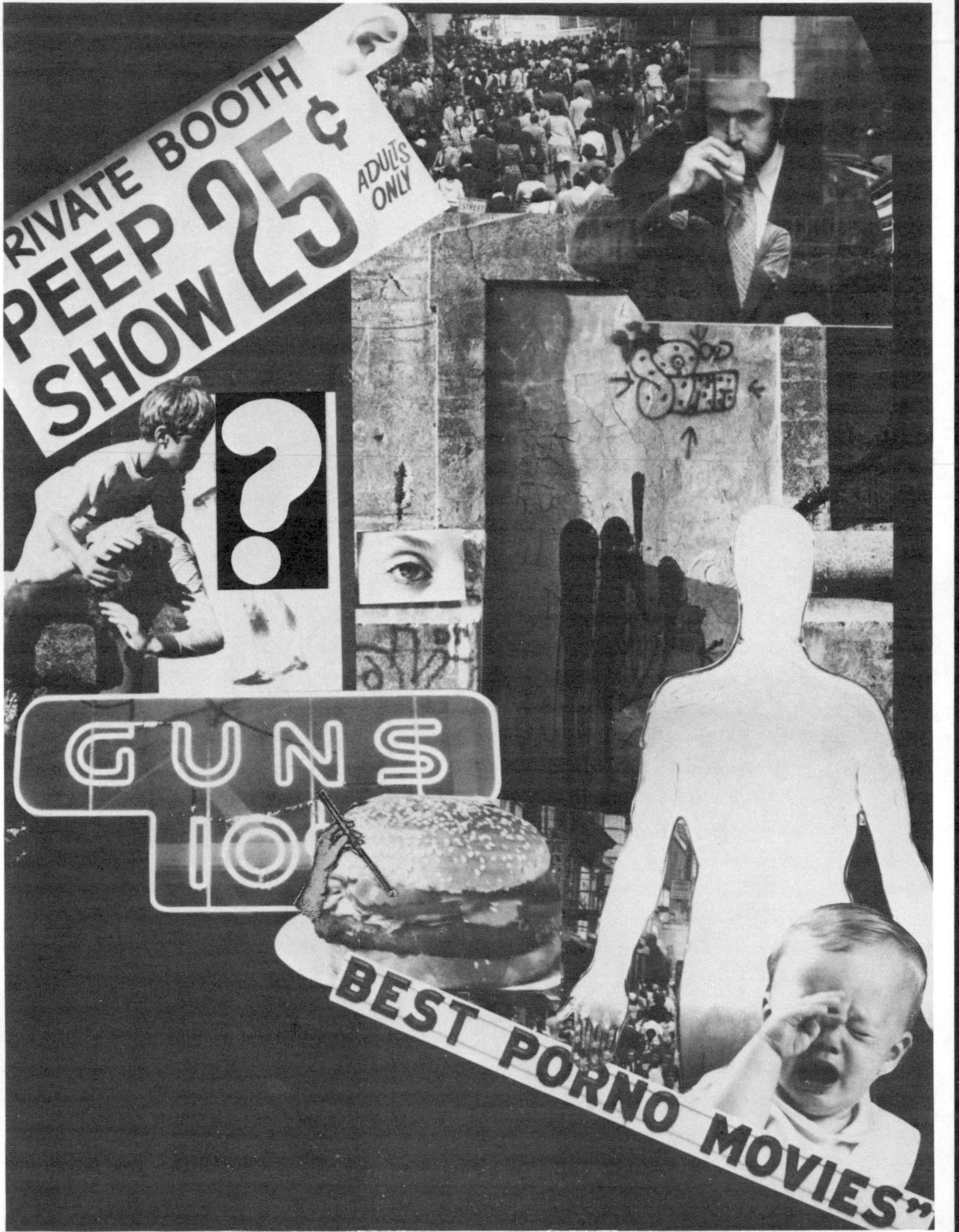
RIVATE BOOTH
PEEP SHOW 25¢
ADULTS ONLY
?
GUNS
BEST PORNO MOVIES"

CHAPTER NINE

COGNITIVE THEORIES AND HUMAN MOTIVATION

In the last chapter we considered Piaget's analysis of cognitive development, which concerns how the individual comes to have knowledge of the environment and himself. In this chapter we will consider several cognitive approaches to human motivation, each of which assumes that the evaluation of the accuracy or consistency of one's knowledge about the world or oneself has significant motivational force.

The course of cognitive development in young children suggests that exploratory tendencies and the increasingly sophisticated ability to make predictions about environmental events are parts of a process in which the child constructs an internal representation of reality. In an adult, this representation of reality can be regarded as a fund of knowledge and powers of reasoning organized into a *cognitive system.* The characteristics of this system can affect behavior through purely cognitive motives, such as the need for consistency between different cognitions or the need for understanding the causation of an event, or the need to predict future events. In this section we shall examine four of the most influential cognitive theories: social comparison theory, balance theory, cognitive dissonance theory, and attribution theory. Each of these theories assume that purely cognitive factors are involved in the motivation of much human behavior.

The Need for Understanding

SOCIAL COMPARISON THEORY

Lewinian Background   The notion that a need for understanding is a basic human motive was advanced long ago by the Gestalt psychologists. *Gestalt psychology* was begun in the years preceding World War I by three German psychologists: Max Wertheimer, Kurt Koffka, and Wolfgang Kohler. They based much of their reasoning about psychological phenomena upon the process of perception, arguing that perception is determined, not by the fixed characteristics of the objects in the perceptual field, but by the relationships among objects in the whole configuration. One of the early associates of the Gestaltists in the years following World War I was Kurt Lewin. Lewin was greatly influenced by the general conceptions of the Gestaltists but felt that their principles should be extended. He became interested in the field concept of physics which had originated in nineteenth century work on electromagnetic fields. Lewin thought that psychological phenomena could be seen as existing in a field analagous to the physical conception and he applied this notion to problems of personality and social psychology (Hall and Lindsey, 1957).

Lewin (1951) defined a field as "the totality of coexisting facts which are conceived of as mutually interdependent" (p. 240). From Gestalt theory, he suggested that certain states in such a field are simpler and more orderly than others and that psychological processes act to make the field as simple and orderly as possible. Lewin felt that the process of understanding simplifies the cognitive system of the individual by categorizing a previously uncategorized stimulus and relating it to other categorized stimuli.

Lewin had a strong influence on the development of social psychology in the United States. He fled to the United States from the Nazi regime in 1932, bringing with him a strong commitment to study experimentally complex human behavior in research projects relevant to social problems. His pioneering studies of leadership styles in the late 1930s were the first studies explicitly called experiments in *group dynamics* (Cartwright and Zander, 1960).

In these studies, matched groups of 10- and 11-year-old children met regularly over a period of several weeks with an adult who followed one of several styles of leadership: democratic, autocratic, or laissez-faire. These styles produced large differences in the behavior of the children. For example, the autocratic leader produced signs of hostility and aggression among some children, including the use of scapegoating against some innocent child or group. Also, there was evidence of more dependence, less individuality, and less friendliness in the autocratic group. Most important to someone living in the late 1930s, there was evidence that the democratic groups could be more efficient than the autocratic group, particularly in terms of work motivation and originality (Lewin, Lippit, and White, 1939; White and Lippit, 1960). Interestingly, when children changed from one group to another, their behavior changed to fit the new group norms. These studies thus provided a dramatic demonstration of the powerful effects of social influence on individual behavior.

Lewin envisioned the eventual construction of a general theory of group dynamics based upon empirical research which could be applied to many seemingly different group situations: work groups, military units, families, committees, the school, the community, and so forth. Under his influence, the Research Center for Group Dynamics was established at the Massachusetts Institute of Technology and later at the University of Michigan. The research stemming from the study of group dynamics has contributed many insights into the complex nature of human motivation, with one of the most direct contributions being the development of social comparison theory.

The Theory   One of the most important aspects of group behavior is the communication between group members. In 1950 Leon Festinger advanced a theory of informal social communication based upon group dynamics research. Festinger posited that much group communication is directed toward instilling uniformity within the group on some issue important to the achievement of group goals. The communication would be directed toward bringing the opinions or beliefs of the group members together, and it would be particularly directed at a deviate who did not agree with the group consensus. If it failed to change the discrepant position of the deviate, Festinger suggested that the group would tend to reject him, and less communication would be directed toward him.

Festinger pointed out that this kind of group influence would be most important when the disputed issue is one that cannot be validated by an objective standard. If a dispute could be settled by some external criterion, there would be little need for communication. However, for most disputed issues, the necessary information is either difficult or impossible to obtain, or no external criterion exists.

In 1954, Festinger extended this analysis from group functioning to individual motivation by suggesting that every person has a desire to validate the correctness of his opinions and also the extent of his abilities. Again, there is little difficulty if the validation can be accomplished by external criteria: one can find which team won the 1949 World Series by simply looking it up. However, most attitudes and opinions cannot be validated so easily. There is no way to know for sure whether American involvement in the Vietnam war would have ended more rapidly if Hubert Humphrey had been elected President in 1968, and even the question of the winner of the 1949 Series could stir much debate if no records were available to the debaters. Although there may be no way to validate conclusively such opinions, they may be quite important to the individual. When one cannot test them against objective reality, his drive for self-evaluation will cause him to use the only available criterion: *social reality* or the opinions and abilities of other people. "The person 'tests himself' against, or more specifically, compares himself with other persons" (Festinger, 1954, p. 95).

Social comparison theory was useful in organizing the findings of many of the experiments on group dynamics, and it has been used to explain the findings of a number of experiments on affiliation, attraction, and attitude change. The most relevant of these studies from our point of view are those suggesting that social comparison affects emotions as well as opinions and abilities: there is evidence that individuals compare their emotional reactions with those of others around them. As a result, one's emotional response can be greatly affected by his cognitions about the emotional reactions of others. This idea has important implications for the theory of emotion, and we shall return to it in Chapter 10.

Cognitive Consistency

Let us now consider a second major cognitive approach: cognitive consistency theory, which also has its roots in Gestalt psychology and was greatly influenced by Lewin's work as well as the work of Fritz Heider. There are a number of cognitive consistency theories, all based on a single, simple premise with many ramifications: that there is a tendency for an individual's cognitions to be related to one another in a logical manner so that, in effect, the human mind has a strong need for consistency. All of the theories involve *cognitive elements* and the *relations* between cognitive elements. These are defined in various ways in the different theories, and these differences in definition give rise to many of the differences between the theories (cf. Brown, 1965). We shall examine balance theory, which was one of the first consistency theories that has influenced many of the others, and cognitive dissonance theory, which has thus far inspired more research than any other cognitive theory.

BALANCE THEORY

Balance theories were put forward independently by Fritz Heider (1944; 1946) and Theodore Newcombe (1953). Abelson and Rosenberg (1958; Rosenberg, Hovland, McGuire, Abelson, and Brehm, 1960) used their insights in constructing their affective-cognitive consistency theory. We shall not dwell on the differences between these approaches but shall simply present Abelson and Rosenberg's model.

Abelson and Rosenberg define cognitive elements as concrete or abstract things which can be persons, groups, institutions, practices, values, opinions, and so on (see Brown, 1965). They are usually named with nouns or noun phrases: examples are "The Arab oil embargo"; "The Soviet Union selling American wheat to Italy"; "Getting good grades"; "The relationship of smoking to heart disease"; "President Nixon." These cognitive elements are the objects of attitudes and are therefore laden with affect: They may be positively valued by the individual (⊕), negatively valued (⊖), or neutral (⊚).

The cognitive elements can be related to one another in a variety of ways. Positive relations associate two cognitive elements and may be equivalent to such statements as: "Likes"; "Owns"; "Is consonant with"; "Causes"; "Supports"; "Is similar to"; and so forth. Negative relations dissociate two cognitive elements: "Dislikes"; "Opposes"; "Is dissonant with"; "Attacks"; and so forth. Null relations indicate an absence of relationship between two cognitive elements: "Is irrelevant to"; "Has no connection with"; and so on (Brown, 1965).

The heart of balance theory is that certain combinations of cognitive elements are *imbalanced,* or cognitively uncomfortable for the individual. When imbalance exists, there will be a tendency to change either one's attitude about one of the elements or the relation between elements so that balance may be restored. Specifically, when something that one likes is positively related to something that one dislikes ($\oplus$——+——$\ominus$), as when one's friend likes one's enemy, imbalance exists. Also, if something that one likes is negatively related to something else that one likes, imbalance exists ($\oplus$——–——$\oplus$), as when two friends dislike one another. In general, the theory states that imbalance exists whenever elements of a like sign are linked by a negative relation and elements of an unlike sign

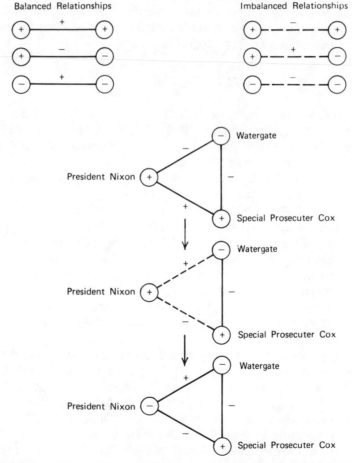

FIGURE 9.1   Illustrations of balanced and imbalanced relationships between cognitive elements.

are linked by a positive relation. The possible balanced and imbalanced relationships between two elements are shown in Figure 9.1.

The predictions of balance theory can be most easily conveyed by an example. Many examples are suggested by the Watergate scandals, and one of these is illustrated in Figure 9.1. Suppose an individual had supported Richard Nixon throughout his term as President, but was troubled by the Watergate break-in and the associated "horrors." However, he initially felt that President Nixon knew nothing about Watergate and would have been strongly opposed had he known. Our individual also felt that Special Prosecutor Archibald Cox, who was appointed by the President, was also strongly opposed to Watergate. In Figure 9.1, we can see that no imbalance existed for this individual: a positively valued President is linked with a positively valued Mr. Cox ($\oplus$———$+$———$\oplus$) and negatively linked to Watergate ($\oplus$———$-$———$\ominus$), and Mr. Cox is negatively linked to Watergate ($\oplus$———$-$———$\ominus$)

However, in the Fall of 1973, President Nixon fired Mr. Cox. The result was an unprecedented flood of angry telegrams and letters to the President and Congress, many recommending impeachment of the President. Many letters came from persons who had previously supported Mr. Nixon. As a result, the House of Representatives began impeachment hearings for the second time in American history.

Balance theory shows how the firing of Mr. Cox could have created strong imbalance in the mind of a supporter of the President. As Figure 9.1 illustrates, the firing created a negative relation between the positively valued President and Mr. Cox ($\oplus$———$-$———$\oplus$), and it may have created the suspicion of a positive relation between the President and Watergate ($\oplus$———$+$———$\ominus$). The resulting state can easily be balanced by becoming negative toward the President, as Figure 9.1 indicates. Thus, the changes in the relationships between the President and other important objects of attitudes can be seen as contributing to the sudden drop in the popularity and credibility of the President, leading to deepening political crisis in the latter months of 1973 and contributing to the ultimate resignation of Mr. Nixon.

Like social comparison theory, balance theory has been very useful in analyzing phenomena in the areas of attitude formation, maintenance, and change. Experiments done to test derivations from balance theories have had mostly positive results, although there have been complications. A full discussion of these issues is beyond the scope of this book, and the interested reader should consult sources such as Insko (1967), Lindzey and Aronson (1968), or Shaw and Costanzo (1970). We shall next examine cognitive dissonance theory which, more than social comparison or balance theory, has inspired a large number of experiments specifically directed at testing the propositions of the theory.

COGNITIVE DISSONANCE THEORY

Origins   Leon Festinger got the essential idea behind dissonance theory when he read of the aftermath of a serious earthquake in India. The report said that there were widespread rumors in the stricken area that more and deadlier earthquakes were imminent. Festinger asked himself why the survivors of an earthquake would predict more earthquakes. On the surface, one might think that the survivors of a disaster would try to comfort each other by assurances that it was all over and that they were safe. But something motivated them to talk about even greater danger in the future.

Festinger hypothesized that this phenomenon may have been due to the fear felt by many of the survivors. Even though the danger was over, most survivors felt frightened and panicky. Festinger reasoned that one's perceptions of one's own state of fear could be a cognitive element analagous to one's knowledge of some outside object. However, the cognition "I am afraid" is not consistent with the cognition that there is no danger. Since the fear could not immediately be suppressed, Festinger suggested that the survivors began to interpret events in the environment in ways that were consistent with their fearful state. They predicted future disaster because it was consistent with their fear (see Figure 9.2).

Like the balance theorists, Festinger based his reasoning on the notion that there is a tendency toward consistency between cognitive elements. However, there are important differences between dissonance theory and balance theory. One of these is that, as the above example illustrates, one of the cognitive elements in dissonance theory is usually a cognition about oneself: one's own behaviors or feelings.

Statement of the Theory   Festinger defines a cognitive element as a unit of knowledge or a belief about the environment or about oneself.

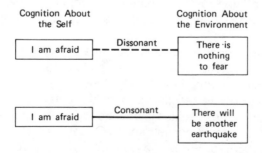

FIGURE 9.2   Illustrations of cognitive dissonance.

Whereas the cognitive elements in balance theory are best expressed in nouns or noun clauses, the elements in dissonance theory are most easily expressed as sentences: "I smoke cigarettes"; "Smoking causes cancer"; "I voted for Spiro Agnew"; and so on (Brown, 1965).

Unlike balance theory, in dissonance theory there are no explicit relations between cognitive elements independent of the elements themselves. Instead, the relations are implied in the elements. Festinger states that dissonance exists between two cognitive elements "if, considering these two alone, the obverse of one element would follow from the other" (Festinger, 1957, p. 13). Thus the proposition "I smoke cigarettes" is in itself *dissonant* with the proposition "Smoking causes cancer." If one cognitive element implies the other, they are said to be *consonant* with one another: "I am afraid" is consonant with "An earthquake is imminent." If one cognitive element implies nothing about the other, they are said to be *irrelevant* to one another. As in other consistency theories, when dissonance exists between two elements, there will be a tendency to change one or the other in the direction of consonance.

This definition of dissonance sounds very neat and straightforward, but it should be noted that it is based upon a complex and elusive kind of psychological implication rather than logical implication. There is nothing logically inconsistent with the propositions "I smoke cigarettes" and "Smoking cigarettes causes cancer." However, the two propositions do violate what we might expect: if you know that a person believes that smoking causes cancer, you would be likely to expect that he would not smoke. One can sense when two propositions will be dissonant for most people, but there are no specific rules for defining dissonance between cognitive elements. Also, one can never be sure that two elements are dissonant for a given individual: a person may hold the cognitions "I smoke cigarettes" and "Smoking cigarettes causes cancer" and experience no dissonance at all as long as he himself is not aware of the inconsistency between them.

The vagueness of the basic dissonance formulation has annoyed many psychologists, but it has not detracted from the ability of the theory to generate research. The theory's vagueness may in fact have been useful, since it has contributed to the controversy that has surrounded the theory. However, the most important reason for this controversy has been the ability of dissonance theory to generate experiments with nonobvious results that, at least at first glance, seem contrary to the commonsense predictions of other theories. One of the areas in which this has occurred is in the analysis of the relationship between attitudes and action. It has long been assumed that one's actions follow from one's attitudes: if you think that something is bad, you will belittle it and avoid doing anything that will support it. However, a major analysis of attitudes and action inspired by dissonance theory suggested that one's actions often create and mold one's attitudes.

Brehm and Cohen's Analysis   Brehm and Cohen (1962) reviewed many experiments on dissonance done between 1957 and 1962 and suggested that the manipulation of psychological implication in many of them involved the roles of *commitment* and *volition.* Commitment occurs after one has publicly made a choice between two alternatives, such as choosing to buy one object rather than another or choosing to do or not do a certain thing. For such commitment to create dissonance, the choice must be voluntary.

Commitment to a voluntary public action incompatible with one's attitudes leads to a particular kind of situation in which one of the dissonant cognitive elements, the action, cannot be altered easily. If one does something voluntarily, in full public view, it is difficult for him to change that action or distort it cognitively. If some internal belief or attitude is dissonant with the action, the attitude is likely to change. Thus one's attitudes may be changed by one's actions.

This position has very important practical implications. For many years it was felt that the key to changing the actions of people was to first change their attitudes. If one wished to get people to eat less desirable cuts of meat in wartime, one must first change their attitudes about the meat. If one wished to change the discriminatory behavior of one social group toward another group, one must first reduce prejudiced attitudes in the former group. Dissonance theory suggested that, if you could induce people to behave differently, their attitudes would eventually follow and become consistent with these altered behaviors. This kind of process may account for some of the success of the civil rights movement in changing the attitudes of white people toward black people in the United States. For decades, a rigidly segregated social structure was accompanied by strongly prejudiced feelings on the part of whites. Many argued that integration was impossible until these prejudiced attitudes were changed: you cannot legislate morality, they claimed. However, as black people gained some of their basic rights, and whites were obliged, under penalty of law, to change their behavior toward black people by allowing them access to restaurants, theatres, hotels, schools, jobs, and the ballot box, public opinion polls showed that verbalized prejudice declined dramatically. Although the goal of a truly integrated society is as yet far in the future, this experience suggests that one of the most effective ways to change attitudes is to change behavior, that morality can indeed be influenced by legislation.

The Forced Compliance Phenomenon   One of the most interesting derivations of dissonance theory concerns this kind of effect of counterattitudinal actions upon attitudes, and specifically the role of external justification in determining when counterattitudinal behavior is or is not dissonance-producing. We have seen that voluntary commitment to behavior contrary to one's attitudes tends to create dissonance that can be reduced only by changing the attitude. However, if there is sufficient external justification for engaging in the counterattitudinal behavior, this dissonance will be minimal and there will be little tendency to change the attitude. For example, if a person does something contrary to his attitudes for pay, he will experience little dissonance if he is paid well but considerable dissonance if he is paid poorly. This leads to one of the nonobvious predictions of dissonance theory: if a person has little justification for doing something contrary to his attitudes, he will show more dissonance-reducing attitude change than if he has sufficient justification.

Festinger and Carlsmith (1959) tested this proposition in an experiment in which subjects were induced (seemingly voluntarily) to behave in a manner that was inconsistent with their attitudes. This kind of study has come to be called a *forced compliance* experiment. Subjects were required to spend an hour doing a series of tedious and boring tasks, such as turning the pegs on a large pegboard ¼ turn to the right, and then ¼ turn to the left, over and over again. The subject was then asked to convince another person, ostensibly the next subject, that the experiment had been, in fact, interesting and enjoyable. In one condition, the subject was offered $20.00 for this bit of perjury, in another condition he was offered only $1.00. The subject was then introduced to the next subject, who was actually a confederate of the experimenter trained to make sure the subject publicly committed himself to saying that the experiment was interesting and enjoyable. In a third, control, condition, the subject was not asked to laud the experiment. All subjects were then told that the Psychology Department was checking up on all of the experiments being conducted, and the subject was asked to rate the interest and scientific value of the experiment he had just participated in.

The results of the rating indicated that, as expected, the control group rated the experiment as rather boring and dull. The subjects paid $20.00 for lying also rated the experiment as dull: telling the lie had not produced attitude change when the subject got $20.00 for lying. However, in the $1.00 condition, the experiment was rated as being fairly interesting. This was in accord with dissonance theory predictions, as Figure 9.3 illustrates. In all three conditions, it is presumed that the subjects initially experienced the experiment as boring. In the control condition, they did nothing incompatible with this attitude. In the $20.00 condition, they engaged in counterattitudinal behavior by telling the next subject that the study was interesting, but they had sufficient external justification to do this without creating much dissonance. Therefore, they did not need to change their attitude about the experiment. However, the subjects in the $1.00 condition engaged in counterattitudinal behavior with relatively little external justification. They therefore experienced dissonance, and to reduce this dissonance they changed their attitude about the experiment so that it became consonant with their behavior.

Dissonance theorists have applied this kind of reasoning to study the cognitive effects of the threat of punishment. Aronson and Carlsmith (1963) showed a child a group of attractive toys and forbade him to play with one of those toys. In one condition, they backed up this prohibition with a threat of strong punishment if he disobeyed, in another condition there was no threat. The child was then left alone to play and was secretly observed to make sure that he did not play with the forbidden toy. The experimenters then returned and asked the child to make ratings of the attractiveness of all of the toys. They found as they expected that the forbidden toy was devalued in the ratings of the children who had been mildly threatened but not devalued among the children who had been strongly threatened. Freedman (1965) replicated and extended these results. Instead of asking the children to rate the toys, Freedman had them return to another experiment up to 64 days after the original study. The children were then allowed to play with a number of toys, including the forbidden one. Of the children who had in the past been severely threatened not to play with the toy, 67% played with it in the second experiment.

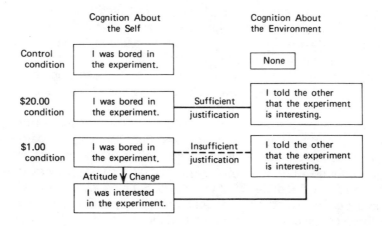

FIGURE 9.3   Hypothesized cognitive changes in the Festinger and Carlsmith (1959) experiment.

Of the children in the mild threat condition, only 29% played with the previously forbidden toy. Freedman's study suggests that the devaluation of the toy in the mild threat condition is a remarkably strong and long-lasting phenomenon. More recent studies have generally been consistent with these results (cf. Zanna, Lepper, and Abelson, 1973).

The presumed cognitions of these children are presented in Figure 9.4. We assume that all of the children initially found the forbidden toy to be attractive. However, they did not play with it. In the severe threat condition, they had sufficient external justification for not playing with it: the experimenter's threatened punishment. In the mild threat condition, however, dissonance existed between the cognition that the toy is attractive and the cognition that he did not play with it. To reduce the dissonance, the child changed his attitude about the toy to be consistent with his action.

Other studies of forced compliance have generated similar nonobvious results. For example, subjects who are induced to eat a disliked food (fried grasshoppers) will report liking the food more if the person who induced them to eat it is unpleasant (Smith, 1961; Zimbardo, 1965). Apparently subjects who obeyed the unpleasant person felt less justified and therefore experienced more dissonance when they ate the grasshoppers than did subjects who obeyed a pleasant person. Similarly, subjects induced to eat a disliked vegetable who thought they would get more of the vegetable in the future, reported liking the vegetable more if they were told that it had little nutritive value. If the vegetable is thought to be nutritious, the subjects evidently felt more justified in eating it and had less need to reduce dissonance by saying that the vegetable was good tasting. Also, a number of studies have suggested that if one expends much effort in

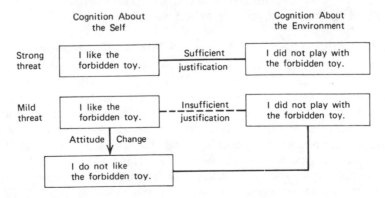

FIGURE 9.4   Hypothesized cognitive changes in the Aronson and Carlsmith (1963) and Freedman (1965) experiments.

engaging in some counterattitudinal behavior, he will experience more dissonance and manifest more attitude change than if he expends little effort (Cohen, 1959; Aronson, 1961; Lawrence and Festinger, 1962; Zimbardo, 1965). As Festinger has commented, we seem to come to accept and value that which we suffer for.

The experiments of forced compliance suggest that the optimum amount of threat or reward is that which is just strong enough to cause the desired counterattitudinal behavior. If the threat or reward is too weak, the person will not perform the counterattitudinal action and no dissonance will be produced. Any more threat or reward than this minimum, and the threat or reward will serve as an external justification to reduce the dissonance between the attitude and action. There are important practical applications to these results. For example, they suggest that a mild threat may be most effective if one wishes to keep a child from running out into the street or sticking objects into electric outlets. Indeed, there is evidence that some brainwashing techniques use this principle of "as little justification as possible" in manipulating attitudes. Interrogators have been known to encourage a prisoner to admit privately that he participated in some war crime, with a reward such as a clean bed or mail from home for compliance. Before compliance, the interrogator will magnify the justification ("You deserve this letter from home") and minimize the importance of compliance ("No one will know you told me you committed war crimes"). However, if the prisoner takes the bait the interrogator will later be able to maximize the dissonance between the prisoner's attitude ("I did not participate in war crimes.") and his action ("I told the interrogator that I participated in war crimes.") by magnifying the importance of the action and deprecating the amount of justification. "You wouldn't tell such a lie just for a letter from home, because you are an honorable man. You must have told the truth that you committed war crimes."

The Incentive-Theory–Dissonance-Theory Controversy   The dissonance theorists' predictions and findings that the less justification for an action, the more effect the action had upon attitudes started a lively controversy between dissonance theorists and reinforcement or incentive theorists whose ideas about attitude change evolved from learning theory. In the 1950s, Carl Hovland and his associates at Yale University carried out studies of attitudes and attitude change begun during World War II (cf. Hovland, Janis, and Kelley, 1953). They analyzed attitudes as being altered according to reinforcement principles: attitude-relevant behavior should strengthen or weaken attitudes to the extent that the behavior provides rewards or punishments to the individual. If a person engages in a behavior contrary to his attitude, he will begin to believe what he is saying, and thus change his attitude, to the extent that he gains rewards or avoids punishments for engaging in that behavior. Hovland et al. (1953) feel that a person engaging in counterattitudinal behavior (i.e. arguing a point that he does not believe) may persuade himself that the argument against his initial position has its merits and adopt new beliefs about the attitude object. They feel that the more reward he receives from engaging in the counterattitudinal behavior, the more he will come to accept it and the more he will change his initial attitude.

This analysis was supported by experiments on *role playing,* in which a person takes a viewpoint different and often conflicting with his usual viewpoint. Role playing has evolved into a useful tool for changing behavior (cf. Friedman, 1972). For example, Janis and Mann (1965) used role playing to help alter cigarette smoking. A smoker plays the role of a lung cancer patient going through the discovery and treatment of the disease. Ideally, the person gets highly involved in a detailed role: coughing and feeling pain, going to the doctor, waiting in dread for the X-rays, looking at the X-rays, responding to the news of cancer, waiting for the operation, undergoing the operation, and so forth. Many persons found this an intense, emotionally arousing experience, and Janis and Mann report in a six-month follow-up that it was more effective in reducing smoking behavior than other techniques.

Although the results from studies of role-playing are not in themselves inconsistent with the dissonance theory analysis of counterattitudinal behavior, the implications regarding the effect of the reward for counterattitudinal behavior do seem to conflict, at least at first glance. The incentive theorists feel that the more counterattitudinal behavior is rewarded, the more persuasive it will be to the individual and the more the attitude change. In fact, Janis has found that if the person is given more money for his performance, or if the audience praises his performance, there is more attitude change (Janis and Gilmore, 1965).

The apparent conflict between the dissonance theory prediction and the incentive theory prediction set off a great number of experiments on both sides, each trying to disprove the other. Interestingly enough, both theories were able to muster a considerable amount of support, but in different kinds of experiments. William McGuire, a psychologist highly regarded for his thoughtful and perceptive essays on difficult theoretical problems, attempted to resolve the controversy by showing that both theories were correct, but that each applied to a limited part of the process that occurs when one engages in counterattitudinal behavior (McGuire, 1968). Let us examine his solution.

McGuire assumes that engaging in counterattitudinal behavior involves first a commitment to engage in such behavior, and then the behavior itself. The sequence of events is illustrated in Figure 9.5. He suggests that dissonance theory is concerned with the effect of justification for committing oneself to engaging in the counterattitudinal behavior, while reinforcement theory is concerned with the effect of rewarding the counterattitudinal behavior itself. McGuire assumes that commitment causes dissonance and that any reinforcement that preceeds the commitment to engage in the behavior constitutes a justification for commitment. The more the commitment is justified, the less the dissonance and the less the attitude change. Thus the more the reward, or the less the threat of punishment, the less the attitude change, as long as the reward or threat preceeds commitment. However, once the person is committed and is actually engaging in the counterattitudinal behavior, the more the counterattitudinal behavior itself is rewarded, the more the person will accept it and the more the attitude change. Thus the more the reward or the less the punishment, after commitment, the more the attitude change.

As McGuire acknowledges, his solution does not account for all of the numerous and complex findings in the area. However, it does predict that one should be able to demonstrate both the dissonance effect and the incentive effect in the same experiment by manipulating whether the individual is being reinforced for committing himself to the behavior or for the behavior itself. Several experiments have done this. For example, Linder, Cooper, and Jones (1967) asked students to write an essay supporting a law which the students strongly opposed: banning the taking of the 5th amendment. In one experiment, the students were simply told to write the essay: they were given no sense of having made a choice. In another condition, the students were told that writing the essay was up to

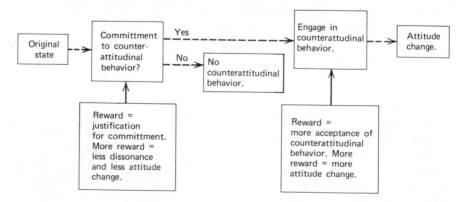

FIGURE 9.5   Illustration of McGuire's (1968) analysis of the effect of reward on counter-attitudinal behavior.

them: they could choose to write the essay or not. The students were paid either $.50 or $2.50 for writing the essay. After they wrote the essay, they gave their own opinions about the law. The results of the experiment are presented in Table 9.1. When they were given a choice about writing the essay, the students had to specifically commit themselves to doing something contrary to their attitudes. In this condition, the more money they got, the less the dissonance and the less their attitude change, as dissonance theory would predict. Apparently the money served as a dissonance-reducing justification for the commitment to write the essay. However, when they were not given any choice, the students experienced no dissonance about writing the essay. You will recall that Brehm and Cohen specified that the subject must feel that his actions are voluntary for dissonance to occur. Thus the money evidently served as a reward for writing the essay, and the more reward, the more their attitude change, just as incentive theory would predict. Linder, Cooper, and Jones' findings have been repeated by other investigators using a variety of research designs (Holms and Strickland, 1970; Sherman, 1970a; 1970b).

Motivation and Cognitive Dissonance   We began the last chapter with a consideration of drive theory and noted the difficulty the drive concept encountered in explaining exploratory and stimulus-seeking behavior. We then discussed White's effectance motivation and Piaget's analysis of cognitive development, both of which suggested that cognitive development and organization are intrinsically motivated. Much of cognitive theory is based on the assumption that there are intrinsic cognitive motives involved in the development and organization of the cognitive system. However, it has been argued that cognitive consistency phenomena may be motivated by a cognitive motivation analagous to drive.

The motivational basis of consistency theory has been generally ig-

TABLE 9.1 ATTITUDE CHANGE FOLLOWING COUNTERATTITUDINAL BEHAVIOR UNDER FREE-CHOICE AND NO-CHOICE CONDITIONS.

AMOUNT OF PAYMENT	NO CHOICE	FREE CHOICE
$ .50	1.7	3.0
$2.50	2.3	1.6

From D. E. Linder, J. Cooper, and E. E. Jones, "Decision freedom as a determinant of the role of incentive magnitude in attitude change." *Journal of Personality and Social Psychology*, 1967, **6**, 245–254. Copyright 1967 by the American Psychological Association. Reprinted by permission.

nored until recently (Singer, 1966). The notion of balance in Heider's pioneering theory, for example, stems historically from Gestalt ideas of good perceptual organization, but the connection has apparently never been explicitly defended by Heider, and balance has been applied to group as well as individual functioning (e.g., by Cartwright and Harary, 1956). Singer (1966) has suggested that Festinger is the only consistency theorist that deals with the motivational basis of cognitive consistency explicitly and in detail. Festinger regards dissonance as analogous to drive, in that it is an aversive state which can be reduced and which will provoke tension until it is reduced. Thus, in dissonance theory, inconsistency between cognitive elements is accompanied by the experience of an unpleasant state of tension, which will be reduced if the individual changes the incompatible cognitive elements in the direction of consonance.

Although the experience of this aversive motivational state is central to dissonance theory, it has rarely been studied directly. Most studies have inferred the presence of dissonance by experimentally eliminating all but one or two cognitive adjustments that could reduce dissonance and observing whether the remaining cognitive adjustments occur. For example, in the forced compliance experiments we have considered, the subject is induced to act in a way contrary to his attitudes. Since he cannot alter his action, the only dissonance-reducing cognitive adjustment available is to alter the incompatible attitude. The measure of dissonance is made by determining whether the attitude has been altered to correspond with the discrepant action.

As we have seen, this kind of research strategy has demonstrated that dissonance theory can predict nonobvious results. However, as Singer (1966) has pointed out, there is no independent measure of the intervening motivational state in this kind of experiment. This lack of independent verification has opened the whole area of dissonance research into question on motivational grounds. For example, Bem (1967) has suggested that the attitude statements that are measured in dissonance studies may be influenced by the subject's attributions about his own behavior and that the postulated drive for consistency is unnecessary to explain the behavior.

The problem of the motivational basis of consistency theory has attracted increasing attention (cf. papers in Abelson, et al. 1968). In particular, Bem's analysis has sparked a great deal of controversy. One response to it has been to show that situations involving dissonance have effects similar to those of conventional drives. For example, studies have shown that situations involving cognitive inconsistency are associated with arousal on certain physiological measures (Buck, 1970, 1972; Cronkhite, 1966; Gerard, 1967; 1968; Ward and Carlson, 1964). Thus Gerard (1967; 1968) gave subjects a series of choices betweens prints of paintings. The choices were similar or disparate in value. Measures of finger pulse amplitude were taken, reflecting the degree of the sympathetically-mediated constriction in the arterioles of the finger. There was evidence of higher arousal both before and after the choice between similar prints than between disparate prints, and the postdecision arousal could reflect the presence of dissonance.

Other studies have shown that situations involving dissonance have energizing effects on performance similar to those of conventional drives (Cottrell and Wack, 1967; Pallack, 1970; Pallack and Pittman, 1972; Waterman, 1969). For example, Pallack and Pittman (1972) created high or low dissonance conditions by offering subjects high or low choice in performing a dull task. The subjects then performed a verbal task which was irrelevant to the dissonance task. The high dissonance seemed to have an energizing effect upon verbal behavior in a way analagous to the effect of a high level of a conventional drive. This energizing effect could be due to a drive-like state associated with the dissonance. Other investigators, however, have failed to find evidence that dissonance is associated with an energizing drive state (Suedfeld and Epstein, 1971).

These experiments seem to indicate that a drive-like state of arousal often accompanies a state of dissonance, but this is not the same thing as saying that a drive-like state is a motivating factor in dissonance-reducing behavior. To do this one would have to show that there is a functional relationship between the drive state and dissonance-reducing behavior—that as dissonance-reducing behavior occurs, the drive state declines. Otherwise, the drive state could be a result of some motive aroused by the dissonant situation but independent of dissonance arousal and reduction per se. One experiment has attempted to study relationships between dissonance-reducing behaviors and physiological measures of arousal: subjects were led to believe that they were volunteering to give intense shocks (high dissonance), mild shocks (mild dissonance), or harmless tones (no dissonance) to an innocent victim (Buck, 1970; 1972). Heart rate and skin conductance responses showed arousal in the high dissonance conditions, but this arousal was unrelated to later dissonance-reducing behavior. On the other hand, self-reported conflict was negatively related to dissonance-reducing behavior: subjects who reduced dissonance by minimizing the painfulness of the shock or denying the suffering of the victim reported having less conflict about giving the shocks. The finding that verbal behavior is related as expected to dissonance-reducing behavior, while physiological responding is not, casts some doubt on the idea that a drive state reflected in the physiological responses was involved in the motivation of the dissonance-reducing behavior.

It is possible that the motivation associated with cognitive dissonance is purely cognitive and unrelated to conventional drives. Thus Pepitone (1968) has suggested that one of the motives underlying cognitive consistency is a tendency to "seek and maintain valid cognitive structures" (p. 323). Perhaps cognitive consistency is a result of a purely cognitive tendency to acquire structured, organized, and valid knowledge about reality, and the analogy between this purely cognitive motivation and drive may be misleading.

The Attribution of Causality

ATTRIBUTION THEORY

Attribution theory is a relatively new cognitive approach with implications for human motivation and there is evidence that it will be an important and fruitful one. Broadly conceived, *attribution* is one of the central processes involved in giving meaning to external and internal events. Attribution concerns how people explain the causation of events, particularly the causation of the behavior of other persons (*social perception*) and of one's own behavior and feelings (*self-perception*). Accurate causal attributions are useful to the individual for the prediction and control of future events.

Attribution involves how people answer questions beginning with "why" (Kelley, 1973). Attribution in social perception involves the attempt to answer questions like: "Why did boy *A* hit boy *B* with the baseball?" The attempt to find an answer may take many sources of information into account: the previous behavior or disposition of boy *A* (Is he a friendly child or a bully?), the relationship between boy *A* and boy *B* (Are they friends or enemies?), one's perception of the event itself (Did boy *B* turn away from boy *A* just before or just after the ball was thrown?), others' reactions to the event, and so forth. Attribution in self-perception is involved in explaining the causation of one's own behavior and feelings. In Chapter 2 we discussed Schachter's theory of emotion, which stated that emotion involves both physiological arousal and cognitions about the reasons for that state of arousal. When in an aroused state, the individual asks himself "Why do I feel this way?" The answer again involves complex information about oneself (When did I feel this way in the past? How did I act and what happened?), about the situation (What caused me to feel this way?), and about the reactions of others (How are other people reacting to this situation?). Different answers to these questions may result in vastly different emotional behavior. Schachter (1964) found that the same state of arousal could be attributed to an emotional state of anger or euphoria; we shall

speculate (in Chapter 11) that attributions about one's arousal state could determine whether one heckles or helps a potential suicide.

Attribution theory has been at the center of a number of interesting and exciting projects in social psychology, only a few of which we can consider here. For example, Weiner (1972) has offered an attributional analysis of achievement motivation. Also, a number of investigators have emphasized the importance of the attribution that one's behavior is free (cf. Steiner, 1970). We have seen that Brehm and Cohen (1962) stressed that the subjective perception of free choice is necessary for an act to result in cognitive dissonance. Brehm later (1966) suggested that everyone has a need to see himself as free and able to control events and that, if his freedom is threatened, a motive to restore freedom called *reactance* is aroused.

All of these concerns are related to the basic concern of attribution theory: the perception of causality. We shall first consider the perception of causality and Heider's theory about the perception of whether behavior is caused by internal forces (i.e., personality dispositions) or external determinants (i.e., situational factors). We shall then examine individual differences in the tendency to make internal or external causal attributions. We shall then consider a recent application of this kind of analysis to the perception of personality dispositions, and the question of whether such dispositions really exist.

The Perception of Causality   Like other cognitive theories, attribution theory assumes that human beings are motivated to acquire organized and valid knowledge about the environment. Attribution theory emphasizes the importance of correctly perceiving the causal relationships between events in the acquisition of such knowledge: One must know why an event has occurred to "attain a cognitive mastery of the causal structure of (the) environment" (Kelley, 1967, p. 193).

The French psychologist A. Michotte has demonstrated the prevalence of causal attributions in a classic study in which subjects were shown two inanimate objects, a red disk *A* and a black disk *B*, moving on a screen. Disk *A* approaches and bumps disk *B*. If disk *B* immediately moves, the observer has the impression that *B's* movement is due to *A*. Michotte calls this the launching effect. If *B* moves off with *A* after impact, it is seen to be carried or dragged along by *A*. This is termed the carrying effect. Thus even inanimate objects are seen to be causal agents, but only under certain circumstances. If a short (¼–½ second) delay is introduced between the moment *A* touches *B* and *B* begins to move, the perception of causality disappears.

Piaget and his colleagues have made extensive observations about the development of the concept of causality in children (Piaget, 1954; 1955). His analysis includes both an account of the ontogeny of causal attributions in children and an analysis of the logic of causality. For example, Piaget (1955) suggests that young children assume that a meaningful cause-and-effect-like relationship exists between any events that occur together (recall the child who blinked at the light switch to turn off the light). This blanket assumption that contiguous events are related to each other lasts until about six years of age. Piaget suggests that children must learn that some contiguous events are less causal than others and that some are due to chance. DeCharms (1968) has observed that Piaget's position stands in interesting contrast to the position of empiricist philosophers (i.e., Hume, 1739), who assumed that children must learn that some events are causally related. Piaget suggests that they must learn that some events are *not* related.

It might be noted parenthetically that Piaget's theory is a rich lode that has yet to be mined by cognitive social psychologists. Cognitive theory in social psychology has been notoriously ahistorical, largely discounting development and concentrating on the individual's contemporary cognitions. This may in part stem from an early reaction against the psychoanalytic doctrine that the personality is formed in childhood. However, Piaget's account of cognitive development should be of great relevance to theories of social comparison, cognitive consistency, and particularly attribution. The integration of Piagetan ideas with social psychological cognitive theories should be extraordinarily exciting and rewarding, leading to a much fuller view of human cognitive functioning.

Heider's Attribution Theory   Fritz Heider is generally acknowledged to be the founder of attribution theory, stating in an early paper that people tend to attribute events to central unitary cores which cause surface events (Heider, 1927). Such attributions should aid in the prediction and control of future events. In his major statement of his position, *The Psychology of Interpersonal Relations,* Heider notes as an example that if he found sand on his desk, he would want to find out the underlying reason for this unusual event:

> *I make this inquiry not because of idle curiosity, but because only if I refer this relatively insignificant offshoot event to an underlying core event will I attain a stable environment and have the possibility of controlling it. Should I find that the sand comes from a crack in the ceiling and that this crack appeared because*

of the weakness in one of the walls, then I have reached the
layer of underlying conditions which is of vital importance for
me. The sand on my desk is merely a symptom, a manifestation
that remains ambiguous until it becomes anchored to disposi-
tional properties—cracks and stresses in this case (Heider,
1958, P. 80).

Heider theorizes that people also look for the underlying causes of the behavior of other persons, building up a "naive psychology" to aid in developing an orderly and coherent view of the behavior of others. In this naive analysis, the central unitary cores are termed *dispositional proper-*
ties and include such things as abilities, needs, intentions, wishes, emotions and so forth. Thus a trembling person who makes supplicatory statements with a soft voice may be perceived as relatively weak, frightened, and wishing to flee; while a frowning person who makes hostile statements with a loud voice may be seen as relatively strong, angry, and willing to fight. Often, such attributions are mediated by fairly subtle nonverbal facial, gestural, and voice-quality cues.

Heider pays particular attention to the naive analysis of overt actions. He points out that action can be attributed to causal factors within the person or to causal factors in the environment. The factors within the person include the person's *ability* and his *motivation.* Motivation is further analyzed into *intention* (what the person is trying to do) and *exertion* (how hard he or she is trying to do it). The perception of the relative importance of personal and environmental factors in causing a given action will determine the attribution of personal responsibility for that action. Generally, the more the action is seen to have been caused by personal factors, the more the responsibility (Shaw and Costanzo, 1970).

Heider notes that the concept of responsibility is used differently at different stages of cognitive development.* In the earliest stage, the actor is held responsible for any outcome connected with him in any way, that is, even for actions of his ancestors. In the second stage he is held responsible for any outcome in which he played a necessary part, regardless of his intentions or ability to prevent the outcome. Thus a child might blame someone for stepping on and breaking a toy even though the child had placed it where it would be stepped on. In stage three the actor is held responsible for an outcome regardless of his intentions, but only if he could have foreseen and prevented the outcome. Thus a driver will be

---

* Heider's analysis has interesting parallels with Piaget's (1932) version of moral development, which we shall examine below.

seen as responsible if his car runs out of gas by mistake. In stage four the actor is held responsible for intended outcomes, but little attention is given to extenuating circumstances. A man who steals is wrong whether he does it for personal gain or to save his sick child. In stage five, the actor will be held less personally responsible if external environmental circumstances are judged to provoke or coerce his actions.

The ascription of responsibility for an action to personal or environmental influences affects one's understanding of the actor and predictions about his future behavior. This is equally true when the actor is oneself. Thus if we attribute our success on a test to personal factors, such as our own ability, we might feel more pride, raise our occupational and academic aspirations, enroll in more difficult courses, study less hard, and so on. (Weiner,1972). Conversely, if we attribute our success to environmental factors ("It was an easy test." "I just happened to study the right things."), our success tells us nothing about our ability. The validity of our attributions of responsibility is critical. As Heider puts it (1958): "In order to profit from our experience, one has to analyze the events correctly into the underlying invariables, otherwise no adaptation to the environment is possible . . . " (p. 151).

Heider's attribution theory has drawn growing attention in recent years (see De Charms, 1968; Jones, et al., 1972; Kelley, 1967; Weiner, 1972). In the next chapter we shall examine studies of the effect of attribution processes on emotional behavior and eating. For the present, we shall examine individual differences in the tendency to attribute the responsibility for events to the environment or to oneself.

Individual Differences in Causal Attribution   A number of investigators have pointed out that a person's perception that he is responsible for the outcomes that occur or that he is helpless in the face of environmental events will have widespread consequences, possibly affecting the individual's sense of competence, self-esteem, achievement orientation, perception of situations as challenging or threatening, ability to work for intrinsic motivation, and so forth. An early theory of this type was proposed by Julian Rotter (1966), who suggested that there are individual differences in the tendency to attribute outcomes to skill (internal or personal factors) or luck (external or environmental factors). He constructed an external–internal locus of control scale to measure such differences. De Charms (1968) has advanced a similar distinction between an origin, who is a person who perceives his behavior to be determined by his own choosing and a pawn, who sees his behavior to be determined by external forces.

Studies based upon these approaches suggest that persons who see themselves as responsible for their behavior differ in a number of ways from persons who attribute their fate to external forces. In particular, internal individuals seem to get higher grades in school. However, these individual differences in causal attribution are more complex than one might first imagine. For example, an intellectual achievement responsibility scale developed by Crandall and his colleagues suggests that a student who attributes his success to his own efforts may or may not also attribute his failure to personal factors. This suggests that causal attribution to external or internal factors is not a unidimensional construct (Weiner, 1972). Also, Gurin, Gurin, Lao, and Beattie (1969) have distinguished between one's attributions about the locus of control of one's own fate (personal control) and one's beliefs about how much control most people possess (control ideology). Thus, one could feel in control of his own destiny and yet believe that the environment (the system) is responsible for the fate of most people. In a study of black youths, they found that a personal locus of control is related to success in school: higher grades, confidence, educational aspirations, and so forth. However, this was independent of control ideology, and in fact an ideology that attributed the major control of events to external factors was positively related to innovative social action (civil rights activity). As Lao (1970) suggests, "internality in a personal sense relates to competent behavior in the academic domain; externality in an ideological sense relates to innovative behavior in the social arena"(p. 270).

Wiggens et al. (1971) point out that the perception of an internal personal locus of control may vary from situation to situation. Thus a youth who grows up in a poor neighborhood might learn a sense of competence and personal control from his physical strength, sexual accomplishments, and general skill at "making it" in the neighborhood, while an affluent youth may find that academic accomplishment brings desired outcomes from his environment. Both may develop habits of internal causal attribution with a sense of personal control and a high level of self-esteem, but in quite different settings and with quite different skills. If the affluent youth were to suddenly move to an environment which emphasized physical strength, and so on, he would be likely to experience a sense of helplessness, a loss of self-esteem, and a general feeling that he is not in control of his fate. The same is true of the poor youth who moves to an environment, such as a college, where academic excellence produces the desired outcomes. In both cases, there would be a period in which the individual would be compelled to adjust his expectations and behaviors so that he could produce the outcomes rewarded in the new environment.

It should also be noted that there is a pervasive difference in the typical experience of females and males in the encouragement of a sense of competence and personal control. Generally, girls are encouraged to develop competence only in behaviors appropriate to the female sex role, and boys are taught to be competent only in the male sex roles. In addition, there are often expectations that males should *not* be competent in female role behaviors, and vice versa. A woman is not supposed to know anything mechanical, a man is expected to be helpless in the kitchen. It might be expected that the causal attributions of males and females would vary accordingly.

The concept of individual differences in causal attribution has been very useful in stimulating the development of significant personality measures and encouraging research, but many more questions have been raised than answered. It is clear that locus of control is not a simple, unidimensional personality variable (cf. Collins, Martin, Ashmore, and Ross, 1973). More research is needed to clarify the complex nature of individual differences in causal attribution.

Causal Attribution by Actor and Observer   Jones and Nisbett (1972) have pointed out one important determinant of causal attribution: whether the attribution is made by the person doing the action or by an observer watching the action. They suggest that observers usually attribute the causes of actors' behavior to internal personality dispositions, while the actor himself usually attributes the causes of his own behavior to situational factors. Nisbett and his colleagues have conducted several experiments illustrating this phenomenon (Nisbett, Caputo, Legant, and Marecek, 1973). They demonstrated for example that male college students tend to describe the cause of their friend's choice of girlfriend and college major in terms of the dispositional qualities of their friend, while they describe the causes of their own similar choices in terms of the properties of the girlfriend or the major.

Jones and Nisbett cite this phenomenon in support of a rather radical suggestion that stable transsituational personality dispositions are not real properties of individuals, that in effect personality traits do not really exist. Since only the behavior of other persons is explained in terms of personality dispositions, it may be that such dispositions exist "more in the eye of the beholder than in the psyche of the actor" (Jones and Nisbett, 1972, p. 89). They suggest that attributions about personality dispositions in the actor is in large part a function of biases and deficits in the information available to the observer: the observer generally does not know the true range of behavior in the actor, the situational pressures impinging on the actor, and so forth. It is for these reasons that the observer forces the actor into a personality mold that does not really fit.

This is consistent with the position of Mischel (1968; 1969), who started a lively controversy in personality theory when he argued that the concept of transsituational personality traits is obsolete. Mischel contended that personality tests are poor predictors of behavior and that any consistency that does appear in an individual's behavior can be explained by similarities between situations and role demands. Bem (1972), in defending Mischel's position, acknowledged that there was nothing wrong with the original assumption of personality psychologists that there are stable personality traits, or in Bem's words that "everything is glued together until proven otherwise." However, he writes, "since it has now proved otherwise, it seems only fair to give a sporting chance to the counterassumption that nothing is glued together until proved otherwise" (Bem, 1972, p. 25).

This insinuation that personality dispositions are not real brought forth strong counterarguments (Alker, 1972; Averill, 1973b). Averill conceded that Mischel's argument is useful in helping to correct the long neglect of situational factors in personality theory. However, Averill argues that the absolute denial of the usefulness of personality dispositions in explaining behavior goes too far: "As the pendulum starts to swing, there is a danger of overcompensation" (Averill, 1973b, p. 275).

Jones and Nisbett (1972) argue that observers attribute causality to personality dispositions because their knowledge of the actor is imperfect and that the actor, with his greater information, can see that situational factors are the true cause of his behavior. However, there is evidence that actors may explain their own behavior in terms of situational factors simply because they are in a poor position to judge their own personality dispositions. In a study by Storms (1973), an actor engaged in a brief spontaneous conversation with a partner while he was videotaped and observed by an observer. As Jones and Nisbett have predicted, the actor attributed more of his own behavior to the situation (i.e. the behavior of the partner) than did the observer, both without watching any videotape and after watching a videotape taken from their original perspective (i.e. after the actor saw a videotape of his partner and observers saw a videotape of the actor). However, after seeing a videotape taken from a different perspective, that is after the actor saw a videotape of himself and the observer saw a videotape of the partner, the actor attributed more of his behavior to his own dispositions than did the observer (see Figure 9.6).

Storms suggests that this result indicates the importance of simple visual orientation in determining the attributional biases of actors and observers. Actors watch the environment and pay little attention to their own behavior, both because they physically cannot observe their behavior and because it is difficult to attend to one's own behavior and still deal with the situation: people soon learn that acting self-consciously is not func-

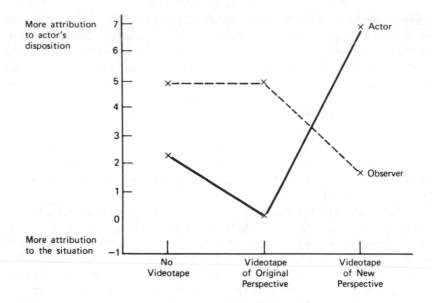

FIGURE 9.6   Total dispositional minus situational attribution scores from three points of view. Adapted from data presented in M. D. Storms, "Videotape and the attribution process: Reversing actors' and observers' points of view." *Journal of Personality and Social Psychology*, 1973, 27, 165–175. Copyright 1973 by the American Psychological Association. Reprinted by permission.

tional. Thus perhaps it is the actor who has a deficit of information about himself. The observer, on the other hand, spends more time watching the actor's behavior than the actor's situation, perhaps partly because he finds it more efficient in understanding and making predictions about the events.

Storms' result appears to indicate that people will attribute their own behavior to personality traits if allowed to view their behavior from an observer's point of view. This does not prove, of course, that personality traits exist, or, more properly, that personality traits are useful in understanding and making predictions about behavior. However, it does appear to refute the implication that observers see personality dispositions in others because of deficits in information about the actor: it is hard to imagine that Storms' actors had deficits of information about themselves.

It is nevertheless true that psychologists and lay persons alike have greatly underestimated the strength of situational influences upon behavior. In Chapter 11, we shall examine the role of cognitive and situational factors in moral and aggressive behavior. This will illustrate again that, while it is useful to take the development of individual dispositions into account in understanding human behavior, the influence of situational factors is stronger than most of us realize.

Summary

We have considered several kinds of cognitive motives—motives which involve the striving for accuracy or consistency in one's knowledge about the world and about oneself. These have included social comparison theory, balance theory, cognitive dissonance theory, and attribution theory.

In terms of our schema of motivation and emotion, these theories demonstrate how the internal dynamics of the cognitive system generate motives such as needs for understanding, cognitive consistency, accurate causal attribution, and so forth. The status of these motives *vis a vis* other kinds of motives such as learned drives is unclear. Some have argued that motives like cognitive consistency are similar to other learned drives while others argue that they are purely cognitive motives that should not be confused with the concept of drive. Thus while some would say that the need for understanding is a learned drive based upon the child's realization that understanding something is a rewarding state and that not understanding something can be punishing. Others would argue that the need for understanding is "built in" to the cognitive system and that rewards and punishments external to the cognitive system are not necessary to explain it.

CHAPTER TEN

THE COGNITIVE—PHYSIOLOGICAL INTERACTION

We saw in the last chapter that purely cognitive motives—the need for understanding, cognitive consistency, and so on—affect much human behavior. These cognitive processes do not work in isolation from the physiological mechanisms discussed earlier in the book. In fact, as we saw in Chapter 2, many regard emotion as an interaction of physiological arousal and cognitions associated with that arousal. Thus fear involves both a state of arousal and cognitions about why one is afraid, joy involves a fairly similar state of arousal but a quite different set of cognitions for explaining that arousal, and so forth.

In this chapter we shall consider this relationship between cognition and physiological responding in more detail. Most of the studies in this chapter involve the manipulation of cognitive factors by controlling the information available to the subject, and they measure the resulting effect upon the emotional or motivational response. We shall discuss experiments stemming from Schachter's theory of emotion and his analysis of obesity, cognitive dissonance theory, and Lazarus' theory of coping with stress. We shall also briefly examine the potential theraputic applications of these experiments.

Schachter's Self–Attribution Theory of Emotion

THE THEORY

We discussed Schachter's self–attribution theory of emotion in detail in Chapter 2. It will be recalled that Schachter feels that there are two interacting components in emotion: peripheral physiological arousal and the cognitions associated with that arousal. If either the physiological or cognitive element is not present, the emotion will be incomplete. If the physiological component is present without the cognitive component, that is if the subject feels the tense stirred-up state associated with arousal without knowing why, he will tend to search the environment to find reasons for his state of arousal. If an appropriate explanation is found, the subject will interpret or label the arousal accordingly, and the emotion will be experienced and expressed as a whole (see Figure 2.6).

Schachter's theory makes a number of assumptions about the nature of emotion. First, it assumes that peripheral autonomic arousal is important in determining the emotional state, a position reminiscent of the James–Lange theory of emotion (see Chapter 2). Second, it assumes that the meaning of this arousal is determined cognitively. In addition, it assumes that emotion may often involve an information-search, in which the responder searches the environment for an appropriate explanation for his arousal, and a labeling process, which determines the quality of the emotion. There are experiments relevant to each of these points, and we shall consider them in turn.

PERIPHERAL AROUSAL IN EMOTION

We saw in Chapter 2 that peripheral physiological events are probably not *essential* to either emotional behavior or emotional experience. Activity in certain parts of the brain can produce both emotional behavior and experience in humans without the obvious involvement of either peripheral physiological responses or cognitions. For example, electrical stimulation of the amygdala has produced angry feeling and reactions in subjects who know they have no reason to be angry. Also, the angry reactions come and go with the stimulation at a speed which peripheral physiological responses could never match (King, 1961). This indicates that there are central physiological processes in emotion that are outside the range of Schachter's theory.

On the other hand, there is evidence that peripheral physiological responses do *contribute* to normal emotional experience. Schachter (1964) cited a study of paraplegics and quadriplegics conducted by Hohmann (1962). This study assessed the reported change in sexual excitement, fear, anger, grief, and sentimentality following the spinal cord lesions that had deprived the subjects of their peripheral somatic and visceral sensation. With the exception of sentimentality, Hohmann found that the higher the lesion and thus the greater the loss of peripheral sensation, the greater the decrease in emotionality. Many subjects reported acting emotional but not feeling emotional in the way they had before the lesion. As one said about anger, "It's sort of a cold anger. Sometimes I act angry when I see some injustice. I yell and cuss and raise hell, because if you don't do it, I've learned people will take advantage of you, but it just doesn't have the heat to it that it used to. It's a mental kind of anger." Another said, "Seems like I get thinking mad, not shaking mad, and that's a lot different" (Schachter, 1964, pp. 165–166). Another study, cited by Grossman (1967), attempted to carefully investigate the time course of the subjective reaction of normal subjects to emotional stimuli. The subjects reported an initial experience that occurred too quickly to be due to peripheral responses. However, this was followed by a fuller, more complete experience that could well have been due to peripheral factors (Newman, Perkins, and Wheeler, 1930). Thus, the assumption that peripheral arousal is important in determining the emotional state may be justified when applied to most normal emotions, but it clearly is not a necessary factor in all emotional experience and this fact limits the scope of Schachter's theory.

COGNITIVE INFLUENCES ON THE INTERPRETATION OF AROUSAL

Schachter's second assumption concerns whether or not the meaning of the peripheral arousal is determined and can be manipulated cognitively. The experiment with Singer seems to support this notion: subjects who had no ready explanation for their arousal could be manipulated into the disparate emotions of euphoria and anger. A study by Schachter and Wheeler (1962) is also relevant to this point. In that experiment, subjects received injections of either epinepherine, saline, or chlorpromazine. The latter is a tranquilizer which, among other things, tends to block sympathetic nervous system activity. All subjects were told that the drug was a vitamin that would have no side effects. They then watched a segment of an amusing film, and their visible reactions were recorded every 10 seconds along the following scale: neutral–smile–grin–laugh–big laugh. As expected, epinepherine subjects showed the most amusement, and chlorpromazine subjects showed the least.

Even critics of these studies agree that they demonstrate that both physiological arousal and cognitive factors are important determinants of emotion (Plutchik and Ax, 1967; Shapiro and Schwartz, 1970). But Schachter's theory also implies that a state of sympathetic arousal may be common to all emotion and that subjects in similar states of sympathetic arousal may experience very different emotions, or no emotions at all, depending on the cognitions available to them. Schachter suggests that this may be why it has been so difficult to demonstrate large differences in peripheral physiological responding between different emotional states. This notion has been more controversial. Plutchik and Ax (1967) and Shapiro and Crider (1969) both note that this conclusion should not be taken too far. They point out that there is no support for the notion that all emotional states are physiologically identical and differentiated only by cognitions. In fact, Schachter clearly recognizes that there are limits to the extent that cognitive factors determine how bodily conditions are interpreted. As he puts it, "It is unlikely that anyone with undiagnosed peritonitis could ever be convinced that he was euphoric, high, or anything but deathly ill" (Schachter, 1964, p. 170). The disagreement seems to center on how widely these limits of cognitive determination extend. Schachter suspects that they may be very wide. He notes as an example that vomiting, which seems unpleasant to us, was apparently regarded by Roman gourmets as pleasurable.

On reflection, the question of the cognitive versus the physiological determination of emotion is extremely complex and full of implications. For example, it is probable that central physiological processes, which are not considered by Schachter's theory, are involved very heavily in the determination of the quality of emotion. However, the possible relationships between these central processes and cognitive factors are, to put it mildly, unclear. Perhaps on that level there is no difference between cognitive and physiological factors. Ultimately, future research must determine the extent to which emotions are differentiated by cognitive, as opposed to physiological, factors. In the process, the meaning of what one denotes when one says cognitive processes and physiological processes must be clarified considerably.

THE ENVIRONMENT-SEARCH PROCESS

Another of the implications of self-attribution theory of emotion is that, given an ambiguous situation, the quality of the emotion may be determined by a search of the environment for relevant information. Such an information-search process has been investigated in studies by Valins (1966) and Barefoot and Straub (1971).

Valins showed his male subjects a series of 10 pictures of female nudes while they listened to what they were told was their heartbeat. Actually, the heart rate feedback was false and controlled by the experimenter. It was manipulated to change on 5 pictures and remain constant on 5 others. Afterward, the subjects judged the pictures paired with the false heart rate change to be more attractive than those associated with no change. Since the changes occurred on different pictures for different subjects, the preference must have been determined by the change.

Valins' preferred explanation for this finding was that, when the subject heard his heart rate change, he searched the picture for attributes that might have caused such a dramatic heart rate reaction. Such attributes were present in all the pictures, but the subject attended to them particularly when he heard the heart rate change. This search affected his perception of the picture, creating a relatively permanent cognitive reorganization in which the picture was seen as particularly attractive.

Another explantation could account for Valin's results without requiring a process of information-search. Perhaps the subjects simply told themselves that they must like the picture because they responded to it physiologically. Thus they might say the picture is more attractive without actually changing their perception of it. However, a study by Barefoot and Straub (1971) seems to support the information-search interpretation. They also showed 10 nude pictures to male subjects. Instead of using contrived biofeedback, they simply showed each subject the 5 pictures that had supposedly produced the largest physiological responses in him.

In one condition, the subject was given a total of only 10 seconds to look at these critical pictures. The authors reasoned that this time was insufficient for the subject to change his perception of the pictures, although he would know that they had supposedly affected his physiological response. In two other conditions, the subject was given a total of 25 seconds to view the critical pictures, supposedly long enough for the cognitive reorganization to occur. As expected, the subjects became more positive to the critical pictures in the 25-second conditions, but not the 10-second condition. Evidently, some time in viewing the critical picture is necessary for the effect demonstrated by Valins to occur, and this seems consistent with the information-search interpretation of the phenomenon. This, in turn, is quite consistent with Schachter's (1964) formulation.

THE LABELING PROCESS

Another implication of self-attribution theory of emotion is that the information-search process ultimately results in a labeling process that reduces the subject's uncertainty and determines the quality of the emotion. This labeling process has been investigated in experiments that manipulate the available explanations for an existing state of arousal.

Some of these experiments have shown that it is possible to make subjects believe that their internal state of arousal is caused by some artifical factor. For example, Nisbett and Schachter (1966) gave their subjects instructions that they were to receive a series of painful and unpleasant (high fear) or harmless and not unpleasant (low fear) shocks. They then gave the subjects a placebo pill. Half were told that the pill would cause signs of arousal, such as palpitation, tremor, increased respiration, and visceral upset. The other half were led to expect side effects unrelated to arousal, such as itching and headache. Actually, of course, the pill had no effects. The subjects were then given a series of electric shocks to establish a pain threshold. In the low-fear condition, subjects who believed themselves to be in artificial arousal state caused by the pill tolerated more shock and rated it as less painful than did subjects who were led to expect pill effects unrelated to arousal.

Nisbett and Schachter interpret this result as follows. The pain threshold test creates a certain amount of arousal which, allowing for individual differences, is about the same for all low-fear subjects. However, some of these subjects have been led to expect similar arousal as a side effect of the pill. Of the total amount of arousal they feel, they attribute some to the shock and some to the pill. In effect, they label only part of their arousal as fear of shock. The subjects led to expect side effects irrelevant to arousal, on the other hand, attribute all of the arousal they experience to the shock. Therefore, all else being equal, the latter subjects label more arousal as fear and thus feel that the shock is more painful. This pattern did not apply to the high-fear condition, however. Questionnaires indicated that the high-fear subjects attributed all of their arousal to the shock, regardless of the condition. Presumably, the intensity of the initial fear in those subjects made it more plausible for them to attribute their arousal to the shock regardless of the instructions about the pill (Nisbett and Schachter, 1966).

Using a similar manipulation, Davison and Valins (1969) gave their subjects a shock threshold test, then a placebo, then a second threshold test with the shock intensities surreptitiously halved so that all subjects' threshold performance was changed. Then half the subjects were told that the drug was a placebo. Presumably, these subjects had to attribute their apparently increased threshold performance to themselves. The other half were told the drug had worn off. They were given another threshold test at the original intensities. The placebo subjects, who attributed their performance on the second test to themselves, tolerated more shock and rated it as less painful than the drug-worn-off subjects, who attributed their performance on the second test to the drug.

Ross, Rodin, and Zimbardo (1969) also attempted to change emotional behavior by causing their subjects to attribute natural arousal to a nonemotional source. Subjects were threatened with the anticipation of possible electric shock. Simultaneously with the threat, they were bombarded with high intensity noise. In one condition, the subjects were told that the side effects of the noise would be similar to the symptoms of fear, including palpitations, tremor, visceral upset, and increased respiration. In the other condition, the side effects of the noise were purported to be different from those of fear (e.g., dizziness, ringing of the ears). The measure of fear was the time at which subjects worked on a puzzle whose solution would avoid the threatened shock, as opposed to a second puzzle whose solution would be rewarded by money. As expected, the subjects worked less hard on the shock puzzle when they had had the chance to reattribute their arousal to the effects of noise.

In another study relevant to labeling, Dienstbier and Munter (1971) reported that subjects given a placebo pill that supposedly causes arousal are more likely to cheat when given a chance. Presumably, they did not label the arousal experienced with the initial temptation to cheat as fear or guilt, and thus had fewer inhibitions about cheating (Dienstbier, 1972). In still another study, London and Monello (1969) rigged a clock to go either 10 minutes or 30 minutes while their subjects did a task for 20 actual minutes. Subjects in the 10 minute condition reported being more bored with the task than 30 minute subjects, presumably because the natural arousal they felt, when combined with the cognition that only ten minutes had passed, was labeled as boredom.

In recent years, self-attribution analyses have been applied to a wide variety of emotional situations, including sexual intercourse (Hanson and Blechman, 1971), the menstrual cycle (Koeske and Koeske, 1975), smoking behavior (Nesbett, 1973), and the extinction of conditioned emotional (skin conductance) responses (Loftis and Ross, 1974a; 1974b), and a book on the area has appeared (London and Nisbett, 1974).

DEVELOPMENT OF THE LABELING PROCESS

It might be noted that there has not been, as yet, any systematic attempt to approach Schachter's theory of emotion from a developmental point of view. In Chapter 8 we considered how the child gradually gains an inner representation of the external world from his experiences in the world. In Chapter 11 we shall see that a similar analysis has been applied to the development of moral judgment: the child gains a conception of right and wrong from his experiences in interaction with other people. A similar kind of analysis could be applied to the development of the self-attribution of emotion. A young child would presumably not label his arousal in the same way as an adult. There may well be a process by which a child constructs an inner representation of emotional reality as well as physical reality and moral reality.

The child may develop a set of labels by which to identify and categorize his subjective experience through a process of associating his private experiences with cognitive interpretations and verbal labels. For example, a child may learn to correctly identify and label his feelings of anger by repeated direct and vicarious experiences in situations that arouse such feelings and label them appropriately. When he is overtly expressing his anger, a parent might say "I see that you are angry," or he may see others angry and hear them describe their feelings as anger.

It is possible that such labeling of subjective experience may be inappropriate or erroneous. While a child can model the overt behavior of others quite directly, he has no direct access to their subjective experience, and they have no direct access to his. Learning about subjective events must take place indirectly, via the verbal reports and descriptions of subjective experience that the child gains from others, and the reports that he gives to others. This lack of direct access makes incorrect labeling possible. A child who is fed whenever he expresses anger could conceivably learn to label the subjective experience associated with anger as hunger, or a child who is fed when anxious might label anxiety as hunger.

These possibilities must await the appropriate observation and experimentation in young children.

The studies we have considered suggest that emotional behavior can be greatly affected by altering the explanations available for labeling a person's state of arousal. Taken together, they indicate that Schachter's theory has stimulated much experimental work, the results of which are largely consistent with the original formulation. In addition, the theory has led to important applications, particularly to the study of obesity.

Schachter's Self-Attribution Theory of Obesity

INTERNAL VERSUS EXTERNAL CONTROL OF EATING

The major point in Schachter's analysis of obesity is that obese individuals label the state of hunger in a different way than do nonobese persons. Normal-size persons seem to label their hunger according to bodily need. When the body is in need of nourishment, normal-size persons experience a state that they label as hunger. This does not seem to be as true for obese persons. They seem to regulate their food intake according to external stimuli associated with food, such as the sight and taste of food.

This idea first developed from the results of a study by Stunkard and Koch (1964; reported in Schachter, 1970). These investigators studied the gastric contractions and self-reports of hunger in subjects who had gone without breakfast. The experiment lasted from 9:00 A.M. to 1:00 P.M. They found that, for normal-size subjects, self-reports of hunger coincided with gastric contractions. For obese subjects, in contrast, there was much less correspondence between stomach contractions and self-reports of hunger.

To study this phenomenon further, Schachter, Goldman, and Gordon (1968) conducted a study disguised as a taste experiment. Obese and normal-size subjects were asked to do without a meal preceeding the experimental session, so presumably they were all initially hungry. After they came in, half the subjects were fed roast beef sandwiches and the other half remained hungry. Each subject was then given five kinds of crackers and asked to rate each kind along a long set of rating scale dimensions (such as salty, cheesy, garlicky, etc.). The subject was instructed to eat as few or as many crackers as he wanted so long as his ratings were as accurate as possible. Actually, the experimenters were not interested in the ratings, just the number of crackers eaten by the subjects. As expected, the normal-size subjects who had eaten roast beef sandwiches ate fewer crackers than normal-size subjects who had not eaten.

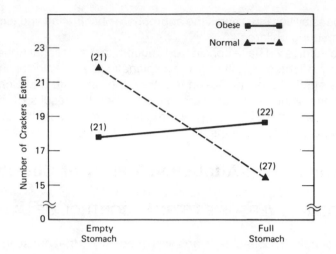

FIGURE 10.1   The effects of previous feeding on eating. From S. Schachter, "Some extraordinary facts about obese humans and rats." *American Psychologist*, 1971, 26, 129–144. Copyright 1970 by the American Psychological Association. Reprinted by permission.

In contrast, the prefeeding with roast beef sandwiches did not affect the cracker-eating behavior of obese subjects. They ate as much regardless of whether their stomach was empty or full. Evidently the bodily state associated with food deprivation was labeled as hunger by normal-size subjects, but not by obese subjects.

If eating by the obese is little related to the internal visceral state associated with food deprivation, the question arises as to what factors are responsible for the triggering of eating behavior among obese persons. Schachter suggests that external stimuli related to food, such as the sight, smell, and taste of food, and the passage of time since last eating, are the cues used by obese persons to regulate their eating (Schachter, 1970).

A study by Nisbett (1968a) investigated the effects of the sight of food. Normal-size and obese subjects who had not eaten lunch were presented with one or three roast beef sandwiches. As the experimenter left the room, he told the subjects that they could help themselves to more from a nearby refrigerator. When the subjects had three visible sandwiches, the obese ate more than did the normal-size. When they had only one sandwich, and had to go to the refrigerator to get more, the obese ate less than the normal size. Nisbett reasoned that, since the eating of the obese subjects is controlled by external factors such as the sight of food, the obese will tend to eat just so long as food is in sight regardless of whether they need food or not. When these visible cues are consumed, they should stop eating, even if their internal need for food is not yet satisfied. In such a case, obese persons may well eat less than normal-size persons. The normal-size person depends on his physiological need for food. If this is unsatisfied when the visible food is consumed, he will forage for more.

A study by Decke (1971) examined the effects of another external stimulus related to food—taste. She gave her subjects either a good vanilla milkshake or a milkshake spiked with bitter quinine. As expected, obese subjects drank more of the good milkshake but less of the bitter milkshake, than normal-size subjects. This replicated the result of an earlier study by Nisbett (1968b) which used good and bad-tasting ice cream. Nisbett found that underweight persons showed the greatest tendency to eat the bad-tasting ice cream, while obese subjects ate the most of the good ice cream.

The physiological need for food appears to alter the taste for food more in normal than in obese subjects. Cabanac and Duclaux (1970) showed that, for fasting normal-size subjects, a stomach-loading of glucose solution changed the taste sensation of a sweet sucrose solution from pleasant to unpleasant. Obese subjects reported the solution to be pleasant regardless of the internal state, suggesting a decreased sensitivity to internal food cues among the obese.

An experiment by Schachter and Gross (1968) studied another external food-related cue—the passage of time. Subjects entered the experiment at 5:00 P.M. and physiological recording electrodes were attached. This necessitated the removal of the subject's watch. The subjects then sat for 40 minutes while their physiological baseline was monitored. A clock in the room with them was rigged to go either too slow or too fast, so at 5:40 the clock read 5:25 in one condition and 6:10 in the other. The subjects were then given crackers to eat. As expected, the obese subjects ate more crackers when they thought it was 6:10 than when they thought it was 5:25. The normal subjects actually ate fewer crackers when they thought it was 6:10, apparently because they didn't want to spoil their dinner.

Goldman, Jaffa, and Schachter (1968) report several clever studies based on the notion that obese subjects are responsive to external food-related cues, but not to internal cues associated with food deprivation. One study involved religious fasting on Yom Kippur, the Jewish Day of Atonement for which fasting is commanded by Biblical Law. It was reasoned that, since obese persons are relatively unaffected by internal cues, they should have an easier time fasting than normal-size persons. It was therefore predicted, and found, that among Jewish subjects who reported being at all religious, the obese were more likely to fast than the normal-size. In addition, it was predicted that, among obese subjects, fasting should prove easier if they avoided external food-related cues. Since there are relatively few food-related cues in synagogues, spending a lot of time in synagogue should make fasting easier for obese subjects, but not for the normal-size subjects who carry their hunger cues around with them. As predicted, time in synagogue was significantly negatively correlated with the rated unpleasantness of fasting for obese ($r = -.50$) but not normal-size ($r = -.18$) subjects.

Another study reported by Goldman et al. (1968) involved the choice of eating places. Since taste is more important to obese persons, they should be drawn to good food and repelled by bad food more than normal-size persons. Dormitory food is generally considered to be bad food, and there is evidence that such was the case at Columbia University when the study was conducted. Most freshmen at Columbia signed up for a meal contract at the beginning of the school year, but many dropped it later for a $15.00 penalty. The investigators reasoned that obese freshmen should have a greater tendency to drop the contract. The prediction was supported: 86.5% of the obese freshmen dropped the contract, as opposed to 67.1% of the normal size freshmen.

The final study reported by Goldman et al. involved the adjustment to time zone changes on transatlantic flights. Long-distance high-speed East-to-West travel creates a great discrepancy between the traveler's physiological state and the locally acceptable eating time. A person taking off from Paris at noon arrives in New York at 8.00 P.M. Paris time but only 2.00 P.M. New York time. The investigators guessed that this should be harder on normal-size and thinner persons, since they are more affected by internal cues. They discovered that Air France had height and weight data, plus spontaneous complaints of eating difficulty experienced by 236 of their personnel on East-to-West flights. Few of these employees were seriously overweight, but they were ordered along a scale from under-weight, through normal weight, to moderately overweight. As expected, the more the tendency toward overweight, the fewer the complaints about time-zone effects on eating.

Goldman et al. concluded, on the basis of their data, that "fasting, fat, French freshmen fly farther for fine food" (p. 123). While the alliteration of this statement is unassailable, recent data have cast doubt on one of its implications: that obese persons work harder for food. On the contrary, it appears that obese persons may not work as hard as normal-size persons for food.

THE FAT RAT ANALOGY

The source of this hypothesis is noteworthy. It was generated because of a number of fascinating similarities between the behavior of obese persons and the behavior of rats with lesions in the ventromedial nucleus of the hypothalamus. We saw in Chapter 2 that the ventromedial (VM) nucleus of the hypothalamus has been described as a satiety center because stimulation in that area tends to stop eating behavior, and lesioning of the area tends to result in gross overeating. The overeating of the VM lesioned rat when allowed ad lib food follows a certain pattern. The animal has fewer meals per day than normal rats, but he eats faster, he eats more per meal, and he eats more food per day. He eats more good, tasty food than his normal counterpart, but when quinine is added to the food to make it bitter, the VM lesioned rat eats *less* than a normal rat. Interestingly enough, the behavior of obese persons parallels the behavior of VM lesioned rats in each of these respects (Schachter, 1970).

To further explore the similarities between obese humans and VM lesioned rats, Schachter turned to the animal literature to find the outstanding characteristics of the eating behavior of fat rats. One such characteristic is that a VM lesioned rat will not work as hard for food as a normal animal. For example, if a VM lesioned rat is given a food pellet on each bar press, he will press more rapidly than will a normal rat. As the payoff rate decreases, the VM lesioned animal will work less and less until he stops getting any food at all, while the normal rat will continue to work (Teitelbaum, 1962; reported in Schachter, 1970). Schachter tested this phenomenon in humans in an experiment whose simplicity should be celebrated in every psychology text. Obese and normal-size subjects were asked to sit at a desk and fill out a series of questionnaires. A bag of almonds was on the desk. The experimenter invited the subject to help himself and left the room for fifteen minutes. In one condition the nuts were shelled, in the other condition they were not. The experimenters assumed that it took more work to eat an unshelled nut than a shelled nut. As expected, the presence or absence of shells had no significant effect on the nut-eating behavior of normal-size subjects. For the obese subjects, only one of twenty ate any unshelled nuts, and only one of twenty *failed* to eat shelled nuts (Schachter, 1971).

THE STIMULUS BINDING HYPOTHESIS

Schachter (1970) speculated that this failure to work for food may be integrated with the other findings on obesity by using a simple theoretical scheme. Perhaps the obese humans (and rats) are more reactive to prominent cues and less reactive to remote cues than normal-size persons. The response of the obese may thus be bound to the prominence of the cue. This assumes that the important aspect about having to work for food is that the more the work, the more remote are the food cues. If one accepts this assumption, it is true that in the studies of human eating behavior, obese persons eat more than normal-size persons when food cues are prominent but less when food cues are remote.

Schachter (1970) cited two studies that test this hypothesis directly. In one, it was found that obese persons worked harder for food when food cues were relatively prominent—the food was wrapped in transparent wrap and the subject had initially had a taste of a good sandwich. When the food was wrapped in nontransparent paper and the subject tasted plain bread, the normal-size subjects worked harder (Johnson, 1970). In the second experiment, subjects sat at a bowl of shelled nuts under high or low illumination. Under high illumination, the obese ate more than normal-size persons. Under low illumination, this finding was reversed with normal-size persons eating more than the obese (Ross, 1969).

Schachter (1970) also cited evidence that eating behavior is only a special case of a general state of overreactivity to prominent cues and underreactivity to remote cues among the obese (see Figure 10.2). In general, he feels that the obese are generally stimulus bound, their behaviors are governed by external stimuli, to a greater extent than normal-size persons. In fact, he points out that this stimulus binding may not always lead to obesity. Under certain environmental circumstances, as where food cues are remote, it could lead to emaciation (Schachter, 1968). For example, Schachter (1968) considered the eating behavior of extremely obese persons who were hospitalized to lose weight. Hashim and Van

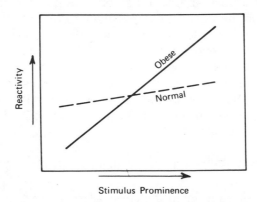

Stimulus Prominence

FIGURE 10.2 Theoretical curves of relationship between reactivity and stimulus prominence. From S. Schachter, *Op. Cit.* Copyright 1970 by the American Psychological Association. Reprinted by permission.

Itallie (1965) reported on a clinical experiment in the nutrition clinic of a New York hospital. Six grossly obese patients and five normal volunteers were given a bland, unappealing liquid diet and allowed to eat as much as they wanted whenever they wanted. The results were striking. The normal volunteers maintained their normal caloric intake on the bland diet. The obese patients went precipitately from an abnormally high caloric intake to an incredibly low intake. One woman went from a prehospital intake of about 3500 calories to an intake of about 500 calories per day. Under the program, the obese patients lost great amounts of weight. In the restricted hospital environment, with unpalatable food, and few prominent food-related cues, they spontaneously ate much less than normals. Sadly, when they left the hospital and returned to a world of food-related cues, none proved capable of restricting their diets and they all returned to their original weights.

The aforementioned similarities between the behavior of VM lesioned rats and obese humans suggests the tentative hypothesis that the ventromedial nucleus of the hypothalamus is involved in human obesity. Although clearly recognizing that they are reasoning by analogy, both Schachter (1970) and Morosovsky (1971) suggest that the VM nucleus is quiescent in obese animals, including obese humans. If this is true, and if Schachter is right about obese humans being overreactive to prominent stimuli and underreactive to remote stimuli, it is conceivable that the VM nucleus of the hypothalamus is somehow involved in this stimulus binding.*

Schachter's theories and experiments on emotion and obesity demonstrate that cognitive influences play a direct part in emotion and that the kind of information an individual uses to interpret and label his emotional and motivational state has important implications, even for such a basic behavior as eating. In the next section, we will consider experiments that suggest that a different kind of cognitive control may be exercised over basic motives.

Effects of Cognitive Dissonance on Motivation

DISSONANCE EFFECTS ON HUNGER, THIRST, AND PAIN MOTIVATION

We saw in the last chapter that the notion of cognitive imbalance, or dissonance, has motivational implications of its own. In this section, we

---

It should be noted that Schachter's reasoning has been challenged by others. cf. Nisbett (1972), Singh (1973), and Singh and Sikes (1974).

shall review a series of studies that attempt to demonstrate how such basic motives as hunger, thirst and pain may be modified by cognitive dissonance manipulations. These studies are based on the dissonance prediction that, if a person voluntarily commits himself to undergoing an unpleasant task with little justification, he will be motivated to minimize the unpleasant aspects of that task. If the task involves a motivational state such as hunger, thirst, or pain, the subject will minimize that motivational state. Thus, the investigators hope to show that the motivational state itself is affected by the attempt to restore cognitive balance.

The studies in this tradition have been brought together by Zimbardo (1969a). Like many dissonance experiments, these studies contain individual inadequacies caused by such factors as subject loss and analysis of only part of the available data due to insufficient dissonance in some groups. Also, we shall see that some of them contain questionable manipulations and measures of motivation. However, the studies taken as a whole are fairly persuasive, since they illustrate the same kind of effect under a variety of conditions using a variety of dependent measures.

An example of a dissonance effect on hunger is provided by Brehm's (1962) study. Subjects were asked to forgo breakfast and lunch on the day of the experiment. At the afternoon experimental session, the subjects rated their hunger and were asked to commit themselves to further food deprivation. Half were given no payment (high dissonance); half were promised $5.00 (low dissonance). They then rerated their hunger and ordered food for the evening test session. As expected, the hunger ratings of the high dissonance subjects tended to go down after commitment, while those of low dissonance subjects went up. Also, the high dissonance subjects ordered less food. Brehm suggested that the high dissonance subjects may have actually reduced their hunger drive by a cognitive process.

Brehm (1962) also reported a similar study on thirst. Subjects were asked to refrain from drinking from the evening before the day of the study until the experimental session in the afternoon. At the experiment, they rated their thirst and were then asked to commit themselves to deprivation for either $1.00 (high dissonance) or $5.00 (low dissonance). They then rated their thirst again. Subject loss in this experiment was high, with 29 out of 69 refusing to continue the deprivation. Of the 40 remaining, 8 more were deleted because they did not rate themselves sufficiently thirsty. Thus, out of 69 original subjects, the data of only 32 were analyzed. The results supported Brehm's expectation that high dissonance subjects would decrease their thirst ratings after commitment. However, this was found only when a pitcher of water and cups were furnished in the experimental room. Again, Brehm suggested that the motivational state of thirst itself was affected.

Another study of dissonance effects on thirst tested the subjects' performance on a variety of tasks designed to assess thirst motivation (Mansson, 1969). Unfortunately, thirst was aroused by the rather dubious means of inducing students to eat a hot sauce. Dissonance was aroused by asking subjects to continue their deprivation for a long (24-hour) or short (4-hour) period with high or low justification. Subjects in the low-justification conditions were told that the experiment was relatively unimportant and that the experimenter was "just trying something out." High-justification subjects were told that the experiment was important and had applications to the space program. This created four conditions; one high dissonance (long deprivation, low justification), one low dissonance (short deprivation, high justification), and two in between.

After the subjects agreed to further deprivation, Mansson measured their thirst motivation by a variety of clever methods. For one measure, pairs of words were presented to the subjects for brief (1/10 sec) exposure times, and the subjects were asked which word they preferred. Some of the words were thirst-related, such as "lake," "wet," and "soup"; others were not, like "cheese" and "mountain." The measure of thirst motivation was the number of thirst-related words preferred. For a second measure, the subjects learned a paired-associate list that contained thirst-related words. The measure of thirst motivation was the speed in learning the list. As a third measure, the subjects were given TAT pictures and asked to make up stories. The measure of thirst motivation was the amount of thirst-related imagery in the TAT. Other measures of thirst motivation were more direct: the subject's self rating of thirst and his water consumption at the end of the experiment.

The high, medium, and low dissonance groups were compared on these measures to two control groups that had not committed themselves to further deprivation. One of the control groups was thirsty (i.e., had eaten the hot sauce), the other was not. The results of the experiment are presented in Table 10.1. They indicated that, as expected, the higher the dissonance the more subjects behaved like the nonthirsty control group on all of these tasks. The less the dissonance, the more their behavior resembled the thirsty control group.

Other studies have attempted to measure the motivational state involved by physiological measures. Brehm, Back, and Bogdonoff (1964) replicated Brehm's (1962) study of hunger using similar manipulations, and they extended it by using measures of the concentration of plasma-free fatty acids (FFA) in the blood stream taken after the commitment to further deprivation. The FFA level rises with fasting (and also with central nervous system arousal), so if cognitive dissonance really lowers hunger motivation, it should lower the FFA level as well. The experiment successfully replicated Brehm's (1962) result using self-ratings, but the FFA meas-

TABLE 10.1   EFFECTS OF COGNITIVE DISSONANCE ON MEASURES OF THIRST

		NO. OF THIRST-RELATED WORDS CHOSEN	LEARNING SPEED (NO. OF TRIALS)	NO. OF THIRST-RELATED TAT RESPONSES	SELF-RATING OF THIRST	C.C. WATER CONSUMED
	High	5.60	6.50	6	29	128
Dissonance	Mod.	8.50	6.85	10	47	138
	Low	9.80	5.00	12	50	155
Control	Not thirsty	7.75	5.95	3	18	106
	Thirsty	9.75	4.95	10	40	152

Adapted from figures in H. M. Mansson, "The relation of dissonance reduction to cognitive, perceptual, consummatory, and learning measures of thirst." In P. G. Zimbardo (Ed.) *The Cognitive Control of Motivation.* Glenview, Ill.: Scott, Foresman, 1969.

Note. Numbers are approximate.

ure worked only among subjects with high ratings of hunger before commitment. In the high dissonance condition, subjects who had high initial ratings of hunger had FFA levels equal to or lower than subjects who had initially rated themselves not hungry. In the low dissonance condition, in contrast, high-rated hunger was associated with a high FFA level. The authors argued that a high precommitment rating of hunger was necessary for true dissonance to occur in this experiment and that the relatively low FFA level among those subjects may have been due to the lowering of the hunger drive by cognitive factors. They admit, however, that this finding is marginal and based on an internal analysis and that replication is necessary.

A study by Zimbardo, Cohen, Weisenberg, Dworkin, and Firestone (1966) used both physiological and learning speed measures to study the cognitive minimization of pain, and it compared the dissonance conditions with control conditions in which the intensity of pain was actually lessened. Subjects were first given a series of painful shocks, and their self-report, skin resistance, and speed of learning a serial-anticipation task while being shocked were measured. They then were asked to undergo a second series of shocks, with either low choice (control), choice with high justification (low dissonance), or choice with low justification (high dissonance). The control group was subdivided into groups which took painful shocks during the entire experiment (Hi–Hi), mild shocks during the entire experi-

TABLE 10.2   EFFECTS OF COGNITIVE DISSONANCE ON MEASURES OF PAIN

	CHANGE IN GSR (OHMS) PRE- TO POSTCOMMITMENT	CHANGE IN LEARNING SPEED (# TRIALS) PRE- TO POSTCOMMITMENT	POSTCOMMITMENT LEARNING SPEED (# TRIALS TO CRITERION)	CHANGE IN SELF-REPORTED PAIN. PRE- TO POSTCOMMITMENT
High	−1200	−1.1	7.30	−9
Dissonance Low	+ 500	+0.2	9.00	−2
Hi-Mod.	−1100	−1.3	7.75	−26
Control Hi-Hi	+1200	+0.3	8.80	− 3

Adapted from Figures in P. G. Zimbardo, A. Cohen, M. Wersenberg, L. Dworkin, and J. Firestone, "The cognitive control of pain." From THE COGNITIVE CONTROL OF MOTIVATION by Philip G. Zimbardo. Copyright © 1969 by Scott, Foresman and Company. Reprinted by permission of the publisher.

Note. Numbers are approximate.

ment (Lo–Lo), or painful shocks during the first part but moderate shocks during the second (Hi–Mod). The intensity of the shock was determined individually for each subject. Subjects then underwent a series of shocks while doing a learning task, as they had done before. The authors predicted that the high dissonance condition should resemble the Hi–Mod control group, in which pain was actually lessened.

The results reproduced in Table 10.2 indicated that the high dissonance group was in fact similar to the Hi–Mod control group in that learning was enhanced and skin resistance responses lowered during the postcommitment trials. They differed significantly from the low dissonance and Hi–Hi control groups, which in turn resembled each other. The self-ratings of pain showed a similar but nonsignificant trend.

This well-controlled study with a relatively low subject dropout rate (6 out of 86) gives fairly persuasive evidence that the motivational state of the subjects may indeed be alterable by cognitive adjustments. Unfortunately, it is the only study in the series that is methodologically adequate. Brehm's studies are called into question by insufficient measurement of hunger motivation, high subject dropout rates, and, in the study with Back and Bogdonoff, the necessity for internal analyses. Mansson's otherwise well-designed study, with proper control groups and multiple measures of thirst motivation, used a very questionable method of inducing thirst peripherally without altering the organism's water balance. Nevertheless, these studies taken as a whole do seem to illustrate the same kind of effect under a variety of conditions and using a variety of measures. Hopefully, more convincing experiments such as that by Zimbardo et al. (1966) will be done on this phenomenon in the future.

Both the Schachter research and the studies stemming from cognitive dissonance theory that we have reviewed have demonstrated relationships between cognitive factors and motivational and emotional processes. We shall now turn to a body of work that has approached these relationships from a different point of view.

Lazarus's Studies on Coping with Stress

Lazarus's research program has addressed a number of important issues in the area of the psychophysiological response to emotion. He and his colleagues have studied the effect of how a threatening event is interpreted or appraised by the subject and how this appraisal is a function of both situational factors and personality and cultural variables that create enduring dispositions to respond to threat. He has also studied how various psychophysiological, self-report, and behavioral measures of stress and emotion relate to each other. (See Chapter 2.)

Lazarus defines appraisal as the "evaluation by the individual of the harmful significance of some event" (Lazarus and Opton, 1966, p. 244). He points out that the same stimulus may or may not be stressful, depending on the person's cognitive appraisal. The nature of this appraisal is determined both by situational and personality-cultural factors.

SITUATIONAL FACTORS

Situational influences involving the context of an event were demonstrated by a series of studies employing gruesome films, including one showing a circumcision-like ritual performed on adolescent boys in an Australian aboriginal culture (subincision film) and another depicting a series of relatively gory industrial accidents (accident film). Lazarus, Spiesman, Mordkoff, and Davidson (1962) reported that the scenes on the subincision film that they had defined a priori as threatening were associated with high arousal on heart rate and skin conductance measures. In the first study of appraisal, Speisman, Lazarus, Mordkoff, and Davidson (1964) created three sound tracks to accompany this film. One track denied the harmful features of the rite and stated that the event was actually a happy one (denial commentary). The second track described the scene technically, encouraging intellectualization (intellectualization commentary). The third track emphasized the horror and pain experienced by the boys (trauma commentary). The study found that the first two tracks significantly reduced autonomic arousal as compared to the silent control film, while the third track increased arousal. A second study by Lazarus and Alfert (1964, see Figure 10.3) showed that denial orientation, or denial information presented before the film showing, was more effective in reducing stress than when it was presented on the sound track. The third study of appraisal by Lazarus, Opton, Nomikos, and Rankin (1965) showed that this "short circuiting" of threat also occurred to the accident film, demonstrating that the principle could be extended to other kinds of film-induced threats in less esoteric settings.

Other studies have shown that situational influences involving the time sequence prior to the threat is an important determinant of the subject's reaction, presumably because the process of appraisal varies with time. Rankin, Nomikos, Opton, and Lazarus (1965) demonstrated that long periods of suspense (30–60 seconds) in anticipation of the accidents on the accident film produced more autonomic arousal than short (5–10 seconds) periods. Similarly, Folkins (1970) reported that a moderate (1 minute) anticipation period is more arousing than short (5–30 seconds) or long (3–20 minutes) periods when subjects are threatened with the prospect of taking an electric shock. Lazarus's theory suggests that the lesser response in the extremely short intervals is due to the fact that there is

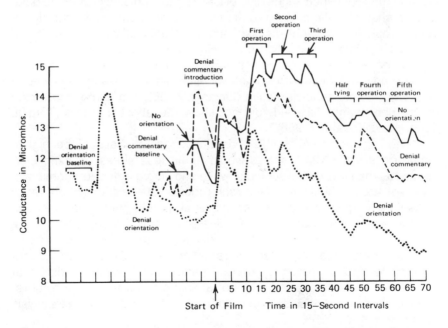

FIGURE 10.3   Skin conductance curves for the denial orientation, denial commentary, and no denial film conditions. From R. S. Lazarus and E. Alfert, "Short circuiting of threat by experimentally altering cognitive appraisal." *Journal of Abnormal and Social Psychology.* 1964, 69, 195–205. Copyright 1964 by the American Psychological Association. Reprinted by permission.

no time to assimilate and comprehend the nature of the harm. With moderate warning, there is time to appraise the significance of the harm but insufficient time to develop effective ways of coping with it. With more time, the subject can fully appraise the threat and also self-generate ways of coping with it. Folkins's data is consistent with these expectations. At the short and long anticipation times, he found a low incidence of ego failure and a high incidence of coping in detailed content analyses of the subjects' self-reported reactions. At the moderate anticipation times, in contrast, coping was less prevalent than ego failure (Folkins, 1970).

PERSONALITY AND CULTURAL FACTORS

The study of self-generated coping behavior and its personality and cultural correlates represents another aspect of Lazarus's research. Lazarus has investigated possible personality correlates of the response to threat from the beginning of his work, with varying success. The Speisman et al. (1964) study contained suggestive evidence that subjects inclined to denial as a characteristic mode of defense were more calmed by the denial sound track and that subjects disposed to intellectualization were helped more by the intellectualization track. However, an experiment that contrasted the responses of college students and nonstudents, who presumably differed in their tendency to intellectualize, did not show the anticipated interaction to the subincision film (Lazarus, 1966), and a later replication of the Speisman et al. study did not show the effect (Lazarus, Tomita, Opton, and Kodama, 1966).

The Lazarus and Alfert (1964) results suggested that subjects high in denial on several MMPI scales would admit less stress on self-report measures than low-denial subjects, while showing greater autonomic evidence of stress. The finding of less self-reported stress among high-denial subjects was replicated in the Lazarus et al. (1966) study and extended in a reanalysis of six experiments (Weinstein, Averill, Opton, and Lazarus, 1968). The latter showed that high-denial subjects, or "repressors," showed greater autonomic than self-report arousal, while low-denial "sensitizers" tended to show the opposite pattern. The original finding that high-denial subjects showed a higher absolute level of physiological response than low-denial subjects was not replicated in the reanalysis (Weinstein et al., 1968).

Several experiments by investigators outside Lazarus's group are relevant to this suggestion that some high-denial persons (repressors) show a greater tendency to respond on physiological than self-report measures, while low-denial sensitizers show the opposite pattern. Using the Byrne (1964) R–S scale, Parsons, Fulganzi, and Edelberg (1969) formed five-person discussion groups containing majorities of repressors or sensitizers. They found that, compared to sensitizers, repressors had greater skin conductance responding but reported themselves as being less aggressive in the discussion. This appears to fit nicely with Lazarus's finding that repressors are relatively more reactive on physiological measures, but less reactive on self-report measures. In addition, Parson, et al. took a measure of overt aggression: the groups were rated by observers using the Bales categories of behavior. Interestingly, the repressors were rated as *more* aggressive than sensitizers. Thus, in this situation, repressors appeared to be relatively high on overt behavioral and physiological measures, but low on self-report measures, of emotional responding.

A study by Taylor (1967) attempted to demonstrate differences between overcontrollers and undercontrollers on overt aggressive behavior and skin conductance responding. Undercontrollers were defined as subjects admitting impulsive overt expression of aggression on a self-report inventory, while overcontrollers were subjects acknowledging inhibition of their hostile feelings. The study included a control group of subjects that admitted neither expression nor inhibition of aggression. As predicted, undercontrollers showed more overt aggression than overcontrollers or control subjects. However, contrary to expectation, overcontrollers did not show higher physiological responding than undercontrollers. Instead, control subjects showed higher skin conductance responding than either overcontrollers or undercontrollers. A possible explanation for this finding that is consistent with the other results may be found in the fact that, while the overcontrollers were low in overt behavioral responding, they were high in reporting subjective experiences of hostility. The control subjects, in contrast, acknowledged neither overt nor subjective hostility and may have thus been high in denial.

We saw in Chapter 7 that several recent studies have demonstrated a negative relationship between skin conductance responding and facial expressiveness (Buck et al. 1969, 1972, 1974; Lanzetta and Kleck, 1970). Following a distinction proposed by Jones (1935), persons high in skin conductance responding but low in facial expressiveness were labeled internalizers, while those showing the opposite pattern were termed externalizers. Together with the results of Lazarus' group, these experiments suggest that high-denial subjects are high in physiological but low in facial and self-report responses to emotion. More generally, these studies demonstrate that individuals differ in their tendencies for responding on overt behavioral, self-report, and physiological measures of emotion, and they suggest that these response tendencies may be related to important personality dispositions.

Despite some success in analyzing personality factors in the autonomic response to stress and emotion, Opton and Lazarus (1967) note that most efforts in this field yield disappointingly small and unstable relationships. A major reason, they note, is the occurrence of great individual differences in neuroanatomy and neurophysiological functioning. It may be meaningful to speak of a large skin conductance change as mirroring a more important psychological event than a small skin conductance change when one is dealing with a single person, but such a comparison between persons is subject to so much error that it is extremely unreliable. As a consequence, Opton and Lazarus (1967) and Alfert (1967; 1968) suggest that research designs using an idiographic, or intraindividual strategy be used in this area.

As an example, they discuss an experiment that contrasted a subject's physiological response to the threat of shock with his response to the accident film. Subjects who responded to the film more than to the shock described themselves on personality questionnaires as being more socially inhibited, introverted, submissive, suggestible and obedient, insecure, passive, anxious, not caring about friends, and lacking in impulse expression. In contrast, a nomothetic, or between subjects, analysis yielded no more discriminating personality items than would be expected by chance. Opton and Lazarus concluded that the idiographic design "can control much of the extraneous variance which probably is responsible for the weak and ephemeral relationships between personality and psychophysiological response commonly found in studies using (nomothetic) designs" (1967, p. 291).

Just as personality factors lead to enduring dispositions for coping with stress, so should cultural factors. Unfortunately, few cross-cultural studies have been done. One of these studied the reactions to the subincision film among Japanese students and adults. Lazarus et al. (1966) found that Japanese subjects showed high skin conductance responding to both the stressful film and a control film on rice farming. The self-reported distress ratings of the Japanese subjects, however, was similar to those of comparable American subjects. Lazarus et al. suggest that the Japanese subjects were stressed by the whole experimental situation, because of cultural differences in the experience of being observed and evaluated. Perhaps cultural training encourages the Japanese to be repressors, at least in this kind of experimental situation.

THE THEORETICAL ANALYSIS OF COPING

Lazarus and his colleagues have recently offered theoretical analyses of stress and emotion based in part on their studies (Averill, Opton, and

Lazarus, 1969; Lazarus, Averill, and Opton, 1968; Lazarus, 1966). Their general approach represents a kind of systems analysis that conceives of emotions as response systems, or interrelated processes that are distinguished from other psychological phenomena primarily on the basis of response characteristics. They distinguish emotions from other phenomena (such as motives) by saying that emotions tend to interrupt and monopolize ongoing behavior and that the emotional response system is relatively independent of external feedback control (Averill et al., 1969).

The major components of the emotional response system (ERS) are illustrated in Figure 10.4. These include input variables (stimulus properties), the appraiser subsystem, and output variables (response categories). Stimulus properties include intrinsic, extrinsic, and response-determined properties. Intrinsic properties convey information specific to the object, extrinsic properties convey nonspecific information (i.e., novelty, ambiguity), and response-determined properties are stimulus elements created by the subject's own prior response. Response categories include instrumental and expressive responses, which involve overt activity, and also purely cognitive responses. The latter are cognitive modes of coping termed "reappraisals" which can be invoked when no overt action is possible because of internal or external inhibitions. They are a function of ego response mechanisms and include the traditional defense mechanisms (e.g., repression, projection, denial, etc.) Thus, they often involve distortion of reality (Averill et al., 1969; Lazarus, 1966).

The heart of the ERS is the appraiser subsystem. Stimuli are first evaluated by a cognitive process of primary appraisal. This process is not specific to emotional contexts but plays a general discriminative role. It is compatible with an individual's self-concept and his values and goals, and it is open to normal change through environmental control and reinforcement. The primary appraisal process is involved in the first appraisal of stimuli as threatening. This first appraisal is a function of the stimulus properties in the situation, and also the psychological structure of the individual and his cultural norms and values.

Once a stimulus has been appraised as threatening, coping strategies are initiated to deal with it. The selection of these coping strategies is a function of the cognitive processes of secondary appraisal. Whereas primary appraisal is concerned with the original evaluation of threat, secondary appraisal functions to evaluate what can be done to cope with the threat. It is more likely to depart from the usual values and goals of the person, because habitual modes of cognition become less useful the more dangerous and immediate the threat. The processes of secondary appraisal will result in one of the three kinds of response categories outlined

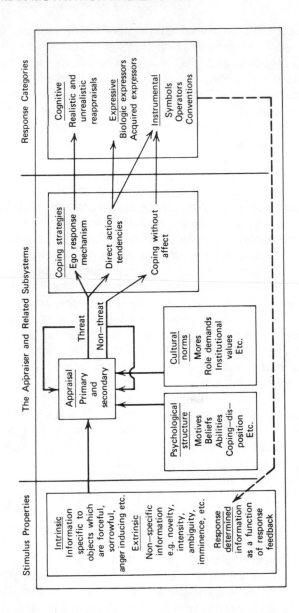

FIGURE 10.4   Outline of the emotional response system. From J. R. Averill, E. M. Opton, and R. S. Lazarus, "Cross-cultural studies of psychophysiological responses during stress and emotion." *International Journal of Psychology*, 1969, 4, 83–102. Copyright © 1969 by the International Journal of Psychology. Reprinted by permission.

earlier: cognitive, expressive, and instrumental responses (Averill et al., 1969).

It is clear from this summary that Lazarus and his colleagues regard cognition as the central process from which emotional phenomena should be studied. They feel that "cognitive processes create the emotional response out of the organism-environment transaction" and that biological and cultural influences are thus filtered through the individual psyche (Lazarus et al., 1968). They admit, however, that their theory of emotion is at this point merely a statement of a frame of reference and that the details of how cognitive factors are involved in emotion are almost entirely unknown and subject to conjecture.

Lazarus and his colleagues present their theory as a general theory of emotion. Shapiro and Shwartz (1970), however, regard it as a relatively small and circumscribed theory of coping with threat, in comparison with Schachter's broad formulation. There seems to be some justification in this view. Lazarus's theory seems most reasonable and acceptable when negative emotions are considered, that is, when the subject is responding to some threat. Lazarus and his colleagues do not give examples in terms of positive emotions such as joy or love, and it is difficult to imagine how such phenomena could be covered in their terms.

In addition, Lazarus's theory regards the usual physiological and self-report indicants of emotion as outcomes of a cognitive state of appraisal. While this view may be useful in analyzing some kinds of emotional processes, it ignores the possibility suggested by conditioning studies that strong emotional responses may be conditioned to stimuli in situations with little or no cognitive mediation. While cognitive factors might play an important role in determining the integrated response of the whole organism, it could be argued that the first kind of response to threat in many situations would be physiological and that the organism's own conditioned emotional response would be a major stimulus factor on which any appraisal would be based. In the extreme case of phobia, the emotional response as measured by the subject's physiological arousal or self-report might be the only element in the subject's preceptual field that could be regarded as indicative of threat. He might be frightened even though he knows that there is no real threat in the situation. Thus, any attempt that treats cognitive factors as *central* in the development of an emotional state must be regarded as limited in scope.

We have considered a number of processes that go on during emotion and motivation whose relationships with each other, at the present state of knowledge, are unclear. We have seen that peripheral autonomic, somatic, and endocrine processes may be altered directly by arousing stimuli by conditioning. The same processes also seem affected by cognitive factors such as appraisal. At the same time, these peripheral responses form part of the stimulus complex that is being appraised. Finally, there are central nervous system mechanisms of emotion and motivation in the limbic system and hypothalamus whose relationships with both the peripheral physiological responses and the cognitive factors are unknown. A complete theory of emotion and motivation must account for all of these processes.

Therapeutic Implications of the Cognitive-Physiological Interaction

Writers in both the Schachter tradition and dissonance theory tradition have become intrigued with the therapeutic possibilities of their findings. For example, Valins (1966; Valins and Ray, 1967; Davison and Valins, 1969) has suggested that cognitive manipulations of the perceived level of arousal may have therapeutic applications. He suggests that phobic subjects may be desensitized by simply giving them manipulated information about the level of their internal response to events (Valins, 1966). In a study with Ray (1967) he demonstrated that leading subjects to believe via false heart-rate feedback that snakes did not affect them internally increased approach behavior to live snakes. He used this result to question the physiological incompatibility theory upon which desensitization therapy is based. However, other investigators have been unable to replicate the Valins and Ray results (Sushinsky and Bootzin, 1970; Kent, Wilson, and Nelson, 1972; Rosen, Rosen, and Ried, 1972).

The Valins and Ray (1967) study used false biofeedback to alter the perceived *level* of arousal. Other studies have used reattribution techniques similar to those of Nisbett and Schachter (1966) and Ross et al. (1969) to alter the perceived *source* of arousal. Storms and Nisbett (1970) report an attempt to treat insomnia by such a reattribution technique. Insomniac subjects took placebo pills before going to bed. Some were told the pills would cause arousal (arousal condition), others were told that they would reduce arousal (sedation condition). As predicted, arousal subjects went to sleep *more* easily than usual, and sedation subjects went to sleep *less* easily. Presumably, the arousal subjects attributed their own arousal to the pill, while sedation subjects attributed it to themselves and were more affected than usual because they were led to expect sedation.

The finding by Lazarus and his colleagues on personality differences in patterns of emotional responding is relevant to an interesting experiment with medical implications. Janis (1958) studied the postoperative recovery of surgical patients and found evidence that a moderate level of preoperative fear and concern was more closely associated with a satisfactory postoperative recovery than either a very high or low level of fear. He suggested that the person who experiences moderate preoperative fear is more able to cope with unpleasant postoperative experiences than the person who feels little fear, mainly because the latter person has gathered little information about what to expect following surgery. Janis suggested from this that hospital personnel should warn all patients about what to expect following their surgery since the normal person will lack the motivation to inform himself (Janis, Mahl, Kagan, and Holt, 1969). This advice has been followed by some physicians, apparently with positive results (Egbert, Battit, Welch, and Bartlett, 1964; Healy, 1968; Vernon and Bigelow, 1974). Egbert and his colleagues, for example, found that patients for abdominal surgery required fewer pain-killing drugs and a shorter hospital stay when informed than when not informed about the operation (Egbert, 1966).

However, a study by Andrew (1970) suggests that this procedure may not be beneficial if the patient is one who prefers to use avoidant defenses. Andrew classified patients hospitalized for inguinal hernia surgery as having avoidant defenses, sensitizing defenses, or no defensive preference. She gave some patients a factual statement about the nature of inguinal hernia and the surgical procedures. The informative statement was beneficial to the patients with no defensive preference, as measured by faster recovery. However, it had no effect on the patients who used sensitizing defenses, and the patients who preferred avoidant defenses had slower recovery and required more medication when they had received the information.

DeLong (1970) gave patients either specific information about their illness, what to expect from the operation, the reasons for surgery, and so on, or nonspecific information about the rules of the hospital, hospital facilities, and so forth. The type of information did not affect the recovery of patients with no defensive preference, who recovered quickly under both conditions, or the recovery of patients with avoidant defenses, who recovered poorly. The patients who used sensitizing defenses recovered more quickly after being given specific than general information. As Averill (1972) concludes in his discussion of these studies, the Andrew and DeLong results are not entirely consistent with one another, and more research is needed in this area. However, they do demonstrate how the information a person receives about a threatening event interacts with his characteristic style of defense in determining his response to stress.

Summary

This chapter has considered Schachter's theory of emotion and the experiments growing out of it, with particular reference to the ideas that peripheral physiological arousal plays a role in the subjective experience of emotion, that the meaning of this arousal is determined cognitively, and that emotion under some circumstances may involve an information-search process, in which the responder searches the environment for an appropriate explanation for his arousal, and a labeling process, which determines the quality of the emotion. All of these ideas have led to experiments whose results are largely consistent with the original formulation, and the theory has been applied with success to a wide variety of motivational and emotional situations. One of the latter is Schachter's theory of obesity, which suggests that obese humans label their hunger according to external food-related cues, while normal-size persons label hunger according to their internal need for food.

The chapter also reviewed studies demonstrating that such basic drives as hunger, thirst, and pain are modifiable by cognitive dissonance manipulations, and Lazarus' studies on the process of coping with stress. These again demonstrated the importance of cognitive factors in motivation and emotion. The potential therapy applications of the studies in the chapter were also reviewed.

In terms of the schema presented in Chapter 1, this chapter focused on the cognitive-physiological interaction in some detail. With the material from this chapter, a more elaborate picture of this interaction can be presented. Figure 10.5 shows the affective stimulus, after being filtered

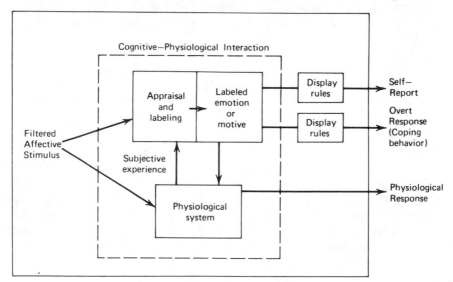

FIGURE 10.5   Elaborated schema showing the cognitive-physiological interaction in motivation and emotion.

through the appropriate innate mechanisms and learned reactions, impinging upon the cognitive and physiological systems. The cognitive system will gather information from the filtered affective stimulus and also from the subjective sensations arising from the reaction of the physiological system. If this information is insufficient to understand or label the affective state, the individual will be motivated to gain more information. If the state is labeled, the label will serve as a basis for making overt behaviors and self-reports consistent with that state and the relevant display rules learned in that situation. The label may also itself affect the physiological system—there may be additional need for bodily adaptation following labeling.

CHAPTER ELEVEN

SOCIAL INFLUENCE AND HUMAN MOTIVATION

It was mentioned in Chapter 1 that, to this writer, the most important single finding in psychology since World War II is the extent to which human behavior is subject to social and situational influences. We saw in Chapter 9 that a number of investigators have argued that situational factors are more important than an individual's personality or disposition in determining his behavior, even to the extent that some doubt the reality of trans-situational personality variables. In this chapter we shall briefly examine the experiments on conformity which first demonstrated the surprising power of social pressure and situational influences. We will then discuss the influence of the individual's cognitive development and situational factors on moral judgment and behavior: the judgment of right and wrong and the taking of the appropriate action. We shall then examine the role of social and situational variables in aggressive behavior, pointing out a kind of socially based aggression quite different from the kinds of aggression examined in Chapter 5.

Experiments on Conformity

One of the first experiments to call attention to the power of social influence was the famous study by Solomon Asch (1952). Asch had ten subjects make simple perceptual judgments involving the lengths of lines. They gave their judgments verbally and in succession. The first nine subjects were actually confederates of the experimenter. On certain trials, these subjects unanamously gave an incorrect judgment. About one-third of the naive subjects conformed to the group and gave an obviously incorrect judgment.

A large literature has derived from Asch's experiment. *Social influence* has been found to have powerful effects on the behavior of individuals. In one experiment, college students were asked if they agreed with the statement "society should suspend free speech whenever it feels itself threatened." In a control condition only 2% of the students agreed with this statement, but under unanamous group pressure, over half of the students indicated agreement. Some experiments have attempted to find personality differences between conformers and subjects who resist group influence to remain independent. On the whole, few relationships have been found between personality and conformity, although one scale —the F scale of authoritarianism—has been found to be higher among conformers in a number of experiments. Also, many studies have indicated that, at least among college-age subjects, women tend to conform more than men. We shall return to these findings below.

Moral Judgment and Behavior

The moral capacity has been studied by two major research traditions: one focusing on moral judgment, or the ability to judge right from wrong, and the other focusing on moral behavior, or the tendency to act in accordance with moral prescriptions. This literature offers important insights into the relationship between transsituational personality dispositions and social and situational influences in the determination of behavior.

Jean Piaget has applied his unique methodology and theoretical perspective on cognitive development to the study of the development of moral judgment. His 1932 book, *The Moral Judgment of the Child,* remains his major statement of this work: although Piaget has referred to moral development in later works, he has not attempted any detailed revision of his 1932 theory. However, Lawrence Kohlberg has developed Piaget's basic ideas and approach into a very useful theory of the development of moral judgment. We shall briefly consider Piaget's ideas and then examine Kohlberg's theory and some of the research it has inspired.

PIAGET'S THEORY OF MORAL JUDGMENT

Methodology   Piaget began his study of the development of moral judgment by asking children about their conceptions of the rules of the game of marbles, a popular pastime among the children of Geneva. Piaget pretended to be a naive adult interested in learning how to play marbles, and he asked children to play a game with him to show him how to play. To put the child at his ease, Piaget played "in a simple spirit (letting) the child feel a certain superiority at the game (while not omitting to show by an occasional good shot that (he was) not a complete duffer)." (Piaget, 1932; quoted by Bernstein, 1971).

A second method employed by Piaget was to ask children questions about stories designed to assess hypotheses developed from the observations of the marble games. For example, to assess whether the child regards the magnitude of the damage committed or the intentions of the actor as more important in judging the seriousness of a crime, he constructed stories in which one actor commits great damage accidentally and another causes small damage through mischief:*

---

*From Bronfenbrenner, U. *The role of age, sex, class, and culture in studies of moral development.* Religious Education Research Supplements,*1962,* 57, *S3-S17.*

A little boy who is called John is in his room. He is called to dinner. He goes into the dining room. But behind the door there was a chair, and on the chair there was a tray with fifteen cups on it. John couldn't have known that there was all this behind the door. He goes in, the door knocks against the tray, bang go the fifteen cups and they all get broken!
Once there was a little boy whose name was Henry. One day when his mother was out he tried to get some jam out of the cupboard. He climbed up on to a chair and stretched out his arm. But the jam was too high up and he couldn't reach it and have any. But while he was trying to get it he knocked over a cup. The cup fell down and broke (Bronfenbrenner, 1962, pp. 2–3).

After the stories, the child would be asked: "Are these children equally guilty?" "Which of the two is naughtiest and why?" Similarly, as a means of distinguishing what type of punishment the child thought appropriate, the following kind of story and questioning were used:

A boy has broken a toy belonging to his little brother. What should be done? 1. Should he not be allowed to play with any of his own toys for a week? (expiation); 2. Should he give the little fellow one of his own toys? (reciprocation); 3. Should he pay for having it mended? (restitution). (Bronfenbrenner, 1962, p. 3).

The Theory   On the basis of the childrens' answers, Piaget distinguished two stages of moral judgment. The first stage of *moral realism* develops about the age of 4 and lasts to about 8 years. It is thought to be based upon adult authority: rules are regarded as absolute and unchangeable, and the letter, rather than the spirit, of the law is emphasized. Guilt is defined on the basis of the seriousness of the objective damage caused without regard to the intentions of the actor. Justice is administered by harsh expiatory punishment, and there is a belief in immanant justice: that nature or physical things will punish a wrongsdoer (Kohlberg, 1963a).

The second, more mature, stage of moral judgment is termed the *morality of cooperation*. This is characterized by an ethic of mutual respect: rules are seen as agreed upon by equals in the common interest of all and can be changed by mutual consent. Guilt is defined with consideration of the intentions and motives of the actor. Justice is seen as best served by reciprocation or restitution so that the harm is repaired (Bronfenbrenner, 1962; Kohlberg, 1963a; 1964).

Piaget feels that these stages of normal judgment are based upon two factors: cognitive development and social experience. The young 4–8 year-old child has cognitive limitations that cause him to confuse moral rules and physical laws. His egocentrism makes him unable to understand that others have different perspectives, resulting in an inability to judge intentionality in others. He also confuses subjective phenomena with objective things, and this *realism* makes him view rules as eternal things rather than subjective expectations.

These cognitive limitations are combined with the child's relationship with adults to produce *moral realism.* Piaget believes that, just as cognitive development is accomplished by experience with objects and actions in the real world, the development of moral judgment is accomplished by experience with people. The kind of relationship spontaneously established between adults and children is an authoritarian relationship in which the adult knows more, has more power, and directs the child as to what is right and wrong. This encourages the acceptance of conventional rules and obedience to authority characteristic of moral realism.

Moral realism represents an adequate equilibrium in moral judgment, given the cognitive skills and the unilateral nature of the social relationships dominant in the life of the preoperational child. However, with greater social experience and increasing cognitive skills, disequilibrium increases. The child is motivated to achieve a new cognitive organization that will encompass these new experiences and abilities into a consistent framework for a more equilibrated system of moral judgment: the *morality of cooperation.* This depends first of all upon the loss of egocentrism, which makes it possible for the child to judge intention which is basic to the morality of cooperation.

Along with cognitive changes, the child has increased experience in peer group interaction and less dependence upon one-sided relationships with adults. The cooperative relationships spontaneously established between peers develops a natural morality of mutual respect and solidarity. The child begins to "feel from within the desire to treat others as he himself would wish to be treated" (Piaget, 1932, p. 196).

Experiments   A number of aspects of Piaget's theory have been supported in later work. Thus there is evidence that many of the characteristics of normal realism—judging guilt on the basis of objective damage, belief in absolute and unchangeable rules and values, expiative punishment, and immanant justice—do decrease regularly with age in a variety of cultures, as Piaget would predict. However, it has become clear that moral judgment is more complex than Piaget's theory suggests and that important developments take place during adolescence as well as in childhood (see Bronfenbrenner, 1962; Kohlberg, 1963a; 1964; and Lickona, 1969, for reviews of research relating to Piaget's theory). Kohlberg has accepted the broad outlines of Piaget's approach in his more extensive and detailed work on moral judgment.

KOHLBERG'S THEORY OF MORAL JUDGMENT

The Six-Stage Model   Kohlberg (1963b) began his analysis using older subjects than Piaget had used: 72 boys living in suburban Chicago, aged 10, 13, and 16. Kohlberg gave the boys a 2-hour interview in which they were asked about a series of 10 moral dilemmas. The dilemmas were considerably more complex than the stories employed by Piaget: in each, an act of obedience to legal rules or authority was in conflict with the welfare of human beings. For example, in one of the stories laws against stealing were in conflict with the needs of a cancer victim:*

> *In Europe, a woman was near death from a special kind of cancer. There was one drug that the doctors thought might save her. It was a form of radium that a druggist in the same town had recently discovered. The drug was expensive to make, but the druggist was charging ten times what the drug cost him to make. He paid $200 for the radium and charged $2000 for a small dose of the drug. The sick woman's husband, Heinz, went to everyone he knew to borrow the money, but he could only get together about $1000 which is half of what it cost. He told the druggist that his wife was dying and asked him to sell it cheaper or let him pay later. But the druggist said: "No, I discovered the drug and I'm going to make money from it." So Heinz got desperate and broke into the man's store to steal the drug for his wife. Should the husband have done that?*

After extensive analysis of the responses of the 72 boys to these

*From Kohlberg, L. The development of childrens' orientations toward a moral order. I. Sequence in the development or moral thought. Vita Humana 1963, 6, 11-33.

stories, Kohlberg defined six types of value-orientation grouped into three levels in the development of moral judgment and labeled them as follows:

> LEVEL I.   Premoral level.   Impulses are controlled by the influence of rewards and punishments.

> TYPE 1.   Punishment and obedience orientation.

> TYPE 2.   Naive instrumental hedonism.

> LEVEL II.   Morality of Conventional Role-Conformity. Conduct is controlled by the anticipation of social praise and blame.

> TYPE 3.   Good-boy morality of maintaining good relations, approval of others.

> TYPE 4.   Authority maintains morality. Law-and-order orientation.

> LEVEL III.   Morality of self-accepted moral principles. Conduct is regulated by ideals that enable a person to act in a way that seems to him right regardless of the praise or blame of his immediate social environment.

> TYPE 5.   Morality of contract and of democratically accepted law.

> TYPE 6.   Morality of individual principles of conscience.

The nature of these types can be better appreciated by reference to Table 11.1, which defines and details the stance of the various types on two aspects of morality: the motivation for rule obedience and the conception of human rights. Kohlberg defines each type of value-orientation on the basis of its stance on these and 29 other aspects of morality (i.e. universality of moral judgment, basis of respect for social authority, orientation toward punitive justice, etc.) (cf. Kohlberg, 1963b; 1964).

Kohlberg feels that these stages form an invariant developmental sequence, such that the "use of a more advanced stage of thought depends upon earlier attainment of each preceding stage and that each involves a restructuring and displacement of previous stages of thought"

TABLE 11.1   DEFINITION OF KOHLBERG'S STAGES OF MORAL JUDG-MENT.

STAGE 1.   Punishment and obedience orientation. Egocentric deference to superior power. *Obey rules:* to avoid punishment by another. *Human rights:* No real conception of rights. "Having a right" equated with "being right."

STAGE 2.   Naive instrumental hedonism, or instrumental relativism. Right action is that which satisfies one's needs. Aware of relativism of value to each actor's needs and perspectives. Naive egalitarianism and orientation to exchange and reciprocity. *Obey rules:* to manipulate goods, gain rewards from others. *Human rights:* Rights are factual ownership rights. Everyone has a right to do what they want with themselves and their posessions, regardless of the rights of others.

STAGE 3.   "Good-boy" orientation to pleasing, helping, and winning the approval of others. Conforms to stereotyped images of role behavior. *Obey rules:* to avoid disapproval of others. *Human rights:* as above, but qualified by the belief that no one has the right to do evil.

STAGE 4.   Law and order orientation. Morality and the social order maintained by authority. Oriented toward doing one's "duty," respecting authority, and maintaining the social order for its own sake. *Obey rules:* to avoid censure by legitimate authorities, subsequent guilt. *Human rights:* A right is an earned claim, for example, for payment for work.

STAGE 5.   Social contract orientation. Recognizes an arbitrary starting point in rules and agreements. Duty is defined in term of a contract. Avoids the violation of the rights of others, recognition of majority will and welfare. *Obey rules:* To maintain community respect. *Human rights:* Conceives of universal unearned human rights as well as rights linked to a role or status.

STAGE 6.   Individual principles. Orientation to universal principles of conscience as well as social rules. *Obey rules:* To avoid self-condemnation. *Human rights:* as above with notions of respecting the individual life and personality of others.

Adapted from Kohlberg (1964; 1967).

(Kohlberg, 1964, p. 404). Thus in studying other samples of American children and adolescents with his methods, Kohlberg has found that the preconventional or premoral types of reasoning decrease with age, the conventional types increase until age 13 and then level off, and the post-conventional types increase with age (see Figure 11.1). Furthermore, studies have suggested that the higher stages are not simply added to the lower stages: children who use higher stages tend to avoid using the reasoning appropriate to lower stages (Kohlberg, 1963a). Also, Turiel

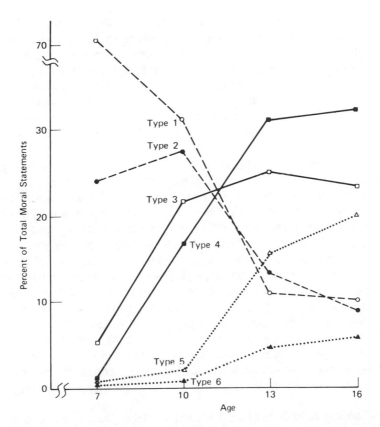

FIGURE 11.1   Mean percent of total moral statements of each of six moral judgment types at four ages. From "Development of moral character and moral ideology," by Lawrence Kohlberg from *Review of Child Development Research*, Volume I, by Martin L. Hoffman and Lois Wladis Hoffman, Editors, © 1964 by Russell Sage Foundation. Reprinted by permission of the publisher.

(1964) has found that children are more influenced by an argument using reasoning one step above their own than they are by an argument using less advanced reasoning. Turiel also found that children seem to have difficulty assimilating moral reasoning two levels above their own. Perhaps reasoning that is a little advanced, but not too advanced, from the child's own serves as the best aliment to the development of moral judgment.

Kohlberg (1968) has investigated the development of moral reasoning in a number of cultures around the world. He argues that the basic structure of moral reasoning found in his six stages can be found in all cultures, although there are differences in content. Thus in responding to why a man should save the life of his wife, a child from the town of Atayal in Malaysia said that he should save her because if she died there would be an expensive funeral. A child from a village in Taiwan answered by saying that if she died there would be no one to cook for the husband. Kohlberg notes that these answers differ in content according to cultural factors: the people of Atayal have very expensive funerals while those of Taiwan do not. However, the structure behind the answers is similar. Both children define the worth of human life in Stage 2 terms: the wife's life is seen as valuable because it is instrumental to the satisfaction of the needs of the husband.

In these cross-cultural studies, Kohlberg found that moral reasoning was more advanced in some settings than others. For example, boys from urban areas of Mexico and Taiwan showed patterns of development roughly similar to that shown in Figure 11.1: a decline with age in premoral reasoning, a rise and leveling off in conventional reasoning, and a steady rise in postconventional reasoning. However, boys from isolated villages on Taiwan and the Yucatan in Mexico showed a higher level of premoral reasoning which declined with age, a steady rise in conventional reasoning with age, and almost no postconventional reasoning. Kohlberg suggests that the reasoning of the isolated boys was delayed because they had less extensive experience in social participation than the urban boys and therefore had less chance to develop "role-taking ability," which is necessary to the development of moral reasoning. However, Kohlberg pointed out that the isolated boys still went through the sequences as the theory would predict, with conventional reasoning replacing premoral reasoning.

Role-Taking and Moral Judgment   Like Piaget, Kohlberg considers moral judgment to be a joint function of cognitive development and experience in social relationships: a spontaneous product of the child's attempt to make sense out of his experience in a complex social world, using his cognitive abilities to the fullest. However, rather than seeing moral development as a single step occurring in childhood and based only upon one's interaction in peer groups, Kohlberg sees the development of moral judgment as a long and complex process extending into adolescence.

Kohlberg feels that children who have extensive social participation and experience will reach mature stages of moral judgment more quickly because their *role-taking* ability—their ability to view the world and themselves from the perspective of another person—will be accelerated. In his initial study, Kohlberg (1958) found that more socially active boys showed accelerated development. This result has been repeated by Keasey (1971), who found that the stage of moral development is positively associated with a number of measures of social participation. Other recent studies have focused on the analysis of role-taking *per se* (i.e. Flavell, 1968; Selman, 1971). Selman (1973; Selman and Byrne, 1973) has offered a detailed analysis of 5 stages in the development of role-taking which he links theoretically to both Piaget's theory of cognitive development and Kohlberg's stages of moral judgment.

This kind of analysis points out possible relationships between the development of moral judgment and the ability of an individual to make accurate attributions, descriptions, evaluations, and so on about other people. One might expect that individual differences in person perception might reflect an individual's social sensitivity or empathy which may in turn underlie his role-taking ability. Many psychologists have long considered the process of person perception to be a most basic issue in the field of social psychology, and it has been the focus of much research (cf. Bruner and Tagiuri, 1954; Tagiuri, 1968). Unfortunately, the work on individual differences in the accuracy of perceiving others has been so plagued by methodological problems that few firm conclusions can yet be drawn (Secord and Backman, 1964; Kanekar, 1972). Some have concluded that there is no general ability to make accurate judgments about others, while others have argued that the inconsistent findings in the area are due to the lack of reliable measures of the accuracy of judging others (Cline, 1964).

We have seen that nonverbal behavior is a particularly important source of information in social interaction (cf. Secord and Backman, 1974), and it is possible that one's ability to receive or decode nonverbal information is an important component of social sensitivity. Several attempts are currently being made to develop tests of nonverbal sensitivity. Ekman (1972) has developed the Brief Affect Recognition Test (BART) which involves slides of posed facial expressions judged to represent happiness, anger, fear, and so forth. Subjects are given a very brief exposure to each slide and required to judge which emotion was represented. Ekman reasons that the brief exposure given the slide approximates the brevity of spontaneously emitted facial cues. Rosenthal and his colleagues (1974a; 1974b) are developing the Profile of Nonverbal Sensitivity (PONS), in which a filmed actor portrays different situations (i.e. asking forgiveness, expressing jealous anger, etc.) both verbally and nonverbally. The subject sees a series of 220 scenes including all possible combinations of facial cues, bodily cues, and distorted vocal cues. He is required to choose which of two situations is represented by each scene. The scoring procedure allows the computation of accuracy scores based on facial, bodily, and distorted vocal cues, plus combinations of the three. Buck (1976) is also developing the communication of affect receiving ability test (CARAT) based upon the spontaneous facial expressions of college student senders to emotionally loaded color slides. Unknown to them, the senders' facial expressions were videotaped as they watched and described their reaction to sexual, pleasant, unpleasant, and unusual slides. The subject watches selected sequences of expressions and attempts to judge what kind of slide was shown and whether the sender's reaction to it was pleasant or unpleasant. This instrument will allow the analysis of the relative importance of facial and distorted or nondistorted vocal cues in judgment accuracy.

There is some evidence that these instruments constitute reliable and valid tests of nonverbal sensitivity. If they do, they may provide useful measures of an important aspect of the social sensitivity and they may show how this is related to role-taking ability and, perhaps, moral judgment.

MORAL BEHAVIOR

From a casual look at Piaget's and Kohlberg's theories of moral judgment, one might expect that once an individual has reached a given stage of moral reasoning, he will behave accordingly. This is not necessarily the case. We have seen moral judgment to be based largely upon the level of the individual's cognitive development and his accumulated social experience or role-taking ability. These are transsituational characteristics which the individual carries with him. Moral behavior is undoubtedly influenced by these transsituational characteristics to some extent, but it is also determined by a multitude of situational factors. We saw in the Asch conformity experiment and other studies that people will modify their behavior to a surprising extent to fit situational pressures. Moral behavior is no exception to this finding. People will often do things in response to situational influences that violate their stated moral judgments. A study that illustrates the influence of situational factors on moral behavior is the early but very sophisticated study of morality by Hartshorne and May (1928–30).

The Hartshorne and May Study   This first systematic study into the nature of morality was commissioned by a religious group which apparently wished to prove that children who went to Sunday School and participated in scouting were more virtuous than children who did not. It was an ambitious study employing over 1000 children and covering both moral knowledge and moral conduct. Moral knowledge was assessed by a variety of paper-and-pencil measures. Moral conduct was studied by giving the children opportunities to steal, cheat, lie, and so on in circumstances where, although they felt safe from discovery, their behavior could be observed. The opportunities were given in a variety of settings: at school, at home, in games and athletic contests, and so forth.

The major result of this study was that the morality of conduct in a given situation was not strongly related to the morality of conduct in another: the average correlation was about +.34 (Brown, 1965). A child who cheated in one situation often showed honesty in another, and participation in Sunday School and scouting were not guarantees of virtue. Hartshorne and Mays's basic result has often been repeated: different measures of moral behavior are often related by low positive correlations, sometimes by no correlations, and only rarely by large correlations (cf. Brown, 1965).

Given that situational factors have a substantial effect upon moral behavior, one must then inquire about the nature of the situational factors and the mechanisms of their effect. In a review of the literature on altruism, Krebs (1970) concludes that the existence of positive affective states associated with competence, success, and so on are associated with increased altruism. Also, negative affective states associated with harming another person have led to increased altruistic behavior. Apparently if one feels good or guilty he is more likely to help someone. Altruism is greater if one likes or is otherwise attracted to the recipient. Observing altruistic models also increases altruistic behavior. Note that none of these factors should greatly affect the extent to which a person would judge that helping behavior is morally justified or deserved in a given situation: one's liking for a potential recipient of help should not greatly affect the judgment of whether or not he deserves help.

Helping Behavior in Emergency Situations   Some of the most dramatic examples of the effects of situational factors on moral behavior have involved situations in which people have failed to respond to help someone who is in critical need of help. The study of this problem was initiated by a number of highly publicized real-life incidents. The best known of these is the murder of Kitty Genovese, who was attacked outside her apartment building as she came home from work at 3:00 a.m. Thirty-eight of her neighbors watched as her assailant attacked her with a knife, retreated, and came back to attack again. Despite her cries for help and despite the fact that it took over 1/2 hour for the assailant to kill her, no one from the apartment intervened, even to anonymously call the police or an ambulance.

Such events are evidently not uncommon. John Darley and Bibb Latane, the psychologists who began experiments based upon this phenomenon, have reported that dozens of such incidents have been called to their attention since they began their research (Darley and Latane, 1968b). They cite the case of the 17-year-old boy who was stabbed in the stomach as he rode the subway and bled to death as 11 other riders watched without offering aid, even though the assailants had left the car; the case of the woman who broke her leg on a busy sidewalk and called for help for 40 minutes until someone finally came to her aid, and so forth.

Darley and Latane suggest that one of the reasons that these events occur is that there are so many people around. They noted that responding to an emergency requires that people (1) notice that a potential emergency is occuring, (2) define that event as an actual emergency, and (3) decide that it is their personal responsibility to act. They suggest that the presence of other people may inhibit a helping response in an emergency by making it less likely that people will notice an event, define it as an emergency, and feel a personal responsibility to act.

They designed several experiments to test these propositions. In one, Latane and Darley (1968) had subjects fill out a questionnaire in a room, either alone or with others. While the subjects worked on the questionnaires, smoke began to pour into the room through a vent in the door. The measure of response was whether or not and how quickly the subjects came out of the room to investigate the smoke. They found that subjects waiting with another person were significantly slower to respond than subjects waiting alone. Upon questioning, it was discovered that the subjects waiting with others took longer to notice the smoke. Apparently, when waiting together, each subject tended to focus his attention on his questionnaire and didn't look around the room, perhaps out of consideration for the privacy of the other subject. In contrast, when a subject waited alone, he tended to glance and look around the room while he worked, and he was therefore more likely to notice the smoke quickly. Thus, the presence of other people may reduce one's scanning of the environment and make it less likely that an emergency will be noticed.

There were indications that, even after they had noticed the emergency, people waiting with others seemed less concerned: they did not define the event as an emergency. Latane and Darley suggested that the individuals in a group may be genuinely concerned about an event and they may look to others to compare their feelings and reactions. However, there is a tendency to remain outwardly cool and seemingly indifferent in public, particularly with strangers. Since no one shows his concern openly, each comes to the conclusion that no one else is concerned: no one responds because all appear less concerned than they are in fact. In this way, the presence of others may create a state of pluralistic ignorance which makes it less likely that an emergency, once noticed, will be interpreted as an emergency.

To test this proposition, Latane and Rodin (1969) used as an emergency an event that was impossible not to notice. Male undergraduates waited for an experiment alone or with another person. As the subjects filled out some questionnaires, the female experimenter went into an adjacent room. After a few minutes, she turned on a tape recording of herself climbing onto a bookcase to retrieve a stack of papers, and then falling with a loud crash and a scream calling for help: "Oh, my God, my foot . . . I . . . I . . . can't move it. Oh . . . my ankle . . . I . . . can't get this . . . thing . . . off me." (Latane and Rodin, 1969, p. 192). Again, the measure was whether or not and how quickly the subjects came out of the room to help. Among subjects waiting alone, nearly 70% came out to help. However, if the subject was waiting with an experimental confederate who did not respond to the cries, only 7% intervened. The subjects in this condition seemed upset and confused, and they often glanced at the confederate. However, the other simply kept working on the questionnaire, and the real subject usually did not intervene. Postexperimental interviews disclosed that many of the subjects who did not intervene had decided that the emergency was not too serious: the presence of an apparently unresponsive other may have enabled the subject to resolve his uncertainty and conflict about helping by deciding that it was not a real emergency.

A second study suggested that pairs of friends may be better able to communicate their concern to one another than pairs of strangers. Rather than employing a confederate, Latane and Rodin used real subjects either individually or in pairs. Half the pairs were friends, half were strangers. When the woman fell, nearly 70% of the pairs of friends versus 40% of the pairs of strangers responded, and the strangers responded more slowly. The difference may have been based on the more accurate nonverbal communication of concern among the friends: "Strangers . . . seemed noticeably confused and concerned . . . they often glanced furtively at one another, anxious to discover the other's reaction yet unwilling to meet eyes and betray their own concern. Friends, on the other hand, seemed better able to convey their concern nonverbally" (Latane and Rodin, 1969, p. 200).

The importance of the nonverbal communication of concern is shown in two other experiments. Piliavin, Rodin, and Piliavin (1969) performed a field experiment on the New York City subway in which a passenger staged a collapse. Unlike the other studies we have been considering, the number of people nearby had no effect on the amount or speed of helping behavior. Darley, Teger, and Lewis (1973) noted that the face-to-face seating arrangement on a subway increases the likelihood that people will see the initial involuntary responses of others to the emergency: their startle response, orienting toward the event, facial expressions of concern, and so forth. Thus the people will know that others besides themselves are concerned, and they will be less likely to inhibit and mask their own expressions of concern. To test this, they repeated the study in which someone falls in the next room, but varied the seating arrangements so that some subjects faced each other. They found that the subjects facing each other responded about as often and as quickly as subjects waiting alone, while subjects who did not face each other did not respond or were slow to respond because they did not define the event as an emergency.

The effects we have been discussing—the tendency to notice fewer things in the environment and to interpret potential emergencies as benign —both depend upon the close physical presence of other persons. The other has to be present if he is to be seen as unconcerned. Darley and Latane (1968a) termed this *direct group inhibition,* and suggested that it does not affect a third factor inhibiting group response in emergencies. The *diffusion of responsibility,* or the interpretation that since there are other people present, one does not have personal responsibility to take action, depends only on the knowledge that others are present. For example, when Kitty Genovese was murdered, few of the 38 bystanders could directly assess the reactions of other bystanders: they were separated into different apartments. They therefore could not have been affected by direct group inhibition. Their lack of response must have been due primarily to the diffusion of responsibility.

Darley and Latane (1968a) attempted to create an experimental situation that would simulate the conditions present when Kitty Genovese was murdered. Subjects were told that they would take part in a discussion about personal problems. Each subject sat alone, speaking over an intercom system to guarantee anonymity. He was told that each person would speak in turn into a microphone, and others would listen. The intercom worked so that each speaker could speak into it at his appointed time, but at other times he could not be heard or hear from others except the one taking his turn to speak. The experimenter stated that he would not listen in to any of the conversation. Actually, the entire discussion that the subject heard was presented via a tape recorder: there were no other subjects, but he was led to believe that he was talking to one other person, two others, or five others. During the ensuing discussion, one of the other subjects underwent what appeared to be a very serious seizure:

I–er–um–I think I–I need–er–if–if could–er–er somebody er–er–er– er–er–er–er give me a little–er–give me a little help here be- cause–er–I–er–I'm–er–er–h–h–having a–a–a real problem–er–right now. . . . (growing increasingly louder and incoherent, it

concluded). . . . help–er–uh–uh–uh (choking sounds). . . . I'm
gonna die–er–er–I'm . . . gonna die–er–help–er–er–seizure–er
(Chokes, then quiet) (Darley and Latane, 1968, p. 379).

The experimenters determined whether and how long it took for subjects
to seek help for the seizure victim.

The results are presented in Figure 11.2. As it indicates, subjects who
thought that only they heard the call for help all eventually responded.
However, among subjects who thought that others besides themselves
had heard the call for help, fewer intervened and those who did acted
more slowly. Thus, even in a situation where the subject could not see the
reactions of others, the perception that others were present reduced
helping behavior, apparently because the subject felt less personal responsibility to respond.

This does not mean that the subjects were apathetic or indifferent to
the fate of the victim. In fact, Darley and Latane reported that the subjects
who did not respond seemed, if anything, more upset than subjects who
reported the emergency. "When the experimenter entered the experimental room to terminate the situation, the subject often asked if the victim was
'all right.' . . .Many of these subjects showed physical signs of nervous-

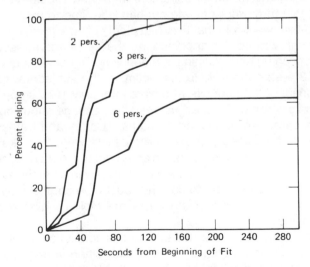

FIGURE 11.2   Cumulative distribution of helping responses. From J. Darley
and B. Latane, "Bystander intervention in emergencies: Diffusion of responsibility." *Journal of Personality and Social Psychology*, 1968, 8, 377–383. Copyright 1968 by the American Psychological Association. Reprinted by
permission.

ness; they often had trembling hands and sweaty palms" (Darley and Latane, 1968a, p. 382). Why then had they not responded? Darley and Latane suggest that the subjects were in a state of indecision and conflict between their tendencies to help the victim and their fear of overreacting; they did not wish to ruin the experiment or destroy the anonymity of the situation, and they did not want to appear foolish. If they knew that other persons were present, the need to help the victim was not so acute and the subjects vacillated in conflict between two undesirable alternatives: allowing the victim to suffer and the costs of rushing to help.

A study by Darley and Bateson (1973) illustrates another situational factor that can influence helping behavior: whether or not the potential helper is in a hurry. The experiment attempted to recreate the situation presented in the Biblical parable of the Good Samaritan, in which a Samaritan helped a man who had been robbed and beaten on the road from Jerusalem to Jericho. Subjects were students at the Princeton Theological Seminary, whom one would expect would not be persons apathetic to the needs of others or indifferent to moral strictures. Half read a discussion of future job opportunities for seminarians, the other half read the parable of the Good Samaritan. They were then asked to go to another building to record a short talk on what they had read: one-third were told that they were late for the appointment there and should hurry, one-third were told that they were not late but had little time to make the appointment, one-third were told that they had plenty of time to make the appointment. On the way to the appointment, the seminarian passed a victim slumped coughing and moaning in a doorway. Of the subjects with plenty of time, 63% stopped to help the victim; of the subjects with little time, 45% stopped; of the subjects who were late, only 10% stopped. It made no difference whether they had just read the passage about job opportunities or the parable of the Good Samaritan. Darley and Bateson suggest that some of the subjects under time pressure were less likely to notice the victim or interpret the event as an emergency; others noticed the victim but chose not to stop because it would conflict with what the experimenter wanted and expected them to do. Thus again the conflict between allowing the victim to suffer and the costs of helping inhibited action in a potential emergency.

Staub (1970; 1971) has studied how this conflict over helping a victim develops in young children. He found that, when young children heard another child fall and call for help from the next room, their helping behavior increased from kindergarten to second grade, but then *decreased* from second to sixth grade. This decrease in helping behavior was unexpected, for it was felt that children would help more as their capacity for role-taking increased with age. Staub suggested that around the age of the second grade, in our culture, children may begin to experience conflict about helping others: they learn that one should not interfere in the concerns of others, one should mind his own business, and so forth. This increasing concern about socially inappropriate behavior begins to interfere with the child's impulse to help others: "Older children, having learned rules of appropriate social behavior as a part of their socialization, may be inhibited from helping by fear of disapproval for potentially inappropriate conduct" (Staub, 1971, p. 137). Thus, learning about one kind of moral judgment—that one should not interfere in the affairs of others—may conflict with another kind—that one should help persons who are in need of help.

We have considered only a few of the many situational factors that may influence moral behavior independently of one's moral judgment about what is the right or wrong thing to do in a situation. However, this should not be taken to mean that one's level of moral judgment has no effects on behavior. On the contrary, it has been shown that high levels of moral judgment are associated with less cheating (Krebs, 1967; Brown, Feldman, Schwartz, and Heingartner, 1969). Also, Kohlberg (1969) showed that persons who used some Stage 6 moral reasoning were more likely than conventional or Stage 5 subjects to refuse to injure another person in the Milgram-type obedience experiment which will be discussed in the next section. Some of the most interesting studies relating moral judgment and behavior have concerned political ideology and behavior.

Moral Judgment and Political Ideology   One of the most impressive demonstrations of the relationship between Kohlberg's stages of moral judgment and morally relevant behavior has concerned the moral reasoning of persons arrested at the Free Speech Movement sit-in at Berkeley in 1964. Haan and his colleagues found that the persons arrested tended to be either postconventional (Stages 5 and 6) or preconventional (Stage 2) in their level of moral reasoning. Few persons at the conventional level of development were represented among the arrestees (Haan, Smith, and Block, 1968; Haan, 1972). Haan et al. suggested that the postconventional arrestees were concerned with basic issues of civil rights and civil liberties and were committed and responsive to others, while the preconventional arrestees were less committed to others and more concerned with self-referenced conflict between individual rights and the power of the university.

Fishkin, Kenniston, and MacKinnon (1973) studied this apparent relationship between moral reasoning and political ideology by relating Kohlberg's measure to agreement or disagreement with a series of political slogans. Some of the slogans were violent and radical in nature (kill the pigs; bring the war home; etc.), some were peaceful-radical (make love not war; give peace a chance; etc.), while others were conservative (America —love it or leave it; better dead than red, etc.). They found that subjects who reasoned at the conventional moral level had conservative political beliefs: there was a particularly strong relationship between reasoning at Stage 4 (law-and-order orientation) and the acceptance of conservative, and rejection of radical, slogans. Preconventional subjects agreed with the violent radical slogans. The postconventional students disagreed with the conservative slogans but did not strongly endorse the radical slogans.

Both Haan et al. (1968) and Fishkin et al. (1973) point out that, since all of the subjects in their studies were well-educated and advantaged young people, it is likely that the preconventional moral orientation manifested by some of them was not due to a lack of experience with the reasoning at higher levels. Instead, they suggest that these students experienced and rejected conventional moral reasoning by a regression back to Stage 2. Thus the new experiences and settings of late adolescence may create temporary or permanent regressions in moral reasoning, as well as progressive changes. The circumstances determining whether progressive or regressive changes occur have yet to be explored: it would be interesting to apply Erikson's (1950) ideas to this question.

The Social Bases of Aggression

We have seen that people will modify their moral behavior in ways that violate their stated moral principles in response to situational pressures. We shall now examine the effects of situational and social pressures upon aggressive behavior. In Chapter 5 we saw that there are different kinds of aggression which may have little or nothing in common with one another except the superficial similarity of the overt behavior of injuring another. Thus Moyer's typology shows how some aggressive behavior is bound up with innate preprogrammed response tendencies that differ from species to species, other aggressive behavior is more closely linked with emotion, stress, frustration, and associated physiological mechanisms, and still other aggressive behavior is wholly learned and has no physiological basis other than that which underlies all learning. A given aggressive response, for example a knifing during a fight between gangs of adolescent boys, could be a kind of intermale aggression or fear-induced aggression based on innate response tendencies similar to those seen in animals, or it could be associated with passionate anger and a desire to kill fueled by deprivation and frustration, or it could be an instrumental act coldly calculated to obtain money or some other reward. However, another explanation is possible—the aggressor's response could be an act of conformity with the norms of his group.

All of the types of aggression outlined by Moyer and others that we considered in Chapter 5 reside within the individual. The innate dispositions, the passions, the learning processes are all characteristics of the individual. Indeed, the Western tradition has long assumed that the motivation for most human behavior arises within the individual. However, we have seen that individual behavior is influenced to an unexpected degree by social and situational factors, and aggressive behavior is no exeption to such influence.

OBEDIENCE AND AGGRESSION

Milgram's Experiment   In 1963, Stanley Milgram published an experiment which demonstrated dramatically that social influence can affect aggressive behavior as well as perceptual judgments and statements of opinion (cf. Milgram, 1963; 1965; 1974). Middle-aged men of varying occupations served as subjects. Two subjects were brought together and told that the experiment concerned the effects of punishment on learning. One of the men was actually a confederate of the experimenter, and he was designated to be the "learner" in a rigged drawing. The naive subject was the "teacher," and he was to present the learner with a series of stimulus words. The learner was to associate the stimulus word correctly with another word. If he made a mistake, the teacher was told to punish him by pressing a switch to deliver an electric shock.

The shock apparatus was equipped with 30 level switches which supposedly delivered increasing intensities of shock. The switches were labeled with voltage readings ranging from 15 to 450 volts in 15-volt increments. In addition, groups of four switches were labeled with increasingly disagreeable verbal descriptions: slight shock, moderate shock, strong shock, very strong shock, intense shock, extreme intensity shock, danger: severe shock. The last two switches were marked XXX. The subject was told to give the learner a more intense shock every time the learner made a mistake.

The learner was led to a separate room and, as the teacher watched, strapped into an electric chair which made it impossible for him to escape from the shock electrodes. Electrode paste was applied "to avoid blisters and burns." The learner asked whether the shocks could be dangerous since he suffered from a heart condition. The experimenter replied that "although the shocks can be extremely painful, they cause no permanent tissue damage."

Once the experiment began, the learner gave many wrong answers, so the teacher soon found himself giving strong shocks. At 75 volts the learner began to grunt and moan when the shock was given. At 150 volts the learner demanded to be let out of the experiment, saying that he did not want to take any more of the shocks. His demand became more and more insistent, and he began to complain that his heart was bothering him. At 180 volts he cried out that he could no longer stand the pain. At 300 volts the learner ceased to react to the shock and he stopped responding to the stimulus word: the shocks were suddenly met by silence. The experimenter than told the teacher to count a nonresponse as a wrong response and to continue to give increasingly intense shocks.

Most of the teachers attempted to resist giving further shocks as the learner demanded to be freed. The experimenter told the teacher that he must continue, using a series of prepared prods: "Please continue," "The experiment requires that you continue," "You have no other choice, you must continue." If the teacher continued to resist after the last prod, the experiment was discontinued.

The real purpose of the experiment was to see how far subjects would go in injuring another person in obedience to the commands of the experimenter: no shocks were actually delivered. The results showed much more obedience than anyone expected. To illustrate the extent to which the behavior of the subjects differed from intelligent expectation, Milgram asked 40 psychiatrists to predict how far subjects would go. The results of their predictions and the actual results of the experiment are presented in Figure 11.3. The psychiatrists predicted that over half would stop at the 150-volt level at which the learner first asked to be freed, that only 3.73 percent would go beyond the 300-volt level, and that only 0.125 percent would go to the highest 450-volt level. Actually in this experiment, Milgram found that over 60 percent of the subjects complied fully with the experimenter and went on to give the 450-volt shock.

Milgram emphasized that most subjects clearly did not want to shock the learner. They showed signs of extreme tension and stress, including sweating, trembling, stuttering, and groaning. Many subjects had bizarre fits of nervous laughter, and several had uncontrollable seizures. However, despite this extreme reluctance, most of the subjects continued to comply with the experimenter. Milgram (1965, pp. 253–534) presented the following transcript of the remarks of one of the obedient subjects:*

> *150 VOLTS DELIVERED.*   You want me to keep going?
> *165 VOLTS DELIVERED.*   That guy is hollering in there.

* From Milgram, S. Some conditions of obedience and disobedience to authority. In I.D. Steiner and M. Fishbein (Eds), Current Studies in Social Psychology. New York: Holt, Rinehart, and Winston, 1965.

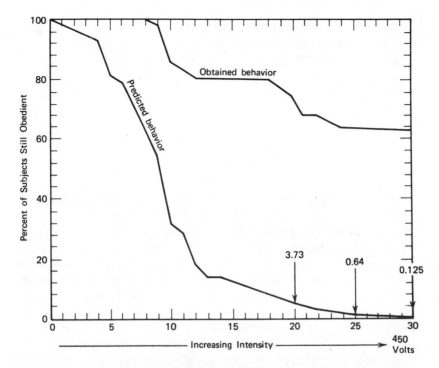

FIGURE 11.3   Predicted and obtained behavior, voice feedback condition. From S. Milgram, "Some conditions of obedience and disobedience to authority." In I. D. Steiner and M. Fishbein (Eds.) *Current Studies in Social Psychology.* New York: Holt, Rinehart, and Winston, 1965. Copyright © 1965 by Holt, Rinehart, and Winston. Reprinted by permission.

There's a lot of them here. He's liable to have heart condition. You want me to go?

180 VOLTS DELIVERED.   He can't stand it! I'm not going to kill that man in there! You hear him hollering? He's hollering. He can't stand it. What if something happens to him?. . .I'm not going to get that man sick in there. He's hollering in there. You know what I mean? I mean I refuse to take responsibility. He's getting hurt in there. He's in there hollering. Too many left here. Geez, if he gets them wrong. There's too many of them left. I mean who is going to take responsibility if anything happens to that gentleman? [The experimenter accepts responsibility.] All right.

195 VOLTS DELIVERED.   You see he's hollering. Hear that. Gee, I don't know. [The experimenter says: "The experiment re-

quires that you go on."] I know it does, sir, but I mean—huh—
he don't know what he's in for. He's up to 195 volts.
210 VOLTS DELIVERED.
225 VOLTS DELIVERED.
240 VOLTS DELIVERED.   Aw, no. You mean I've got to keep
going up with the scale? No sir. I'm not going to kill that man!
I'm not going to give him 450 volts! [The experimenter says:
"The experiment requires that you go on."] I know it does but
that man is hollering in there, sir. . . .

Despite all of these objections, this subject obeyed the experimenter fully and proceeded to give the 450 volt shock.

Milgram found this obedience effect in other experiments even when the laboratory was moved to an office building and identified with a fictitious research organization with no ties to any university. In another extension of the experiment, the learner sat in the same room with the teacher with his hand resting on a shock plate. After the 150-volt shock, the learner refused to place his hand on the plate. The experimenter ordered the teacher to forcibly hold the victim's hand on the plate. Most complied, and 30 percent continued to comply until they had given the 450-volt shock.

Milgram's experiments demonstrate dramatically that under social influence an individual may engage in aggressive behavior for reasons that may not be associated with aggressive tendencies within himself and indeed may be contrary to his wishes and values. Such aggressive behavior in response to social influence does not fit any of the categories suggested by Moyer and other aggression theorists, and it may be quite independent of any individual motives and goals beyond those motives associated with obeying an authority figure. This conclusion is supported by the pattern of sex and personality differences in obedient aggression.

Sex and Personality Differences in Obedient Aggression

We have seen in the experiments of Bandura and others that young boys generally show more aggressive behavior than girls. Experiments by Buss and Brock (1963; Brock and Buss, 1964) similarly show that college-age men are more aggressive than women when shocking fellow students without direct social pressure. On the other hand, studies of social influence generally show more conformity behavior among women. This raises the question of the nature and direction of sex differences in obedient aggression—will obedient aggression be higher among males, reflecting the cultural and/or constitutional factors that make males more aggressive, or will it be higher among females, reflecting their greater tendencies to conform?

There is evidence that women may be put in a greater state of conflict than men when ordered to shock another person. Buck (1970; 1972) took measures of skin conductance while subjects gave intense shocks, mild shocks, or painless signals to a same-sex partner. Women giving shocks showed a larger physiological reaction than men both when initially given the instructions about shocking the other and when they delivered the shocks.

Despite this evidence of greater conflict among women, there is little evidence that women are less likely to show obedient aggression. Milgram found no evidence of a sex difference in his experiments (reported in Sheridan and King, 1972). In a more recent study, Larsen and his colleagues studied the amount of shock a subject would give to a victim under various conditions of social influence (Larsen, Coleman, Forbes, and Johnson, 1972). They found that samples of women estimated that they would give less shock than did samples of men when the experiment was described to them. However, they found no evidence of such a sex difference in the actual experiment—both men and women, but particularly women, gave more punishment than the estimates (See Table 11.2).

Sheridan and King (1972) studied the willingness of male and female subjects to give increasingly intense shocks to a small furry puppy. The procedure was adapted from that of Milgram: Subjects shocked the puppy for mistakes on an (actually insoluble) learning task. The increasingly intense shocks first produced foot flexion, then running and barking, and finally continuous yelping and howling. In this study, women showed more obedient aggression than did men. Six of the 13 male subjects broke off before reaching the end of the shock scale, but *none* of the 13 women broke off. All continued to shock the puppy to the end of the scale.

These experiments, in demonstrating that women show as much or

TABLE 11.2   MEAN MAXIMUM VOLTAGE ADMINISTERED TO LEARNER (MAXIMUM POSSIBLE = 390 VOLTS).

SEX OF TEACHER	PREDICTED	ACTUAL (CONFORMITY CONDITION)
Female	80	328
Male	147	295

Adapted from data presented in K. Larsen, D. Coleman, J. Forbes, and R. Johnson, "Is the subject's personality or the experimental situation a better predictor of a subject's willingness to administer shock to a victim?" *Journal of Personality and Social Psychology,* 1972, **22,** 287–295. Copyright 1972 by the American Psychological Association. Reprinted by permission.

more obedient aggression than men, suggest that obedient aggression is more an act of conformity than it is an act of aggression. Experiments on the personality correlates of obedient aggression suggest a similar conclusion. Larsen et al. (1972) related a number of personality scales designed to measure aggressiveness with the amount of shock given the victim. No strong relationships were found, and the investigators suggested that obedient aggression may be related more strongly to personality measures assessing conformity. In fact, Elms and Milgram (1966) did find that the F scale of authoritarianism, a measure related to high confirmity, was indeed higher among obedient subjects.

The Power of Obedience—An Example
It is hard to understand the behavior of the subjects in these obedience experiments without appreciating how difficult it is to disobey an established authority figure. Milgram has illustrated the power of social influence in another and more easily appreciated way: by showing how difficult it is to go against common and apparently trivial social expectations by asking for someone's seat on the subway (Tavris, 1974).

Milgram suggested that students in his class go up to someone on the New York City subway and, courteously but without explanation, ask for his seat. The class recoiled *en masse* with much nervous laughter—a sign to Milgram that something important was being tapped. Eventually a brave student took on the assignment of making the request to 20 passengers. He found that about one-half the passengers complied without question, but he was unable to complete the task, explaining that it was one of the most difficult things he had ever done.

Curious to see why making such a trivial request was such a frightening project, Milgram decided to repeat the experiment himself. He found that as he approached a seated passenger, a paralyzing inhibition overcame him: the words of the simple request seemed lodged in his throat. After several tries, he finally went up to a passenger and choked "Excuse me, sir, may I have your seat?" He felt suddenly overcome with panic, but the man got right up and gave him the seat. Taking it, Milgram reported feeling an overwhelming need to behave in a way that would justify the request: "My head sank between my knees, and I could feel my face blanching. I was not role-playing. I actually felt as if I were going to perish." (Tavris, 1974, p. 72). Significantly, he found that as soon as he left the train (at the next stop), the tension went away.

Milgram suggests that this experience points up the enormous anxiety, ordinarily unnoticed, that prevents us from breaching social norms. Once the norm is breached, it illustrates the powerful need to justify that breach (by appearing sick or exhausted in this case). Milgram stresses that this was not acting, but was a "compelled playing out of the logic of social relations." Finally, the experience shows that the intense feelings were created in, and limited to, the particular situation, illustrating the power of the immediate situation on behavior and feelings.

Milgram states that the experience gave him a better understanding of the behavior of some subjects in the obedience experiment. He stated: "I experienced the anxiety they felt as they considered repudiating the experimenter. That anxiety forms a powerful barrier that must be surmounted, whether one's action is consequential—disobeying an authority —or trivial—asking for a seat on the subway." (Tavris, 1974, p. 72). If you don't believe this, try singing—loudly—the next time you are on a bus.

The Origins of Obedience   Given the surprising power of social expectations, one might ask how the susceptibility to such social influence develops in the individual. Generally it is assumed that conforming behavior is a product of socialization, developing as one aspect of the general process of moral development. It is often assumed that there is a fundamental antagonism between the child's natural behavior tendencies and this socialization process: society is often seen as either repressing natural human potential (if one's conception of human nature is positive) or inhibiting anarchic human impulses (if one's conception is negative). However, the demonstrated power of social influence suggests that another possibility be considered—that conformity to social influence is itself a central fact of human nature, an innate response tendency that will appear naturally if supportive experiences are provided. Certainly, it is true that nonhuman primates are social animals and that the situation of early man was probably such that social organization was necessary for survival. Thus it is conceivable that one heritage of evolution is an innate responsiveness to social influence.

This view is compatible with the ethological-evolutionary model of social development proposed by Bowlby (1958;1969;1972). It suggests that the infant has innate tendencies to orient toward, and later to promote contact and proximity with, other persons. These tendencies gradually focus upon the most familiar other—generally the mother. Ainsworth and her colleagues suggest that such infant-mother attachments provide safeguards against the possible dangers of exploratory behavior. Obedience— the compliance with maternal signals—appears at about the same time as locomotor exploration and the formation of attachment. Stayton, Hogan, and Ainsworth (1971) suggest that the attachment bond seems to "foster a willingness to comply with parental signals" (p. 1067). Such obedience may reflect the adaptive advantage conferred upon infants whose actions in a hazardous environment can be controlled by their mothers.

If this is true, it would suggest that whether or not conformity to social demands is in conflict with some aspects of human nature, it is also an important aspect of human nature in its own right. This would help to explain some of the contradictions of human behavior. Human nature may not be good or evil but simply quite flexible and responsive to immediate social and situational influences. This social responsiveness may be responsible for the survival of the human species, and it may underlie much human cooperation and constructive social enterprises. Ironically, it may also play a major role in the most dangerous and destructive human crimes.

Obedience and Group Aggression   The finding that many individuals can be induced to engage in aggressive behavior contrary to their wishes and personal values is extremely important when we consider aggression as a social issue. Some of the most destructive and unacceptable manifestations of aggression—lynchings, massacres, pograms—involve attacks by members of a group upon relatively weak and defenseless individuals and groups. Such occurrences generally require that large numbers of "normal" people be induced to participate or at least acquiesce in the aggressive actions, and this inducement involves conformity and obedience.

Group aggression is often seen as the result of the summation of the aggressive tendencies of the individuals making up the group. We saw in Chapter 5 that a group can encourage its members to be aggressive by providing a wide range of aggressive models to imitate and by reinforcing aggressive behavior. Such a group may well be more likely to engage in group aggression than a group which does not encourage individual aggressiveness. Also, it has been found that members of a group may be made aggressive by frustration. Group aggression tends to increase in times of dissatisfaction with social and economic conditions. For example, Hovland and Sears (1940) analyzed the lynchings of blacks by whites in the southern United States between 1880 and 1930 and showed that such lynchings were more common in times of economic difficulty. Economic difficulties similarly contributed to massacres of Jews in Europe (Campbell, 1947) and Armenians in Turkey (Dadrian, 1971). It is theorized that economic and social dissatisfaction creates conditions of frustration and deprivation affecting a large number of people and increasing the probability that each will be aggressive.

Milgram's experiments have shown how group aggression might occur even if the members of the group are not personally inclined to be aggressive. Many persons who become involved in group aggression may do so only because they are unable to resist conformity pressures. Their conformity in turn increases the apparent uniformity of the group and further increases the power of conformity.

The massacre of South Vietnamese civilians by American troops at My Lai provides a tragic example of the role played by obedience and conformity in group aggression. According to published reports, some of the soldiers were extremely reluctant to obey the orders of superior officers to kill defenseless villagers. Some were reported to have taken prisoners out of the area so that they would be spared, another apparently shot himself in the foot so that he could be evacuated and leave the situation, another was observed to be crying as he fired into groups of civilians (cf. *Newsweek,* Nov. 30, 1970, p. 16; *Life,* Dec. 5, 1969, p 43). However, none actively resisted the orders or the subsequent killing.

The history of the short reign of Nazism in Germany is replete with examples of official directives, chains of command, and orderly procedures which led to the destruction of millions of people. The ordeal of the Jews was only the beginning of Nazi planning. After the war, documents were discovered showing that the entire population of industrial Russia—many millions of people—were marked for systematic death by starvation (Shirer, 1959). Hardly anyone in Germany actively resisted these activities at the time, and those who were directly involved in the killing of innocent and defenseless people maintained later that they were only following orders and were not responsible for their actions.

The view of the development of obedience outlined above can also take into account the sociopathic individual who seems incapable of normal conformity. The tendency toward obedience, like other innate response tendencies (i.e. the facial display of affect in the rhesus monkeys discussed in Chapter 7), may develop abnormally or not at all in the absence of a proper social environment. If the social environment is not responsive to the child, strong attachment bonds may not be formed and the tendencies toward conformity may well be lost. This may also happen to a normally socialized individual if he feels that his behavior is not being monitored by others—that he is anonymous and will not be held responsible for his actions. This brings us to another factor that has been held to underly aggression in group situations: deindividuation. Rather than involving slavish conformity to social influences, deindividuation involves a breakdown of normal social restraints.

DEINDIVIDUATION AND GROUP AGGRESSION

According to Zimbardo (1969b), deindividuation is caused by a sense of anonymity and a lack of responsibility which minimizes one's concern about the social evaluation of one's behavior. This weakens socialized controls and increases the expression of inhibited behavior, particularly aggressive behavior.

Zimbardo uses the concept of deindividuation to analyse the vandalism of automobiles. A large number of cars abandoned on the streets of certain large cities are quickly looted and vandalized by passers-by. At one time Zimbardo counted 218 vandalized cars in the 20 miles between his home in Brooklyn and the campus of New York University in the Bronx. To study the pattern of such vandalism, Zimbardo left a ten-year-old Oldsmobile on a street in the Bronx with license plates removed and the hood up, and watched. The first strippers arrived in ten minutes—a middle-class couple with an 8-year-old boy. The mother acted as lookout while father and son searched the trunk and glove compartment and removed the radiator and battery. Within 26 hours, a steady stream of looters had removed all of the usable items: hubcaps, air cleaner, windshield wipers, a good tire, and so forth. Random destruction of the car then began, with youngsters breaking the windshield, lights, and windows. Zimbardo noted that most of the looting and destruction was done in broad daylight and that the adult looters were "all well-dressed, clean-cut whites who would under other circumstances be mistaken for mature, responsible citizens demanding more law and order" (1969b, p. 290).

Zimbardo reports that similar looting has been observed with planted cars located in Milan and Paris. However, the fate of a car abandoned in Palo Alto, California was quite different. Zimbardo left a car in Palo Alto at the same time the car was abandoned in the Bronx. Only one passer-by touched it during the observation period—when it began to rain, someone lowered the hood to keep the engine dry!

Zimbardo attributes the difference in the treatment of the cars in the Bronx and Palo Alto to the feelings of anonymity learned in a large city like New York. He suggests that such feelings of anonymity may both increase aggressive behavior and decrease discrimination so that innocent as well as deserving victims will be attacked. To test this, he told groups of female subjects that they were to shock another girl every time a signal was given. They could see the (feigned) pained reactions of the victim through a one-way mirror. In the deindividuation condition, the subject gave the shocks in total darkness, no names were used, and the subjects wore bulky lab coats with a hood over their faces. In the individuation condition, the lights were turned on, regular clothes were worn, and large name tags emphasized identifiability.

Each subject shocked two victims. One was presented as sweet and altruistic, the other as conceited, self-centered, and obnoxious. As predicted, subjects in the deindividuation condition were more aggressive, giving longer shocks to both victims, and there was evidence of less discrimination between nice and obnoxious victims among deindividuated subjects.

Zimbardo argues that deindividuation is fostered when the individual feels that he cannot be recognized and identified by others. Watson (1973) reasoned that cultures that change the appearance of warriors prior to battle may be fostering deindividuation. He measured the incidence of special face and body painting, hair cutting, the wearing of masks, and so on associated with battle in selected cultures. He related this to reports of extreme forms of aggression in warfare, such as torturing, mutilating, and sacrificing the enemy and killing without quarter. He found that the cultures that scored high on deindividuation prior to battle also scored high on extreme forms of aggression.

EMOTIONAL AROUSAL AND GROUP AGGRESSION

There is another aspect to group aggression which may be related to deindividuation: an extreme and unreasoning emotional excitement that often leads to uncontrollable behavior. Some of the soldiers at My Lai apparently went wild for a time, shooting people, animals, and inanimate objects repeatedly and indiscriminately. According to the account of Sgt. C. West, "the guys were hollering about 'slants.' It wasn't just the young guys, older ones were shooting too. They might have been wild for awhile, but I don't think they were crazy. . . . If these men had been crazy, they would have gone on killing people" (*Life*, Dec. 5, 1969, p. 43). Apparently the situation at My Lai not only forced the participation of men not personally disposed to kill, but it disinhibited and perhaps greatly excited aggressive behavior in other men.

In an analysis of the My Lai massacre, an Army psychiatrist suggested that this excitement is due to an essential enjoyment of killing: "What people don't like to believe is that there is a real thrill in killing people. And in a combat situation, in the passions of the moment, there is the feeling that none of the rules count" (Bourne, quoted in *Newsweek*, Dec. 8, 1969, p. 35). Zimbardo too prefers to treat this excitement as a result of deindividuation, and, if deindividuation is defined as a process which releases socialized restraints and controls on behavior, it implies that this uncontrolled destructive excitement must be natural behavior that is inhibited by the process of socialization. This suggests a distinctly Hobbesean view of man—remove the controls and *homo homini lupus!*

However, another interpretation is possible. Deindividuation may be a necessary, but not sufficient, condition for the occurrence of this excitement. The uncontrollable excitement may be a result of the high arousal created by the situation. We considered above the possibility derived from Schachter's (1964) self-attribution theory that general arousal may increase aggression if it is labeled or interpreted to be aggressive arousal.

As we saw in Chapters 2 and 10, Schachter suggested that when one is aroused in a novel and unstructured situation, he may be unsure of the reason for that arousal. He is then motivated to search for a reason for his aroused state, and he may well compare his state with the behaviors of other people. The reactions of others can give us more knowledge and understanding of our own reactions (cf. Schachter, 1959; 1964).

Under certain circumstances, such emotional comparison may lead to uncontrollable aggressive excitement. A frightened and frustrated soldier might be experiencing an extremely high state of arousal. If he sees others around him being aggressive, he could well label this arousal as anger and hostility, and his aggressive behavior would gain strong and perhaps uncontrollable emotional force.

This analysis is quite speculative, but it would account for the great diversity of human group behavior. It is true that groups can be brutally and cruelly aggressive. It has been noted in several instances that groups witnessing a person contemplating jumping to his death may begin to laugh and joke and urge him to jump. Perhaps the high arousal in the novel situation of witnessing a potential suicide was defined as amusement for that group because of a few sociopathic individuals. On the other hand, groups have reacted to similar situations constructively with courage and self-sacrifice. A group once waded into a raging flooded stream holding hands to save trapped occupants of a car. Perhaps their arousal was defined as concern and courage in this case because of the actions of a few concerned and courageous individuals. Thus the same kind of arousal state can be channeled into constructive or destructive paths by the actions of a few.

We have seen that there are neural circuits in humans which are closely associated with aggressive behavior. They can be activated abnormally by disorders such as tumor, certain rare forms of epilepsy, upsets in endocrine balance, and so forth. They are perhaps also affected by particular releasing stimuli, such as a stare from a stranger or unwonted intrusion upon one's familiar territory. These circuits can also be sensitized by frustration, deprivation, and stress. However, some of the most dangerous forms of human aggression may be quite unrelated to these circuits. Aggressive behavior can be a coldly calculated means to an end, or it can be a reluctant act of obedience to authority.

We began Chapter 5 with the question of whether human nature is good or evil. One can find examples of human behavior to support virtually any answer to this question. Human beings are passionate creatures who are powerfully oriented toward distant goals and strongly influenced by their fellows. From these qualities come much that is good in humanity, and much that is evil.

Summary

This chapter has shown that, to a surprising extent, people act as if they were passive pawns in the service of the influences around them. They act out the expectations that others have of them: they stand on the subway without demanding seats from others; they do not sing loudly in public places; they go about their business without interfering in the affairs of others, even when the other might desperately need their help; they kill defenseless women and children when ordered to do so. It is suggested that this remarkable susceptibility to social influence may be based upon an innate disposition to obey derived from the evolution of the human being as a social animal. Whether or not this is true, there seem to be two sides to this disposition: it may underlie tendencies toward constructive cooperation between people as well as tendencies toward destructive obedience.

The chapter began with a consideration of the process by which the individual learns to judge right and wrong. The development of moral judgment has been analysed as a universal phenomenon based upon experiences in social relationships. As Piaget puts it, we learn to feel from within the desire to treat others as we ourselves would wish to be treated. However, this desire can easily be short-circuited by social and situational pressures. Darley and his colleauges found that we cannot rely on feelings of compassion and pity to assure that the individual will help another in need, even when that individual is a divinity student who has just read the parable of the Good Samaratan. Milgram found that such feelings will not stop an individual from doing the bidding of malevolent authority.

The Milgram experiment helps to explain how ordinary people can be induced to cooperate in the commission of monstrous crimes. It does not explain the uncontrollable aggressive behavior that is occasionally observed in normal-appearing people who are free of any sign of organic disorder which might explain such behavior. Zimbardo has suggested that people lose their learned inhibitions of aggression in situations where they feel anonymous and free of responsibility. It was also suggested that diffuse emotional excitement stemming from various sources—fear, anxiety, frustration—may be labeled as anger and contribute to uncontrollable aggression.

Social influence does not really appear in the schema introduced in Chapter 1. The schema involves the interaction of emotional and motivational forces within the individual. Although such processes are undoubtedly activated in the conflicts created in the kinds of social influence situations we have considered, those processes do not really determine the individual's behavior (unless he sucessfully resists the influence). In following social influence, the individual in effect surrenders his responsibility and his freedom in choosing his own behavior. His behavior is determined by forces outside himself.

APPENDIX

THE PHYSIOLOGICAL BASES OF EMOTION AND MOTIVATION

APPENDIX

Physiological Bases of Emotion and Motivation

This appendix will consider some of the facts of neuroanatomy, neuro-chemistry, and physiological methodology that can serve as a background to an understanding of the physiological bases of motivation and emotion. We shall first examine the nature of the neuron and the chemical substances that carry nerve impulses from one neuron to another, the synaptic transmitters. We shall then examine the somatic and autonomic branches of the peripheral nervous system and how these can be measured through the psychophysiological measures. We shall then consider the endocrine system and the complex feedback relationships between the hormones and the nervous system. The appendix will then examine the research methods used to study the depths of the brain: those regions of the central nervous system which seem most directly linked with emotional and motivational phenomena. These include the *reticular formation* and *diffuse thalamic system*, the *hypothalamus*, and the *limbic system*.

The Neuron and Synaptic Transmission

THE NEURON

The *neuron* or nerve cell is a basic unit in the organization of the nervous system. Although they come in many sizes and shapes (many are several feet long), a typical neuron is composed of dendrites, a cell body, and an axon that terminates in a number of synaptic knobs (see Figure A.1). Each neuron receives influences from other neurons that either excite or inhibit it. These influences are passed from one neuron to another by chemical *transmitter substances* across a microscopic space (about 1/10,000,000 of a millimeter) that separates the synaptic knob of one neuron from the dendrite or cell body of another. This is called a synaptic junction or *synapse.*

If the net excitation is strong enough, the neuron receiving the influence is fired. A nerve impulse travels down its axon until it reaches the (usually numerous) synaptic knobs at the end of the axon. There the impulse apparently functions to activate or liberate the chemical transmitter substance into the synaptic space separating the discharging *presy-*

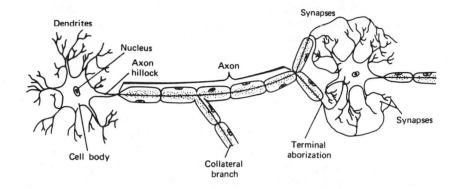

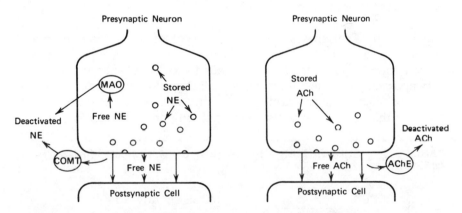

FIGURE A.1   Simplified diagram of a neuron (*above*), an adrenergic synapse (*left below*), and a cholinergic synapse (*right below*). In the adrenergic synapse, norepinepherine (NE) is broken down by monoamimine oxidase (MAO) within the neuron and catechol-O-methyl transferase (COMT) in the synaptic space. In the cholinergic synapse, acetylcholine (ACh) is broken down by acetylcholine esterase (AChE) in the synaptic space. See text for further description.

naptic neuron from the *postsynaptic* neuron. The transmitter substance delivers an excitatory or inhibitory influence to the postsynaptic cell. A given neuron may be influenced by scores or even hundreds of other neurons, and it may in turn influence many neurons.

SYNAPTIC TRANSMITTER SUBSTANCES

Only a few substances are regarded with confidence as transmitters. They are released at the synapse in such minute amounts that it is extremely difficult to study them, particularly in depths of the brain. One of the earliest identifications of transmitters was made by Otto Loewi. Loewi found that stimulation of sympathetic nervous system fibers produced a substance that excited or accelerated cardiac muscle, while parasympathetic nervous system fibers secreted a substance that inhibited it. The acceleratory substance was subsequently shown to be *norepinepherine* (once called noradrenalin), while the inhibitory substance turned out to be *acetylcholine* (Grossman, 1967). Norepinepherine and acetylcholine (*ACh*) are the major transmitter substances in the peripheral nervous system, and there is evidence that they are important transmitters in the central nervous system as well. Other substances suspected of being central nervous system transmitters include dopamine and serotonin. We shall consider in some detail the way a transmitter substance works, using the best known examples: *cholinergic* transmission based on ACh and *adrenergic* transmission based on norepinepherine.

Cholinergic Transmission   ACh is synthesized in the neuron and stored in sacs in the synaptic knob (see Figure A.1). When an impulse arrives down the axon, the ACh is released into the synaptic space where it temporarily alters the membrane of the postsynaptic neuron. If the alteration (termed depolarization) is strong enough, an impulse is produced in the axon of the postsynaptic neuron (for an introductory discus-

TABLE A.1   SUBSTANCES THAT AFFECT CHOLINERGIC TRANS-MISSION.

DRUG	MODE OF ACTION
A. Cholinergic drugs Carbachol Muscarine Nicotine	Imitate the action of ACh at certain cholinergic synapses—cause depolarization (synaptic transmission).
B. Anticholinesterase drugs Physostigmine Neostigmine Organophosphates (Includes the insecti- cide parathion, the nerve gasses sarin, soman, tabun, DFP.	Cause ACh to accumulate in the cholinergic synapse by blocking AChE—cause depolarization (synaptic transmission).
C. Anticholinergic drugs Curare Atropine Scopalamine	Block the depolarizing effect of ACh at certain cholinergic synapses—inhibit depolarization (synaptic transmission).

sion of this depolarization process, see Eccles, 1965). As the ACh remains in the synaptic space, it is quickly destroyed by the enzyme *acetyl-cholinesterase* (AChE) and the membrane becomes repolarized.

A large number of substances excite or inhibit the actions of ACh and AChE, and these can be used experimentally to study the functions of that part of the nervous system in which ACh is the transmitter. Table A.1 names some of these substances, many of which are discussed in the book.

An important drug that acts on the cholinergic synapse is curare, a substance long used as a poison by native South Americans. Curare blocks the action of ACh at certain synapses, including the connections between the somatic motor neurons and the skeletal muscles. This prevents normal muscle contractions, resulting in paralysis. As is discussed in Chapter 4, curare has been used experimentally to rule out skeletal muscle movement artifacts in studying the control of autonomic responding. In such studies the experimental animal must be artificially respirated until the curare wears off. Curare has also been used in humans in carefully monitored amounts to treat tetanus or lockjaw, a disorder in which the skeletal muscles contract uncontrollably.

Another important class of substances acting on the cholinergic synapse are the anti-AChE drugs. These inhibit AChE and thus allow ACh to accumulate in the synaptic space. This causes the membrane of the postsynaptic cell to remain depolarized so that it fires uncontrollably. Shortly before World War II, substances were discovered which irreversibly inactivate AChE. These were developed into the extremely toxic nerve gases, soman, sarin, tabun, and DFP. Small amounts of these substances have lethal effects, causing weakness, twitching, and finally paralysis of the muscles; involuntary defecation and urination; and paralysis of the respiratory muscles. Exposure leads to death by suffocation in from 5 minutes to 24 hours (Koelle, 1971). An antidote for this kind of nerve gas is atropine, an anti-ACh which apparently works by affecting the postsynaptic membrane in such a way that it is more difficult for ACh to depolarize it.

Adrenergic Transmission   Adrenergic transmission involves a family of chemical substances that are of major interest to psychologists, the amines. The amines are divided into two broad categories, the *catecholamines,* including dopamine, norepinepherine, and epinepherine, and the *indole amines,* including serotonin (also called 5-hydroxy-tryptamine or 5-HT) and histamine. There is evidence that these substances are closely related to mood and emotion (see Schildkraut and Kety, 1967; Jouvet, 1969), and they are considered at several points in Chapters 2 and 3.

Understanding of adrenergic transmission has greatly increased in recent years, due in part to the introduction of new experimental techniques such as fluorescence methods (Axelsson, 1971). Formaldehyde and certain other compounds condense with a variety of biologically important amines giving fluorescent products whose strength and color varies with the particular amine involved. This reveals the precise distribution and density of specific amines important in adrenergic transmission (Angelakos and King, 1968).

Norepinepherine is synthesized within the neuron in a sequence beginning with the dietary amino acid tryosine. Tryosine is converted via an enzyme to dopa, dopa is converted via another enzyme to dopamine, and dopamine is converted to norepinepherine via a third enzyme. The local concentration of norepinepherine probably helps control the synthesis of further norepinepherine by controlling the enzyme that acts on tryosine (Lipton and Udenfriend, 1968; Spector, 1968). Norepinepherine is inactivated within the neuron by MAO (monoamine oxidase) which is found in structures called mitochondria (see Figure A.1).

Norepinepherine is stored within the neuron in granules, and like ACh, it is released into the synaptic space by nerve impulses. Unlike ACh, which acts on the membrane of the postsynaptic neuron, norepinepherine may act by entering and initiating biochemical reactions in the other cell (Costa and Weiss, 1968). There is evidence that these biochemical reactions involve the extremely important and ubiquitous substance, cyclic AMP, which has widespread effects on many bodily functions (Axelsson, 1971). The deactivation of norepinepherine seems to be accomplished both by an enzyme COMT (Catechol-O-methy-transferase) in the synaptic space and by reuptake into the presynaptic neuron (Schildkraut, Davis and Klerman, 1968).

This introduction to cholinergic and adrenergic transmission will be useful in understanding the functioning of the autonomic nervous system and the actions of certain drugs on a cellular level. It is also relevant to some new and very interesting research into the functioning of the brain, which are considered in Chapters 2 and 3.

The Peripheral Nervous System

The peripheral nervous system includes *afferent* nerves entering the brain and spinal cord from various sense organs and *efferent* nerves leaving the brain and spinal cord going to various effectors, such as the muscles and glands. It is organized into 12 pairs of cranial nerves attached to the brainstem and 31 pairs of spinal nerves which connect to the spinal cord between the spinal vertebrae. The peripheral nervous system is divided

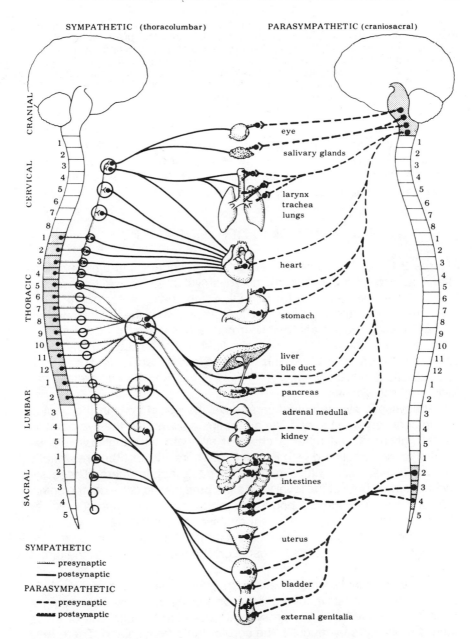

SYMPATHETIC (thoracolumbar)   PARASYMPATHETIC (craniosacral)

CRANIAL

CERVICAL

THORACIC

LUMBAR

SACRAL

eye
salivary glands
larynx
trachea
lungs
heart
stomach
liver
bile duct
pancreas
adrenal medulla
kidney
intestines
uterus
bladder
external genitalia

SYMPATHETIC
.... presynaptic
——— postsynaptic
PARASYMPATHETIC
- - - presynaptic
▬▬▬ postsynaptic

FIGURE A.2   The autonomic nervous system is customarily divided into two components: the sympathetic and parasympathetic systems. The motor pathways of both usually have two neurons: the first (presynaptic) neuron exits the spinal cord and synapses with a second (postsynaptic) neuron which innervates the target organ. The presynaptic neurons of the sympathetic nervous system typically synapse in ganglia some distance from the target organ. They may influence a number of long postsynaptic neurons. The presynaptic neurons of the parasympathetic system are relatively long, synapsing on a short postsynaptic neuron close to the target organ. See text for further discussion. Reprinted from BIOLOGICAL SCIENCE by William T. Keeton. Illustrated by Paula DiSanto Bensadoun. By permission of W. W. Norton & Company, Inc. Copyright © 1967 by W. W. Norton & Company, Inc.

into the *somatic nervous system,* including the sensory nerves from most receptors and motor nerves serving the skeletal muscles, and the *autonomic nervous system,* including the sensory and motor nerves serving heart, glands, and smooth muscles of the viscera. Most of our concern will be with autonomic functioning.

THE AUTONOMIC NERVOUS SYSTEM

Figures 2.1 and A.2 illustrate many of the important anatomical neurochemical facts of the autonomic nervous system. Figure A.2 shows the paths of the autonomic motor nerves. Sympathetic motor nerve fibers leave from the middle portions of the spinal cord, while the parasympathetic fibers emerge above and below, from the brainstem and tail region of the spinal cord. These autonomic motor fibers synapse between the spinal cord and end organ. The organization of these synapses is different for sympathetic and parasympathetic nerve fibers, and this difference has functional implications.

Presynaptic sympathetic fibers leave the spinal cord in the ventral root in company with the somatic motor fibers. However, the sympathetic fibers branch off and enter a chain of sympathetic ganglia which run parallel to the spinal cord (see Figure 2.1). There, most of the presynaptic fibers synapse, each with a number of postsynaptic fibers. These synapses may be both at the level where the presynaptic cell exits the spinal cord and one or two levels above and below. One presynaptic cell may affect a number (perhaps 20 or 30) postsynaptic fibers that may be at a considerable distance above or below its level in the spinal cord. The postsynaptic cells then leave the ganglion chain and proceed to the target organ.

Other presynaptic sympathetic neurons go through the ganglion chain and synapse on postsynaptic cells in one of three sympathetic ganglia outside the chain. Still other presynaptic fibers go through one of these ganglia to the adrenal medulla, the core of the adrenal gland. There they stimulate the secretion of the hormone *epinepherine* into the bloodstream. The effects of circulating epinepherine on the body are very similar to the effects of the sympathetic nervous system, and it has been suggested that the adrenal medulla evolved because it provides a useful hormonal backup to the sympathetic nervous system. In fact, the cells of the adrenal medulla evolved from postsynaptic sympathetic neurons. It may be that the sympathetic nervous system provides a fast-acting, but relatively short-term response to stress and emergency, while the circulating epinepherine provides a slower acting but longer-lasting response. Whatever the reason, the sympathetic nervous system and adrenal medulla act in concert to such an extent that Cannon (1928) termed them the sympathetico-adrenal system (Sternbach, 1966).

In summary, most presynaptic cells of the sympathetic nervous system are relatively short, synapsing in ganglia near the spinal cord and far from their target organs. Each presynaptic cell connects with a number of postsynaptic cells. An exception is the collection of presynaptic cells that affect the adrenal medulla. Because of these facts, Cannon suggested that the sympathetic nervous system is organized to act in a diffuse, unitary fashion on the body. If a presynaptic sympathetic neuron is stimulated, it may affect dozens of postsynaptic neurons that spread widely over the body. Similarly, when the adrenal medulla is stimulated, circulating epinepherine carries sympathetic-like effects throughout the body.

In contrast to the sympathetic nervous system, the organization of the parasympathetic nervous system suggests that its effects are more focused. Presynaptic parasympathetic neurons are relatively long, exciting the brainstem or spinal cord and traveling directly to the target organ. There they synapse and a short postganglionic cell stimulates the organ. Thus, stimulation of a presynaptic parasympathetic neuron has an effect on only one bodily structure.

There is another important distinction between sympathetic and parasympathetic functioning. The presynaptic neurons throughout the autonomic nervous system are cholinergic, so that ACh is the transmitter substance. This is also true of the postsynaptic parasympathetic neurons, but most of the postsynaptic sympathetic neurons are adrenergic. Their transmitter substance, norepinepherine, points out another affinity between the sympathetic nervous system and the adrenal medulla, and it supports the view that the action of the sympathetic nervous system is relatively diffuse. Norepinepherine is very similar chemically to epinepherine, and they have similar effects on most bodily functions. In fact, the presence of circulating epinepherine may release norepinepherine from the synaptic knobs of the sympathetic neurons without the need for nerve impulses in the postsynaptic sympathetic neurons. Also, the action of norepinepherine as a transmitting substance is more diffuse than the action of ACh. We have seen that ACh is rapidly destroyed in the synaptic space by the enzyme AChE. Thus, the release of ACh has brief effects on a limited area. Norepinepherine is not broken down as quickly and most is disposed of by relatively slow reabsorption into the presynaptic neuron.

Thus, norepinepherine from one synapse may spread rather widely. In the junctions between the postsynaptic sympathetic neurons and smooth muscle fibers, only about 1 in 100 muscle fibers are directly innervated. The others are apparently activated by norepinepherine that spreads from the synapse over the tissues.

There are some exceptions to the rule that postganglionic sympathetic neurons are adrenergic. One important exception is the sweat glands. These are innervated solely by postsynaptic sympathetic fibers, but the transmitter substance involved is ACh. The sweat glands do not respond to epinepherine or norepinepherine, but their activity is blocked by the anti-ACh atropine (Lader and Montagu, 1962). This fact is frustrating to psychophysiologists who measure sweat gland activity via skin conductance (GSR) measurement and would like to relate this measure to sympathetic nervous system activity. Another exception to the adrenergic rule are the blood vessels. These are also innervated only by sympathetic fibers, and in general the fibers that cause vasoconstriction (constriction of the blood vessels) are adrenergic while those causing vasodiliation are cholinergic (Netter, 1962).

The fact that postsynaptic parasympathetic fibers are cholinergic and sympathetic fibers are adrenergic has implications for the effects of certain drugs. For example, atropine can be applied to the eye to block the constricting parasympathetic influences, leaving the competing sympathetic influences free to dilate the pupil. Similarly, epinepherine can be given in some cases of asthma, since it excites the sympathetic fibers that inhibit the formation of mucus.

We have been concentrating on the motor functions of the autonomic nervous system, but both the sympathetic and parasympathetic have sensory functions as well. Pressure, stretch, and pain receptors, which we shall call *interoceptors,* are present throughout the viscera. Sensory fibers from the interoceptors on their way to the spinal cord mix with autonomic motor fibers. In the sympathetic nervous system, the sensory fibers pass through the chain of sympathetic ganglia before they mix with somatic sensory fibers and enter the spinal cord through the dorsal root (see Figure 2.1).

The Psychophysiological Measures

One of the most fascinating aspects of the autonomic nervous system is that its activity can be monitored in humans, albeit indirectly, through the measurement of bodily electrical activity. Certain activities of the somatic and central nervous systems can also be monitored in this way. Collectively, these measures are termed the psychophysiological measures. The measures of autonomic activity include electrodermal measures (skin conductance, skin potential) and measures of the circulatory system (heart rate, blood pressure, and vasomotor responses). The electromyograph (EMG) reflects skeletal muscle tension, and the electroencephalograph (EEG) reflects arousal in the central nervous system. These measures are normally taken by a polygraph which monitors bodily electrical activity and converts it into voltage changes that are written out on a moving sheet of paper.

ELECTRODERMAL MEASURES

Various terms have been used for the electrical phenomena of the skin, including the galvanic skin response (GSR) and the psychogalvanic response (PGR). We shall use terms which specify the technique used to measure the response: skin conductance (SC) and skin potential (SP). Skin conductance and skin potential can be measured both as basal levels of conductance and potential and as responses superimposed on these levels.

The characteristic waveforms for skin conductance and potential responses as they appear on the polygraph record are shown in Figure A.3. The skin conductance response is a unidirectional drop in resistance (or rise in conductance) while the skin potential response is a biphasic wave with an initial negative component followed by a positive component. Skin

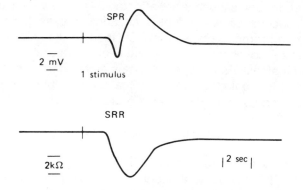

FIGURE A.3   Characteristic skin potential (SPR) and skin resistance (SRR) response curves. Skin conductance is the reciprocal of skin resistance: when it is measured the SRR curve seen above is typically inverted. From P. H. Venables and I. Martin, "Skin resistance and skin potential." In P. H. Venables and I. Martin (Eds.) *Manual of Psycho-physiological Methods*. New York: Wiley, 1967. Copyright © 1967 by John Wiley and Sons, Inc. Reprinted by permission of the publishers.

conductance and potential levels may be conveniently abbreviated as SCL and SPL, while their respective responses may be called SCR and SPR (Venables and Martin, 1967).

Skin conductance is obtained by applying a weak electric current through the skin and measuring the resistance of the skin to the flow of current. The resistance measures are transformed into conductance units by taking their reciprocals. (Conductance in mhos = 1/Resistance in ohms). The resistance of the skin varies with sweat gland activity. You may recall from above that the sweat glands are innervated by cholinergic sympathetic fibers. Activation of these fibers appears to cause temporary changes in the membranes of the sweat glands that decrease the resistance (or increase the conductance) of the skin.

Skin potential is obtained by measuring the difference in potential between two points on the skin. The physiological mechanism underlying skin potential responding is unclear, but it is probable that the initial negative component of the response involves the same changes in sweat gland activity that underly skin conductance changes (Martin and Venables, 1964). The later positive component may be based upon the filling of the sweat gland ducts, but this is uncertain (Venables and Martin, 1967).

Measures of electrodermal responses have been called "the most sensitive physiological indicator of psychological events available to the psychologist" (Montagu and Coles, 1966, p. 261.) They are also among the oldest, having a rich history of experimentation dating back to their discovery in the late nineteenth century (see Neumann and Blanton, 1970). Electrodermal responses are affected by a wide variety of arousing situations. Emotional stimuli, both pleasant and unpleasant in nature, elicit more SCRs and larger increases in SCL than do neutral stimuli. Also, sudden, intense, novel, and unusual stimuli elicit larger changes than do mild or familiar stimuli (Berlyne, 1966). Thus electrodermal changes have been said to reflect both the *affective* (pleasant or unpleasant) and *collative* (uncertain and surprising) aspects of a situation.

THE CIRCULATORY SYSTEM

The circulatory system is responsible for the supply of oxygen and nutrients to every cell in the body. It responds to the control of the autonomic nervous system, and thus measures of circulatory functioning are indirect measures of autonomic activity. However, the circulatory system is also a hydraulic system in which every change affects the functioning of the whole system. Measures of circulatory functioning may reflect changes in other circulatory functions as well as general autonomic activity. The impressive complexity of the regulation of circulation is illustrated in the work of Guyton, Coleman, and Granger (1972), who have presented a systems analysis of overall circulatory regulation which contains over 200 variables and over 400 mathematical equations, each describing some facet of circulatory functioning.

Heart Rate   The muscle potentials associated with heart action can be picked up by electrodes placed on the body surface on both sides of the heart. The resulting electrocardiogram (EKG) record reveals a characteristic waveform with a sharp spike (R-wave) associated with each heartbeat. The number of these spikes in a given time can be used to obtain heart rate, which is usually expressed in beats per minute. Like skin conductance, heart rate can be measured over an extended period of time (over 30 seconds or so) as *tonic* heart rate, or quick *phasic* changes in heart rate can be measured.

Often, a psychologist interested only in heart rate will use a device called a cardiotachometer that measures the time between each R-wave and records the speed of the heart at each beat. Figure A.4 illustrates the skin conductance and heart rate response to an unexpected buzzer. The top line shows the raw EKG record with the spikes, and the bottom line is the beat-by-beat heart rate as indicated by the cardiotachometer.

The heart is innervated by both the sympathetic and parasympathetic branches of the autonomic nervous system, with symptathetic activation increasing heart rate and parasympathetic activation decreasing it . An increase in heart rate thus might reflect an increase in sympathetic activation, or a decrease in parasympathetic activation. The autonomic effects on heart rate are controlled through cardiovascular regulatory centers in the brainstem. These centers receive information from chemical-sensitive and pressure-sensitive receptors in the blood vessels and in two structures in major arteries near the heart—the carotid sinus and aortic arch. These receptors sense such things as blood pressure and the amount of oxygen (O_2) and carbon dioxide (CO_2) in the blood. Increases in CO_2, decreases in O_2, or lowering of blood pressure stimulates the cardioacceleratory center in the brainstem which increases heart rate via sympathetic fibers. The opposite changes in the blood stimulate the cardioinhibitory center and result in lower heart rate via parasympathetic fibers. The third cardiovascular regulatory center in the brainstem is the sympathetic vasoconstrictor center which causes vasoconstriction in certain blood vessels and a consequent rise in blood pressure (Brener, 1967).

You may notice in Figure A.4 that, before the buzzer sounded, the cardiotachometer showed a rhythmic pattern of rising and falling. This is called *sinus arrythmia* and it is associated with respiration. Heart rate increases as the subject breathes in and decreases as he breathes out.

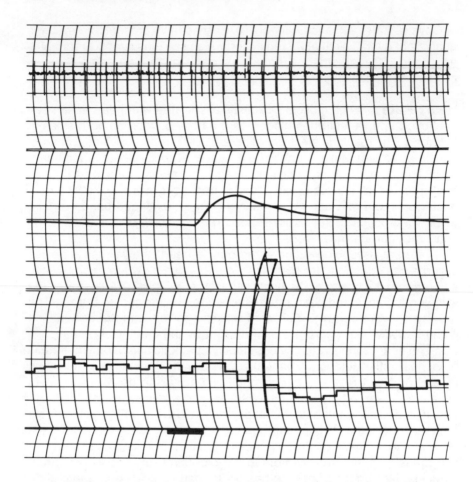

FIGURE A.4   Heart rate and skin conductance response to an unexpected buzzer. The extra spike appearing eight beats after the buzzer is an artifact. *Top line* the electrical wave caused by the heart measured directly. *Second line*: skin conductance (note the delay in response). *Third line*: cardiotachometer record (note the interference caused by the artifact). *Bottom line*: 2.5 second duration buzzer.

This is an example of an effect upon heart rate that is caused by internal factors within the circulatory system that does not reflect the activity of the autonomic nervous system as a whole. The physiological mechanisms underlying sinus arrythmia involve reflex actions on the cardioacceleratory and cardioinhibitory centers in the brainstem.

Vasomotor Responses   The dilation and constriction of the blood vessels have two functions: to maintain body temperature and to direct blood to body areas where local metabolic demands require increased blood flow. Vasomotor responses are regional—arterioles simultaneously dilate in active organs and constrict in inactive ones.

The control of vasomotor responses differs according to the area of the body and the type of tissue involved. The responses of vessels in the skin are very different from those in the muscles. In the fingers, for example, the blood supply is mainly to the skin and changes in blood flow appear to function to maintain skin temperature. The innervation of these vessels is fairly simple, involving only adrenergic sympathetic vasoconstrictor fibers. Vasodilation is accomplished by a reduction in this vasoconstrictor tone (Lader, 1967). The control of vasomotor responses in large muscles is much more complex. For example, adrenergic vasoconstrictor fibers also exist in the arm muscles, but vasodilation is an active process. During exercise, the local accumulation of metabolic wastes triggers vasodilation. During stress, cholinergic vasodilator fibers and circulating epinepherine cause vasodilation and large increases in blood flow (Lader, 1967).

Vasomotor responses underlie familiar changes in the appearance of the skin. Blushing in the face is caused by vasodilation, while pallor indicates vasoconstriction (Brown, 1967). This change in coloration is the basis for one technique of measuring vasomotor responses, the photoplethysmograph, which operates by passing a beam of light through living tissue to a photocell. Living tissue is relatively transparent and blood is relatively opaque to red and infrared light, so that the amount of light of this type passed through the tissue to the photocell is inversely proportional to the amount of blood in the tissue (Weinman, 1967).

Another major technique for measuring vasomotor responses is the volume plethysmograph. This takes advantage of the fact that vasodilation tends to increase the blood supply of an organ, and this increase is associated with an increase in the volume of the organ. Volumetric changes are recorded by enclosing the organ (such as a finger) in a rigid container filled with liquid, so that changes in volume will result in measurable displacements of the liquid.

Blood Pressure   Blood pressure reflects both vasomotor responding and cardiac output. The more blood pumped by the heart, and the more resistance the blood encounters in the vessels due to vasoconstriction, the higher the blood pressure. Sympathetic activity tends to increase blood pressure by increasing heart rate and causing vasoconstriction in some vessels.

The pumping action of the heart creates a pressure wave with a high point at systole, the peak of the heart's ejection pulse, and a low point at diastole, the trough of the pulse. The high point of blood pressure is thus called *systolic blood pressure* and the low point is *diastolic blood pressure.*

The most accurate way to record blood pressure is through a cannula inserted into an artery. This technique is much too uncomfortable and hazardous to use for routine monitoring of blood pressure. A variety of indirect techniques have been developed, most of them derived from the methods described by Korotkoff and others at the turn of the century (Lywood, 1967). The basic technique involves placing an inflatable cuff around the upper arm and inflating it so that the arteries in the arm are pressed closed and circulation is stopped. The pressure is then let off slowly, and the operator listens with a stethescope at the brachial artery below the cuff. When blood flow is completely stopped in the artery the operator hears nothing. When the pressure in the cuff falls below systolic blood pressure, blood flows through the artery when the pressure is near the systolic peak, but it is stopped when the pressure is near the diastolic trough. The resulting discontinous flow of blood can be heard through the stethescope as characteristic pulses or Korotkoff sounds. The operator notes the pressure at which he first hears these pulses as the systolic blood pressure, and he continues to let off pressure in the cuff. When the pressure falls below diastolic pressure the flow of blood through the artery becomes continuous, and the Korotkoff sounds dissappear. The operator notes the pressure at which he stops hearing the sounds as diastolic blood pressure.

A number of automatic techniques based on this general method have been devised (See Lywood, 1967; Olmstead, 1967). Some use microphones to pick up the Korotkoff sounds and signal a pump to inflate and deflate the cuff, and finger cuffs have been developed to provide freedom of movement.

MUSCLE TENSION

Muscle tension involves the measurement of somatic, rather than autonomic, nervous system activity. Skeletal muscles are usually arranged in antagonistic flexor–extensor pairs which maintain a balanced state of tension. This tension is lowest during sleep, rises during alertness, and increases in the appropriate muscles with the intent to move even when there is no overt movement (Grossman, 1967; Jacobson, 1938; 1951). Muscle tension varies, of course, across different muscle groups depending on the responder's activity. The muscle tension in irrelevant muscles, those not engaged in the specific task at hand, seems to increase with anxiety. Symptoms caused by the abnormally prolonged contraction of particular muscle groups are common in patients with high anxiety (Lippold, 1967). For example, long term contraction of the neck muscles can result in a type of tension headache (see Chapter 4).

Muscle tension can be measured by an electromyograph (EMG): this involves placing electrodes over a muscle group which pick up the electrical changes associated with muscle activity. These changes can be recorded raw or their frequency and intensity can be integrated to show tension changes more clearly.

THE ELECTROENCEPHALOGRAPH (EEG)

Unlike the other measures we have considered in this section, the EEG is a direct measure of central nervous system activity. Electrodes placed on the scalp can pick up voltage changes from the brain that seem to vary with the alertness of the organism (see Figure A.5). An alert animal normally shows fast (30–60 Hz) unsynchronized waves of low amplitude. Rest and relaxation is often associated with slow (8–12 Hz), synchronized, higher amplitude *alpha waves.* States of drowsiness and sleep show waves of increasing irregularity, with the appearance of 12–15 Hz sleep spindles and very slow (1–2 Hz), high amplitude *delta waves.* Interestingly, the deepest stage of sleep (as defined by the difficulty of arousing the organism) is associated with fast low-amplitude waves in the cortex similar to those seen during full alertness. This has been called paradoxical sleep. It is often accompanied by rapid eye movements (REM), deep relaxation in the neck muscles, regular 4–8 Hz *theta waves* from subcortical structures, and reports of dream activity upon waking (Dement and Kleitman, 1957; Jouvet, 1967).

If a sudden stimulus is presented to a relaxed or sleeping animal, the animal orients toward the stimulus and the EEG changes from slow synchronized activity to the fast low-amplitude activity associated with alertness. This is variously known as EEG arousal, desynchronization, or alpha blocking. If the stimulus is presented again and again, the EEG arousal generally becomes smaller and the animal ceases to orient toward the stimulus. This decrease in response with stimulus repetition is termed habituation.

The Endocrine System

The endocrine glands are ductless glands which release chemical substances, called *hormones,* directly into the bloodstream. These participate with the autonomic nervous system in the functions of adaptation and the

EXCITED

RELAXED

DROWSY

ASLEEP

DEEP SLEEP

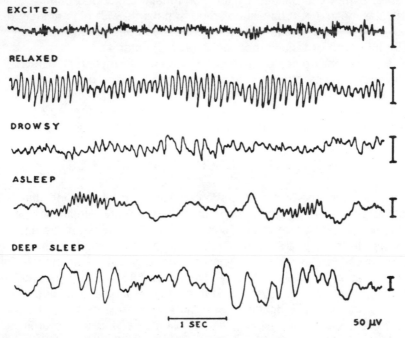

1 SEC   50 μV

FIGURE A.5   Electroencephalographic (EEG) records during excitement, relaxation, and varying degrees of sleep. Note that excitement is characterized by a rapid frequency and small amplitude and that varying degrees of sleep are marked by increasing irregularity and by the appearance of slow waves. Alpha waves are most prominent in the relaxed state. In the fourth strip runs of 14/sec rhythm superimposed on slow waves are termed sleep spindles. From H. Jasper, *Epilepsy and Cerebral Localization*. New York: Charles C. Thomas, 1941. Copyright © 1941 by Charles C Thomas.

maintenance of homeostasis. Table A.2 presents a summary of the hormones released by some endocrine glands and their effects on the body. The central nervous system controls the endocrine system by way of neurochemical feedback loops involving the hypothalamus and the pituitary gland. We are most concerned with the pituitary gland and its relationships with the adrenal cortex and the gonads. The feedback system involving the pituitary and the adrenal cortex is known as the *pituitary-adrenal axis,* and that involving the gonads is the *pituitary-gonadal axis.* The essential components of this feedback process and the actions of the pituitary-adrenal axis are described in Chapter 2. Here we will discuss the pituitary-gonadal axis and the complex feedback process involved in the control of the female estrus or menstrual cycle.

TABLE A.2   SOME IMPORTANT MAMMALIAN HORMONES.

SOURCE	HORMONE	PRINCIPAL EFFECTS
Adrenal medulla	Adrenalin (Epinepherine)	Stimulates syndrome of reactions commonly termed "fight or flight"
	Noradrenalin (Norepinepherine)	Stimulates reactions similar to those produced by adrenalin, but causes more vasoconstriction and is less effective in conversion of glycogen into glucose
Adrenal cortex	Glucocorticoids (corticosterone, cortisone, hydrocortisone, etc.)	Stimulate formation (largely from noncarbohydrate sources) and storage of glycogen; help maintain normal blood-sugar level
	Mineralocorticoids (aldosterone, deoxycorticosterone, etc.)	Regulate sodium-potassium metabolism
	Cortical sex hormones (adrenosterone, etc.)	Stimulate secondary sexual characteristics, particularly those of the male
Anterior pituitary	Growth hormone	Stimulates growth
	Thyrotrophic hormone	Stimulates the thyroid
	Adrenocorticotrophic hormone (ACTH)	Stimulates the adrenal cortex
	Follicle-stimulating hormone (FSH)	Stimulates growth of ovarian follicles and of seminiferous tubules of the testes
	Luteinizing hormone (LH)	Stimulates conversion of follicles into corpora lutea; stimulates secretion of sex hormones by ovaries and testes
	Prolactin	Stimulates milk secretion by mammary glands
Intermediate lobe of pituitary	Melanocyte-stimulating hormone	Controls cutaneous pigmentation
Posterior pituitary	Oxytocin	Stimulates contraction of uterine muscles: stimulates release of milk by mammary glands
	Vasopressin	Stimulates increased water reabsorption by kidneys; stimulates constriction of blood vessels (and other smooth muscle)
Testes	Testosterone	Stimulates development and maintenance of male secondary sexual characteristics and behavior
Ovaries	Estrogens	Stimulate development and maintenance of female secondary sexual characteristics and behavior
	Progesterone	Stimulates female secondary sexual characteristics and behavior, and maintains pregnancy

THE PITUITARY-GONADAL AXIS

Like the pituitary-adrenal axis, the pituitary-gonadal axis is under the direct control of the hypothalamus. The hypothalamus directs the pituitary in the release of gonadotropic hormones, including luteinizing hormone (LH) and follicle-stimulating hormone (FSH). In both males and females, puberty begin when the hypothalamus triggers the release of increased LH and FSH from the pituitary. These hormones induce the gonads to begin secreting sex hormones, *testosterone* from the male testes and *estrogen* and *progesterone* from the female ovaries. The adrenal cortex is also involved, producing *cortical sex hormones.* The sex hormones stimulate the development of the secondary sex characteristics and the maturation of the reproductive organs.

   The *menstrual cycle* of the female illustrates a complex interaction between the hypothalamus and several hormones in the endocrine system. The first event in the cycle is that, under the control of the hypothalamus, the pituitary releases FSH (see Figure A.6). FSH (follicle-stimulating hormone) causes the development of a follicle in an ovary. The growing follicle begins to secrete estrogen. As the level of estrogen increases, it apparently inhibits the hypothalamic FSH center and the level of FSH begins to drop. At the same time, the estrogen excites the LH center of the hypothalamus and the level of LH begins to rise.

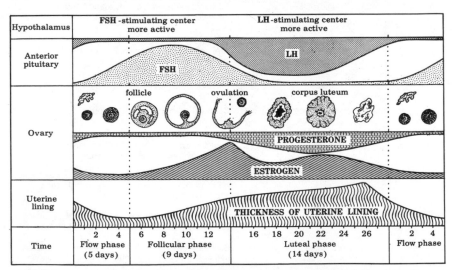

FIGURE A.6   The sequence of events in the human menstrual cycle. Reprinted from BIOLOGICAL SCIENCE by William T. Keeton. Illustrated by Paula DiSanto Bensadoun. By permission of W. W. Norton & Company, Inc. Copyright © 1967 by W. W. Norton & Company, Inc.

When the LH concentration reaches a critical level, the follicle ovulates, releasing an egg or ovum. Ovulation ends the follicular phase of the cycle, which lasts approximately 9 days.

After ovulation, LH (leuteinizing hormone) acts on the old follicle, converting it to a corpus luteum. The corpus luteum still secretes estrogen, although less than before ovulation. It also begins to secrete progesterone. Progesterone causes thickening and development of the uterine lining, and with the estrogen it continues the inhibition of the FSH center. If no fertilization occurs, progesterone begins to inhibit the LH center as well. When the LH level falls, the corpus luteum begins to atrophy and ceases to release estrogen and progesterone. The thickened lining of the uterus is sloughed off with some bleedng, ending the approximately 14-day luteal phase and beginning the 5-day flow phase. The lack of estrogen and progesterone frees the FSH center of inhibition, thus the FSH level rises, beginning another cycle. Birth-control pills, containing compounds similar to estrogen and progesterone, prevent the release of FSH and thus prevent follicular growth and ovulation.

In most species of mammals, these hormonal rhythms result in *estrus cycles.* Females are said to be in estrus or in heat for a brief period near the time of ovulation, and they normally are sexually receptive only at these times. In primates and humans, this period is not as pronounced and the female is receptive to some degree throughout most of the cycle. As is discussed in Chapter 7, sexual behavior in general becomes less dependent upon hormonal mechanisms the higher one goes on the phylogenetic scale.

The Central Nervous System: Methods of Study

We shall now turn to the regions of the central nervous system that are most directly linked to emotional and motivational phenomena. These regions are largely located in the depths of the brain, and special techniques are required to study them. The development of these techniques, occuring mainly since World War II, has been responsible for much of the recent revolution in the understanding of motivation and emotion.

Some cautionary statements should be made about the practice of associating emotional and motivational functions with particular locations in the brain. It is convenient, at least in the present state of knowledge, to break the central nervous system into anatomical structures such as the hypothalamus, limbic system, and so on and to break these structures into their anatomical parts. We can then consider the functions that these parts seem to have in mediating emotion and motivation. Some of them may seem to have such definite functions that they have been labeled "centers" of activity, such as the FSH and LH centers of the hypothalamus described above. This is a convenient way to approach the awesome complexity of the physiological systems underlying emotion and motivation, but it carries with it the danger that it may imply that different functions are isolated within specific anatomical structures. This is not true. Some degree of localization of some functions exists, but the nervous system is so interconnected that no structure works in isolation. All structures are involved together in determining behavior. It is only because of our ignorance and the difficulty of comprehending this immensely complex process that we must proceed one structure at a time in seeking to understand it.

In considering the anatomical features of the central nervous system, we shall make repeated use of anatomical terms that describe the location of of structures within the body. These terms are summarized in Figure A.7. *Dorsal* refers to the back of the body while *ventral* means the front of the body. In most animals, the top of the brain is toward the back, while in upright animals like monkeys and men the top of the brain is at right angles to the back of the body. To maintain consistency, anatomists refer to the top of all brains as *dorsal,* the bottom as *ventral,* the front as *anterior,* and the back as *posterior. Medial* means toward the middle, and *lateral* means toward either side. Thorough learning of these terms will help you to visualize the positions of structures in the three-dimensional world inside the brain. Thus, it will be easy to remember that the ventromedial

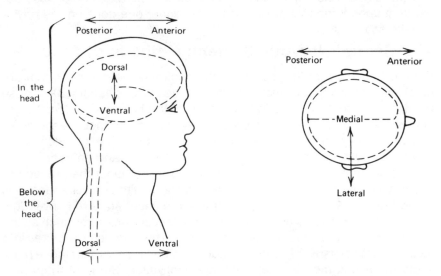

FIGURE A.7   Anatomical terminology used to describe position and location in reference to the axes of the body.

nuclei of the hypothalamus are located toward the middle in the bottom of the hypothalamus, and the lateral nuclei are located to either side. Inspection of Figure A.8 will clarify this.

LESIONS

One of the oldest techniques for studying the central nervous system is by lesioning or destroying a structure and observing the changes in behavior that result. It is usually assumed that any resulting behavior change is due to the destruction of that particular tissue, but this assumption may not always be warranted.

Destroying the surface cortex of the brain is called *ablation*. It is often accomplished by suction. The destruction of underlying structures is usually done by placing an electrode into the structure and applying current which cauterizes the tissue. Such lesions may sometimes cause problems by producing irritation and abnormal behavior in the surviving tissue surrounding the lesion. Behavior changes may result from this abnormal activity instead of the inactivity of the lesioned tissue. This problem is lessened when certain precautions are observed in the lesioning procedures (Milner, 1970).

Reversible lesions can be produced by cooling brain tissue below 25°C but above 0°C. This stops conduction in most neurons without destroying them. When they warm up, they can again become active. Such lesions are usually accomplished by inserting a tube into the brain and allowing a refrigerant gas to vaporize at the tip. Reversible lesions have been made clinically in humans to determine whether a given area of the brain is malfunctioning. Once discovered, the disturbed area can be lesioned permanently (Milner, 1970).

BRAIN STIMULATION

The *electrical stimulation* of specified areas of the brain has been one of the most productive techniques in physiological psychology. In the late nineteenth century, it was found that electrical stimulation of certain areas on the surface of the cerebral cortex elicited muscular movements. Later, stimulation of nearby regions in conscious human patients undergoing brain surgery elicited reports of sensations. These findings led to the mapping of the sensory and motor regions of the cerebral cortex.

In the mid-1920s, W. R. Hess invented a device to stimulate the deeplying subcortical regions. Thin wire electrodes were implanted deep

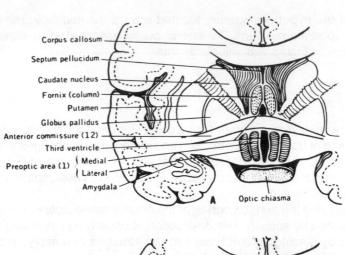

Corpus callosum
Septum pellucidum
Caudate nucleus
Fornix (column)
Putamen
Globus pallidus
Anterior commissure (12)
Third ventricle
Preoptic area (1) { Medial, Lateral }
Amygdala
Optic chiasma

A

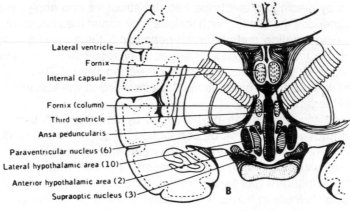

Lateral ventricle
Fornix
Internal capsule
Fornix (column)
Third ventricle
Ansa peduncularis
Paraventricular nucleus (6)
Lateral hypothalamic area (10)
Anterior hypothalamic area (2)
Supraoptic nucleus (3)

B

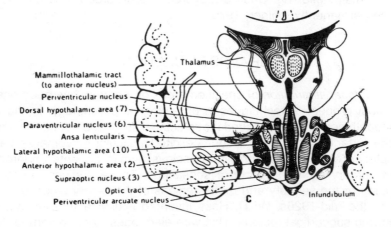

Thalamus
Mammillothalamic tract (to anterior nucleus)
Periventricular nucleus
Dorsal hypothalamic area (7)
Paraventricular nucleus (6)
Ansa lenticularis
Lateral hypothalamic area (10)
Anterior hypothalamic area (2)
Supraoptic nucleus (3)
Optic tract
Periventricular arcuate nucleus
Infundibulum

C

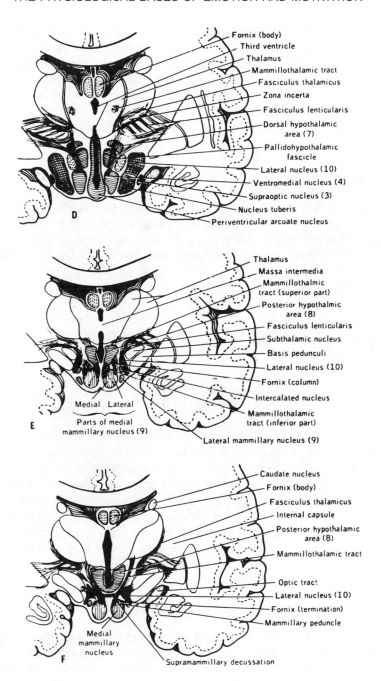

into the brain and attached to a platform which was screwed to the skull. The electrodes were activated by detachable flexible wires which permitted the animal considerable freedom of movement. This basic technique is used today, with refinements such as the use of telemetry to stimulate the brains of freely moving animals with no need for wires. Electrical stimulation techniques are being increasingly applied clinically to humans for the diagnosis and treatment of a number of disorders.

Techniques involving the *chemical stimulation* of subcortical regions have recently been developed. A tube is inserted into the region to be stimulated in the same way as an electrode is implanted, and chemicals in solid or liquid form are introduced through the tube. Chemical stimulation has a potential advantage over electrical stimulation because the latter affects all the neurons in the surrounding area while chemical stimulation may affect only those that are sensitive to the particular chemical. This is important in some brain areas where neurons serving quite different functions may lie in the same area (Fisher, 1964; Miller, 1965). For example, electrical stimulation of certain areas of the hypothalamus often leads to mixed effects of eating and drinking. Grossman (1960) found that an animal will tend to eat when this area is chemically stimulated by norepinepherine and drink when it is stimulated by ACh, suggesting that an adrenergic eating center and a cholinergic drinking center may exist in the same area.

BRAIN RECORDING

There are a number of techniques for recording the electrical activity of the brain, ranging from the gross measurement of thousands of cells with the electroencephalograph (EEG) to the measurement of the activity within a single functioning neuron. With the EEG, voltages generated by the brain are picked up from electrodes placed on the surface of the cortex, or, in humans, on the scalp. Electrical activity can also be recorded from small regions of the brain using the same kind of electrode attachments used to stimulate the brain. Such electrodes can be placed to record the activity of a single neuron. Smaller electrodes can be made to enter a cell and record the electrical changes within it.

Central Nervous System Mechanisms

In this section we shall describe the anatomical locus and major incoming and outgoing connections of some of the central nervous system mechanisms most concerned with motivation and emotion. Studies detailing the functions of these mechanisms are covered in Chapters 2 and 3.

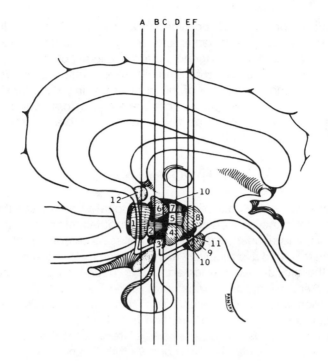

FIGURE A.8   General topography of the hypothalamus. The drawing above indicates the planes for the vertical sections. (1) preoptic nucleus; (2) anterior hypothalamic area; (3) supraoptic nucleus; (4)ventromedial nucleus; (5)dorsomedial nucleus; (6) paraventricular nucleus; (7) dorsal nucleus; (8) posterior hypothalamic area; (9) mammillary body; (10) lateral nucleus; (11) intercalated nucleus; (12) anterior commissure. From E. L. House and B. Pansky, *Neuroanatomy,* New York: McGraw-Hill, 1960. Copyright © 1960 by McGraw Hill. Reprinted by permission of the publisher.

THE RETICULAR FORMATION AND DIFFUSE THALAMIC SYSTEM

The importance of the reticular formation and diffuse thalamic system for our purposes lies in their involvment in the control of arousal, attention, and sleep. The placement of these structures is well suited to their apparent function of monitoring the reaction of the central nervous system to sensory input. The reticular formation is a collection of nuclei and scattered fiber tracts located in the core of the brainstem extending from the spinal cord to the hypothalamus and thalamus (see Figure 2.8). Its name derives from its resemblance under the microscope to a fishnet or reticulum. The reticular formation is surrounded by ascending sensory and descending motor fibers. It receives input from most, if not all, of the primary sensory systems. It sends ascending fibers to the cortex and to subcortical structures, including the thalamus and hypothalamus, and descending fibers to the spinal cord. The diffuse thalamic system lies within the thalamus along the midline of the brain, involving the intrinsic nuclei of the thalamus. It receives fibers from the reticular formation and some sensory pathways, and it sends fibers to the cerebral cortex along a number of indirect routes.

THE HYPOTHALAMUS

The hypothalamus is a collection of nuclei located below the thalamus. Figure A.8 shows the location of the major hypothalamic nuclei. The hypothalamus has the richest supply of blood vessels of any structure in the nervous system, and it is relatively easy for chemicals in the bloodstream to cross the blood-brain barrier and enter neural tissue in the hypothalamus. Also, the hypothalamus borders the third ventricle, a cavity in the brain filled with cerebrospinal fluid. Thus, the hypothalamus is well situated to receive chemical information from bodily fluids.

The hypothalamus receives large fiber tracts from the limbic system through the *fornix, medial forebrain bundle* (MFB), and *stria terminalis.* It also receives fibers from the *frontal cerebral cortex,* the *diffuse thalamic system,* and the *brainstem* and *spinal cord.* The latter include many fibers from autonomic nuclei. The hypothalamus sends fibers to the *anterior thalamus* and thence to the *cingulate gyrus* of the limbic system via the *mammillothalamic tract.* It also sends fibers and chemical influences to the *pituitary gland.* The *periventricular system* (PVS) arises from hypothalamic nuclei and sends fibers to the thalamus and to the brainstem and spinal cord. The latter include many autonomic motor fibers.

THE LIMBIC SYSTEM

There is some disagreement about what structures should be included in the limbic system. Some broad definitions include the hypothalamus, thalamus, and parts of the neocortex often including the prefrontal cortex. We shall follow Grossman (1967) in including only paleocortical structures (cortical structures with fewer than six layers) plus one noncortical nucleus, the amygdala, in our definition of the limbic system.

These structures are illustrated in Figure A.9. It is difficult to visualize the structures of the limbic system because most of them are buried in the depths of the brain. The *amygdala* are large nuclei embedded near the tips

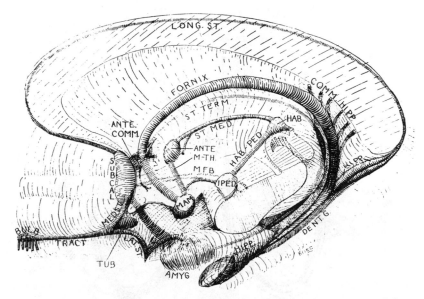

FIGURE A.9   Medial view of the human limbic system. Amyg., amygdala; Ante. comm., A. C., anterior commissure; Ante., anterior nucleus of thalamus; Bulb, olfactory bulb; Comm. hipp., hippocampal commissure; Dent. g., dentate gyrus; Diag. bd., diagonal band of Broca; Hab., habenula; Hab.-ped., habenulopeduncular tract; Hipp., hippocampus; Iped., interpeduncular nucleus; Lat. st., lateral olfactory stria; Long. st., longitudinal stria; Mam., Mammillary body; Med. st., medial olfactory stria; MFB, medial forebrain bundle: M.-th., mammillothalamic tract; St. Med., stria medullaris; St. term., stria terminalis, Subcal., subcallosal gyrus; Tract, olfactory tract; Tub., olfactory tubercle. From W. J. S. Krieg, *Functional Neuroanatomy*. Evanston, Illinois: Brain Books, 1942. Copyright © 1942 by Brain Books, Inc. Reprinted by permission of the publisher.

of the temporal lobes. Just behind the amygdala, also deep in each temporal lobe, is the long tubelike *hippocampus*. The amygdala and hippocampus are reciprocally connected with the hypothalamus through long arching pathways called, respectively, the *stria terminalis* and the *fornix*. These rise out of the temporal lobes, turn and come together at the midline of the brain, and then fall and separate before terminating in the hypothalamus. Figure A.10 shows the approximate structure of these paths as they would appear if the rest of the brain were cut away. The fornix sends fibers to many structures. A major offshoot connects with the septal area and the medial forebrain bundle. Others fibers enter the hypothalamus where most go to the mammillary bodies, but others connect with other parts of the hypothalamus, the thalamus, and the midbrain region of the brainstem. The stria terminalis from the amygdala sends fibers into the

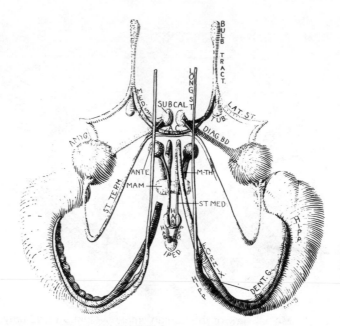

FIGURE A.10 The human limbic system viewed from above. See Figure A.9 for legend. From W. J. S. Krieg, *Op. Cit.* Copyright © 1942 by Brain Books, Inc. Reprinted by permission of the publisher.

medial regions of the hypothalamus. Another large projection system from the amygdala sends fibers to the septal area and the lateral portions of the hypothalamus (Nauta, 1960; Nauta and Haymaker, 1969). These fiber routes are illustrated in Figure 3.4 in Chapter 3.

Other important paleocortical structures surround these circuits. These include the *cingulate gyrus, hippocampal gyrus,* and *pyriform gyrus.* The mammillary bodies are indirectly connected to the cingulate gyrus through the *mammillothalmic tract.* This connects the mammillary bodies with the anterior thalamus, which then connects with the cingulate gyrus.

Two important descending pathways from the limbic system are the medial forebrain bundle (MFB) and the periventricular system (PVS). The MFB is a massive pathway passing through the lateral hypothalamus and connecting the forebrain-septal area to a region in the midbrain called the limbic midbrain area (Nauta, 1960). The PVS courses parallel to the MFB, only it lies toward the midline of the brain from the MFB. It arises from hypothalamic structures, passes medial to most nuclei of the hypo-thalamus, and ends up in the limbic midbrain area. Its course runs near the perifornical region to central grey route that studies of the hypo-thalamus have implicated in aggression (see Chapter 3). The MFB and PVS have assumed great importance in the analysis of positively and negatively reinforcing systems in the brain.

THE NEOCORTEX

The neocortex is the layered covering of grey matter that envelops the outside of the two large cerebral hemispheres. It is the newest brain structure to evolve, and many believe that it is responsible for the complex psychological functions that distinguish humans from other animals. The neocortex is divided into four major lobes, the occipital, temporal, parietal, and frontal. Beneath the neocortex lies the corpus striatum (striped body), so named because the white fibers running between the neocortex and lower centers interspersed with grey masses of cell bodies give the area a striped appearance. Also beneath the neocortex is the corpus callosum, which consists of fibers passing between the two cerebral hemispheres (see Figure A.8 and A.9).

Several areas of the neocortex are particularly concerned with senso-ry and motor functioning, including the visual cortex in the occipital lobes, the auditory cortex in the temporal lobes, and the somatic sensory-motor cortex at the top of the brain. There is an area in the left hemisphere that appears to be important in verbal communication in humans. Injuries to this area in adulthood can lead to communication dysfunctions known as aphasias.

The area of the neocortex most closely associated with motivation and emotion is the frontal cortex, which has many reciprocal connections with the limbic system and hypothalamus. It is these connections which are severed in the frontal lobotomy operation, which was widely practiced on persons with emotional difficulties before the widespread clinical use of psychoactive drugs.

There is evidence that the right hemisphere has different functions from the left hemisphere in humans. The corpus callosum has been sev-ered in a number of persons to control the spread of epileptic seizures. These people can live entirely normal lives after such an operation, with no change in their personalities or life styles. However, controlled tests reveal that they have, in effect, two brains which are independent of one another. This becomes clear when only one hemisphere is presented with a certain piece of information. For example, if a person picks up a hidden object (i.e. a hairbrush) with his left hand, only the right hemisphere of the brain is able to receive the sensory impressions of the object. If the person is asked to pick up a similar object with his right hand he is unable to do so, because the left hemisphere controlling the right hand has no way of knowing what the object is.

Studies with these patients have shown that the two separated hemispheres are really two brains, each separately capable of a high order of psychological functioning (Gazzaniga, 1972). However, the left and right hemisphere have different kinds of cognitive abilities. The left hemisphere is normally dominant and seems to excel in tasks involving verbal transformations. The right hemisphere is superior in the perception and manipulation of spatial relations, the ability to generate the percept of a whole from parts, and the visualization of complex stimuli that have no verbal label (Nebes, 1974).

Gazzaniga (1972) cites a particularly interesting illustrative experiment. The word *heart* was flashed across the visual field of the person in such a way that the *he* was in the left part of the visual field, going to the right hemisphere, and the *art* was in the right part of the visual field going to the left hemisphere. When asked what word was presented, the patient said *art*, the portion presented to the dominant left hemisphere responsible for speech. However, if asked to point the left hand to the word that was presented—*art* or *he*—the patient would point to *he*. Gazzaniga concludes that "both hemispheres had simultaneously observed the portions of the word available to them . . . the right hemisphere, when it had the opportunity to express itself, had prevailed over the left" (1972, p. 121).

The analysis of the different cognitive abilites of the two cerebral hemispheres has only begun, but a tentative model describing these differences has emerged. The left hemisphere is seen to analyze input sequentially, associating the most relevant details with verbal labels in order to more efficiently manipulate and store the data. The right hemisphere is more of a synthesizer that organizes input into complex wholes rather than analyzing it into parts. (Nebes, 1974).

Author Index and List of References

Works cited in this book are listed alphabetically by author (or senior author) and year of publication. Numbers in boldface type following each entry refer to the pages on which the works are cited.

Abelson, H., Cohen, R., Heaton, E., and Suder, C. National survey of public attitudes toward and experience with erotic materials. *Technical report of the commission on obscenity and pornography,* Vol. 6. Washington, D.C.: U.S. Government Printing Office, 1970. **218, 219, 220**

Abelson, R. P., Aronson, E., McGuire, W. J., Newcombe, T. M., Rosenberg, M. T., and Tannenbaum, P. H. (Eds.) *Theories of cognitive consistency: A sourcebook.* Chicago: Rand McNally, 1968. **323, 336**

Abelson, R. P., and Rosenberg, M. J. Symbolic psychologic: A model of attitudinal cognition. *Behav. Sci.,* 1958, *3,* 1–13. **323**

Akert, K., Koella, W. P., and Hess, R., Jr. Sleep produced by electrical stimulation of the thalamus. *Am. J. Physiol.,* 1952, *168,* 260–267. **57**

Akimoto, H., Yamogushi, M., Okabe, K., Nakagawa, T., Nakamura, I., Abe, K., Torii, H., and Masahashi, I. On the sleep induced through electrical stimulation of dog thalamus. *Folia Psychiatr. Neurol. Jap.,* 1956, *10,* 117–146. **56**

Alexander, F. *Psychosomatic medicine.* New York: Norton, 1950. **37, 38, 230**

Alfert, E. Comparison of response to a vicarious and direct threat. *J. Exp. Res. Pers.,* 1966, *1,* 179–186. **372**

Alfert, E. An idiographic analysis of personality differences between reactors to a vicariously experienced threat and reactors to a direct threat. *J. Exp. Res. Pers.,* 1967, *2,* 200–207. **372**

Alker, H. A. Is personality situationally specific or intrapsychically consistent? *J. Exp. Res. Pers.,* 1971, *40,* 1–16. **345**

Allport, F. H. *Social psychology.* Boston: Houghton-Mifflin, 1924. **251**

Amoroso, D. M., Brown, M., Preusse, M., Ware, E. E., and Pilkey, D. W. An investigation of behavioral, psychological, and physiological reactions to pornographic stimuli. *Technical reports of the commission on obscenity and pornography,* Vol. 8. Washington, D. C.: U. S. Government Printing Office, 1970. **223, 224**

Anand, B. K., and Brobeck, J. R. Hypothalamic control of food intake in rats and cats. *Yale J. Biol. Med.,* 1951, *24,* 123–140. **65**

Anand, B. K., Chhina, G. S., and Singh, B. Studies on Shri Ramanand Yogi during his stay in air-tight box. *Indian J. Med. Res.,* 1961, *49,* 82–89. **133, 134**

Anand, B. K., and Dua, S. Feeding responses induced by electrical stimulation of the hypothalamus in cat. *Indian J. Med. Res.,* 1955, *43,* 113–122. **64**

Andrew, J. M. Recovery from surgery, with and without preparatory instruction, for three coping styles. *J. Pers. Soc. Psychol.,* 1970, *15,* 223–226. **377**

Angell, J. R. A reconsideration of James's theory of emotion in the light of recent criticisms. *Psychol. Rev.,* 1916, *23.* **44**

Arafat, I. S., and Cotton, W. L. Masturbation practices of males and females. *J. Sex Res.,* 1974, *10,* 293–307. **209**

Ardrey, R. *The territorial imperative.* New York: Dell, 1966. **13**

Arnold, M. *Emotions and personality* (2 volumes). New York: Columbia University Press, 1960. **28**

Aronoff, J., and Litwin, G. Achievement motivation training and executive advancement. *J. Appl. Behav. Sci.,* 1968. **313**

Aronson, E. The need for achievement as measured by graphic expression. In J. W. Atkinson (Ed.) *Motives in fantasy, action and society.* Princeton: Van Nostrand, 1958. **311**

Aronson, E. The effects of effort on the attractiveness of rewarded and unrewarded stimuli. *J. Abnorm. Soc. Psychol.,* 1961, *63,* 375–380. **332**

Aronson, E., and Carlsmith, J. The effect of severity of threat on the devaluation of forbidden behavior. *J. Abnorm. Soc. Psychol.,* 1963, *66,* 584–588. **330, 331**

Aryapetyants, E. Sh., Lobanova, L. V., and Cherkasova, L. S. Materials on the physiology of the internal analyser in man. *Tr. Inst. Fiziol. Pavlova,* 1952, *1,* 3–20. **116, 118, 119**

Asch, S. *Social psychology.* Englewood Cliffs: Prentice Hall, 1952. **251, 382**

Atkinson, J. W. Motivational determinants of risk taking behavior. *Psych. Rev.,* 1957, *64,* 359–372. **302, 303**

Atkinson, J. W. (Ed.) *Motives in fantasy, action, and society.* Princeton: Van Nostrand, 1958. **301**

Atkinson, J. W. *An introduction to motivation.* Princeton: Van Nostrand. 1964. **303**

Atkinson, J. W., and Cartwright, D. Some neglected variables in contemporary conceptions of decision and performance. *Psych. Rep.,* 1964, *14,* 575–590. **304**

Atkinson, J. W., and Feather, N. T. (Eds.) *A theory of achievement motivation.* New York: Wiley, 1966. **303**

Atkinson, J. W., and McClelland, D. C. The projective expression of needs. II. The effect of different intensities of the hunger drive on thematic apperception. *J. Exp. Psychol.,* 1948, *38,* 643–658. **300**

Averill, J. R. Personal control over aversive stimuli and its relationship to stress. *Psychol. Bull.,* 1973(a), *80,* 286–303. **377**

Averill, J. R. The dis-position of psychological dispositions. *J. Exp. Res. Pers.,* 1973(b), *6,* 275–282. **345**

Averill, J. R., Opton, E. M., Jr., and Lazarus, R. S. Cross-cultural studies of psychophysiological responses during stress and emotion. *Int. J. Psych.,* 1969, *4,* 33–102. **372, 373, 374**

Avis, H. H. The neuropharmacology of aggression: A critical review. *Psychol. Bull.,* 1974, *81,* 47–63. **186**

Ax, A. F. The physiological differentiation between fear and anger in humans. *Psychosom. Med.,* 1953, *15,* 433–442. **35**

Axelsson, J. Catecholamine functions. *Annu. Rev. Physiol.,* 1971, *33,* 1–30. **422**

Bagchi, B. K., and Wenger, M. A. Electro-physiological correlates of some yogic exercises. *Proceedings of the First International Congress of Neurological Sciences.* Brussels, 1957. **134**

Baker, J. W., II, and Schaie, K. W. Effects of aggressing "alone" or "with another" on physiological and psychological arousal. *J. Pers. Soc. Psychol.,* 1969, *12,* 80–96. **179**

Balasubramanian, V., and Ramumurthi, B. Stereotaxic amygdalectomy in behavior disorders. *Confin. Neurol.,* 1970, *32,* 367–373. **144**

Baldessarini, R. J. Biogenic animes and behavior. *Ann. Rev. Med.,* 1972, *23,* 343–354. **66, 103, 105**

Baldwin, A. L. *Theories of child development.* New York: Wiley, 1967. **184, 292**

Bandura, A. Vicarious processes: A case of no-trial learning. In L. Berkowitz (Ed.) *Advances in experimental social psychology,* Vol. 2. New York: Academic, 1965(a). **165, 167, 177**

Bandura, A. Influence of models' reinforcement contingencies in the acquisition of imitative responses. *J. Pers. Soc. Psychol.,* 1965(b), *1,* 589–595. **165, 167**

Bandura, A. *Principles of behavior modification.* New York: Holt, Rinehart, and Winston, 1969. **114, 165**

Bandura, A. *Aggression: A social learning analysis.* Englewood Cliffs: Prentice-Hall, 1973. **165, 173, 184**

Bandura, A., Ross, D., and Ross, S. A. Transmission of aggression through imitation of aggressive models. *J. Abnorm. Soc. Psychol.,* 1961, *63,* 575–582. **164**

Bandura, A., Ross, D., and Ross, S. A. Imitation of film-mediated aggressive models. *J. Abnorm. Soc. Psychol.,* 1963, *66,* 3–11. **164, 167**

Bandura, A., and Walters, R. H. Adolescent aggression. New York: Ronald, 1959. **163**

Bandura, A., and Walters, R. H. *Social learning and personality development.* New York: Holt, Rinehart, and Winston, 1963. **163, 166, 173, 217**

Bard, P. A diencephalic mechanism for the expression of rage with special reference to the sympathetic nervous system. *Am. J. Physiol.,* 1928, *84,* 490–515. **70**

Bard, P. The hypothalamus and sexual behavior. *Ass. Res. Nerv. Dis. Proc.,* 1940, *20,* 551–579. **66**

Barefoot, J. C., and Straub, R. B. Opportunity for information search and the effect of false heart-rate feedback. *J. Pers. Soc. Psychol.,* 1971, *17,* 154–157. **353**

Barker, R., Dembo, T., and Lewin, K. Frustration and regression: An experiment with young children. *University of Iowa studies in child welfare,* 1941, *18,* (Whole No. 386). **162**

Baron, R. A. The aggression-inhibiting influence of heightened sexual arousal. *J. Pers. Soc. Psychol.,* 1974, *30,* 318–322. **174n**

Barry, H., Bacon, M. K., and Child, I. L. A cross-cultural survey of some sex differences in socialization. *J. Abnorm. Soc. Psychol.,* 1957, *55,* 327–332. **315**

Basmajian, J. Electromyography comes of age. *Science,* 1972, *176,* 603–609. **142**

Bateson, G. The frustration-aggression hypothesis and culture. *Psych. Rev.,* 1941, *48,* 350–355. **162**

Bauer, H. G. Endocrine and other clinical manifestations of hypothalamic disease. *J. Clin. Endocrinol.,* 1954, *14,* 13–31. **62, 77**

Beach, F. A. A review of physiological and psychological studies of sexual behavior in mammals. *Physiol. Rev.,* 1947, *27,* 240–305. **211, 212, 216**

Beach, F. A. *Sex and behavior.* New York: Wiley, 1965. **213**

Beach, F. A. It's all in your mind. *Psych. Today,* 1969, *3,* 33–60. **211, 212**

Beach, F. A., Noble, R. G., and Orndoff, R. K. Effects of perinatal adrogen treatment on responses of male rats to gonadal hormones in adulthood. *J. Comp. Physiol. Psychol.,* 1969, *68,* 490–497. **213**

Bem, D. J. Self perception: An alternative interpretation of cognitive dissonance phenomena. *Psych. Rev.,* 1967, *74,* 183–200. **336**

Bem, D. J. Constructing cross-situational consistencies in behavior: Some thoughts on Alker's critique of Mischel. *J. Pers.,* 1972, *40,* 17–26. **345**

Benson, H. Yoga for drug abuse. *New Engl. J. Med.,* 1969, *381.* **135**

Benson, H., Shapiro, D., Tursky, B., and Schwartz, G. E. Decreased systolic blood pressure through operant conditioning techniques in patients with essential hypertension. *Science,* 1971, *173,* 740–742. **139**

Berger, A. S., Gagnon, J. H., and Simon, W. Urban working class adolescents and sexually explicit media. *Technical reports of the commission on obscenity and pornography,* Vol. 9. Washington, D. C.: U. S. Government Printing Office, 1970. **220**

Berkowitz, L. Aggressive cues in aggressive behavior and hostility catharsis. *Psych. Rev.,* 1964, *71,* 104–122. **170**

Berkowitz, L. Some aspects of observed aggression. *J. Pers. Soc. Psychol.,* 1965(a), *2,* 359–369. **170**

Berkowitz, L. The concept of aggressive drive: Some additional considerations. In L. Berkowitz (Ed.) *Advances in experimental social psychology*, Vol. 2. New York: Academic, 1965(b). **93**

Berkowitz, L. Simple views of aggression. *Am. Sci.*, 1969(a), *57*, 372–383. **159, 160**

Berkowitz, L. (Ed.) *Roots of aggression: A re-examination of the frustration-aggression hypothesis.* New York: Atherton, 1969(b). **163**

Berkowitz, L. The contagion of violence. In W. J. Arnold and M. M. Page (Eds.) *Nebraska Symposium on Motivation.* Lincoln: University of Nebraska Press, 1970. **165**

Berkowitz, L. The "weapons effect," deviant characteristics, and the myth of the compliant subject. *J. Pers. Soc. Psychol.*, 1971(a), *20*, 332–338. **174**

Berkowitz, L. Sex and violence: We can't have it both ways. *Psychol. Today*, 1971(b), *5*, 14–23. **230**

Berkowitz, L. The case for bottling up rage. *Psychol. Today*, 1973, *7*, 24–31. **230**

Berkowitz, L., and Geen, R. G. Film violence and the cue properties of available targets. *J. Pers. Soc. Psychol.*, 1966, *3*, 525–530. **170**

Berkowitz, L., and Le Page, A. Weapons as aggression-eliciting stimuli. *J. Pers. Soc. Psychol.*, 1967, *7* 202–207. **174**

Berlyne, D. E. *Conflict, arousal, and curiosity.* New York: McGraw-Hill, 1960. **283**

Berlyne, D. E. Curiosity and exploration. *Science,* 1966, 25–33. **428**

Berlyne, D. E., and Slater, J. Perceptual curiosity, exploratory behavior, and maze learning. *J. Comp. Physiol. Psychol.*, 1957, *50*, 228–232. **281**

Berninghausen, D. K., and Faunce, R. W. Some opinions on the relationship between obscene books and juvenile delinquency. Unpublished manuscript, University of Minnesota, 1965. **218**

Bernstein, H. The development of morality from a Piagetian point of view. Special Area Examination, Carnegie-Mellon University, 1971. **323**

Bexton, W. H., Heron, W., and Scott, T. H. Effects of decreased variation in the sensory environment. *Can. J. Psychol.*, 1954, *8*, 70–76. **281, 282**

Birdwhistell, R. L. *Kinesics and context.* Philadelphia: University of Pennsylvania Press, 1970. **248**

Bishop, M. P., Elder, S. T., and Heath, R. G. Intracranial self-stimulation in man. *Science,* 1963, *140,* 394–396. **91, 98**

Black, A. H. The operant conditioning of heart rate in curarized dogs: Some problems of interpretation. Paper presented at the meeting of the Psychonomic Society, St. Louis, October 1966. **126**

Block, J. A study of affective responsiveness in a lie detection situation. *J. Abnorm. Soc. Psychol.,* 1957, *55,* 11–15. **262**

Blurton-Jones, N. G. Criteria for describing facial expressions in children. *Hum. Biol.,* 1971, *43,* 365–413. **254**

Bowlby, J. The nature of the child's tie to his mother. *Int. J. Psychoanal.,* 1958, *39,* 350–373. **407**

Bowlby, J. *Attachment and loss* (2 volumes). London: Hogarth, 1969, 1972. **407**

Boyanowsky, E. O., Newtson, D., and Walster, E. Effects of murder on movie preference. *Proceedings, 80th Annual Convention, APA,* 1972, 235–236. **178**

Brady, J. V. and Nauta, W. J. H. Subcortical mechanisms in emotional behavior: Affective changes following septal forebrain lesions in the albino rat. *J. Comp. Physiol. Psychol.,* 1953, *46,* 339–346. **89**

Bradley, P. B. Effects of atropine and related drugs on EEG and behavior. *Prog. Brain Res.,* 1968, *28.* **55**

Brain, P. F. Mammalian behavior and the adrenal cortex—A review. *Behav. Biol.,* 1972, *7,* 453–477. **34**

Bramel, D., Taub, B., and Blum, B. An observer's reaction to the suffering of his enemy. *J. Pers. Soc. Psychol.,* 1968, *8,* 384–392. **182**

Brehm, J. W. Motivational effects of cognitive dissonance. In M. Jones (Ed.) *Nebraska symposium on motivation.* Lincoln: University of Nebraska Press, 1962. **364, 365**

Brehm, J. W. *A theory of psychological reactance.* New York: Academic, 1966. **339**

Brehm, J., Back, K., and Bogdonoff, M. A physiological effect of cognitive dissonance under stress and deprivation. *J. Abnorm. Soc. Psychol.,* 1964, *69,* 303–310. **365**

Bremer, F. Cerveau "isole" et physiologie du sommeil. *C. R. Soc. Biol.,* 1935, *118,* 1235–1241. **53**

Brehm, J. and Cohen, A. *Explorations in cognitive dissonance.* New York: Wiley, 1962. **328, 339**

Bremer, J. *Asexualization: A follow-up study of 244 cases.* New York: Macmillan, 1959. **212**

Brener, J. Heart rate. In P. H. Venables and I. Martin. *Manual of Psychophysiological Methods.* New York: Wiley, 1967. **429**

Brener, J., and Hothersall, D. Heart rate control under conditions of augmented sensory feedback. *Psychophysiology,* 1966, *3,* 23–28. **132**

Brobeck, J. R., Larsson, S., and Reyes, E. A study of the electrical activity of the hypothalamic feeding mechanism. *J. Physiol. (Lond.),* 1956, *132,* 358–364. **64**

Brobeck, J. R., Tepperman, J., and Long, C.N.H. Experimental hypothalamic hyperphagia in the albino rat. *Yale J. Biol. Med.,* 1943, *15,* 831–853. **64**

Brock, T. C., and Buss, A. H. Dissonance, aggression, and evaluation of pain. *J. Abnorm. Soc. Psychol.,* 1962, *65,* 197–202. **404**

Bronfenbrenner, U. The role of age, sex, class, and culture in studies of moral development. *Relig. Ed. Res. Suppl.,* 1962, *57,* 53–517. **383, 384, 385, 386**

Brown, B. *New body, new mind.* New York: Harper and Row, 1974. **135**

Brown, C. C. (Ed.) *Methods in psychophysiology.* Baltimore: Williams and Wilkins, 1967. **431**

Brown, M., Feldman, K., Schwartz, S., and Heingartner, A. Some personality correlates of conduct in two situations of moral conflict. *J. Pers.,* 1969, *37,* 41–57. **399**

Brown, P., and Elliott, R. Control of aggression in a nursery school class. *J. Exp. Child Psychol.,* 1965, *2,* 103–107. **167**

Brown, R. *Social psychology.* New York: Free Press, 1965. **16, 297, 306, 323, 327, 393**

Brozek, J. Recent developments in Soviet psychology. *Ann. Rev. Psychol.,* 1964, *15,* 493–594. **121, 136**

Brudny, J., Grynbaum, B., and Korein, J. Spasmodic torticollis: Treatment by feed-back display of EMG. *Arch. Phys. Med. Rehab.,* 1974, *55,* 403–408. **142**

Brugger, M. Fresstreib als hypothalamisches symptom. *Helvet. psysiol. pharmacol. Acta,* 1943, *I,* 183–198. **65**

Bruner, J. S. and Tagiuri, R. The perception of people. In G. Lindzey (Ed.) *Handbook of social psychology,* Vol. 2. Reading Mass. : Addison-Wesley, 1954. **391**

Buck, R. W. The effects of film-induced excitement and expectation to retaliate upon an aggressive response. Unpublished Master's thesis, University of Wisconsin, 1965. **174**

Buck, R. W. Relationships between dissonance-reducing behaviors and tension measures following aggression. Unpublished doctoral dissertation, University of Pittsburgh, 1970. Paper presented at the meeting of the Midwestern Psychological Association, Cleveland, 1972. **264, 336, 337, 405**

Buck, R. Nonverbal communication of affect in children. *J. Pers. Soc. Psychol.,* 1975, *31,* 644–653. **259, 270**

Buck, R. A test of nonverbal receiving ability: Preliminary studies. *Human communication research,* 1976, *2,* 162–171. **391**

Buck, R., and Miller, R. E. A measure of sensitivity to facial expression. Videotape screening and demonstration. Anthropological and Documentary Film Conference, Temple University, 1972. **391**

Buck, R. W., Miller, R. E., and Caul, W. F. Heart rate and skin conductance responding during three attention-direction tasks. *Psychonomic. Sci.,* 1969, *15,* 291–292. **52**

Buck, R. W., Miller, R. E., and Caul, W. F. Heart-rate and skin-conductance responding during three attention-direction tasks under distraction conditions. *Psychonomic Sci.,* 1970, *20*(6), 355. **52**

Buck, R. W., Miller, R. E., and Caul, W. F. Sex, personality and physiological variables in the communication of emotion via facial expression. *J. Pers. Soc. Psychol.,* 1974, *30,* 587–596. **258, 259, 265, 371**

Buck, R., Savin, V. J., Miller, R. E., and Caul, W. F. Nonverbal communication of affect in humans. *Proceedings, 77th Annual Convention,* APA, 1969, 367–368. **257, 258, 259, 371**

Buck, R., Savin, V. J., Miller, R. E., and Caul, W. F. Nonverbal communication of affect in humans. *J. Pers. Soc. Psychol.,* 1972, *23,* 362–371. **257, 258, 259, 264,**

371

Buck, R., Schiffman, T., and Siegel, D. The relationship between nonverbal expressiveness and skin conductance responding in preschool children. Paper presented at the meeting of the Eastern Psychological Association, New York, 1975. **259**

Buck, R., Worthington, J., and Schiffman, T. Nonverbal communication of affect in preschool children. *Proceedings, 81st Annual Convention, APA,* 1973, 103–104. **270**

Budzynski, T. H., and Stoyva, J. M. An instrument for producing deep muscle relaxation by means of analogue information feedback. *J. Appl. Behav. Anal.,* 1969, *2,* 231–237. **141**

Budzynski, T., Stoyva, J., and Adler, C. Feedback induced muscle relaxation: Application to tension headache. *J. Behav. Ther. Exper. Psychiatr.,* 1970, *1,* 205–211. **139**

Budzynski, T., Stoyva, J., Adler, C., and Mullaney, D. EMG biofeedback and tension headache: A controlled outcome study. *Psychosom. Med.,* 1973, *35,* 484–496. **139, 143**

Burnham, J. C. The origin of Freud's instinctual drive theory and its cultural uses. History of Science colloquium, Carnegie-Mellon University, December 1972. **195**

Buss, A. H., Booker, A., and Buss, E. Firing a weapon and aggression. *J. Pers. Soc. Psychol.,* 1972, *22,* 296–302. **174**

Buss, A., and Brock, T. Repression and guilt in relation to aggression. *J. Abnorm. Soc. Psychol.,* 1963, *66,* 345–350. **404**

Butler, R. A. Discrimination learning by rhesus monkeys to visual-exploration motivation. *J. Comp. Physiol. Psychol.,* 1953, *46,* 95–98. **281**

Butler, R. A. The differential effect of visual and auditory incentives on the performance of monkeys. *Am. J. Psychol.,* 1958, *71,* 591–593. **281**

Butler, R. A., and Harlow, H. F. Discrimination learning and learning sets to visual exploration incentives. *J. Gen. Psychol.,* 1957, *57,* 257–264. **281**

Byrne, D. Repression-sensitization as a dimension of personality. In B. A. Maher (Ed.) *Progress in experimental personality research,* Vol. 1. New York: Academic, 1964. **371**

Cabanac, M., and Duclaux, R. Obesity: Absence of satiety aversion to sucrose. *Science,* 1970, *168,* 496–497. **359**

Caggiula, A. R. Analysis of the copulation-reward properties of posterion hypothalamic stimulation in male rats. *J. Comp. Physiol. Psychol.,* 1970, *70,* 399–412. **74**

Caggiula, A. R., and Hoebel, B. G. "Copulation-reward site" in the posterior hypothalamus. *Science,* 1966, *153,* 1284–1285. **67**

Cannon, W. B. *Bodily changes in pain, hunger, fear, and rage.* New York: Appleton, 1915. **27**

Cannon, W. B. The James-Lange theory of emotion: A critical examination and an alternative theory. *Am. J. Psychol.,* 1927, *39,* 106–124. Reprinted in M. Arnold (Ed.) *The nature of emotion.* Baltimore: Penguin, 1968. **43, 46**

Cannon, W. B. The mechanism of emotional disturbance of bodily functions. *New Engl. J. Med.,* 1928, *198,* 877–884. **425**

Cannon, W. B. *The wisdom of the body.* New York: Norton, 1932. **27, 122, 127**

Cannon, W. B., and Britton, S. W. Studies on the conditions of activity in endocrine glands. XV. Pseudoaffective medulliadrenal secretion. *Am. J. Physiol.,* 1925, *72,* 283–294. **70**

Cannon, W. B., Lewis, J. T., and Britton, S. W. The dispensability of the sympathetic division of the autonomic nervous system. *Boston Med. Surg. J.,* 1927, *197,* 514. **43**

Campbell, A. A. Factors associated with attitudes toward Jews. In T. M. Newcombe and E. L. Hartley (Eds.) *Readings in social psychology.* New York: Holt, 1947. **408**

Campos, J. J. and Johnson, H. H. Affect, verbalization, and directional fractionation of autonomic responses. *Psychophysiology,* 1966, *3* (3), 285–290. **52**

Campos, J. J., and Johnson, H. J. The effect of affect and verbalization instructions of directional fractionation of autonomic response. *Psychophysiology,* 1967, *3,* 245–290. **52**

Carpenter, C. R. *Naturalistic behavior of nonhuman primates.* University Park: Pennsylvania State University Press, 1966. **13**

Cartwright, D. and Harary, F. Structural balance: A generalization of Heider's theory. *Psych. Rev.,* 1956, *63,* 277–293. **336**

Cartwright, D., and Zander, A. *Group dynamics,* 2nd ed. Evanston: Row, Peterson, 1960. **321**

Chapman, R. M., and Levy, N. Hunger drive and the reinforcing affect of novel stimuli. *J. Comp. Physiol. Psychol.,* 1957, *50,* 233–238.

Chapman, W. P. Depth electrode studies in patients with temporal lobe epilepsy. In E. R. Ramey and D. S. O'Doherty (Eds.) *Electrical studies on the unanesthetized brain.* New York: Paul B. Hoeber, 1960. **83, 86**

Chatrian, G. E. and Chapman, W. P. Electrographic study of the amygdaloid region with implanted electrodes in patients with temporal lobe epilepsy. In E. R. Ramey and D. S. O'Doherty (Eds.) *Electrical studies on the unanesthetized brain.* New York: Paul B. Hoeber, 1960. **86**

Chorover, S. The pacification of the brain. *Psychol. Today,* 1974, *7,*(12) 59. **144, 145**

Claridge, G. S., and Harrington, R. N. Excitation-inhibition and the theory of neurosis: A study of the sedation threshold. In H. J. Eysenck (Ed.) *Experiment with drugs.* New York: Pergamon, 1963. **268**

Cleeland, C. Behavior techniques in the modification of spasmodic torticollis. *Neurology,* 1973, *23,* 1241–1247. **142**

Cline, V. B. Interpersonal perception. In B. A. Maher (Ed.) *Progress in experimental personality research,* Vol. 1. New York: Academic, 1964. **391**

Cline, V. B., Croft, R. G., and Courrier, S. The desensitization of children to television violence. Unpublished manuscript. University of Utah, 1972. **178**

Cochran, W. G., Mosteller, F., and Tukey, J. W. Statistical problems of the Kinsey report. *J. Am. Stat. Assoc.,* 1953, *48,* 673–716. **201**

Coe, M. R., Jr. Fire-walking and related behaviors. *Psych. Rec.,* 1957, *7,* 101–110. **131**

Cofer, C. N., and Appley, M. H., *Motivation: Theory and research.* New York: Wiley, 1964. **154, 194, 195, 212, 278, 279**

Cohen, A. Communication discrepancy and attitude change. *J. Pers.,* 1959, *27,* 386–396. **332**

Coleman, J. C. *Abnormal psychology and modern life.* Chicago: Scott, Foresman, 1956. **81, 85**

Costa, E., and Weiss, B. The present understanding of subsynaptic and postjunctional monoamine receptors. In D. H. Eron (Ed.) *Psychopharmacology,* Washington, D. C.: National Institute of Mental Health, 1968. **422**

Cottrell, N. B., and Wack, D. L. The energizing effect of cognitive dissonance. *J. Pers. Soc. Psychol.,* 1967, *6,* 132–138. **337**

Cox, V. C., and Valenstein, E. S. Attenuation of aversive properties of peripheral shock by hypothalamic stimulation. *Science,* 1965, *149,* 323–325. **74**

Craig, K., and Lowrey, H. J. Heart rate components of conditioned vicarious autonomic responses. *J. Pers. Soc. Psychol.,* 1969, *11,* 381–387. **264**

Crandall, V. C., Katkovsky, W., and Crandall, V. J. Childrens' beliefs in their own control of reinforcement in intellectual-academic achievement situations. *Child Dev.,* 1965, *36,* 91–109. **343**

Crandall, V. J. Achievement. In H. W. Stevenson (Ed.) *Child psychology.* Chicago: University of Chicago Press, 1963. **301**

Crider, A., and Lunn, R. Electrodermal lability as a personality dimension. *J. Exp. Res. Pers.,* 1971, *5* (2), 145–150. **263, 264**

Crider, A., Schwartz, G. E., and Shnidman, S. On the criteria for instrumental autonomic conditioning: A reply to Katkin and Murray. *Psych. Bull.,* 1969, *71,* 455–461. **129**

Cronkhite, G. Autonomic correlates of dissonance and attitude change. *Speech Monogr.,* 1966, *33,* 392–399. **336**

Dadrian, V. N. Factors of anger and aggression in genocide. *J. Hum. Relat.,* 1971, *19,* 394–417. **408**

Dalal, A. S., and Baber, T. X. Yoga, "yogic feats," and hypnosis in the light of empirical research. *Am. J. Clin. Hypn.,* 1969, *11,* 155–166. **131**

Dalton, K. *The premenstrual syndrome.* Springfield, Ill.: Charles C. Thomas, 1964. **188**

Dana, C. L. The anatomic seat of the emotions: A discussion of the James-Lange theory. *Arch. Neurol. Psychiat.* (Chic.), 1921, *6,* 634–639. **44**

Darley, J. M., and Bateson, C. D. "From Jerusalem to Jericho": A study of situational and dispositional variables in helping behavior. *J. Pers. Soc. Psychol.,* 1973, *27,* 100–108. **398**

Darley, J., and Latane, B. Bystander intervention in emergencies: Diffusion of responsibility. *J. Pers. Soc. Psychol.,* 1968(a), *8,* 377–383. **396, 397, 398**

Darley, J., and Latane, B. When will people help in a crisis? *Psych. Today,* 1968(b), *2,* 54–71. **394**

Darley, J. M., Teger, A. I., and Lewis, L. D. Do groups always inhibit individuals' responses to potential emergencies. *J. Pers. Soc. Psychol.,* 1973, *26,* 395–399. **395**

Darrow, C. M. Differences in the physiological reactions to sensory and ideational stimuli, *Psych. Bull.,* 1929, *26,* 185–201. **51**

Darwin, C. *Origin of species.* New York: Modern Library, 1936. **153** (First published 1859.)

Darwin, C. *The descent of man.* London: Murray, 1872. **153**

Darwin, C. *The expression of emotions in man and animals.* London, 1872.

Das, N. N., and Gastant, H. Variations de l'activité electrique du cerveau, du coeur et des muscles squélettiques au cours de la méditation et de 'l'extasé yoguique. *Electroencephalograph Clin. Neurophysiol.,* 1955, *Suppl. 6,* 211–219. **133**

Davidson, J. M., and Levine, S. Endocrine regulation of behavior. *Ann. Rev. Physiol.,* 1972, *34,* 375–408. **34, 214**

Davies, E. What happened to the Minoans? *Psychol. Today,* 1969, *3,* 43–47. **311**

Davis, K. E., and Braucht, G. N. Reactions to viewing films of erotically realistic heterosexual behavior. *Technical reports of the commission on obscenity and pornography,* Vol. 8. Washington, D. C.: U. S. Government Printing Office, 1970. **223**

Davison, G. C., and Valins, S. Maintenance of self-attributed and drug-attributed behavior change. *J. Pers. Soc. Psychol.,* 1969, *11,* 25–33. **355, 376**

Davitz, J. R. The effects of previous training on postfrustrative behavior. *J. Abnorm. Soc. Psychol.,* 1952, *47,* 309–315. **168**

DeCharms, R. *Personal causation.* New York: Academic, 1968. **302, 340, 342**

DeCharms, R. C., Morrison, H. W., Reitman, W. R., and McClelland, D. C. Behavioral correlates of directly and indirectly measured achievement motivation. In D. C. McClelland (Ed.) *Studies in motivation.* New York: Appleton Century Crofts, 1955. **301**

Decke, E. Effects of taste on the eating behavior of obese and normal persons. Cited in S. Schachter, *Emotion, obesity, and crime.* New York: Academic, 1971. **359**

Deets, A., and Harlow, H. F. Early experience and the maturation of agonistic behavior. Paper presented at the convention of the American Association for the Advancement of Science, New York: Dec. 28, 1971. **235, 236, 237, 238**

Delgado, J. M. R. *Physical control of the mind.* New York: Harper and Row, 1969. **44, 88, 89, 91**

Delgado, J. M. R., Mark, V. H., Sweet, W. H., Ervin, F. R., Gerhardt, W., Bach y Rita, G., and Hagawara, R. Intracerebral radio stimulation and recording in completely free patients. *J. New. Ment. Dis.,* 1968, *147,* 329–340. **83, 87**

Delgado, J. M. R., Roberts, W. W., and Miller, N. E., Learning motivated by electrical stimulation of the brain. *Am. J. Physiol.,* 1954, *179,* 587–593. **95**

De Long, D. R. Individual differences in patterns of anxiety arousal, stress-relevant information and recovery from surgery. Unpublished doctoral dissertation, University of California, Los Angeles, 1970. **377**

Dement, W., and Kleitman, N. Cyclic variations in EEG during sleep and their relation to eye movements, body motility, and dreaming. *Electroencephalography. Clin. Neurophysiol.,* 1957, *9,* 673–690. **433**

Deutsch, J. A. Learning and electrical self-stimulation of the brain. *J. Theor. Biol.,* 1963, *58,* 1–9. **98**

Deutsch, J. A. Brain reward: ESB and ecstasy. *Psychol. Today,* 1972, *6,* 45–48. **97, 98**

Deutsch, J. A., and Deutsch, D. *Physiological psychology.* Homewood, Ill. Dorsey, 1966. **97**

DeVore, I. *Primate behavior: Field studies of monkeys and apes.* New York: Holt, Rinehart, and Winston, 1965. **156**

DeWeid, D. Inhibitory effects of ACTH and related peptides on extinction of conditioned avoidance behavior in rats. *Proc. Soc. Exp. Biol. and Med.,* 1966, *122,* 28–32. **34**

DeWeid, D. Opposite effects of ACTH and glucocorticoids on extinction of conditioned emotional behavior. In L. Martini et al. (Eds.) *Hormonal Steroids.* Netherlands: Moulton and Co., 1967. **34**

DiCara, L. V. Learning in the autonomic nervous system. *Sci. Am.,* 1970, *222,* 30–39. **133, 137**

DiCara, L. V. Introduction. In L. V. DiCara et al. (Eds.) *Biofeedback and self control: 1974.* Chicago: Aldine, 1975. **128**

DiCara, L. V., Braun, J. J., and Pappas, B. A. Classical conditioning and instrumental learning of cardiac and gastrointestinal responses following removal of neocortex in the rat. *J. Comp. Physiol. Psychol.,* 1970, 208–216. **127**

DiCara, L. V., and Miller, N. E. Long term retention of instrumentally conditioned heart-rate changes in curarized rats. *Commun. Behav. Biol.,* 1968(a), *2,* 19–23. **126**

DiCara, L. V., and Miller, N. E. Changes in heart rate instrumentally learned by curarized rats as avoidance responses. *J. Comp. Physiol. Psychol.,* 1968(b), *65,* 8–12. **126**

DiCara, L. V., and Miller, N. E. *Commun. Behav. Biol.,* 1968(c), *1,* 209. **126**

DiCara, L. V. and Miller, N. E. Instrumental learning of systolic blood pressure responses by curarized rats. *Psychosom. Med.,* 1968(d), *30,* 489–496. **127**

DiCara, L. V., and Miller, N. E. Instrumental learning of vasomotor responses by rats: Learning to respond differentially in the two ears. *Science, 159,* 1485–1486. **127**

Dienstbier, R. The role of anxiety and arousal attribution in cheating. *J. Exp. Soc. Psychol.,* 1972, *8,* 168–179. **355**

Dienstbier, R. A., and Munter, P. O. Cheating as a function of the labeling of natural arousal. *J. Pers. Soc. Psychol.,* 1971, *17,* 208–213. **355**

DiGiusto, E. L., Cairncross, K., and King, M. G. Hormonal influences on fear-motivated behavior. *Psych. Bull.,* 1971, *75,* 432–444. **30, 32, 33, 34**

Dollard, J., Doob, L., Miller, N., Mower, O., and Sears, R. *Frustration and aggression.* New Haven: Yale University Press, 1939. **162, 163, 231**

Doob, A. N., and Climie, R. J. Delay of measurement and the effects of film violence. *J. Exp. Soc. Psychol.,* 1972, *8,* 136–142. **174**

Doob, A. N., and Kirshenbaum, H. M. The effects of arousal of frustration and aggressive films. *J. Exp. Soc. Psychol.,* 1973, *9,* 57–64. **174**

Doob, A. N., and Wood, L. Catharsis and aggression: The effects of annoyance and retaliation on aggressive behavior. *J. Pers. Soc. Psychol.*, 1972, 22, 156–162. **160, 182**

Duffy, E. Emotion: An example of the need for reorientation in psychology. *Psychol. Rev.*, 1934, *41*, 184–198. **49**

Duffy, E. The psychological significance of the concept of "arousal" or "activation." *Psychol. Rev.*, 1957, *64*, 265–275. **49**

Duncan, S. Nonverbal communication. *Psych. Bull.*, 1969, *72*, 118–137. **248**

Dunn, G. W. Stilboestrol-induced testicular degeneration in hypersexual males. *J. Clin. Endocrinol.*, 1941, *1*, 643–648. **188**

Eccles, J. The synapse. *Sci. Am.*, 1965, *212*, pp. 56–66. **421**

Egbert, L. D., Battit, G. E., Welsh, C. E., and Bartlett, M. K. Reduction of postoperative pain by encouragement and instruction of patients. *New Engl. J. Med.*, 1964, *270*, 825–827. **377**

Eggar, M. D., and Flynn, J. P. Effects of electrical stimulation of the amygdala on hypothalamically elicited attack behavior in cats. *J. Neurophysiol.*, 1963, *26*, 705–720. **72**

Eibl-Eibesfeldt, I. *Ethology: The biology of behavior.* New York: Holt, Rineholt, and Winston, 1970. **76, 78, 154, 158, 161, 205, 230, 235, 239, 240, 252, 253**

Eibl-Eibesfeldt, I. *Love and hate.* New York: Holt, Rinehart, and Winston, 1972. **239, 252, 253**

Ekman, P. Communication through nonverbal behavior: A source of information about an interpersonal relationship. In S. S. Tomkins and C. Izard (Eds.) *Affect, Cognition and Personality.* New York: Springer, Press, 1965. **257**

Ekman, P. Nonverbal behavior and psychopathology. In R. J. Friedman and M. M. Katz (Eds.) *The phychology of depression: Contemporary theory and research.* Washington, D. C.: U. S. Government Printing Office, 1972. **391**

Ekman, P., and Friesen, W. V. Constants across cultures in the face and emotion. *J. Pers. Soc. Psychol.*, 1971, *17*, 124–129. **252**

Ekman, P., Friesen, W. V., and Ellsworth, P. *Emotion in the human face.* New York: Pergamon, 1972. **250, 251, 252, 255, 256**

Ekman, P., Friesen, W. V., and Malmstrom, E. J. Facial behavior and stress in two cultures. Unpublished manuscript, Langley Porter Neuropsychiatric Institute, San Francisco, 1970. **255**

Ekman, P., Friesen, W. V., and Tomkins, S. S. Facial affect scoring technique: A first validity study. *Semiotica,* 1971, *3,* 37–58. **254**

Ekman, P., Liebert, R. M., Friesen, W., Harrison, R., Zlatchin, C., Malstrom, E. J., and Baron, R. A. Facial expressions of emotion while watching televised violence as predictors of subsequent aggression. In G. A. Comstock, E. A. Rubenstein, and J. P. Murray (Eds.) *Television and social behavior,* Vol. 5. Washington, D. C.: U. S. Government Printing Office, 1971. **176**

Ekman, P., Sorenson, E. R., and Friesen, W. V. Pan-cultural elements in the facial displays of emotion. *Science,* 1969, *164,* 86–88. **252**

Elkind, D. Cognitive growth cycles in mental development. In J. K. Cole (Ed.) *Nebraska Symposium on Motivation.* Lincoln: University of Nebraska Press, 1971. **293**

Elliott, R. Tonic heart rate: Experiments on the effects of collative variables lead to a hypothesis about its motivational significance. *J. Pers. Soc. Psychol.,* 1969, 12(3), pp. 211–228. **52**

Elliott, R. The significance of heart rate for behavior: A critique of Lacey's hypothesis. *J. Pers. Soc. Psychol.,* 1972, *22,* 398–409. **52**

Elliott, R., Bankart, B., and Light, T. Differences in the motivational significance of heart rate and palmar conductance: Two tests of a hypothesis. *J. Pers. Soc. Psychol.,* 1970, 14(2), pp 166–172. **52**

Ellsworth, P. C., Carlsmith, J. M., and Henson, A. The stare as a stimulus to flight in human subjects: A series of field experiments. *J. Pers. Soc. Psychol.,* 1972, *21,* 302–311. **162**

Elmadjian, F., Hope, J. M., and Lamson, E. T. Excretion of epinepherine and morepinepherine in various emotional states. *J. Clin. Endocrinol.,* 1957, *17,* 608–620. **35**

Elms, A. C., and Milgram, S. Personality characteristics associated with obedience and defiance toward authoritative command. *J. Exp. Res. Pers.,* 1966, *1,* 282–289. **406**

Engel, B. T. and Bleeker, E. R. Application of operant conditioning techniques to the control of the cardiac arrhythmias. In P. A. Obrist, et al (Eds.) *Cardiovascular psychophysiology.* Chicago: Aldine, 1974. **138**

Engel, B. T., and Chism, R. A. Operant conditioning of heart rate speeding. *Psycho-physiology*, 1967, *3*, 418–426. **132**

Engel, B. T., and Hansen, S. P. Operant conditioning of heart rate slowing. *Psycho-physiology*, 1966, *3*, 176–187. **132**

Engel, B. T., Nikoomanesh, P., and Schuster, M. Operant conditioning of rectos-phincteric responses in the treatment of fecal incontinence. *New Engl. J. Med.*, 1974, 646–649. **140**

Engel, G. L., and Schmale, A. H. Psychoanalytic theory of somatic disorder. *J. Am. Psychoanal. Assoc.*, 1967, *15*, 344–365. **136**

Epstein, A. N. Reciprocal changes in feeding behavior produced by intra-hypo-thalamic chemical injections. *Am. J. Physiol.*, 1960, *199*, 969–974. **65**

Erikson, E. *Childhood and society*. New York: Norton, 1963. **299, 400** (First Published 1950.)

Eron, L., Huesmann, L. R., Lefkowitz, M., and Walder, L. Does television violence cause aggression? *Am. Psychol.*, 1972, *27*, 253–263. **176, 177**

Ervin, F. R., Mark, V. H., and Stevens, J. R. Behavioral and affective responses to brain stimulation in man. In J. Zubin and C. Shagass (Eds.) *Neurological aspects of psychopathology*. New York: Grune and Stratton, 1969. **57, 83, 91, 92**

Estes, W. K., and Skinner, B. F. Some quantitative properties of anxiety. *J. Exp. Psychol.*, 1941, *29*, 390–400. **112**

Everitt, B. J., and Herbert, J. Adrenal glands and sexual receptivity in female rhesus monkeys. *Nature*, 1969, *222*, 1065–1066. **211**

Everitt, B. J., and Herbert, J. The maintenance of sexual receptivity by adrenal androgens in female rhesus monkeys. *J. Endocrinol.*, 1970, *48*, xxxviii. **211**

Everitt, B. J. and Herbert, J. The effects of dexamithasone and androgens on sexual receptivity of female rhesus monkeys. *J. Endocrinol.*, 1971, *51*, 575–588. **211**

Eysenck, H. J. *The dynamics of anxiety and hysteria*. New York: Praeger, 1957. **267**

Eysenck, H. J. *Mandsley personality inventory*. San Diego, Calif.: Educational and Industrial Testing Service, 1959. **264**

Eysenck, H. J. Conditioning, introversion-extraversion, and the strength of the nervous system. *Proc. XVIIIth Int. Congr. Exper. Psychol.,* Moscow, 9th Symposium, 1966, 33–45. **285**

Eysenck, H. J. *The biological basis of personality.* Springfield, Ill.: Charles C. Thomas, 1967. **260, 263, 267, 268**

Eysenck, H. J., and Levy, A. Conditioning, introversion-extraversion and the strength of the nervous system. In V. D. Nebylitsyn and J. A. Gray (Eds.) *Biological bases of individual behavior.* New York: Academic, 1972. **268**

Feldman, S. M., and Waller, H. J. Dissociation of electrocortical activation and behavioral arousal. *Nature,* 1962, *196,* 1320–1322. **55**

Felipe, N., and Sommer, R. Invasions of personal space. *Soc. Relat.,* 1966, *14,* 206–214. **161**

Fenichel, O. The counterpholic attitude. *Int. J. Psychoanal.,* 1939, *20,* 263–274. **177**

Feshbach, S. The stimulating versus cathartic effects of a vicarious aggressive activity. *J. Abnorm. Soc. Psychol.,* 1961, *63,* 381–385. **170**

Feshbach, S. The function of aggression and the regulation of aggressive drive. *Psych. Rev.,* 1964, *71,* 257–272. **185**

Feshbach, S. Dynamics of morality of violence and aggression: Some psychological considerations. *Am. Psychol.,* 1971, *26,* 281–291. **185**

Festinger, L. Informal social communication. *Psych. Rev.,* 1950, *57,* 271–282. **321, 322**

Festinger, L. A theory of social comparison processes. *Hum. Relat.,* 1954, *7,* 117–140. **48, 322**

Festinger, L. *A theory of cognitive dissonance.* Stanford: Stanford University Press, 1957. **326, 327**

Festinger, L., and Carlsmith, J. Cognitive consequences of forced compliance. *J. Abnorm. Soc. Psychol.,* 1959, *58,* 203–210. **329, 330**

Finley, W. W. Reduction of seizures and normalization of the EEG following sensorimotor biofeedback training. In N. E. Miller et al. (Eds.) *Biofeedback and self control.* Chicago: Aldine, 1974. **141**

Fisher, A. E. Maternal and sexual behavior induced by intracranial electrical stimulation. *Science,* 1956, *124,* 228–229. **68**

Fisher, A. E. Chemical stimulation of the brain. *Sci. Am.* June 1964. **68, 440**

Fishkin, J., Keniston, K., and MacKinnon, C. Moral reasoning and political ideology. *J. Pers. Soc. Psychol.,* 1973, *27,* 109–119. **399, 400**

Flavell, J. *The development of role-taking and communication skills in children.* New York: Wiley, 1968. **391**

Folkins, C. H. Temporal factors and the cognitive mediators of stress reaction. *J. Pers. Soc. Psychol.,* 1970, *14,* 173–184. **369, 370**

Ford, C. S., and Beach, F. A. *Patterns of sexual behavior.* New York: Harper, 1951. **217**

Freedman, J. Long-term behavioral effect of cognitive dissonance. *J. Exp. Soc. Psychol.,* 1965, *1,* 145–155. **330, 331**

French, E. G. *Development of a measure of complex motivation.* Lackland Air Force Base, Texas: Res. Rep. AFPTRC-TN-56-48, Air Force Personnel and Training Research Center, April 1956. **301**

Freud, S. Instincts and their vicissitudes, 1915. In *Collected papers of Sigmund Freud,* Vol. IV. (Joan, Riviere transl.) London: Hogarth Press, 1949. **195**

Friedman, P. H. The effects of modeling, roleplaying, and participation on behavior change. In B. A. Maher (Ed.) *Progress in experimental personality research.* New York: Academic, 1972. **333**

Funkenstein, D. H. The physiology of fear and anger. *Sci. Am.* May 1955, 2–6. **35**

Funkenstein, D. H., King, S. H., and Drolette, M. E. *Mastery of stress.* Cambridge: Harvard University Press, 1957. **35**

Furman, S. Intestinal biofeedback in functional diarrhea: A preliminary report. *J. Behav. Ther. Exp. Psychiatr.,* 1973, *4,* 317–321. **140**

Gale, A., Coles, M., Kline, P., and Penfold, V. Extraversion-introversion, neuroticism and the EEG: Basal and response measures during habituation of the orienting response. *Br. Psychol.* 1971, *63,* 533–548. **268**

Gallistel, C. R. Electrical self-stimulation and its theoretical implications. *Psych. Bull.,* 1964, *61,* 23–34. **97**

Gallistel, C. R. The incentive of brain stimulation reward. *J. Comp. Physiol. Psychol.,* 1969, *69,* 722–729. **97**

Gallistel, C. R. Self-stimulation: The neurophysiology of reward and motivation. In J. A. Deutsch (Ed.) *The physiological basis of memory.* New York: Academic, 1973. **74**

Gambaro, S., and Rabin, A. I. Diastolic blood pressure responses following direct and displaced aggression after anger arousal in high and low-guilt subjects. *J. Pers. Soc. Psychol.,* 1969, *12,* 87–94. **179**

Garlington, W. J., and Shimota, H. E. The change seeker index: A measure of the need for variable sensory input. *Psychol. Rep.,* 1964, *14,* 919–924. **286**

Gazzaniga, M. S. The split brain in man. In *Altered states of awareness,* San Francisco: Freeman, 1972. **49, 448**

Geen, R. G. *Aggression.* Morristown, N. J.: General Learning Press, 1972. **169**

Geen, R. G., and Berkowitz, L. Name-mediated aggressive cue properties. *J. Pers.,* 1966, *34,* 456–465. **170**

Gellhorn, E. *Principles of autonomic-somatic integrations.* Minneapolis: University of Minnesota Press, 1967. **36**

Gerard, H. B. Choice difficulty, dissonance, and the decision sequence. *J. Pers.,* 1967, *35,* 91–108. **336**

Gerard, H. B. Experimental investigation of mediational events. In R. P. Abelson et al. (Eds.) *Theories of cognitive consistency: A sourcebook.* Chicago: Rand McNally, 1968. **336**

Gibson, W. E., Reid, L. D., Sakai, M., and Porter, P. B. Intracranial reinforcement compared with sugar-water reinforcement. *Science,* 1965, *148,* 1357–1359. **98**

Glickman, S. E., and Schiff, B. B. A biological theory of reinforcement. *Psychol. Rev.,* 1967, *74,* 81–109. **76, 92, 288**

Gliner, J. A., Horvath, S. N., and Wolfe, R. R. Operant conditioning of heart rate in curarized rats: Hemodynamic changes. *Am. J. Phys.,* 1975, *228,* 870–874. **128**

Glusman, M., Won, W., and Burdock, E. I. Effects of midbrain lesions on "savage" behavior induced by hypothalamic lesions in the cat. *Trans. Am. Neurol. Assoc.,* 1961, *86,* 216. **72**

Goldman, R., Jaffa, M., and Schachter, S. Yom Kippur, Air France, dormitory food, and the eating behavior of obese and normal persons. *J. Pers. Soc. Psychol.,* 1968, *10,* 117–123. **359, 360**

Goldstein, J. H., and Arms, R. L. Effects of observing athletic contests on hostility. *Sociometery,* 1971, *34,* 83–90. **160**

Goldstein, M. J., Kant, H. S., Judd, L. L., Rice, C. J., and Green, R. Exposure to pornography and sexual behavior in deviant and normal groups. *Technical report of the commission on obscenity and pornography,* Vol. 7. Washington, D. C.: U. S. Government Printing Office, 1970. **220, 221**

Goldstein, M. J., Kant, H., Judd, L., Rice, C., and Green, R. Experience with pornography: Rapists, pedophiles, homosexuals, transexuals, and controls. *Arch. Sex. Behav.,* 1971, *1,* 1–15. **220, 221**

Goodall, J. New discoveries among Africa's chimpanzees. *Nat. Geogr.,* 1965, *128,* 802–831. **238, 239, 240**

Goodall, J. In P. C. Jay (Ed.) Primates: *Studies in adaptation and variability.* New York: Holt, Rinehart & Winston, 1968. **238, 239, 240**

Goranson, R. Media violence and aggressive behavior: A review of experimental research. In L. Berkowitz (Ed.) *Advances in experimental social psychology,* Vol. 5. New York: Academic, 1970. **171**

Graham, D. T., and Stevenson, I. Disease as a response to life stress. I. The nature of the evidence. In H. I. Lief, V. G. Lief, and N. R. Lief (Eds.) *The psychological basis of medical practice.* New York: Harper and Row, 1963. **39**

Graham, L., Cohen, S., and Shamavonian, G., Sex differences in automatic responses during instrumental conditioning. *Psychosom. Med.,* 1966, *28,* 264–271. **264**

Grant, E. C. Human facial expression. *Man,* 1969, *4,* 525–536. **254**

Gray, G. W. Cortisone and ACTH. *Sci. Am.,* 1950, *182,* 30–37. **33**

Gray, J. A. *Pavlov's typology.* New York: Macmillan, 1964. **285**

Gray, J. A. *The psychology of fear and stress.* New York: Mc Graw-Hill, 1971. **242**

Gray, J. A. The psychophysiological nature of introversion- extraversion: A modification of Eysenck's theory. In V. D. Nebylitsyn and J. A. Gray (Eds.) *Biological bases of individual behavior.* New York: Academic, 1972. **268, 269**

Green, J. D. Electrical activity in the hypothalamus and hippocampus of conscious rabbits. *Anat. Rec.*, 1954, *118*, 304. **69**

Green, J. R., Duisberg, R. E. H., and McGrath, W. B. Focal epilepsy of psychomotor type. A preliminary report of observations on effects of surgical therapy. *J. Neurosurg.*, 1951, *8*, 157–179. **85**

Grohmann, J. Modifikation oder funktionsreifung? *Z. Tierpsychol.*, 1939, *2*, 132–144. **154**

Gross, K. *The play of man.* New York: D. Appleton, 1901. **288**

Grossman, S. P. Eating or drinking elicited by direct adrenergic or cholinergic stimulation of hypothalamus. *Science,* 1960, *132*, 301–302. **66**

Grossman, S. P. Chemically induced epileptiform seizures in the cat. *Science,* 1963, *142*, 409–411. **86**

Grossman, S. B. *A textbook of physiological psychology.* New York: Wiley, 1967. **63, 65, 70, 79, 86, 89, 97, 351, 420, 432, 444**

Gubar, G. Recognition of human facial expressions judged live in a laboratory setting. *J. Pers. Soc. Psychol.,* 1966, *4*, 108–111. **257**

Gurin, P., Gurin, G., Lao, R. C., and Beattie, M. Internal-external locus of control in the motivational dynamics of Negro yough. *J. Soc. Issues,* 1969, *25*, 29–53. **343**

Guyton, A. C., Coleman, T. G., and Granger, H. J. Circulation: Overall regulation. *Ann. Rev. Physiol.,* 1972, *34*, 13–46. **429**

Haan, N. Activism as moral protest: Moral judgments of hypothetical moral dilemmas and an actual situation of civil disobedience. In L. Kohlberg and E. Turiel (Eds.) *The development of moral judgment and action.* New York: Holt, Rinehart, and Winston, 1972. **399**

Haan, N., Smith, M. B., and Block, J. H. Moral reasoning of young adults: Political-social behavior, family backgrounds, and personality correlates. *J. Pers. Soc. Psychol.,* 1968, *10*, 183–201. **399, 400**

Hall, C. S., and Lindzey, G. *Theories of personality.* New York: Wiley, 1970. **199, 320**

Hall, E. *The hidden dimension.* New York: Doubleday, 1966. **161, 248**

Hall E. *The silent language.* Garden City: Doubleday, 1959. **161, 248**

Hall, M. H. A conversation with Masters and Johnson. *Psychol. Today.*, 1969, *3*, 50–58. **203**

Hamburg, D. A. Psychobiological studies of aggressive behavior. *Nature*, 1971, *230*, 19–23. **157, 167**

Hanson, L. R., and Blechman, E. The labeling process during sexual intercourse. Cited in E. E. Jones et al. (Eds.) *Attribution: Perceiving the causes of behavior.* Morristown, N.J.: General Learning Press, 1971. **356**

Hardt, J. Effects of breathing alterations and of drugs on the abundance of EEG alpha activity. Unpublished paper, Carnegie-Mellon University, 1970. **130, 134**

Harlow, H. F. Learning and satiation of response in intrinsically motivated complex puzzle performance in monkeys. *J. Comp. Physiol. Psychol.*, 1950, *43*, 289–294. **280**

Harlow, H. Mice, monkey, men, and motives. *Psych. Rev.*, 1953, *60*, 23–32. **288**

Harlow, H. F. Love in infant monkeys. *Sci. Am.*, 1959, *200*, 68–74. **232, 235**

Harlow, H. F. The heterosexual affectional system in monkeys. *Am. Psychol.*, 1962, *17*, 1–9. **233**

Harlow, H. F., Blazek, N. C., and McClearn, G. E. Manipulatory motivation in the infant rhesus monkey. *J. comp. physiol. Psychol.*, 1956, *49*, 444–448. **280**

Harlow, H. F., Gluck, J. P., and Suomi, S. J. Generalization of behavioral data between human and nonhuman animals. *Amer. Psychol.* 1972, *27*, 709–716. **231**

Harlow, H. F., Harlow, M. K., and Meyer, D. R. Learning motivated by a manipulation drive. *J. Exp. Psychol.*, 1950, *40*, 228–234. **280**

Harlow, H. F., McGaugh, J. L., and Thompson, R. F. *Psychology.* San Francisco: Albion, 1971. **233, 234, 246**

Harlow, H. F., and Zimmerman, R. R. The development of affectional responses in infant monkeys. *Proc. Am. Phil. Soc.*, 1958, *102*, 501–509. *232*

Harmon, D. K., Masuda, M., and Holmes, T. H. The social readjustment rating scale: A cross-cultural study of Western Europeans and Americans. *J. Psychosom. Res.*, 1971, *14*, 391. **39**

Hart, B. L. Gonadal androgen and sociosexual behavior of male mammals: A comparative analysis. *Psychol. Bull.*, 1974, *81*, 383–400. **211**

Hart, J. T. Autocontrol of EEG alpha. *Psychophysiology,* 1968, *4,* 506 (Abstract). **135**

Hartmann, D. P. Influence of symbolically modeled instrumental aggression and pain cues on aggressive behavior. *J. Pers. Soc. Psychol.,* 1969, *11,* 280–288. **171, 172, 173**

Hartshorne, H., and May, M. *Studies in the nature of character.* 3 volumes. New York: MacMillen, 1928–1930. **392**

Hashim, S. A. and Van Itallie, T. B. Studies in normal and obese subjects using a monitored food dispensing device. *Ann. N. Y. Acad. Sci.,* 1965, *131,* 654–661. **362, 363**

Hawke, C. C. Castration and sex crimes. *Am. J. Ment. Defi.,* 1950, *55,* 220–226. **188**

Heath, R. G. Electrical self-stimulation of the brain in man. *Am. J. Psychiatr.,* 1963, *120,* 571–577. **100, 101**

Heath, R. G. (Ed.) *The role of pleasure in behavior.* New York: Hoeber Medical Division Harper and Row, 1964a. **83, 90, 91, 99, 101**

Heath, R. G. Pleasure responses of human subjects to direct stimulation of the brain: Physiologic and psychodynamic and considerations. In R. G. Heath (Ed.) *The role of pleasure in behavior.* New York: Hoeber Medical Division, Harper and Row, 1964b. **90, 91, 100, 101**

Heath, R. G. Pleasure and brain activity in man. *J. Nerv. Ment. Dis.,* 1972, *154,* 3–18. **91**

Heath, R. G., and Mickle, W. A. Evaluation of seven years' experience with depth electrode studies in human patients. In E. R. Ramey and D. S. O'Doherty (Eds.) *Electrical studies on the unanesthetized brain.* New York: Paul B. Hoeber, 1960. **86, 90**

Hebb, D. O. Drives and the C. N. S. (Conceptual nervous system). *Psychol. Rev.,* 1955, *62,* 243–254. **49, 280, 284**

Heider, F. Ding und medium. *Symposium,* 1927, *1,* 109–157. **340**

Heider, F. Social perception and phenomenal causality. *Psychol. Rev.,* 1944, *51,* 358–374. **323**

Heider, F. Attitudes and cognitive organization. *J. Psychol.,* 1946, *21,* 107–112. **323**

Heider, F. *The psychology of interpersonal relations.* New York: Wiley, 1958. **341, 342**

Heimburger, R. F., Whitlock, C. C., and Kalsbeck, J. E. Stereotaxic amygdalectomy for epilepsy with aggressive behavior. *J. Am. Med. Assoc.,* 1966, *198,* 741–745. **82, 144**

Herberg, L. J. Seminal ejaculation following positively reinforcing electrical stimulation of the rat hypothalamus. *J. Comp. Physiol. Psychol.,* 1963, *56,* 679–685. **67**

Heron, W. The pathology of boredom. In S. Coopersmith (Ed.) *Frontiers of psychological research.* San Francisco: Freeman, 1966. **282**

Hess, W. R. Stammgarglien-reizversuche. *Ber. Ges. Physiol.,* 1928, *42,* 554. **70**

Hess, W. R., and Brugger, M. Das subkortikale zentrum der afektiven abwehrreaktion. *Helv. Physiol. Pharmacol. Acta,* 1943, *1,* 33–52. **72**

Hetherington, A. N. and Ranson, S. W. The spontaneous activity and food intake of rats with hypothalamic lesions. *Am. J. Physiol.,* 1942, *136,* 609–617. **64, 70**

Hicks, D. J. Imitation and retention of film-mediated aggressive peer and adult models. *J. Pers. Soc. Psychol.,* 1965, *2,* 97–100. **165**

Hinkle, L. E. Ecological observations of the relations of physical illness, mental illness, and the social environment. *Psychosom. Med.,* 1961, *23,* 289–297. **39**

Hinkle, L. E., and Wofff, H. G. Ecologic investigations of the relationship between illness, life experiences, and the social environment. *Ann. Intern. Med.,* 1958, *49,* 1373. **39**

Hnatio, M. and Lang, P. J. Learned stabilization of cardiac rate. Psychophysiology, 1965, *1,* 330–336.

Hobbes, T. *Leviathan.* New York: Macmillan, 1904. (First published 1650.) **152**

Hobbs, A. H. and Lambert, R. D. An evaluation of sexual behavior in the human male. *Am. J. Psychiat.,* 1948, *104,* 758–764. **201**

Hofstadter, R. *Social Darwinism in American thought.* New York: George Braziller, 1959. **153**

Hohmann, G. W. The effect of dysfunctions of the autonomic nervous system on experienced feelings and emotions. Paper read at the Conference on Emotions and Feelings, New School of Social Research, New York, 1962. **44, 351**

Hokanson, J. E. Psychophysiological evaluation of the catharsis hypothesis. In E. I. Megargee and J. E. Hokanson (Eds.) *The dynamics of aggression.* New York: Harper and Row, 1970. **180**

Hokanson, J. E., and Burgess, M. The effects of three types of aggression on vascular processes. *J. Abnorm. Soc. Psychol.,* 1962(a), *64,* 446–449. **179**

Hokanson, J. E., and Burgess, M. The effects of status, type of frustration, and aggression on vascular processes. *J. Abnorm. Soc. Psychol.,* 1962(b), *65,* 232–237. **179**

Hokanson, J. E., Burgess, M., and Cohen, M. F. Effects of displaced aggression on systolic blood pressure. *J. Abnorm. Soc. Psychol.,* 1963, *67,* 214–218. **179**

Hokanson, J. E., and Edelman, R. Effects of three social responses on vascular processes. *J. Abnorm. Soc. Psychol.,* 1966, *3,* 442–447. **179**

Hokanson, J. E., and Shetler, S. The effect of overt aggression on physiological arousal. *J. Abnorm. Soc. Psychol., 1961, 63,* 446–448. **179**

Hokanson, J. E., and Stone, L. Intensity of self-punishment as a factor in intropunitive behavior. Unpublished manuscript. Florida State University, 1969. **182**

Hokanson, J. E., Willers, K. R., and Koropsak, E. The modification of autonomic responses during aggressive interchange. *J. Pers.,* 1968, *36,* 386–404. **180, 181**

Holmes, D. S. Effects of overt aggression on level of physiological arousal. *J. Pers. Soc. Psychol.,* 1966, *4,* 189–194. **179**

Holmes, J. G., and Strickland, L. H. Choice freedom and confirmation of incentive expectancy as determinants of attitude change. *J. Pers. Soc. Psychol.,* 1970, *14,* 39–45. **335**

Holmes, T. H., and Rahe, R. H. The social readjustment rating scale. *J. Psychosom. Res.,* 1967, *11,* 213–218. **39**

Horner, M. S. Sex differences in achievement motivation and performance in competitive and non-competitive situations. Unpublished doctoral dissertation, University of Michigan, 1966. **315**

Horner, M. S. Woman's will to fail. *Psych. Today,* 1969, *3,* 36–62. **315**

Hothersall, D., and Brener, J. Operant conditioning of changes in heart rate in curarized rats. *J. Compl. Physiol. Psychol.,* 1969, *68,* 338–342. **136**

House, E. L., and Pansky, B. *Neuroanatomy.* New York: McGraw Hill, 1960. **441, 442, 443**

Howell, R. J., and Jorgenson, E. C. Accuracy of judging emotional behavior in a natural setting—A replication. *J. Soc. Psychol.,* 1970, *81*(2), 269–270. **257**

Hovland, C. I., Janis, I., and Kelley, H. *Communication and persuasion.* New Haven: Yale University Press, 1953. **332, 333**

Hovland, C. I., and Sears, R. R. Minor studies of aggression VI. Correlation of lynchings with economic indices. *J. Psychol.,* 1940, *9,* 301–310. **408**

Huber, E. *Evolution of facial musculature and facial expression.* Baltimore: The John Hopkins Press, 1931. **251**

Hume, D. *A treatise on human nature* (First published 1740.) Oxford: The Clarendon Press, 1896. **340**

Hunsperger, R. W. Affektreaktionen auf elektrische reizung in hirnstamm den katze. *Helv. Physiol. Acta,* 1956, *14,* 70–92. **70, 71**

Hyman, H., and Barmack, J. E. Special review: Sexual behavior in the human female. *Psych. Bull.,* 1954, *51,* 418–427. **201, 208**

Inhelder, B., and Piaget, J. *The growth of logical thinking from childhood to adolescence.* New York: Basic, 1958. **298**

Insko, C. A. *Theories of attitude change.* New York: Appleton Century Crofts, 1967. **325**

Ippolitov, F. V. Interanalyser differences in the sensitivity-strength parameter for vision, hearing, and cutaneous modalities. In V. D. Nebylitsyn and J. A. Gray. *Biological bases of individual behavior.* New York: Academic, 1972. **286**

Itani, J. On the acquisition and propagation of a new food habit in the troop of Japanese monkeys at Takasakiyama. *Primates,* 1958, *1,* 84–98. (In Japanese with English summary.) **231**

Izard, C. The emotions as a culture-common framework of motivational experiences and communicative cues. Technical Report No. 30, Contract Nonr 2149(33), Office of Naval Research, 1968. **251**

Izard, C. *The face of emotion.* New York: Appleton Century Crofts, 1971. **253**

Jacobson, E. *Progressive relaxation.* Chicago: University of Chicago Press, 1938. **141, 432**

Jacobson, E. Muscular tension and the estimation of effort. *Am. J. Psychol.,* 1951, *64,* 112–117. **432**

Jacobson, E. *You must relax.* New York: McGraw-Hill, 1962. **141**

Jacobson, E. *Modern treatment of tense patients.* Springfield, Ill. Charles C. Thomas, 1970. **141**

Jaffe, Y., Malamuth, N., Feingold, J., and Feshbach, S. Sexual arousal and behavioral aggression. *J. Pers. Soc. Psychol.,* 1974, *30,* 759–764. **174n**

James, W. What is an emotion? *Mind,* 1884, *9,* 188–205. Reprinted in M. Arnold. *The Nature of emotion.* Baltimore: Penguin, 1968. **42, 43**

Janis, I. L. *Psychological stress.* New York: Wiley, 1958. **376**

Janis, I., and Gilmore, J. The influence of incentive conditions on the success of role playing in modifying attitudes. *J. Pers. Soc. Psychol.,* 1965, *1,* 17–27. **333**

Janis, I., and Mann, L. Effectiveness of emotional role-playing in modifying smoking habits and attitudes. *J. Exp. Res. Pers.,* 1965, *1,* 84–90. **333**

Jasper, H. H. Unspecific thalamocortical relations. In J. Field, H. W. Magonn, and V. E. Hall (Eds.) *Handbook of physiology: Neurophysiology,* II. Washington, D. C.: American Physiological Society, 1960. **57**

Jennings, J. R., Averill, J. R., Opton, E. M., and Lazarus, R. S. Some Parameters of heart rate change: Perceptual versus motor task requirements, noxiousness, and uncertainty. *Psychophysiology,* 1970, *7*(2), 194. **52**

Johnson, H. J., and Campos, J. J. The effect of cognitive tasks and verbalization instruction on heart rate and skin conductance. *Psychophysiology,* 1967, *4,* 143–152. **52**

Johnson, H. J., and Schwartz, G. E. Suppression of GSR activity through operant reinforcement. *J. Exp. Psychol.,* 1967, *75,* 307–312. **132**

Johnson, R. N. *Aggression in man and animals.* Philadelphia: Saunders, 1972. **183**

Johnson, W. G. The effect of prior-taste and food visibility on the food-directed instrumental performance of obese individuals. Unpublished doctoral dissertation, Catholic University of America, 1970. **362**

Jones, E. *The life and work of Sigmund Freud.* Edited and abridged by L. Trilling and S. Marcus. New York: Basic, 1961. **151**

Jones, E. *The life and work of Sigmund Freud,* Vols. I–III. New York, Basic, 1953–1957. **194**

Jones, E. E., Kanouse, D. E., Kelley, H. H., Nisbett, R. E., Valins, S., Weiner, B. *Attribution: Perceiving the causes of behavior.* Morristown, N. J.: General Learning Press, 1972. **342**

Jones, E. E., and Nisbett, R. E. The actor and observer: Divergent perceptions of the causes of behavior. In E. E. Jones *et al.* (Eds.) *Attribution: Perceiving the causes of behavior.* Morristown, New Jersey: General Learning Press, 1972. **344, 345**

Jones, H. E. The galvanic skin response as related to overt emotional expression. *Am. J. Psychol.,* 1935, *47,* 241–251. **260, 371**

Jones, H. E. An experimental cabinet for physiological study of emotions. *Child Dev.,* 1936, *7,* 183–188. **261**

Jones, H. E. The study of patterns of emotional expression. In M. Reymert (Ed.) *Feelings and emotions.* New York: McGraw-Hill, 1950. **260, 262, 270**

Jones, H. E. TheLongitudinal method in the study of personality. In Iscoe and H. W. Stevenson (Eds.) *Personality development in children.* Chicago: University of Chicago Press, 1960. **260, 261, 263**

Jouvet, M. The states of sleep. *Sci. Am.,* February, 1967. **433**

Jouvet, M. Biogenic amines and the states of sleep. *Science,* 1969, *163,* 32–41. **103, 421**

Kagan, J., and Moss, H. A. *Birth to maturity.* New York: Wiley, 1962. **247**

Kanekar, S. Accuracy in person perception. *Psychologia,* 1972, *15,* 76–88. **391**

Kamiya, J. Conditional discrimination of the EEG alpha rhythm in humans. Paper presented at the meeting of the Western Psychological Association, San Francisco, 1962. **133**

Kemiya, J. Conscious control of brain waves. *Psychol. Today,* 1968, *1,* 56–60. **133, 134, 135**

Kaplan, B. J. EEG biofeedback and epilepsy. In N. E. Miller el al. (Eds.) *Biofeedback and self control.* Chicago: Aldine, 1974. **37, 141**

Kasamatsu, A., and Hirai, T. An electroencephalographic study on the Zen meditation (Zagen). *Folia Psychiatr. Neurol. Jap.,* 1966, *20,* 316–336. **133, 134**

Katkin, E. S., and Murray, E. N. Instrumental conditioning of autonomically mediated behavior: Theoretical and methodological issues. *Psychol. Bull.,* 1968, *70,* 52–68. **123, 127, 128, 129, 132**

Katkin, E. S., Murray, E. N., and Lachman, R. Concerning instrumental autonomic conditioning: A rejoinder. *Psych. Bull,* 1969, *71,* 462–466. **129**

Kawamura, S. The process of sub-cultural propagation among Japanese Macaques. In C. H. Southwick (Ed.) *Primate Social Behavior.* Princeton: Van Nostrand, 1963. **231**

Kawai, M. Newly acquired pre-cultural behavior of the natural troop of Japanese monkeys on Koshima Island. *Primates,* 1965, *6,* 1–30. **231**

Keasey, C. B. Social participation as a factor in the moral development of preadolescents. *Dev. Psychol.,* 1971, *5,* 216–220. **390**

Keeton, W. T. *Biological science.* New York: Norton, 1967. **33, 423, 424, 435, 436**

Kelley, H. H. Attribution theory in social psychology. In D. Levine (Ed.) *Nebraska Symposium on Motivation.* Lincoln: University of Nebraska Press, 1967. **339**

Kelley, H. H. The processes of causal attribution. *Am. Psychol.,* 1973, *28,* 107–126. **290, 338**

Kent, R. N., Wilson, G. T., and Nelson, R. Effects of false heart-rate feedback on avoidance behavior: An investigation of "cognitive desensitization." *Behav. Ther.,* 1972, *3,* 1–6. **376**

Kessler, M. M. Spontaneous and reflex emotional responses differentiated by lesions in diencephalon. *Proc. Soc. Exp. Biol. Med.,* 1941, *47,* 225–227. **70**

Kety, S. S. The biogenic amines in the central nervous system: Their possible roles in arousal, emotion, and learning. In F. O. Schmitt (Ed.,) *The neurosciences.* New York: Rockefeller University Press, 1970. **102, 103**

Kimble, G. H. *Hilgard and Marquis' conditioning and learning,* 2nd Ed. New York: Appleton Century, 1961. **122**

King, H. E. Psychological effects of excitation in the limbic system. In D. E. Sheer (Ed.) *Electrical stimulation of the brain.* Austin: University of Texas Press, 1961. **83, 88, 351**

Kinsey, A. C., Pomeroy, W. B., and Martin, C. E. *Sexual behavior of the human male.* Philadelphia: W. B. Saunders, 1948. **200, 212**

Kinsey, A. C., Pomeroy, W. B., Martin, C. E., and Gebhard, P. H. *Sexual behavior in the human female.* Philadelphia: W. B. Saunders, 1953. **200, 208, 209, 222**

Klausner, S. Z. *The transformation of fear.* Washington, D. C.: Bureau of Social Science Research, 1966. **177**

Klinberg, O. Emotional expression in Chinese literature. *J. Abnorm. Soc. Psychol.,* 1938, *33,* 517–520. **251**

Kluver, H., and Bucy, P. C. "Psychic blindness" and other symptoms following bilateral temporal lobectomy in rhesus monkeys. *Am. J. Physiol.,* 1937, *119,* 352–353. **79**

Kluver, H., and Bucy, P. C. An analysis of certain effects of bilateral temporal lobectomy in the rhesus monkey with special reference to "psychic blindness." *J. Psychol.,* 1938, *5,* 33–54. **79**

Kluver, H., and Bucy, P. C. Preliminary analysis of functions of the temporal lobe in monkeys. *Arch. Neurol. Psychiatr. Chic.,* 1939, *42,* 979–1000. **79**

Koelle, G. B. Anticholinesterase agents. In L. S. Goodman and A. Gilman (Eds.) *The pharmacological basis of therapeutics.* New York: Macmillan, 1971. **421**

Koening, O. Das aktionssystem der Bartmeise (*Panurus biarmicus L*). Oesterr. *Zool. Z.,* 1951, *3* 247–325. **78**

Koeske, R. and Koeske, G. An attributional approach to moods and the menstrual cycle. *J. Pers. Soc. Psychol.,* 1975, *31,* 473–478. **356**

Kohlberg, L. The development of modes of moral thinking and choice in the years 10 to 16. Unpublished doctoral dissertation, University of Chicago, 1958. **390**

Kohlberg, L. Moral development and identification. In H. W. Stevenson (Ed.) *Child psychology.* Chicago: The University of Chicago Press, 1963(a). **384, 385, 386, 388**

Kohlberg, L. The development of children's orientations toward a moral order. I. Sequence in the development of moral thought. *Vita hum.* 1963(b), *6,* 11–33. **386, 387**

Kohlberg, L. Development of moral character and moral ideology. In M. L. Hoffman and L. W. Hoffman (Eds.) *Review of child development research.* New York: Russell Sage Foundation, 1964. **385, 386, 387, 388, 389**

Kohlberg, L. The child as moral philosopher. *Psychology Today.* Sept 1968. **389, 399**

Kohlberg, L. The relations between moral judgment and moral action: A developmental view. Paper presented at the Institute of Human Development, Berkeley, 1969. **399**

Kolb, D. Achievement motivation training for underachieving high-school boys. *J. Pers. Soc. Psychol.,* 1965, *2,* 783–792. **314**

Komaroff, A. L., Masuda, M., and Holmes, T. H. The social readjustment rating scale: A comparative study of Negro, Mexican, and White Americans. *J. Psychosom. Res.,* 1968, *12,* 121. **39**

Konecni, V. J., and Doob, A. N. Catharsis through displacement of aggression. *J. Pers. Soc. Psychol., 1972, 23,* 379–387. **160, 182**

Kortlandt, A. Experimentation with champanzees in the wild. In D. Starck, R. Schneider, and H. Kuhn (Eds.) *Neue ergeb. primatol.* Stuttgart (Fisher), 1967. **239, 240**

Krasne, F. B. General disruption resulting from electrical stimulus of ventromedial hypothalamus. *Science,* 1962, *138,* 822–823. **64**

Krebs, D. L. Some relationships between moral judgment, attention, and resistance to temptation. Unpublished doctoral dissertation, University of Chicago, 1967. **399**

Krebs, D. L. Altruism: An examination of the concept and a review of the literature. *Psych. Bull,* 1970, *73,* 258–302. **393**

Krieg, W. J. S. *Functional neuroanatomy.* Evanston, Ill.: Brain Books 1942. **445, 446**

Kutchinsky, B. The effect of pornography: A pilot experiment in perception, behavior, and attitudes. *Technical report to the commission on obscenity and pornography,* Vol. 8. Washington, D. C.: U. S. Government Printing Office, 1970. **222, 223, 224**

LaBarre, W. The cultural basis of emotions and gestures. *J. Pers.,* 1947, *16,* 49–68. **251**

Lacey, J. I. Psychophysiological approaches to the evaluation of psychotherapeutic process and outcome. In E. A. Rubenstein and M. B. Parloff (Eds.) *Research in psychotherapy.* Washington, D. C.: American Psychological Association, 1959. **51**

Lacey, J. I. The evaluation of autonomic responses: Toward a general solution. *Ann. N. Y. Acad. of Sci,* 1967 (a), *67,* 123–164. **52**

Lacey, J. I. Somatic response patterning and stress: Some revisions of activation theory. In M. H. Appley and R. Trumbell (Eds.) *Psychological stress: Issues in research*. New York: Appleton Century Crofts, 1967(b). **55, 56**

Lacey, J. I., Kagan, J., Lacey, B. C., and Moss, H. A. The visceral level: Situational determinants and behavioral correlates of autonomic response. In P. Knapp (Ed.) *Expression of the emotions in man*. New York: International Universities, 1963. **51**

Lacey, J. I., and Lacey, B. C. Verfication and extension of the principle of autonomic response stereotypy. *Am. J. Psychol.,* 1969, *71*, 50–73. **52**

Lachman, S. J. *Psychosomatic disorders.* New York: Wiley, 1972. **139**

Lader, M. H. Pneumatic plethysmography. In P. H. Vinatles and I. Martin (Eds.) *Manual of psycho-physiological methods*. New York: Wiley, 1967. **431**

Lader, M. H., and Montagu, J. D. The psycho-galvanic reflex: A pharmacological study of the peripheral mechanism. *J. Neurol, Neurosurg. and Psychiatry,* 1962, *25*, 126. **426**

Lang, P. J. Autonomic control *Psychol. Today,* 1970, *4*, 37–86. **131, 140**

Lang, P. J., and Melamed, B. C. Case report: Avoidance conditioning therapy of an infant with chronic ruminative vomiting. *J. Abnorm. Psychol.,* 1969, *74*, 1. **140**

Lang, P. J., Sroufe, L. A., and Hastings, J. C. Effects of feedback and instructional set on the control of cardiac-rate variability. *J. Exp. Psychol.,* 1967, *75*, 425–431. **132**

Landis, C. The interpretation of facial expressions of emotion. *J. Gen. Psychol.,* 1929, *2*, 59–72. **249**

Landis, C. An attempt to measure emotional traits in juvenile delinquency. In K. S. Lashley (Ed.) *Studies in the dynamics of behavior.* Chicago: University of Chicago Press, 1932. **260**

Lanzetta, J. T., and Kleck, R. E. Encoding and decoding of nonverbal affect in humans. *J. Pers. Soc. Psychol.,* 1970, *16*, 12–19. **257, 259, 371**

Lao, R. C. Internal-external control and competent and innovative behavior among Negro college students. *J. Pers. Soc. Psychol.,* 1970, *14*, 263–270. **343**

Larsen, K. S., Coleman, D., Forbes, J., and Johnson, R. Is the subject's personality or the experimental situation a better predictor of a subject's willingness to administer shock to a victim? *J. Pers. Soc. Psychol.,* 1972, *22*, 287–295. **405,**

406

Latane, B., and Darley, J. Group inhibition of bystander intervention in emergencies. *J. Pers. Soc. Psychol.*, 1968, *10*, 215–221. **394**

Latane, B., and Rodin, J. A lady in distress: Inhibiting effects of friends and strangers on bystander intervention. *J. Exp. Soc. Psychol.*, 1969, *5*, 189–202. **395**

Lawrence, D. H., and Festinger, L. *Deterrents and reinforcement*. Stanford: Stanford University Press, 1962. **332**

Lazarus, R. S. *Psychological stress and the coping process*. New York: McGraw-Hill, 1966. **370, 373**

Lazarus, R. S., and Alfert, E. Short-circuiting of threat by experimentally altering cognitive appraisal. *J. Abnorm. Soc. Psychol.*, 1964, *69*, 195–205. **368, 369, 370**

Lazarus, R. S., Averill, J. R., and Opton, E. M., Jr. Towards a cognitive theory of emotion. Paper presented at the Third International Symposium on Feelings and Emotions. Chicago, October, 1968. **373, 375**

Lazarus, R. S., and Opton, E. M., Jr. The study of psychological stress: A summary of theoretical formulations and experimental findings. In C. D. Spielberger (Ed.) *Anxiety and behavior*. New York: Academic, 1966, 225–262. **368**

Lazarus, R. S., Opton, E. M., Jr., Nomikos, M. S., and Rankin, N. O. The principle of short-circuiting of threat: Further evidence. *J. Pers.*, 1965, *33*, 622–635. **369**

Lazarus, R. S., Speisman, J. C., Mordkoff, A. M., and Davison, L. A. A laboratory study of psychological stress produced by a motion picture film. *Psychological Monographs*, 1962, *76*, 34, (Whole No. 553). **368**

Lazarus, R. S., Tomita, M., Opton, E. M., Jr., and Kodama, M. A cross-cultural study of stress-reaction patterns in Japan. *J. Pers. Soc. Psychol.*, 1966, *4*, 622–633. **370, 372**

Leakey, L. S. B. Exploring 1,750,000 years into man's past. *Natl. Geogr.*, 1961, *120*, 564–589. **157**

Leaky, R. E. Skull 1470. *Natl. Geogr.*, 1973, *143*, 818–829. **14**

Learmonth, G. J., Ackerley, W., and Kaplan, M. Relationships between palmar skin potential during stress and personality variables. *Psychosom. Med.*, 1959, *21*, 150–157. **260, 263**

Lefkowitz, M., Eron, L., Walder, L., and Huesmann, L. R. Television violence and child aggression: A follow-up study. In G. A. Comstock and E. A. Rubinstein (Eds.) *Television and social behavior.* Vol. 3. Washington, D. C.: U. S. Government Printing Office, 1971. **176**

LeGros Clark, W. E., Beattie, J., Riddoch, G., and Dott, N.M. *The Hypothalamus.* Edinburgh: Oliver and Boyd, 1938. **96**

LeMaire, L. Danish experience regarding the castration of sexual offenders. *J. Criminal. Law Criminol.*, 1956, *47,* 294–310. **188**

Levine, S. Sex differences in the brain. *Sci. Am.*, 1966, *214*, 84–90. **215**

Levine, S. Hormones and conditioning. *Nebraska symposium on motivation.* Lincoln: University of Nebraska Press, 1968. **30**

Levine, S. Stress and behavior. *Sci. Am.*, 1971, *224,* 26–31. **29, 30**

Lewin, K. *Field theory in social science: Selected theoretical papers.* New York: Harper, 1951. **320, 321**

Lewin, K., Lippitt, R., and White, R. Patterns of aggressive behavior in experimentally created "social climates." *J. Soc. Psychol., 1939, 10*, 271–299. **321**

Lewis, M. State as an infant-environment interaction: An analysis of mother-infant behavior as a function of sex. *Merrill-Palmer Q. Beh. Dev.* 1972, *18,* 95–121. **246**

Lhermitte, F., Gautier, J. C., Marteau, R., and Chain, F. Troubles de la conscience et mutisme akinétique. *Rev. Neurol.*, 1963, *109*, 115–131. **55**

Lickona, T. Piaget misunderstood: A critique of the criticisms of his theory of moral development. *Merrill-Palmer Q. Behav. Dev.*, 1969, *15*, 337–350. **386**

Liberman, B. *Human sexual behavior.* New York: Wiley, 1971. **201**

Liebert, R. M., and Baron, R. A. Short-term effects of televised aggression on children's aggressive behavior. In J. P. Murray, E. A. Rubenstein, and G. A. Comstock (Eds.) *Television and social behavior*, Vol. 2. Washington, D. C.: U. S. Government Printing Office, 1971. **176**

Liebert, R. M., Neale, J. M., and Davidson, E. S. *The early window: Effects of televison on children and youth.* New York: Pergamon, 1973. **169**

Life, Dec. 5, 1969, 43. **409, 411**

Linder, D. E., Cooper, J.; and Jones, E. E. Decision freedom as a determinant of the role of incentive magnitude in attitude change. *J. Pers. Soc. Psychol.*, 1967, *6*, 245–254. **334, 335**

Lindsley, D. B. Emotion. In S. S. Stevens (Ed.) *Handbook of experimental psychology*. New York: Wiley, 1951. **55**

Lindsley, D. B. Psychophysiology and motivation. In M. R. Jones (Ed.) *Nebraska symposium on motivation, 1957.* Lincoln: University of Nebraska Press, 44–105. **49, 54, 55**

Lindsley, D. B. Attention, consciousness, sleep, and wakefulness. In J. Field, H. W. Magoun, and V. E. Hall (Eds.) *Handbook of physiology, neurophysiology*, III. Washington, D. C.: American Physiological Society, 1960. **54**

Lindzey, G., and Aronson, E. *The handbook of social psychology*, 2nd Ed. 6 volumes. Reading, Mass.: Addison Wesley, 1968. **325**

Lippold, O. C. J. Electromyography. In P. H. Venables and I. Martin (Eds.) *Manual of Psychophysiological Methods*. New York: Wiley, 1967. **433**

Lipton, M. A., and Udenfriend, S. Catecholamines: Synthesis and synthesis inhibitors. In Efron, D. H. (Ed.) *Psychopharmacology*. Washington, D. C.: National Institute of Mental Health, 1968. **422**

Lisina, M. I. The role of orientation in the transformation of involuntary reactions into voluntary ones. In L. G. Voronin *et al.* (Eds.) *Orienting reflex and exploratory behavior*. Washington: American Institute of Biological Sciences, 1965. **123**

Loftis, J., and Ross, L. Effects of misattribution of arousal upon the acquisition and extinction of a conditioned emotional response. *J. pers. soc. Psychol.*, 1974a, *30*, 673–682. **356**

Loftis, J., and Ross, L. Retrospective misattribution of a conditioned emotional response. J. Pers. Soc. Psychol., 1974b, *30*, 683–687. **356**

London, H., and Monello, L. Cognitive manipulation of boredom. Paper presented at the meeting of the Eastern Psychological Association, Philadelphia, 1969. **355**

London, H., and Nisbett, R. E. *Thought and feeling: Cognitive alteration of feeling states.* Chicago: Aldine, 1974. **356**

Lorenz, K. *On aggression.* New York: Harcourt, Brace, and World, 1966. **14, 154, 155, 157, 185**

Luthe, W. Autogenic training: Method, research, and application in medicine. In C. Tart (Ed.) *Altered states of consciousness.* New York: Wiley, 1969. **141**

Lynch, J., and Paskewitz, D. On the mechanisms of the feedback control of human brain wave activity. *J. Nerv. Ment. Dis.,* 1971, *153,* 205–217. **135**

Lywood, D. W. Blood pressure. In P. H. Venables and I. Martin (Eds.) *Manual of psycho-physiological methods.* New York: Wiley, 1967. **432**

MacLean, P. D. Chemical and electrical stimulation of hippocampus in unrestrained animals. II. Behavioral findings. *A.M.A. Arch. Neurol. Psychiatr.,* 1957, *78,* 128–142. **90**

MacLean, P. D. Contrasting functions of limbic and neocortical systems of the brain and their relevance to psychophysiological aspects of medicine. In E. Gellhorn (Ed.) *Biological foundations of emotion.* Glenview, Ill.: Scott, Foresman, 1968. **79, 89, 90**

MacLean, P. D. The hypothalamus and emotional behavior. In W. Haymaker, E. Anderson, and W. J. H. Nanta (Eds.) *The Hypothalamus.* Springfield, Ill.: Charles C. Thomas, 1969. **70, 72, 79**

MacLean, P. D. The limbic brain in relation to the psychoses. In P. H. Black (Ed.) *Physiological Correlates of Emotion.* New York: Academic, 1970. **78, 79, 86, 212**

MacLean, P. D., and Ploog, D. W. Cerebral representation of penile erection. *J. Neurophysiol.,* 1962, *25,* 30–55. **67, 90**

Maddi, S. R. Affective tone during environmental regularity and change. *J. Abnorm. Soc. Psychol.,* 1961, *62,* 338–345. **286**

Maddi, S. R., Propst, B., and Feldinger, I. Three expressions of the need for variety. *J. Pers.,* 1965, *33,* 82–98. **286**

Mágoun, H. W. Central neural inhibition. In M. R. Jones (Ed.), *Nebraska symposium on motivation.* Lincoln:. University of Nebraska Press, 1963. **57**

Mallick, S. K., and McCandellss, B. R. A study of catharsis of aggression. *J. Pers. Soc. Psychol., 1966 4,* 591–596. **182**

Malmo, R. B. Measurement of drive: An unsolved problem in psychology. In M. R. Jones (Ed.) *Nebraska symposium on motivation,* 1958. Lincoln: University of Nebraska Press, 229–265. **49**

Malmo, R. B. Activation: A neuropsychological dimension. *Psychol. Rev.,* 1959, *66,* 367–386. **49**

Malmo, R. B., Kohlmeyer, W., and Smith, A. A. Motor manifestations of conflict in interview. *J. Abnorm. Soc. Psychol.*, 1956, *52*, 268–271. **45**

Malmstrom, E. J., Opton, E., Jr., and Lazarus, R. S. Heart rate measurement and the correlation of indices of arousal. *Psychosom. Med.*, 1965, *27*, 546. **51**

Mandler, G., and Sarason, S. A study of anxiety and learning. *J. Abnorm. Soc. Psychol.*, 1952, *47*, 166–173. **302**

Mangan, G. L., and Farmer, R. G. Studies of the relationship between Pavlovian properties of higher nervous activity and Western personality dimensions. *J. Exp. Res. Pers.*, 1967, *2*, 101–106. **285**

Mann, J., Sidman, J., and Starr, S. Effects of erotic films on the sexual behavior of married couples. *Technical report of the commission on obscenity and pornography*, Vol. 8. Washington, D. C.: U. S. Government Printing Office, 1970. **222, 223, 224**

Mansson, H. H. The relation of dissonance reduction to cognitive, perceptual, consummatory, and learning measures of thirst. In P. Zombardo (Ed.) *The cognitive control of motivation*. Glenview, Ill.: Scott, Foresman, 1969. **365, 366**

Marakov, P. O. A study of interoception in human subjects. *Uch. Zap. Leningr. U., Sem. Biol.*, 1950, *22*, 345–368. **117**

Maranon, G. Contribution a l'étude de l'action émotive de l'adrénaline. *Rev. Fr. d'Endocrinol.*, 1924, *2*, 301–325. **46**

Mark, V. A psychosurgeon's case *for* psychosurgery. *Psychol. Today*, 1974, *8*, No. 2, 28. **144, 145, 146**

Mark, V. H., and Ervin, F. R. Violence and the brain. New York: Harper and Row, 1970. **82, 85, 86, 87, 144, 182**

Marshall, N. B., Barnett, R. J., and Mayer, J. Hypothalamic lesions in goldthioglucose injected mice. *Proc. Soc. Exp. Biol. Med*., 1955, *90*, 240. **64**

Martin, M. J. Muscle-contraction headache. *Psychosomatics*, 1972, *13*, 16–19. **139**

Martin, I., and Venables, P. H. The contribution of sweat gland activity to measures of palmar skin conductance and potential. Paper read to the *Soc. Psychophysiol. Res*., Washington, D. C., 1964 **428**

Mason, W. A. The effects of social restriction on the behavior of rhesus monkeys: III. Tests of gregariousness. *J. Comp. Physiol. Psychol.*, 1961, *54*, 287–290. **238, 240, 241**

Masters, W. H., and Johnson, V. E. *Human sexual response.* Boston: Little, Brown, 1966. **202**

Masters, W. H., and Johnson, V. E. *Human sexual inadequacy.* Boston: Little, Brown, 1968. **202**

Masters, W. H., and Johnson, V. E. The sexual response cycles of the human male and female: Comparative anatomy and physiology. Reprinted in B. Lieberman (Ed.) *Human sexual behavior.* New York: Wiley, 1971. (First published 1965.) **202, 203, 204, 205**

McClelland, D. C. *The achieving society.* Princeton: Van Nostrand, 1961. **306, 308, 310, 311, 312**

McClelland, D. C. Toward a theory of motive acquistion. *Am. Psychol.,* 1965(a), *20,* 321–333. **314**

McClelland, D. C. *N* achievement and entrepreneurship: A longitudinal study. *J. Pers. Soc. Psychol.,* 1965(b), *1,* 389–392. **306**

McClelland, D. C., and Atkinson, J. W. The projective expression of needs. I. The effect of different intensities of hunger drive on perception. *J. Psychol.,* 1948, *25,* 205–222. **300**

McClelland, D. C., Atkinson, J. W., and Clark, R. A. The projective expression of needs. III. The effect of ego-involvement, success, and failure on perception. *J. Psychol.,* 1949, *27,* 311–330. **300**

McClelland, D. C., Atkinson, J. W., Clark, R. A., and Lowell, E. L. *The Achievement motive.* New York: Appleton Century Crofts, 1953. **300**

McClelland, D. C., and Winter, D. G. *Motivating economic achievement.* New York: Free Press, 1969. **302, 306, 307, 312, 314**

McCracken, S. R. Comprehension for immediate recall of time-compressed speech as a function of sex and level of activation of the listener. In Emerson Foulke (Ed.) *Proceedings of the second Louisville conference on rate and/or frequency-controlled speech.* Louisville: University of Louisville, 1971. **264**

McGuire, W. J. The nature of attitudes and attitude change. In G. Lindzey and E. Aronson. *Handbook of social psychology,* Vol. III. Reading, Mass.: Addison Wesley, 1968. **333, 334**

McLeod, J., Atkin, C., and Chaffee, S. Adolescents, parents, and television use: Adolescent self-report measures from Maryland and Wisconsin samples. In G. A. Comstock and E. A. Rubenstein (Eds.), *Television and social behavior.* Vol.

3. Washington, D. C.: U. S. Government Printing Office, 1971a. **176**

McLeod, J., Atkin, C., and Chaffee, S. Adolescents, parents, and television use: Self-report and other-report measures from the Wisconsin sample. In G. A. Comstock and E. A. Rubenstein (Eds.) *Televisions and social behavior*, Vol. 3. Washington, D. C.: U. S. Government Printing Office, 1971b. **176**

Merton, P. A. How we control the contraction of our muscles. *Sci. Am.,* May, 1972. **23**

Meyer, T. P. Effects of viewing justified and unjustified real film violence on aggressive behavior. *J. Pers. Soc. Psychol.*, 1972, *23*, 21–29. **170, 171**

Michael, R. P. Estrogen-sensitive neurons and sexual behavior in female cats. *Science*, 1962, *136*, 322–323. **69**

Michael, R. P. The selective accumulation of estrogens in the neural and genital tissues of the cat. In L. Martini and A. Pecile (Eds.), *Hormonal Steroids*, Vol. 2. New York: Academic, 1965. **69**

Michotte, A. E. *The perception of causality*. New York: Basic, 1963. **339**

Milgram, S. Behavioral study of obedience. *J. Abnorm. Soc. Psychol.*, 1963, *67*, 371–378. **401**

Milgram, S. Some conditions of obedience and disobedience to authority. In I. D. Steiner and M. Fishbein (Eds.) *Current studies in social psychology*. New York: Holt, Rinehart and Winston, 1965. **401, 402, 403, 404**

Milgram, S. *Obedience to authority: An experimental view*. New York: Harper and Row, 1974. **401**

Miller, N. E. Learnable drives and rewards. In S. S. Stevens (Ed.) *Handbook of experimental psychology*. New York: Wiley, 1951. **124**

Miller, N. E. Liberalization of basic S-R concepts: Extensions to conflict behavior, motivation, and social learning. In S. Koch (Ed.) *Psychology: A study of a science*, Vol. II. New York: McGraw-Hill, 1959. **124**

Miller, N. E. Learning and performance motivated by direct stimulation of the brain. In D. E. Sheer (Ed.) *Electrical Stimulation of the Brain*. Austin: University of Texas Press, 1961. **72**

Miller, N. E. Some psychophysiological studies of motivation and of the behavioral effects of illness. *Bull. Brit. Psychol Soc.*, 1964, *17*, 55. **64**

Miller, N. E. Chemical coding of behavior in the brain. *Science*, 1965, *148*, 328–338. **440**

Miller, N. E. The learning of visceral and glandular responses. *Science,* 1969, *163,* 434–445. **122, 124, 125, 126, 127, 133**

Miller, N. E. Biofeedback: Evaluation of a new technic. *New Engl. J. Med.*, 1974, *290*, 684–685. **137, 143**

Miller, N. E., and Banuazizi, A. Instrumental learning by curarized rats of a specific visceral response, intestinal or cardiac. *J. Comp. Physiol. Psychol.*, 1968, *65*, 1–7. **126**

Miller, N. E., and Carmona, A. Modification of a visceral response, salivation in thirsty dogs, by instrumental training with water reward. *J. Comp. Physiol. Psychol.*, 1967, *63*, 1–6. **124**

Miller, N. E., and DiCara, L. Instrumental learning of heart rate changes in curarized rats. *J. Comp. Physiol. Psychol.*, 1967, *63*, 12–19. **125, 126**

Miller, N. E., and DiCara, L. V. Instrumental learning of urine formation by rats: Changes in renal blood flow. *Am. J. Physiol.*, 1968, *215*, 677–683. **126**

Miller, N. E., and Dollard, J. *Social learning and imitation.* New Haven: Yale University Press, 1941. **112, 124, 162**

Miller, N. E., and Dworkin, B. Visceral learning: Recent difficulties with curarized rats and significant problems for human research. In P. A. Obrist, et al. (Eds.) *Cardiovascular psychophysiology.* Chicago: Aldine, 1974. **128**

Miller, R. E. Social and pharmacological influences on nonverbal communication in monkeys and man. Paper presented to the symposium on communication and affect, University of Toronto, March 16, 1973. **258**

Miller, R. E., Banks, J., and Kuwahara, H. The communication of affects in monkeys: Cooperative reward conditioning. *J. Genet. Psychol.* 1966, *108*, 121–134. **240**

Miller, R. E., Banks, J., and Ogawa, N. Communication of affect in "cooperative conditioning" of rhesus monkeys. *J. Abnorm. Soc. Psychol.*, 1962, *64*, 343–348. **240**

Miller, R. E., Banks, J., and Ogawa, N. Role of facial expression in "cooperative-avoidance conditioning" in monkeys, *J. Abnorm. Soc. Psychol.*, 1963, *67*, 24–30. **240**

Miller, R. E., Caul, W. F., and Mirsky, I. A. Communication of affects between feral and socially isolated monkeys. *J. Pers. Soc. Psychol.*, 1967, *7*, 231–239. **241, 242**

Miller, R. E., Murphy, J. V., and Mirsky, I. A. Nonverbal communication of affect. *J. Clin. Psychol.*, 1959, *15*, 155–158. **240**

Miller, R. E., and Ogawa, N. The effect of adrenocorticotropic hormone (ACTH) on avoidance conditioning in the adrenalectomized rat. *J. Comp. Physiol. Psychol.*, 1962, *55*, 211–213. **34**

Milner, P. M. *Physiological psychology.* New York: Holt, Rinehart and Winston, 1970. **55, 66, 68, 69, 97, 439**

Mirsky, I. A. Determinants of psychosomatic disorders. *Proceedings of the third world congress of psychiatry*, 1962. **136**

Mischel, W. *Personality and assessment.* New York: Wiley, 1968. **344**

Mischel, W. Continuity and changes in personality. *Am. Psycholog.*, 1969, *24*, 1012–1018. **344**

Moan, C. E., and Heath, R. G. Septal stimulation and the initiation of heterosexual behavior in a homosexual male. *Behav. Ther. Exp. Psychiatr.*, 1972, *3*, 23–30. **146**

Money, J. Sex hormones and other variables in human eroticism. In W. C. Young (Ed.) *Sex and internal secretions.* Baltimore: Williams and Wilkins, 1961. **66, 211, 212**

Money, J. *Sex errors of the body.* Baltimore: John Hopkins University Press, 1968. **216**

Money, J., and Ehrhardt, A. A. *Man and woman, boy and girl.* Baltimore: The John Hopkins University Press, 1972. **211, 216**

Montagu, A. (Ed.) *Man and aggression.* Oxford: Oxford University Press, 1968. **155, 159**

Montagu, J. D., and Coles, E. M. Mechanism and measurement of the galvanic skin response. *Psych. Bull.*, 1966, *65*, 261–279. **428**

Montessori, M., *Spontaneous activity in education.* Cambridge, Mass.: Robert Bentley, 1964. **293**

Montgomery, K. C. The relation between exploratory behavior and spontaneous alternation in the white rat. *J. Comp. Physiol. Psychol.*, 1951, *44*, 582–589. **281**

Montgomery, K. C. The role of the exploratory drive in learning. *J. Comp. Physiol. Psychol.*, 1954, *47*, 60–64. **281**

Montgomery, K. C. The relations between fear induced by novel stimulation and exploratory behavior. *J. Comp. Physiol. Psychol.*, 1955, *48*, 254–260. **281**

Montgomery, K. C., and Segall, M. Discrimination learning based upon the exploratory drive. *J. Comp. Physiol. Psychol.*, 1955, *48*, 225–228. **281**

Morgan, C. D., and Murray, H. Method for investigating fantasies: The thematic appreciation test. *Arch. Neurol. Psychiatr.*, 1935, *34*, 289–306. **300**

Morosovsky, N. *Hibernation and the hypothalamus.* New York: Appleton-Century-Crofts, 1971. **363**

Morton, J. H., Addition, H., Addison, R. G., Hunt, L., and Sullivan, J. J. A clinical study of premenstrual tension. *Am. J. Obstet. Gynecol.*, 1953, *65*, 1182–1191. **188**

Morris, D. *The naked ape.* London: Constable, 1967. **14**

Moruzzi. G., and Magoun, H. W. Brain stem reticular formation and activation of the EEG. *Electroencephalogr Clin. Neurophysiol.*, 1949, *1*, 455–473. **54**

Mosher, D. L. Psychological reactions to pornographic films. *Technical Report of the commission on obscenity and pornography*, Vol. 8. Washington, D. C.: U. S. Government Printing Office, 1970. **222, 223, 224**

Mowrer, O. H. *Learning theory and behavior.* New York: Wiley, 1960. **112**

Moyer, K. E. Kinds of aggression and their physiological bases. *Commun. Behav. Biol.* 1968, *2*, 65–87. **92, 186**

Moyer, K. E. The physiology of affiliation and hostility. Reprint #70–1, Carnegie-Mellon University, 1970. **92**

Moyer, K. E. A physiological model of aggression: Does it have different implications. Presented at the Houston Neurological symposium on *neural basis of violence and aggression*, March 9–11, 1972. **92, 94, 187**

Moyer K. E., and Brunell, B. N. Effect of injected adrenaline on an avoidance response in the rat. *J. Genet. Psychol.*, 1958, *92*, 247–251. **34**

Moyer K. E., and Korn, J. H. Effect of adrenalectomy and adrenal demedullation on the retention of an avoidance response in the rat. *Psychonom. Sci.*, 1965, *2*, 77–78. **34**

Munroe, R. *Schools of psychoanalytic thought.* New York: Holt, Rinehart, and Winston, 1955. **199**

Murphy, J. V., and Miller, R. E. The effect of adrenocorticotropic hormone (ACTH) on avoidance conditioning in the rat. *J. Comp. physiol. Psychol.*, 1955, *48*, 47–49. **34**

Murray, H. A. *Explorations in personality.* London: Oxford University Press, 1938. **300**

Murray, H. A. Types of human needs. In D. C. McClelland (Ed.) *Studies in motivation.* New York: Appleton-Century-Crofts, 1955. **300**

Myers, T. I. Tolerance for sensory and perceptual deprivation. In J. P. Zubek (Ed.) *Sensory deprivation.* New York: Appleton-Century-Crofts, 1969. **287**

Narabayashi, H. Stereotaxic amygdalectomy for behaviour disorders with or without skull EEG abnormality. Second International Congress of Neurological Surgery, October 1961, *Excerpta Medica International Congress Series*, No. 36, p E125. **82**

Narabayashi, H. Sterotaxic amygdalectomy. In B. E. Eleftheriou (Ed.) *The neurobiology of the amygdala.* New York: Plenum, 1972. **144**

Narabayashi, H., and Uno, M. Long range results of stereotaxic amygdalectomy for behavior disorders. *Confin. Neurol.*, 1966, *27*, 168–171. **82**

Nauta, W. J. H., and Haymaker, W. Hypothalamic nuclei and fiber connections. In W. Haymaker, E. Anderson, and W. J. H. Nauta (Eds.) *The hypothalamus.* Springfield, Ill.: Charles C. Thomas, 1969, **446**

Nawy, H. The San Francisco erotic marketplace. *Technical report of the commission on obscenity and pornography*, Vol. 4. Washington, D. C.: U. S. Government Printing Office, 1970. **220**

Nebes, R. D. Hemispheric specialization in commissurotomized man. *Psych. Bull.*, 1974, *81*, 1–14. **448**

Nebylitsyn, V. D. *Fundamental properties of the human nervous system.* New York: Plenum, 1972. **285**

Nebylitsyn, V. D. and Gray, J. A. *Biologial bases of individual behavior.* New York: Academic, 1972. **285**

Nemiah, J. C., and Sifneos, P. E. Psychosomatic illness: A problem in communication. *Psychother. and Psychosom,* 1970, *18,* 154–160. **265, 266**

Nesbett, P. D. Smoking, physiological arousal, and emotional response. *J. Pers. Soc. Psychol.,* 1973, *25,* 137–144. **356**

Netter, F. H. *Nervous System.* New York: Ciba, 1962. **426**

Neumann, E., and Blanton, R. The early history of electrodermal research. *Psychophysiology,* 1969, *6,* 453. **428**

Newcomb, T. M. An approach to the study of communicative acts. *Psychol. Rev.,* 1953, *60,* 393–404. **323**

Newman, E. B., Perkins, F. T., and Wheeler, R. H. Cannon's theory of emotion: A critique. *Psychol. Rev.,* 1930, *37,* 305–326. **45, 49, 351**

Newsweek, Dec. 8, 1969, 35. **411**

Newsweek, Nov. 30, 1970 16. **409**

Nisbett, R. E. Determinants of food intake in human obesity. *Science,* 1968(a), *159,* 1254–1255. **358**

Nisbett, R. E. Taste, deprivation, and weight determinants of eating behavior. *J. Pers. Soc. Psychol.,* 1968(b), *10,* 107–116. **359**

Nisbett, R. E. Hunger, obesity, and the ventromedial hypothalamus. *Psych. Rev.,* 1972, *79,* 433–453. **363**

Nisbett, R. E., Caputo, C., Legant, P., and Marecek, J. Behavior as seen by the actor and by the observer. *J. Pers. Soc. Psychol.,* 1973, *27,* 154–164. **344**

Nisbett, R. E., and Schachter, S. Cognitive manipulation of pain. *J. Exp. Soc. Psychol.,* 1966, *2,* 227–236. **354, 355, 376**

Obrist, P. A., Webb, R. A., and Stutterer, J. R. Heart rate and somatic changes during aversive conditioning and a simple reaction-time task. *Psycho-physiology,* 1969, *5,* 696–723. **52**

Obrist, P. A., Webb, R. A., Stutterer, J. R., and Howard, J. L. The cardiac-somatic relationship: Some reformulations. *Psychophysiology,* 1970(a), *6,* 569–587. **52**

Obrist, P. A., Webb, R. A., Stutterer, J. R., and Howard, J. L. Cardiac Deceleration and reaction time: An evaluation of two hypotheses. *Psychophysiology*, 1970(b), *6*, 695–706. **52**

Okhnyanskaya, L. G. A study of the conditioned respiratory-vasomotor reflexes: Respiration as the stimulus of vaso-motion. *Fiziol. Zh. SSSR*, 1953, *39*, 610–613. **116, 119**

Okuma, T., Kogu, E., Ikeda, K., and Sugiyama, H. The EEG of Yoga and Zen practitioners. *Electroencephalogr. Clin. Neurophysiol.*, 1957, *Suppl. 9*, 51. **133**

Olds, J. Pleasure centers in the brain. *Sci. Am.* October, 1956a. **94, 97**

Olds, J. Runway and maze behavior controlled by basomedial forebrain stimulation in the rat. *J. Comp. Physiol. Psychol.*, 1956b, *49*, 507–512. **98**

Olds, J. Self stimulation of the brain. *Science*, 1958, *127*, 315–324. **90, 95**

Olds, J., and Milner, P. Positive reinforcement produced by electrical stimulation of septal area and other regions of rat brain. *J. Comp. Physiol. Psychol.*, 1954, *47*, 419–427. **89, 94**

Olds, J., and Olds, M. E. Drives, rewards, and the brain. In T. M. Newcombe (Ed.) *New directions in psychology*, Vol. 2. New York: Holt, 1965. **97**

Olds, M. E., and Olds, J. Approach-avoidance analysis of the rat diencephalon. *J. Comp. Neurol.*, 1963, *120*, 259–295. **95**

Olmstead, F. Measurement of blood flow and blood pressure. In C. C. Brown (Ed.) *Methods in psychophysiology*. Baltimore: Williams and Wilkins, 1967. **432**

Opton. E. M., and Lazarus, R. S. Personality determinants of psychophysiological response to stress: A theoretical analysis and an experiment. *J. Pers. Soc. Psychol.*, 1967, *6*, 291–303. **372**

Opton, E. M., Rankin, N. O., and Lazarus, R. S. A simplified method of heart rate measurement. *Psychophysiology*, 1966 *2*, 87–97. **51**

Orne, M. T. On the social psychology of the psychological experiment. *Am. Psychol.*, 1962, *17*, 776–783. **100**

Page, M. M., and Scheidt, R. J. The elusive weapons effect: Demand awareness, evaluation apprehension, and slightly sophisticated subjects. *J. Pers. Soc. Psychol.*, 1971, *20*, 304–318. **174**

Pallak, M. S. The effects of expected shock and relevant or irrelevant dissonance on incidental retention. *J. Pers. Soc. Psychol.*, 1970, *14*, 271. **337**

Pallak, M. S., and Pittman, T. S. General motivational effects of dissonance arousal. *J. Pers. Soc. Psychol.*, 1972, *21*, 349–358. **337**

Papez, J. W. A proposed mechanism of emotion. *Arch. Neurol. Psychiat.*, 1937, *38*, 725–743. **78**

Patterson, G. R., Littman, R. A., and Bricker, W. Assertive behavior in children: A step toward a theory of agression. *Monographs of the society for research in child development*, 1967, *32*, No. 5 (Serial No. 113). **167**

Pepitone, A. The problem of motivation in consistency models. In Abelson et al., (Eds.) *Theories of cognitive consistency: A sourcebook*. Chicago: Rand McNally, 1968. **338**

Perry, R. B. General Theory of Value, 1926. **43, 44**

Petrie, A. *Individuality in pain and suffering.* Chicago: University of Chicago Press, 1967, **286**

Piaget, J. *The child's conception of physical causality*. London: Routledge and Kegan Paul, 1930. **340**

Piaget, J. *The moral judgment of the child.* Glencoe, Illinois: Free Press, 1948. (First published 1932.) **341, 383, 385**

Piaget, J. *The origins of intelligence in children.* New York: International Universities Press, 1952. **288, 289**

Piaget, J. *The construction of reality in the child.* New York: Basic, 1954. **340**

Piaget, J. *The language and thought of the child.* New York: Meridian, 1955. **340**

Piaget, J. *Piaget's theory.* In P. Mussen (Ed.) *Handbook of child development*, Vol. I. New York: Wiley, 1971. **291**

Piaget, J. and Inhelder, B. *The child's conception of space.* New York: Humanities press, 1956. **297** (First published 1948.)

Piaget, J., and Inhelder, B. *The psychology of the child.* New York: Basic, 1969. **291, 294, 295, 296, 297, 298**

Piliavin, I. M., Rodin, J., and Piliavin, J. A. Good samaritanism: An underground phenomenon? *J. Pers. Soc. Psychol.,* 1969, *13,* 298–299. **395**

Plutchik, R., and Ax, A. F. A critique of "Determinants of emotional state" by Schachter and Singer (1962). *Psychophysiology*, 1967, *4*, 79–82. **352**

Pogrebkova, A. V. Conditioned reflexes to hypercapnia. *Dokl. Akad. Nauk. SSSR*, 1950, *73*, 225–228. **116**

Pogrebkova, A. V. Respiratory intero- and exteroceptive conditioned reflexes and their interrelationship. I. Formation and properties of respiratory intero- and exteroceptive conditioned reflexes. In K. M. Bykov (Ed.) *Voprosy fiziologii interoteseptsii.* Moscow: Akad. Nauk SSSR, 1952(a). **116, 117**

Pogrebkova, A. V. Respiratory intero- and exteroceptive conditioned reflexes and their interrelationship. II. Correlation of respiratory conditioned reflexes. *Tr. Inst. Fiziol. Pavlova*, 1952(b), *1*, 103–115. **116**

Pomeroy, W. B. *Dr. Kinsey and the Institute for Sex Research.* New York: Harper and Row, 1972. **200**

Porter, R. W., Cavanaugh, E. B., Critchlow, B. V., and Sawyer, C. H. Localized changes in electrical activity of the hypothalamus in estrous cats following vaginal stimulation. *Am. J. Physiol.*, 1957, *189*, 145–151. **69**

Prideaux E. The psychogalvanic reflex: A review. *Brain, 43*, 1920, 50–73. **260**

Prokasy, W., and Raskin, D. *Electrodermal activity in psychological research.* New York: Academic, 1973. **264**

Rahe, R. H. Life-change measurement as a predictor of illness. *Proc. Roy. Scc. Med.*, 1968, *61*, 1124–1126. **39**

Rahe, R. H., McKean, J. D., and Arthur, R. J. A longitudinal study of lifechange and illness patterns. *J. Psychosom. Res.*, 1967, *10*, 355–366. **39**

Rankin, N. O., Nomikos, M. S., Opton, E. M., Jr., and Lazarus, R. S. The role of surprise and suspense in stress reaction. Paper presented at the meeting of the Western Psychological Association, Honolulu, 1965. **369**

Razran, G. The observable unconscious and the inferable conscious in current Soviet psychophysiology. *Psychol. Rev.*, 1961, *68*, 81–147. **115, 116, 117, 118, 119, 120, 121, 123, 124**

Reeves, A. G., and Plum, F. Hyperphagia, Rage, and dementia accompanying a ventromedial hypothalamic neoplasm. *Arch. Neurol.*, 1969, *20*, 616–624. **62**

Report of the commission on obscenity and pornography. Washington, D. C.: U. S. Government Printing Office, 1970. **218, 220, 221, 223, 224, 225**

Reynolds, D. V. Neural mechanisms of laughter. Paper given at the Midwestern Psychological Association Convention, Detroit, 1971. **77**

Riddoch, G. The reflex functions of the completely divided spinal cord in man, compared with those associated with less severe lesions. *Brain*, 1917, *40*, 264–402. **66**

Riss, W., Hapern, M., and Scalia, F. Anatomical aspects of the evolution of the limbic and olfactory systems and their potential significance for behavior. Ann. N. Y. Acad. of Sci., 1969, *159*, 1096–1111. **79**

Roberts, W. W. Both rewarding and punishing effects from stimulation of posterior hypothalamus of cat with same electrode at same intensity. *J. Comp. Physiol. Psychol.*, 1958, *51*, 400–407. **72**

Roberts, W. W., and Kleiss, H. O. Motivational properties by hypothalamic aggression in cats. *J. Comp. Physiol. Psychol.*, 1964, *58*, 187–193. **70, 72**

Roberts, W. W., Steinberg, M. L., and Means, L. W. Hypothalamic mechanisms for sexual, aggressive, and other motivational behaviors in the opossum (Didelphis virginiana). *J. Comp. Physiol. Psychol.*, 1967, *64*, 1–15. **67, 70, 72**

Robinson, B. L., and Sawyer, C. H. Loci of sex behavioral and gonadotropic centers in the female cat hippocampus. *Physiologist*, 1957, *1*, 72. **67**

Rodgers, C. M. Hypothalamic mediation of sex behavior in the male rat. Unpublished doctoral dissertation, Yale University, New Haven, 1954. **67**

Roeder, F., Orthner, H., and Muller, D. The stereotaxic treatment of pedophilic homosexuality and other sexual deviations. In E. Hitchcock, L. Laitinen, and K. Vaernet (Eds.) *Psychosurgery.* Springfield, Ill.: Charles C. Thomas, 1972. **145**

Rosen, G. M., Rosen E., and Reid, J. B. Cognitive desensitization and avoidance behavior: A reevaluation. *J. Abnorm. Psychol.*, 1972, *80*, 176–182. **376**

Rosenberg, M. J., Hovland, C. I., McGuire, W. J., Abelson, R. P., and Brehm, J. W. *Attitude organization and change.* New Haven: Yale University Press, 1960. **323**

Rosenblatt, J. S. Effects of experience on sexual behavior in cats. In F. A. Beach (Ed.) *Sex and behavior.* New York: Wiley, 1965. **211**

Rosenthal, R. *Experimenter effects in behavioral research.* New York: Appleton-Century-Crofts, 1966. **100**

Rosenthal, R., Archer, D., Koivumaki, J., DiMatteo, M. R., and Rogers, P. Assessing sensitivity to nonverbal communication: The PONS test. *Division 8 Newslet-*

ter. Washington, D. C.: American Psychological Association, January 1974. **(a)** **391**

Rosenthal, R., Archer, D., DiMatteo, M. R., Koivumaki, J., and Rogers, P. The language without words. *Psychology Today,* 1974b, *8,* 64–68. **391**

Ross, L. D. Cue- and cognition-controlled eating among obese and normal subjects. Unpublished doctoral dissertation, Columbia University, 1969. **362**

Ross, L., Rodin, J., and Zimbardo, P. G. Toward an attribution therapy: The reduction of fear through induced cognitive-emotional misattribution. *J. Pers. Soc. Psychol.,* 1969, *12,* 279–288. **355, 376**

Rosvold, H. E., Mirsky, A. F., and Pribram, K. H. Influence of amygdalectomy on social behavior in monkeys. *J. Comp. Physiol. Psychol.,* 1954, *47,* 173–178. **88**

Rotter, J. Generalized expectancies for internal versus external control of reinforcement. *Psychol. Monogr.,* 1966, *80,* (1, Whole No. 609), 1–28. **342**

Routtenberg, A., and Lindy, J. Effects of the availability of rewarding septal and hypothalamic stimulation of bar-pressing for food under conditions of deprivation. *J. Comp. Physiol. Psychol.,* 1965, *60,* 158–161. **95**

Rubenstein, H. S. *The study of the brain.* New York: Grune and Stratton, 1953. **24**

Rubin, R. T., Gunderson, E. K. E., and Arthur, R. J. Life stress and illness patterns in the U.S. Navy. III. Prior life change and illness onset in an attack carrier's crew. *Arch. Environ. Health.,* 1969, *19,* 753. **40**

Rubin, R. T., Gunderson, E. K. E., and Arthur, R. J. Life stress and illness patterns in the U.S. Navy. IV. Environmental and demographic variables in relation to illness onset in a battleship's crew. *J. Psychosom. Res.,* 1971(a), *15,* 277–288. **40**

Rubin, R. T., Gunderson, E. K. E., and Arthur, R. J. Life stress and illness patterns in the U.S. Navy. V. Prior life change and illness onset in a battleship's crew. *J. Psychosom. Res.,* 1971(b), *15,* 89–94. **40**

Rubin, R. T., Gunderson, E. K. E., and Arthur, R. J. Life stress and illness patterns in the U.S. Navy. VI. Environmental, demographic, and prior life change variables in relation to illness onset in naval aviators during a combat cruise. *Psychosom. Med.,* 1972, *34,* 533–547. **40**

Ruch, L. O., and Holmes, T. H. Scaling of life change: Comparison of direct and indirect methods. *J. Psychosom. Res.,* 1971, *15,* 221–227. **39, 40**

Russell, B. *A history of Western philosophy.* New York: Simon and Schuster, 1945.
152, 153

Russell, B. *An outline of philosophy.* Cleveland: World, 1961. **47**

Rylander, G. The renaissance of psychosurgery. In L. Laitinen and K. E. Livingston
(Eds.) *Surgical approaches in psychiatry.* Baltimore: University Park Press, 1973.
11, 82

Sales, S. Need for stimulation as a factor in social behavior. *J. Pers. Soc. Psychol.,*
1971, *19,* 124–134. **284, 285, 286**

Sales, S. Need for stimulation as a factor in preferences for different stimuli. *J.
Pers. Assess.,* 1972, *36,* 55–61. **286**

Sales, S., Guydosh, R., and Iacono, W. Relationship between "strength of the
nervous system" and the need for stimulation. *J. Pers. Soc. Psychol.,* 1974, *29,*
16–22. **286**

Sales, S., and Throop, W. F. Relationship between kinesthetic after effects and
"strength of the nervous system." *Psychophysiology.,* 1972, *9,* 492–497. **286**

Sands, D. E. Further studies on endocrine treatment in adolescence and early
adult life. *J. Ment. Sci.,* 1954, *100,* 211–219. **188**

Sands, D. E., and Chamberlain, G. H. A. Treatment of inadequate personality in
juveniles by dehydroisoandrosterone. *Br. Med. J.,* 1952, 66–68. **188**

Sano, K., Yoshika, M., Ogashiva, M., Ishijima, B., and Ohye, C. Posteromedial
hypothalatomy in the treatment of aggressive behaviors. *Confin. Neurol.,* 1966,
27, 164–167. **82**

Sargent, J., Green, E., and Walters, E. D. Preliminary report on the use of autogenic
feedback training in the treatment of migrane and tension headaches. *Psychosom. Med.* 1973, *35,* 129–435. **139**

Saul, L. J., Rome, H., and Lenser, E. Desensitization of combat fatigue patients.
Am. J. Psychiatr., 1946, *102,* 476–478. **178**

Sawyer, C. H. Neuroendocrine blocking agents and gonadotropin release. In A. V.
Nalbandov (Ed.) *Advances in neuroendocrinology.* Urbana: University of Illinois
Press, 1963. **69**

Sawyer, C. H. Regulatory mechanisms of secretion of gonadotropic hormones. In
W. Haymaker, E. Anderson, and W. J. H. Nanta (Eds.) *The hypothalamus.*
Springfield, Ill.: Charles C. Thomas, 1969. **66, 67, 68, 69**

Schachter, J. Pain, fear, and anger in hypertensives and normotensives. *Psychosom. Med.,* 1957, *19,* 17–29. **35**

Schachter, S. *The psychology of affiliation.* Stanford: Stanford University Press, 1959. **412**

Schachter, S. The interaction of cognitive and physiological determinants of emotional state. In L. Berkowitz (Ed.) *Advances in experimental social psychology,* vol. 1. New York: Academic, 1964. **43, 44, 46, 173, 334, 351, 352, 354, 412**

Schachter, S. Obesity and eating. *Science,* 1968, *161,* 751–756. **362**

Schachter, S. Some extraordinary facts about obese humans and rats. *Am. Psychol.,* 1970, *26,* 129–144. **357, 358, 361, 363**

Schachter, S. *Emotion, obesity, and crime.* New York: Academic, 1971. **361**

Schachter, S., Goldman, R., and Gordon, A. Effects of fear, food deprivation, and obesity on eating. *J. Pers. Soc. Psychol.,* 1968, *10,* 91–97. **357**

Schachter, S., and Gross, L. Manipulated time and eating behavior. *J. Pers. Soc. Psychol.,* 1968, *10,* 98–106. **357**

Schachter, S., and Singer, J. Cognitive, social and physiological determinants of emotional state. *Psych. Rev.,* 1962, *69,* 379–399. **47**

Schachter, S., and Wheeler, L. Epinepherine, chlorapromazine, and amusement. *J. Abnorm. Soc. Psychol.,* 1962, *65,* 121–128. **352**

Schildkraut, J. J. *Neuropsychopharmacology and the effective disorders.* Boston: Little, Brown, 1969. **103**

Schildkraut, J. J., Davis, J. M., and Klerman, G. L. Biochemistry of depressions. In D. H. Efron (Ed.) *Psychopharmacology.* Washington, D. C.: National Institute of Mental Health, 1968. **422**

Schildkraut, J. J., and Ketty, S. S. Biogenic amines and emotion. *Science,* 1967, *156,* 21–30. **35, 45, 103, 104, 421**

Schill, T. R. Aggression and blood pressure responses of high- and low-guilt subjects following frustration. *J. Couns. Clin. Psychol.,* 1972, *38,* 461. **179**

Schon, M., and Sutherland, A. M. The relationship of pituitary hormones to sexual behavior in women. In H. G. Biegel (Ed.) *Advances in sex research.* New York: Harper and Row, 1963. **211**

Schultz, J. h., and Luthe, W. *Autogenic training.* New York: Grune and Stratton, 1959. **141**

Schwab, R., Sweet, W. H., Mark, V. H., Kjellberg, R. N., and Ervin, F. R. Treatment of intractible temporal lobe epilepsy by stereotoxic amygdala lesions. *Trans. Am. Neurol. Ass.,* 1965, *90,* 12–19. **82**

Schwartz, G. Biofeedback as therapy. *Am. Psychol.,* 1973, *28,* 666–673. **142**

Schwartz, L. A. Group psychotherapy in the war neuroses. *Am. J. Psychiatr.,* 1945, *101,* 498–500. **178**

Scott, J. P. *Aggression.* Chicago: University of Chicago Press, 1958a. **246**

Scott, J. P. That old-time aggression. In M. F. Ashley Montagu (Ed.) *Man and aggression.* Oxford: Oxford University Press, 1968b. **159, 160**

Scoville, W. B., and Milner, B. Loss of recent memory after bilateral hippocampal lesions. *J. Neurol. Neurosurg. Psychiatr.,* 1957, *20,* 11. **82**

Sears, R. R., Maccoby, E., and Levin. H. *Patterns of child rearing.* Evanston; Ill. Row, Peterson, 1957. **165, 315**

Sears, R. R., Whiting, J. W. M., Nowlis, V., and Sears, P. S. Some child-rearing antecedents of aggression and dependency in young children. *Genet. Psychol. Monogr.,* 1953, *47,* 135–234. **165**

Secord, P. F., and Backman, C. W. *Social psychology.* New York: McGraw-Hill, 1964. **391**

Selman, R. The relation of role-taking to the development of moral judgment in children. *Child Dev.,* 1971, *42,* 79–92. **391**

Selman, R. A structural analysis of the ability to take another's social perspective: Stages in the development of role-taking ability. Paper presented to the Society for Research in Child Development, Philadelphia, 1973. **391**

Selman, R., and Byrne, D. Manual for scoring stages of role-taking in moral and non-moral social dilemmas. Unpublished paper, Harvard University, 1973. **391**

Selye, H. *The physiology and pathology of exposure to stress.* Montreal: Acta, 1950. **30**

Selye, H. *The stress of life.* New York: McGraw-Hill, 1956. **30, 31, 32**

Sem-Jacobson, C. W. *Depth-electroencephalographic stimulation of the human brain and behavior.* Springfield, Ill.: Charles C. Thomas, 1968. **77, 99, 100**

Shagass, C., and Malmo, R. B. Psychodynamic themes and localized muscle tension during psychotherapy. *Psychosom. Med.,* 1954, *16,* 295–313. **45**

Shapiro, D., and Crider, A. Psychophysiological approaches in social psychology. In G. Lindzey and E. Aronson (Eds.) *Handbook of social psychology,* Vol. 3, Reading, Mass.: Addison-Wesley, 1968. **47, 352**

Shapiro, D., and Schwartz, G. E. Psychophysiological contributions to social psychology. *Annu. Rev. Psychol.,* 1970, *21,* 87–112. **375**

Shapiro, D., Tursky, B., Gershon, E., and Stern, M. Effects of feedback and reinforcement on the control of human systolic blood pressure. *Science,* 1969, *163,* 588–589. **132, 138, 139**

Shapiro, D., Tursky, B., and Schwartz, G. E. Differentiation of heart rate and systolic blood pressure in man by operant conditioning. *Psychosom. Med.,* 1970, *32,* 417–423. **132**

Sharma, K. N., Anand, B. K., Dua, S., and Singh, B. Role of stomack in regulation of activities of hypothalamic feeding centers. *Am. J. Physiol.,* 1961, *201,* 593–598. **64**

Sharpless, S., and Jasper H. H. Habituation of the arousal reaction. *Brain,* 1956, *79,* 655–680. **57**

Shaw, M. E., and Costanzo, P. R. *Theories of social psychology.* New York: McGraw-Hill, 1970. **325, 341**

Sheridan, C. L., and King, R. G. Obedience to authority with an authentic victim. *Proceedings, 80th Annual Convention, APA,* 1972, 165–166. **405**

Sherman, S. J. Effects of choice and incentive on attitude change in a discrepant behavior situation. *J. Pers. Soc. Psychol.,* 1970a, *15,* 245–252. **335**

Sherman, S. J. Attitudinal effects of unforseen consequences. *J. Pers. Soc. Psychol.,* 1970b, *16,* 510–520. **335**

Sherrington, C. S. Experiments on the value of vascular and visceral factors for the genesis of emotion. *Proc. Roy. Soc. (Lond.), B,* 1900, *66,* 390–403. **43**

Shirer, W. *The rise and fall of the Third Reich.* New York: 1959 **409**

Shmavonian, B., Yarmat, A., and Cohen, S. Relations between the automatic nervous system and central nervous system in age differences in behavior. In *Behavior, aging, and the nervous system.* Springfield, Ill: Charles C. Thomas, 1965. **264**

Sigusch, V., Schmidt, G., Reinfeld, R., and Sutor, I. Psychosexual stimulation: Sex differences. *J. Sex Res.,* 1970, *6,* 10–24. **223, 224**

Silverman, A. J., and Cohen, S. I. Affect and vascular collrelates to catecholamines. In L. J. West and M. Greenblatt (Eds.) *Explorations in the physiology of emotions.* Psychiatric Research Reports of the A.P.A., No. 12, January 1960. **35**

Simon, H., and Newell, A. Models: Their uses and limitation. In L.D. White (Ed.) *The state of the social sciences.* Chicago: University of Chicago Press, 1956. **16**

Simon, W., and'Gagnon, J. On psychosexual development. In D. A. Goslin (Ed.) *Handbook of socialization theory and research.* Chicago: Rand, McNally, 1969. **209**

Singer, J. E. Motivation for consistency. In S. Feldman (Ed.), *Cognitive consistency: Motivational antecedents and behavioral consequents.* New York: Academic, 1966. **366**

Singer, J. L. The influence of violence portrayed in television or motion pictures upon overt aggressive behavior. In J. L. Singer (Ed.), *The control of aggression and violence.* New York: Academic, 1969. **174**

Singh, D. Role of response habits and cognitive factors in determination of behavior of obese humans. *J. Pers. Soc. Psychol.,* 1973, *27,* 220–238. **363**

Singh, D., and Sikes, S. Hunger motivation in obese human: Role of previous experience. *J. Comp. Physiol. Psychol.,* 1974. **363**

Skinner, B. F. *The behavior of organisms: An experimental approach.* New York: Appleton-Century, 1938. **122**

Skultety, F. M., and Chamberlain, M. D. The effects of lateral midbrain lesions on evoked behavioral responses. *Neurology,* 1965, *15,* 438. **72**

Smith, E. The power of dissonance techniques to change attitudes. *Publ. Opin. Q.,* 1961, *25,* 626–639. **331**

Smith, K. Conditioning as an artifact. *Psychol. Rev.,* 1964, *61,* 217–225. **123**

Snyder, C., and Noble, M. Operant conditioning of vasoconstriction. Paper presented at the meeting of the Psychonomic Society, St. Louis, October 1966. **132**

Snyder, C., and Noble, M. Operant conditioning of vasoconstriction. Paper presented at the meeting of the Midwestern Psychological Association, Chicago, 1965. **132**

Sommer, R. *Personal space.* Englewood Cliffs: Prentice-Hall, 1969. **161, 248**

Spector, S. Regulation of norepinepherine systhesis. In D. H. Efron (Ed.) *Psychopharmacology.* Washington, D. C.: National Institute of Mental Health, 1968. **422**

Spies, G. Food versus intracranial self-stimulation reinforcement in food-deprived rats. *J. Comp. Physiol. Psychol.,* 1965, *60,* 153–157. **95**

Spiesman, J. C., Lazarus, R. S., Mordkoff, A. M., and Davidson, L. A. Experimental reduction of stress based on ego-defense theory. *J. Abnorm. Soc. Psychol.,* 1964, *68,* 367–380. **368, 370**

Staub, E. A child in distress: The influence of age and number of witnesses on children's attempts to help. *J. Pers. Soc. Psychol.,* 1970, *14,* 130–141. **398**

Staub, E. A child in distress: The influence of nurturance and modeling on children's attempts to help. *Dev. Psychol.,* 1971, *5,* 124–132. **398, 399**

Stayton, D. J., Hogan, R., and Ainsworth, M. D. S. Infant obedience and maternal behavior: The origins of socialization reconsidered. *Child Dev.,* 1971, *42,* 1057–1069. **407**

Stein, L. Reciprocal action of reward and punishment mechanisms. In R. G. Heath (Ed.) *The Role of Pleasure in Behavior.* New York: Hoeber, 1964. **96**

Stein, L. i1Reciprocal action of reward and punishment mechanisms. Washington, D. C.: U. S. Government Printing Office, 1968. **105, 106**

Stein, A. H., and Friedrich, L. K. Television content and young children's behavior. In J. P. Murray, E. A. Rubinstein, and G. A. Comstock (Eds.) *Television and social behavior,* Vol. 2. Washington, D. C.: U. S. Government Printing Office, 1971. **175**

Steiner, I. D. Perceived freedom. In L. Berkowitz (Ed.) *Advances in experimental social psychology,* Vol. 5. *New York: Academic, 1970. 339*

Stellar, E. The physiology of motivation. *Psychol. Rev.,* 1954, *61,* 5–22. **72, 73**

Sterman, M. B. Neurophysiologic and clinical studies of sensorimotor EEG biofeedback training: Some effects on epilepsy. *Seminars in Psychiatry,* 1973, *5,*

507–524. **135**

Sterman, M. B., Macdonald, L. R., and Stone, R. K. Biofeedback training of the sensorimotor electroencephalogram rhythm in man: Effects on epilspey. *Epilepsia.* 1974, *15,* 395–416. **141**

Sternbach, R. A. *Principles of psychophysiology.* New York: Academic, 1966. **11, 27, 53, 425**

Stevens, J. R., Sacdev, K., and Millstein, V. Behavior disorders of children and the electroencephalogram. *Arch. Neurol.,* 1968, *18,* 160–477. **86, 87**

Stone, L., and Hokanson, J. E. Arousal reduction via self-punitive behavior. *J. Pers. Soc. Psychol.,* 1969, *12,* 72–79. **180**

Storms, M. D. Videotape and the attribution process: Reversing actors' and observers' points of view. *J. Pers. Soc. Psychol.,* 1973, *27,* 165–175. **345, 346**

Storms, M. D., and Nisbett, R. E. Insomnia and the attribution process. *J. Pers. Soc. Psychol.,* 1970, *16,* 319–328. **376**

Strelau, J. Nervous system type and extraversion-introversion: A comparison of Eysenck's theory with Pavlov's typology. *Pol. Psychol. Bull.,* 1970, *1,* 17–24. **285**

Strongman, K. T. *The psychology of emotion.* New York: Wiley, 1973. **6**

Stunkard, A., and Koch, C. The interpretation of gastric mobility: I. Apparent bias in the reports of hunger by obese persons. *Archives of General Psychiatr.,* 1964, *11,* 74–82. **357**

Suchowski, G. K. Sexual hormones and aggressive behavior. Proceedings of the *Symposium on the Biology of Aggressive Behaviour, Milan, May 1968.* Amsterdam: Excerpta Medica, 1969. **188**

Suedfeld, P. Theoretical formulations II. In J. P. Zubek (Ed.) *Sensory deprivation.* New York: Appleton-Century-Crofts, 1969(a). **284**

Suedfeld, P., and Epstein, Y. Where is the "D" in dissonance. *J. Pers.,* 1971, *39,* 178–188. **337**

Sushinsky, L., and Bootzin, R. Cognitive disensitization as a model of systematic desensitization. *Behav. Res. and Ther.,* 1970, *8,* 29–34. **376**

Sweet, W. H., Ervin, F. R., and Mark, V. H. The relationship of violent behavior to focal cerebral disease. In S. Garratini and E. B. Sigg (Eds.) *Aggressive behavior.* Amsterdam: Excerpta Medical, 1969. **184**

Tagiuri, R. Person perception. In G. Lindzey and E. Aronson (Eds.) *Handbook of social psychology,* Vol. 3. Reading, Mass.: Addison Wesley, 1968. **391**

Tavris, C. A conversation with Stanley Milgram. *Psychol. Today,* 1974, *8,* 71–80. **406, 407**

Teitelbaum, P. Disturbances of feeding and drinking behavior after hypothalamic lesions. In M. R. Jones (Ed.), *Nebraska symposium on motivation.* Lincoln: University of Nebraska Press, 1961. **64, 361**

Teitelbaum, P., and Cytawa, J. Spreading depression and recovery from lateral hypothalmic damage. *Science,* 1965, *147,* 61–63. **65**

Teitelbaum, P., and Epstein, A. N. The lateral hypothalmic syndrome. *Psychol. Rev.,* 1963, *69,* 74–90. **64**

Teitelbaum, P., and Stellar, E. Recovery from the failure to eat produced by hypothalmic lesions. *Science,* 1954, *120,* 894–895. **65**

Television and growing up: The impact of televised violence. Report to the Surgeon General. Washington, D. C.: U. S. Government Printing Office, 1971. **174, 175, 176, 177**

Teplov, B. M. The problem of types of human higher nervous activity and methods of determining them. In V. D. Nebylitsyn and J. A. Gray (eds.) *Biological bases of individual behavior.* New York: Academic, 1972. **286**

Terman, L. M. Kinsey's *sexual behavior in the human male: Some comments and criticisms.* Psych. Bull., 1948, *45,* 443–459. **201**

Terzian, H., and Dalle Ore, G. Symptoms of Kluver and Bucy reproduced in man by bilateral removal of the temporal lobes. *Neurology,* 1955, *5,* 373–380. **81**

Thomas, A., Chess, S., and Burch, H. G. The origin of personality. *Scientific Am.,* 1970, *223,* 102–109. **242, 243, 244**

Tinbergen, N. On war and peace in animals and man. *Science,* 1968, *160,* 1411–1418.

Tomkins, S. Affect, imagery, and consciousness: *The positive affects,* Vol. 1. New York: Springer, 1962. **250, 251, 253**

Tomkins, S. Affect, imagery, and consciousness: *The negative affects,* Vol. 2. New York: Springer, 1963. **250, 251, 253**

Trowill, J. A. Instrumental conditioning of the heart rate in the curarized rat. *J. Comp. Physiol. Psychol.,* 1967, *63,* 7–11. **125**

Turiel, E. Sequentiality of developmental stages in the child's moral judgments. *J. Pers. Soc. Psychol.,* 1966, *3,* 611–618. **388, 389**

Ursin, R., Ursin, H., and Olds, J. Self-stimulation of hippocampus in rats. *J. Comp. Physiol. Psychol.,* 1966, *61,* 353–359. **95**

Valenstein, E. S. *Brain control.* New York: John Wiley, 1973. **10, 11, 144, 145, 146, 147**

Valenstein, E. S., Cox, V. C., and Kakolewski, J. K. Reexamination of the role of the hypothalamus in motivation. *Psychol. Rev.,* 1970, *77,* 16–31. **74, 75, 92**

Valins, S. Cognitive effects of false heart rate feedback. *J. Pers. Soc. Psychol.,* 1966, *4,* 400–408. **353, 376**

Valins, S., and Ray, A. Effects of cognitive disensitization on avoidance behavior. *J. Pers. Soc. Psychol.,* 1967, *7,* 345–350. **376**

Vanselow, K. Meditative exercises to eliminate the effects of stress. *Hippokrates,* 1968, *39,* 462–465. **135**

Vantress, F. E., and Williams, C. B. The effect of the presence of the provocator and the opportunity to counteraggress on systolic blood pressure. *J. Gen. Psychol.,* 1972, *86,* 63–68. **179**

Van Twyer, H. B., and Kimmel, H. D. Operant conditioning of the GSR with concomitant measurement of two somatic variables. *J. Exp. Psychol.,* 1966, *72,* 841–846. **132**

Vasilevskaya, N. E. Interoceptive conditioned reflexes of the second order. *Dokl. Akad. Nauk. SSSR.,* 1948, *61,* 161–164. **116**

Vasilevskaya, N. E. The formation of second-order interoceptive conditioned reflexes with exteroceptive reinforcement. *Nauch. Byull. Leningr. Gos. U.,* 1950, *26,* 21–23. **116**

Vaughan, E., and Fisher, A. E. Male sexual behavior induced by intracranial electrical stimulation. *Science.* 1962, *137,* 758–760. **67**

Venables, P. H., and Martin, I. Skin resistance and skin potential. In P. H. Venables and I. Martin (Eds.) *Manual of psycho-physiological methods.* New York: Wiley, 1967. **427, 428**

Vernon, D. T. A., and Bigelow, D. A. Effect of information about a potentially stressful situation on responses to stress impact. *J. Pers. Soc. Psychol.,* 1974, *29,* 50–59. **377**

Von Holst, E., and Von Saint Paul, U. Electrically controlled behavior. *Sci. Am.* March. 1962. **76, 88, 93**

Wallace, R. K. Physiological effects of transcendental meditation. *Science,* 1970, *196,* 1751–1754. **134**

Waller, A. D. Periodic variations of conductance of the palm of the human hand. *Proc. R. Soc.,* 1919, B, *91,* 32–40. **260**

Walters, R. H., Bowen, N. V., and Parke, R. D. Experimentally induced disinhibition of sexual responses. Unpublished manuscript, University of Waterloo, 1963. **217**

Walters, R. H., and Llewellyn Thomas, E. Enhancement of punitiveness by visual and audiovisual displays. *Can. J. Psychol.,* 1963, *17,* 244–255. **169**

Walters, R. H., Llewellyn Thomas, E., and Acker, C. W. Enhancement of punitive behavior by audiovisual displays. *Science* 1962, *136,* 872–873. **169**

Ward, W. D., and Carlson, W. A. Cognitive dissonance, opinion change, and physiological arousal. *J. Gen. Psychol.,* 1964, *71,* 115–124. **336**

Washburn, S. L. *Social life of early man.* Chicago: Aldine, 1961. **14**

Wasman, M., and Flynn, J. P. Directed attack elicited from hypothalamus. *Am. Med. Assoc. Arch. Neurol.,* 1962, *6,* 220–227. **72**

Waterman, C. K. The facilitating and interfering effects of cognitive dissonance on simple and complex paired-associate learning tasks. *J. Exp. Soc. Psychol.,* 1969, *5,* 31–42. **337**

Watson, J. B., and Rayner, R. Conditioned emotional responses. *J. Exp. Psychol.,* 1920, *3,* 1–14. **113**

Watson, R. I. Investigation into deindividuation using a cross-cultural survey technique. *J. Pers. Soc. Psychol.,* 1973, *25,* 342–345. **411**

Weiner, B. The effects of unsatisfied achievement motivation on persistence and subsequent performance. *J. Pers.,* 1965, *33,* 428–442. **305**

Weiner, B. New conceptions in the study of achievement motivation. In B. A. Maher (Ed.) *Progress in experimental personality research,* Vol. 5. New York: Academic, 1970. **302, 303, 304, 305**

Weiner, B. *Theories of motivation.* Chicago: Markham, 1972. **303, 304, 314, 339, 342, 343**

Weiner, M., Devoe, S., Rubinow, S., and Geller, J. Nonverbal behavior and nonverbal communication. *Psycho. Rev.,* 1972, *3,* 185–214. **249**

Weinman, J. Photoplethysmography. In P. H. Venables and I. Martin (Eds.) *Manual of psycho-physiological methods.* New York: John Wiley and Sons, 1967. **431**

Weinstein, J., Averill, J. R., Opton, E., Jr., and Lazarus, R. S. Defensive style and discrepancy between self-report and physiological; indoces of stress. *J. Pers. Soc. Psychol.,* 1968, *10,* 406–413. **263, 370**

Weiss, J. M., McEwen, B. S., Teresa, M., Silva, A., and Kalkut, M. F. Pituitary-adrenal influences on fear responding. *Science,* 1969, *163,* 197–199. **34**

Weiss, T. and Engel, B. T. Operant conditioning of heart rate in patients with premature ventricular contractions. *Psychosom. Med.,* 1971, *33,* 301–321. **137, 138**

Welgan, P. R. Learned control of gastric acid secretions in ulcer patients. *Psychosom. Med.,* 1974, *36,* 411–419. **140**

Welsh, B. L., and Welsh, A. S. 69 **103**

Wenger, M. A., and Bagchi, B. K. Studies of autonomic functions in practitioners of yoga in India. *Behavo. Sci.,* 1961, *6,* 312–323. **130, 131, 133, 134**

Wenger, M. A., Bagchi, B. K., and Anand, B. K. Experiments in India on "voluntary" control of the heart and pulse. *Circulation,* 1969, *24,* 1319–1325. **130, 131, 134**

Whalen, R. E. *Sexual motivation. Psych. Rev.,* 1966, *72,* 151–163. **207, 212**

Wheatley, M. D. The hypothalamus and effective behavior in cats: A study of the effects of experimental lesions, with anatomic correlations. *Arch. Neurol. Psychiatr.,* 1944, *52,* 296–316. **70**

White, J. C. Autonomic discharge from stimulation of the hypothalamus in man. *Res. Publ. Assoc. Res. Nerv. Ment. Dis.,* 1940, *20,* 854–863. **77**

White, K. D., Mangan, G. L., Morrish, R. B., and Siddle, D. A. T. The relation of visual after-images to extraversion and neuroticism. *J. Exp. Res. Pers.,* 1969, *3,* 268–274. **285**

White, R. K., and Lippitt, R. Leader behavior and member reaction in three "social climates." In D. Cartwright and A. Zander. *Group Dynamics,* 2nd ed. Evanston, Ill.: Row, Peterson, 1960. **321**

White, R. W. Motivation reconsidered: The concept of competence. *Psych. Rev.,* 1959, *66,* 297–333. **288, 289, 290**

Wickramasekera, I. E. Temperature feedback for the control of migrane. *J. Beh. Ther. Exp. Psychiatr.,* 1973, *4,* 343–345. **140**

Wiggins, J. S., Renner, K. E., Clore, G. L., and Rose, R. J. *The psychology of personality.* Reading, Mass.: Addison Wesley, 1971. **343**

Wikler, A. Pharmacological dissociation of behavior and EEG sleep patterns in dogs: Morphine, N-allylnomorphine and Atropine. *Proc. Soc. Exp. Biol. (N.Y.),* 1952, *79,* 261–265. **55**

Williams-Ashman, H. G., and Reddi, A. H. Actions of vertebrate sex hormones. *Ann. Rev. Physiol.,* 1971, *33,* 31–82. **216**

Wilson, R., and DiCara, L. V. The effects of previous curare immobilization on Pavlovian conditioned heart rate deceleration in the curarized rat. *Physiol. Behav.,* 1975, *14,* 259–264. **128**

Winick, C. Some observations on characteristics of patrons of adult theaters and bookstores. *Technical report of the commission of obscenity and pornography,* Vol. 4. Washington, D. C.: U. S. Government Printing Office, 1970(a). **220**

Winick, C. A study of consumers of explicitly sexual materials: Some functions served by adult movies. *Technical report of the commission on obscenity and pornography,* Vol. 4. Washington D. C.: U. S. Government Printing Office. 1970(b). **220**

Winterbottom, M. T. The relation of childhood training in independence to achievement motivation. Unpublished doctoral dissertation, University of Michigan, 1953. **308**

Wise, C. D., and Stein, L. Facilitation of brain self-stimulation by central administration of norepinepherine. *Science,* 1969, *163,* 299–301. **105**

Wise, R. A. Hypothalamic motivational systems: Fixed or plastic neural circuits? *Science,* 1968, *162,* 377–379. **76**

Wolf, S., and Wolff, H. G. *Human gastric function,* 2nd Ed. New York: Oxford University Press, 1947. **45**

Wolpe, J. *Psychotherapy by reciprocal inhibition.* Stanford: Stanford University Press, 1958. **141**

Wolpe, J., and Lazarus, A. *Behavior therapy techniques.* New York: Pergram, 1966. **141**

Wurtz, R. H., and Olds, J. Amygdaloid stimulation and operant reinforcement in the rat. *J. Comp. Physiol. Psychol.,* 1963, *56,* 941–949. **95**

Wyler, A. R., Masuda, M., and Holmes, T. H. Magnitude of life events and seriousness of illness. *Phychosom. Med.,* 1971, *33,* 115–122. **39**

Wynne, L. C., and Solomon, R. L. Traumatic avoidance learning: Acquisition and extinction in dogs deprived of normal peripheral autonomic function. *Genet. Psychol. Monogr.,* 1955, *52,* 241–284. **33, 43**

Young, P. T. *Motivation and emotion.* New York: Wiley, 1961. **6**

Zanna, M. P., Lepper, M. R., and Abelson, R. P. Attentional mechanisms in children's devaluation of a forbidden activity in a forced-compliance situation. *J. Pers. Soc. Psychol.,* 1973, *28,* 355–359. **331**

Zetterberg, H. L. The consumers of pornography where it is easily available: The Swedish experience. *Technical reports of the commission on obscenity and pornography.* Vol. 9. Washington, D. C.: U. S. Government Printing Office, 1970. **220**

Zhorov, P. A., and Yermolayeva-Tomina, L. B. Concerning the relation between extraversion and the strength of the nervous system. In V. D. Nebylitsyn and J. A. Gray (Eds.) *Biological bases of individual behavior.* New York: Academic, 1972. **285**

Zillman, D. Excitation transfer in communication-mediated aggressive behavior. *J. Exper. Soc. Psychol.,* 1971, *7,* 419–434. **174**

Zimbardo, P. The effect of effort and improvisation on self-persuasion produced by role-playing. *J. Exp. Soc. Psychol.,* 1965, *1,* 103–120. **331, 332**

Zimbardo, P. G. (Ed.) *The cognitive control of motivation.* Glenview, Ill.: Scott, Foresman, 1969(a). **364**

Zimbardo, P. G. The human choice: Individuation, reason, and order versus deindividuation, impulse, and chaos. In W. J. Arnold and D. Levine (Eds.) *Nebraska symposium on motivation.* Lincoln: University of Nebraska Press, 1969(b). **409, 410**

Zimbardo, P. G., Cohen, A. Weisenberg, M., Dworkin, L., and Firestone, I. Control of pain motivation by cognitive dissonnance. *Science,* 1966, *151,* 217–219. **366, 367**

Zimbardo, P. G., and Montgomery, K. C. The relative strengths of consummatory responses in hunger, thirst, and exploratory drive. *J. Comp. Physiol. Psychol.,* 1957, *50,* 504–508. **281**

Zimbardo, P., Weisenberg, M., Firestone, I., and Levy, B. Communicator effectiveness in producing public conformity and private attitude change. *J. Pers.,* 1965, *33,* 233–255. **331, 332**

Zubek, J. P. Sensory and perceptual effects. In J. P. Zubek (Ed.) *Sensory deprivation.* New York: Appleton-Century-Crofts, 1969(a). **282**

Zubek, J. P. Physiological and biochemical effects. In J. P. Zubek (Ed.) *Sensory deprivation.* New York: Appleton-Century-Crofts, 1969(b). **283**

Zuckerman, M. Hallucinations, reported sensations, and images. In J. P. Zubek (Ed.) *Sensory deprivation.* New York: Appleton-Century-Crofts, 1969(a). **282**

Zuckerman, M. Theoretical formulations I. In Zubek, J. P. *Sensory deprivation.* New York: Appleton-Century-Crofts, 1969(b). **282, 284**

Zuckerman, M., Bone, R. N., Neary, R., Mangelsdorff, D., and Brustman, B. What is the sensation seeker? Personality trait and experience correlates of the sensation-seeking scales. *J. Consult. Clin. Psychol.,* 1972, *39,* 308–321. **287**

Zuckerman, M., Kolin, E. A., Price, L., and Zoob, I. Development of a sensation-seeking scale. *J. Consult. Psychol.,* 1964, *28,* 477–482. **286**

SUBJECT INDEX